Penguin Books
Spare Rib Reader

'*Spare Rib* set out, ten years ago now, to be the magazine that "put women's liberation on the news stands". An early proposal declared: "There is the most urgent need for a magazine that will reach A L L women – that is, women who are frustrated by the limitations of existing magazines. Commercial journalese gives unrealistic solutions to problems, thus increasing loneliness and isolation."

'It was to be a forty-eight page news magazine published monthly at fifteen pence. Great emphasis was placed on regular, "professional" production: this was partly in reaction to the unreliability of alternative publications and partly to prove women's capability and efficiency. In July 1972, the first issue went on the news stands – and sold out. In those early days two editors and six women with specific job designations steered the magazine on an exciting and sometimes contradictory course. The magazine ran regular columns on Law, Sex, Health, Work, and the Arts, had a do-it-yourself page called "Spare Parts", offered wholesome recipes, the occasional knitting pattern, and a men's page.

'Over the next few years many changes took place. The masthead of *Spare Rib 18* announced that the magazine was to become a collective – all jobs and skills would be shared; "big names" disappeared (along with contributors' payments) in favour of encouraging many more "ordinary" women to describe their lives in words, illustrations or photos – although people like Jane Fonda continued to provide hard-sell cover material.

'Bedevilled by problems of distribution and fluctuating sales, *Spare Rib* nervously altered its image: having started with the proud logo, "the new women's magazine", it retreated to plain "news magazine", then veered over the next few years between "women's magazine" and "women's news magazine", and then left a description off altogether. With its fourth birthday, it came out at last a "women's liberation magazine".

'A decade later and we're still at it. Something like sixty women have worked on the *Spare Rib* collective since its first issue, and many hundreds more have written, drawn, photographed, designed and helped out in the office. In these ten years, the way the magazine looks and the issues it covers have changed in as many ways as the women who make it, on and off the collective, have changed. And with another hundred issues it will be different again. The *Spare Rib Reader* offers a glimpse of those first hundred issues and reflects the vision that *Spare Rib* originally set for itself – to be a magazine for all women, directed towards changing all our lives.

'Marsha Rowe, one of *Spare Rib*'s two founding editors and collective member until the mid seventies, has chosen the anthology with the collaboration of members of the collective. She now lives in Leeds, and is part of a socialist feminist women's group which has been meeting for six years.'

Spare Rib Reader

EDITED BY MARSHA ROWE

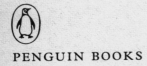

PENGUIN BOOKS

Penguin Books Ltd, Harmondsworth, Middlesex, England
Penguin Books, 40 West 23rd Street, New York, New York 10010, U.S.A.
Penguin Books Australia Ltd, Ringwood, Victoria, Australia
Penguin Books Canada Ltd, 2801 John Street, Markham, Ontario, Canada L3R 1B4
Penguin Books (N.Z.) Ltd, 182–190 Wairau Road, Auckland 10, New Zealand

This collection first published in Penguin Books 1982
Reprinted 1984
This collection copyright © Spare Ribs Ltd, 1982
Copyright in each contribution is held by its contributor
All rights reserved

Printed and bound in Great Britain by
Cox & Wyman Ltd, Reading
Set in Monophoto Plantin

Acknowledgements

Spare Rib wish to thank all contributors for permission to reprint their material in this collection. We have made every attempt to contact contributors, but in some cases were regrettably unable to do so.

Contents

Introduction

Rereading seventy-seven copies of *Spare Rib* magazine, from the first issue to the December issue of 1978, has been a strange journey back into the past for me. I was unprepared for the replay of experience which the reading provoked. As the memories surfaced they had the vivid quality that old people talk about when they recall childhood; they evoked feelings more far-reaching than reading old letters and more disturbing than nostalgia. I lived again the four years when I worked on *Spare Rib*. I remembered my first feminist involvement in the early seventies as a time which felt like being reborn in slow stages, and I relived anguish, bitterness, embarrassment, exhilaration, determination and hope. The emotions faded as I began to see a structure for ordering the mass of material, of articles, news reports and reviews, out of which to select for this anthology. I have chosen themes to reflect, as far as possible, the issues brought into focus by the women's movement during the decade, although often the divisions seemed false, as the areas constantly flowed into one another.

Spare Rib was begun because of the impetus of the women's liberation movement, but it was also a daughter of the underground press. It was a product of the counter-culture and a reaction against it. The newspapers and magazines that sprouted up as part of the youth culture of the sixties included *IT*, *OZ* and *Frendz*, all based in London. Their production was made possible by the technical development of offset litho printing, which did not entail expensive metal blocks for photo and type. Offset litho also meant that designers had more free play in layout. Colour could spread over margins, pictures could be stuck down at odd angles, and the page could be assembled so that print and colour superimposed upon each other, the psychedelic result resplendent with the excitement of experimenting with symbols, words and technique.

The visual effect of *OZ* magazine especially was often spectacular, like a cubist painting done by a surrealist, an attempt to deny the dimensions of the flat page, not by the single viewpoint realism of a photograph, but by simultaneously representing as many different perspectives as possible. It was a graphic exploration of the youth-culture aesthetic, the expansion of consciousness, affirming the power of the imagination, and posing the validity of subjective experience against establishment values. The underground press offered an alternative outlet, a more authentic voice for the concerns and mood of the youth movement than the mass media.

The editorial content was eclectic, covering ecology, sexuality, communal living, drugs, music, Third World politics, food, health, mysticism, psychology amongst others. Germaine Greer described the freewheeling inclinations and interests of the underground in the July issue of *OZ* in 1969: 'The political character of the underground is still amorphous, because it is principally a clamour for freedom to move, to test alternative forms of existence to find if they were practicable, and if they were more gratifying, more creative, more positive, than mere endurance under the system.'

These aspirations were given shape in the music of the sixties, which drew on a host of sources: folk, blues, soul, jazz, country and western, rock and roll. The music, at small events, or combined with 'happenings', or at enormous festivals which drew thousands of young people together, integrated the counter-culture more than any other single element, and also revealed its emphasis. The cultural radicalism had energy and vision but it was also a dream world, dependent on the prosperous, consumerist society it criticized. A young woman interviewed in *Spare Rib* No. 4 said that, on looking back, she felt betrayed: 'At first, the alternative way of life was great, back in the days of flower power, but when the initial enthusiasm wore off, most people didn't make the effort needed to actually plan and work for an alternative society.'

But the disintegration had begun earlier, partly because the rhetoric of free love and dope was legally unacceptable. These two were twin births – the sexual and the spiritual – of the counter-culture's reaction against repression of libido. Mind-expanding drugs, as the means for heightened spiritual awareness which would release creative potential and radicalize the person, became 'the politics of ecstasy'. However, of course, the drugs were illegal and those who took them were subject to criminal law.

The flaunting of a defiant sexuality also provoked legal prosecution. *IT* (*International Times*) was taken to court for publishing small ads for homosexuals, despite the legalization of homosexuality between 'consenting adults in private'. Police seized *OZ* magazine's 'School Kids'

Issue', produced by a guest editorial team of twenty young people. The charge brought, not against the school kids, but the three *OZ* editors, was the first time the Obscene Publications Act, 1959, was combined with a moral conspiracy charge. The three were convicted and given jail sentences. During the trial, the prosecuting barrister accused the community of which the magazine was a part of being without love. Richard Neville responded that, on the contrary, *OZ* was against the guilt and obsession of repressed sexuality and that '*OZ* was trying to redefine love, to broaden it, extend it and revitalize it, so it could be a force of release and not one of entrapment'.

The irony of this was that, while this may have been true for men, it was rarely the case for women. The underground press used sex-objectifying images which had developed from being fairly romantic to stridently sadistic. The women who worked on its magazines and newspapers served the men and did the office and production work rather than any editorial work. After a time on *OZ* I had worked for the defence in the *OZ* trial, and the cover of that issue was a montage of pictures of a naked woman in erotic display. In November 1971, three months after the trial, I went to the women's liberation demonstration outside the Albert Hall, the second against the Miss World competition, and was beginning to feel contradictions exploding inside my head. One of the banners read, 'Stop Miss World we want to get off', and Gay Liberation did a street show, with people dressed up as 'Miss Laid' and 'Miss Used'.

By the end of the sixties there had been a change in the underground press itself. Many of the journals were struggling to survive financially. The alternative-lifestyle communities had begun to shrink and retreat, and newer, more politically based activity had developed. Release, originally organized in Notting Hill, London, to assist people on drug busts, had become more like a community law centre, helping on a wide variety of issues, including the rights of squatters. In 1968 the Claimants' Union had started up in Birmingham and subsequently spread throughout the country. The gay liberation and the women's liberation movements had formed. By January 1972 the women in Gay Liberation had broken away to form their own autonomous gay movement. The alternative newspaper *INK*, which had been planned as a 'bridge between the underground and the straight press' by some of the people associated with *OZ* magazine and others in 1970, had shifted from this liberal position. Its new perspective was to serve as a 'national liberation paper' and it was run by an editorial collective. Its politics were on the homefront, linked to different radical groups, and devoting whole issues to subjects such as Ireland, or romantic love.

There was a strong international element to the underground, and copies of the radical American press arrived regularly at the *OZ* office. One day *RAT* had appeared, transformed into *Liberation*, and I read that women had taken over the running of the newspaper as a protest gesture against male supremacy. These women were no longer willing to serve or to remain appendages to men. Feelers began to tendril their way round my imagination and I wondered whether such an action could happen in Britain. Then Michelene Wandor, who was poetry editor on *Time Out* magazine, suggested to a friend, Louise Ferrier, who had helped on *OZ*, *INK* and the *OZ* trial, that we call a meeting of women who worked in the underground press.

The first meeting was held in December 1971 and about fifty women came, including women from *Time Out* (which had started a news section in competition with *INK*). Some of the women did work on editorial, but the majority did not. The main impression that has stayed in my mind is of women voicing the other side of sexual permissiveness, talking of pain and anxiety about abortions, the problems of obtaining an abortion earlier in the sixties, and in one case of a woman having gone through pregnancy as a teenager only to see the child adopted. The discussion about work took second place to the one about sexuality. So much of our lives had been concealed from each other, it was as if we had been strangers. Other impressions were the way the room seemed to swirl with emotion so long suppressed and that I was frightened. After everyone left, Louise and I couldn't sleep and sat up for hours feeling terribly shaken, nervous and near hysteria, clinging to each other every now and then for reassurance.

The meetings continued and I met Rosie Boycott who worked on the Notting Hill newspaper *Frendz*. At the third meeting we suggested the idea of producing an alternative magazine for women.

This was prompted by all we had learned on the underground press, which included the notion that self-organizing was possible, as well as familiarity with the mechanics of production and distribution. Rosie had some journalistic experience on *Frendz*, while my editorial experience was limited to research and helping on layout. Different groups forming the London Women's Liberation Workshop at the time were taking turns to produce the newspaper *Shrew*, but we had not found it easy to obtain copies. Three issues of the *Women's Newspaper* had also been published, although we had not heard of it then. We wanted to produce something which would reach out to women and which would also use and test our own capabilities.

We held two meetings shortly after that to discuss the idea. Lots of women came with advice and suggestions. Rosie and I set off the next week to see a distributor and rashly committed ourselves to producing the first issue six months hence, in June 1972 (which we did). We stencilled off a questionnaire to find out what other women wanted, and handed it out at a conference organized by *Time Out* and The Other Cinema at the Roundhouse on 'Repression and Responsibility in the Media' in February 1972. Women suddenly disrupted the conference in the early afternoon, parading with placards, one of which read, 'With brothers like these who needs chauvinists'. They took over the microphones and assembled on the stage to protest against the way the conference ignored discrimination against women, the sexism of the alternative press and the structure of the conference itself. I was confused but crept out of my seat to join them.

We raised a fairly small sum, £2,000 (which we nevertheless hoped would cover costs until sales money began to come in), from various sympathetic individuals who were probably worried about our lack of editorial experience and supported our enthusiasm more than anything else. By this time, *INK* had collapsed because of economic difficulties, and the whole idea of national press alternatives had dissolved like the 'Day the Music Died'. We formed a limited company for *Spare Rib* and allocated shares.

The suggestion to call the magazine *Spare Rib* was originally a joke but it stuck. Kate Hepburn designed the logo and the layout grid. When *Spare Rib* started Kate did the artwork with Sally Doust, who had been art editor for *Vogue* magazine in Australia when I worked there as secretary/production assistant. Marion Fudger came to do the advertising and Rose Ades production. Rosie Parker visited the office after reading about *Spare Rib* in the *Guardian* and in a short time became a contributing editor. We worked as a hierarchy initially because Rosie Boycott and I were the only ones with experience of magazines. This gradually broke down as everyone learned more and as ideas about collective organization from the women's movement filtered through to us. Rosie Boycott and I were criticized by the others for being so competitive with each other that we did not give anyone else a chance to talk or to discuss the content of the magazine democratically.

By the end of 1973 the magazine was produced collectively. This meant that the office work was shared on a rota system, with each woman in turn taking the responsibility for a day. Different aspects of the work were still particular responsibilities, but the editorial and design were discussed at collective meetings and everyone learned to do their own paste-up for articles, co-ordinating with the designer. We shared tasks like cleaning the office as well as the editorial work. We also tried to recognize individual skills and interests, and the collective gave women a chance to concentrate on work they found most rewarding.

I was aware of a change in the political atmosphere around the time of starting *Spare Rib*, which seemed to be one of coming down to earth. This was reflected in how we approached *Spare Rib*'s design and production. Instead of the irregular, anarchic production of *OZ* which had been published according to people's time and energy, we aimed to produce a magazine on a regular, monthly basis. This was in response to the demands of the distributor, the way commercial women's magazines are published, and because we felt a need to prove that we could be professional and efficient. This revealed our lack of confidence. It was also to do with the way the relaxed optimism of the sixties had faded and the fact that being 'cool' and 'laid back' had existed for the men, but not for the women who had handled the nitty-gritty work in the underground. The layout of the magazine was meant to be calmer, clearer and easier to read. We felt it had to be grounded in a style which would reflect the manner in which we were redefining ourselves as women. Instead of seeing ourselves in a world set apart, we were beginning to connect with the lives of other women. It was part of a broadening out of our political awareness. The Night Cleaners Campaign had started in 1970 – 'It was the first time, in London at least, that women's liberation became actively involved in a struggle among working women to organize themselves'* – and women went out to leaflet office buildings after all the office workers had gone home, when the women cleaners started work.

When Rosie Boycott and I planned the original questionnaire, it was in candlelight with candle grease dripping over the typewriter, because of the miners' strike. We were vulnerable to pressure from all sides because we were so unsure. Looking back over our notes for the original questionnaire, I find them direct and simply put. But when we came to type them up for the stencil, we inserted coy copy, stilted phrases and advertising jargon. This extended to the magazine itself. Until one contributor, Lilian Roxon, pointed out the omission, we did not even preface articles with introductions.

After the first three issues of *Spare Rib* there was a row with some men we knew who thought we should address the magazine to them as well as to women. This divided our loyalties, and when we reasserted ourselves as women producing a magazine for women, a new relationship began to develop amongst us. My feelings towards other women began to take on the deep significance I had previously recog-

* Sally Alexander, 'The Night Cleaners', *Red Rag* No.6.

nized only in relationships with men. My heterosexual orientation remained but the depth of my feelings towards the women with whom I worked each day were as powerful as the emotions of sexual love.

Spare Rib was beset with economic crises. Not relying on advertising revenue freed the magazine workers from the subtle self-censorship which occurs in commercial women's magazines and allowed for more editorial independence, but it also meant survival depended on sales. The magazine was baled out of crises by generous donors and also by benefits we organized to which many people came and through which we felt the women's movement as a supportive presence. The first music benefit was at the Marquee, London, in June 1974. That night I was aware of a warmth and creativity, like the feelings at similar events in the sixties, but this time I felt it included my whole being. It did not entail the earlier distortion and caricaturing of the self.

When *Spare Rib* began, we saw it as an activity and consciousness-raising process combined. We were a bit prickly and oversensitive about how much there was to learn, but the advantage of that position was that we did not set ourselves up as feminists superior to readers. From the beginning we invited contributions from readers, including women not active in the women's movement, and, as time went on, we developed this, seeing the magazine in a two-way role, sifting information and ideas and continually making alterations according to response. In this way the style and the content of *Spare Rib* changed. We had originally decided to publish a magazine rather than a newspaper since we thought women would find that more approachable. We had to think how and why *Spare Rib* would be different from other women's magazines. At that time *Nova* (now defunct) was the newest magazine on the market. It had a reputation as the women's magazine read by men, and added current affairs to the usual fashion, food and homemaking of the monthly magazines. But it carried no alternative values, and since the underground culture had been about a new way of being, it was remote to us. We were also consumers, but we thought our manner of consumption was different. We decided to incorporate the traditional elements of women's magazines into *Spare Rib*, but to express them in other ways. The first issue had a double-page spread on jeans, with photos of fat, thin, tall and short people, none of whom were models. Friends did cookery columns from their own recipes, often emphasizing cheapness. We had cosmetic columns about alternatives, such as cucumber cleanser. We were still concerned with beauty, although we also tried to pan it and to examine it. A regular 'Looks' column once featured a man taken to a hairdresser, given a facial and made up by a beautician (but its lampooning was taken seriously by some readers); another explored the women characters' obsessive preoccupation with appearance in Jean Rhys's novels. There was a man's page, not only to make a satirical comment on the tokenism of women's pages in newspapers, but because we wanted men to write exploring their feelings. There was a page for children and a demystifying do-it-yourself column, 'Spare Parts', on technical topics such as changing electric plugs, car maintenance, shoe repairs and printing. These interests were dropped over the first two to three years.

A more articulate feminist editorial content emerged from the early *Spare Rib* format, which had been a jumble of articles from established women journalists and novelists, feminists and women learning to write for the first time. The early photos and illustrations often presented women with controlled, passive faces, or echoed titillating, clinical or anti-women attitudes, and this also changed as the women's movement grew, as *Spare Rib* became more identified as a part of it, and as more feminist photographers and illustrators appeared.

The women's magazines from the big publishing houses strike me now as carrying contradictory messages in a similar way to the first issues of *Spare Rib*, although it has never had the bulk of their advertising, nor is it published for profit. Their feature content both reflects and informs social awareness of changes in women's legal and economic position through the seventies. Previously taboo subjects like abortion or sexuality are now included. Questions such as how to combine childcare and work, accepting infertility, male fear of women's independence, the legal rights of women cohabitees, 'mature students', are discussed. But they are also accompanied by both editorial and advertising content which undermine the stance of these topics and conjure up a world where women's consciousness is unchanging. Their political comment is confined to views expressed in reviews, to the occasional interview with a woman politician, or to warnings about where it may be dangerous to travel on holiday. Although some columnists are more feminist, many of the magazines still have men columnists propounding views about the 'real' woman, who does not fuss her pretty head with ideas, who is mystified in her 'feminine glory'; or there are health columns written by doctors who perpetuate paternalistic attitudes. Articles on women and work tend to concentrate on the ability of the exceptional woman to succeed in a career despite discrimination, and are aimed at the middle-class rather than the working-class woman. Cosmetics and underwear are advertised as merchandise which women can buy to discover and express their essence, their individuality, their real selves. Occasionally there is a hint of masochism. We used to joke that the only advertisements showing women as active were those for sanitary protection, but now there is a fashion market for clothes like jumpsuits to jog in, and tampons have become 'the key to freedom'.

To reflect the diversity of *Spare Rib*'s content over the years would have taken an anthology twice as long as this one. Overall, I have chosen articles to illustrate both the development of ideas in the women's movement and the development of *Spare Rib*. There are inevitable gaps. There are many campaigns, arguments about strategies and aims, and debates about theory which are not included and there are specific areas of interest, such as religion, or anthropology or community organizing which have had to be left out. I have aimed for a balance within sections between articles which describe personal experience, articles which give a feminist analysis and articles which show how women have organized for change. In these areas there are historical examples, although most of the selection is from the seventies, a past so recent it feels part of the continuing present. The emphasis is on first-hand accounts, written by the women involved rather than by journalists observing events from the outside. This is where *Spare Rib* is a part of a broad feminist concern to find forms by which women can communicate perceptions to oppose the ideology of oppression, of race, class or sex. The longest section is on paid work, since this is the area most consistently covered by *Spare Rib*, demonstrating how basic and important a place it holds in women's lives. Many sections illustrate the way events have overtaken and modified a number of the early demands of the women's movement. Whereas at first it seemed possible for demands on the state and for self-organizing to exist side by side, to use and to learn from each approach, activities have been curtailed or changed direction because of the economic crisis, government policy and cuts in public spending, but the anthology shows that these changes have not been limited to defensive action. Most of the articles are about women living in Britain. There are some from outside Britain which show how local conditions produce particular insights and methods of organizing, and of international similarities and differences. The perspective, of some sections especially, is peculiar to the seventies without losing relevance now – for instance, the health section concentrates on reproduction although the health movement had a broader scope by the end of the decade. The different writings in this anthology show that there is an intricacy and range to women's experience, a resilience of spirit despite the harshest of lives, capacities for courage, love, intellect and humour and for resistance and action.

None of the articles has been altered from the original published but some have been cut for length, or excerpts chosen for quotes and if so it is indicated by. . . . A group on the *Spare Rib* collective revised the anthology so that the final choice is the result of our collaboration. I'd like to thank Ruthie Petrie for all the work she put into co-ordinating at each stage and for her support.

I would also like to thank Barbara Charles for suggesting some changes in placement, Tina Reid who helped to edit my long introductions, and Julia Vellacott who was editor at Penguin when the work began. Thanks too to many people for encouragement and understanding, including Caroline Bond, Lee Comer, Rosie Graham, Stef Pixner and Chris Rawlence particularly over the introductions, and to Sian Dodderidge, Alison Fell, Sarah Perrigo, Rachel Peto and Sheila Rowbotham.

MARSHA ROWE, *Leeds*

NOTE

The selection of articles from *Spare Rib* 1 to 77 was made by Marsha Rowe, and the selection from issues 78 to 100 was later made by four members of the present *Spare Rib* collective: Susan Hemmings, Sue O'Sullivan, Ruthie Petrie and Ruth Wallsgrove.

1 IMAGE

In the imagery of everyday life – films, television, radio, newspapers, magazines, books – women are depicted as inferior to men. Produced within a male-dominated culture, these images confine women to stereotyped roles, such as the mother who nurtures, the wife who nags, the object of male desire, or the jealous, overbearing mother-in-law. Although there have been some breakthroughs during the last ten years, these are exceptions and the same overall impression remains. Such images make up the pictorial language of how we are seen in society and how we see ourselves.

To overcome women's subordinate position, it is just as necessary to understand and to change these images as it is to change the outward circumstances of women's lives. This is complicated by the way our society stresses sexual difference, attaching particular value to characteristics which are supposedly either feminine or masculine. We connect certain images with certain ideas and feelings. Ruth Wallsgrove in *SR.72* illustrated a spectrum of her self-images. She described how she associated romance and being sexually attractive with the feminine stereotype: 'I imagine myself smaller, softened and rounded, graceful.' But she had an opposite picture when she imagined herself as capable and brave, one which was not concerned with passive appearance. It emphasized function over appearance and could be read as more 'masculine' – she saw herself 'admired not for how I *look* but for what I *do*'. The contradictions in these images, between 'doing' and 'being', the 'masculine' and the 'feminine', meant that when she came to describe her day-to-day self, trying to combine and express both qualities, her feelings became ambiguous. She said: 'I hope I look tough and friendly: I'm afraid I look rather large and clumsy.' She began to explore a space which women are not supposed to occupy because it stretches the frontiers of the 'feminine' and goes into the world of 'masculine' assertiveness and independence. It is easy to feel we have become too big for our boots rather than gaining confidence, since we are susceptible too to the caricatured social image given to feminism. This caricature both allays the fear feminism arouses and attempts to contain the threat it poses to established patterns.

When we think of our self-image, we also include our gestures and the way we talk. Our consciousness of ourselves and of others is affected by our class background and by the particular culture we inherit. Women have begun to explore these dimensions of image, in order to see how the experience of class or race is communicated. This means we can look at women's role in reproducing these images and challenge aspects which are oppressive. In one issue of *Spare Rib* a woman talked about the competitiveness of her academic education. This brought a continual pressure to prove one's personal superiority over others: 'Everybody grades each other, there's a combination of arrogance and self-confidence, and talking about other people in the most clever terms possible by which you also subtly put people down.' She recognized that her middle-class family life had prepared her for this in the way it maintained aloof relationships: 'Talk at my parents' home had to be interesting, or civilized, or important. Now I talk more about what I would have considered either boring or slightly embarrassing details, which I was always suppressing' (*SR.30*). The images of women show the tangible connection between our imagination and the world outside ourselves, and the new images we produce represent the changes we experience and hope for. A feminist photographer, Jo Spence, put it this way: 'What we need to do with our own pictures and with our own self-image if you like is to shift the emphasis back to a point where we understand that everything we do as women has a validity – not just the perfect moments' (*SR.68*).

SR.64, November 1977

A Weight Off My Head

KAREN DURBIN

Excerpts from a diary:

27 August. I'm going to get my hair cut off. I'm tired of it. Have to find a good place that won't leave me feeling miserable.

31 August. Spent four pounds and two hours at one of the fanciest hairdressers in London yesterday and came out looking like a suburban matron, circa 1962. Awful. Bought some clippers and finished the job myself. It now looks properly boyish. I'm at last glad I got it cut . . . Spirits have risen considerably . . . I really feel like working again. Amazing what a new head will do for a woman.

4 September. This hair-cutting business means something. Several things, probably, none of which I've been willing to think about. But here goes. Images of shorn heads fill my mind – and, oddly, propel me to the bathroom to take a little more off. The French girls whose heads were shaved in punishment for sleeping with German soldiers. Lavinia in *Titus Andronicus* after she's been raped and mutilated. Help. What's going on here? It feels sexless to have so little hair. And defiant. As if I'm thumbing my nose at the whole idea of trying to be sexy. It also feels satisfyingly unserious. Motives? Well, I wanted to . . . But. Withdrawing. Retreating. Making declarations to myself, to R. Punishing myself and him? Oh, but it does feel good. Parting with vanity. End of earth mama/drug queen era. Simpler and not so heavy to look like this. I'm travelling light.

It was an eventful summer. A long, complicated love affair came unravelled, leaving me completely on my own for the first time in several years. I quit my secure, well-paid government job to take a chance at the insecure, badly paid hustle of freelance writing. And I got my hair cut off.

You mightn't think the third item on the list deserves to be up there with the other two, but it does. Hair is important, a potent symbol dating back to (and doubtless well beyond) the Samson myth. A woman I know said that when she cuts her husband's hair, he gets nervous.

'He likes the way I cut it,' she said, 'but it's a castration thing. It freaks him out a little every time.'

Hair is a symbol of sexuality. Among the more austere sects of Orthodox Jews, a married woman must wear a wig to cover her hair when she appears in public. To go bareheaded would be an insult to her husband, a display of wantonness.

The heroine of Ibsen's play *Hedda Gabler* is considered to be one of the most powerful and difficult roles for an actress to play. Hedda is a dynamo, larger than life, who rages against the stifling bourgeois world of her marriage. But a motif that runs through the play is Hedda's thin hair and her anger at its thinness. It infuriates her that Thea Elvsted, the soft, gentle little lady who competes with her for the affections of a poet-lover, has thick, luxuriant hair. In the play, Thea is the essential female. Hedda, for all her immense force of character, is a sexless creature – stormy and ambitious, more interested in making an impact on the world than in making love.

Finally, take a look at the last fifteen years. I reached puberty in the America of the late 1950s, the era of the post-war togetherness, when the family was glorified out of all proportion, when sex roles were rigidly defined and sex itself was suppressed. The boys I dated had crew-cuts and 'flat-tops'; they came as close to being bald as they could without shaving their heads. The girls I knew had short, neat haircuts or, if their hair was long, carefully set, shoulder-length pageboys. (Manufacturers got rich off hair spray in the fifties the way they're getting rich off vaginal deodorants now.)

We were, of course, Good Girls and Nice Boys, well-behaved, middle-class children, the future leaders of our country. The Bad Boys and Bad Girls had more hair. The boys had duck's ass Elvis cuts, well greased, with a teardrop curl in the front. The girls looked like Jane Russell or Marilyn Monroe – long, looser hair than ours, with slightly frowsy waves falling over one eye. The difference between our styles was one of sex. Bad Boys and Bad Girls were frankly sexy, with their greasy curls and frowsy, flopping waves. We knew about them: they Did It, at drive-in movies, in parked cars. They were going to go blind some day, and they weren't going to be the future leaders of their country.

Then came the sixties, and the previous decade's hard shell of sexual myths cracked wide open. The line between good girls and bad girls began to blur. We were all on the Pill by the middle of the decade. Boys stopped looking like Marine sergeants and started looking like the Beatles. Political protest marches filled the streets, the women's movement erupted, and sex roles started breaking down. Through it all was this amazing sprouting – hair seemed to grow on everybody under thirty. The phrase 'long-hair' in America no longer meant artistic foreigners who played Beethoven, it meant *kids*. We were like so many green weeds, shooting up through the cracks in the concrete. At first, the change was moderate. Girls wore long, smooth, straight hair, ironing it for hours, if necessary. It looked more natural than the elaborate hairdos of the fifties, but if you weren't blessed with long, smooth, straight hair, you had to work at it. Boys' hair remained cautiously Beatle-length, which wasn't so static, since the Beatles appeared on every new album cover with another inch of hair.

By the end of the decade, the vanguard types who started out shaggy had gone into Total Freak. Afros, Isros, great tumbling, tangled clouds of hair emanated from their heads. And the style had filtered back to the straight world. Stockbrokers got their new long locks 'shaped' at special unisex barbers. Young construction workers showed three inches of curl below the edges of their hardhats. It was a very hairy time, memorialized in a musical that's still running in the West End. A restrictive sexual morality had given way to something looser, easier, more fun, and we wore the symbol of the change on our heads.

For women, especially, it was as if we were announcing our sexuality. I remember vividly when I stopped setting my long hair. I'd gone to the country with some friends, and we got caught Saturday afternoon in a summer shower. For me, that meant waist-length instant frizz. I was about to hide the mess in a scarf when our host, a photographer, asked if he could take some pictures of it. He put me in front of bright lights, sat me on rocks out in the sun, generally made me feel like Verouschka. 'You've got wonderful hair,' he kept rhapsodizing. 'God, it does so many things.' My lover looked on, grinning. We'd had a running battle for six months over the issue of my 'ugly' hair, and now he'd found an ally.

I wore my hair like that for almost four years. It was, as they say, my most distinctive feature. I never did think it was pretty, just wild and woolly. Earth mama/drug queen. It became a litmus test: uptight people didn't like it, hang-loose hippies did. My lover loved it; he found it sexy. My mother hated it. She probably found it sexy, too. I found it inconvenient. It had a way of getting caught in car doors and other people's coat buttons. It took an hour to wash and brush and a half-day to dry. It got in my eyes when I rode my bicycle.

I put up with it, anyway. My only real doubts about it had to do with feminism. I was active in the women's movement, and it always struck me funny to go to a meeting and see all us activist women, in our jeans and teeshirts and sturdy boots, talking about the hassles of being sex objects, and yet, with no more than one or two exceptions at every gathering, we all had outrageous heads of hair. Impractical, inconvenient, downright counter-revolutionary. A good thing we weren't guerrilla fighters in Bolivia. Two yards into the jungle, and we'd all have been hopelessly tangled up in the underbrush.

To be fair, I don't think it was simply vanity. We were making a statement with all that hair. That we weren't nice girls any more. That we were wild and woolly and out of control. The movement in America has been dominated largely by middle-class women, and we had myths to break.

Fay McTavish, *SR.56*, March 1977

However, change is in the wind. Very short hair is beginning to look attractive again, on women (although I don't ever want to see another crew-cut again, on man or woman, as long as I live). Our eyes have probably been prepared for this by the advent of the shag. The shag, which became popular in New York a year or so ago, was the definitive compromise haircut, half-long, half-short. Three men I knew turned up in as many weeks then with suspiciously short hair, not very short, but they didn't look freaky any more. Oh, my god, I thought. Here it is, the backlash. The fifties all over again. Nixon. Apathy. Good girls. Bad girls. And all the rest of that dreck.

'No, man, that's not it,' said one newly shorn friend. 'It's just that all that hair was getting to be a drag to take care of. This is easier.' I watched him for signs of incipient fascism, but there haven't been any. He goes on being an idealistic radical lawyer for lost causes. Whew.

It may just be that we've made our point, and we don't need to make it any longer. Short hair *is* easier to live with, and it feels as natural and appropriate to my way of life as blue jeans and comfortable shoes. But apart from the issue of announcing one's freedom from convention, there's the not-so-simple matter of sex. And since I'm human (and heterosexual) as well as feminist, I can't pretend it's not important to me to know that I can attract men who attract me. At the same time I enjoyed the freedom from all those hours of washing and untangling and drying. I couldn't help wondering if I'd be sexless without my plumage.

Fortunately, these questions have a way of answering themselves. There was this party, see, where I met this man . . . He says I look like a pineapple when I wake up in the morning with my three inches of hair standing up in spikes. But it's OK. Turns out he likes pineapple.

SR.18, December 1973

Marilyn Monroe

MARGARET WALTERS

. . . Her death has been called a Hollywood tragedy, an American tragedy, even a tragedy of civilization. I think it's a *feminine* tragedy. Her life is frightening to women simply because she's so familiar to us; she sums up all the contradictions of a particular feminine stereotype. She reminds us of the death wish that's hidden in our narcissism, the dark other face of glamour.

In her public image Marilyn is everything we're told we want to be; in her private life she's everything we fear we probably are.

SR.3, September 1972

Images of Janis Joplin

MARGARET WALTERS

. . . One of the most exciting things about Janis was the way she broke through the conventional feminine image. She was singing in the six-ties, when women were only beginning to come together and question their possibilities. At a time when most women performers were still neat, composed, careful of their looks, Janis had the courage to appear as she was – spotty, pudgy, haggard – and beautiful. She's beautiful because her face is always changing, because it's so expressive, because she's able to forget it, and herself, in the music. She enjoyed the fact that she offended all the nicely brought up, properly feminine girls, in their panty girdles and make-up: 'That's the way I was raised, man, I know exactly what's on those bitches' minds, they don't like me, man.' She didn't want to be passively pretty, so she often acted hard and butch; she could be hostile to other women because, I think, she feared and hated her own 'femininity'. She had affairs with women, but if Peggy Caserta* is telling anything like the truth, they seem to have repeated the careless, exploitative power games of straight sex. Everything in the rock world tended to isolate her from other women; one of the saddest things about her life is that she never really realized how much her music meant to other women, how much she illuminated our lives.

Watching her on film, I'm struck by things I didn't see so clearly back in the sixties. Janis constantly shifts – between songs, almost between bars – from one conventional feminine role to another. One moment she dances gaily, a small girl – wilful, mischievous – trying to charm the grown-ups in her borrowed finery. The next moment she's a honky-tonk lady, tough, generous, comforting; everybody's 'sweet-talkin' sweet-lovin' momma bear'. In yet another mood she comes on like a cheap hooker, hips swaying, tongue between her lips. She hustles, provokes, does a sexy, knowing rap to introduce a song: 'Honey, if you've had your eye on a piece of talent and that chick down the road is getting all the action, then you know what you gotta do – *Try*, just a little bit harder.' Then she ends the set with an act that's as aggres-sively macho as Mick Jagger, stomping round the stage, playing con-temptuously with the mike, kicking the sound into silence. Like the rest of us, Janis was all those things – and none of them. Isolated as she was, living in a man's world, there was no way she could get beyond them, find out what else she could be.

* Peggy Caserta, *Going Down with Janis*.

But seeing her like that, I started to hear her blues rather differently. Like the Black blues singers she admired, Janis had the gift of making the most banal songs sound intensely personal. All her songs, and not just the ones she actually wrote, came across with the kick of auto-biography. They all work the same ground, over and over again: Women is Losers, A Woman Left Lonely, Little Girl Blue, Cry Baby, I Need a Man to Love. She stays within the familiar circle of blues complaint; she sings about loneliness, the endless search for a good man, who's bound to do you wrong in the end. She protests, endlessly, the unfairness of love, of life, of being a woman. But she can use even a commonplace song to feel her way into her most disturbing emotions. She takes Ma Rainey's great blues song – 'Love is draggin' me down/ Just like a ball and chain' – and plays with it, broods on it, stretches it out and slows it down, until it's a complex musical drama that focuses and explores her own pain and anger, and her sense of being trapped, in the end, by her own emotions.

And just sometimes, she seems to dig way beneath the old theme of sexual disappointment and frustration, to the most primitive layers of feeling. Sometimes, it's as if she manages to draw on, and voice some primary, primal depression; she's like a child screaming to be filled, to be loved, to be consoled, a child terrified of its own impossible de-mands, its own rage.

> I once had a daddy,
> He said he'd give me everything in sight,
> Yes he did.
> So I said, hon, I want the sun,
> And the stars out of the night.
> Come on, give it to me, baby,
> And I want it right now.
> (Joplin, 'Turtle Blues')

Her songs are disturbing, sometimes, because she does tap some depth of pain and anger that it's almost impossible to confront, in her, in oneself. Janis never escapes from the frightening and predictable circle of feminine suffering and anger. She's 'buried alive in the blues', trapped in the painful contradictions of being a woman, unable to escape because she's fighting alone. But she expresses, communicates, clarifies a pain that most of us know. . .

SR.37, July 1975

Being Jewish: Anti-Semitism and Jewish Women

ROZSIKA PARKER

... You learn that you suffer and are persecuted for being called 'The Chosen People' – you feel guilty at the arrogant superiority that implies and at the same time guilty for not living up to the name.

Michelene Wandor ascribes the guilt to 'the lack of geographical and political roots – it produces all sorts of things and I think guilt is a mixture of knowing you can't be fully Jewish because you don't quite know what it is, or if you know what it is, you can rarely be it.'

Another arena of guilt is in relation to the suffering of your parents: 'Their childhood and their suffering, the difficulties they had in going to medical school, how they had to work their way through anti-Semitism. I felt there was nothing I could do,' says Sheila Y, 'which would be as good as what they had done because I hadn't had to overcome anything.'

And yet so much is expected of you. You have to prove that your parents' suffering was worthwhile. Perhaps this creates the excessively self-sacrificing behaviour parodied in the stereotype of 'The Jewish Mother'. Some of us were afraid of behaving like Jewish Mothers. Others were afraid of contributing to the stereotype rather than dissecting it, because we had experienced our Jewish mothers as 'Jewish Mothers' who intimate that all their suffering on our behalf would be justified if only we would live happily ever after with Mr Jewish Right and give them all the grandchildren they deserve. But as Gail says, 'The stereotype bears about as much relation to the majority of Jewish women as the mother-in-law jokes bear to most mother-in-laws.' It's therefore important to understand the precise history of the Jewish family and women's changing place within it...

SR.79, February 1979

What Katy Didn't Do

CAMILLA NIGHTINGALE

Many women I know remember the hunt for suitable heroines to identify with. We longed for books about women pilots, women divers, women explorers, climbers and space travellers, or even about girls who were unrepentantly naughty and rebellious. It wasn't just that we couldn't identify with boys in stories, we also wanted to be reassured that we were not to be excluded from the world of action. We ended up reading Biggles and William, and like other girls, we soon got the message that the people who have the adventures and scope to determine the course of their own lives, are men.

. . . Boys' adventures take place in all-male societies of motor-racing circuits, the Services, cargo boats. The selection I looked at were about smuggling, rallying, motor racing and trapping. The stories roved all over Europe, America, northern Canada, and the China Seas. Extraordinary feats of physical endurance and skill were involved and the resources of the hero were stretched to the limit. One thing common to them all was the hero's high degree of technical competence in his particular field – the technicalities of motor cars, explosives or traps were all described in detail, and the adventures, though hair-raising enough to be satisfying, were based on a firm grasp of real life.

Books especially for girls are set in predominantly female societies like schools, pony clubs, ballet school, and among secretaries, nurses or air hostesses. Adventures are reduced to a kind of social extravaganza. In a school setting this could be the achievement of Angela Brazil's 'sunshine of popularity', by the proper exercise of feminine qualities. In the more sophisticated stories for older girls the aims are social success in the adult world and the capture of the inevitable husband. Lorna Hill has written a whole string of books about different girls at Sadlers Wells. Dance, however, plays a minor part in the stories, which are concerned with the social lives of the characters. There are illustrations of the girls doing various ballet steps, but no real sense is given of the rigorous life a dancer leads, and the technical detail, so emphasized in boys' books is studiously avoided. The difficulties are entirely in adapting to the rarefied world of balletomanes. Other 'girls only' books describe the girls overcoming their desires for adventure and feelings of rebellion (described as their capriciousness and wilfulness) and transforming them into acceptable feminine qualities like inner strength and imagination. Remember Jo in *Little Women*, and Katy of *What Katy Did*. Another common plot tells how the girl heroine overcomes the motiveless malice of another girl. These female Iagos appear surprisingly frequently, and encourage the belief subscribed to by women themselves, that there is a suspect quality in all women.

Current booklists promoted by publishers as 'for girls' show a preponderance of books about love, dating and romance, with a sideline in problems, like spots, glasses and so on, which interfere with romance.

Dating is a teenage and subteenage preoccupation, and should be considered in children's books, and so should the physical problems which manifest themselves in the teens. However, the implication in these books is that romance is the purpose of a girl's life, and problems exist in so far as they hinder romance. Boys are interested in dating too, but they are not expected to read books about it.

Illustration by S. Van Abbe for *Little Women*

. . . The following quotations are typical:

'A girl confident that with A certificate typing, her ugly mug would not impede her career.' – *Juliet in Publishing*.

Daddy: 'I know it's a bit of a bore, but shorthand typing never comes amiss' – and later –

Julian: 'I think it would be silly for you to give up this job of yours.

Obviously you like it. It's going to get you out and about all over the world and teach you to stand confidently on your own two feet. But maybe in say four years time you might feel that you've got all you can get out of being a ship's officer and that a home of your own might be a good idea?' – *Hester, Ship's Officer*.

Broadly speaking, books for boys extend the child's desire for adventure and involve him closely with the technical aspects of the development of the plot. Girls' books minimize adventure to social play acting and skate over the technicalities of adult life, clouding them in romance. I think that the great popularity of the school story must lie in the fact that the girl heroine is allowed considerable scope for adventure and rebellion against authority. There are no men present, indeed within the terms of reference of the story, men hardly exist, except in the very menial capacity of gardeners and grooms. There is no need therefore to inhibit the girls to maintain a standard of femininity. Even in school stories however, the girl does not rebel for the sake of rebelling, or because she questions the authority imposed upon her. It is always revealed that she was acting to uphold the honour of the school.

. . . The family or group adventure story [books] represent a supposedly balanced view of reality, which the single-sex books manifestly do not, but all this means sexual role playing is more subtle. Girls often play a crucial part in the adventure, but the leader and final decision maker is always a boy. The male and female roles are invariably stereotyped when it comes to physical prowess. Boys and girls of similar ages vary a great deal in physical accomplishment, but it is always the girl who jeopardizes the safety of the gang by falling over a tree root, or by her strength giving out halfway up a rope. And it is always a boy, not another girl, who comes back and rescues her. Emotionally, too, girls are a liability in a group adventure. They may, like Anne in the *Famous Five*, be crybabies who need constant encouragement from the others, or their impulsiveness may thwart the plans of the boy leader, or their extra sensitivity may allow them to sympathize with the other side too much. In all cases, girls become an extra hazard, an old man of the sea for the boys to deal with.

. . . An interesting concession to young girls' rebellion is the tomboy. She appears in the younger age range, when little girls are still unsure about accepting female status, and do many of the same things that little boys do, like playing rough games and climbing trees. Tomboys are allowed to play a prominent part in an adventure, even to take over the leadership for part of the time, to be tough, resourceful and to make decisions. They also openly attack the female role that outside people like parents and relations expect them to play. George in the

Famous Five is openly scornful of the idea that girls are in any way weaker than boys. Nancy in *Swallows and Amazons* fiercely defends a girl's ability and right to do anything a boy can do. Unfortunately the tomboy's scorn for the trappings of femininity extends to girls themselves. George treats Anne in exactly the same way that the boys do, patronizing her weakness, and kindly looking after her. Anne maintains the feminine ideal, while George is considered as a boy. Peggy and Susan in *Swallows and Amazons* spend their time in the galley being good girls, allowing Captain Nancy to have her abberrations. The tomboy seems to be a kind of safety valve for girls who are unsure of their role. She allows free rein to their fantasies of adventure, but at the same time she is sternly contrasted with the real girls. She is allowed no concessions to femaleness, dressing, acting and looking like a boy, and while she herself will not accept the fact she is a girl, she is not totally accepted by the boys. Her world is ultimately unsatisfactory. Perhaps it is better after all to be a real girl.

It is interesting to note that the roles are never reversed the other way . . .

SR.23, May 1974

Round in a Flat World

TESSA WEARE

. . . Everywhere I go, it goes before me, this round full womb. When I sit it nests heavily on my thighs; as I turn my body, my arms brush against it. My skin is unbelievably stretched into this large gourd, this drum, this container. The baby curled inside kicks at my ribs, my pelvis, each side of my body. In about two weeks it will be born.

When I walk into a room of people I see them noticing this protruding part of me first, and me second. The more honest stare at it with fascination as they talk to me, others glance furtively pretending they haven't noticed. Many are uneasy, some even physically withdraw from me.

Meanwhile in the London streets I'm surrounded by advertising hoardings: thin models displayed across their flat surfaces. And women in the streets, their hips encased in tight jeans, hip-hugging skirts. I find myself staring at their flat bellies, unable to imagine that mine once looked like theirs. And the men too: everyone with bones and protruding genitals. I feel out of place.

Sometimes it seems as if I have an invisible seal around my body that both protects me and pushes me apart from everyone else . . . Pregnancy has no place in the sexuality that pervades everything.

Once you are pregnant you are 'obviously' another man's property, and rape – physical or verbal – has so much to do with the threat of impregnating the innocent, the vulnerable, or with punishment for being available – and I'm not. So for a long time I've been free from sexual innuendos, grabs at my tits, attempted pick-ups. Men who walk up to me turn away from my womb with a mixture of guilt, fear and disgust on their faces. Strangely, once I was no longer bombarded with sexist sexual advances, it struck me how in one way they gave me a sense of power, of attractiveness, and more importantly, a sense that I existed.

SR.78, January 1979

Why Not Slip into Something a Little More Comfortable?

LISA TICKNER

Woman's dress, too – how perfectly it describes her condition! . . . from the bonnet string to the paper shoe, she is the hopeless martyr to the inventions of some Parisian imp of fashion. Her tight waist and long, trailing skirts deprive her of all freedom of breath and motion. No wonder man prescribes her sphere. She needs his aid at every turn. He must help her up stairs and down, in the carriage and out, on the horse, up the hill, over the ditch and fence, and thus teach her the poetry of dependence. (Elizabeth Cady Stanton, 1857)

After the relative freedom of the Regency period, Victorian woman found herself again restricted to quite a severe degree by at least three different aspects of her fashionable dress: by the dignity and expansive graciousness of her heavy skirts, and later crinoline, which hampered her movements and slowed her gait; by the very low set sleeve which prevented her from raising her arms; and by the tightly laced corset which assisted the display of an eighteen-inch waist, restricted her lungs, displaced her internal organs, caused her to faint in warm or tiring circumstances, and generally endangered her health.

Fashionable women's clothing had of course been both cumbersome and restricting in the past: no Victorian crinoline was any more ridiculous than the Elizabethan farthingale, or the eighteenth-century panniers it resembled; but the very impracticality of court dress contributed to its ceremonial and hierarchical effect. Far larger numbers of middle-class women, and even cooks and housemaids, were now struggling to survive the day's activities whilst blinkered by their bonnets, trussed up in their corsets, and surrounded by petticoats and whalebone hoops which had to be squeezed through doorways, cautiously manoeuvred up and down staircases, and perched precariously on the edges of armless chairs.

Throughout the nineteenth century the criticisms grew, as women realized that their dress was completely unsuitable for anything but the most limited social role. It was no exaggeration to speak of skirts sweeping the streets. Paxton's specially invented floor cleaners were apparently not required at the Great Exhibition after all – the floors were kept swept and polished by the ladies' trains; and there are many other comments and anecdotes which refer to the dust they raised and the piles of litter left at the kerb by a skirt and train as the wearer stepped into a carriage after a short walk.

The artist G. F. Watts emphasizing the selfishness endemic in fashionable female dress pointed out that it also prevented women from functioning properly. Crinolines and trains were extravagant in form, inconvenient for the wearer and inconsiderate of others. Tight sleeves and gloves made arms and fingers look like rigid sausages, useless for clasping the hand of another in friendship, or for snatching a child suddenly out of danger. But the point was that women were not expected to move quickly or freely, nor to shake hands with vigour, but to combine dignity with delicacy in crinolines and trains which set off the fragility of a narrow waist and tiny hands and feet.

The clothing worn by all the newly fashionable sections of society was so exaggerated that it provoked an almost unique phenomenon: a deliberate, and sporadically organized attempt to reform dress and even to abolish vagaries of fashion itself. Why, as Lady Harberton put it, should it be supposed 'that the male form came perfect from the hands of the Creator, while that of the female needs constant tinkering and screwing into shape to make it presentable'?

Raising these kinds of questions meant taking on a much wider issue than the cut of a sleeve or the length of a hem, and so the movement for dress reform was inevitably and intricately bound up with the development of nineteenth-century feminism, although not always in an entirely predictable manner. To struggle for women's rights – a fight already under way in the 1850s and 1860s – was by definition to reject the whole contemporary concept of femininity, since ladies did not 'fight' for anything. It was also, and almost automatically, to invite the accusation of 'unwomanliness', which was the alleged consequence of the hardening influences of public life.

The 'strong-minded' or 'platform' woman was the Victorian equivalent of the modern media image of the bigoted and bra-burning 'libber'. Both were convenient stereotypes, identikit pictures to which few if any actual people approximated, which served as a warning backed up by the implied threat of social disapproval and even ostracism. Just as the popular contemporary picture of the feminist is fixed at scruffy denims, a generally unkempt and (in media terms) unappetizing appearance, so the Victorian platform woman was illustrated in *Punch* with short hair and dark, severely tailored, masculine clothing.

There are isolated instances of nineteenth-century women, like George Sand and Helen Weber, who were courageous, extrovert, and perhaps desperate enough to adopt for everyday wear a modified version of masculine dress. Nevertheless, it was hardly likely that in the face of social ostracism, a large number of women would suddenly do so. A less dramatic but a more influential decision was that reached by Elizabeth Smith Miller, working long hours in her garden during the spring of 1851:

I became so thoroughly disgusted with the long skirt, that the dissatisfaction, the growth of years, suddenly ripened into the decision that this shackle should no longer be endured. The resolution was at once put into practice. Turkish trousers to the ankle, with a skirt reaching some four inches below the knee, were substituted for the heavy, untidy, exasperating old garment.

She had spent her honeymoon travelling through Europe, and according to other accounts was influenced by the clothing worn in Swiss sanatoria, where women were recovering from the effects of tight lacing, and the lack of physical exercise. Shortly afterwards, she went to visit her cousin, Elizabeth Cady Stanton, in Seneca Falls, and Mrs Stanton copied the new costume with immediate delight, feeling as she wore it 'like a captive set free from his ball and chain'.

> The question is no longer, *rags* how do you look?
> But *woman*, how do you feel?

Amelia Bloomer was a neighbour and involved in editing the feminist/temperance magazine *Lily*:

At the outset, I had no idea of fully adopting the style; no thought of setting a fashion; no thought that my action would create an excitement throughout the civilized world, and give to the style my name and the credit due to Mrs Miller. This was all the work of the Press. I stood amazed at the furore I had unwittingly created.

The circulation of the *Lily* increased dramatically, and women from all parts of America wrote for details of the pattern. *The Times* quoted from Amelia's article in the May issue of *Lily* under the heading 'A Lady Resolved To Be Free And Easy'; the *Illustrated London News* published a picture of her in the new costume in July; and soon Bloomers were seen in England: at the Crystal Palace, in Piccadilly, and even on six wax models at Madame Tussauds.

No. VI.—SOMETHING MORE OF BLOOMERISM.
(BEHIND THE COUNTER THERE IS ONE OF THE † INFERIOR ANIMALS.)

Punch, 1896

In February 1853, Amelia Bloomer attracted over 3,000 people to a temperance meeting and the *New York Tribune* correspondent described the dress which made her famous:

Mrs Bloomer was attired in a dark-brown changeable tunic with a kilt descending to just below her knees, the skirt of which was trimmed with rows of black velvet. Her pantaloons were of the same texture and trimmed in the same style. She wore gaiters. Her head-dress was cherry and black. Her dress had a large, open corsage, with bands of velvet over the white chemisette in which was fixed a diamond stud pin. She wore flowing sleeves, tight undersleeves, and black mitts. Her whole attire was both rich and plain in appearance.

Most of the dresses were made with loose waists and no whalebone, and this kind of scrupulous attention to style and trimming seems to have been part of a conscious effort to forestall the criticism aroused by something otherwise so unconventional.

The Bloomer became notorious, and for the popular press, the topic of the year. Small Staffordshire china figures of Amelia were manufactured; there were at least three farces in West End theatres; a Bloomer polka, waltzes and quadrilles; and the costume was mercilessly lampooned, in *Punch* and elsewhere, by those who had in the previous months bemoaned instead the stupidity of women's trailing skirts. Satirical cartoons, rhymes and music-hall sketches on role-reversal flourished: Bloomerism in the ballroom, with women asking men to dance, and Bloomered women 'popping the question', joining the police force, or smoking tobacco. This was the exposing of a raw nerve. Victorian society, even more rigidly than our own, believed the separate roles of men and women to be distinctive, and 'complementary'. For a woman to display initiative outside the home, to express opinions, to hope for a measure of independence, or to suggest any of these by the adoption of 'masculine' attire, was to threaten the natural balance of male and female, and with it the whole social structure.

> As the husband, shall the wife be. He will have to wear a gown
> If he does not quickly make her put her Bloomer shortcoat down.

Despite all this, the Bloomer was never intended to appear masculine. The costume of an oriental harem was hardly a suitable source for progressive reform, but trousers or breeches had for so long been worn exclusively by men that they had become the visible symbol of masculine domination. *That* was why the few women who dared adopt them provoked heated accusations of unwomanliness and gross immodesty. The Bloomer represented a real, though short-lived challenge to the standards of conventional dress, and by implication to the values of contemporary society. It was significant because of the publicity it received; because it became by association a kind of feminist battle dress for women like Sarah and Angeline Grimke, Susan B. Anthony, Lucretia Mott and Lucy Stone; but most of all because it grew out of women's own consciousness of what restricted them and how they might be free.

Ironically, these were the very same factors which prevented it from being taken up on a more serious scale.

If the Bloomer dress had come from a Paris milliner, it would have been welcomed in Boston, New York, and Philadelphia; but . . . it is the only dress which has ever been adopted from principle – *from a desire in woman to fit herself for daily duty*.

But in the end, as Elizabeth Cady Stanton observed, the 'tyranny of custom' was so strong,

that to escape constant observation, criticism, ridicule, and persecution, one after another gladly went back to the old slavery, and sacrificed freedom of movement to repose. I have never wondered since that the Chinese women allow their daughters' feet to be encased in iron shoes, nor that the Hindoo widows walk calmly to the funeral pyre.

The originator of the costume (Elizabeth Smith Miller) gave it up after six or seven years; and so did Amelia Bloomer, who was sufficiently tired of the expense and inconvenience of keeping up two wardrobes to adopt the crinoline, believing that 'my influence would be greater in the dress ordinarily worn by women than in the one I was wearing'. In various statements she made it quite clear that she was a feminist first and on principle, and a dress reformer second, and for the sake of personal convenience. She wrote:

We all felt that the dress was drawing attention from what we thought to be of far greater importance – the question of woman's right to better education, to a wider field of employment, to better remuneration for her labour, and to the ballot for the protection of her rights. In the minds of some people the short dress and woman's rights were inseparably connected. With us, the dress was but an incident, and we were not willing to sacrifice greater questions to it.

Long after the Bloomer costume had itself been dropped, a general interest in dress reform continued. The subject was discussed at a convention in Syracuse in 1857, and at the 1868 Council of German Women in Stuttgart, where a motion was passed in favour of a 'reform in dress' which would resist the 'tyranny and vagaries of fashion'. However, it was not really until the 1870s that there were consistent and organized attempts at reform.

By this point there were three separate precedents for an alternative convention: a long tradition of medical invective against tight lacing, which stretched right back (through Rousseau) to German physicians of the mid eighteenth century; the example of the Bloomer costume of 1851/2; and in England the eccentrically picturesque and often quasi-medieval clothing common in some artistic circles, worn particularly by the Pre-Raphaelite women – Christina Rossetti, Elizabeth Siddal, Jane Morris, and Effie Ruskin. A modified version of this sort of clothing, usually a little fussier and more self-conscious, formed the basis of 'Aesthetic Dress', lampooned by *Punch* and in Gilbert and Sullivan's *Patience*, and commercially produced by the newly established Liberty's in the later 1870s and 1880s.

Meanwhile the fashionable silhouette had itself been changing: the symmetrical crinoline was suddenly abandoned in 1868, and replaced almost immediately by the misleadingly named 'Watteau Toilette'. This demanded a 'Grecian' or 'S'-bend posture from the wearer, the breasts thrust forward, the buttocks pushed back and emphasized with

a mass of bunched-up fabric and ribbons. As Stella Mary Newton
shows, by the late 1880s the image of woman had become

compact and smooth as a hedgerow bird and as distinct in outline . . . her dress
. . . gave no hint of soft flesh beneath, curiously utilitarian. The vulnerable
nakedness was compressed into a mould that looked resistant, as the blackbird
looks resistant. It was this woman, rather than the melting artistic lady, who
really proclaimed, with a cool precision, the victory of her sex.

Fashion is here unconsciously reflecting the changing social circumstances of women, whilst simultaneously restricting and inhibiting the
individual concerned. Aesthetic dress in its loose floppiness and
Liberty prints, although physically liberating, is visually associated
with a traditional femininity, whilst the image of fashionable dress
implies a new toughness and capability despite its conventionally repressive construction.

Punch, 1896

An interest in dress reform continued into the 1880s and 1890s. In
England the Rational Dress Society was founded in 1881, as the result
of a meeting between Viscountess Harberton and Mrs E. M. King,
both of whom were already interested in clothing reform and had

written independently on the subject. Lady Harberton herself was firmly in favour of trousers, if necessary in combination with a skirt.

The trouser is not only more comfortable, healthy and clean, but also more decent ... The prevailing idea of decency, which exposes the whole of the upper part of a woman's body for the mere sake of display when she is in full dress, but shrouds her legs in layer upon layer of material is a very strange one, and it is time that it was altered. Let us combine to do this, ladies, and prove to the world that union is strength.

In 1883 the Rational Dress Society mounted an exhibition in Piccadilly and contributed to the clothing section of the International Health Exhibition the following year.

The couturier Worth is supposed to have designed a costume for one of its members consisting of knee breeches and a short full skirt halfway between waist and knee, together with a blouse frilled at neck, wrists and hem. But more typical was the commercial view expressed in a trade journal that 'there is no need for a woman to be able to do more than use her limbs in a feminine fashion'. The aim of the Rational Dress Society was, in contrast, 'to promote the adoption, according to the individual taste and convenience, of a style of dress based upon considerations of health, comfort and beauty and to deprecate constant changes of fashion that cannot be recommended on any of these grounds'.

The Society was anxious to emphasize that it advocated a reformed, and not a masculine dress for women. For those who did not wish to adopt divided skirts, divided petticoats were recommended. But even these provoked the *Lancet* in 1879 into speaking out against 'bifurcated garments'. Medical reformers on the whole had very conventional views about the nature and status of women; though in favour of healthier wives and mothers they could not conceive of any basic alteration to the status quo.

By the 1890s the diffuse influences of Romantic socialism and Kate Greenaway nostalgia contributed to an enthusiasm for picturesque outlines and humble materials, much embellished with hand embroidery. This fashion, although not particularly logical, expressed the mingled socialist and artistic preoccupations peculiar to certain late nineteenth-century circles. The new graceful, healthy and rational dress became the uniform of a wealthy and artistic clique; and rebellion was transformed into style. Perhaps it could be argued that a point had been made, and some degree of relaxation achieved? For the less conventional, possibly; for the followers of high fashion, not at all. Artistic dress was robbed of its power to change, by its adoption as an optional fantasy. Late Victorian and Edwardian corsets were as tightly laced as they had ever been. The fashionable Lily Langtry figure was a buxom and artificial 38-18-38. The hobble skirt was still to come.

For all the effort, it is hard to say who or what was finally responsible for the end of the corset: the feminists, the doctors, Paul Poiret (for so he claimed), the craze for bicycling, or the First World War. And one further question remains unanswered. If clothes are a useful expression of social rebellion, are they a wise one?

Amelia Bloomer was throughout her life an active and influential champion of women's emancipation, but she never considered her clothing a significant part of her political stance, and tactfully switched to skirts when she addressed the Nebraska legislature. Some writers have assumed that her costume gave the cause 'great impetus, and advanced the fulfillment of its aims by many years'; others, that it damaged the furtherance of female suffrage for the rest of the century. Certainly this controversy of ends and means was discussed at the time. Should women (or any other group struggling for social change) adopt the uniform of an 'emancipated' dress, or stay relatively unobtrusive? Was it to be the role of the uniformed soldier, or of the secret agent? Perhaps there was then, and remains now, a need for both.

In the photographs that I have seen, the Pankhursts wear fashionable and not 'artistic' or 'rational' clothing. But my own sympathies are with Ada Ballin, who summed up for the opposing view in 1885: 'Tight lacing must be banished from the mind and body of the woman who would ride the iron steed.'

She meant the bicycle: but it is quite a good metaphor for life.

SR.51, October 1976

Alice Plinth – a woman haunted

1973 - her First Dungarees...

a liberating experience, which leads to others.... a regenerated Alice gives her all to the women's movement....

hmmm...

we'd like something light and humourous, but deep and meaningful, which says everything about women's oppression, o.k.? i've had this marvellous idea, see, you have this woman standing there, looking kept down but dignified, right, and she's wearing an apron to show she's working class, and one leg is shackled to the kitchen sink and the other leg is attached by a great heavy chain to a pram with ten kids in it and one arm is being twisted behind her back by a man who looks like a capitalist, you know, a bowler hat and a cigar, and there are three men on her back, symbolising the working, middle and upper class male establishment, but.... you'll love this bit.... she's got her other arm raised and her fist clenched to show she's still struggling.... actually, we were going to have her crucified on a clothes horse, and crowned with nappy pins, but we didn't want it to be too heavy....

Jo Nesbitt, *SR.79*, February 1979

You Don't Know What is Happening Do You, Mr Jones?

LAURA MULVEY

To decapitate = to castrate. The terror of the Medusa is thus a terror of castration that is linked to the sight of something. The hair upon the Medusa's head is frequently represented in works of art in the form of snakes, and these once again are derived from the castration complex. It is a remarkable fact that, however frightening they may be in themselves, they nevertheless serve actually as a mitigation of the horror, for they replace the penis, the absence of which is the cause of the horror. This is a confirmation of the technical rule according to which a multiplication of penis symbols signifies castration. (Freud, *The Medusa's Head*)

In 1970 Tooth's Gallery in London held a one-man show of sculptures by Allen Jones which gained him the notoriety he now enjoys throughout the women's movement. The sculptures formed a series, called 'Women As Furniture', in which life-size effigies of women, slave-like and sexually provocative, double as hat-stands, tables and chairs. The original of *Chair* is now in the Dusseldorf home of a West German tycoon, whose complacent form was recently photographed for a *Sunday Times* article, sitting comfortably on the upturned and upholstered female figure. Not surprisingly, members of women's liberation noticed the exhibition and denounced it as supremely exploitative of women's already exploited image. Women used, women subjugated, women on display: Allen Jones did not miss a trick.

Since 1970 Allen Jones's work has developed and proliferated in the same vein. His paintings and sculptures are exclusively images of women. He has won increasing international acclaim, with exhibitions in Italy, Germany, Belgium and the United States, as well as Britain. He is one of the shining properties in the stable of Marlborough Fine Art, the heaviest and most prestige conscious of the international art traders. He has expanded his interests beyond painting and sculpture proper into stage design, coffee-table books, luxury editions, film and television. The Allen Jones artistic octopus extends its tentacles into every nook and cranny where the image of woman can be inserted and spotlighted.

At first glance Allen Jones seems simply to reproduce the familiar formulas which have been so successfully systematized by the mass media.

His women exist in a state of suspended animation, without depth or context, withdrawn from any meaning other than the message imprinted by their clothes, stance and gesture. The interaction between his images and those of the mass media is made quite explicit by the collection of source material which he has published. *Figures* is a scrapbook of cuttings, out of magazines, both respectable (*Nova, Harpers Bazaar, Life, Vogue, Sunday Times* supplement, etc.) and non-respectable (*Exotique, Female Mimics, Bound, Bizarre*, etc.). There are also postcards, publicity material, packaging designs and film stills (*Gentlemen Prefer Blondes, Barbarella, What's New Pussycat?*). *Projects*, his second book, records sketches and concepts for stage, film and TV shows, including *Oh Calcutta!* and Kubrick's *Clockwork Orange* (some unfinished) and includes more source material as an indication of the way his idea developed. By publishing these clippings Allen Jones gives vital clues, not only to the way he sees women, but to the place they occupy in the male unconscious in general. He has chosen images which clearly form a definite pattern, which have their own visual vocabulary and grammar. The popular visuals he reproduces go beyond an obvious play on the exhibitionism of women and the voyeurism of men. Their imagery is that of a fetishism. Although every single image is a female form, not one shows the straight female genitals. Not one is naked. The cunt (yoni) is always concealed, disguised or supplemented in ways which distract attention from it. *The achievement of Allen Jones is to throw an unusually vivid spotlight on the contradiction between woman's fantasy presence and real absence from the male unconscious world.* The language which he speaks is the language of fetishism, which speaks to all of us every day, but whose exact grammar and syntax we are usually only dimly aware of. Fetishistic obsession reveals the meaning behind popular images of women.

It is Allen Jones's mastery of the language of 'basic fetishist' that makes his work so rich, and compelling. His use of popular media is

important not because he echoes them stylistically (pop art) but because he gets to the heart of the way in which the female image has been requisitioned, to be re-created in the image of man. The fetishist image of women has three aspects, all of which come across clearly in his books and art objects. First: woman plus phallic substitute. Second:

woman minus phallus punished and humiliated, often by woman plus phallus. Third: woman *as* phallus. Women are displayed for men as figures in an amazing masquerade which expresses a strange male underworld of fear and desire.

The nearer the female figure is to nakedness, the more flamboyant the distraction. The only example of frontal nudity in his work, a sketch for *Oh Calcutta!*, is a history of knickers, well-worn fetishist items, in which the moment of nakedness is further retrieved by the fact that the girls are carrying billiard cues and an enormous phallus is incorporated into the scenery. In the source material, a girl from *Playboy* caresses a dog's head on her lap; another, on the cover of a movie magazine, clutches an enormous boa constrictor as it completely and discreetly entwines her. Otherwise there is an array of well-known phallic extensions to divert the eye: guns, cigarettes, erect nipples, a tail, whips, strategically placed brooches (Marilyn Monroe and Jane Russell in *Gentlemen Prefer Blondes*), a parasol, etc., and some, more subtle, which depend on the visual effect of shadows or silhouettes.

Women without a phallus have to undergo punishment by fetish objects ranging from tight shoes and corsetry, through rubber goods to leather and torture. Here we can see the *sadistic* aspect of male fetishism, but it still remains fixated on objects with phallic significance. An ambiguous tension is introduced within the symbolism. For instance, a whip can be simultaneously a substitute phallus and an instrument of punishment. Similarly, the high heel on high-heeled shoes, a classic fetishist image, is both a phallic extension and a means of discomfort and constriction. Belts and necklaces, with buckles and pendants, are both phallic symbols and suggest bondage and punishment. The theme of *woman bound* is one of the most consistent in Allen Jones's source material: at its most vestigial, the limbs of pin-up girls are bound with shiny tape, a fashion model is loaded with chains, underwear advertisements, especially for corsets, proliferate, as do rubber garments from fetishistic magazines. Waists are constricted by tight belts, necks by tight bands, feet by the ubiquitous high-heeled shoe. For the TV show illustrated in *Projects* Allen Jones exploits a kind of evolved garter of black shiny material round the girls' thighs, which doubles openly, in one case, as a fetter. The most effective fetish both constricts and uplifts, binds and raises, particularly high-heeled shoes, corsets or bras, and, as a trimming, high neck bands holding the head erect.

In *Projects* the theme of punishment can be seen in the abandoned plan for the milkbar in the film of *Clockwork Orange* (infinitely more subtle in detail than the kitsch design Kubrick finally used for the movie). The waitress is dressed from neck to fingertip to toe in a rubber garment with an apron, leaving only her buttocks bare, ready for discipline, while she balances a tray to imply service. The same theme can be traced in his women as furniture sculptures and, in *Figures*, the background to these is made clear. Gesture, bodily position and clothing are all of equal importance. *Hat Stand* is based on the crucial publicity still from *Barbarella*, which unites boots, binding, leather and phallic cache-sexe, in the image of a girl captive who hangs ready for torture, her hands turned up in a gesture which finally becomes the hat peg. A similar design for an *hors-d'œuvre* stand derives from a Vargas drawing of a waitress who sums up the spirit of service and de-personalization.

Another aspect of the theme of punishment is that the subject phallus-less woman should suffer spanking and humiliation at the hands of the man-woman, the great male hope. Characterized in Eneg's drawings for *Bound* (reproduced in *Figures*) by tight belt, tight trousers, mask and constricted neck (while a female woman carries a soon-abandoned handbag), the man-woman emerges with full force of vengeance in *Projects* as Miss Beezley in *Homage to St Dominic's* ('to be played by a 7-foot woman – *or a man would do*. With 6-inch platform heels "she" would be 18 inches taller than the school "girls"'). And again in *The Playroom* (another abandoned stage project) where the transvestite owner, 'an elderly "woman"', chases the children. A whole series of paintings show sexually ambiguous images in which a man walks into female clothing to become a woman or male and female legs are locked as one.

Finally, in *Männer Wir Kommen*, a show for West German Television, which is illustrated in *Projects* by stills, notes and sketches, Allen Jones adds yet another dimension to his use of fetishistic vocabulary. The close-ups and superimpositions possible on television give him the chance to exploit ambiguities of changed scale and proportion. The spectator is stripped of normal perceptual defences (perspective, normal-size relationships) and exposed to illusion and fantasy on the screen. As sections of the female body are isolated from the whole and shown in close-up, or as the whole body shrinks in size and is superimposed on a blown-up section, Allen Jones develops even further the symbolic references of woman to man and subjects her form to further masculinization.

His previous work preserved the normal scale of the female body physically, although it distorted it symbolically. *Männer Wir Kommen* contains some imagery of this kind: *Homage to Harley* uses the motorcycle and the nozzle in their classic roles as phallic extensions, with the women in natural proportion to them (women clad in black bands around their thighs, boots and bound necks). But by far the most striking image is that of the entire figure of one girl, shrunk in scale though symbolically erect, superimposed as a phallic substitute on the tight black shiny shorts of another. A series of freeze-frames from the show, female manikins strategically poised, makes Allen Jones's point blindingly clear.

More close-ups in the television sketch carry the female body further into phallic suggestion. Girls supporting a boxing-ring like human pillars have bared breasts divided by a shiny pink material fastened to their necks. A single frame, from breast to neck only, gives the breasts a look of testicles with the pink material functioning as a penis. Female bodies and fragments of bodies are redeployed to produce fantasy male anatomies. A similar emphasis on breasts divided by a vertical motif can be seen in the source material: the torture harness in the *Barbarella* still, Verushka's single-strap bikini in a fashion photograph. There is a strong overlap between the imagery of bondage and the imagery of woman as phallus built into fetishism. The body is unified to a maximum extent into a single, rigid whole, with an emphasis on texture, stiffness caused by tight clothing and binding, and a general restriction of free movement.

In *Figures* there is a consistent theme of women as automata, with jerking, involuntary, semaphore movements, suggestive of erection of the phallus. These automata often have rhythmic movements (Ursula Andress dancing in a series of stills, like an animated doll, the Rockettes, Aquamaid water-skiers in Florida), uniforms in which the conception of duty and service is combined with strictness and rigidity (for instance, a cutting from the *Daily Express* in which 'Six Model Girls Step Smartly Forward For Escort Duty') and, most important of all, the stiffness induced by wearing tight clothes which constitute a second slithery skin (rubber garments transforming the body into a solid mass from fingertip to toe, one-piece corsets, synthetic garments ranging from perspex to nylon). An identification develops between the phallus and woman herself. She must be seen in her full phallic glory.

To understand the paradoxes of fetishism, it is essential to go back to Freud. Fetishism, Freud first pointed out, involves displacing the sight of woman's imaginary castration on to a variety of reassuring but often surprising objects – shoes, corsets, rubber goods, belts, knickers, etc. – which serve as signs for the lost penis but have no direct connection with it. For the fetishist, the sign itself is the subject of his fantasy – whether actual fetish objects or else pictures or descriptions of them – and in every case it is the sign of the phallus. It is man's narcissistic fear of losing his own phallus, his most precious possession, which causes shock at the sight of the female genitals and the fetishistic attempt to disguise or divert attention from them.

A world which revolves on a phallic axis constructs its fears and fantasies in its own phallic image. In the drama of the male castration complex, as Freud discovered, women are no more than puppets; their significance lies purely in their lack of penis and their star turn is to symbolize the castration which men fear. Women may seem to be the subjects of an endless parade of pornographic fantasies, jokes, day-dreams, etc., but fundamentally most male fantasy is a closed-loop dialogue with itself, as Freud conveys so well in the quotation about the Medusa's head. Far from being a woman, even a monstrous woman, the Medusa is the sign of a male castration anxiety. Freud's analysis of the male unconscious is crucial for any understanding of the myriad ways in which the female form has been used as a mould into which meanings have been poured by a male-dominated culture.

Man and his phallus is the real subject of Allen Jones's paintings and sculptures, even though they deal exclusively with images of women on display. From his work we see how the mass media provide material

for a 'harem cult' (as Wilhelm Stekel describes the fetishist's penchant for collections and scrapbooks in his classic psycho-analytic study) in which the spectre of the castrated female, using a phallic substitute to conceal or distract attention from her wound, haunts the male unconscious. The presence of the female form by no means ensures that the message of pictures or photographs or posters is about women. We could say that the image of woman comes to be used as a sign, which does not necessarily signify the meaning 'woman' any more than does the Medusa's head: the harem cult which dominates our culture springs from the male unconscious and woman herself becomes its narcissistic projection.

Freud saw the fetish object itself as phallic replacement so that a shoe, for instance, could become the object on which the scandalized denial of female castration was fixated. But, on a more obvious level, we could say with Freud in 'The Medusa's Head' that a *proliferation* of phallic symbols must symbolize castration. This is the meaning of the parade of phallic insignia borne by Allen Jones's harem, ranging from precisely poised thighs, suggestive of flesh and erection, through to enormous robots and turrets. Castration itself is only rarely alluded to in even indirect terms. In one clipping an oriental girl brandishes a large pair of scissors, about to cut the hair of a man holding a large cigar. In another, a chocolate biscuit is described in three consecutive pictures: *c'est comme un doigt* (erect female finger), *avec du chocolat autour* (ditto plus chocolate), *ça disparait très vite* (empty frame), then larger frame and triumphal return, *c'est un biscuit: Finger de Cadbury* (erect biscuit held by fingers).

There is one exception to this: the increasingly insistent theme of women balancing. Female figures hang suspended, at their peak, on the point of coming down (the phallic reference is obvious). Anything balanced upright – a woman walking a tightrope or balancing a tray or poised on the balls of her toes – implies precariously a possible catastrophe that may befall. The sculptures of women as furniture, especially the hat-stand, imply erectness and suspension at the same time, hung motion and hanging in space. In addition, the physical structure of some of his earlier paintings – three-dimensional flights of steps leading steeply up to two-dimensional paintings of women's legs poised on high heels – in itself implies ascending to a point, erect posture and suspension and balance, fused into one image by the illusionistic effect.

In his most recent paintings, exhibited this summer at the Marlborough Galleries, Allen Jones develops the theme of balance much further. A number of the paintings are of women circus performers, objects of display and of balance. Here the equation 'woman = phallus' is taken a step further, almost as if to illustrate Freud's dictum that 'the remarkable phenomenon of erection which constantly occupies the human phantasy, cannot fail to be impressive as an apparent suspension of the laws of gravity (of the winged phalli of the ancients).' In *Bare Me*, for instance, the phallic woman, rigid and pointing upwards, holding her breasts erect with her hands, is standing in high-heels on a tray-like board balanced on two spheres. She is on the way up, not down. Loss of balance is possible, but is not immediate.

But in other paintings in the same show this confidence is undercut. The defiance of gravity is more flamboyant than convincing. The same devices – high-heels, walking on spheres – which compel an upright, erect posture can also point to its precariousness. In the painting *Whip*, derived from a brilliant Eneg drawing of two women, castrator and castrated, a woman lassooed by a whipcord is slipping off a three-legged stool: in the painting we can see only the toppling stool, but there can be no doubt from comparison with the Eneg source, that her real absence – symbolic castration – is intended. In another painting, *Slip*, both figures from the same Eneg drawing are combined into one and loss of balance becomes the explicit theme. Dancers on points, waitresses carrying trays, women acrobats teetering on high-heels or walking the tightrope – all are forced to be erect and to thrust vertically upwards. But this phallic deportment carries the threat of its own undoing: the further you strive up, the further you may fall.

In *Männer Wir Kommen* the reverse side of the phallic woman, the true horror of the fetishist, can be seen in one startling sequence. The female body, although still bound in a tight corset and with a snake necklace wound round her neck, has a flamboyant, scarlet scar over her genitals. The surrounding *mise-en-scène* consists of enormous eggs, containing bound women rising from a foetus-like position while, in another sequence, maggot-like women's limbs emerge from equally enormous apples. The scar breeds the putrescence of pregnancy and nothing but decay can come out of the apple. The apple and the egg are the only non-fetishistic images of women to appear in Allen Jones's work. Infested by manikin maggots, they are the eternal companion of the scar.

Most people think of fetishism as the private taste of an odd minority, nurtured in secret. By revealing the way in which fetishistic images pervade, not just specialized publications, but the *whole of the mass media*, Allen Jones throws a new light on woman as spectacle. The message of fetishism concerns not woman, but the narcissistic wound she represents for man. Women are constantly confronted with their own image in one form or another, but what they see bears little relation or relevance to their own unconscious fantasies, their own hidden fears and desires. They are being turned all the time into objects of display, to be looked at and gazed at and stared at by men. Yet, in a real sense, women are not there at all. The parade has nothing to do with woman, everything to do with man. The true exhibit is always the phallus. Women are simply the scenery on to which men project their narcissistic fantasies. The time has come for us to take over the show and exhibit our own fears and desires.

SR.8, February 1973

Censored

ROZSIKA PARKER

There is increasing media uproar over who the Arts Council chooses to support, but not surprisingly we hear few complaints about the Arts Council's censorship.

Press attack on public patronage began in London last summer with Carl André's bricks at the Tate Gallery, continued with Mary Kelly's 'Post-Partum Document' at the Institute of Contemporary Arts in October and reached a crescendo the following month with Coum's exhibition 'Prostitution', also at the I C A. Tax payers' money, we were told, was being spent on dirty nappies, Tampax and pornography. Attention was briefly diverted from the cuts and the falling pound by self-righteous articles trivializing the artists' intentions instead of trying to explore the relationship between art and audience. But at least we were able to look at the artists' work and draw our own conclusions. Not so with Suzanne Santoro's art. The Arts Council decided to suppress her book *Towards New Expression*. Selection is sometimes necessary but on what grounds?

The story begins last February, when the organizers of an Arts Council touring exhibition of books made by artists rang *Spare Rib*. They had been impressed by feminist artist Suzanne Santoro's book and wanted to include it in 'Artists' Books'. Could we supply her address?

Soon afterwards Suzanne, an American living in Rome, received a letter saying that her book was wanted for the show and the organizers 'must have five copies by mid February'.

Suzanne was in England when 'Artists' Books' opened at the I C A in August. Arriving at the exhibition, she noted that her book was entered in the catalogue as Number 103. She browsed through the show – out of the 119 books by individual artists, only ten were by women – but she couldn't find her book. There was no Number 103. Her work had been excluded though it had originally been selected and entered in the catalogue.

Suzanne's sparse, carefully produced, black and white volume was published by the Italian women's liberation group Rivolta Feminile. Suzanne is one of a number of women artists whose work is based on images of women's genitals. For example there's Ann Severson's film *Near the Big Chakra*, and Judy Chicago's work in paint and porcelain.

For most feminists vaginal imagery signifies a rejection of images by men of women, and an exploration and affirmation of their own identity. It attacks the idea of women's genitals as mysterious, hidden and threatening, and attempts to throw off a resulting shame and secrecy. Suzanne begins by demonstrating the way women's genitals have been portrayed in the history of art – 'annulled, smoothed down and in the end idealized'.

Suzanne established herself as an artist in the 1960s. Her art was taken seriously, she was professionally successful. 'I built huge things out of rope. I did a lot of heavy, difficult sculpture. I worked with sheet metal and things like that,' she says, 'then I got involved with feminism – with a group called Rivolta Feminile. For three years we talked about sex.'

It was 1970. In Italy the debate over vaginal and clitoral orgasm was well underway. Suzanne reacted as a person working with shape and form: 'I had never really looked at myself, so I decided to take a cast of myself. We were learning how important it was for women to know how they were made. I took a cast and I was amazed by the structural solidity of it – the very precise construction and form.'

She went on to photograph genitals and in *Towards New Expression* she juxtaposes the photographs with illustrations of flowers and shells. The photos are a refined examination of structure, desexualized and isolated in the centre of a blank page.

She carefully points out that the juxtaposition of flowers, shells and genitals is not intended to confirm the old identification of women with nature as against culture. She writes: 'The placing of the Greek figures, the flowers and the conch shell near the clitoris is a means of understanding the structure of the female genitals.' And she adds: 'I just wanted to make the point that I had found structural identities, not symbolic identities.'

In *The Second Sex* Simone de Beauvoir underlines the importance of knowing the structure: 'The feminine sex organ is mysterious even to the woman herself . . . Woman does not recognize herself in it and this explains in large part why she does not recognize its desires as hers.'

Similarly, Suzanne sees demystification as a prerequisite for sexual self-expression: 'The placing of the flowers and the conch shell near the clitoris . . . is also an invitation for the sexual self-expression that has been denied women till now', and which, she believes, leads to greater self-knowledge in other areas of our lives. 'Expression begins with self-assertion and the awareness of the difference between ourselves and others.'

By 'expression' she means creative or artistic self-expression. The whole book condemns the image of women in art which damages our ability to see ourselves as creative people. The female nude – passive, available, devoid of individual desires, her body a blank canvas for men's creativity – is a major subject of art in our culture. And it's easy to take the image at face value and believe we're destined to be always the model and never the maker. Suzanne concludes: 'We can no longer see ourselves as if we live in a dream or an imitation of something that just does not reflect the reality of our lives.'

In Italy Suzanne's work has been widely exhibited and discussed. Some women feel that isolating a woman's genitals confirms the split between sexuality and other social relations. Others feel that we have been identified for too long by our biology, and even though Suzanne is using a biological/natural imagery to criticize the way we've been perceived in the past, it's dangerously open to misunderstanding.

She has received criticism but never censorship. *Spare Rib* asked the Arts Council why they'd suppressed *Towards New Expression*. 'On the grounds that obscenity might be alleged,' replied Director of Art Robin Campbell. 'We are willing to defend obscenity on the grounds of artistic excellence but considered that in this case the avowed intention of the book was primarily a plea for sexual self-expression.'

But if it was not considered artistically excellent, why, we wonder, was it selected for the show in the first place? And what sort of 'obscenity' is the Arts Council prepared to defend? The answer is women used, women subjugated, women on display – in other words, Allen Jones's *Projects*, which did appear in 'Artists' Books'.

. . . Some years ago Suzanne said, 'As a child I used to go to bed and pinch myself to feel if I was alive. Am I real? That feeling of not being, not living a full enough life is still with me. I think it's a female thing.' Her recent experience at the hands of the Arts Council must have increased her feeling of 'not being' but it's certainly shown the subversive quality of works like hers.

SR.54, January 1977

JUICY, FRUITY, FRESH & CHEAP

WELLS Jaffa Orange Drink

CHEMISTRY OF WOMEN

Symbol – Wo   Atomic Weight – Light but heavy

Physical Properties

1. Surface usually found with film of painted oxide.
2. Boils at nothing, freezes without reason.
3. Unpolished specimens turn green in presence of polished ones.
4. All varieties melt when given proper treatment.
5. Bitter if used incorrectly.
6. Density varies from great to infinity.
7. States: from virgin metal to common ore.
*Pure specimen turns rosy when discovered in natural state.

Chemical Properties

1. Highly explosive except in experienced hands.
2. Attracted by gold and silver.
3. Ability to absorb quantities of liquid substance.
4. May explode spontaneously when left with male.
5. Insoluble in liquid but activity greatly increased.
6. Yields to pressure.
7. Ages vary rapidly.

Uses

Chiefly ornamental.
Reducing agent (see Bank Balance).
Illegal to possess more than one married specimen but a certain amount of exchange is permitted.

From *King's College*, London's rag magazine
Sent in by Catherine Ebenezer, London SW17

Tooth & Nail

PLEASE KEEP SENDING SEXIST CUTTINGS, PHOTOS, QUOTES AND ADVERTISEMENTS TO "TOOTH AND NAIL", INCLUDING ALL DETAILS WHICH MAY BE NEEDED BY PEOPLE WANTING TO FIGHT BACK.

WHO TO ATTACK ABOUT SEXIST ADS:
the manufacturers of the product advertised and/or the agency who make up the ad.
WHO TO COMPLAIN TO:
The Independent Broadcasting Authority, for ITV ads and programmes, 70 Brompton Road, London SW3.
The Advertising Standards Authority, though notoriously unresponsive to complaints about sexism, 15 Ridgemount Street, London WC1.
WHO TO WORK WITH:
AFFIRM (Alliance For Fair Images and Representation in Media). A group acting against sexism and offensive stereotyping, can be contacted at 35 Colehearne Road, London SW10.

From *Radical Philosophy* No.16 Sent in by Stef Pixner, London E8

Throughout the sixties and early seventies English academic Marxism lay back with its legs open. We experienced the successive thrills of penetration by the giants of continental European Marxist philosophy.

Judge warns rapist, 68

A JUDGE at Leeds Crown Court yesterday gave a warning to a 68-year-old pensioner who pleaded guilty to raping a 70-year-old widow.

Mr Justice Thesiger, said: "With your state of health, with your high blood pressure, I warn you not to behave like this. You may overtire your heart and die in mostunfortunate circumstances." Then he gave Mr George Dickinson, a widower, of Woodhouse Hill Road, Leeds, a two year suspended sentence.

The Guardian March 1977   Sent in by Hilary Cannon, Bristol

Manchester Evening News March 1977
Sent in by Gaby Porter, Salford

A letter from *The Lady* magazine to an advertiser
Sent in by A. Miconi, London SE3

The Lady
PUBLISHED EVERY THURSDAY

39-40 BEDFORD STREET, STRAND, LONDON WC2E 9ER

Telephone 01-836 8705 Telegrams: LADINEWS LONDON WC2

Our Ref: Sit/QC   22nd March 1977

Mrs A. Miconi,
Flat 17, Lyncourt,
The Orchard,
Blackheath,
London SE3

Dear Madam,

We thank you for your letter and payment of £3.80, received on 21st March.

Before proceeding, we must ask whether you would agree to a slight amendment of the wording in order that the advertising conforms to our normal style. The words "Socialist feminist" we would prefer to read "friendly, motherly," thereby allowing the wording to conform.

We now look forward to your further instructions, whilst advising you that our next issue is 7th April for which we close for press upon receipt of the first post Tuesday 29th March.

Yours faithfully

CLASSIFIED ADVERTISEMENT DEPARTMENT

Women's liberation?

A busy housewife may find she's never really free — from responsibility, from worry, from sheer hard work. She gets few chances to relax, little opportunity to eat properly; and that's when vitamin deficiency can arise.

When you start to feel increasingly tired, out of sorts, hemmed in, it may be through a temporary lack of vitamins.

Pharmaton Capsules can help restore the balance, because they contain the vitamins essential for healthy living, plus many important minerals and trace elements. They're the easiest way of making sure of your daily vitamin requirements.

Try them – just ask your chemist for Pharmaton Capsules.

Pharmaton Capsules
The Swiss combination of vitamins, minerals and Ginseng

For further information please write to The Pharmaton Information Bureau, Stimney House, Church Street, Liverpool L1 3AU.

A Day in the Life of . . . Janice

. . . When Ben can't find clean socks which are staring him in the eye or flounders helplessly in front of a cooker, I have caught myself thinking, 'Men, they are useless when it comes to looking after themselves' – and up pop images of the wise, motherly wife and the rather silly husband – images employed again and again in advertisements. I think women in the home are particularly vulnerable to role suggestion, because they are not interacting with the outside world in a work situation where they would have to assert their personality and forge some sort of separate identity for themselves. This is how I feel, anyway, and because of that vulnerability am happier not watching much television . . .

SR.65, January 1978

Disabled Women
ANNA BRIGGS INTERVIEWS MURIEL

. . . Muriel is in her fifties, and is wheelchair-bound with severe arthritis . . . 'People are peculiar about the disabled – they think we don't have emotions and feelings like them, that we don't fall in love. Eighteen years ago, when we married (we both had disabilities then) people would say: "What are you getting married for?" My husband was mild-mannered, and would get upset, but I would throw their dirty minds back at them: "Why do you think?" People invade your privacy in a way they wouldn't with a non-disabled person. But the disabled are now fighting back – especially in the last ten years.'. . .

SR.80, March 1979

Speaking Out on Age
PAULINE LONG

. . . Women who understand my feelings will know how angry I am.
. . . Ageism is the assumption that older people are not real people: not only are their needs fewer, and in some important areas such as sexuality, non-existent; but it is considered that their experience is of

little account and is to be avoided. Given the chance, older people will get boring about the past. In fact, older people are O K if they are dead, since death gives the 'in' generation a chance to look at and evaluate their work in an historical context. In addition, contact – that is, real contact – with older people is feared because they mirror in their changing looks the common condition of humanity – a tendency to get older. This equates with less beautiful, less strong, and ultimately with death. Death is something that must always happen to others, and must not be allowed to impinge on a personal consciousness. Any contact with age, experience and death is therefore to be shunned.

. . . Today in Britain women have an average of fifteen to twenty years between post-menopause and death. The period is lengthening all the time. Nobody knows what 'to do' with such women. Experienced, survivors, skilled, healthy, energetic and beautiful. There is no place for them in our society. And in the women's movement? The answer was made by a younger woman. When I first thought of going into a women's group she encouraged me: but I demurred because of my age (fifty). She said: 'We can learn from you and you can learn from us.' I came in, and she was right. Let hers be the last words.

SR.82, May 1979

Put a Her in Your Hertz
ANNA COOTE

Sister, if you ever rent a car from Hertz (though women, of course, are seldom in a position to do so) I sincerely hope you will rent it from one of their male representatives and that you will have a button missing from your coat.

Let me explain. You may have been lucky enough to miss the Hertz advertisement which appears in the national press occasionally. It shows a slightly balding man standing by a blackboard. In front of him are three young girls in mini skirts, listening attentively and taking notes. He is pointing to words on the blackboard which say: 'Hertz says Yes!' Beneath the picture is a slogan: 'Teaching a girl about Hertz is teaching her to say Yes'. Beneath that, the smaller print declares:

Before every new Hertz girl meets her public, she has to learn to always say Yes to a customer.

It's easy when you work for Hertz because there's no limit to what Hertz has to offer. In fact, it takes us six weeks to fill her pretty head with all the facts and figures.

What we don't spell out in the book, we know a Hertz girl can handle naturally. We choose her because she's the kind of girl who enjoys solving all the little things that don't seem very little at the time.

Yes, I'll phone your wife to tell her you'll be late.

Yes, I'll find the briefcase you left in the car.

Yes, I'll sew the button on your coat.

The next time you want to rent a car, ask a Hertz girl. You'll see how well she's learned her lessons.

If this has reduced you to spluttering fury, you'll understand why our women's group decided we couldn't let it go by without registering a protest.

So we wrote two letters: one to the *Guardian*, which featured the ad regularly, and one to Hertz. We told them we took the strongest possible exception to the advertisement and detailed our grievances: (1) the sexual overtones of 'teaching her to say Yes'; (2) the patronizing implication that the Hertz girl is so stupid it takes six weeks to 'fill her pretty head', while she needs to have a totally facile concept spelled out on a blackboard; and (3) the reinforcement of the misconception that women are best suited for jobs of a servile nature. We asked the Editor of the *Guardian* whether he would include such ads in future. We asked the Managing Director of Hertz whether men were employed in the same job and, if so, whether they were given the same training. Ten of us signed each letter.

One week later we received a letter from G. P. Taylor, Advertising Director of the Guardian. He had taken the trouble to write us two pages, which made me suspect he hadn't been inundated with letters like ours. 'I understand', he said, 'why you take this exception and I have a great deal of sympathy with your point of view'; the *Guardian* probably would include such advertisements in future; it was not their policy to censor advertising. 'We believe that the advertiser should be free to advertise what he has to sell and say what he has to say within the limits of the law.' He apologized for causing us offence.

A week after that, we received a letter from Robin Crawshaw, Managing Director of Hertz. Dear Ladies, he said, he could not agree with our criticism and he wished to make these observations:

1. It is complete nonsense to suggest that the advertisement had any sexual overtones.

2. Our girls are in fact pretty, they are not dumb and the campaign slogan can only be conveyed effectively by emphasizing the kind of service we expect a rental representative to perform.

3. With regard to your comment that sewing on buttons is a servile duty, I cannot agree at all. In fact, what we offer is nothing more than a helpful service to the desperate business man who is unlikely to carry needle and thread with him.

Susie Courtauld

As to whether men are employed as representatives, the answer is yes. However, as far as I know, we do not employ any young ladies as mechanics or car washers, so perhaps we do succumb to the traditional 'misconception' that there are certain jobs for which our charming Hertz ladies are less well suited than their male counterparts.

In short, I believe that your objections are totally without foundation.

See what I mean? Get the Hertz boy to sew up the neck of the boss's stuffed shirt while he's got his needle out . . .

SR.8, February 1973

'What Offends One of Us Won't Offend the Next Chap': The Advertising Standards Authority's Line on Sexism

JILL NICHOLLS AND PAT MOAN

I am alone in the underground waiting for a train. All around me are huge images of female parts: giant rubber peach-tone breasts, wet lips, denim bums, damp-looking stomachs, long legs in high-heels ('Hundreds of women take them off for us every day'). I don't know where to look that doesn't make me feel angry or vulnerable. A man comes into the tunnel and looks me up and down. All these ads are like his gang – telling him I am a cunt-thing, a leg-thing, a breast-thing and that I am waiting for him. He is psyched up to think that he has a right to me. (The Lovable bra ad, his hand resting lightly but oh so firmly on her naked waist – his territory.)

My mother used to say it was a great relief to her being an old woman because men left her alone. So I am careful to conceal my youth, never to look like those ads. When it is hot I don't wear shorts because it isn't safe: I become a leg-thing. Even in a T-shirt one becomes a tit-thing, ogled, mocked, prodded. Winter means armour of boots, coat, hat and relative safety, but there are no summer clothes behind which to hide your body . . .

The Advertising Standards Authority, 'editors of our streets' as they see themselves, hotly deny that sexist images are a *general* representation of women. They don't have anything to do with *us*, now do they? As they say in their letter rejecting the complaint against Wells 'juicy, fruity, fresh and cheap' orange juice ad, it 'plainly was not making a statement about women in general, or seeking to suggest to any individual woman who saw the poster that she was required to identify herself with the woman depicted in it'.

But even if you don't identify yourself with those ads, men *do*. Advertising is an incredibly powerful agent of male supremacy, a fact which the ASA glosses over with platitudes like 'You have your views and other people have theirs.' Of course we have our views but the advertisers have the power and pay a fortune to buy space to push their products. The rest of us are left speechless.

'I stand in the underground station coming to work in the morning with the pictures on the wall of girls in bathing costumes. *Extremely* pretty girls. And I stand there and I enjoy them thoroughly. I come into the office and there's a letter of complaint about the very advertisement that I'd been enjoying,' says Tony Painter, deputy director of the A S A. 'That just proves the point that we've all got our own views. What offends one of us won't offend the next chap.'

Geoffrey Williams, new boy at the A S A, is sure that a lot of men 'really *like* lascivious advertising'. Pushed, he does admit that the use of women in ads reflects their position in society (it may not seem much but it sounded really advanced during our interview in their boardroom!). But the A S A, *not* a government body but the self-policing arm of the advertising industry, financed by a 0.1 per cent surcharge on display advertising, is obsessed with antiquated notions of 'taste and decency' which are totally defined by what they conceive majority views to be, based of course on their own.

The A S A waits for complaints to come in, rather than taking initiatives themselves, though they do pre-vet ads in certain areas – cigarettes and slimming aids for instance. They cover only press and poster advertising – cinema, T V and radio are not their responsibility.

The council of twelve members appointed by the chairman, himself appointed by the advertising industry, considers complaints behind closed doors. They meet once a month to decide on cases prepared for them by a secretariat (nearly forty-strong) which services both the A S A and the Code of Advertising Practice (C A P) Committee, a trade association to which most advertisers and publications belong. The C A P committee writes the code – with its empty call for ads to be 'legal, decent, honest and truthful', whatever that means – and the A S A supervises its implementation.

Asked about their criteria on sexism, which fits only under their umbrella of 'decency', Painter said, 'Really you're asking me to read the minds of the council and that's very difficult for me to do . . . They're just like everybody else, you've got a group of twelve ordinary people making these judgements. You get another group of twelve and they might take a different view – it's the name of the game.'

Just like everybody else? The A S A boast that two thirds of the council have no connection with advertising and so 'our independence is assured by the independence of the members of the council, who have no axe to grind.' What's more – 'they come from all walks of life' and three are 'ladies'. Yes, there are M Ps, company directors, lords, a vicar, even the Baroness of Fulham (just an ordinary housewife?).

They're proud too that their members are answerable to no one – 'We don't want representatives, we want ordinary people, people who make their own judgements.'

In the case of the Wells ad, which received, they say, about twenty complaints, a lot by A S A standards, Painter said: 'The *majority* of the council didn't think that the words could *logically* apply to the caricature of the woman.' One of the arguments was that although the words could apply to the woman, 'they could equally well apply to the orange juice'! (*Who* was talking about logic??)

The fact that the drawing was stylized loomed large for the council – quite why escaped us. They seem to see style and humour as a thing apart from the 'content' or 'meaning' of an ad, which they take clodhoppingly literally. Asked if they'd ever had any complaints about sexual imagery in ads – phallic symbolism (foaming champagne bottles), masturbation scenes like in the Rothmans ad where the uniformed arm reaches for the gear lever – they looked slightly shocked and said, 'No. Well yes. Doubtless from time to time but I can't recall having one. But then I've only been here a short time.' Judging by their response to Wells, the chances of such complaints being understood is pretty low. They can spot a nude when they see one and disapprove, but don't delve much deeper – though they do claim to know the difference between feminist objections to the exploitation of women and puritanical revulsion at nudity as such.

Job ads that are overtly sex discriminatory ('Girl Friday wanted') are relatively easy to deal with because they break the law. (Painter points out that Britain's race relations legislation is stronger than that on sex discrimination, which has nothing comparable to the clause about not 'inciting to racial hatred'.) Ads like those for Green Shield stamps that idealize women as housewives and insist on our role within the family as carers, consumers and dependants, are not illegal – or indecent – they're just sexist, and that doesn't count.

Factual complaints they find easier to deal with (if an ad promises 90 per cent beef when the stuff's made of soya), so we asked about another kind of 'misleading claim' – you'll get a boyfriend if you use this deodorant/cleanser/hair-remover: buy this and he'll buy you.

'The question the council would ask itself is whether a significant number of girls would be silly enough to believe it,' says Painter. So if you're influenced you're silly, if you're not it's a bad ad. And how can women *not* be influenced by the messages screamed from all sides?

Though Painter 'can't remember' a complaint on grounds of sexism being upheld, writing to the A S A is not an utter waste of time. In the case of Wells, which they insist was 'a borderline case', each complaint was passed on to the company and the effect of that is 'to deter Wells from using the same ad again', according to Painter. Unless a complaint is considered too 'trivial' to pursue, they publish the results of their investigations – for or against – in a monthly report, sent out to consumer agencies and the media – this includes the name of company and product and is considered bad publicity. If an advertiser refuses to change an ad against which a complaint has been upheld, the A S A can ask the media not to accept it. As a last resort it could recommend that the advertiser's trading privileges be withdrawn. In any event they do assume that for every complaint they receive, 100 to 1,000 other people are also offended who didn't bother to write. Diplomatically perhaps, they kept urging us to test the system and see how they handle anti-sexist complaints: 'It's difficult to criticize the system if it's not being used, isn't it – you ought to try it out.'

HUNKY, CHUNKY BIG & CRUNCHY

STUART'S Nutz Are Best

Thalia Doucas

If everyone who sent a cutting to *Spare Rib*'s 'Tooth and Nail' – on average two or three a day – or slapped a sticker on some hideous poster, also dashed off a note to the A S A, they'd be overwhelmed!

However, they are sticky about defining how 'representative' opinions are (ironically, given their own constitution). The code is meant to reflect 'the prevailing view of the population of the U K'. They ask if an ad will 'offend the majority of people who will see it . . . We may get a dozen complaints about a particular ad or poster and immediately a new question arises: how representative are these complaints?' Sometimes they are prepared to withdraw an ad if a 'minority' is deeply offended – for instance a Smirnoff vodka ad which made a joke about the Titanic (because it upset relatives of those who drowned) and a Japanese car ad which mentioned Hiroshima.

But angry women don't get this special treatment.

Affirm is a feminist alliance against ads, articles and images that exploit women. Its aim is, simply, to abolish all sexism in the media. As well as using traditional ways of campaigning – writing to the A S A and to T V and radio stations, monitoring newspapers and writing letters to the editor – the women involved also try to work out more imaginative methods. They support direct action, sell stickers and badges and are preparing an action kit for the enraged woman! They're willing to speak at schools, colleges and conferences, and plan to hold a conference of their own in the autumn.

Affirm, they feel, has a huge consciousness-raising function: 'We try to get behind the ads, showing how media images interrelate with a whole ideology. People get used to sexism, they aren't shocked any more. There's a lot of emphasis in ads on the *possession* of women – this relates to violence against women, because if men can't *have* the women they're offered, they take.'

Affirm meets fortnightly in London and functions as a contact point for individuals around the country. It's eager to form new groups and hear from more women.

We have had reports of individual women dreaming up schemes on their own . . . one woman even thought of sticking pins in Wells plastic orange squash bottles in supermarkets (illegal of course).

If you're caught spraying – or tearing down or subverting posters with stickers – sentences can be heavy. You're treated as any ordinary vandal – political motivation seems to come into it only if used against you! If you *do* get caught, cash in on the publicity. When Diane Potter and Maria Schween were tried in London recently for 'defacing property' – posters for *The Stud* and *Emmanuelle* – crowds of women picketed the court and the story made all the local papers.

Even if the ad-men *are* dreaming up ways to incorporate our protests – like the Brook Street ad with leg in plaster cast, complete with empty space just *inviting* passers-by to scrawl a message – graffiti are still one small way of making our voice heard. Any more suggestions?

S.R.72, July 1978

Suffrage Posters
PAULA HARPER

The posters made by members of the women's suffrage movement in the USA and Great Britain between 1900 and 1920 have an unexpected, and perhaps dubious, distinction. Since most of them predate the First World War, they are among the earliest manifestations of a new phenomenon in the twentieth century: the political picture poster.

The suffragists used the format of the advertising posters surrounding them, but they were the first group to adapt this commercial art form, with its dilutions of fine art styles, to a political function. They set the precedent which was quickly followed on a massive scale by the makers of official government propaganda posters during the First World War.

The graphic heirs of the First World War posters are in the style of the 'paid political announcement' which now dominates posters and billboards; images created by professional teams of commercial artists, market researchers and public relations experts. But the suffrage posters were made by convinced individuals with no commercial motives, they supported an anti-establishment cause, and were directed to an audience which did not care so much about art as about the issues.

The posters were published either privately or by local or national women's organizations, among them the National Woman Suffrage Association in New York (NAWSA) and in London by the Women's Social and Political Union (WSPU), the Artists' Suffrage League and the more conservative Women's Franchise League.

The nineteenth-century suffragists Susan B. Anthony, Elizabeth Cady Stanton and Lucy Stone, had made an assault on the ideas and institutions taken for granted by middle-class Americans. They challenged the sanctity of marriage and the family, the roles and responsibilities of men and women as defined by the Scriptures and the privileges due to the 'weaker sex'. In response, the anti-suffragists defined and supported these ideas and institutions more explicitly than ever before. From the turn of the century, when the period of practical action to achieve the vote began and the suffragists found that persuasive techniques were politically necessary to win friends and influence the electorate, they developed new arguments to rebut the anti-suffragist position without undermining traditional ideas about relationships between the sexes. The posters adopt a similar strategy.

For example, 'Give Mother the Vote – We Need It' is a defensive poster, designed to counter a common theme in anti-suffrage literature and imagery; the antithesis between a woman's natural function as directed by the Scriptures, the bearing and rearing of children, and her taking part in political life. Voting would be a burden for a busy mother; it would create dissension in the home, competition between men and women and bring an end to chivalry which was a refining influence on men. Only ugly women wanted political power because they could wield no influence through their charms. The rebuttal to this argument was proposed by Jane Addams in an article, 'Why Women Should Vote', which first appeared in the *Ladies Home Journal* in 1909. She urged women to use the ballot to *preserve* the home, by electing governments which would provide clean milk, sanitary surroundings and good education for their families in the new urban environment. She pointed out that the farm woman could assume personal responsibility for the safety and cleanliness of the milk from her own cow but that in the cities, mothers were dependent on the community for such services. Women's traditional responsibilities were education and the protection of children; they must bring their superior spiritual forces to bear on a materialistic world. A woman must, wrote Jane Addams, even though it was an extra burden, 'bring herself to the use of the ballot'. Many posters emphasized this motivation. Images of motherly suffragists who gently asked for the vote in order to provide better homes for their families offered an analgesia to the anti-suffrage forces and soothed masculine misgivings.

An anti-suffrage article by George Holland in the *Sewanee Review* of 1909 predicted that if the suffragists were successful in gaining the ballot, all women would in time become 'large-handed, big-footed, flat-chested and thin-lipped'. These unfeminine characteristics were often used by caricaturists to satirize feminists. A long tradition of popular prints from the fifteenth century to the cartoonists from *Punch* and *Life* in the early twentieth century mocked the 'over-emancipated' woman by picturing her as stringy, angular and sexless or as self-satisfied and matronly with an enormous, overwhelming bosom and bottom. Role reversal is a common caricatural device in this tradition; men are shown caring for the squalling baby, cleaning and washing up, while the women laze about, congregate in saloons, smoke cigars or write novels. The pro-suffrage poster artists countered with images of the 'Womanly' woman, whose sources in the history of art were traditional madonna or classical goddess types. These images, in general, suppressed the sexual characteristics of woman and presented her as a creature somewhere between a nun and a nineteenth-century nature goddess.

The style of posters as well as their content, carries the message. The 'how' is part of the 'what'. The choice of a style for the suffrage posters which communicated to the right public with the right voice was a crucial part of the process of making them.

The poster artists for Women's Suffrage seem to have chosen styles appropriate to their intentions. In general they followed the stylistic tradition of persuasive art by using modes of either illusionism or stylized realism. But unlike most political poster makers they drew inspiration from the romantic Pre-Raphaelite and decorative Art Nouveau styles. These styles influenced commercial art and the design of home furnishings and arts and crafts even into the 1920s, but they were generally considered unsuitable for political posters. The Pre-Raphaelite and Art Nouveau styles have this advantage, however; they romanticize women. They are 'feminine' styles not created by women but carrying connotations of what constitutes femininity from a masculine point of view. Posters in these styles were designed to counteract anti-suffrage images which showed women as aggressive harridans.

The suffrage posters are also influenced by magazine and book illustration, an intentionally 'innocent' and even 'cute' style. The colours of the posters tend to be pastel, the lines pliant; the emphatic colour contrasts and aggressive forms of most twentieth-century political posters are avoided.

The posters, by their peculiar lack of forcefulness, their gentility and timidity, visually illustrate the dilemma of the suffragists. They wanted political power and freedom from an oppressive social status but hesitated to part with their traditional sexual identity (even though it was one which had been defined by men), perhaps for fear of being left sexless.

The women who made the posters faced this problem in concrete terms; they had no tradition of image-making to draw upon except the masculine one in which they were embedded as second-class citizens. This tradition did not serve them; it provided few images of women except male-created ones. The poster artists could only make a selection from this available tradition and fit the suffragist image, more or less uneasily, into it. The Pre-Raphaelite woman was graceful, elegant, idolized, and above all, ladylike. It was an image which connoted sexual and social privilege and with which, most probably, many of the suffragists found it pleasant to identify. But was it a self-image which, once adopted, may have impeded the suffragists from clearly challenging a political system which denied women equality in exchange for giving them privilege, and a social system which emphasized the superiority of an educated cultivated minority? In other words, if one wishes to oppose the status quo, can one use the artistic conventions acceptable to that status quo without self-contamination? A conviction that one cannot is behind the present-day search of many women artists for new forms and content – new self-images – which are truly their own and not selected or modified from available, primarily masculine, tradition. But the suffragists looked into the Mirror of Art and believed they saw themselves. This belief may have conditioned not only the style of their posters but their style of political action.

The differences between posters produced in Great Britain and the United States seem to reflect the differences in the political realities and the ideology of suffragists in the two countries. On the whole the British posters tend to be more aggressive than the American, occasionally on the attack rather than on the defensive. In England, militancy was greater and reaction stronger. The British posters, like the American, mainly addressed themselves to a well-educated, middle-class audience. However, there are some English posters which plead the special cause of working-class women, a group almost totally ignored in the American suffrage movement.

The British posters also seem to place far more stress on the intellectual achievements and professional accomplishments of women and less on the importance of motherhood and 'womanly nature'. The anonymous poster 'Polling Station' probably refers to a parade held in London on 13 June 1908, in which 13,000 women marched in groups; professional women, university graduates, artists, writers and actresses among them. Homemakers brought up the rear of this parade and motherhood has been treated with some ambivalence by the poster designer. The mother is shown front and centre – the most important figure in the placement – but her position of bending down to the child lowers her in relation to the erect figures of the professional women flanking her on both sides.

Aileen Kraditor in her book *Ideas of the Women's Suffrage Movement 1890–1920* notes that up into the 1890s the suffrage movement in the USA was educational, basing its appeal on the equality of men and women and on the justice of suffrage for both. But as the movement took on a more activist stance, new and more politically sophisticated arguments were introduced, based not on 'justice' but on 'expediency'. Suffragists campaigning in northern cities, for example, pointed out that the male, lower-class, immigrant vote could be outbalanced by the female, middle-class, 100 per cent American vote. These tactics led to less emphasis on the principle of equality, in contrast to the British poster of 1908 'Justice Demands the Vote' which pleads the simple fairness of suffrage for women.

But British poster makers were willing to use arguments based on 'expediency' also. 'Polling Station' shows distinguished professional women outside a voting place which is being freely entered by a motley crew of males. The appeal of this poster and also of 'Convicts, Lunatics and Women Have No Vote' of 1901 is based on the superiority of the educated woman to some men and the loss to society of the benefit of her contribution to government. The idea for 'Convicts, Lunatics and Women Have No Vote' is in fact taken from a post-card-sized photomontage which was widely circulated in the United States in the 1890s ('American Woman and Her Political Peers'). In the centre of this curious image the refined and respectable face of Frances Willard, President of the International Women's Christian Temperance Union, appears. In the four corners are representatives of the other groups in American society who also cannot vote: clockwise from upper left, the congenital idiot, the lunatic and the Indian. The message, however, is certainly not that male Indians and idiots should be allowed to vote.

The women's posters showed a decided reluctance to attack and caricature the opposition. If the little boys in the poster 'Now you greedy boys I shall not give you anymore until I have helped myself', for example, had been shown as grossly fat and ugly as well as aggressively greedy (the way Gillray might have pictured them) and the mother obviously undernourished and needy, the poster would carry its message with more force and clarity. This lack of audacity may account for the missing theme in the posters of the women's suffrage movement. There are no attacks on men.

In other visual propaganda campaigns by politically insurgent groups fighting dominant groups (the Protestants versus the Catholics in the sixteenth century, the Republicans against the Monarchists in nineteenth-century France, and the Socialists versus Capitalists in the later nineteenth and twentieth centuries, for example) the enemy was always specifically defined and clearly attacked through mockery, exaggeration of his animal or sub-human nature, or by associating him with the devil or satanic powers. But where, for example, is the suffragist poster depicting a monstrous male with his cruelly booted heel grinding down on the neck of the voteless, helpless female? Not to be found. The poster makers for women's suffrage avoid attacking men in favour of presenting a positive image of women. Perhaps it was distasteful to women to lose dignity by admitting their oppression. Perhaps they feared losing advantages they already had. Perhaps there was a natural reluctance on the part of the weaker half of the human race to define the stronger half as the enemy. It was only men after all who could *give* women the vote; posters which antagonized them were apparently not believed to be good political strategy.

In the First World War posters made at almost the same time (mostly by men), women are cast in another role. They are shown as strong, capable, engaged in manual labour, in heroic 'masculine' poses or as powerful allegorical figures. The contrast between the timid, self-deprecating woman in 'Won't you let me help you John?' and the glamorous operetta heroine in the poster for the National League for Women's Service of the First World War is startling. Which image helped win the vote for women? The result (if not the aim) of both kinds of propaganda was the same; to convince men that women were harmless, that they would not threaten the social status quo and that they believed in and would work for the same ends as men. Women's efforts in the First World War substantiated this. Patriotism and the 'americanization' of aliens were specific war aims of NAWSA.

Without the proof women gave in the First World War that they could make a contribution to the national war effort it is doubtful that they would have received the vote, either in the USA or in Britain. The campaign of the British suffragists resulted in partial victory in 1919, when university graduates over thirty, women householders and householders' wives over thirty were granted the vote. Full suffrage on an equal basis with men did not come until 1928. In the USA all women citizens over twenty-one were given the vote in 1920.

As it turned out, women were harmless. The vote was conceived of as an end, not a means to an end, by most suffragists, and after winning it women rarely used it to their own advantage.

SR.41, November 1975

2   FAMILY

The ultimate source of pleasure, fulfilment and sense of social
usefulness for women is meant to lie in their role in the family. This
role as homemaker is more insular and the emotional responsibilities
more intense than they were before industrialization. As work and
home have become more separate, so other responsibilities of the
family, like education and health, now belong to the state. The home
has become a refuge from work, a sanctuary from the rest of the
world. Woman's role as keeper of this sanctuary was described by
Michelene Wandor in an early issue of *Spare Rib*:

> Her functions are distinct but often simultaneously demanded of her so that she
> has to be an actress switching deftly from role to role; mother to baby, mother
> to husband, psychologist and teacher to baby, pupil to husband. Somewhere
> within this labyrinth is her 'self' if only she can find it. The odds on her finding
> it are minimal, since she never makes the choice of which role she is playing.
> That is always determined by either her husband or her children, or both in
> conflict with each other. (*SR.5*)

This stress has contributed to the breakdown of the nuclear family
reflected in divorce statistics and the increase in single-parent
families.

We do need the close relationships, the tenderness, care and
empathy which we seek from the family. However, in the nuclear
family women not only experience loss of identity and isolation, but
are legally and economically dependent on the husband as
breadwinner and head of the household. This inequality and the
nuclear family itself are upheld by state policy on housing, in
education, in the system of welfare provision and in the processes of
the law.

Women's work in the family includes the bearing and nurturing of
children and housework. Yet women today have fewer children,
spend a reduced proportion of their lives in childrearing and often
return to work while they are still involved in childcare. As women

have gained a measure of independence they have had to face the contradiction of their status as legally and financially dependent. This has highlighted women's criticisms of their role in the nuclear family. Within the family itself, women have questioned the male assumptions of control and ownership, described by one woman in an interview in *Spare Rib*: 'See, it's like jumping out of the frying pan into the fire when you get married; you might as well go back to being fifteen again and have to ask your bloody parents every time you want to go out.' But the independence of earning a wage that is less than a man's is limited: 'There's always somebody that you have to justify yourself to and when you go home to that you know that it's like Cinderella; you were only pretending to be free for the evening' (*SR.76*). Feminists have argued that women's biological capacity to bear children should not be used to justify confining women to the maternal role or to domestic work.

Some women have consciously sought alternatives to the nuclear family in collective or communal households, not only for a more equal sharing of the practical work but for closer relationships with women, or more equal and mutually supportive relationships between men and women, or for sharing childcare. But the past bears down on the present and changing the way we live does not automatically release us from patterns of feeling learned within the nuclear family in the first place. The psychic upheaval which can be involved in trying to change those relationships shows that the private world of the family and the public world of work are not completely separate. The family helps to shape the world outside it. The way we learn our gender identity and our psychological development are linked to the form of our family life, to the authority of the father and especially to women's primary role in mothering. Lisa Vine commented on the significance of understanding the mother–child bond and a woman's identity as a mother when she reviewed the film *Riddles of the Sphinx* in *Spare Rib*:

The 'real' world of unions, work, campaigning for a nursery, do not always seem in touch with her central problems. The former have their place in the patriarchal world, whereas the silent mysteries of a woman's life at home, in the house alone with her child, are unvoiced both in the 'real' world and to herself: only, it seems, in women's collective identity is the silence beginning to break. (*SR.59*)

Poem

OLIVE SCHREINER

I saw a woman sleeping. In her
sleep she dreamt Life stood
before her, and held in each
hand a gift – in the one Love,
in the other Freedom. And she
said to the woman, 'Choose!'
And the woman waited long:
and she said, 'Freedom!'
And Life said, 'Thou hast
well chosen. If thou hadst said,
"Love," I would have given
thee that thou didst ask for;
and I would have gone from
thee, and returned to thee no
more. Now, the day will come
when I shall return. In that
day I shall bear both gifts in
one hand.'
I heard the woman laugh in
her sleep.

SR.29, November 1974

Lucy

INTERVIEWED BY HER DAUGHTER LIZ

. . . When I left school I knew nothing, so I went into the Civil Service.
I made the tea for a bit, then I got in as a typist. In those days it was all
women. Two thousand women in that building, Waterloo Bridge
House. You could see them all gradually getting older and older and
older. And us younger ones used to really despise them as they hadn't
got married. There were a lot of them because, in that generation, all
the men had been killed in the war. We used to think, 'We're not going
to stay here till we're sixty, like those spinsters.'

So everybody did their damnedest to get a bloke. It didn't matter
who it was as long as it wore trousers. Then they used to come in

and flaunt their engagement rings. We had little celebration parties. They'd be flashing this diamond and all the others would be as jealous as hell. It was terrible. There were six of us friends. They all gradually got engaged, and then there was me left. People used to think I was peculiar. I felt awful, like some strange, weird monster.

The supervisor was a spinster. She was a cow! In her fifties. We thought she was ghastly, fancy being a miss. We were horrible, but that was the pattern. In those days you really despised anyone who wasn't married by at least twenty-five. These poor souls. It was pitiful really. There was one – she was always writing to Lonelyhearts clubs. Rather like Jean Rhys, that type of person. She was always heavily painted – rouge, lipstick, ginger hair. Just to try and get a man. I don't think she ever got anybody. It was terribly sad. But, of course, we used to laugh at her. When I joined women's liberation, and I thought back to all those things, I felt terribly ashamed. But a lot of it still goes on, right?

I was very tall, and whenever I went to a dance I always used to get midgets who hung round my waist and laid their heads on my bosom. I felt absolutely awful. The only way to pick up a boy was to go to a dance. We used to go to the Lyceum Ballroom, which I thought was, oh my dear, the absolute ultimate in sophistication. We'd all stand round like the cattle market – just stand there. All my friends would get blokes – but when they saw how tall I was I never got a partner. They'd look you up and down. Most humiliating. I felt really sad, really down. I thought I'd never get a bloke.

I was twenty-six when I met Dad. I was really on the back of the shelf, covered in dust, beginning to give up hope. My elder sister had said, 'Look, Luce, it's time you got married, and if you don't hurry up, you've had it.' People used to say to my mum, 'Isn't it terrible Lucy's not married.' I think my poor old Mum felt a bit funny about it. She'd say, 'Well, she doesn't like men.' It was just something to say. But, of course, it was the worst thing she could've said.

Then there was that famous occasion on Wood Street Station when I met Dad. The worst day of my life. Why I ever did it, I'll never know. Mind you, I was twenty-six. I'd just got over typhoid fever and I was bald. My head was covered in down! I used to wear hats all the time. Dad didn't care tuppence what I looked like, as long as I was tall. When Dad asked me out, I thought it was wonderful. At long last! That was the beginning of the end, of the rot. But I wouldn't have had you and Joy, otherwise, would I?

Dad was a male chauvinist pig – as were most of his generation. I can remember my mum cleaning out my father's shoes. There she was, putting the blacking on. His slippers were always ready for him although he was a right bastard. But it was the recognized thing. The women waited on men hand and foot.

With Dad I did the same. You didn't expect them to do anything. Of course you hadn't done anything all day, except slog and wash and iron and cook and clean. But Dad was always saying how stupid women were. They couldn't be very good mothers, let alone anything else. He thought the women in his office were silly. It was only in the last year of his life that he admitted one or two women comptometers in his office in Smithfields were quite bright. But grudgingly.

He had a very low opinion of women and, of course, it rubs off on you in the end. I knew I knew more than Dad, or different things anyhow. He didn't know French, for example. But he said it to me so often that I really thought I was stupid. It wasn't really till women's liberation that I changed my mind a bit. Silly, isn't it? All those years. Even now I've got no confidence in myself. Never will have now. It's amazing – men are doing that all the time. But now, with some women, the fact that they've gone out to work has given them a bit of confidence, just from doing a job. But on the other hand, when you see some women, especially young ones, how they take everything from men – but everything – it makes you weep. They run around, wait on the men, even some married ones in women's liberation groups.

Dad started drinking soon after we were married. He had always been waited on hand and foot by his mother. He never did a thing there. Of course, his father was a drunk too. Grandma [Lucy's mother-in-law] sometimes had both of them lying on the kitchen floor, drunk father and son. But Grandma thought Dad was the cat's whiskers, right to the end, no matter what he did. He thought I was going to carry on where she left off. Which, of course, I did. I used to have the meal ready every evening. He never came in till midnight. Every night there was meat and two veg. In the end, I didn't bother to cook it, do you blame me?

I waited up every night in terror. For thirty years you sit there with your heart thumping. That's going to affect your body in the end, isn't it? Wears it out, you can't cope. Maybe that's why I had that heart attack recently. Hearing his footsteps coming up the road – an accumulation of that for years and you don't have that high an opinion of men and marriage.

. . . Women's liberation was such a revelation to me. Let's be free, be somebody in our own right, not just an adjunct to a man. That, to me, was marvellous. That first march we went on on my birthday. I really enjoyed that, walking. 'What do we want? LIBERATION.' To me that was absolutely the ultimate. A woman of my age, walking down the Strand, shouting 'Liberation'. Cor! Blimey!

We were really downtrodden, our generation. I wish they could all come now.

SR.31, January 1975

Thursday, 21 August

ANN TALKS TO LYNN PEARSON

Ann *lives with her husband Terry and their baby Karen on a Midlands council estate. They've been married three years. Their flat is eight floors up in one of the six highrise blocks on the estate, overlooking the near-by car works where Terry works as a drilling machine operator. Ann told Lynn Pearson about a day in her life – a day shared by millions of women.*

Linda Cooper

What do I do all day? Well, I don't have any set routine except for getting the baby to bed, and getting her meals – apart from that I just do things when I feel like doing them. We've lived here two and a half years – we just wanted a place, nowhere special, and they gave us this one – we'd have taken anywhere. We're going to move soon, though, to another part of the city, where there's a ground-floor maisonette with a garden.

I have breakfast with Karen at about 8.30, and then get out to do the shopping. I take Karen with me – I shop each day of the week, as that's the only time I get out. If I bought everything in one big lot, I'd have nothing to buy during the week . . .

I get home about 10.30 and put Karen to bed, then I make a cup of coffee, a piece of toast and read the *Mirror*. People here don't seem to want to talk even when you do see them – I think it's because of the flats, people are all shut up; you can be inside your flat, and you don't know what's going on outside. I can't stand the peace and quiet, I'd much rather have a noisy place with people around. You never see anybody from one day to the next, and the baby, she's terrified of other kids, she never sees any.

When the children get bored, it gets the parents down, so the parents get depressed. Most of the mothers here are more worried about their kids than themselves, as they are going to be the parents of the future; mothers can get over being depressed. I'd like to see some sort of playschool, but something that the mothers could join in with. There is a playschool at the school across the road, but it's only for one day a week and there's a waiting list for it. The community centre is quite near, but all I use it for is the welfare – I take Karen there. The only other thing they have there is bingo, and I won't go to that. I'd like to see a play area nearer to the community centre, connected with it. And I'd like a library a bit nearer than the one we've got now. But the main thing wrong with the area is too many flats – I'd like to see more houses built, not flats.

After I have my coffee I do the housework – ironing, washing, you know. I wouldn't want to go back to working full time; I don't regret giving it up at all. What I did like about it, though, was seeing people – I'm not even seeing much of Terry at the moment because he's working for my brother-in-law at the weekends, on their house, apart from his other job. He's practically living over there at the moment . . .

I get Karen up at 12.30 and give her some dinner while I'm having mine listening to Radio 1. I play with Karen, and then take her out to the play area for half an hour. She plays on the slide and frames – this is fine in the summer, but unpleasant in the winter, when the wind sweeps across between the blocks. I put her to bed about 3.00 and then do some more housework. I have a cigarette and a cup of coffee about 3.30, and watch the racing on TV, if there's any on. I give Karen her tea at 4.30, and then she has a bath. She goes to bed about 6.00. Terry gets home about 6.30, so I get his tea ready for him, and we have tea together when he gets home. The TV's on all the time, but we don't always watch it.

Terry sometimes goes out in the evenings, but I can't get a baby-sitter, and we can't afford a proper babyminder, so I don't go out. I don't mind too much, but I'd like to be able to go out occasionally – it's depressing being in all the time. I miss things we used to do before I had the baby – we used to go for a meal, or a drink, or to a club if there was something special on. We used to go to discos before we got married, but after that, we just stopped. I watch TV in the evenings, and I have a couple of puzzle books I like doing.

I thought about getting a job at home, as I get so depressed, but if you send off for lists of jobs, all you get is lists of addresses you're supposed to write to. And most of the jobs involve selling – I don't like that, making your friends buy things. I like filling forms in – the moment the tax form comes through the door, I sit down and fill it in. I suppose that's why I like crosswords and puzzles, I can do them while I'm watching the television. I watch TV until the programmes finish, or go to bed a bit before that, about 11.00.

This area's got shops, a good bus service, pubs, social clubs, plenty of green space – it's all nice except the factory – it's just the women in the flats . . . During the holidays, it would be good to have somewhere the kids could go in the mornings – it's the eight, nine, ten-year-olds, twelve-year-olds who do all the vandalism – they're just bored, they shouldn't be at that age. The council have bought a big area which used to be the factory apprentices' playing fields, but they haven't done anything with it. There's a play area down there, but if something happens, if they fall over and crack their heads, it's too far down – by the time you've got out of the door, got the lift and got down there, it's too late. I don't know how to find out if there's a playschool where we're moving to – but just being out of the flat will make it better, Karen will be able to play outside in the garden. I think kids ought to be able to enjoy themselves while they're young . . .

SR.60, July 1977

Caring for the Disabled

ANNA BRIGGS

. . . Pat is in her late thirties and looks after Vicky who is mentally handicapped and spastic after whooping cough at five months. She is now eight.

'She's in hospital for a week (the thirtieth time in two years), partly because I can't cope and partly because she wasn't eating for no apparent reason. In the last eight weeks she's had two upper respiratory infections, three urinary tract infections and she's been fitting a lot because she suddenly won't take the anti-convulsant tablets. It just got me down and I couldn't see an end. Three times a day I was having a battle feeding her . . . We can't leave her with babysitters because of fits, so Ken and I never go out together. He sometimes goes out on his own but I don't because there's nowhere to go on my own . . . I just felt the other day that I couldn't go on. Every time I leave her she cries, when she's poorly. Ken has to bath her because I have a worn disc and sciatica and she's already heavy to lift. I'm always amazed by the fuss people make over a problem with a possible solution, when there are problems like this with no solution. I sometimes wonder if it's worth bothering – you don't live a normal life at all – you can't plan anything in advance – you don't even know if you're going to get a good night's sleep – some of the things no one can help you with' . . .

SR.81, April 1979

Living with a Difference: Cypriot Stories

AYSE, MARIA AND ZEYNEP

. . . I was brought up to think the one aim in life is to grow up and get married. Nothing like most of you, probably, when you can grow up and fall in love and marry. You see, my marriage will be arranged. They will introduce me to a man and if I like him, and him me, we will probably get engaged and within months be married.

The first time a man was introduced to me was when I was fourteen – I was at a party when a mother and her son approached us. But my mum turned them away saying I was too young.

At a few other weddings mums would come up to my mum and say, 'I have got a lovely son and what a nice match he would be for your daughter.' This made me feel a bit sick knowing that all these mothers wanted me to marry their sons. But what got me extra mad was that they asked my mum – it wasn't *her* that they were going to marry their sons to, it was *me* (not that I wanted to marry them, but still they might ask *me*).

This carried on for a few years until I was sixteen when one of my mum's cousins came to visit and asked my mum if he could speak to her in private. Well, I knew what it was going to be about when I heard that he wanted to speak to her alone. When my mum returned and told me he was going to bring a certain family to visit us I said to her that I didn't want to meet one of their stupid boys and I didn't want to get married, I told her I just couldn't fall in love like that and I didn't want to end up like her.

For the first time ever my mum listened to me and said, 'I understand what you mean and don't worry. I won't let you get married.'

Two weeks later a knock came at the door. My sister answered it and took whoever it was into the front room to my mum. Then she came running to the kitchen and said, 'They're here.' I said, 'Who's here?' and she said, 'You know, that family – that boy Mum's cousin wants you to marry.'

I started to laugh. Then my mum came in and said, 'Quick, let's make the tea so they can hurry up and go.' I asked my mum if I had to go in and she said, 'Yes, just present yourself, give out the tea and just sit there.'

I knew I wasn't going to enjoy myself but we made the tea and went in. I gave it out and noticed I was being watched by the mother and the family. I thought to myself, 'Now I know what it's like when the cows are at the market being sold.' I felt just like them. I sat down and just listened to the conversation and of course let off the occasional smile. By then I was beginning to wonder where on earth was the boy they wanted me to meet. And what a shock I get when I was told who it was – he was no boy, he must have been twenty-six or twenty-seven. It was terrible. My every move was being watched. So when I heard the mother say, 'Well, we must be going now', what a big smile the words put on my face.

They said goodbye and left, but before they left his mother said to my mum, 'What a nice daughter you have.' We didn't hear from them till the next week and they told us that the 'boy' wanted to marry me. 'How stupid,' I thought. 'He doesn't even know me and he wants to marry me.'

Well, they were waiting for my reply and said that I could have a few days to think it over but I said I didn't need another second, my answer was *no*. A few weeks later I heard that this man was getting married to a girl whose father had a factory. 'How awful,' I thought, 'he doesn't even know her, he probably doesn't love her, but he wants to marry her. I suppose it's her money he wants more than her.'

My next one was a rich man. My brother-in-law works for this man, and he invited me and my sister down for a meal. But he also said to my sister to make sure I looked older, and extra special. Myself, I didn't have a clue what he was up to until we arrived. My brother-in-law was sitting at a table laid for four. We sat down and my sister said, 'Right. When are we going to eat?' My brother-in-law said, 'Not yet, we are waiting for someone to come.' Then he dashed up to go to the door – anyone would have thought the Queen was coming.

Then, when I saw the man I knew what I'd really been invited down for. I felt awful, as if I was *after* him, and that was why I was there. I didn't feel hungry any more and neither did my sister. She knew I was uncomfortable so she suggested we went to wash our hands. When we were doing this I said to her, 'You should have told me that was the real reason we came here.' She said that she didn't know, that he probably never told me because he knew that then I wouldn't come. We went back up and they were still talking. I noticed that he kept watching me but I didn't even so much as look at his face. I said to myself, 'I bet I could pick up a better man in the streets.'

We had a drink, then he drove us home. He came in and my mum made him a cup of coffee – all this time I was playing with my niece. When he had finished his coffee my brother-in-law called me and told me to take his cup. I just took it and put it on the tray. A few minutes later he left. My brother-in-law asked me what I thought of him; I said I hated him. He said, 'You mean you wouldn't have him? But what about all his money, his car, and his business?' I said, 'He can stuff his money etc. down his throat and if he is out to buy a wife he can look elsewhere because he isn't getting me.' A few days later I heard that he wanted me, so I just said, 'Hard cheese, I am not up for sale.'

Now every time I hear anything about arranged marriages or one of my relatives saying some boy is very nice I just feel sick and say I don't want anyone.

Since I never had a father my uncle acted like one. When he heard that I was staying on at school for the sixth form his first question wasn't 'Are you staying on for a better job and grades?' it was 'Is there a boy or teacher you love, is that why you're staying on at school?' One of my real reasons was that if I left I probably would have got married.

Not that I would have been forced. I just would probably have got so fed up saying no that I would have eventually taken the next man available, just to get myself out of the house.

My uncle told me to watch the boys at school and not to fall for any. But this I couldn't obey. You can't help liking a boy – you can't stop yourself just because your uncle says so. I liked this certain boy for three months. I tried my best to talk to him but every time I did I remembered my uncle, so it was hopeless. I remember once when a boy I had liked for ages tried to kiss me and I wouldn't let him – he probably thought I didn't like it but how could I explain to him about my family life and my uncle who always told me it was wrong to do a thing like this?

Now that I've left school I know I won't get another chance to go out to school dances or anything. But I've already told them that I shall be joining evening classes at my school, then at least I can go out. It isn't anywhere special but at least it's somewhere.

In the past few weeks I've liked another boy, and now that I have left school I probably won't see him any more unless I bump into him on the street. I have still not got over him.

I hope one day I find a Turkish boy and fall for him straight away. But until then I'm saying *no* to all these other pigs . . .

To protect the writers of this article, all names have been changed.

SR.39, September 1975

Devil Children

MARGARET WALTERS

There's one genuinely terrifying scene in *The Omen*. Katherine (Lee Remick) is standing on a chair in her hall gallery to water some hanging plants; her small son, riding his tricycle ferociously, slams into the chair, and with dizzying slowness, she falls over the banister to the floor below. He stands and watches.

As you've probably gathered, *The Omen* is about a child who's not just possessed, but perhaps the devil himself. Despite desperate efforts by his father – Gregory Peck not wholly convincing as the American Ambassador in London – first to understand then to destroy him, the devil-child wins hands down. At the end of the movie, his parents and three other people who got in his way, are gorily dead; the boy has been adopted by daddy's old buddy who just happens to be president of the U S.

This thriller – skilfully made but altogether predictable – grossed over $25 million in its first six months in the States, and is cleaning up in England. It's partly due to clever publicity – it was released in the States on the 6th day of the 6th month, '76, which you'll remember was a devilishly significant date in the movie. But *The Omen* – like its predecessors *Rosemary's Baby*, recently shown again on TV, or the block-busting *The Exorcist* – clearly touches on some sensitive nerve in audiences. I suspect we're going to see many more movies in this genre: indeed, *Exorcist II* is already in the works.

Despite all the sensational publicity about levitation and head-turnings in *The Exorcist*, the scenes I remember are the early ones where the tough, working mother, who's bringing up her daughter alone, realizes something is wrong with her child. During her mother's smart party, the girl gets out of bed and pisses on the floor in front of the startled guests; she's sullen, inaccessible and destructive. And similarly *The Omen* hooks us, not by the scary sequences – melodramatic storms, a pack of wild dogs in a deserted Italian cemetery – but during the quiet domestic scenes that open the film.

At some level, all those films are concerned, not with black magic, but the ambivalent feelings between parents and children. The fantasy of a child possessed by the devil is rooted in doubts and contradictions we're all familiar with. Thus Katherine in *The Omen* is jealously over-protective of her son. (Her too-desperate need of a child, it's suggested, is the source of all the trouble: when her own baby dies at birth, her husband, fearing for her sanity substitutes a foundling.) As the family walks by the river, the small boy maliciously scares his careful parents by hiding from them; later, forced into his best clothes, he refuses hysterically to be dragged into a smart church wedding. Proofs of a diabolic nature – or perfectly ordinary acts of childhood rebellion?

Again, Katherine's growing uneasiness about her child is only too familiar. Though her whole life is built around her love for her son, she's irritated by his noisiness, resents his demands and fears his wild energy. Consumed by guilt, she confesses to a psychiatrist her hatred and her fantasy that he's not really 'her' child. He treats her as a perfectly 'normal' neurotic – which she *is*.

I'm convinced that the real power of movies like *The Omen* and *The Exorcist* lies in the skill with which they play, subliminally, on the whole complex of mixed and painful feelings within the family. They evoke the guilty resentment beneath maternal love, and the anger, known by the most loving parents, at the way a child disrupts their lives. They hook into the woman's fantasy that she might give birth to a monster, terrifying and alien – but a monster that externalizes everything dark and evil within herself. The films hint that these evil children are a punishment on the parents – and at the same time suggest that, since the evil is satanic, supernatural, the parents are not really responsible after all. *The Exorcist* certainly implied that the sexy, independent mother was being punished for her lifestyle – *and* it offered the audience the sadistic spectacle of the child being battered back to normality. And at the climax of *The Omen*, the father actually tries to kill his own child: to exorcise the devil – or his own overwhelming fear and hatred?

It's easy to dismiss these films as merely fashionable and implausible fantasies dreamed up by a cash-conscious Hollywood. But only recently, and here in England, a man and woman were tried for murdering their small daughter believing that she was inhabited by the devil, that they were ridding the world of an evil and destructive force. That terrifying, but by no means unprecedented incident, perhaps suggests that we should try more seriously to understand the success of these devil movies and the fantasies – in all of us – that they exploit so skilfully.

SR.53, December 1976

-Well, as long as you don't try to get away, you can hardly feel it.

Liz Mackie, *SR.19*, January 1974

Out of the Closet into the Courts

ELEANOR STEPHENS

There have always been children brought up by parents who are homosexual, but until recently their homosexuality has been a closely guarded secret. More and more women are now choosing to live openly as lesbians in relationships with their lovers, and if they have children they are also asserting their right to be lesbians and mothers. It is a risk anyway to come out as a homosexual and, because of prejudice in the law involving custody of children, lesbian mothers are finding that the risk involves losing their children.

When a woman who is a lesbian is unlucky enough to have to go to court to fight for custody she has at the moment no chance of winning. The judge always awards custody to the father. The most the mother can hope for is 'access' – the right to visit the children who have lived with her from birth and often for long periods since separating from her husband. (Recently in America cases have been won, usually on appeal.)

The assumption of the courts and the judges, who alone make this decision, is that a lesbian cannot by definition be a good mother, so it must always be in the interests of the children to live apart from her. Normally in 'tug-of-love' cases the courts would give custody to the mother since childcare is assumed to be the woman's role. The husband may participate in major decisions, contribute financially and have access at weekends and holidays. The judge will only separate children from their mother if there are over-riding factors like the mother's health, or actual neglect or cruelty. Such considerations are obviously relevant to the children's welfare.

The mother's sexual orientation is taken to be just such a factor, and no other evidence has to be produced to disqualify her from bringing up her children. One judge, considered to hold relatively liberal views, went to some lengths to explain that while he did not attribute blame to the mother for her lesbianism, and could even go so far as to sympathize with her, it was vital that the court distinguish between understanding and approval. To approve of homosexuality, he said, would mean the decay of society as we know it and could only corrupt others.

A lesbian with openly feminist ideas poses a double threat. She is seen as a direct challenge to family life and the traditional sexual roles which the courts uphold. A head-on political clash takes place with all the power on one side. (A few cases have been lost by women only because of their feminist involvement, without the added stigma of lesbianism.)

In one of the early cases, much was made of the mother having subversive feminist literature in her home – magazines like *Spare Rib* and *Shrew* were used as evidence against her – and she was accused of exposing her children to 'an exotic atmosphere in which intellectual opinions expressing themselves as an eagerness for total feminine freedom, sexual and otherwise, will have a marked influence'. The judge declared that her 'passionate interest in the women's liberation movement' was likely to mean that her daughters would grow up with 'little or no respect for the ordinary obligations of family life' and 'be exposed to propaganda about sexual morality which could expose them to quite extraordinary risks in adolescence'. Having painted this picture of life in what he described as an unhealthy 'milieu of feminine fanaticism' he then felt quite justified in 'protecting' the children involved by separating them from their mother.

The fact of women living together and raising children without men poses the most extraordinary threat to these guardians of the status quo. The court functions like a male club whose ageing members wield absolute power over people's lives and who automatically sympathize with the husband. An American judge spelt this out only too well:

It is difficult to conceive of a more grievous indignity to which a person of normal psychological and sexual constitution could be exposed than the entry by his spouse upon an active and continuous course of homosexual love with another. Added to the insult to sexual loyalty per se (which is present in ordinary adultery) is the natural revulsion arising from the knowledge of the fact that the spouse's betrayal takes the form of a perversion.* Common sense and modern psychiatric knowledge concur as to the incompatibility of homosexuality and the subsistence of marriage between one so afflicted and a normal person.

Some judges may pay lip service to more liberal views, but these are the kind of attitudes underlying courtroom debate. The choice is seen to lie between the stigmatized, afflicted deviant, and the 'normal' husband who presents the very picture of decent, solid virtues, often with new wife and mother-substitute in tow. The verdict comes as no surprise.

But the courtroom is not just a theatre of the absurd. It has terrible implications for the women and children concerned. Gillian, who has no chance at all of winning custody, said to me: 'If I had known when I left my husband how it would turn out with my children, I sometimes wonder if I would have gone through with it.' None of the women I spoke with regretted making this change but they all questioned that

* The law does not define a homosexual relationship during marriage as *adultery*. It is considered 'unreasonable conduct'.

they should pay so high a price for their right to live and love as they chose.

Sue lives with her five-year-old son John and her lover Mary in the West Country. They have been living together for two years since Sue left her husband. Their home would appear to be everything a court could ask for, an idyllic place to raise a young child; they have many acres of woodland with streams running through, and have lots of friends and relatives, so John has plenty of contact with people of both sexes.

When Sue, after five years of marriage, told her husband about her relationship with Mary, he explained that he had been having a long-term affair which Sue knew nothing about, and asked that John live with him and his girlfriend. Sue agreed because she knew she had little chance of winning a contested custody case. But very soon the girl-friend left and John's father couldn't cope without female help, so he returned John to his mother. This to-ing and fro-ing happened again, and Sue decided it was best for John to make his home and with her and Mary.

'John's father agreed with him living with us, and relations between us were quite friendly to begin with; I made sure John saw his father regularly. Then I had the impression that he got worried and rushed around to find a new woman. He found someone very competent and impressive whom he married two days after our divorce. Once she appeared on the scene, it was obvious they would fight to take John away, and everything became very strained and unpleasant. We first went to court last year. The judge said he didn't like tug-of-love cases and sent us outside to work it out. To our surprise the two barristers agreed to keep the status quo and leave John, who was only just four, with us. That's why it's all the more infuriating to lose now.'

Sue went to court last month with what looked to be a very strong case. She had an excellent team of feminist lawyers and very good reports from welfare workers, psychiatrists, character witnesses and all the rest. The very young age of the child made it less likely that he would be removed from his mother. Against this was the fact that the father offered a mother-substitute in a heterosexual family with the possibility of new brothers and sisters. While the judge allowed that all four contenders were 'attractive personalities' he approved par-ticularly of the new wife. 'She is the only adult without psychiatric blemish.' (The judge even reprimanded Sue for not having made friends with this fine woman who was trying to take her child away! Incidentally, Sue and Mary's only 'psychiatric blemish' was their homosexuality.)

The judge granted that there was little to choose between the two homes, and that John had an excellent relationship with his mother, so the judgement was based on the 'problem' of the mother's sexual orientation. Both parties produced psychiatric reports on the possible effects of a child brought up in a lesbian household and the judge chose to accept the negative conclusions of the husband's witness, a psychiatrist who wrote: 'John's mother practises statistically abnormal sexual acts which can be looked upon either as a deviation from normal or frankly perverted. I have no evidence before me to state that this environment will not affect John's future emotional and psycho-sexual development. In the absence of a father or father-figure, male identification is not possible unless a substitute father is provided and this, within the setting of a homosexual environment, would not be satisfactory. The only person or persons John would be able to identify with would be his mother and her cohabitee and sooner or later he must learn that they engage in unnatural acts. It would be difficult to imagine that this young boy could go through his adolescent period of development without feeling shame and embarrassment, of having a mother who has elected to engage in sexual practices which are statistically abnormal. I think it would be agreed by a large body of practising clinical psychiatrists that persons who engage in homosexual patterns of behaviour have personality difficulties.'

Most of these assertions are just that – unfounded assertions – but *they* carried weight in court rather than the report from the mother's psychiatrist which was much more moderate and emphasized the quality of the mother–child relationship. (As Sue said afterwards, do they think John is going to grow up to be a statistician?!)

Unfortunately there is no documentation on children raised in homosexual families so there is nothing with which to counter the traditional prejudices on their own terms. Sue thought this could have made a difference in her case: 'We desperately need some research on all this. If we could have said in court, "Look, here is a study of fifty children who've grown up with lesbian mothers and they're no different from other kids" (heterosexual, whatever, since we have to fight this on their terms at present), I believe this would have had a tremendous effect. It would undermine some of the statements they make which are based on nothing but prejudice and ridiculous myths about homosexuals. We also need people who've been brought up by homosexual parents to come out and say so. Our judge ended his summing up, "These are uncharted waters which I'm not prepared to sail on." Instead he chooses to remove a young child from the home where he's happy and place him in a new situation. We have to have these waters seen to be charted, that's a priority.'

By the time you read this, John will have left his mother's home and been moved to his father. Sue is allowed access once a fortnight and part of school holidays, although the ex-husband said in court that he may not be able to afford his half of the travel expenses for John to visit his mother. The judge insisted that John be 'protected from the lesbian relationship' and that when he visits, the two women must sleep apart and be 'just friends'. Such an invasion of privacy is quite common; a couple who, out of fear of losing what little they had, followed this injunction found that the children were upset by the change. They assumed their mother and lover had quarrelled and that something was wrong for them to be more distant.

After the judgement, Sue wrote: 'I really do not know how to find words to express my reaction to this delicate queer-bashing. Anyone would think that the sexual aspect of our relationship is the be-all and end-all. I love John and can't envisage life without him but it seems that at the moment there is nothing we can do; we have been advised that it would be pointless to appeal. I suppose we have paid the price for our love and we are both very sore at the cost. We shall never lose these battle scars completely and the judgement will stick in our throats

Alison Fell, *SR. 65*, December 1977

every time we try to swallow it – like trying to swallow a whole ostrich egg. If we can fight to make things different for other people in the future we shall do so. And we certainly do not intend to be ostriches.'

The obsession with the mother's sexuality is striking in many cases and the husband may dwell on details designed to reinforce the court's phobia of lesbianism. One man, for instance, described how he had found marks on the pillows of his wife's double bed showing they had been depressed by two heads! The courts apply a double standard to the question of the lesbian couple showing any physical affection to each other with children around: in a heterosexual relationship this is thought to be good for the children by contributing to a loving, secure atmosphere, but it is considered detrimental – almost obscene – in a homosexual relationship.

The myth of lesbians as child molesters is often in evidence and the courts may ask the mother how she will manage if her women friends make sexual advances to her daughters. It is hard to believe that the judge would voice his concern about a woman's new husband seducing her daughter – though it is far more likely to happen.

As Sue's case showed, the new wife, although often a complete stranger to the children, plays an important part in strengthening her husband's claim for custody, particularly if she has children herself. His lawyers paint her as the picture of respectability and draw maximum contrast between her and the 'deviant' mother. One such woman who made an excellent impression on the judge, exploited her conventionality to the full: 'I'm really just a Marks and Sparks sort of person', was how she described herself in court.

Although the custody battle is assumed to be between the mother and the father who both wish to bring up the children, once the father has custody he often plays a minimal part in their daily lives. If he has not remarried, the children may be cared for by relatives or a succession of housekeepers. A woman who has lost custody told me that one of the saddest things was the fact that her children had been looked after by ten au pairs in fifteen months. By taking the children away from their mother, the court may be depriving them of any close parental relationship whatsoever.

Gillian is unable even to get regular access to see her two young children. She has no chance at all of custody. During the last two years since she left her husband and children, there have been a succession of court orders for access which her husband consistently obstructs. From the moment she told him about her feelings for Jane, who was also married with a young child, his attitude has been vindictive and punitive using the children as weapons. He immediately gave her an ultimatum to leave ('I don't want my children touched by a lesbian') or to stop seeing Jane, give up her job and never go out without him. Under this pressure she and Jane decided to leave for London straight away. 'Looking back, we should have taken the kids with us. I would advise women to do that if they possibly can – but how could we? We were both under incredible strain, set off at once and slept the first nights in the car. We knew no one in London – we even went to sex shops in Soho to find out about gay organizations!'

Jane's husband was already having an affair with a woman who he later married and he has been relatively co-operative about their child. She goes up to see her every fortnight and the child comes to stay with them in the holidays.

Gillian had hoped for a similar arrangement with her husband but she has had to fight all the way. 'My case was badly mishandled by my solicitors, who didn't bother to go for custody at the time of the divorce. It's very important to do this or later it's used as evidence that you didn't care about your children. Now it's a struggle just to see them at all. My daughter, who I was very close to, has been turned against me by her father and says now that she doesn't want to see me. He's told her I'm abnormal and don't want to be her mother. Once I managed to talk to her on the phone while he was out. He punished me for this by not bringing the children to meet me after I'd driven a long way to see them. He has become completely vindictive, while maintaining that he's trying to protect the children from being contaminated by me. When you remember that two years ago, Jane and I spent all our time together with the children, we even had plans to go on holiday together; now I can't even see them without a chaperone! I think he's hoping that if he makes life hard enough we'll give up. But we won't, we'll fight it to the House of Lords if necessary.'

Of course many women never do fight their cases because they know they have no chance of winning, so these injustices remain invisible. The cases that have come to court reveal a phobia not just of lesbianism but of nonconformity in general: people who deviate from society's ideas of what is normal are penalized. They show a striking resemblance to American custody cases involving inter-racial marriages – the non-white, minority-group parent loses custody.

Time and again fears that the children will grow up homosexual and be influenced in its favour, and that the social stigma against homosexuality will harm the child, are taken as facts to be used as evidence. One American judge of the Pennsylvanian Supreme Court did try to counter these biases, but he is an exception: 'If the children are raised in a happy and stable home, they will be able to cope with prejudice and hopefully learn that people are unique individuals who should be treated as such.' Perhaps this can give us some hope for English court decisions, though at the moment it seems to me that the backlash of intolerance which is growing in the present crisis makes the outlook grim.

Homosexuality is not a crime, a sin or a disease; it need not even be a problem if society did not make it so for many. What is meant to be at issue in a custody case (and I believe the entire custody system needs to be challenged) is the interest and wellbeing of the children, some-

From *Up from Under*, 1973, *SR.42*, December 1975

thing the recent Children's Act emphasized. So the crucial factor is what the person is like as a parent. Neither heterosexuality nor homosexuality are in themselves guarantees of good parenthood; how the parent defines herself (or himself), her religion, politics, lifestyle or sexual preference is irrelevant. If the court is to question someone's 'fitness' to be a parent it must be on grounds that would apply to anyone – lesbian or heterosexual, Black Muslim or macrobiotic.

A pressure group, Action for Lesbian Parents (ALP), is working to publicize this injustice in the legal system and to promote research on children growing up in homosexual families. It is crucial that all of us who feel strongly about this blatant anti-woman prejudice make our voices heard. We urge you to contact ALP c/o *Spare Rib* if you can help in any way.

Minor details have been changed in this article to preserve anonymity. Court quotes are from notes written in court, not from official transcripts.

SR.50, September 1976

'I Keep Digging Our Relationship Up'

SUE COX

John and I aren't married, although we've been living together for a couple of years. I used to be fairly proud of that – escaping the legal but meaningless bonds and so on – now I'm not so sure. Getting married is largely an outdated and hypocritical business – and yet people still do it all the time. And looking at a lot of them it seems to me that their marriages were at least a declaration of confidence in the future; a declaration of sureness of feelings that I envy.

John and I have never felt a security or confidence in each other. Or to be precise – *I* have never felt a security or confidence in my feelings for John. They wax and wane, that's the trouble. Sometimes I feel so close to him and sometimes I hate him. Sometimes I am alive to his every move, and sometimes I am indifferent to him. And I know that these changes are brought about by my expectations which are so often disappointed. I want so much out of the relationship. I want a truly deep understanding and liking which will reassure me constantly that we are the best of friends, and I want a lover who is both passionate and tender. I want to be able to read his mind and his heart and I want him to read mine. To this end, I often lay my mind and heart out on a plate for him and then feel frustrated because he can't or won't or doesn't need to do the same.

Perhaps, in spite of my conscious rejection of the *Woman's Own* ideal relationship, I am bogged down and wallowing in romantic hangovers that men don't have. I have had a 'good job', and neither wanted marriage nor, so far, children, always a career and equality, and yet, even so, a relationship with a man has always been the thing of central importance in my life. But I can't just let it happen. I worry at it. As John puts it – I keep digging it up to see if it's growing.

If anybody is the wronged party in our relationship it's John. Because I don't behave consistently towards him he is developing a guardedness and nervousness towards me. He can't be sure what my reactions to anything will be and he can't be sure whether I'll come home at the end of the day with a smile or a scowl for him, and so he seems to hide himself so as not to get hurt, I suppose. And can you blame him?

You may wonder at this mutual oppression. We have talked about splitting up, but as yet the ties are too tight. I'm sorry if this sounds like romantic mush, but I haven't lived with John for two years and not known the good times. When I reach a phase of hardness and decide I must break the bonds for both our sakes, a phase of softness and affection follows close on its heels and no change results. Does this strike a chord with any of you? Notice that I say *I* must break the bonds. John wouldn't, partly because he now has a new job in this town while I have just given one up, making it easier for me to move, and partly because he doesn't make decisions easily. In fact, he's even more laboured than me. I think he waits in the hope that some miracle cure will steady my temperament and all will end happily. I've hoped and I'm growing old waiting.

If things aren't so good, why don't we try spreading our wings without talking about cataclysmic farewells and complete breaks? I don't feel free enough to experiment. My freedom isn't curtailed consciously by John; it's curtailed more by my own temperament, conditioning and hang-ups. I believe in my head that living exclusively with one person of the opposite sex, with or without children, is a restricting and neurosis-producing business, but I am still light years from doing anything about it. I wonder if I set my sights too far. I have been looking for something high and wild. Should I recognize my own limitations imposed partly by my uneventful, middle-class, fairly spoiled upbringing, or should I strive for something I can't yet identify – some soaring freedom perhaps, some strength that will bolster my spirit and make life a joy to wake up to every day?

Kate Hancock, *SR.26*, August 1974

To come back to John and me. Sex, is predictably enough, a potential hang-up as well as a pleasure in this situation. John could

fancy it any time. I can fancy it when and if the moment is right –
usually when it arises out of a feeling of closeness through the sharing
of something else. Because I know it's frustrating for a bloke to be
refused, and because I'm liking him well enough, even if not fancying
him, I try to oblige. When I try to oblige I usually can't. One tension
brings on another. And the tension of my not really wanting him inside
me makes it difficult for him. We both end up frustrated; physically
because we've struggled for it like it's a Big Money Prize. The
Consumer Society. Other times, it's just John who's frustrated because
I'm spark out when I hit the pillow.

If two people share the same bed every night of the year, it strikes
me as hardly surprising that their separate beings can't always achieve
a perfect union. When we make love, when we get that far, it's usually
great for both of us, and I wonder then why we don't do it more often.
I can't get the hang of the warm-up. The transfer from feelings of
warmth and gentleness to feelings of energy and desire is a hard one.
And I have found myself often making this transfer by silently telling
myself as we play with each other that I'm going to like this, aren't I?
Oh yes, if I can just stick with it a while how well rewarded will I be.
So much for the Act of Love. John believes that if we made love more
often our relationship would settle down. I believe that our sex life is a
symptom of the disease.

I am diverted by the phrase 'settle down'. An expression that is
totally abhorrent to me. I have a horror of settling down if it means
banality, ordinariness, predictability. And I wonder if that is why I
keep digging our relationship up to see if it's growing. To create some
trouble and drama? To shake it about so it doesn't get boring? And yet
– I really don't want this upset to go on. I am exhausted by my own
inconsistency. What I really want, I suppose, is for the relationship to
settle on a plane that is deeper and more fulfilling and exciting than
what I take to be the norm behind the front doors down our road. But
I am full of contradictions – I just said that I believe that one-to-one
relationships are not ideal anyway. Please can I be excused my contradictions in a world that changes so fast?

If John and I keep living together it may be because we have found
some peace, or because change is too difficult. If we split up I may join
a commune or I may get right down to the straight and narrow and
acquire a smart hat and a regular bed time when I'm forty-five.

One thing's for sure – it's a great strain living with a man whom you
admire on one hand for his ability to shake off many of the accepted
and odious norms of his sex, and whom you resent on the other hand
with an unreasonable but ever present resentment for his maleness –

for the fact that he and his like have it easier than us. It seems to me that from this resentment comes a general anti-male feeling which I often find in *Spare Rib*, and it disturbs me. I think that women's liberation is a prerequisite for people's liberation, but if we come to hate our 'oppressors' in the process of freeing ourselves, what sort of world will we have made for ourselves? Is a world divided into opposing sexual camps more preferable than a world divided into the haves and have-nots?

I love John. I hate him. I admire him. I resent him. But I want to be on the same side as him fighting the other buggers. And so, perhaps, I am holding back from the freedom of individuality. A cop out?

SR.47, June 1976

Life on Social Security

JANE HUTT AND MARY GILES TALKED TO 'MARY'

... It's not 'life' on Social Security (S S), it's 'existence'. People in the government, whatever party, just don't know what it's like to be in the supermarket and have to add everything up as you go along to make sure you have enough money in your purse to pay the bill at the cash-desk. Single parents should get a lot more bloody money.

... I remember telling the woman from the S S that I had to cut down my own clothes to fit my eldest son. She said how lucky I was that I could save money in that way. Since then I've got a bit cheekier. I got money from the S S to buy a second-hand cooker recently. But I don't bother now with grants for the children because they make you feel you're begging ...

SR.85, August 1979

3 CHILDCARE

Women have been bound to their function in the family by the assumption that mothers bear the sole responsibility for looking after children and by the lack of alternative care.

The attitude of successive governments towards nursery provision has been both punitive and cynical: women 'ought' to stay at home with young children – unless and until they are needed to join the work force. Thus, an unprecedented number of nursery places were founded and funded during the war years, and in the sixties spending curbs were relaxed to create places for the children of, ironically enough, teachers and nurses. Many more mothers now work than did during the war years. But the state's policy on care of the under-fives is based neither on the mothers' interests, nor on the welfare of the children.

Enforced isolation with each other produces depression in both children and mothers – in the extreme, battering or suicide. A different desperation is experienced by mothers who go out to work, as do more than a quarter of women with pre-school age children. For most, finding childcare is not a once-and-for-all thing, but a constant, nerve-wracking juggling of arrangements which, as one mother put it, would defeat any pragmatic politician: 'One morning to her mother, two to her father, two mornings with a neighbour; one afternoon to her mother, another to her father, two to a neighbour who takes her to a playgroup, one to another neighbour. And every week these sessions have to be reviewed and altered' (*SR.47*).

But the availability of part-time work shows that it is often in the interests of production to employ women and to fit working hours around childcare. Four out of five part-time workers are women. As Sarah Benton pointed out, employers say women should be grateful for part-time work whereas in fact part-time work is profitable for the employer: 'They put out a lot of P R about how it suits women particularly with children. What they don't say is productivity is considerably increased by having two separate four-hour shifts' (*SR.11*).

Free full-time care is provided in state nurseries for just a tiny handful of children. Mothers and children have to be in the most desperate circumstances to gain a nursery place: they are selected by social workers on the grounds of relative misery and danger, and hundreds of 'high priority' children are still on council waiting lists. Full-time care in the few workplace nurseries is not free and is solely designed to recruit female labour; it is not available to men and has all the drawbacks of tied housing.

Working mothers frequently have to turn to childminders: a case of the exploited exploiting the exploited. Childminders work long and tiring hours for a very low wage and without the benefit of paid holidays, sick leave, pension rights or any industrial protection. Many women childmind because it is the only work available to them. Childminders in Sutton formed an action group and formulated demands to transform their work. They proposed that they be employed by the local authority, receive 'basic training in childcare' and join the National Union of Public Employees (*SR.28*). There are other moves to alter the status of childcare, from being a maternal responsibility to being professionally recognized as work which can be done by either sex. Playgroups, adventure playgrounds and one o'clock clubs have all transformed the private, domestic nature of childcare into a community concern. Nurseries like Dartmouth Park Hill in North London and communal meeting places like Laurieston Hall in Scotland have challenged the idea of childcare as women's work, insisting that men participate on an equal basis – not as highly qualified 'experts' – and spreading anti-sexist, anti-authoritarian methods beyond the private efforts of individual feminists.

Over the last few years workers in these groups have also challenged the notion that community childcare is voluntary work, by demanding better pay, working conditions and facilities for the children.

Some nurseries have been criticized for being 'institutionalized, unjoyful places without strong attachments . . . organized in a very hierarchical way; with matrons in a mother/teacher/nurse role, inducing fear in the hearts of workers, children and parents' (*SR.36*). The majority of facilities are still only available to children aged four and over for short sessions during a school year and virtually exclude all children under two. They are not much help to the beleaguered mother of younger children and no use at all to mothers who go out to work.

What women need and have been campaigning for at local, regional and national levels for the last decade is free childcare for all children, flexibly available for whatever hours mothers require. This basic demand does not mean that women are not concerned with how nurseries are run.

Changing Childcare

MARSHA ROWE

Collective childcare is a creative commitment which has absorbed the energy of many women in the women's movement who do not have children themselves. Often their involvement began as an inspiration to help single or unsupported mothers. Alison, who now lives in a collective household in Leeds, recalled how her involvement began: 'I was living in Oxford in an area where there were a lot of people I knew, with Hugo and Roger, and then a woman arrived from London who was pregnant and had nowhere to live.' Sometimes it was battering which provoked a wife to search for a new life. Jenny, from London, became involved with Babs and her children in this way: 'A group of us had taken a decision to live together. Babs was a battered wife we met a couple of years previously in the Claimants' Union. She had Andy and another boy.'

. . . At times the response of the women without children was spontaneous: 'I don't remember making any decision to say, yes, I'd be involved in collective childcare; it was all based on trust and naivety.' It was something they felt fitted in with the particular directions of their own lives, so that their needs and the needs of the mothers appeared to meet in the collective form of life. There was the desire for kinship with other women, to share domestic labour between the sexes, to work for more equal and supportive relationships between each other. And it was combined with a collective solution to economic inequality in one of the Manchester households when everyone shared their money, which gave the collective childcare a financial foundation.

There were already two children in Jodie's household when Fran decided to move in. Inexperienced, she had assumed that babysitting would not mean any alteration in the pattern of her existence. Subsequently it brought a profound personal change in her, a tie of feeling which, she puzzled, might not have happened if the children 'had been younger, and if they went to bed earlier'. The children played their part: 'Christine in particular makes a lot of fuss. At the best of times she doesn't go to bed before 9.30 to 10.30. She goes through whole acts of sabotage, like putting vinegar in the honey.' Fran feels that now her identity is bound up with the children and it is impossible to extricate herself from the relationship.

Women's susceptibility to taking on a nurturing role was also a motive, as when two of the women, Wendy and Jenny, agreed to help

BABYSita-
nita-week sit on an adult
NOW ACTION
ACTION
NOW EQUAL RIGHTS
FOR MOTHERS
I want my mum
make new (little) friends
sit on a grown-up

Sara Fay, *SR.51*, October 1976

after they became unemployed: 'I thought what an altruistic thing it would be to look after other people's kids.' The duty to care, the old duty of femininity, lay hidden underneath their feminist aim to find a new form for the family. The contradiction only revealed itself to Jenny after she returned to her job: 'I was unemployed at the time so I had more time to relate to the kids, and I think it was quite a mistake really because I haven't got the time now and I've still got the emotional bond.'

For Alison, who at the time thought procreation was repugnant, collective childcare was a chance to be close to children without pregnancy. When she decided to help bring up a friend's baby two weeks after the birth, she realized the memory of her own upbringing initiated the idea of changing the parent–child relationship: 'My mother was a very active, energetic woman and yet she felt she should stay at home and look after me, so there was all this energy going on to me. It was claustrophobic.' To Alison and the others in her household, the relationship of love in childcare presented itself as an area of personal politics. They decided to set up a creche to share the work and to change the nature of parental love, to divide and share the emotional labour: 'It was getting away from the idea of nuclear relationships where the children have to get their whole satisfaction and emotional support from just one person.'

Rotas are a 'practical necessity' in most of the households and are usually sorted out into specific tasks rather than days of the week. In one household it is 'Getting them up, dressing, taking them to school or nursery, picking them up, and being around until other people get in from work, then feeding them and putting them to bed.' The week-end rota stays the same but people don't put their names on a list: 'It depends on who's around and mucking in.'

Rota systems have dangers. Jenny expressed worry that the children lose their identity as growing human beings and become mere extensions of a timetable, fragments of the housework. 'Children are part of the *housework* rota.' She feels divided against herself in going along with the mothers' distance from the children: 'I'm thinking of these children as a duty but it's part of the whole definition of this house.'

However, without a structure, Jodie doesn't know where she is at times, and it produces hesitation and worry in her relationship to the mother of the child. She feels torn between anxiety that she doesn't contribute enough to the childcare, and that if she did more she'd be 'intruding' on Louise's relationship to the child: 'I put Susan to bed if Louise is going out early, or if I want to, or if Susan wants me to. It's difficult because I don't think I can take any initiative over it.' She is hesitant, reluctant in the face of the authority of the mother. But she stresses too, that it's not a personal problem between her and Louise but part of the wider issue of having responsibility without control which is the cause of her conflict: 'Sometimes I *have* to put her to bed, but without deciding how, why, or when.'

The activity of childcare calls on women without children in the same way as it does mothers, absorbing their being and dissolving their identity: 'No matter what you plan, a child's needs can just override all effort at organization.' A full day's childcare is 'mind-deadening', 'grinding', the day is 'bitty', divided into many distracting facets and it seems impossible to find the space or concentration even to write a letter. The childless woman's existence can, like the mother's, flee from her control, her sense of self vanish, to be replaced by the meaningless, moody reflection of an unceasing flow of demands and tasks.

It is in the context of their feelings about children and the transformation of themselves during childcare that women find themselves in particular conflict. The women who are not mothers but who have devoted endless energy to childcare have found themselves past the point of detachment from the children. Unlike nursery workers or childminders, their care for the children extends over twenty-four hours and they become non-biological parents. There is a passionate presence to their commitment which they feel parents and outsiders have not understood or have disregarded. They learn a parent's responses to the children: 'We worry about the kids being ill, etc., just the same', and grief over the loss of a child expresses the intensity of the relationship, undefined yet deeply loving.

Parents have asserted their proprietorial rights over children and taken them away from collective households without considering this relationship. The pain expressed by Alison was tumultuous and engulfing: 'Cass left just over a year ago. After being with a group of us for three and a half years, he suddenly disappeared. It was really terrible. I experienced Cass being taken away as much worse than my mother dying, much worse than any sexual relationship being broken up. A lot of summer is blanked out because the feeling was so bad. If I had been the biological mother everyone would have been very understanding. People don't understand how you can feel about a child who didn't come out of your own body.'

The sense of renewal, the joy, fascination and revival of wonder which comes at the birth of a baby are not merely the prerogative of maternity. The birth can also be a tender, shared rediscovery of energy for non-biological parents. The mothering can be undertaken by a group from the child's first weeks of life. In Alison's household this happened twice and she talks about the children with the familiar, confident knowledge usually only associated with a mother: 'She had the baby in hospital and came out after forty-eight hours. She only breastfed for two weeks so we were all taking turns to get him up at night. Cass was a very easy baby, he slept lots, woke up and was fed and went back to sleep. He was pretty cheerful. He was thirteen and a half months when Maya was born. Maya wasn't breastfed because Penny couldn't manage it and so that meant everyone shared it as before. When she was a tiny baby she slept in a carrycot in different people's rooms.'

This particular group formed a creche which operated between two households after a time, with two different adults out of a total of eight men and women looking after four children a day: 'depending on different people's jobs, commitment and preference'. Wendy described their rota system with some amusement: 'All the kids stayed at our house at some point. One night there'd be no kids and the next night two kids. We had these immense rotas. One time we had a six-colour coded rota as to where all the kids were. They didn't necessarily spend the night at the same place as they spent the day, so there was swapping around at 5.30. The first week I moved in was a nightmare. We had creche meetings once a fortnight, and there'd be all these adults sitting round talking about a kid shitting on the floor. There were these problems. All the nappies would end up in the same place, or all the trousers, and there were never enough to go round.'

The meetings were necessary for the survival of the creche, because of the complexities of organization, and to ensure a communal, concerned exchange of information about the children. 'Childcare in general is not a boring thing, but the minute details of whether little Jane is eating an apple or not are very dull.' The non-biological parents depended on the meetings for support. Their deep sense of responsibility for the children needed reassurance against cynical observations flung out by those who 'feel they have an absolute right to barge in and criticize what you're doing. People would never behave so crassly and insensitively to parents in a family set-up, or to unsupported mothers or to fostering/adopting parents. Because it's an unusual structure they think you're strange people who don't have feelings.'

Mothers who have had sole responsibility during their child's early years, who have gone through the frightening discovery that mothering is not all instinctive, feeling bewildered, unsure and insecure, feel also a sense of achievement. Their strength flows from their relationship with the children. When this particular relationship to their children changes and the constancy of their children's dependence begins to lose its hold, they can feel alone in a new anxiety. Their child's affection might disappear. This is an undertow of dread which is hard to reveal to the non-biological parents and which, in the delicacy of creating trust between parents and non-parents, can institute itself as defensiveness. At the creche meetings, Moira was always 'reticent' about asking for special time with her child in her own house because her suggestion was interpreted as 'possessiveness', an 'incorrect' emotion, and met by a hurried reassurance that the other adults would be 'nice' to her child. The issue of her identity as a mother was 'swept under the carpet'.

On the other hand, there is the question of mothers expecting the women to take responsibility while at the same time denying them real control. When this is raised, mothers can evade it by deflecting the question back on to their feelings. Fran gave an example from her household:

'Like over teatime, I think if I'm cooking the tea, it ought to be up to me to decide whether or not the kids can have a sandwich beforehand, but when they go and ask their mother, she'll say yes or no regardless of me making the tea. And she just seems to get defensive when she's confronted about it, she just gets this guilty thing about "I'm a bad mother".'

The extreme of forcing relationships to fit into a newly ordained order within the collective is, however, uselessly destructive. At one point in Fran and Jodie's household 'We had agreed to abolish parenthood. James had been living with his mum for two years before that but if he called her mum someone would say "Her name is Rose".' Four years later Jodie comments wryly that they had 'unrealistic expectations'. The mother's practical experience of the child was rejected, and at times she had felt 'put down just for being the mother'. When the mother and child remained emotionally dependent on each other, some of the other adults had felt rejected. They reacted by rejecting the child themselves and almost blaming the mother for the situation.

Caroline's experience of collective living in London has led her to the conclusion that the mother is always a central figure in collective households and the childless women peripheral. 'The exigency the kids had was absolute, the two mothers had a great deal of power in the collective.' She felt this was because the intense emotion and physical effort of childcare – despite a fairly even distribution of work between the parents and non-parents – was out of balance when control stayed with the parents: 'In all the collectives I've known the parents have had the ultimate responsibility or pleasure.' Her response has been to have a child of her own because, finally, it seemed impossible to disentangle the love and labour: 'Childcare is a very fine, exciting and volatile mixture of love and housework.'

Her desire was echoed by some of the other women confronted by the ultimatum of mother-right and the imminent departure of children from their lives. 'From my experience mothers just want someone to help them out and they don't really want to give up control, and I feel now I would have to have kids myself to get that sort of relationship' was the despair and defeat felt by Jodie. Wendy and Alison thought that 'parents can treat their kids like shit but they're still theirs.' For Fran it was hard to live with the fear of loss: 'Louise and the children are moving out to a co-op house, and this means that after years I am not going to be living with them any more, and last week I started getting really upset because I thought that when Louise no longer needs me to help out I won't be seeing them any more.'

... Jenny brought out the particular contrast between her job in a London council nursery and the oddity of being a non-biological parent in private life. 'There I'm being paid as a nursery worker, the children go back to their parents in the evening and I don't feel all those responsibilities. It's a more clearly defined role as opposed to being this strange person who looks after other people's kids.' For her the comparison is heightened when parents press for help with their children and overlook the love; 'It's like saying children are just a burden. We wouldn't say that about a sexual relationship. We choose all the time to get dependent. There are a lot of good, positive things about being a parent that people deny. Parents get a lot of emotional reward from having a child. When I am with Andy I feel my life is far more structured and real in the same way you do when you have a sexual relationship.'

. . . The women who are non-biological parents feel like the governess of old – no one knows quite how to treat them. In seeking deeper understanding and clarification of their position, they are asking for recognition of their feelings as well as of their contribution to the work involved in childcare: 'We do not want to load even more criticism on to already pressured mothers. What we are saying is that it is also difficult for childless people in our society, and that unless we all try to work out these conflicts and recognize each other's difficulties, then successful collective childcare will never be a reality. The role of non-parents needs to be more clearly defined both within the collective and in the outside world, and our rights, needs and emotions must be recognized as valid.'

SR.66, January 1978

Leeds Animation Group *SR.64*, November 1977

Not So Much a Day Nursery

DARTMOUTH PARK HILL, LONDON

. . . As our society is structured at the present time, a mother is generally responsible for the daily activities of her child until the age of five. Many women feel isolated and frustrated in this situation: the only training we receive for this parental role is the experience of our own lives.

Many mothers would like to work, others must for financial reasons – all are faced with the practical burden of arranging for suitable childcare. All are faced with the more intolerable emotional burden of guilt placed on them by a society which has built a myth around motherhood and dumped it on all women regardless of their individuality.

The women's liberation movement has long been aware of these problems and has recognized that the childcare available in this country does not fulfil the needs of most mothers. After much discussion and argument, the demand for free twenty-four-hour nurseries for children from nought to five was formulated for the first women's demonstration in March 1971. Twenty-four hours for women who had to work at night – nurses and cleaners, etc.

This demand proved unrealistic and unworkable.

On 30 March 1971, Camden Council in London held a meeting on Childcare, two members of the women's liberation movement attended and complained about the existing childcare facilities in Camden. Following this meeting, two women were approached by the Director of Social Services and asked for positive suggestions as to how the problem might be tackled.

With some reservations they agreed to discuss the position among themselves. Several meetings were held with members from twelve North London groups attending.

At these meetings it was decided we would ask the council to:

A: Supply us with twelve empty short-life houses in redevelopment areas.

B: Renovate these houses.

C: Give us a grant for one full-time worker and running costs for the house.

We in return would:

A: Organize and run twelve full-time nurseries.

B: Supply free labour on a voluntary rota basis (in the belief that free education is the right of every child).

We insisted that the nurseries should be free, and that we should have complete control and autonomy in the running of them, and of all activities connected with the nurseries.

The group felt that the hours the nurseries were open must suit mothers who work full-time. We must be open at least from 8.30 to 6.00 p.m. We were also anxious that men should be involved, believing that childrearing is the responsibility of both men and women.

The large group of women's liberation members slowly dwindled to a small core. This group then became involved with local women not in the movement and a working group of seven was finally formed. This group negotiated with the council for eighteen long and disheartening months. How long can a pre-school child wait?

On 11 May 1971 our proposals were accepted by the Director of Social Services and we started to look for suitable housing.

We chose the Highgate New Town area primarily as it was local to most of us, and several in the group already had contact with the local community. The community was in flux: half the residents had been moved out during the redevelopment programme, and other homeless families moved in for short stays in condemned houses. So we particularly wanted our Centre to be a caring friendly place for people old and young.

We searched the area and gave the council long lists of empty houses, many of which they did not know they owned.

Eventually we agreed upon a house, No. 123 Dartmouth Park Hill. We drew up plans for the conversion and had many meetings with the council about money, organization, and just getting things started.

At this time we realized that one of our greatest mistakes was never to get any of the council promises in writing. This made it extremely difficult to put pressure on them as all dates and agreements were verbal – delay followed exasperating delay. Finally we became so frustrated that we wrote them a threatening letter saying that unless we were given a definite completion date we would demonstrate publicly and take our story to the media. The council outsmarted us by releasing their own press statement. However, as a result of our letter we got a completion date of 12 August, also a pledge published in the *Daily Mail* that we should be rehoused once our house was demolished.

We got the keys in September and were shocked at the state in which the contractors had left the place. Foolishly, we had said we would do the decorating, hoping to get local people involved in this work, so that they would really feel that it was their Centre. The amount of work left for us to do was staggering, and as time was so short and everyone fed up we felt unable to ask for local help.

There followed desperate weeks of carpentry, plumbing, plastering and painting.

We also learnt at this stage that we would not be allowed to accommodate babies.

This was a blow as we felt strongly that mothers of very young children desperately need a few hours to themselves during the week.

More weeks of ordering, organizing and buying equipment followed. Finally, on 4 December 1972, we opened.

The Centre is run in a four-storey house with a flat at the top occupied by a mother and child. We have discovered several good things about having a Centre for children in a house rather than a church hall or a purpose-built nursery school. First the children can relate to the size of the rooms and it is more like their own homes. Secondly it is flexible. We can change things around if we like, paint it how we (and the kids) want it, use it in the evenings and weekends and, what's more, both of us – kids and grown-ups – feel that it's OUR Centre, it doesn't belong to the church or the education authority.

We have separate rooms for different activities namely an art room (paint, clay, water-play, cutting and pasting), imaginative play room (house corner, dressing up, building materials), 'quiet' activities room and eating room (books, table toys), sleeping room and office.

We were given £15,000 initially to equip the Centre throughout, and managed to get several things second-hand or free; and we get £3,000 a year running costs, to include salaries of the paid workers. We have one qualified full-time worker and one part-time worker, both having experience with pre-school children, and a cleaner worker in the evenings, all of them having been chosen by us.

There is a rota of people who work at the Centre, consisting of paid workers, parents who are able to give time and volunteers who do not have children at the Centre but who want to work there. We have actively encouraged men to work on the rota if they can and there are now four who do. We have found that they are capable of doing more than just mending the toys, but they have often felt unsure of themselves, and it's been hard for them entering a world where, to date, women are a majority and have more experience.

The children are being cared for by, and are learning from, a group of people, not just a single parent or teacher, in a stimulating and loving environment. This allows a much greater range of experiences and relationships for the child than the often stifling and exclusive mother–child bond, and enables us to care for our children together in a supportive situation where problems can be shared. It also means that we have more time of our own to work if we want or have to, and to develop ourselves in other ways. Both the children and the grown-ups are benefiting from the collective care of our children.

There is a journal written daily in which the events, progress and problems of the day are recorded, plus any other information or questions one wants to pass on to others. This means that parents who usually work at the Centre once a week can read it and find out what has been happening on other days. It is also very useful as a record of the children and the Centre, and we have been able to trace changes and developments since we began. Anyone who wants to can write in it, and writing in it makes you really think about what has happened.

There are twenty-one children who come to the Centre, but only fifteen at any one time because of space limitations. Some are at the Centre all day, some only in the morning or the afternoon, and the age range is two to five years. Six of the children who come are those of the original organizers, but our priority now is to take children from the immediate neighbourhood.

We are open from 8.30 until 6 p.m. to meet the needs of those parents who have full-time jobs and therefore cannot work on the rota. Some of the parents have part-time jobs and others work at home (housework and care of babies). Both of the latter are expected to work on the rota. There is always a wholesome meal midday, plus morning and afternoon snacks, and the younger children sleep in the afternoon if they want to.

Many of us are trying to work out different ways of relating to children. We don't want to be authorities always telling them what to do and commenting on whether they are good or bad. We want to recognize them as human beings and to treat them as such. There are many ways in which we have been attempting to turn these ideas into practice and to translate the theory into something more than words and hot air. We encourage the children to be independent and to do as much for themselves as they can and we have been continually surprised at how capable they are. The lunchtime procedure is a good example of this. They serve themselves from central bowls on the table, pour their own drinks (and wipe up the spills!), clear away their own dishes and collect their own dessert from the kitchen. In the beginning we all had to restrain ourselves from always doing things for them, although it may be quicker and cleaner to do so in the short term. It took a great deal of thought, trial and error before things ran anything like smoothly and we are still learning. We had to buy jugs that they could handle easily, bowls that they could see into, and we are trying to get child-size brooms that really work so that they can sweep up afterwards and not just 'play' at sweeping in the house corner.

All the toys and most of the art materials are on open shelves at child height so that the kids can always help themselves to things they want to use and they are encouraged to put things back when they have finished with them. The basic activities mentioned earlier are always available, but in addition we plan special activities around a weekly theme, in order to increase the number of different experiences we can offer the children. Examples of themes include living things, colour, how things work, shape and size, the senses, printing, etc. Whenever possible we go out with the children to try and link what they experience at the Centre with the world outside. The same local park can illustrate colour one week and plants the next. Having a theme helps to bring continuity from one day to another and it also makes us feel more secure when we work at the Centre if we know there are activities planned. One day the kids painted the leaves of the runner beans we were growing in the yard, bright red and yellow, and were terrifically pleased with the result. A few weeks later they saw that the leaves died because the sun and air couldn't get to them. They learnt something, but even so they will probably do it again!

Alison Fell, *SR.36*, June 1975

Whenever possible we try to involve the children in everything that happens at the Centre. They help to shop for the food, they go to the launderette to do washing, they help in preparation of food (cutting up fruit, grating cheese, making rice pudding or jelly), they put out chairs and set the tables. It does not always run smoothly. They don't always want to do it. But on the whole they respond to responsibility and appear to thrive on it. Grown-ups are always available to help them, to talk to them, to cuddle and love them, and very often they comfort and hug each other. They are encouraged to help and care for one another and to be aware of each other's needs. This can be done in many small but important ways, e.g. asking them to help each other on and off with coats, pointing out when another child is crying and asking them why they think she is crying, noticing when children are away and discussing where they might be. It isn't happening overnight, but we do believe things are changing and the kids are growing more sensitive to one another and are better able to work together, asking each other for help rather than always asking the adults. Like the adults they are learning that things get easier when they are shared.

We believe that girls and boys should have the same opportunities. We do not want the girls to be always in the house corner with the dolls preparing for motherhood while the boys are enjoying rough and tumble games in the yard. We interest the boys in doing traditionally female things like cooking and setting tables and encourage girls to hammer nails and saw wood, although no one is forced to do anything. We don't want our children to be channelled into very rigid roles according to their sex, which would limit their choices now and continue to do so all their lives.

One of the central problems of education is contact between home and school. In one sense, we have no problem – the workers are employed by the parents, and are hardly likely to exclude them. But how to relate what goes on in the Centre to what goes on in the home? The weekly Sunday meeting provides an essential link. As a rule, one or two children are discussed each week – people are notified beforehand, and the discussion only takes place if the parent or parents of the child are there.

Here parents can voice any anxieties or suggestions they may have about their children – not, as it were, to a group of 'professionals', but to a group made up largely of other parents, who know their children and work with them, and whose children in turn are known to all. So discussion is based, not on asking the advice of experts, but on the exchange of experience and common problems. How does the child relate to other children in the Centre? Or to brothers, sisters or parents? What happens in the home or out shopping? Has the child changed since coming to the Centre, or do the parents have difficulty in relating their behaviour there to their behaviour in the home?

Not all parents are used to handling a lot of children at once, and many of us feel the need to discuss some of the problems we encounter. In the meeting there's the opportunity to learn from each other as a group – from successes and failures – and of basing our learning on our practice, and vice versa.

The meeting, in fact, is fundamental to the organization of the Centre. In a situation where most parents work, there is no other regular opportunity for all to get together. It's not just a question of 'participating' in the running of the Centre – the parents run it, and the meeting is the place where the policies and daily routines are worked out.

Subjects for discussion include children's books, and the almost in-soluble problem of finding ones which don't cast children into the old stereotypes. Or aggression among the children: should they be left to fight it out, or should we intervene? And if so, at what stage? And what do the children expect of us? Or again, the problem of sex-roles: if a girl *wants* to do the washing up and help with the food, why shouldn't she? But if she monopolizes these activities, will she be preventing a boy from learning? On other occasions we've used films – i.e. other people's ideas about childcare – to stimulate our own discussions.

We don't want to make it sound as if we don't have problems: we do. There are personal and political differences between people, as in all groups, and we can't claim that everyone in the neighbourhood looks favourably on us. Many older residents, who were forced to bring up their children without free facilities of any kind, are understandably resentful.

It's not always easy for new parents coming into the Centre to realize that it's not only their Centre, but their responsibility to run. In the meetings, some people talk a lot, and some hardly at all. It's important that we're sensitive to everyone, and don't allow one group to dominate. Perhaps more important, however, is the inability or unwillingness of some parents to come to the meeting at all. We've argued a lot about this, but we've finally come to the conclusion that in an organization in which responsibilities should be shared by all, we should insist that parents come to at least one meeting a month.

Transport, too, is a problem: several of us have vans or cars, but we regard outings as an essential part of the learning process, and we need to find ways of getting hold of the money for a mini-bus.

We have had many discussions about publicizing the work and aims of the Centre. Some members of the group feel that work in this field diverts much-needed energies from the practical business of running the Centre. This is a very real problem, as all are pressed for time.

Others feel that it is of vital importance that we make our information and experience available to others trying to organize in similar ways, and that we should try to spread our ideas in the hope of showing people what is possible.

All feel, however, that any publicity given to the Centre should be controlled by us. Those in the women's movement have good reason to be wary of the media. In general we try to relate our publicity to some activity.

Naturally we did our best to make the opening known, particularly in the immediate neighbourhood, and on 5 March this year we held a press conference. The response from the members of the press who turned up was sympathetic.

Later we held a public meeting for groups and individuals interested in setting up centres in their own areas. This meeting was very successful, and gave us all a great sense of solidarity and achievement. The opportunity to discuss the Centre with new interested people was especially rewarding and hopeful.

A film is being made about the Centre with the object of showing it to people as a basis for discussion.

We do not want to remain an isolated experiment, but to become part of a much wider movement of local collective action.

SR.17, November 1973

Alison Fell, *SR.36*, June 1975

A Playgroup Called Freedom

WOMEN FROM ARMAGH

For working-class women in Northern Ireland there is no escape from the presence of the British army, from the day-to-day struggle in the streets. No escape either from the drudgery of housework and childcare. Here a group of women from Armagh, a county town thirty-five miles south-west of Belfast, describe their fight to form a playgroup on their housing estate. The playgroup, which opens in December [1975], will be called 'Saorise' – 'Freedom' in Irish.

... At a cursory glance our estate appears ideal, surrounded by pleasant green fields with a river running close by. Closer inspection shows that it is far from ideal, and any of the women living here can testify to that.

The estate is built on a very steep hill which should have been levelled – instead large concrete steps join one level to another. There are over 400 of these steps, not counting those at the front and back of houses, as many as thirty up to one house. Dangerous unfenced walls mask drops of up to fifteen feet in places. The one supermarket, very expensive, is situated in the middle of the estate. To reach it from the bottom you have to climb eighty-three feet. Picture that with a shopping bag, toddlers and perhaps a pram! Old age pensioners live in bungalows at the bottom of the estate; none of them have ever seen the shop. The estate is a mile and a half from the town centre; there is no bus service, and a taxi costs 35p.

Most of the people living here are newly married, so the percentage of pre-school children is very high. The structural dangers are a constant nightmare to mothers continually 'on guard' with playing kids. The planners have erected a 'play area' – we call it a death trap – which is totally unsuitable for any child under ten. It is built beside the only entrance to and exit from the estate, and the swings, slide and steel climbing frame have already claimed many pre-school victims, some of whom required hospitalization.

With the constantly high male unemployment figures, Armagh like most towns has followed the traditional pattern with plenty of social outlets and meeting places for the men, like pubs and bookies, while the women stay at home, isolated, with nothing but the bingo, some pubs or the recently opened cinema.

One woman who moved here from Belfast where she had been involved with other women called a few of us together one evening,

primarily to talk about the problems we had living here. The major thing
discussed was childcare. We came to realize that by running a nursery or playgroup on a co-operative basis we would not only be helping
our kids but we'd be going a long way in alleviating some of our own
problems. The question was where to hold it and how to finance it.

A large community centre had been built on the estate in 1972, but
had stood empty since then because no official body was prepared to
take financial responsibility for opening and running it. It had cost
£48,000. It's around this centre that our fight has revolved. We decided
that its minor hall was an ideal site for the playgroup, but the centre
was not available to the community.

The Unionist-dominated Armagh District Council has refused to
take over responsibility for it, although under the Youth and
Recreational Service Order Act (1973) N.I. they were entitled to. The
council gave various excuses as to why they would not take it on – 'Rise
in rates' or 'If we give you a community centre, everyone will want
one'. We think every estate like this should have one.

The council's decision is generally accepted as sectarian – the
Unionist council discriminating against the anti-Unionist citizens by
refusing them access to the community centre. A battle raged over this,
but the Tenants' Association and the Community Association soon
bowed out of the fight.*

In April 1975 the Housing Executive of Northern Ireland told the
press they were going to brick up the centre in a bid to combat vandalism. But the Housing Executive had previously refused to spend
money either to secure the building or to make it usable. For the older
kids the centre had become a symbol of sectarianism. We have always
maintained that if the place had been used from the start the vandalism would not have occurred.

We decided to form a strong committee to combat the council. We
called an emergency meeting of women interested in the nursery. At
that meeting we decided to move in, clean up the place and take it over
as it stood, in order to show the council and the Housing Executive
that they would not get out of things so lightly. We issued a press
statement laying the blame for the damage to the centre at the feet of
Armagh District Council.

In an effort to identify people in the area with what should be *their*
community centre we organized a grocery sale in May this year, collecting groceries throughout the town and selling them for next to

* The Tenants' Association is just for the estate. The Community Association covers a
whole area – five estates. Each Tenants' Association has a representative on the overall
Community Association, which manages the community centre.

nothing. This was the first time the centre had been used. We made £75 for the playgroup and planned to start it as soon as possible, either by fixing up the minor hall ourselves or by squatting the first available house on the estate.

All this time the Tenants' Association did nothing except engage themselves in a smear campaign against the women, calling us Provies (members of the Provisional wing of the Irish Republican Army), troublemakers and lefties. The Tenants' Association was dominated by Stickies (members of the official I R A) and we were exposing their inadequacy and ineffectiveness.*

We'd all become aware that by directly associating us with a particular organization, in this case the Provisional I R A, they were really saying that as women we were not capable of doing all this ourselves – there must be some men in the background pushing us. And these are people who call themselves socialists and talk of women's rights.

We kept on using the hall to raise funds, expose the council and pressurize everyone in authority. The Housing Executive didn't even try to brick up the hall. We had women planted all over the estate in case they did, and the teenagers who helped us clean the place up kept an eye on it in case of further vandalism or moves from 'above' to close it.

The weekly meetings went on. We were not restricted to playgroup matters, as we had come to be seen on the estate as the only group interested in or capable of solving people's problems. The teenagers came to us for help, because with the daily sectarian assassinations – directed mostly against Catholics – they couldn't leave the estate day or night and had nothing to do.

We advised them to identify their own problems and think of ways to solve them, promising help when required. We thought it important that the teenagers learn to make decisions on their own. As kids continually kept down by authority figures at home and in school this was difficult, but things have smoothed themselves out.

There is a youth committee which runs discos and games nights, with minimal help from the women. We were able to get some equipment from the Department of Education and when the weather is bad kids play in the centre. We also use it one night a week for a keep-fit class for women. This is popular and attracts women not just from this area but from all over the town.

But the playgroup still needs a finished building and proper finance.

---

* In 1970 the I R A split into two factions. The breakaway faction, the Provisionals, believe in a military solution to the present Irish crisis. The Official wing believes it should play only a defensive role militarily, while politically educating the working class. Both say they are fighting for a united socialist republic.

Some people thought we should buy the centre ourselves but we didn't agree that working-class people should have to pay for such facilities. So when local businessmen and the Chamber of Commerce organized a Civic Week Festival in May we decided to cash in on it to publicize our needs. We 'invaded' various displays and events, distributed leaflets and talked to people about the playgroup and community centre.

At the end of the festival the Chairman of the District Council was to attend a Vintage Car Cavalcade in the centre of Armagh. We thought we would publicly embarrass him and the council by picketing with a banner we'd made: 'Civic Pride, Civic Responsibility: Armagh District Council – We Need A Play Centre'.

Like the centre of most towns in the North, the Mall in Armagh is considered Unionist territory. It's of Georgian design with a well-kept green for playing *cricket*. The only women's prison in Northern Ireland stands at one end and the court-house at the other. Some women were afraid to go on the picket but a few of us brazened it out.

It was a frightening experience. We sneaked through the crowd into the middle of the road and unfurled the banner. This stopped the cavalcade for fifteen minutes, much to the annoyance of the crowd and the RUC (the Royal Ulster Constabulary, the predominantly Protestant police force in Northern Ireland), who couldn't give us the usual 'booting' because of all the press and TV people around.

We then went through the crowd giving out the leaflets. Most people refused even to take one, and some threatened us, calling us 'Catholic bastards'. The sad thing was that some people there wouldn't identify with our demand because of the sectarian block in their minds.

The exercise was worthwhile for apart from all the TV coverage it proved to other women that when organized nothing is impossible for us.

The government was forced to take an interest, and a stop-gap measure was found. The Department of Education agreed to pay for the damage to and renovation of the centre, and the Housing Executive agreed to lease the hall to the Community Association for six months.

On 14 September we met some bigwigs (architects, ministries of this and that) and they agreed to renovate the minor hall first so that we can open the playgroup while the rest of the reconstruction is still going on. We put in our plans for small toilets, washbasins, etc., and we'll now have a community centre with a purpose-built room for a nursery.

. . . The project has started to break down the isolation felt acutely by women living in a family set-up on estates like this.

SR.41, November 1975

South Oxford Nursery Stays

OXFORD CITY NURSERY CAMPAIGN, NEWSHORT

Last July a Council Working Party secretly decided to close South Oxford Nursery. The County Council Education Committee, consisting of country squires, antique dealers and led by Brigadier Streatfield, were delighted to save a measly £8,000 a year. 'No babyminding on the rates!' said the Brigadier. Since then, the class has had its waiting list closed and so last term only thirteen children remained. This is the only city centre nursery provision and the children came from all over Oxford – many from Asian, Egyptian, Spanish, Italian and Chilean families, where English is not the first language, and some from one-parent families where the mother is out at work.

We were all aware that here was a good state nursery class with potentially thirty full-time places, being closed for no reason. It was no substitute to be offered part-time places in other nurseries. At a meeting called by the Nursery Campaign, it was decided that the only thing to do was for the parents to occupy the building when they went to collect their children. The parents were acutely aware of their small numbers, language problems and lack of confidence to take such a radical action; nevertheless they went ahead and occupied the nursery. The occupation has since been successfully maintained with the support of the Nursery Campaign and other groups. The children have been involved throughout the occupation.

Our campaign is not only concerned with the loss or reduction of nursery education for the children now at the school, but is fighting to save thirty full-time places for the city and to expand nursery provision. We are now running a happy and efficient nursery with trained staff. The trades council have given their support and public sector workers have refused to cut off our essential services ... However, we are aware that unless public opinion both locally and nationally stays with us, the council will get a possession order from the courts. When they think we are an abandoned cause, no longer news-worthy, they will try to send in the bailiffs. It would be a bitter loss if all the energy, co-ordination and caring created through the occupation were to be wasted. Many of us have realized for the first time what can be achieved by taking action and fighting together for our rights. This action is of national importance as it is the first occupation of a nursery since the passing of the Criminal Trespass Law. It is vital for us to win this fight against particularly vicious education cuts.

SR.70, May 1978

Oxford Nursery Plays On

OXFORD CITY NURSERY CAMPAIGN, NEWSHORT

South Oxford Nursery . . . was evicted on 28 April, but is still going strong in a building just over the road. The council is now complacent that the 'problem' is solved, but with the violence of the eviction, people are angrier than ever and even more determined to show that they're not finished.

So the children and their friends played all day in the nursery, and some of them stayed all night as well. And the brigadier stamped and swore.

BUT . . .
One day, as the children played, they heard a terrible noise . . . CLUMP CLUMP CLUMP.

And Brigadier Streatfield, the terrible giant, came stamping into their playground.

Oxford County Council took them to court on 27 April and got a possession order. Anne Marie Sweeney, one of the parents, explains: 'We got a tip-off from the County Court that the bailiffs would come at seven the next morning, expecting no press or children. So we rang round the papers and got everyone there at 7 a.m.! It was full when the bailiffs arrived so they panicked and fled. The stupid fools came back at 11.30, right in the middle of a class – we had sixteen kids there, and some press still. We refused to open the door so they smashed it in, breaking flowerpots and really upsetting the kids. There were forty of them there – bailiffs, council officials, police – intimidating the kids, saying, "You'd better come with us or we'll put you in jail."

'We had to decide whether to resist and be carried out – two Chilean parents were anxious not to because of the danger of being arrested, so we decided to leave together, singing.' They went straight to the new premises they'd arranged – given them by the church.

At the end of July the council plans to close a middle school in the same building as the nursery: 'We see this as an attack on our whole community,' says Anne Marie, 'which just happens to be a prime development area.' . . .

SR.71, June 1978

New Creche

ANGELA PHILLIPS

For a few parents in London, the dream of co-operatively controlled, cheap childcare has become a reality. The Kingsway Children's Centre opened at the beginning of September for about thirty children, ranging from a few months to school age. The centre is the result of eighteen months of planning and organizing by a joint trade union committee initiated by the staff at the T U C.

The centre is unique in several ways. For a start, it is (as far as we know) the only creche to be organized solely by employees of participating firms, independent of any particular management. Secondly, it is the first creche to be financially supported by a number of employers paying two thirds of each child's place while the parents pay one third. The money is to be paid six months in advance, which gives the creche some financial stability.

The creche management committee is made up of the staff, plus one member of each participating organization, irrespective of the number of places paid for. It is expected that representatives will be either from the trade unions involved or parents (preferably one and the same). Again, this ensures that no single organization gains control, and that preference for places will not always go to the larger firms.

The cost of each place is £20 a week, of which parents pay £7. This price reflects the high staff ratio required for children under two years old. To make the cost reasonably economic for everyone, the number of really young babies will be kept at a proportion of nine to twenty-one.

The staffing also reflects the thinking behind the project: both nursery nurses and nursery teachers have been employed, avoiding the failing of many council schemes which separate creche and nursery facilities, providing the former merely for care and the latter for education (usually part-time). At Kingsway, education is seen as part of the function, and the skills of the staff are expected to overlap. Payment will be on the higher teaching scale rather than the abysmally low rates for nursery nurses.

Money to get the scheme going was raised in loans and grants from participating organizations. Camden Council provided a loan of £5,000. The luckiest find was the centre itself, a disused nursery attached to the Kingsway Mission in Holborn, a place conveniently close to work for all the parents involved in the scheme. They have use of it rent free.

The organization of childcare facilities requires planning and capital before it starts, as well as knowledge of all the regulations which govern the public care of children, and a real understanding of the needs of both children and parents. Kingsway proves that it is economically possible for even small firms to provide childcare facilities. It should provide a useful example for all those of us trying to negotiate with employers for creches.

SR.64, November 1977

Editorial

SPARE RIB COLLECTIVE

'For most families these [childcare] services are not appropriate. If they are made available at public expense too readily they can all too easily be seen as the expression of a philosophy which preaches that parents may do what they like and it is the duty of the state to look after children . . . Increasing state intervention carries with it the risk of eroding the responsibilities of individual parents.' Patrick Jenkin, Tory Social Services Secretary, laid Conservative policy for women firmly on the line in this speech to the National Children's Bureau. Mothers (not parents) are the best people to care for children, he said, and they should stay at home full-time.

. . . Telling women their place is 'kitchen, children and church' is meant to make us feel guilty about things that are not our fault. Whenever children suffer from cramped housing, no play space, over-worked childminders, horrible schools, it's mothers who are blamed. 'Irresponsible parents should be fined and punished by law,' said Marion Roe, a GLC councillor, at the Tory Party Conference. She attacked 'the women's liberation philosophy' as the root cause of the increase in juvenile crime and vandalism, because according to her it has 'brainwashed' us into being ashamed of looking after our children properly. It's up to us to fight back against restrictions on our rights, and also to provide alternative propaganda to destroy the myth that feminists are uncaring child haters. Neither children nor women will gain if we're forced to choose between being childless 'career women' or full-time housewives.

SR.88, November 1979

4   HOUSEWORK

Women's labour in the home is taken for granted. It is not seen as work that should be paid for, but something that women will do automatically, 'naturally'. Women who are thrown out of paid work are assumed to disappear back into the category of 'housewives'. An unemployed man does not slip back into being a 'househusband'. Yet housework is essential. It includes shopping, preparing meals, washing up, cleaning, washing clothes, ironing and mending, as well as emotional servicing. In 1970 – a decade ago – it was estimated by Chase Manhattan Bank in the USA that it would cost as much as $257 (about £100) a week to pay someone else for all the components of a housewife's job.

Housework is tied up with loving care and as such its frontiers are interminable. It is not measurable by conditions which have been laid down in paid work, like an eight-hour day. A loved family is a well-fed, comfortable family. A husband gives some of his wage to his wife for shopping, but she works for him 'for love'. Women compensate for low wages or for the effects of inflation by the amount of work they do at home – when school meals are cut it is the house-wife who puts in extra time and makes economies to replace them.

Men have power in the world which women do not have and it is harder for women to challenge men in the one-to-one relationship at home than when women are working together and can organize. But improvements in the position of women at work will not give women social equality with men unless the sexual division of labour between home and work is taken into account. Most women who work outside the home take on a dramatically increased work load. They have the 'second shift' of their domestic responsibilities in addition to their jobs. Alternatively, where a man's work is located in the home, women are often involved but their work is identified as 'helping out' and not given independent status. In 1978 *Spare Rib* reported that an industrial tribunal had ruled that a woman's book-keeping and telephone work for her husband's business was 'only an extension of her household duties'. But in the same year a doctor's wife succeeded in winning her case that the work of wives in the doctor's surgery should be paid.

While housework remains the sole responsibility of women, its tasks stay tied to the motivation of guilt, and housewives feel they don't have the right to any rest, peace or solitude. Persuading men to participate in housework often brings out male anxiety and the fear of being henpecked, as if housework represents all that is feminine. It also, however, brings out the amount of thought and planning which domestic work entails, as Jennifer Coates pointed out: 'Teaching people, for instance, to buy food – to recognize signs of good and bad quality – is an exhausting process because it demands rationalizing and articulating a mass of perceptions that one is unaccustomed to talk about.' (an early *SR*) But men's *help* will not change the sexual allocation of work. For men to *take on* housework, mothering, care of the sick or disabled and the old, would be a fundamental shift of responsibility and transform the world as we know it.

History of the Housewife

CATHERINE HALL

To be a housewife in fourteenth-century England meant something very different to what it does today, when it has been decisively separated from the productive and industrial sphere. It still involved domestic work and the care of children, and it was still unpaid: but for a large proportion of women it would also involve many other kinds of work besides – brewing, baking, looking after the poultry, and so on. Part of the reason for that was the fact that the family itself, both among the peasants and in the town, was a productive unit.

The family means in this context father, mother, often unmarried brothers and sisters, possibly grandparents, children, servants and – in an urban situation – apprentices. In this family the labour power of each individual member is only a definite portion of the labour power of the family. Women were, therefore, themselves centrally related to production, and not only through their husbands. The pre-industrial family was a self-sufficient economic unit and consequently domestic work had a much wider definition than it does now. It might well involve brewing, dairy work, the care of poultry and pigs, the production of vegetables and fruit, the spinning of flax and wool and also medical care – nursing and doctoring. These areas were roughly defined as 'women's work': but there is much more flexibility in the drawing of lines around women's work and men's work – work was done on the basis of task-orientation rather than by way of a rigid and formalized division of labour.

There were some jobs which were always specifically connected with one sex. The higher manorial officers were always men and the dairymaid, for example, was always a woman. A thirteenth-century manual on 'The Duties of Manorial Officers' gives us an account of the dairymaid's work:

The dairymaid ought to be faithful and of good repute, and keep herself clean, and ought to know her business and all that belongs to it. She ought not to allow any under-dairymaid or another to take or carry away milk, or butter, or cream, by which the cheese shall be less and the dairy impoverished. And she ought to know well how to make cheese and salt cheese, and she ought to save and keep the vessels of the dairy that it need not be necessary to buy new ones every year.

The two most powerful medieval theories about women were the creations of the church and the aristocracy. The church's view of women was heavily influenced by St Paul and saw women as the creation of the devil and as both inferior and evil. Marriage was an institution set up to contain the unavoidable sin of sexuality; as Our Lord put it in a vision to Margery Kempe, the fifteenth-century mystic, 'for though the state of maidenhood be more perfect and more holy than the state of widowhood, and the state of widowhood more perfect than the state of wedlock, yet, daughter, I love thee as well as any maiden in the world.' The aristocracy on the other hand developed the counter-doctrine of the superiority of women. This was connected with the cult of the Virgin Mary, the adoration of the Virgin in Heaven and the lady on earth. Though the two theories were at different poles, in one sense both combined to give women another worldly role – they were seen as in no way central to political or economic life. This split between the wicked and the divine, the prostitute and the saint, represents an ideological split and projection by men which has recurred in many forms. Women provided either an explanation for evil or a haven of good. Neither view had much to do with reality. In Chrétien de Troyes' romance *Lancelot*, the hero gets into Queen Guinivere's bedroom but Lancelot 'holds her more dear than the relic of any saint' and 'when he leaves the room he bows and acts precisely as if he were before a shrine.' Neither of these theories were taken at face value outside the Church and the aristocracy; but what was clearly already accepted was that women were secondary and inferior.

Because of the need for their labour, women in the village were in a better position than aristocratic women, in the sense that they were involved in productive relations. What this means in fact is that they were free to be exploited in an equal way with men. The feudal economy was based on the ownership of land, which was the major source of power, by a relatively small number: the land was worked by both free and unfree peasants. Few received money wages – the unfree worked on the lord's land in return for renting some of the lord's land. Every peasant was subject to a lord and in a hierarchical society every lord was subject to another who was ultimately subject to the king. Supposedly there was a system of rights and obligations at each level but at the bottom of the ladder the obligations which the lord owed to the peasant were absolutely minimal whereas his rights were extensive.

Peasant women were able to hold land though the normal assumption was that heads of households would be male – the position of widows in particular has long been recognized as of importance, both because of their longevity and their established rights. Manorial records, as Rodney Hilton has shown, do record a substantial number of women holding land – even as minors. It seems that unmarried women with holdings would usually quickly marry – the labour of the man was as important to the woman as vice versa. However, their right to hold land was only because the holdings were small and would not affect the distribution of power on the feudal estate. Aristocratic women, with few exceptions, could not hold land since land was the key to the feudal economy and once the property rights of a family or aristocratic line came into question women were simply a marriageable commodity. It is clear that peasant women did do heavy work on the land as can be seen from the illustrations of clod breaking and there is evidence that at some points they got equal pay. The question as to whether women labourers were paid the same as their male counterparts seems to have something to do with job definition and bargaining power. Female domestic servants were low paid, for example, because they were subject to non-economic compulsion since they tended to live in the lord's household and could have all kinds of personal pressure put on them. But it would be wrong to associate the respect given to women's labour with a society free from discrimination. Distinctions were of course made in the law, education, the Church and in political and property rights between men and women. Peasant women could not assume the limited rights to property which men had – their rights were much less clear and would probably depend on the customs of a particular locality.

Women were, furthermore, subject to particular kinds of exploitation by the feudal lord. At Pattingham in Staffordshire in April 1369, Juliana, the daughter of Roger Baroun, was 'deflowered' by a Welshman and had to pay a five-shilling fine to the lord of the manor. A woman who was not a virgin had less monetary value to her feudal lord since a well-to-do peasant might refuse to marry her and consequently the cut of the marriage settlement which the lord got would be less. In 1388 Agnes, the daughter of Juliana Prynce, had to pay ten shillings to the lord of the manor to be able to marry and go as a free woman with her goods.

But abstract theories about the proper role of women were not allowed to stand in the way of meeting familial and social needs. Peasant women were able to play a relatively independent role in day-to-day economic life – they were open to the same kind of exploitation by the feudal lord as were men whereas at other times the appropriation of women's labour has been effected in a more indirect way. This means that women were likely to organize themselves politically in the same way as men. In Halesowen in Worcestershire in 1386, 'A certain John atte Lythe and Thomas Puttewey, serfs, by the advice, procurement and maintenance of a certain Agnes, wife of John Saddler, assembled an illegal conventicle of unknown rebels against the abbot ... saying openly that they did not wish any more to be considered as serfs of the abbot and would not do any of the previously owed services.'

The social, political and ideological dominance of the male was clear, however, at the local level. Women were not the heads of tithings, they didn't sit on local juries, they didn't fill the office of constable or reeve. Women with a legal title to a holding could often be obliged to marry and they had to suffer a regular barrage from the Church about their evil influence. Women played a variety of economic roles within the village – they were not all housewives and housewife had a much wider definition than it does now. They were not all housewives because there was a much smaller number of households to the population and there might be several women living in a household whose jobs were as domestic servants or labourers. Peasant women might, according to their age and marital status, be doing a variety of different jobs. They might be doing specifically women's work, such as spinning and carding or in the dairy; they might be doing work which was not rigidly defined as men's or women's – in the fields – ploughing or harvesting; they might be working centred around their own household – cooking, brewery and caring for children – or as domestic servants either in the lord's house or in the house of a richer peasant.

'Housewife' in fourteenth-century England tended to mean the coordinator and organizer of an establishment and of a centre of production. The condition of being wedded to a house was a more substantive one than it is now because the fourteenth-century house had a different function and meaning from the twentieth-century equivalent. It did imply a status which was, however, considerably limited by the current ideology on the position of women. This reminds us that the ideological forms do not merely reflect the economic but have a life and relative autonomy of their own which can even serve in certain instances to limit and restrict the economic sphere. The economic and ideological demands on women in the village were to a considerable degree in contradiction to each other.

The situation was very similar in the towns – being a housewife was recognized as a particular job but it involved a wide range of domestic activity. Generally there were no frontiers between professional or business life and private life. These activities all tended to go on in the same living/working area. The household was the centre both of domestic activity and mercantile activity. This integration of work and home contributed to the fact that it was not necessary to regard the socialization of children as one of the most important functions of the family. Children were not seen as a special group – once they were past infancy they were absorbed into the adult household and were educated by the process of life and work going on around them. Domestic service and apprenticeship were two of the major ways of educating and these applied to boys and girls alike (though the evidence as to girls being formally apprenticed is unclear, they certainly were apprenticed and trained informally).

In a feudal society the notion of service was central to the relations between lord and master, parents and children, lover and mistress. Transmission of a way of life from one generation to another was ensured by the everyday participation of children in adult life. In the towns, as in the villages, women were engaged in a wide range of economic activities connected with the family as a unit of production. Women figure in guild records as barbers, furriers, carpenters, saddlers, joiners, and in many other trades. There are relatively few trades which explicitly exclude women. All the female members of a merchant's household would be engaged in some form of economic activity – the housewife herself might spend a good deal of her energies organizing other men and women to fulfil the necessary domestic tasks so that she would be free to engage in mercantile activities. Women in smaller scale households might take up one of the entrepreneurial activities which were often associated with women because they were extensions of domestic activity – Margery Kempe who was the daughter of one of Lynn's leading citizens describes how 'she now bethought herself a new housewifery' and went in for milling. This was after the failure of her brewing enterprise which she ascribes to God's disapproval of her involvement in such activities:

Then for pure covetousness, and to maintain her pride, she began to brew, and was one of the greatest brewers in the town of N. for 3 years or 4, till she lost much money . . . For, though she had ever such good servants, cunning in brewing, yet it would never succeed with them.

But the degree to which it was considered the duty of the good wife to look after her husband should not be underestimated. *The Goodman of Paris*, a late fourteenth-century text, instructs the wife:

Wherefore love your husband's person carefully, and I pray you keep him in clean linen, for that is your business, and because the trouble and care of outside affairs lieth with men, so must husbands take heed, and go and come, and journey hither and thither, in rain and wind, in snow and hail, now drenched, now dry, now sweating, now shivering, ill-fed, ill-lodged, ill-warmed and ill-bedded. And naught harmeth him, because he is upheld by the hope that he hath of the care which his wife will take of him on his return, and of the ease, the joys and the pleasures which she will do him, or cause to be done to him, in her presence, to be unshod before a good fire, to have his feet washed and fresh shoes and hose, to be given good food and drink, to be well served and well looked after, well bedded in white sheets and nightcaps, well covered with good furs, and assuaged with other joys and desports, privities, loves and secrets whereof I am silent. And the next day fresh shirts and garments . . . Wherefore, dear sister, I beseech you thus to bewitch and bewitch again your husband that shall be, and beware of roofless house and of smoky fire, and scold him not, but be unto him gentle and amiable and peaceable. Have a care that in winter he have a good fire and smokeless and let him rest well and be well covered between your breasts, and thus be with him . . . And thus shall you preserve and keep your husband from all discomforts and give him all the comforts whereof you can bethink you, and serve him and have him served in your house, and you shall look to him for outside things, for if he be good he will take even more pains and labour therein than you wish, and by doing what I have said, you will cause him ever to miss you and have his heart with you and your loving service and he will shun all other houses, all other women, all other services and households.

. . . In the fourteenth century, the Church provided the ideology of feudalism – it deified hierarchical relations. With the crisis in the Catholic Church, the Reformation and the development of Puritanism, the Anglican Church no longer combined within itself religious, educational and cultural functions. Consequently the family became much more formative in the socialization of children. As a prayer in the primer of 1553 put it, 'To have children and servants is thy blessing, O Lord, but not to order them according to thy word deserveth thy dreadful curse.' The woman's role in this was limited. She was her husband's lieutenant and ultimately he made all the decisions of importance in most households.

Meanwhile the wives of the bourgeoisie were becoming less and less involved in domestic and productive activities, and increasingly the desired image was that of the lady of leisure. Housewifery seems to continue to be a valued skill amongst families of middling status where the labour of the woman was still needed. For those who can afford it, however, the ideal is the old, aristocratic one of passivity and dependence – a living demonstration of the wealth of the husband or father. Whereas in the medieval village at least women had a crucial economic function which was recognized, by the seventeenth century women are deprived both economically and ideologically as secondary – as people who care for and support others rather than themselves being active in the world. There is less tension between the economic and the ideological spheres than there was in pre-capitalist society because the woman's two main economic functions have become firstly, the organization of a household which is no longer the central unit of production, and secondly, the provision of a cheap supply of labour.

. . . In the nineteenth century the pattern established in the seventeenth century with the development of the capitalist mode of production was strengthened and extended with the formation of industrial capitalism. As the division of labour becomes more refined and job specialization increased so the sexual division of labour rigidifies. The bourgeoisie make their wives into ladies in a position of complete dependence economically and complete subordination ideologically and then use lower-middle-class and working-class women to service their households and produce their textiles.

The emergence of monopoly capitalism has not fundamentally altered the sexual division of labour. Two of the main functions of women with twentieth-century capitalism could be described as the provision of unpaid labour in the home and the provision of a reserve labour force which is predominantly unskilled and low paid.

. . . Women buy packaged foods and consumer durables thus cutting down considerably on the time taken in running a house but also providing an ever-expanding market. But, however many gadgets and aids exist, housework can in no sense be abolished without fundamental social change, and women still work extremely long hours in the home.

SR.26, August 1974

Memories of My Mother-in-Law

MERLIN CLARKE

My mother-in-law was born in August 1909 at Plaistow when Edward VII was king. She was the second child in a family of four children, three sisters and the youngest child a brother.

She was brought up in a three-bedroomed house together with her paternal grandparents. She considers she had an extremely happy and settled childhood, due partly to the fact that her father had regular employment as a clerk in Henley's Cable factory in Woolwich. To get to work he travelled a 2d tram journey (4d return) but would always walk the first part of the way as to tram this as well would have cost him another 1d (2d return). His hours were 9–5.30 p.m. Mon–Fri and 9–12 noon Sat. His wages were £2 per week and his father received 5s pension from Tate & Lyle, 5s OAP and his mother also received a 5s OAP. Her father's job was a non-union one and she has no recollections of him ever being on strike.

Another strong influence in the stability of her upbringing was the unquestioning respect of parents and the Church. Her father never swore at the children or ever hit them, he never rowed or shouted with her mother, at least not in front of the children. The grandparents, on the other hand, did argue and this was very upsetting, also the drunken fights of a few neighbours.

The furniture of her house was much as of the time. The parlour had a piano, a mahogany table, lino and mats and a low, open fireplace with fire irons. The kitchen had a scrub-top table, wooden chairs (her father's chair was the holy of holies), rag rugs and a large kitchen range for cooking on. Lighting in the kitchen was by an oil lamp which was attached to the ceiling and went up and down. Her mother would turn the oil lamp off in the winter to save the oil and they would all sit in the firelight, singing songs and hymns until her father came home when the lamp would be relit. The parlour was lit by a portable oil lamp which her parents sometimes used in their bedroom, but normally it was candles for the bedroom.

At mealtimes, as far as possible, all the family sat down to a meal together, but as children they were not allowed to talk whilst eating and they were certainly not allowed to 'get down' until everyone had finished. A typical breakfast would be porridge and toast, with sandwiches taken to school for lunch. She thought nothing of having jam or mashed potato sandwiches. If they did come home for lunch for some reason they would have jacket potatoes. Tea would be bread and jam and often bread pudding. Her mother, more often than not, would have a pot of broth on the range in the winter made from a marrow bone and split peas. During the 1914–18 war, margarine and butter were unavailable at one point and she remembers having bread and lard with salt and pepper. Whilst she does remember having meat, eggs, bacon and cheese, they were obviously less in evidence than the starchy, filling foods. The family kept chickens for meat and eggs during 1914–18.

There was the usual corner shop and it was the children's job to run errands. A cup would be taken for a pennyworth of mustard pickle, beetroot jam, or the like. Her mother always bought tea in ¼-lb bags. Normally they all ate margarine but with 2 oz butter for father. If any of the children were ill, he would nurse them while he ate and feed them titbits off his plate. During the 1914–18 war you had to register where you would buy your groceries and the children would take it in turn to queue early, then their mother would come and take their place and whichever child it was would run off to school. During Christmas week the stalls in the markets would be left up decorated and you could buy oranges, forty for 1s. Presumably oranges couldn't have been so available during the war.

Washing and cleaning in the home really were heavy chores. To do the washing you first had to save everything that would burn to stoke up the stove and copper, or the stove and cast-iron copper. My mother-in-law remembers that her mother was friendly with the owners of the corner shop who would give her wood in the shape of boxes. Once you had your fuel, you had to fill your copper by hand and when the water was hot you ladled it out into a tin bath when you would use a rubbing board and blocks of soap. Once all the washing had been rubbed it went back into the refilled copper together with bleaching soda and ordinary soda and would be left to boil for twenty minutes. It was a steamy job, pushing it down every so often with a copper stick. As the children went out to work and there was a little more money, her mother would use Hudson's Soap Powder instead of the two sorts of soda. When the wash had finished boiling it would be lifted out into a bath of clean water to be rinsed, all 'whites' would be 'blued' with a Reckitts blue bag, or starched, and finally it would all be wrung out through a hand-operated mangle. After the wash had been dried it would be ironed on the kitchen table on an old piece of blanket with a sheet or piece of cotton over that. The irons would be hot irons heated by the fire and the only sure way to see if they were hot enough would be to spit on them. In 1923, her mother had to have an operation for breast cancer and a neighbour, whose husband was a dock worker, and more often than not, was not chosen to work, came in and did all the washing, not the ironing, for 2s 6d. The neighbour came at 8 a.m. and left at 1 p.m. and would only stop for a glass of beer and bread and cheese half-way through the morning. Apparently this neighbour also took in washing and thought nothing of pawning the clean laundry on Tuesday until payday. My mother-in-law only ever went into a pawn shop once and she had such a telling off from her mother that she was too frightened ever to go again, even though she had only gone with a friend. The hearth had to be hearthstoned and blackleaded, the fenders rubbed with Brasso. The step and sills would be rubbed with a donkey stone. Lace curtains starched and pulled.

Children started school much earlier then than now, it seems. My mother-in-law started school at four and a half, but her elder sister started at three. There were forty-five to fifty pupils in a class and lessons were done on a slate with a slate pencil. The poor children would go to school early at 8 a.m. and have a breakfast of porridge and bread and margarine, but for them to receive this their parents would have to have undergone a means test and to have sold any furniture or goods that weren't really essential to living. The receiving officer would then issue five tickets for breakfasts for a week. She has no memories of school lunches. She was taught the three Rs and also how to knit. When you became an older pupil you were taken swimming. If, as a pupil, you became 'high' in the hot weather, the teacher would arrange to take you to the public baths where you had a free bath and you became socially more acceptable. It was only the neglected children who had to suffer this fate. To have a bath at home, the copper ritual would have to start all over again, the tin bath would be placed on two kitchen chairs in front of the fire, the eldest child had the cleanest water with the water being topped up down to the youngest.

Emily Pankhurst told me not to wash his clothes too

SR.2, August 1972

For clothes the girls always wore a white pinafore over a thick winter dress or in the summer a calico dress. Under this would be either a flannelette or calico petticoat, flannel stays, liberty bodice, a vest and calico drawers. In winter this would be topped off with a coat and knitted hat. Her mother made all of their clothes but after the eldest it was all hand-me-downs. As they all wore button boots, the girls always fought as to who would have the button hook first. Straight hair was curled in 'rag crackers' for special occasions and as most Sunday School parties were on a Friday evening you had to present a note at school asking permission to keep your 'rags' in during the day.

. . . If you needed a doctor but had no money you went to the relieving office doctor and then received any medicine you needed off him. Her brother once had an abcess in his groin and the doctor charged 1s for calling, and then lanced the abcess while her brother was on the kitchen table.

A milkman called and he took a measure from his can and ladled it into your own jug. The baker also came, and weighed each loaf on a pair of scales before he sold it to you as, if it was under weight, you had a make-weight piece.

Her few recollections of the 1914–18 war include remembering brown paper stuck to the windows as black out and sitting under the kitchen table for a shelter.

Whilst I think she had remembered fairly accurately and not made things seem too rosy, I do wonder what her father's working hours were as they seem much too short compared to other workers of the time.

Another reason for their completeness as a family may have been that her mother was half German and may have been subject to ill-feeling from neighbours, and if they kept themselves to themselves perhaps they felt more secure.

SR.29, November 1974

Daffodils, Cards – and Wages

JILL NICHOLLS

'All of us are housewives and mothers – we do the work of mothering other people. We're tired of doing it for free.' Suzie Fleming of Bristol Wages for Housework Campaign was addressing about one hundred women and a BBC camera crew in London's Gate Cinema on 20 March, Mother's Day. We'd all come in free, and been given a daffodil each.

'Few of us can get time off even on Mother's Day. We appreciate the cards and the flowers but they're just not enough – we want a wage for our work,' she went on, showing a stack of petitions for a higher family allowance and wages for housework which were taken to Mr Healey at the end of the afternoon. Then the cameras went away and there were songs and their film *About Time*.

> We'd have some money and some wages too
> Ain't it amazing what wages do . . .

The speeches that followed referred to the Iceland strike, where women withdrew their labour for one day with the slogan 'When women stop, everything stops', and explained the campaign's position: all women are housewives – gay and straight, black and white, married, single, prostitute – and all women's work is essentially housework; as housework is a labour of love, so all women's work is low paid and low status. If housewives were paid by the state they'd have higher status and more bargaining power – they could refuse their work.

. . . The assumption was that no woman would choose to live with a man if she could afford not to. Assuming that, Wages for Housework means money for women so they can live apart from men, bring up their children in their own homes and not have to do jobs they don't like (the assumption being that women go out to work only for money; given the chance they'd stay home).

CAZ, *SR.4*, October 1972

That's what speakers at the meeting implied, but it can come across rather differently – 'We appreciate the cards, the flowers, the love, but we want the money too.' This need not challenge woman's role as wife, housewife and mother, or the way housework is organized. Wages for Housework campaigners do question the idea that housework and childcare are 'naturally' woman's work, and that the family is the best place for them – they see a wage as the way to start changing this. But they sometimes suggest that if the economics change, the rest will follow and don't face up to the way Wages for Housework can be used by people who don't want women's situation to change.

A Finnish nursery worker, at the meeting with three Swedish women, had a familiar left–feminist reaction against the idea: 'I am amazed that you are campaigning for women to stay at home. In Sweden where I live, the right-wing government is trying to get women to accept money to do that. In the crisis they want the men to have the jobs. The women's liberation movement is united against this. It's the *last* thing women want. It's a way of keeping us out of society. You have to have the right to have a job. The right wing is saying that women are only fit to look after a family.' . . .

SR.58, May 1977

'Our Food Co-op Knows the Best Place'

ALISON FELL AND JILL NICHOLLS

In the last months of 1973 one of the prime problems of living, for everyone, was rising food prices. It was hard to combat this in any practical way, let alone to attack the causes of the inflation. By Christmas people felt angrier and yet even more powerless than before. It was around then that a group of active women from East London decided that a food co-op might be one way women could organize together about something which affected them so basically. A few were women from a political group – East London Big Flame. The others were housewives and working women from Lincoln Estate in Bow. Together they visited the 'Red Market', a kind of co-op which had been operating with some success on a West London estate, discussed this, and set about writing a leaflet which local children helped distribute around Lincoln Estate. Although the shopping amenities there are meagre – only two corner shops, and those expensive, and the nearest market a $1\frac{1}{2}$-mile walk away – the first leaflet brought no response.

'I got a leaflet through my door, the first time I read it but took no notice, the second time I said I'm going to find out what it is, and ever since then I'm in the food co-op.'

However the women took a risk and decided to buy more food than they needed for themselves. They set up a table in front of the estate and sold the surplus.

'I was coming back from shopping and there was a stall and some women over on the green by some of the flats and one of them approached me about the food co-op and asked me if I was interested, and asked me to go and have a look at some of the things they had on display, and I was very impressed. I've been going to the food co-op ever since. I find it makes a vast difference in my money.'

The food co-op began to attract interest and support from other tenants. However, the local shopkeepers, threatening to contact the

GLC and tell them that the women were selling on their property, sent the police round. Because of this harassment the women stopped selling on the green and restricted their buying to the needs of those already in the food co-op and sharing in its work. 'We started sharing the food out at someone's flat, different every fortnight. But it was chaotic with nine or ten people trying to pick up their orders in someone else's sitting room.'

They had approached the local tenants' committee for use of the tenants' hall but the committee wouldn't hear of it being used for food distribution. Luckily a woman living nearby in short-life housing over a semi-derelict shop offered the use of the shopfront, and it's here that food is stored now, and orders shared out on Saturday mornings.

So how does it work? The main organizing and allotting of tasks is done at a fortnightly Wednesday meeting. Order forms are given out and prices discussed; everyone decides what they need for the week, fills out an order form and puts enough cash in the float to cover their order – if they have the lump sum, otherwise they pay when collecting their order. The women organized a jumble sale to provide a cash float to start them off, foreseeing that some people might be too hard up midweek to lay out large sums for advance buying. Up to £100 is handled every week. When it came to finding out where to buy cheaply and in bulk the women drew on their own experience of bargain hunting, and that of friends and relatives who had lived in the area for a long time.

'At first people didn't want to share their special knowledge because they thought it made them better shoppers than the others. But gradually we shared everything we knew about the best places to buy things so that we could all benefit and we found out the best places to buy food wholesale. Now, instead of "I know the best place" it's "Our food co-op knows the best place." Individual fads about certain brands – "I only use Heinz Baked Beans, I wouldn't touch anything else, I'm funny that way" – tended to lose their importance as the collective effort became more absorbing. Now people mostly trust the choice of whoever does the shopping.'

There are three places the women buy their stock. On Thursday mornings two women drive to Wapping warehouse, which takes in supermarket tinned goods with damaged wrappers. On Fridays the eggs, potatoes and apples, which come straight from a farm, are picked up. Also on Friday, two other women visit the Cashmart where they buy all their basic groceries, meat and household goods like toothpaste, bleach, toilet rolls. On Friday evening two people go through all the bulk-bought goods using the order forms and pack each order into a separate box. Meat is wrapped, priced and kept in someone's freezer overnight.

'It takes two to three hours, but it's much more enjoyable than shopping, you have a bit of a natter with whoever's doing it. It's not just walking into a shop and getting served.'

From 10 o'clock on Saturday mornings the shop fills up with people collecting their orders, buying extras from what's left over, perhaps, and checking out the bills. Children play among the tins and boxes. This is one of the few times that men appear on the scene – some husbands pick up their wives' orders but none are directly involved in organizing apart from a couple of the Big Flame men who sometimes help with the driving. Accounts like other tasks are shared as far as possible.

'It may be more efficient keeping the same jobs but it's more fun taking it in turns going to the different places, otherwise it gets to be humdrum, a chore.'

'It's been slow to get the jobs shared out equally, only some of the Big Flame women can drive and though we've planned to teach people to drive we've not got round to it yet.'

But the major problems of organizing such a self-help project have mainly been solved and the People's Food Co-op has kept going where others have folded either from lack of a committed enough group to keep them running, or the absence of real material need among the members.

Apart from the material advantage of cheaper food and the satisfaction to be gained from bypassing some of the middle men in the food distribution racket, the food co-op attracted members for other, more social reasons. The labour connected with feeding the family is usually a lonely, never-ending chore, a matter of tramping round supermarkets getting a stuffy head and bleary eyes, a matter of scrabbling through magazines for recipes which might prove your worth to . . . whom? Yourself, neighbours, husband, kids? These lonely battles for self-respect are not easy for women to win. When these tasks are done communally, they still amount to hard work, but it's sociable work. The women who joined wanted more than cheap food, they wanted to get out of the house, to make friends. Isolation bred suspicion – some were afraid to speak to neighbours in the lifts in case they were criticized for being unmarried mothers; some were so apprehensive about anything new that they answered through the letterbox when the first leafletters came round. They aren't scared any more. A shared project of their own and opportunities for discussing everything under the sun have opened them up.

The energy generated by the food co-op has carried over into other areas – there's a Tuesday afternoon playgroup for the kids and a talk group for the mothers, which has lasted, while a babysitting scheme failed. A small self-help therapy group set up by women in Big Flame meets fortnightly.

But they feel that the food co-op itself could do more, could expand and cater for more people than it does at present. They are making another attempt to get the tenants' hall in order to open out the Wednesday meetings so that women who might have felt that the food co-op was exclusive to a group of friends would find it easier to join in and draw on its resources. Certainly for the ten or so women who have been deeply and consistently involved since the co-op began eighteen months ago, the benefits of this kind of organizing have been tangible and many sided.

'I'd like to live more communally next. You get energy off others. You can't do it alone.'

SR.40, October 1975

Alison Fell, *SR.57*, April 1977

His and Her Housework

WENDY WHITFIELD

. . . A year at college, in a very free environment, clearly underlined my marriage's restrictions on my activities and relationships. I was torn between the two worlds of continuing with my studying and self-development and coping with my domestic responsibilities – washing, shopping, cooking, being home every evening and weekend with my husband. Back in a nine-to-five job, this dilemma was exacerbated. My studying was replaced by unrewarding labour and the same old chores.

I'd been reading a lot of women's literature – *The Female Eunuch, Wedlocked Women, Spare Rib* and the like. We were both becoming involved in left-wing politics. I participated in a strike at my place of work. So it seemed quite natural that I should pursue a course of industrial action in my domestic situation, where I was working long hours while the Boss read or watched the telly.

After the usual nagging, the disguised and undisguised gibes, I decided on an all-out fight. All or nothing. I went on strike. I announced that from now on I would do only *my* shopping, cooking and cleaning. I would not clean up, nor would I keep up my incessant tidying, writing lists, washing and returning milk bottles, putting away the dishes that he left to drain instead of drying them, defrosting the fridge or cleaning the cooker, clearing away the coffee cups or writing to his relatives. In short, I would do no more than a man would do. Dave thought I was joking.

After a few days it ceased to be funny. The battle began in earnest. His reactions and behaviour immediately fell into a recognizable pattern. At first I was treated with humour and affection. Then I was gently admonished, and then firmly dealt with, like a naughty child. When this failed – well, he'd done all a reasonable man could be expected to do, so I'd be left to 'get out of it' by myself.

At this stage, it is important that personalities be kept out of the dispute: all discussion must be based on the assumption that marriage in a capitalist society inevitably produces a conflict of interests, and that it is in the interests of both partners to fight this. We as women must not be afraid to keep bringing up the subject and forcing our partners to reason through their objections. It is up to us to remember that men are conditioned to expect servicing, and even if they acknowledge equality in theory, they will relax all too soon into the role society prepares them for. I learnt that the same applies to us, and I had to reappraise my own attitude to my role. Was it really necessary to keep dusting and cleaning? Wasn't it enough to wait until it really looked untidy? Together, we had to work out a common definition of 'dirty' and 'untidy'. I've read that men *camp*. Certainly, Dave's standards, like most men's had been lower than mine; now I was expecting him not only to keep a reasonable standard, but to emulate the unreasonably high standards set out in magazines and on television.

Eventually Dave was forced to start negotiating, in his own interest. Luckily we both liked each other enough not to take the easy way out and walk out. I suggested a rota, as the only way of reminding him of his commitments. This led to a bid to humiliate me: according to him, the degradation was mine for making such a suggestion – not his for forgetting to wash his own underpants.

Then there were his attempts to bring in support from outside – in the form of friends and, more deadly, the in-laws. This proved a very successful tactic on his part: I'd be lying if I said I didn't have my own doubts about the struggle. Their shock, dismay and disapproval increased these doubts, but I gained fresh strength when I was accused of not being able to love my husband. This sounded all too familiar. Hadn't my psychiatrist persuaded me to ignore my own feelings rather than question the status quo? Why do women have to humiliate themselves in this way to prove their love? Why can't we *enjoy* loving our partners? Isn't it humiliating that men expect this kind of 'devotion' and wouldn't I have left Dave if I didn't love him? All the same, relatives proved to be the deadliest of 'enemies'. And I haven't sorted that one out yet.

It was finally agreed that the major chores were to be done in turns. The first stage was won. It worked well at first, but then Dave slipped into a decline again. He developed certain 'last stands'. He absolutely refused (and still does) to clean the loo. I tried all tactics, ranging from asking, cajoling, joking, teasing to bullying and humiliating. None worked. I have shelved that one for the time being. Maybe I'll have to compromise.

When it came to washing, Dave worked to rule. He never realized the need for tackling the dirty socks under the bed, or the occasional washing like curtains and dressing gowns. I resorted to noticing them for him by popping them into the linen basket at the last moment. Tiresome though it is to do his thinking for him, he's beginning to get the message, and is starting to develop a little professional pride. Similarly, he pretended not to understand the process of sorting out colours. After a few of my pale things had been ruined, I had to start teaching him. *He* never minded if his handkerchiefs were the colour of his Levis.

All this pretence at ignorance, I found, is an exercise in defiance. Men can't really be that stupid. He not only succeeded in making me feel like a tyrant, but also failed to lighten my load, as I had to think about his turn as well as mine. The only way to tackle this obtuseness is to discuss it. Don't be afraid to 'keep bringing it up'. That's all part of the same trick – treating it all as a joke and ignoring the problem.

When Dave saw he really looked like 'losing', he played his best card. He waited until the traditional time for family drama, Christmas. With the extra workload brought by visiting relatives, his share increased somewhat. Well, he left his chores right until Christmas Eve. There he was cleaning the stairs until three in the morning. What he found to do for two and a half hours I'll never know. I think it was to make me feel guilty, as there was a regular chorus of curses going on. But I'd learnt that the best way not to feel guilty was to go out, and so I did.

Next day I regretted it. The in-laws settled down round a cosy fire. Cheer and goodwill? Treason. Judas with barely concealed delight told his mother that he'd been cleaning the stairs. On Christmas Eve. For two and a half hours.

I again considered throwing in the towel. Did he really want me on his terms or not at all? It was a cold New Year.

When I decided to work part-time in order to continue with my studies, I very nearly lost all the ground we'd made. With the novelty of having more time to myself at home, I indulged in orgies of housework, intending always to start studying 'tomorrow'. Dave was delighted. It wouldn't be long before he was enjoying my domestic services again. By the time I came to my senses and realized that I should be separating my domestic and studying activities, the rot had set in. It took quite a while to realize that studying at home involves considerable disadvantages, especially if you are a woman. It is all too easy to fritter away the best hours of the day shopping and cleaning. It took longer for Dave to acknowledge this, as it was against his interests to do so. He preferred the explanation that I really did prefer tidying up his mess left on my drawing board the night before, to studying.

Dave frequently works from home himself, and does not suffer from the same compulsion to tidy up or do the shopping before settling down to work. Here, we women must take the lesson from men and assess our priorities. The problem has been overcome to some extent however now that we have an extra room which has been converted into a workroom . . .

SR.45, April 1976

5 WORK

Today 41 per cent of all employees are women. Since the implementation of the Equal Pay Act in 1975, women's earnings have increased from just over half men's to under three quarters. Employers have used a combination of methods to avoid equality, from altering the job content for men and for women so their work cannot be compared, to restructuring grading systems with women below men. In doing so they called upon the well-worn myths about women's work which stem from the sexual division of labour. A feminist exhibition about women and work reviewed in *Spare Rib* No. 40 showed that 'The male jobs tend to be mobile (often involving the movement of the whole body); the women's jobs tend to be static, fiddly and repetitious.' Manual dexterity is called a woman's talent. Such explanations are used to restrict the work available to women, to classify this work as women's work and, as such, to rationalize paying women less.

However, the militant action of women against the methods used to delay or prevent equal pay has scattered myths. Time and again throughout the seventies, women, often with no previous experience of organizing at work, had to strike over equal pay, and in doing so demanded a new respect for the work they do. The strikes were not always successful and often involved great hardship. And women had to fight, not only their employer, but men's reluctance to support them, and the hostility of individual union organizers.

Women who work in the public sector, whose jobs are an extension of the caring female role, have similarly shown a new militancy. The nurses' strike in 1974 involved hundreds of women around the country, and questioned percentage pay rises which leave the lowest paid with the lowest rise. Women in both the public and private sectors have taken unprecedented action, resisting cuts by government and employers which threatened their livelihood, rebelling against the idea that women should provide a reserve pool of labour, at the same time raising issues beyond the economic. Strikes by cleaners have been concerned with health and asbestos dust. Groups of women workers brought out problems of racism, and of the particularly vulnerable position of women migrant workers in the lowest paid jobs, like hotel chambermaids and domestic workers. Shopworkers, cleaners, hotel workers and clothing workers, went on strike over the right to unionize, challenging the myth of women's reluctance to organize. This myth conceals the way men have been unwilling to organize with women, and the way men have not understood women's particular relation to work: the double responsibility of home and work, a consciousness of the way inflation affects food prices and eats up wage rises, problems of time and exhaustion, childcare which prevents attendance at evening union meetings, and the difficulty of women asserting themselves in the all-male atmosphere of meetings.

Other issues have been raised by the mechanism of the tribunals set up to deal with Equal Pay claims and the Sex Discrimination Act specifically. The tribunals have been difficult for women because an individual often has to act alone, on her own initiative, which requires great determination and confidence. Some of the cases which have been lost show the threat women pose to men when they step outside the symbolic boundaries, like the women entering the male building trades, or even fishing, who have been sacked for reasons like 'swearing', or because they were a 'distraction' to the men.

These instances show the immense obstacles to women entering work on the same terms as men. Yet more women spend more of their lives in paid work than ever before. Although women's work is often structured around the needs of childcare (the number of part-time women workers increased from 29 per cent in 1968 to 35 per cent in 1976) women are often penalized for working part-time. *Spare Rib* No. 77 reported an Appeal Tribunal's ruling that a woman working part-time is not entitled to the same hourly rate as a man working full-time at the same job.

In *Spare Rib* No. 51 the Press Association reported that the government felt that an 'encouraging factor is that in the last three months most of the increase in unemployment was among women'. But most women who work need the money as well as the personal independence of earning wages. Unless there is recognition of the demands of childcare in the form of nurseries, decently paid maternity and paternity leave and the right to resume a career after an absence rearing children, women will not have equality at work.

General Maid

MINNIE COWLEY

*When Minnie Cowley retired, she wrote a detailed account of her childhood
from 1910 to 1923. Her daughter Annette Kuhn, who had always been
fascinated by her mother's stories, sent an extract to* Spare Rib *saying: 'I
should very much like other people to have the opportunity to look at it,
and I think that there are sections which are particularly interesting as
regards the history of women's – and especially working-class women's –
socialization, education and labour during the early years of this century.
I'm sending you the section on my mother's experiences in domestic service,
which was still one of the main sectors of employment for working-class
girls immediately after the First World War – although it is clear that
service was very much disliked.' Minnie Cowley's father was a plasterer.
Her parents, with their seven children, lived in Richmond. The extract
opens with Minnie, aged thirteen and unable to find a job in a shop or
factory, visiting a domestic employment agency.*

A little way past Marble Hill and almost opposite St Stephen's
Church in Twickenham there was a domestic agency whose window
was always full of 'wanted' cards. These were for cooks, 'generals',
parlourmaids, housemaids, kitchen maids, butlers, companions,
nursemaids and married couples, all to live in. I had often stopped
to read these cards, and now I made up my mind to go there and see
if they could find me a job. Making myself as respectable-looking as
possible in the old mauve astrakhan coat my aunt had given me while
I was still at school, a woollen tam-o'-shanter borrowed from my
sister Aggie, and nice clean shoes, I set off for the agency without
telling Mum what I had in mind.

Feeling nervous but determined, I approached the building and
with no hesitation knocked on the door; but I was in such a hurry to
knock that I had not noticed the sign saying 'Please Walk In'. My heart
was thumping and butterflies were chasing each other in my tummy,
but I went in and sat down on one of the hard chairs which were
arranged round the walls. Before long, I heard footsteps nearing the
room and a very severe-looking lady put her head round the door and
said, 'Will you come this way?' She led me across a passage to another
room.

'Good morning. Sit down,' said the person sitting behind the desk.
With its large blotting pad and wooden inkstand, the desk looked to me
just like the one my headmistress used to have.

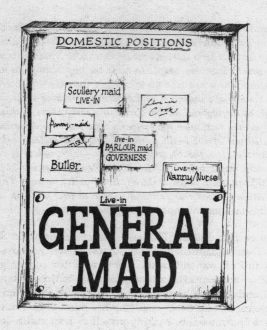

'What can I do for you?' she asked, not looking quite so severe as the lady who had shown me into the room.

'I'm looking for a job to sleep in,' I replied in little more than a whisper.

Opening a big writing book – which I later learned was called a ledger – she proceeded to ask my name, address and age, writing them down as I told her.

Then she asked me what school I had attended and where I had worked; these, she said, were for her to contact about references. She pulled a box of cards towards her, sorted them over and after some hesitation picked one out. 'There's something here that might suit you,' she said, 'I'll telephone the lady and find out.' She did this, and then she looked across the desk at me as I sat there dying to know what had been said, and asked if I would go and see a lady who lived near Richmond Hill and who wanted a 'general' to start as soon as possible. She informed me that if I took the situation I should have to pay her a fee of two shillings and sixpence. This was unexpected, but I agreed, thinking it would be worth that to get a job. By the time I left the agency, it was twelve-thirty and my appointment was for two o'clock. I had no dinner, but there was not enough time to go home.

I found the road and the house I wanted quite easily, and with the time I had to spare weighed up the place in which I might be staying. It looked massive. There was a bay window on each side of the front door, more big windows on the first floor and an attic window high up in the roof. My sister had told me that servants slept either in the basement or the attic, and as there was no basement in this house, I realized that if I did get the job I should have to sleep right up there.

Feeling as if I were going to my doom, I walked up to the house, lifted the fancy latch of the front gate, stepped up the tiled pathway and banged twice on the door. I did not have to wait long before the door was opened by a woman with staring blue eyes.

'Yes, what do you want?' she said, eying me up and down.

'I'm from the agency and I have to see this lady at two o'clock,' I said, handing her the letter I had been given.

'You should have gone round the side,' she said, 'that's the servants' entrance. But you'd better come this way now. I'll tell madam you're here.' Opening the door wider, she made room for me to step into the red-carpeted hall, where just ahead of me I noticed a grandfather clock with a round pendulum swinging back and forth. The 'Hickory, Dickory, Dock' nursery rhyme went through my mind. I was shown into a room and told to wait there 'while I tell the mistress you're here'. On each side of the fireplace was a brown leather armchair studded with buttons of the same colour. The sides of the fireplace and the hearth were tiled in green, and I hoped I could make the tiles as shiny as they were at that moment. The fireplace and overmantel were white, and in the middle of the mantelpiece stood a marble clock which, with its pillars, looked like the front of a building. At each end was a small statue. How different this was to our mantelpiece at home, which was always covered with odds and ends. Having taken note of my surroundings, I was just looking at the clock again to check the time when madam came in, and right then I felt hungry and scared. The interview was not too bad, though. She asked me where I lived, what my dad worked at, how I had done at school, and where she could apply for references. This was Thursday and she wanted me to start on Saturday: she was sure, she said, that my references would be satisfactory. The household consisted of master, mistress, companion, a boy of about four years old named Peter, and the cook.

I accepted gratefully, telling her I had one morning apron and a frock that could be worn in the afternoons. She offered to buy a morning frock and apron, two afternoon aprons and two caps, saying I could pay for them at two shillings and sixpence out of my wages. Maids were usually paid monthly but, like Aggie had done, I asked to be paid weekly, and here my wages were to be seven-and-six a week. I had no alternative but to agree with these terms, since Mum could not help me and Dad would not, even though he was in a position to do so: most of his money still went to the publican.

It was about four-thirty when I eventually arrived home, wondering what Dad and Mum would say about my sleeping in. Almost as soon as I got in the kitchen door, Mum asked me to pick up my baby brother Harry. 'Nurse him a little while', she said, 'while I finish getting your father's tea.' This I did very gingerly, scared that I might drop him. Mum was always saying that he was not a very strong baby and while she was to-ing and fro-ing between kitchen and scullery, I blurted out that I had got a job in service and that they wanted me to start on Saturday.

'You'd better tell your father when he comes in,' said Mum. 'It's up to him.'

'Will you start off about it first, Mum?' I asked. 'You know what he is, especially if it's me that wants to do something.'

But it was not too difficult telling him, after all. He was in a good mood and seemed pleased with the idea, which made me feel a load had been taken off my mind. After he had gone to the pub we scrounged round all the cupboards and drawers, getting together the things I would need for the Saturday.

I mended an old flannelette nightie that Aggie had left behind, raked my black alpaca frock out of the bedroom cupboard to be washed and ironed for the afternoons, and took off the vest and bloomers I had on, to be washed as well, so that I could wear clean clothes when I went and still have some left to change into.

On the Saturday morning, I took a penny bus ride to Richmond Bridge and walked up the Hill. I arrived at the house earlier than arranged, and this time did the right thing by going in at the tradesmen's entrance and knocking at the side door, which was opened by the cook.

'Come in,' she said. 'I'm rather busy now, but I'll show you to your bedroom, then you can come down when you're ready.'

Through the kitchen, the hall, then up the carpeted stairs she led me, passing four doors on the first landing; then up another flight of stairs, which this time were covered with lino. There were only two doors leading off the second landing. One of these the cook opened and told me this was where I should sleep. The room next door, she added, was locked and full of things belonging to the people who owned the house. The first thing I noticed about my room was the sloping ceiling: the attic, I thought, just as Aggie had told me. I had never had so much space all to myself, and certainly nothing as posh as this.

'This must be a mistake,' I thought. 'Perhaps the boy will have to sleep with me.' It didn't seem right that this big room should be for just one person. I had to stop my gaping at all the grandness when the cook's voice broke into my thoughts with 'I can't stay, you can come down as soon as you have unpacked.' A small apron, a lacy cap and a pair of celluloid cuffs were on the bed, and so, guessing they were for me to wear, I changed my frock and put them on.

Then I went downstairs. The quiet was a bit frightening, for it seemed strange after the noise and bustle I had been used to. Nearing the kitchen, I heard voices, and on opening the door saw the lady of the house talking to the cook. She introduced me properly to the cook – whose name was Beatrice – showed me round the house and then let me know the work I had to do.

Once a week each room had to be turned out. There was no Hoover for the carpets: tea leaves were saved and sprinkled on them while they were damp, then swept off with a hard broom. The big windows had to be cleaned, fireplaces blackleaded and tiles washed and polished, loads of silver polished – even though some of it was never used – and the boy taken out for two hours every day. Every morning the kitchen range had to be raked out and the fire lit; then it was blackleaded, the fender cleaned with emery cloth and the hearth hearthstoned. Finally, the front step was swept and cleaned and the breakfast laid. All this was before the cook arrived at eight o'clock.

Middle-class people certainly had their pound of flesh in those days. Up at six-thirty in the morning, I never got to bed much before ten at night. My time off was Wednesdays from 3 p.m. to 9.30 p.m. and on one Sunday in every month after the midday dinner. A good fifteen hours a day at the ready all the time: it was not good by present-day standards, but I still think there is something in the old saying that hard work never killed anybody.

The bill for my uniform came to 15s 11¾d, a little over two weeks' wages.

2 afternoon aprons @ 1/11¾d		3	11½
2 afternoon caps @ 1/0¾d		2	1½
1 morning frock @ 6/11d		6	11
1 morning apron @ 2/11¾d		2	11¾
Total:		15	11¾

The mistress deducted two-and-six out of my first week's wages and asked if I would like her to send the two-and-six fee to the agency at the same time as she sent hers. Whether this was to make sure I paid it, or whether she was really doing me a good turn I never knew, but that week I drew the large amount of two shillings and sixpence for a good ninety hours, either working or at the ready.

There may not have been slavery as such in those 'Good Old Days', but for those fourteen-year-olds who were unlucky enough to become 'generals' in the homes of lower-middle-class or jumped-up working-class families, this was just about one step away from it.

Sleeping alone was very frightening. I felt very lonely and would have given anything to wake up and find my sisters there with me. The smallest noise disturbed me, and I would lie awake for a long time, waiting and wondering. A climax had to come: I was so worked up and frightened when I went to bed, especially as my room was so far up. Then there was the locked room next door – my imagination ran wild about what or who might be in there. A witch? A man being kept prisoner?

One night I was wakened soon after I had finally got to sleep by what sounded like a terrific explosion. Before the echo had faded away, I was out of bed and down the stairs. I dashed pell-mell into the drawing-room without even a thought of knocking and cried out hysterically, 'The Germans are here, they're shooting guns in the road!' The mistress sat me on a chair and told me not to be silly, the war had been over a long time and I should go back to bed. She led me into the kitchen and gave me a cup of coffee from the pot they had finished with. I did not know it then, but coffee was the very worst thing to give to anybody for inducing sleep. It took me much longer to get back upstairs than it had done to come down them, and before getting into bed I knelt down and said my prayers, something I had not done for a long time. Then I got between the sheets and cried myself to sleep.

While I was working at this house, the cook sold Mum two wicker armchairs, padded round the sides and covered in cretonne patterned with large red roses. I remember them well: they creaked enough to wake the house whenever they were sat in. I gave the cook five shillings for a kimono, a kind of Japanese dressing gown. I really needed other things first but just couldn't resist that lovely piece of luxury: it was made of crinkly material, had a pattern of a dragon on the back and wide sleeves trimmed in white.

I eventually left the job in the house on Richmond Hill, or rather I got the sack. I must admit that what I did to cause my dismissal was silly. Instead of taking Peter for his usual walk, I took him home to see my young brother, and when he told the mistress he had been to where I lived, she gave me a week's notice on the spot. The trouble was that while he was playing in the field at the back of our house, he fell and cut his knee and had to have it bandaged with a piece of white rag. And to make things worse, he messed up his jacket. I told Mum about it when I went home on my next half-day, and she said, 'Who the devil does she think she is? If he grows up half as strong as you lot, she won't have much to worry about. Playing in a bit of dirt never hurt anyone – he's got to eat a peck before he dies.' . . .

SR.44, March 1976

Against the 'Gentlemen of Justice': Portuguese Cleaners Unite

NEWS FEATURE

'At the moment we are in the forefront of the struggle for women's rights in Portugal.' Sophia Ganhao of the Domestic Workers' Union was speaking in London in March. 'All our struggle is based in the fight for the rights of domestic workers, but as such it is also a struggle for the liberation of women.'

In the summer of 1974 there was a wave of occupations of workplaces abandoned or threatened with closure by frightened owners. One that women took over was a laundry in Lisbon. They told *Officina Samba*, a left-wing paper, that they wanted 'to run it as a service to working-class women so that they would be liberated from housework'.

At the same time in Porto in the north, women who were once maids

From 'Portugal: A Blaze of Freedom', *SR.40*, October 1975

to the rich occupied a house which they turned into a co-operative for housework, with a creche and canteen. They said: 'We will no longer do useless work in the houses of the bourgeoisie. We want to be of service to other workers, not to parasites.'

Early in 1975 the women from these two occupations started a union for all domestic workers, initially to demand a national minimum wage.

They had meetings in Porto and Lisbon and within six months there were 5,000 in the union – cleaners in houses and hospitals, workers in laundries, nurseries and canteens.

They started a labour exchange in opposition to exploitative employment agencies which openly encouraged prostitution.

In Lisbon they opened a home for domestic workers whose employers had fled the country. Its cheap canteen is used not only for meals but for meetings and music, and it is in direct contact with agricultural co-operatives for supplies.

Under fascism there had been a Catholic Service for the Protection of Servants. Sophia Ganhao said: 'The employers took advantage of the very nature of our work by creating false ties with bribes and paternalistic attitudes. Their sole aim – to keep us apart so they could use us as slaves. The Catholic organization disguised the class conflict with moral and religious preaching. They attempted to justify the "social usefulness" of the domestic servant, and legitimize our exploitation.'

Still representing the interests of the Church, the right wing and the employers, but renamed the Free Union of Domestic Servants, it is now posing as an alternative to the Domestic Workers Union. The DWU is demanding recognition as the *only* union for domestic workers.

They are also presenting these demands to the Ministry of Labour:

i) Guaranteed national minimum wage, the same as the building, steel and ship workers have won.

ii) Paid holidays and sick leave.

They have already won the right to ninety days paid maternity leave.

Many unmarried mothers do domestic work as it's the only work they can get. They are not entitled to social security, state housing or any state health benefits . . .

SR.48, July 1976

Yorkshire Fisherwomen

PETER FRANK

Fishing is a real 'man's job', and examples of women actually going to sea are rare in any culture. This may have been to protect women as child-bearers from the dangers of the sea – it was not because fishing was physically arduous, for women in fishing communities have traditionally done other work which was just as exhausting.

Their work was essential to the family's economy. A fishing marriage was a partnership, and many tasks besides housework were included in the woman's share.

Peter Frank has interviewed some of the older people in Whitby and Staithes on the north Yorkshire coast who were children in the late nineteenth and early twentieth centuries when the whole family still helped with the fishing.

One of the people he spoke to, James Cole, a fisherman from Staithes who died last year aged ninety-three, could remember how, when he was ten, he and his mother carried his father's oilskins down at two in the morning when the boat went out. At Staithes the women went to launch the cobles—fishing boats with high prows – because the water was shallow. At ebb tide especially, they had to wade a long way. Looking back on this, James Cole was grateful: 'Well, to tell you the truth, a woman in Staithes did more work than a man that went off.'

In Whitby the water was deeper so this was not necessary. But it was still a long day.

Maud Hind was born into a Whitby fishing family. Her mother, Jane Harland, died when Maud was twenty-one. Maud describes the rhythm of labour during the five years before she got married – to a bricklayer, not a fisherman – and left home.

'I've seen my father go out (get up, you know) about two o'clock of a morning. He used to go down the pier to see the state of the sea, and then he would come back, and many a time I used to think, oh, I wish t'cobles wouldn't get off today . . . And he used to shout upstairs: "Come on! Come on down, t'tea's ready, we're going off." We had to come down. Get tea, and then, as soon as they went off, we used to bring the mussels in and start – my auntie used to help me a lot – and sometimes they were all froze, you know, you got bad fingers with them.'

The key to comprehending the full extent of the wearying, unremitting repetitiveness of women's work in the fishing community lies in the reference to mussels. They were by far the most popular and effective bait, but they became increasingly costly and difficult to obtain. So it was partly to try to cut down on overhead expenses, but also to meet real shortages of mussels, that there was a growing reliance on limpets (called in the local dialect 'flithers'). Up to the early years of the twentieth century, and sporadically since, flither-picking was a permanent feature in the lives of fisherwomen and girls along the Yorkshire coast.

Once the men had gone off, wives, sisters and daughters set out: 'And they've gone on the scaurs, early morning, and maybe they haven't had a drink or a bite,' Maud recollects her mother telling her. Scaurs are flat, rocky outcrops stretching from the foot of the high cliffs down to, and beyond, low-water mark. The rock is blue-grey shale, slippery and fissured with water-filled gullies and pools. On the seaweed which grows on the rocks browse winkles (in the dialect called 'cuvvins') and limpets. Cuvvins had their importance in the fisherfolk's domestic economy, but it was the flithers which afforded valuable bait.

The women set out dressed only in their ordinary, everyday clothing. In winter the men fished with longlines, each with hundreds of hooks. A huge amount of bait had to be gathered daily; and this in the most bitter months of the year. Many a day there was an icy easterly or northerly wind blowing off the sea, but, providing the boats could get off, the bait had to be gathered. So, be it rain, hail, snow or shine, the women took their wicker baskets (called 'swills') and ventured on to the scaurs.

A pair of men's leather sea boots cost a guinea (a good week's income for a fisherman at that time, and there was many a week if a gale was blowing that his income was 'nowt'). Rubberized Wellingtons had not been invented yet, and all the women had to wear were flimsy shoes or, if they were lucky, lace-up boots or wooden-soled clogs. Ankle-length dresses over a quilted petticoat offered a little warmth and protection from the chapping wind; but when they got wet from the rain or tide, as they almost invariably did, the sodden, heavy material flapping against their legs must have caused intense discomfort. Some wore tight-fitting outer bodices over their dresses, and an apron or pinny; while others donned cast-off men's waistcoats for warmth. Over their heads and shoulders they wore black, woollen shawls which were crossed over their chests and the ends tied behind the back. Hand-knitted, woollen half-mittens completed their dress.

To an observer on the cliffs above, the flither-pickers must have looked rather like rooks pecking in the fields. Moving over the rocks they were continually bent, seeking to spot the limpets, and, finding them, stooping or crouching to slide the blade of a knife between shell and rock. A sharp, prising action and the creature's hold was broken and it was transferred into the swill. Only when the swills were full could the women cover over the flithers with 'dillis', a variety of seaweed, and set off along the scaur back home.

So great was the demand for flithers at Staithes (in the 1870s of much greater importance as a fishing station than Whitby), that stocks locally became exhausted. The flithers on the scaurs at Whitby were needed by that port's fishermen, and so it was not uncommon for Staithes women to go further on to Robin Hood's Bay to gather bait. They would walk to Whitby and spend the night with friends in the fishing community, and early the next day walk to the bay, pick their flithers, carry them on their heads back to Whitby, put the flithers on the carrier's cart for Staithes, and then walk home. It was a round journey of about thirty-five miles.

Once the bait had been gathered and the women had returned home, the flithers or mussels had to be 'skaned'. Skaning is the process of removing the soft part, the actual bait, from the shell. Limpets are univalves and thus the body could be removed from the shell virtually in one movement – the bait could be scooped out of the shell in much the same way as one scoops clean the cap of a boiled egg.

Mussels are bivalves and skaning them requires greater speed, dexterity and considerable strength in the wrists. But it takes only a few seconds, and after practice, skaning becomes a very mechanical and repetitive activity. But a woman might have to skane several thousand mussels daily (and a few still do). Sometimes the mussels are covered with barnacles which can cut the hands. As the shells are forced open a saline liquid flows out, and this and the dirt sticking to the outer shell coarsen the skin, split fingernails, and penetrate cuts or grazes. The skaned mussels were dropped into a jar, and a woman knew from experience how many jars of bait would be needed for the lines: 'You might need three mussels for one hook, but Tees mussels were big and plump and then you only needed one.' When a jar was full the mussels were tipped into a tin bath and cold water poured on them ('the colder the better') to make them swell and grow firm ready for baiting.

Skaning and baiting were done in the home: *houses were workplaces as well as dwellings.* When the cobles returned from the fishing grounds the women went down to the harbour to meet them in, get the lines, coil them on to wicker baskets – skeps – and carry them back home on their heads to start 'caving' and baiting.

Caving is clearing the line of old bait, seaweed and other rubbish. First the line is tipped off the skep on to the table. Then the empty skep is placed on one side and the woman begins to coil the line on to it afresh. Occasionally hooks are missing: 'Some women could put hooks on themselves. Old Walter Corrie's wife, she used to whip all his hooks on for him.' The coils are arranged at one end of the skep, and as each hook is baited it is laid out neatly at the other end. There must be no carelessness: a snagged hook as the line is being shot at sea could be time-wasting and possibly dangerous.

In the meantime, the men would be mooring the cobles and seeing to the selling of the catch. Then they would go home, and after something to eat, would work alongside the women at caving and baiting.

By far the worst job was 'mucking' the lines if the boat had not been able to go off. This happened when there was a storm, and, since the mussels would not stay fresh on the lines for more than a few days after having been skaned, the women had to set to, remove the putrefying bait, and start all over again.

The difficulty of keeping living rooms clean where skaning and baiting were being done can be imagined. In Maud's household the black-leaded fireplace and brasses were covered up on a Monday morning and not unveiled again until Saturday teatime, when all was given a polish ready for Sunday. Maud saw to it that she and the younger children had eaten before their father and two elder brothers came in from sea. After the men had had their dinners all was sided away and two tables pulled out into the middle of the room. At one table worked Maud and her father, and at the other her two brothers, all baiting the lines with the mussels she and her aunt had skaned earlier in the day. Before going to bed, everything had to be left ready for the next morning, particularly father's clothes, sea boots and oilskins, lest the lifeboat should be called out during the night.

Before the advent of the railways and technological innovations such as refrigeration, fish was preserved by salting, pickling or drying in the wind and sun. In 1808 the Revd John Graves observed that at Staithes 'on the fishermen's return home, the fish are cut up and salted by the women, which is not only a disagreeable but a laborious employment'. This type of work is now beyond living memory, although James Cole could still recall fish being split up and laid out on wooden racks, called 'flakes', to dry at Staithes: 'They built them in t'fields, like a bit of fence, maybe two foot frae t'ground, out of sticks out of a wood and that, so that t'wind could get underneath the fish and sun on the top to dry them. Then in winter time the women hawked them all over.'

At Whitby some women had stalls on the quayside from which they sold to the public, while others had regular rounds in the town. Maud Hind as a child was often sent by her grandmother to deliver fish during her dinner break from school:

'And she used to come down to our house when I was going to school . . . She used to say, "When you leave school, Maud, you've got to go for me with some fish to Smailes's" . . . And I used to take that fish at dinnertime . . . She used to buy it on the quay, and they used to order the fish off her; and it had to be up for a certain time, 'cos, you know, Smailes were one of those high-class families in Whitby . . . And many a time they've maybe put you an orange in your hand; and I've had to come back and go to school . . .'

Some women tramped long distances with baskets of fish on their heads up Eskdale to scattered farms and villages. Staithes women went regularly into the ironstone-mining villages of Cleveland and to industrial Teesside. Thus in addition to their many other tasks, some fisherwomen performed an entrepreneurial role, something which on the whole their menfolk avoided, or were unable to do because of the demands of the actual fishing. Thus the women made an additional financial contribution to the family exchequer.

The fisherwomen's arduous lives frequently led to ill-health and premature death. For on top of the irregular hours, exposure to bitter weather, the standing, lifting and carrying of heavy burdens, there was the grind of housework and all the dangers attached to frequent pregnancies. It was a style of life, accepted sometimes consciously and by choice, but often fatalistically. The observer from outside the fishing community, as the photographer Sutcliffe noted, viewed fisherwomen's activity more often than not only superficially: it was 'quaint', 'picturesque', a sentimentalized image with the toil only dimly recognized.

This article is a shortened version of a description of women's work in the Yorkshire inland fishing industry published in Oral History – *journal of the Oral History Society – obtainable from the Dept of Sociology, University of Essex. We are grateful to* Oral History *and to Peter Frank for permission to reprint it.*

SR.46, May 1976

Sweatshop at Home

CHRIS POULTER

Homeworking is about the exploitation of women as mothers tied to the home with toddlers, as daughters left to care for the aged or as immigrants whose vulnerability makes them a cheap and malleable labour force. In the beginning of November Homeworkers Action Groups from all over England met in Birmingham.

There are about a quarter of a million homeworkers in Britain today. They are 'taken on' to assemble toys, pens and furniture; to package stamps, buttons and filters; to fold, envelope and label advertising material; to knit sweaters, to sew gloves, to tassel football scarves, the list is endless. As with most low paid women's work it's dull, repetitive and labour intensive.

A recent Low Pay Unit survey found that 80 per cent of homeworkers interviewed were getting less than 30p an hour. From one South London firm, homeworkers get 89p for sewing 1,000 buttons on to cards which means an hourly rate of between 9 and 10p. Even experienced homeworkers who work at high speed are poorly paid. In Leeds a homeworker with two years' experience now tassels ten scarves an hour. Each scarf is worth 4p in wages. For an eight-hour day or eighty scarves she earns £3.20.

In addition employers often fail to compensate for rent of space, heating, electricity, transport and renting or buying equipment.

Homeworkers have few rights under the law. They are generally considered 'self-employed' and so are not covered by the Employment Protection Act. This means they have no job security and get no holiday pay, sick pay, maternity leave or redundancy pay.

Until the government enacts legislation which clearly recognizes the 'employee' status of these workers, little change is possible.

Some homeworkers are covered by the provisions of the various Wage Councils established to determine wage rates in non-unionized industries. But with no homeworkers directly represented, these bodies have obtained no significant improvement on the inadequate statutory minimum piece rates. Decisions on rates are frequently made in ignorance of the work involved. So the Councils actually sanction and legitimize scandalous rates. The case of the women earning between 9 and 10p an hour sewing buttons on cards is actually covered by a Wage Council agreement!

Homeworkers should also be protected by the 1961 Factories Act which requires employers to register all homeworkers with the local authority. Failure to comply can lead to a £20 fine (no less!). According to the Act, Environmental Health Inspectors are responsible for ensuring that checks are carried out on the health and safety aspects of domestic working conditions. In fact employers mostly ignore the requirement to register and cases of prosecution seem non-existent. In turn local authorities make little effort either to maintain an accurate register or to investigate working conditions.

Historically, the trade union movement has opposed homeworking as a threat to the job security and working conditions of its factory-based members. Homeworkers were seen as a dangerous source of non-unionized, cheap labour. This posture is giving way to a recognition that steps must be taken to improve the status and conditions of homeworkers. The TUC has a Working Party which will soon publish its recommendations for legislative change and trade union action, and a number of unions, particularly the General and Municipal Workers' Union, are exploring ways of recruiting and organizing homeworkers.

This is not easy. The workers themselves are afraid that changes will endanger their earnings whether by upsetting employers, alerting the taxman, or messing up their social security benefits. The work is characteristically isolated and leaves the individual at the mercy of officialdom and the employers, with no collective solidarity. In fact many workers earn too little to pay tax or jeopardize benefits – single parents, for example, can earn up to £6 a week without any reduction in benefit.

In 1975 some community workers in East London started the London Homeworking Campaign to act for better pay and conditions, as well as for social provisions so that those who wish to work outside the home can do so. The organization expanded to include activists from trade unions, women's groups, immigrant organizations, local trades councils, community agencies and law centres. At the first national conference this November we mainly shared information about homeworking activity in our areas and discussed our organizing strategies.

Representatives of Long Eaton and District Trades Council described their work in the piano trade. Using a survey as the means of contact, Trades Council members brought workers together to discuss common grievances. As a result forty of the workers joined the Furniture Timber and Allied Trades Union. They now receive factory rates, the bonuses to which indoor workers are entitled and an additional $7\frac{1}{2}$ per cent to cover overhead costs.

An organizer with the Boot and Shoe Operatives' Union talked about a successful drive for unionization in the Rossendale Valley area. The union has apparently extended its national agreement to cover piece rates for homeworkers.

In Leeds, homeworkers tasseling football scarves are involved in a difficult struggle with their employer, Galaxy Sports. Though some have joined the GMWU, the lack of protective legislation has made it difficult for their union officer to fight the recent sacking of their shop steward. And the employer has exploited the remaining workers' isolation to coerce them into signing an illegal agreement promising never to join a union.

Home-based glovemakers in Torrington (Devon) encountered fewer difficulties. With the support of unionized workers inside the various firms, homeworkers joined the GMWU and have negotiated rate increases. While still not earning the piecework rates paid to indoor workers, their increases total $42\frac{1}{2}$ per cent.

These are the more dramatic achievements. Most organizing work has been much slower. Mainly the Campaign has been gathering basic information on the firms which 'put out' work – rates of pay, methods of distributing work and inter-company connections. At the same time homeworkers are being contacted for details of their work situation and to gauge support for various strategies for change.

One possibility being explored by women's groups in East London, Saltley (Birmingham) and Manchester is the establishment of co-operative enterprises run by homeworkers themselves. These could eliminate the profiteering of the parasitic middlemen.

But the key battle remains, at least in the short term, a legislative one. Without legal protection the efforts of workers such as the Leeds football tasselers may continue to fail, leaving them demoralized. It is up to the unions and the public to pressurize for legislative reform, by exposing this hidden poverty trap.

SR.66, January 1978

Waitress du Jour

JOYCE BETRIES

I've been waitressing about four years. There are good things about it. At the end of the day you always have some money in your pocketbook from tips, and you keep moving (I'm a nervous person, and I like to keep moving), you can kid around and joke – I hate to be serious all the time. Besides, one or two uniforms and a couple of pairs of white shoes are a lot cheaper to buy and keep up than a whole work wardrobe that you have to keep in style. Sometimes you can really get along with the people you work with, and when that happens, it's nice. Waitresses and cooks and busboys have to work together, and when we don't, it's hell.

I always try to stay away from the boss as much as possible. Bosses are always threatening us, and trying to find something wrong with what we do. If we don't have a union, the boss can do whatever he wants. Once when I was desperate for work I applied for a job in a 'hip' coffee-house. They told me I had to work twelve hours a day, and I wouldn't get a salary. I would just get to keep my tips. After ten hours, I walked out. It just wasn't worth it. I had made $5.00. In another non-union place, I was fired at four o'clock Sunday morning after working all Saturday night, because I told the boss I couldn't come in that afternoon. There was a union poster in the subways at the time which showed a boss of seventy years ago saying, 'If you don't come in Sunday, don't come in Monday', and explained how a union had ended conditions like that. Well, such conditions still exist for many waitresses.

Even with a union, waitresses are vulnerable. A union can get us a paid vacation, maybe a set weekly schedule, seniority rights, a pension, sick leave, and some medical benefits, and force our boss to have just cause before firing us, but he still might paw us, treat us like we're stupid, and try to take advantage of us anyway he can, hoping we won't know our rights and complain to the union. Unions aren't often easy to deal with either. Almost all the union leadership is male, and how much they want to help varies from person to person. In one union shop where I worked, now and again the boss would reassign the stations, giving a new woman a station that one of us with more seniority should have had. We would phone the union and usually get results, but our representative treated us like children who had gotten hysterical over nothing, and it was degrading. Still, I'm glad we had a union. At least we had that much. I've helped organize for a union in a non-union shop.

We make most of our salary in tips. No union I know of has seriously tried to get us a decent wage. Many people think that all waitresses make a lot of money. Well, sometimes you do find a job where the tips are very good, but that's rare. Usually, in these jobs, the bosses are especially obnoxious because they know you make good money, and don't want to lose the job. Then it becomes a matter of your human dignity – if the extra money is worth the degradation. Waitresses often make less in so-called 'fancy' places, where the food is expensive. In many places like this, the kitchens are so inefficiently designed that it's impossible to give fast, efficient service, especially when there are three to five courses to serve, so the customers don't think you deserve a tip. I have never known a boss to consult the cooks and waitresses as to how the kitchen should be arranged, although we're the ones who obviously know best, because we work there. In restaurants where the tips are really good (where they automatically add 15 per cent service charge to the bill, for example), they generally employ waiters. Also, with the inflation, people aren't tipping very much. With most people, when the cost of living goes up, their salary remains the same, and even then it's hard. With us, when the cost of living rises, our salary actually goes down.

Last summer I went to New York State Employment Agency for a job. They told me there were no jobs because waitressing was a luxury job, and when money got tight, it was one of the first to go. Sometimes it's a luxury for people to eat out, but it isn't a luxury for the waitresses!

We really work for our money. We run miles every day. Many of us eventually develop varicose veins, box feet, and uneven shoulders from carrying heavy trays on one arm. I worked in Schrafft's chain for a while. We had to carry round trays balanced on one arm, piled with food. It was just too heavy. I wore an elastic wrist support, but even that didn't help. The worst thing was we had to hold the tray on our arm while we cleaned the table, piling it with dirty dishes. We weren't allowed to rest the tray on the table because it 'didn't look nice'. Along with the dishes and silver, we had to clear off enormous water goblets that were very heavy when there was water remaining in them. Then, when the tray was piled up we had to remove the dirty tablecloth with our free hand (pick up the salt, pepper, ashtray and sugar) and often, because it was very busy, tuck the dirty cloth under our arm, and spread a clean cloth, balancing the tray all the time! Sometimes there would be people sitting at the table waiting to be served while we did this. This was a union shop. On top of that, Schrafft's had two sections to the restaurant – a men's lounge for businessmen, where women weren't allowed, and a section for men and women. In the men's lounge, the servings of ice cream and soup were larger for the same price. We were told that it was because 'men eat more'.

Often we are lucky if we get a chance to sit down and take a break, and even then nobody covers our tables for us. That means that I'm in the middle of eating dinner, and a customer sits in my station. I have to get up and wait on him. Sometimes the work is so heavy and so nerve-racking and I'm so busy that I can't take a break, and have to leave a sandwich near my station and take bites as I run by. The boss will push me to handle as many customers as I can – more than is humanly possible, because then he doesn't have to hire as many women. The boss hardly pays us anything; we make most of our salary from tips. It would cost him next to nothing to have another waitress on the floor. When I work like this I go home exhausted and dream about it. The dream is a typical real busy day – we're running out of food, and there are no plates or glasses or silver clean, and orders are packed up in the kitchen, and I'm running around and the customers are demanding the food, and the boss is following me, asking why people aren't served, and the cook is screaming at me because he doesn't have the food to fill the orders, and I have to go back, after people have been waiting a while and see if they want to order something else. I wake up feeling more tired than when I went to bed. The dream was driving me crazy, and I told it to a woman who had been waitressing most of her life. She said, 'Oh that, everybody has that dream.' Since then, I've had other women mention it to me, the waitress dream.

Some kitchens are really dirty. I used to work breakfast at a coffee shop in the richest section of New York. I was there at 7 a.m. The first thing I had to do was walk in the kitchen to get the silverware, and the smell used to make me sick. The employees had to eat downstairs, where it was filthy. There was no ventilation and we had to fight the flies for our food. I worked in a bar-restaurant where they let me work in sandals. I stopped wearing them because I found out that rats lived under the counter where I picked up the food. I was afraid my toes would get bitten. These were both considered 'high-class' places too.

Many waitresses work six days a week, and if we're lucky enough to work only five days, we usually have to work at least one day out of the weekend, and we're lucky if we get both our days off in a row. Most waitresses have to work holidays (Christmas, Thanksgiving, Mother's Day) because that's when people come out to eat. We never get a chance to spend a holiday with our own families.

One thing you can't mind too much if you're waitressing is dirty language. Sooner or later, when it gets real busy, the cook is going to curse you out for something that isn't your fault. I don't like it, and often the cook and I sit around and joke about it later over a cup of coffee when the restaurant is closed and the tension is off, but the joke becomes stale fast. The cook knows I need his co-operation in order to give good service, to make tips, and almost all cooks, because they're men, think they're better than waitresses. When this side of them comes out, there's just no way one woman can set them straight. Most trouble starts between people who work together when somebody thinks they're better than somebody else.

Bosses like to keep some employees thinking they're better than others when it doesn't affect the efficiency of their restaurant. They work hard at keeping the women employees divided, especially hostesses and waitresses. Hostesses have a nicer job than waitresses. They're on their feet all day, but they wear street clothes and usually don't have to do the heavy work of carrying loads of food, the way we do. Sometimes bosses don't like to be bothered directly supervising the waitresses, so they make the hostesses do it instead. In the last place I worked, we waitresses weren't allowed to eat anything without paying for it. None of us had ever before had a job where we weren't allowed to eat, and we knew how unfair this was. The hostess had to enforce this rule, and if she caught us eating, she would yell at us, and sometimes she told the boss. If the boss caught us, not only our job, but the hostess's job would be in danger. The hostesses were also made to enforce the boss's rules on how clean our uniforms and shoes should be, what was the proper length for our skirts, how we should wear our hair and make-up, and how long and how often we should take breaks. Often she was made to check out the bathroom to see if we were 'hiding' there, smoking. Since the boss had more personal contact with the hostesses than with us, he would try to take her into his confidence – complaining about the waitresses, telling the hostess how much better, and even prettier, she was than we were. There is no doubt in my mind that hostessing isn't an easy job, but often hostesses order us around as though they were the boss, when we all know that they are being used by the boss, just as we are. They always make less money than we do, but still they forget what side they're on.

Waitresses are always called 'girls' no matter what our ages. Yet, in a lot of places, the bosses try to pit the older and the younger waitresses against each other. In one restaurant I worked a counter in front of a large picture window. The tips were good and the boss was nice to me. Most of the older women worked the back of the restaurant. I never bothered much about it, but after a while, some of the older waitresses started calling me 'Miss America'. I didn't know why. Slowly I found out, by piecing things together, and with the help of one of the cooks, that the boss had hired me specifically because I was young, so that I could work in front of the window and 'attract customers'. My first reaction was shame, then anger. I had been used as bait for three months.

Almost all customers think they're better than we are. Some can't remember what I look like. Others expect me to smile and ask them how they're feeling, or they won't tip. Some actually tell me to smile. Sometimes, when they catch me in the wrong way, I ask them, 'Is that an order?' But I've gotten into trouble with the boss for that. A lot of people think that if you're a waitress you're automatically stupid, and they treat us like children. I was waiting on three middle-aged men in business suits. One was wearing a button on his lapel that I hadn't seen before and I asked him what it meant. All three of them started laughing and joking about the waitress who wanted to know what the button meant. It was as if I didn't exist. A lot of out-of-town businessmen are like that. If I really tell them what I think of them, I'm in danger of losing my job.

Most customers are completely blind to what a waitress is doing, or how busy she is. I find this especially true of people who have a lot of money. I worked a busy counter in a fancy coffee shop on Madison Avenue in New York. I was always on the run. Every day we ran out of silver in the middle of the lunch rush, and I would have to wash my own and didn't have any time. The neighbourhood was high class and while I was doing all this and trying to wait on more people, customers would call me over and ask me for another cup of coffee, because their cup had a small crack, or a chip! They just couldn't see me. They were completely blind to my racing back and forth right in front of them.

I've found that of all the people who treat me decently, most are other working people. I've checked it out. Clerks, sales people, gas station attendants – they're usually the people who say 'thank you' or have a joke, or tell me not to hurry when it's busy. I guess they know what it's like to work for a living and take orders. The nicest customers I had at the job were two men from the Department of Sanitation who took a break in the middle of the morning to have some pancakes. They treated me like a human being.

Reprinted from Up from Under *Vol. 1, No. 4, New York, USA.*

SR.*12*, June 1973

'Brook Street Bureau Got Big By . . .'

SALLY JONES

Brook Street has built its empire upon a carefully constructed image of professional respectability. It projects itself as the most reputable and ethical of agencies, providing a high-quality service for employers. The Chairman shrugs off any criticism that their operations are unscrupulous or parasitic by deploring 'the questionable activities of a minority of agencies' which have 'brought the whole industry into disrepute'. Brook Street, with its Training School for interviewers and a 'Mind Desk' for those suffering from mental illness, is the Marks & Spencer of the business. Its slick and effective campaign slogan – BROOK STREET BUREAU GOT BIG BY BOTHERING – persuades applicants that their interests are Brook Street's main concern. After all, Margery Hurst was recently awarded the OBE for her services to charity.

I worked as an interviewer for permanent staff. (Dealing with the 'temps' depends on how successful you are with the 'perms'.) And I was soon to discover the reality behind their people-oriented façade. On the face of it, the work I was required to do was legitimate and valuable: to find out and assess the interests, skills and needs of the applicant, to match these with vacancies advertised by the employers and to arrange job interviews. But in fact I found myself involved in a high-powered sales operation, as manipulative as door-to-door commercial selling. The interviewer has two sales to make: she sells the job to the applicant and the applicant to the employer. The techniques for doing this are taught at the Training School where speeches are learned by heart and intensive rehearsals take place with examinations at the end of the course. The pressure was so great that four of the twelve interviewers trained with me dropped out.

Let's examine the format of a typical interview with an applicant who walks in looking for a job (Miss X). It begins predictably enough eliciting qualifications, previous job experience, marital status, home responsibilities, ability to travel. During this stage of the interview the Brook Street interviewer must elicit what's known in the trade as Miss X's Most Important Thing. This knowledge of what matters most to each applicant can be used as the key to selling her a vacancy.

Posy, *SR.5*, November 1972

After these preliminaries, the hard sell begins:

Interviewer (flicking through job cards on desk) 'Of course, Miss X, good jobs are hard to come by but I'm confident we'll find just the right one for you. (Pause to flick through some more, then pulls out one. *Only* one to emphasize the scarcity of openings.) Now here's just the job for you, Miss X. How would you like a job which is only a bus ride from home/pays £2,000 a year/working for a young executive? (The selling line will be tailored to match Miss X's Most Important Thing.) Sounds great, doesn't it (before Miss X can contradict)! I'll call Mr Y straight away.'

Interviewer makes phone call to employer and begins the second part of the sale – to convince Mr Y that Miss X is just the person he needs. To do this she plays up her strong points and minimizes weaknesses: 'Now Mr Y, she hasn't yet done cost analysis but we feel she'd be ideal for you. She's very keen/well groomed/has six 'O' levels (whatever is Mr Y's chief requirement). She would like to come straight away to see you.'

This is often the stickiest point for the interviewer. She knows that immediate interviews are statistically more successful than future appointments; that given more time to think it over, both parties will probably have second thoughts. So she may use her feminine charm on Mr Y to make the immediate appointment – 'Now we don't want her snapped up by someone else, do we?' – and she must also help Miss X to make a phone call telling her present boss she'll be late back from lunch.

Once the interview is arranged, Miss X is given advice on how best to present herself. This may include comments on her appearance, personality, posture, even the offer of acetone for chipped nails. The sales work continues after the interview when Mr Y, the employer, reports that Miss X's speech was appalling, and she looked surly, and Miss X complains that Mr Y was an arrogant bully. The interviewer must try to smooth over these minor difficulties and clinch the deal. If she fails the whole operation begins again.

The desired result is a 'placement' and, of course, a healthy fee for Brook Street Bureau. This sum may in fact be taken into account by the employer when he decides on the salary he will pay, and lopped off his new employee's first year's wages. Although it is impossible to prove this, it may well be that the use of private agencies helps keep staff wages low. The nature of temporary employment is quite different and 'temps' face a different problem: their wages may appear relatively high but this is no real compensation for lack of sick pay, holiday pay, job security and other so-called 'fringe' benefits. Using 'temps' may enable employers to cut down on permanent staff and prevent them creating new permanent posts.

Officially, Brook Street Bureau is opposed to all discrimination on the grounds of race and sex but this is another area where, in my experience, a gap exists between the image and the reality. Certainly they are very careful to remain within the law. All staff are briefed on how to deal with employers who contravene the race and sex legislation and they sign monthly memos supporting this. Explicit racial and sexual requirements are no longer found on job cards but employers use the crudest codes to make their meaning clear. These are the kinds of stipulations I've seen on job cards: 'Must have a hairy chest'. 'Must be able to carry buckets of water up and down stairs', this for a clerical job! 'Size 12'. 'Must speak the Queen's English' (an employer may ask to speak to the applicant on the telephone to check for any accent).

In my opinion, Brook Street often reflects the sexist demands of employers. Women are discreetly advised to look attractive and well groomed. Young men with 'A' levels may be found vacancies in insurance and shipping, while girls with similar qualifications will be advised to return in six months with a secretarial course behind them. Women, even if they have other skills, will usually be encouraged to 'try a little typing on our typewriter' because even a slow speed makes her more acceptable. A man is rarely asked this. Despite the new legislation, girls and women are still channelled into supportive and low-paid jobs, and far from challenging the use of women as a cheap labour force (and a way of boosting the – male – employer's ego), Brook Street goes out of its way to accommodate this.

Racial prejudice is more blatant in some areas than others. Because good shorthand typists are still in short supply, a West Indian or Asian secretary will be less discriminated against than, say, an accounts clerk, where vacancies are highly competitive. Employers will often ask for the applicant's place of birth and length of residence in this country before they agree to an interview. Someone may have worked for years as a clerk in Africa or India but will be refused work because he or she has 'no work experience in this country'. This is another phrase used increasingly as an acceptable form of racism.

Towards the end of my career, interviewers were invited to a Remotivating Lecture with supervisors and regional controllers. One of the procedures discussed was what they called a 'priority situation'. It went something like this: 'You have in reception a Mr Patel, an accounts clerk with no work experience in this country, and an attractive secretary in her lunch hour. The secretary has just walked in, the clerk has been waiting some time. How do you proceed?' Normally interviewers take applicants in the order that they arrive but in the case of a 'priority situation' the regional controller explained that the secretary, the more marketable commodity, should be seen first; the interviewer must explain to Mr Patel that the young lady is in her lunch hour. When I tried to raise the implications of this, they were, of course, completely denied. If, as Brook Street claim, they are the most ethical of employment agencies, I dread to think what goes on in others.

It is not only the applicants who are manipulated by the company. The interviewers themselves are trapped in a hierarchy of pressure and competition, and the need to present a totally false image of dynamic optimism in an increasingly depressing job market. A scoreboard for successful 'placements' is prominently displayed in each branch and competition exists between individual interviewers, and between branches and regions. While there is no direct commission (this, they boast, prevents people being pushed into jobs they don't want), the major pressure is psychological. 'Fraternization' among interviewers is discouraged and the area supervisor frowned on a drink after work as 'unprofessional'. Any solidarity between workers would threaten the competitive system they depend on. There are no luncheon vouchers, no pension scheme, no sick pay for three months. When I worked there, Inner London interviewers were paid just over £1,800 p.a. for 9 a.m.–5 p.m. (6.30 p.m. on Fridays) and much unofficial and unpaid overtime. Since lunch hour was our busiest time we usually worked straight through it. An extract from my diary of that period goes like this:

'Conditions here are dreadful. Nowhere to eat, so, since eating at desks is not allowed, we stand up behind a screen to wolf down a sandwich – if there's time. This week I survived on coffee and cigarettes. Today the regional controller came in and asked me how I was. Purely a rhetorical question since the reply must always be, "Absolutely brilliant!" One is expected to bounce around full of confidence and dynamism, we can never be quiet and act normally.'

Brook Street operates with a high turnover of staff to bring in new energy, so there is no permanent core of employees to organize improvements. People either leave or are promoted to managerial level where their interests become identified with the company's. The unions, who disapprove of employment agencies, are indifferent; it's too difficult to organize a floating population of mainly women. And since most interviewers are ex-salesmen, bored secretaries, air hostesses, they are not among the most militant of workers.

Brook Street Bureau owns seven subsidiary companies in England, one in Scotland, three in the USA, one in Australia – which itself owns five subsidiaries, including one in Hong Kong. It's not hard to see how it makes money. Its fees for office workers in Central London range from 8½ per cent to 15 per cent of the employee's annual salary. For a secretary earning £2,500 p.a. the fee is 12½ per cent – about £312. If one interviewer makes five placements a week, the company makes around £1,500. (Temping fees work differently, and while these are a closely guarded secret, a 1975 rates card showed that Brook Street takes an average of 42 per cent of the wages paid to the employee.)

In 1973, net profits, after tax, were £886,324 – this, according to the Chairman was 'an exceptionally buoyant year'. 1974 showed net profits of £621,886. In 1975, Brook Street suffered from 'the severity of the world-wide recession and the consequent decline in business confi-

dence' (Chairman's statement), and so its net profit was a mere
£293,081. The economies made by the company mean that the wages
of interviewers stay the same but the pressure of work increases with
unemployment and more applicants chasing fewer jobs. So even in the
recession, Brook Street keeps its head well above water by exploiting
its own staff and people's desperate need for work. Despite Brook
Street's clever whitewash job, the essential nature of the agency game
remains unchanged. Certainly Brook Street has grown big by bothering: by bothering about profits and very little else.
[*'Sally Jones' was a pseudonym for Cheryl Hicks. Ed.*]

SR.54, January 1977

Are You a Typewriter?

CLARE CHERRINGTON

What is this job that's many teenage girls' dream? For although there
are other types of secretary than the 'personal' – shared secretaries,
pooled typist – most girls at secretarial school hope to be a private
secretary, the pinnacle of most women's rise in the office world.

It's a combination of a variety of jobs: the skilled work of shorthand,
audio or copy typing, administrative routines and tasks and on-the-
spot errands for the boss. What these jobs have in common is that they
are all servicing the boss. Put another way, he does all the 'difficult',
'responsible', interesting things like meeting people, making decisions,
getting projects going or pursuing a specialist activity, like law or
medicine. She does the follow-up work: typing letters, filing records,
making appointments, etc. So there's a horizontal division: he takes the
top half, she the bottom. Hers is a dead-end job, characteristic of the
business world where men get trained to advance in the executive or
specialist level and women may get as far as the nebulous 'personal
assistant', but rarely further. They were never meant to. This division
of labour has existed since women entered the office world – barely
seventy-odd years ago! Shorthand in the nineteenth century was a
male concern: Dickens at eighteen, taking down parliamentary debates
for the press, remarked that he was probably the fastest shorthand
writer in the world. This was before the typewriter, when clerks were
less than 1 per cent of paid workers – which they were still in 1851.
Discounting those relatives of the family who became clerks to learn
the business the hard way, it seems likely that whether the clerks got

promotion or stayed put depended on class. But with the entrance of women into the office, an absolute barrier was raised.

Some of the first women in the office were 'type-writers' – American women using the newly popular machines in the 1870s. Within a decade or so, a torrent of propaganda was sweeping Victorian England. Pamphlets such as 'Should Young Ladies Learn Phonography?' introduced the middle classes to the idea that shorthand might be good for their daughters. In short, there was work for them; businesses were being scientific about profit-making, growing larger and, heavens above, here was an endless supply of cheap labour to save the manager's time and trouble. And the creation of the modern dogsbody secretary and highflying executive followed the pattern of another doer-assistant pair: the doctor/nurse. It was, after all, before women had the vote.

HE WAS TOO FRESH.
A TYPEWRITER BRINGS A CHARGE OF ASSAULT AGAINST HER EMPLOYER.

SR.6, December 1972

Yet, through the seventy-odd years of this century, the job hasn't changed much. There has been a recent patchy increase of part-time work: for instance, between 1973 and 1974 the number of women employed part-time in public administration and defence, insurance, banking, finance and business services, went up by a third as much again as the number of women employed full-time. This is not necessarily progress: otherwise homebound women, desperate for extra cash or self-fulfilment are not in a position to question the conditions of part-time work, which offers disproportionately less security/legal protection compared with full-time work.

The other change, made much of in the early seventies, namely the increase in electronic equipment, has slowed down some since women's labour is still on the whole cheaper. But the main effect of gadgets such as memory typewriters has been to slightly increase the number of women in pools, or of shared, as opposed to one-to-one secretaries.

Some people now claim secretaries aren't necessary. Robert Townsend, the man who turned the American Avis Rent a Car business from a tiny firm into a rival of Hertz, claims in his book *Up the Organisation* (Michael Joseph, 1970) that secretaries should be abolished as time-wasters. Letters should be replied to mostly by hand, work delegated to lower ranking executives wherever possible, telephoning rationalized into short periods . . . and any needed typing and servicing of the executives done by the pool and switchboard. Apart from the worse place this particular 'rationalization' leaves women in, Townsend's theories slipped up some when it came to getting the various drafts of his book typed up: a reliable authority says he had to make use of someone else's secretary!

A rival theory put out in the *Harvard Business Review* by Lane Tracey, claims that secretaries are what makes business work. Starting off from the 'Peter Principle' – widely known in management circles – which states that everyone in the business world is promoted up to the level at which they do the job badly, and stays there, he asks why business works at all?

The obvious conclusion is that our organizations somehow are able to retain a cadre of competent people to whom the 'Peter Principle' does not apply. These people cannot be part of the organizational hierarchy, for there the 'Peter Principle' operates in full force. And yet, to be in a position to carry out the necessary functions of planning, directing and controlling the enterprise, such people must reside at all levels of the administrative hierarchy. What class of people fits this description? The obvious answer is *secretaries*. (AC and LK, 7:23)

. . . Essential or irrevelant, secretaries are here; how do they deal with their second-class position, and what does it do to them?

Running as a refrain through the comments of secretaries about their work, is that it's a fall-back job: 'It's a filler, a filler that may last the rest of my life. If I didn't look at it as a filler, I'd go crazy.' 'It's not a career; it's marking time.' The second woman, incidentally, was the secretary to a Managing Director, with a year's secretarial college and four and a half years' experience behind her. A woman doing the graduate course for secretaries at the City of London Polytechnic said: 'Everybody on the course – all graduates – said the same thing. This is something to fall back on; I can always temp . . . But what did they all do when they finished? They all became secretaries in a panic' (AC and LK, 2:14).

This isn't to say the job has nothing going for it. It can be interesting and rewarding; it's cleaner and pays better than factory or shop work; it can end at the dot of five with no responsibility; it has some perks – and it's easy. But too often it's unbearably boring, there's overwork with no overtime pay, there's responsibility for mistakes but no credit, and there are conditions and pay scales no man would accept. Yet this isn't the point here: the terrible thing about secretaryism is that for too many women *there is no alternative*. This easy path which teenagers think they chose turns out to be a prison they have been prepared for from birth.

Working-class girls want to get out of factory or shop work; they have no real chance of the choice – however limited – offered to boys. Middle-class girls fall into it more through doing what they're told, being what they're wanted to be. An American survey showed that girls under thirteen wanted a wide variety of careers; at adolescence suddenly conformity was more important and their ambitions became more traditional. As the time to choose approaches, the influence of parents, teachers and careers advisers increases. 'It was the usual thing – nursing, teaching or secretarial work. My parents felt very strongly that it wasn't worth educating a girl . . . "You'll find a nice job, dear," they would say, "and in three or four years you'll get married" ' (AC and LK, 2 : 1). The girls are brainwashed into having low expectations of themselves, and teachers are largely unhelpful, scared for the child or ignorant of wider possibilities. And a 1973 report notes that careers guidance given to sixteen-year-old girls was 'particularly unsuccessful' and characterized by 'automatically thinking in terms of clerical work or going in for apprenticeships in hairdressing' (AC and LK, 2 : 5).

Besides the pressure from home and school, the media shower glittery images about secretarial work on young girls – images the polar opposite of any real situation the girl is likely to encounter. Magazine stories promise marriage with the boss, the colleges promise interest, the ads as always promise everything. It's unlikely, however, that the girls believe all this; their acquiescence in the dream is maybe partly a deliberate and humorous attempt to find compensation for what they're beginning to realize they'll never get. And once in the job, it doesn't take long to see you're in a dead-end street: roughly four times more boys got day release than girls in 1975 . . . just the same as in 1971. What do you do when the shutters go down?

The chief personnel officer at the London HQ of a large industrial company put it precisely: 'Let's face it, after you've been a secretary for more than two years, you're no good at being anything else. It's a

support role, and it breeds a support attitude' (AC and LK, 3 : 9).
How? To begin with, the work is monotonous and routine. Townsend
claims that 'Modern organizations are only getting people to use about 20
per cent – the lower fifth – of their capacities. And the painful part is that
God [sic] didn't design the human animal to function at 20 per cent. At
that pace it develops enough malfunctions to cause a permanent shortage
of psychoanalysis and hospital beds.' He says that if the work isn't above
'the psychic subsistence level' the workers will put all their energy into
their private lives! Secretarial magazines are about leisure, not work.

Most of the work is not only below the 'psychic subsistence level' –
after all, most factory work is that, too – but has other destructive
qualities. While the factory worker just sells her labour, the secretary
sells labour plus behaviour. And there seems to be a very particular
mental alienation going on too. There was an ad in the window of an
office electronics suppliers which read: FROM THOUGHT (picture of
man speaking into dictaphone) TO WORDS (woman typing) TO ACTION
(man again). The secretary can compose letters just as well as her boss;
she can make many of the decisions herself, but she must repress her
initiative and creative energy to serve his. Her situation is analogous to
that of the slave woman who had to look after her master's children in
place of her own. Apparently one of Bernard Levin's secretaries who
typed out 200,000 words of a draft of a book of his *in her spare time*
used suddenly to burst out, 'I am a mole and I live in a hole.' In this
context it seems an accurate representation of her mental state; she has
made her mind a reflection of his and her energy has gone underground.
And so she develops a sense of worthlessness while her boss gets an
overdeveloped ego.

This development is helped by other factors. Because his random
needs are more important than her work, she cannot even develop a
sense of pride in her small tasks, or impose a pace or order of her own
on her work. She is trapped in a timeless, static world; bored, she
'switches off'. And lastly, should she doubt her inferiority, the men are
constantly around to remind her, for 'The image that men have created
for the secretary deprives her of her individuality, reduces her to a
physical object, and keeps her firmly in her place' (AC and LK, 5 : 14).
She's the spectator of a world she can't enter; yet her work is precisely
to construct this world.

And she does it uncomplainingly, even to the extent that she acqui-
esces in lying for him as a matter of course. What sense of identity is a
person left with at the end of this process? 'Sometimes I sit here typing
and think that's all I'm good for' (AC and LK, 2 : 15) – this secretary's
words are like a recurrent echo to the clacking of typewriter keys.

The most powerful single reason for secretaries' inaction is that any protest, any attempt to change the pay, conditions, and promotional chances of the work, runs them the risk of getting fired by the boss they have been hired to get along with. And as clerical work is the best-paid area of mass employment for women, who would willingly step back into the manual or service work in which so many working-class and minority women are trapped? The *New Earnings Survey of 1977* shows that within the field of clerical work only supervisors get more than the average £50.9 for secretaries; clerical workers get an average of £47.6 compared to £42.5 for manual work and £36.6 for selling jobs. Without union backing against unfair dismissal and the vaguer 'constructive dismissal' (conditions changed so the job becomes intolerable) not much can be done.

And paradoxically there is quite a bit of resistance among the secretaries themselves to the idea of unionization. As Anna Coote and Laura King put it: 'Her job exists because he exists. Consequently she tends to identify herself with the boss and with management, rather than recognize herself as a worker whose interests may well be at odds with those of her employer' (AC and LK, 4:17).

Although unionization is evidently the basis for change, with the exception of TASS, union policy towards secretarial and other office workers is little more than lipservice. To begin with, it is difficult because there is no specific union for secretaries and typists; scattered as low-grade parts of bigger unions, there is virtually no documentation of a workforce that numbers three quarters of a million! The Association of Professional, Executive, Clerical and Computer Staff, APEX, comes closest to being a secretary's union; they have no specific programme for secretaries; they have pamphlets with fine statements in the abstract, but when asked to be more specific on equal pay and equal opportunity issues, can let drop views like 'I don't think the problem is so great on the non-manual side anyway' (Kathie Dickson, Research Dept). Secretaries who belong to or once joined APEX have nothing good to say about it; complained that 'it was all talk ... I wished I hadn't joined it and I couldn't get out.' CPSA and ASTMS both said they had almost no secretaries in their membership and no special programme; CPSA claimed to have equal pay already, whatever that means, for secretaries. Open hostility towards temporary secretaries was exhibited by NALGO in the early seventies' attack on government use of employment agencies. On the whole, young women are not seen as serious workers, and there is little indication this attitude is changing.

The only union to make a breakthrough into this difficult area is

TASS, as part of their Rights for Women campaign. 'We believe in positive discrimination, because unless special attention is paid to the problems of women, their position is usually ignored,' says Women's Organizer Judith Hunt. They begin, in their literature for women, by asking such questions as, 'Are you satisfied with the pay structure in your company?' and 'What are the channels of promotion at your company?', and 'Do you think you are worth more money than you are getting?' (*A New Deal For Office Staff*).

After creating an awareness that all may not be well, and union membership is essential for change, there comes the difficult problem of how to achieve equal pay in jobs where there is no comparable man's work. TASS have done this by setting up target figures of what they would expect a man doing the same work to get paid; at present this stands at £69 for a secretary, £64 for a shorthand typist, and £60 for a copy typist. There's naturally a gap between ideals and achievements, but some results, like doubling the office staff wages in a Dumbarton office since the women joined in 1974, are quite spectacular.

They are also fighting for the recognition of the skills of the secretary, and for better conditions on the job. But besides this, they are trying to make equal opportunity a reality. As we have seen, the cards are stacked against girl school leavers. TASS is campaigning for the availability of day release and other training schemes for women to learn the skills needed for promotion. They're also trying to get eighteen months' paid maternity leave accepted as basic, and there is talk, but as yet no action, on trying for creches.

While TASS's campaign marks the beginning of women's struggle in the office, its main drawback is that few women can join TASS as it is basically an engineering workers' union. And there is a paradox in unionization of women office workers in that their status and area of work is thereby regularized. This is why TASS feel that it is essential to fight for promotional opportunities and training – but little energy goes into that as yet. And unionization into less aware unions could well be a double-edged weapon that will only keep the secretary more firmly in her place. But it is essential, because without it women have no power.

A sketch of what offices might be was made by Anna Coote and Laura King, who pictured the future office as a place where people were 'self-servicing'. Everyone would type, for example, and everyone be taken into the firm as an apprentice to be trained for the firm's business. In the rare case of a genius needing an assistant to function, the assistant would be rewarded as being as necessary as the genius . . . and if there were typing specialists, they would be treated as specialists.

This utopian picture largely cuts out the servicing side of the picture which, as long as it continues, will probably be done by women.

There was, in 1976, in New York, an organization called Women Office Workers (WOW). Numbering 300 members, they agitated against boredom, low wages, age discrimination, lack of overtime pay, and non-person status. They helped various women in individual struggles, took five age-discrimination cases to the NY Human Rights Court, did some research into office worker unemployment and began to open a Pandora's box of problems at a 'speakout' where half the women's speeches were anonymous . . . for the one thing that emerged repeatedly was that any protest ended in firing.

WOW may have folded; a group of women office workers in Boston recently got a new organization off the ground, the Alliance Against Sexual Coercion. They deal in appropriate fashion with anything from verbal harassment to rape on the job, with a crisis centre, job listings, help with unemployment pay and legal cases. One woman has won 16,000 dollars in back pay because she was fired for refusing her boss's sexual advances! Sounds all right!

In this country, a small group could do a lot, without needing to jeopardize jobs: try to fight racism, research into the area, re-educate teachers and careers advisers, inquire what goes on in secretarial colleges, try to change the media image of women in the office, pressurize the Equal Opportunities Commission to get off its arse, and so on. It would evidently also make a terrific difference if secretaries could begin to meet together to discuss how to deal with the most outrageous infestations of sexism on the job, and begin to retrieve their stolen self-confidence. But unionization is the main tool for change, and so perhaps the most urgent task facing women who want to change their role in offices would be to compel a union or variety of them to effectively serve *all* women office workers, or create a new one.

In the labour-scarce office market of the seventies, secretaries (and office workers) have tremendous power: it is extraordinary it has hardly been used. But perhaps it is not extraordinary; perhaps a lot of energy has gone into convincing the secretary of her powerlessness; perhaps her power has been made invisible. Whatever the case, the consequences of women office workers beginning to demand their rights will be momentous. Is it possible that the sexist structure of the business world, so far virtually untouched by the women's movement, is less impregnable than it seems?

Essential in the writing of this article, although not answerable for any errors and not necessarily similar in views, was a long unpublished paper by Anna Coote and Laura King. Thank you both very much for allowing me such free use of your work.

    SR.69, April 1978

Poster from the See Red Collective, *SR.50*, September 1976

I am Your Automatic Worker

JANE BARKER

Current developments in microelectronics have major implications for the future employment of women – in terms of the number of jobs likely to be available, the level of skill required, the amount of control over the job and new health hazards such as severe eyestrain.

    The development of the 'silicon chip' (this is the size of a thumbnail and has thousands of electronic circuits etched on, which saves wiring up thousands of individual transistors to make a computer circuit) means that it is becoming more profitable for many jobs to be automated. The new word processors (like computerized typewriters) are already putting many typists out of work and bringing down the wages of others.

Two areas of women's employment likely to be affected are office work and light assembly work. A report by Siemans, a large German company, predicts that 40 per cent of present office jobs will no longer exist by 1985. A French report estimates that 30 per cent of jobs in banking and insurance will be lost in the next ten years.

Many women are employed in light assembly of goods with electric and electronic components – these are now being replaced by a smaller number of components, 'silicon chips'. Women have already been laid off in this sector, notably in telephone equipment and TV manufacture.

At a conference organized by TASS, the technical section of the engineering union, on 16 September to discuss 'Computer Technology and Employment', Carmen Wootten from the National Women's Committee said that lack of social facilities such as nurseries would mean that employers would try to discriminate against women in selection for retraining, and that women, especially part-timers, would be the first to be made redundant. The only defence, she said, is for women to be in strong trade unions and play a major role in them.

This whole issue needs to be widely discussed and action taken to ensure that the likely change in employment patterns is to *our* benefit.

Newshort, *SR*.76, November 1978

Danger: Women's Work

WOMEN AND WORK HAZARDS GROUP

Women in factories, offices and shops everywhere risk disease and injury to their health from exposure to noise, dust, fumes, heat, stress, vibration, radiation and poisonous chemicals.

The Women and Work Hazards Group was set up to give working women information on health hazards and to support them in challenging management on technical issues. Here they give an outline of the risks women run.

. . . If we could get complete current statistics they would paint a picture of disease and chronic illness as horrifying as conditions in the sweatshops of the nineteenth century. Workers are still exposed to many of the same old hazards like asbestos and lead. But even more worrying is the fact that 19,000 chemicals are now in common industrial use, with thousands of new ones introduced into the workplace every year – and the health risks of all of them are virtually unknown. Legal limits or standards have been set for only 500 of these toxic substances and for only sixteen of the 2,400 chemicals suspected of causing cancer. The standards which have been set are based on tests geared to the young, fit, male worker – usually U S Marine 'volunteers'. Hazards to fertility or risks of female cancers (breast, uterus) are not criteria that scientists or the government have considered when setting limits of exposure to chemicals at work.

The women's liberation movement has always made health a priority issue. Many of us have through self-examination and self-help learnt not only to understand our menstrual cycle, but also how to identify 'women's complaints', and sometimes cure them with natural remedies. But we've made little of the necessary link between women's health and work. Stress, for example, which may cause tension, digestive disorders, depression and heart disease, occurs at high rates in women who are under pressure from two jobs: one paid and one unpaid. Or take menstrual upsets: some Eastern European studies have revealed that disturbances in the monthly cycle were very common in women whose jobs had a rhythm set by machines, like for example assembly-line work in electronics factories. Our environment as well as our biology affects our health. Where we can show that sickness is related to work, we can demonstrate that as such it is preventable. As feminists we are struggling for the right to information on our health, and rights over our own fertility, but we must include control over our own body in the workplace.

Women are now 40 per cent of the paid workforce and concentrated by and large in low-paid, dead-end jobs, doing boring, repetitive tasks – increasingly on a part-time basis, with little security. Many of these low-paid workers are immigrants who don't speak English well. Often they run more risk of damaging their health at work because management makes no attempt to help them either with language classes or with interpreters.

The more obvious occupational hazards like dusts, which harm the lungs, and noise, affect both male and female workers, and men traditionally have had some of the most dangerous jobs like mining and construction.

But women work in their millions in certain unhealthy occupations and it's these which need a closer look here. In light engineering, such as the manufacture of electrical components, women are mainly employed to do fast repetitive tasks which cause inflammation of tendons in the hands and forearms. Women packing and processing drugs are at risk from many chemicals ranging from hormones to vaccines.

Hairdressers can damage their lungs and skin using toxic sprays and dyes, and harmful detergents. Office workers, too, are exposed to many untested chemicals in photocopiers and stencil fluids. The very nasty trichloroethylene (trike) is used as a base for solvents in correcting fluids, inks, adhesives and dry-cleaning agents. It causes headaches, fatigue, dermatitis, and at high levels, nausea, vomiting and confusion. Several bottles of correcting fluid open at the same time in a typing pool could result in an unsafe level of trike in the air. It can also be addictive. Office workers also suffer the hazards of noise, dermatitis, bad lighting and seating.

Many women are hospital workers. They risk infections, radiation, exposure to dangerous chemicals like formaldehyde, and they often suffer from varicose veins and backache from being on their feet for long periods. Catering workers share many of these problems. Stress from the irregular hours of shift work is also common.

Women working in the home have traditionally suffered from 'housemaid's knee' and 'washerwoman's elbow'. Nowadays, in addition to severe levels of stress from doing housework and looking after children, women working at home may be at risk from unsafe wiring or dangerous chemical sprays (aerosols) such as pesticides and polishes. In many cases it is the same sort of chemical that women are exposed to at home as out at work. For example 62 per cent of workers in the cosmetic industry are female. The harmful effects of various combinations of chemicals inhaled or applied to the body are virtually unknown (note that some commercial talcum powders contain asbestos).

Women with a double workload are doubly at risk. Some have got severe dermatitis by handling substances when at work, and then detergents at home. Women washing men's contaminated overalls at home have contracted asbestosis and beryllium poisoning. Two jobs mean an early shift and a late one. It means working a far longer week than most men. It means stress and exhaustion. Of the 20 million prescriptions dispensed for tranquillizers in 1974, three quarters were for women.

It's a woman's right to choose whether or not to have a child and when. Yet great numbers of women abort, produce abnormal children or are made sterile every year due to exposure to anaesthetics, radiation and a host of chemicals. We must understand reproduction in a wider context than at present, and fight for our rights as women to retain our fertility if we choose.

. . . In Britain, because of known dangers to the foetus, special protective regulations prohibit employment of women in the manufacture of some lead and radiation processes. However the vast majority of chemicals are used by employers with no thought to the health risks to foetuses, pregnant women or anyone else.

The response of some North American companies to this problem (Dow Chemicals, Esso, Dupont) has been simply to refuse employment to all fertile women. Norma Smith kept her job at a Canadian General Motors lead-battery plant by getting herself sterilized. She was forced to do this after the company decided only sterilized or non-fertile women could work in the plant. This attitude threatens all women's jobs.

The British government too is currently recommending a new standard for exposure to lead and recommends that pregnant and all fertile women be banned from working with it.

. . . Making pregnant or fertile women a special category of 'worker at risk' is not the answer to the use of dangerous substances and practices. The only solution is to clean up the workplace so that it's safe for all.

The Health and Safety at Work Act 1974 provides for every unionized workplace to have a trade union safety representative. She's like a workers' inspector, having the right to inspect, investigate hazards and complaints and attend health and safety courses. She can also carry out health surveys – asking fellow workers about their symptoms, thus uncovering shared health problems. More women need to become safety reps if women's health needs at work are to be improved. Go on, become a safety rep!

SR.78, January 1979

I'm Gonna be an Electrical Engineer

MARGARET CHARMAN, SECOND-YEAR ELECTRICAL FITTER AT THE GOVERNMENT TRAINING CENTRE FOR THE PORTSMOUTH NAVAL BASE DOCKYARD, INTERVIEWED BY ANGELA PHILLIPS

'Two years ago I had one "O" level, in cookery. I hated school and just wanted to get out, but I didn't know what to do. It was my father who suggested this apprenticeship. He and my brothers work in the Dockyard, and they saw it advertised.'

. . . There are a few women working in the Dockyard now, as up until two years ago one or two applied and were accepted each year.

Five girls started in Margaret's year, and six last year. But this year, since the Sex Discrimination Act came into force, the number has leapt up to eighty-one applicants, of whom about twenty will probably get through. The overall figure for boys and girls applying this year was double the previous year, 1,050 applying for the 200 apprenticeship places, 900 actually taking the exam. A spokesman at the Dockyard job training centre attributed this increase to the dramatic growth of unemployment amongst school-leavers and the relative security of the job. The ratio of girls applying has risen startlingly – last year one out of sixty applicants was a girl, whereas this year the figure is one in eleven.

'. . . When we started the boys were always waiting for us to make mistakes. They thought we should be at home helping mum. The majority have changed now. As long as we do our fair share it's O K. One problem was the way the instructors treated us. They couldn't do enough to help. They helped us more than they helped the boys, pointing out our mistakes more clearly. We don't really need the extra help. They even tried to make the boys be polite to us, stop swearing and things. It made them resent us. Really, it hasn't helped us get on good terms with the boys. There are always some boys who are quick to find out our bad points. They think their male ego is suffering because a girl is doing the same job as them.

'I came second in the Apprentice of the Year Awards [in the Portsmouth Dockyard] last year. Some boys thought it was favouritism. I got pretty upset when they said "One of you girls had to get it." I wouldn't like to think that I'm only getting anywhere because I am a girl.

'At first it was easier making friends with the boys than with the girls. I suppose we were competing for the boys' attention. They are fun to work with but you can't have a serious conversation with them. At dinnertime the girls get together and talk. I'd like to see more girls here.'

What about the work itself?

'In the first year we had a three-month probationary period learning to use hand tools, mostly filing metals. Then we had a six-week basic fitting course, learning to construct and read diagrams from a small bell circuit, and a light circuit in series. In the last part of the year we learned to draw, strip down and build up starters, motors and armatures [the mechanism that drives motors].

'In the second year we have been divided into groups of twenty-five and spend two months in five different shops. There is the machine shop, where you practise simple cutting jobs with different metals.

Then shore insulation; bending and handling the conduits, the casing
for electrical cables. Then electronics, where you make a radio and a
speaker. Then car electronics, where you strip the electrical system of
a car and rewire it. Lastly, "pre-afloat" where you work on a model of
a ship needing to be fitted, and do all the jobs which go into that. I'm
working on car electronics at the moment. After this year I will be a
mate to an electrical fitter in the Dockyard.' . . .

   SR.48, July 1976

'So Long as It's Red and Going Where They're Going They'll Get on'

DORIS PITTS, BUSDRIVER, INTERVIEWED BY
JILL NICHOLLS

*After one job in a biscuit factory and another in the army, a short stint as
a conductress and a whole string of driving jobs, Doris Pitts, a thirty-two-
year-old Scots Jamaican, applied to be a busdriver last November. London
Transport's original plan was for women to drive only when there was no
work for them as conductresses. Then in 1973, after five years of negotia-
tion between London Transport and the Transport and General Workers'
Union, women were given the same opportunity to drive as men. But
London Transport recruits men from outside while women have to train as
conductresses first. The union says this is to give women who are already
conducting the first chance to apply and train. But there is no date set for
an end to this protective period, which obviously stops most women from
applying.*

*So Doris had to do nine months as a conductress first, then reapplied
and was accepted. She's been driving for two months now – one of fifteen
women drivers in London, the only one at her garage in Putney.*

   What do you think of the recruiting policy?
   My idea is that men should go conducting first too, because then
they'd have an insight into the job. I'm driving now and to me it's easy.
I know where the bus stops are, where the routes go – you can imagine
how difficult it must be for someone who's never been on the buses
before. For instance, I always stop short of a stop so a conductress has
got time to see how many's there and then bring on as many as she
wants. If we stop right at the stop everyone's just going to *dive* on. You
get to know the routes and believe it or not you know how many's

going to get off and on. So if you're busy and you think only a few's going to get on here then you run *past* the bus stop. You can work these things out if you've been conducting. I mean it is a team isn't it, you've got to help each other. So I think it would be a good idea for men to conduct first too.

Is that likely to happen?
(Laughing) No.

Why did you want to go on the buses?
Well, money. There's equal pay so you get a reasonable amount. It's at least a five-day week and I'm not making a fortune, but I'm making a lot more than I did on any other job. There's always been equal pay on the buses, but when women had no chance of becoming drivers they were stuck at less. Drivers get £50–55 a week on average. It's different every week according to what shifts you do – sometimes it's more but I wouldn't say it's ever less. For late shift you get extra because they're called unsociable hours. They don't call early shift unsociable, though I do – I hate getting up early. If you work weekends you get more again, time and a half. And they've introduced this new bonus too – you get about 2p in the pound from the fares you collect – that's the driver as well as the conductor. You get more on omos – that's one man buses – but only if you're working as a driver-operator, and they mostly have crews on them now because they're not efficient as one-manners, and the police don't like them. There's no women driving them because it goes by seniority, and we haven't been driving long enough yet.

Do you think it's enough money for the work you do?
I know it's going back to women and men again, but there's not many women can earn the type of money we can. It's not that you have to have any qualifications either, not as a conductress anyway – just a wee test. As a driver you have to be able to drive, obviously. I learned a hell of a lot in the three weeks' training.

Do people ever say the work's too heavy for women?
No, I'm a big lassie anyway but it's nothing to do with strength. We're all driving the same buses and if they were too heavy for women they'd be too heavy for men too – it's a difficult enough job with the responsibility and the traffic without it being heavy physically too. In fact I sometimes think it's easier driving a bus than a car because you're high up and can see a situation well ahead of you and the steering is power-assisted – that's if you get a decent one, they're getting a bit shoddy at the moment with the shortage of spares. But if you do get a good bus and a good conductor it's a real treat.

I've been driving a long time, I like to drive and I wouldn't say I was worse than any of the men – in fact I think sometimes better. And they're not going to take just anyone are they. When I say anyone I mean I've seen men with heavy goods licences fail the test, and they've been driving for years and years. London Transport's got a strict standard and if you don't come up to it they don't pass you, no matter how many licences you've got. So you've got to feel proud if you do get through.

Obviously as time goes on you learn to handle the bus better. The first day I went out the sweat was pouring off me, and my nerves! I don't mean they went to such an extent that I couldn't drive, but I felt as though everyone was looking at me. Of course no one even bothers who's up front. So long as it's red and going where they're going they'll get on. When I first went out there was a woman conducting and she was telling everyone about me because she was ever so pleased. In the mirror I could see them all running up to look – the men even, but especially the women, old girls running up and waving to you and saying good for you. But otherwise I don't suppose they'd even have known that I was a woman up there driving. And the women drivers are so spread out that people say to me they've never seen any.

Do you have the same promotion prospects?

We have now. At one time there were no women inspectors but now women can go through the grade just as men can. They're saying to me, 'Now you're driving why not go and inspect', but it's not my scene at all, I'd hate it, though you get more money.

Can women do all the same overtime as men?

Yes, it's all the same, it's got to be. If you think you're getting the least bit – what's the word – discriminated, all you've got to do is go to the union.

How much overtime do you do on average?

A restday a week, which makes it a six-day week, and two other chunks. That's all you're allowed by law.

It's a lot of work – are you expected to do that much?

With the staff shortage I suppose they'd like you to, but they can't force you. It's a question of come and go – if you ever want a favour it does help if you're up with them. It's the same with the shifts. There's a fixed rota and if you want to change you have to apply well in advance – it's a bit like the army, everything's got to be in writing. But you can get a mutual exchange – that has to go through the office too but it's automatically granted as long as you've got a replacement. I mean if you ask for an exchange and they say no, then the next time they ask you to do overtime you'll say to hell with it won't you?

How do the shifts work?

Early shift is from roughly 5.30 to 12.30, middle shift from 11.30 to 7.00, late shift from 2.30 to any time after midnight. You have to do seven hours a day, except perhaps on the early shift. I drive the 30s, 14s and 37s. Number one in the 30s is the best job in the garage: it starts at 6.30 and finishes at 10.00. It's something everyone looks forward to because you've got the whole day ahead of you. The early shift on the 14s starts about 5.45 and doesn't finish till 1.30.

If you do early shift and finish say at one then after you've had forty minutes off you can do another couple of hours overtime. It's no worse than doing a spreadover – that's what we call split shift, when you work so many hours, then have a long break and do some more. Not that I do overtime straight after a full shift. Once I've done my day's work that's it.

Is that because you get tired?

You do get tired, especially on early shift, because you've just woken up and there's the crowds – everyone going to work. With this job you don't get the same days off at weekend as everyone else anyway. Sometimes it's Sunday and Monday but usually it goes Sunday–Monday, then Tuesday–Wednesday, then Wednesday–Thursday. Other times you'll work about ten days in one go and then have four days off. So you can't really talk about weekends. Your friends just have to fit in with it. If they're in straight jobs, they ring up and ask what shifts I'm on the next week, and I tell them if I can go out. We all do these shifts and we all do overtime, the conductresses as well.

It must be incredibly difficult for women with children.

They must be able to get round it somehow or they couldn't be on the job. I don't have any ties, no husband or children, so there's no big problem for me. A lot of married couples work on the buses and between them they manage the shifts so they can see the children – though that means they hardly see each other. Let's face it, it's not a very human life on the buses. You get used to the shifts, but when you start it's difficult. You're getting your dinner when you should be eating your tea. The early shift's bad because you do a lot of work before you have your breakfast, and you're starving by then.

Has there been any attempt to introduce childcare facilities at garages?

I've never heard of any. People have to find their own solutions. A lot of women at my garage have been on the buses for years. They might leave for a few years if they get married and have children, then come back when the kids are school age.

Do you think that one of the reasons more women don't drive is that the shifts clash with their work at home?

It can't just be that because they have to come from the back, and conductresses do the same hours. We won't be able to tell till they start taking women from outside and we see how many they recruit. I think it's because it's a big jump from driving a car – and most women don't even drive cars.

The men in charge were a bit dubious about taking women on at all. After I'd passed my test I was out route-learning and the instructor said they were worried about women because of periods and that. Most women do feel a bit that way, though I don't myself. Then women are inclined to be a bit more temperamental than men, and they took all that into consideration.

And the union men were worried that women wouldn't be active trade unionists. Are you in the union?

Oh yes, everyone's got to be in it, the T and G W U. You can't go against the union and I think it's a good thing in this job.

Are you involved in it at all?

No, not particularly interested. They've got their representative, so if I had a beef about anything I'd probably go and have my say. Every Friday we have to pay our dues, 25p a week in cash. If you've got anything to complain about you tell the official and if he thinks it's worth taking up he'll say so, if not he'll say forget it. They're sort of lawyers really. They know whether you're going to win or lose, whether it's worth the bother. Because it costs them money to take action – it all comes out of funds.

When are the meetings?

I haven't a clue, I think they're every week. It's impossible to arrange them to suit all the different shifts.

Did you join in the stoppage six months ago?

Yes, the whole of London Transport came out in protest when a conductor got killed. That was over a fare, a dog's fare. There'd been a lot of violence on the buses, and you can't do anything as an individual so they thought, if everyone gets together, even if just for one day, it would be our way of saying that we wouldn't let it happen again.

Has anything ever happened to you?

No, maybe I've been lucky. There's often racial tension in it. London

Transport's run by coloureds really – we've only got a couple of coloured girls at our garage, but the men sometimes get abuse. I'm lucky there too because I'm a bit of a novelty, being coloured and a woman and being Scots. Wherever I go people are tickled pink. You do hear stories of kids goading Pakistani conductors and that – it's not nice, but there's not much you can do about it, except clout them round the earhole and then you're in trouble.

It's a real strain conducting in the rush-hours. You feel sorry for people – you know they've been waiting and want to get home, but you can't decide who's jumped the queue. You get the situation where you've let so many on and the bus is full and someone runs along the side and jumps on. I won't let them on. I stop the bus and say get in the queue like everyone else. Of course then they start but you've got to bluff it, you're scared of course but you don't want to start using force against them. So you just stand there and you usually find the public are for you and they start on him and he gets so embarrassed he gets off.

Did you feel the public was against you last time the fares went up?

Well, they moan regardless – if they're not moaning about the busfares they're moaning about how long they've waited for the bus. You just say yes and no – humour or ignore them. I understand really, it just gets a bit monotonous. You've got to tell someone how you feel, and who else can they speak to if not the conductor. If you run out of the garage late or there's a couple of buses missing in front of you, you know fine there's going to be all hell let loose. You stand there poised ready for it. I much prefer driving to conducting. I didn't mind so much the first time because there was no chance, but once I knew I could I wanted to drive. It's supposed to be interesting conducting because you meet people, but you meet them and all sorts – sometimes you wish you hadn't met them. Anyway you only meet them to take their money, that's all there is to it really.

Did you get any woman-driver jokes from the blokes at work when you started?

No, they were fantastic, absolutely fantastic. I'm a bit quiet at work and when you first go to a garage not many people talk to you. But since I passed I'm like one of the guys. I've never had so many hand-shakes and cuddles and kisses. Everyone was so excited and pleased – I suppose it was quite an achievement – for myself and for the garage.

I didn't fight to be able to do it. I'm not one for campaigning – for making speeches – though I'll always give my opinion if I'm asked. And I didn't do it to compete with men. I just thought why not do a

job you enjoy doing and get paid for it. I believe in all the things
women are fighting for – equal opportunity and that – I just wouldn't
fight myself. I know people had to push to get women driving the
buses, and I'm glad they did. I mean I'm benefiting from it aren't I.

SR.42, December 1975

Probation Officer

JEAN MCCRINDLE

*Jean McCrindle worked as a probation officer in London in the 1960s
until the shortcomings of the job forced her to give it up.*

... I began to feel part of an authoritarian régime and also that the
machine was so big, so oppressive, that anything I could do would only
minimally effect change. The personal contradiction was borne on me
most in my relations with my probationers. At one level I had to play
the role demanded of me by my job in which I had to ask them certain
questions: how was the job going, did they have money, and at another
I was genuinely interested in them as human beings and trying to
establish a human contact with them. Social case workers are supposed
not to get emotionally involved but to play a supportive role, to 'help
them to help themselves'; at the same time the role places an obligation
on you to make friends with people so that they tell you their personal
problems. I never found it possible to remain emotionally uninvolved:
I reacted to my probationers and they reacted to me. I couldn't see any
way round this, it seemed part of any human relationship. On the one
hand I was a probation officer with the law behind me, so my probationers lied to me as they had to, and some of them used me purely as a
social service. On the other, if I kept entirely within the role, I would
never make the contact required. I suspect this is the experience of
most probation officers, if they are honest. It is a very difficult job. If
you are in any way concerned about your probationer you simply have
to deny the role you are put in, for you can't – or I couldn't – do the job
any other way, except at a purely technical level of getting them money
and keeping them out of scraps with the law.

This ambivalence made me feel very badly. Because anything I was
told I had to write up in my reports, and I was sometimes told things
on the basis of a genuine liking which, if put in the report, would tell
against the woman. I had one girl with two children and a husband in

prison who had maintained all along that she wasn't living with another
man. One day she came to me and said she was feeling very badly
about having kept up this pretence. I really didn't know what to do.
Whether to discuss it with her, to find out whether it was a good thing
for her – which I think it was – and then report it; in which case the
Children's Officer would have to know because the children were still
under a court order. Or simply to leave it. The paradox was that her
admission came only as the result of having created a very good relationship with her, which is what you are supposed to do as a probation
officer . . .

SR.*41*, November 1975

'Being a Woman Doctor'

BARBARA JACOBS

. . . I began to feel solidarity with (instead of shame and contempt for)
my own sex for the first time as I saw the way nurses were treated
(ordered around and condescended to), the way ward aides would melt
away from the gaze of doctors as they entered the wards, the slapping
of physiotherapists' bottoms. The contradictions were reinforced by
my discovery that my identification with nurses was not welcome (they
were suspicious of women playing at doctors, just as they felt disgust at
the thought of male nurses doing work normally considered fit only for
females). I saw the other women medical students take on a veneer of
toughness (thus making themselves laughable) or hop desperately from
bed to bed (thus exposing themselves to ridicule), or just drop out with
depression. The supposedly benevolent nature of medicine was belied
daily on the wards as patients were not listened to, were talked down
to, made the subject of long, irrelevant discussions (usually just within
earshot) and sometimes used as research material without their full
understanding. Jobs such as being friendly, rescuing patients from off
bed pans before the consultant arrived, or simply explaining to a patient
what it was that a doctor had mumbled (or failed to say at all), were left
to student nurses, or a medical student, still too fresh to understand
whose role was what . . .

SR.*26*, August 1974

Nursing and Racism

AMRIT WILSON

'It is true that nurses are bitchy about each other, that we gossip, spy on each other and carry stories to ward sisters. But it is not because we are women that we are bitchy, not because we are women that we gossip. It is because we are servants. We might like to say nursing is a profession but most of us know that nurses, even senior nurses, are just servants as far as doctors are concerned.'

Mary, who said that, works in a well-known London hospital. Like many other overseas student and pupil nurses whose experiences and opinions this article is based on she didn't want her real name revealed – overseas nursing students can't afford to complain or even comment about their situation.

. . . Black nurses who had had children and had not married told me of remarks such as, 'You should have left behind your tribal behaviour when you came to Britain.' A nurse from Guyana who married an English doctor told me how the ward sister had taken the piece of news. 'She looked quite disturbed; she said "Really! Don't you think you are marrying a bit above your station, do you think you'll be happy?" ' Others told of questions about the men they lived with such as, 'Are you sure he'll be able to support you if you get pregnant?' A nurse from Barbados (*Race Today*, 1974) recalled how when, as a student she had been living in the Nurses' Home and had worn clothes which she had brought with her from Barbados, 'Matron said to me, "Where are you going dressed like a tart?" They used to do things like going through your clothes and then ask how you could afford certain things.'

Of course these attitudes are faced by Black nurses from Britain as well as from overseas, but there is a difference: Black women settled in Britain are no longer prepared to tolerate such paternalism; for overseas student and pupil nurses there is no way out. They are not in a position to fight back. Although in some hospitals they constitute the bulk of the workforce, they have no power as workers and more than anything else they are conscious of the insecurity of their position in Britain. In the end many feel like the Nigerian student nurse who commented bitterly, 'In our hospital you don't notice racism. You begin to accept it because you begin to think that Black student nurses who are insulted and ill-treated are just stupid. You only notice racial prejudice when white students are there, when there is a departure from the normal. If a white student is five minutes late they don't get told off. They call it "personality".' 'Personality' of course is very important in nursing. As a ward sister told me, 'The sort of personality I like to see is polite, well-spoken and obedient, and girls from your part of the world so often are, dear.' The fact is that student nurses from 'my part of the world' have to be, otherwise they'd lose their jobs.

. . . The following [is one case of a Black nurse] settled in Britain who experienced the wrath of the hospital hierarchy. Many overseas nursing students in similar positions have had to leave the country.

Mary, a nurse originally from Guyana: 'I worked very very hard at XXXX hospital. One day about seven months after I had been working there, I was in charge of a postnatal ward. A patient complained that her leg was hurting. I told her that I would draw the screen and bandage up her leg. I went off to get the bandage when matron said she wanted to do the ward round with me. I told her that I was about to bandage up a patient's leg. She opened the curtain and the patient had her right foot on the bedside table, the table she usually had her dinner on. It was nearly dinnertime. Matron just wiped the floor with me, said how incompetent I was, what a terrible nurse I was. Seven months of work just went down the drain just like that. In front of the patient she said, "Don't you ever ask me for a reference. I shall never give you one." Later on that day she repeated this.' As a result, for years Mary was unable to find a job which required references. She became an agency nurse.

. . . If an overseas student does in fact manage to get through her training without ever giving offence to anyone, she may still find herself facing deportation when she passes her exams. Under the 1971 Immigration Act no reason need be given by the Home Office; she is merely told that she has passed her exam, stopped being a student and must now leave the country, like any other university or college student. In fact they are defined as students for a specific purpose: to provide the Health Service with a large low-paid and easily exploitable work force. The total numbers of student and pupil nurses as compared to the total number of nurses show the scale of this exploitation (SRNs 99,606, student nurses 54,670; SENs 52,494, pupil nurses 21,594). What it amounts to is not only a policy of oppression for these nurses as individuals but for the Third World countries they come from. In fact the plight of overseas nurses here shows clearly how Britain continues to exploit these countries by using them as a pool of cheap labour which can be drawn upon when required and got rid of when the market no longer needs it.

. . . Back home the conditions often just do not exist for them to go on as nurses. In Guyana, for example, there are no mental hospitals; in Mauritius the hospital structure is self-sufficient, ensuring that vacancies will never be available. In various countries from which nurses are recruited (for example the Philippines and Singapore) the S E N quali-fication is not recognized, a fact the British authorities are well aware of. For the men and women returning to their countries after two years' hard work, and to their families who were looking forward to the result of this hard work in the form of increased financial support, it is a bitter economic set-back.

But the dumping is still being done rather discreetly. Often the decision as to whether overseas students should be offered jobs in the hospitals they are training in is left to the Local Area Health Authority, sometimes even to the District Management Team. But the Department of Health and Social Security (D H S S) is always there to guide these decisions with its directives. In Hounslow, according to Christine Potter, secretary of the N A L G O sub-branch: 'In April last year the District Nursing Officer for that area wrote to the Joint Shop Stewards' Committee saying that in the future they would register all posts with the Department of Education and Science instead of offering them to students. The Shop Stewards protested, but in many hospitals in this area it is still happening. My feeling is that it is the cuts, what they are trying to do is not fill vacancies. The District Management Team said that their action was not based on a change in policy; it was just that the D H S S had drawn it to their attention that there were now a number of unemployed nurses in the resident labour force.'

Implicit in this argument is that overseas nursing students, although living and working in Britain, are not even to be considered a part of the resident labour force. Because they come from the poor countries of the world, because they are Black, when it comes to their rights they can be simply ignored. Every stage in their lives, in their histories, shows the effect on the one hand of sexual oppression and on the other of the continuing exploitation of British imperialism. And yet women's groups have so far shown little interest in their plight, something which perhaps tells us a little about the position of white feminists in Britain.

SR. 70, May 1978

What Happened at Heywood

MARSHA ROWE

'When we go back we'll find out who our friends are. We are thought very militant, me and you. We are called the ring leaders in our room.'
'This is making me militant.'

The 400 women at Salford Electrical Instruments factory stayed out on strike for equal pay for eleven weeks, from August to October this year. The factory's in Heywood, a 12p bus ride from Manchester, the fare being cheaper outside of peak hours.

The two women quoted above are unusual in that they knew each other well before the strike.

'You go in to get your work done, but you don't know someone down the room, until this.'

'We feel more together since the strike, don't we.'

Both women were brought up by their fathers. 'My mother went off to London when I was twelve. It's funny how things stick with you. I remember my dad filling the tub with water, with all the clothes in it, and a little primus underneath, and the rubbing board.'

The Claimants' Union went down to the Social Security office with nine of the women in Rochester, the next town, who were either unmarried mothers or whose husbands had left them. No one received any SS benefit whatsoever. Strike pay was £6.25. 'My rent is £6.99.'

So was the rent of another woman, whose husband was working at the same factory, S E I, 'It's a woman's place, this', employs 200 men. The men continued working during the strike. She said rather flatly how could she pay the rent if she and her husband split up.

There was a grim understanding developing about the men. 'I've always wanted to be on strike. I was picketing for my husband and he was off to the football. It learns you a lot of things.'

'In our job we use ice, and when the men came out we refused to use it, even if it came through the pickets. But the men here, you know, they are getting stuff out so they must be using it.'

Some of the blokes were ironic, 'When I came out tonight Brian sang "Onward Christian Soldiers"', without menacing the women's resistance. And the women were kind and sympathetic, 'It's hard on the husbands, they get fed up', and not averse to knocking them back, 'He said so you've done in here today, love. I said, *Yeah*. A quick hoover and a dust and it looks a lot different when you haven't done it for a bit.' Everyone laughed. There is too the grinding responsibilities of married women, the learned distrust. A woman with soft, haggard eyes couldn't attend the rally on Saturday afternoon, 19 October, which was organized by the Manchester Working Woman's Charter Group to extend awareness of the strike, 'Get my old man around the supermarket and he will be bringing home I don't know what.'

Understanding was deepening between women in the same family. After meeting a woman whose young daughter, she announced, worked in the same room at SEI as she did, I recognized them both when they sat together on a bench at the rally. 'Although you do the same work as the women, you get less pay when you're sixteen. It doesn't go up till you're eighteen.' Her flat rate is not quite £10. Another had said, 'My daughter's fifteen and she wasn't very interested in the strike. She came down to the picket line to see me. "Oh, Mum," she said, "it's awful you shouting at those women going in." I talked to her about how it concerned her, her future.'

Quite conscious is a blank anger towards enemies within the factory. On Saturday morning, after there'd been a few trips downstairs to the toilet, it was my turn to go there to wash the tea cups. The key wouldn't go in. The previous day the door hadn't shut at all. It was only that morning it kept on being closed mysteriously. 'Big . . .', as he was called, had stuffed the lock with paper. 'Nasty.' 'That's what they're like.'

In desperation that the strike could not be successful if the men did not come out, at the beginning of October the women occupied the factory, sneaking past the security guards to take over the switchboard and the reception office. 'We put a chain and a padlock, and barbed wire, on the back gate to lock the men in,' said Pat McMahon, who'd helped to chat up the security guards to divert their attention. '£3 for a padlock for half an hour,' said Bella Fullard drily. The men cut it through at 5.20 p.m., the end of the day shift. Bella was the leader of the strike. She's worked at SEI for twenty-four years, returning a few years after each of her three daughters was born, and she was exhausted to the point of dropping her head on to the desk and falling asleep amidst our chatter. All the women were tired.

'My nerves are gone, can't sleep and you're turning over and over. It's on your mind all the time. Last week I thought I'm not going this morning and I said I wasn't, and I cried all morning. I kept wondering who was at the picket line. Though it was hard when the others broke.'

After a strike meeting two weeks before, twenty-four women returned to work. Bored by calling out 'scabs' on Friday evening, when the 5.25 to 9 p.m. shift started, the picketing women sang out, 'Dah di dah, dah di dah' – a Laurel and Hardy ditty – to the women who dwindled in groups down the lane into the factory, carefully keeping their faces turned away under their umbrellas.

Some of those who went back were said to be new workers. Towards a couple of them there was bitterness, 'She was a spy on the committee. We worked it out, how our plans were getting back.' And an old recognition that any woman whose husband was connected to management was going to be loyal to him and not to the women she worked with.

Jostling came up sometimes, 'No aggro like, all in fun.'

'Nothing personal to you, but I have gone back to work.'

'Mightn't be personal to you, but I take it bloody personal.'

They enjoyed poking at the arrogance of men who escorted the scabs. 'The Production Manager used to come out for his cigar. We used to slow clap him. Then we went right up close. He doesn't come out any more.'

Fears threatened their toughness – worry about how long the striking women could keep it up, and about victimization when they returned to work. 'I heard some of them talking outside the wages room yesterday. I think they are getting a bit tired and frightened.' The women had to be brave to carry on – no one expected the strike to last so long.

. . . The work is graded as light engineering. There is a basic wage each week. The women's basic is £18.25 which is lower than the men's.

'Down the yard there's a press shop and women working next to the men and not paid the same as the men.'

'They are taking women off some jobs and putting men on and they get more money. We don't know how much.'

'I've never seen a man do my job. I don't think men would have the patience.'

Considering the way the women are paid for their work, they have to reach through skin-crawling obstacles towards each other to strike together in the first place. On top of the basic rate, there's a bribe. The official word for it is a bonus rate. The bonus rate differs, according to sex and according to the job – it's a jungle of private incentives. The maximum bonus for the women could not be more than 85 per cent – the men's can be as much as 150 per cent.

Women are timed against each other and against the clock. 'Over us there are the supervisors – they're out – and over them are the charge hands. The charge hands aren't out. They come round with a clock which they put in front of you. They say, "This will help you get it done faster." You have one eye on your work and one eye on the clock. They come back and say, "Oh, six minutes, that's good." '

'There is too many bosses.'

'There is always too many bosses. The supervisor will tell me to do one thing, then the charge hand will come around and she will say the supervisor isn't right and then the charge hand will come back and say the same thing.'

'Sometimes when you're working you think what are you doing here.'

Both men and women also receive threshold payments, the cost of living increase begun under the Tory Phase 3 legislation. Neither the men nor the women are getting anything like the £4 announced by the government in the middle of October. Before the strike the threshold payment to the women was £1.60.

After the skilled men took successful action inside the factory in April/May this year, the A E U W proceeded with the women's claims for equal pay in July. 'We were working on go slow and the management came round and said do we want to work normal, and we said, "What do you mean?" He said, back to bonus work or we would not get paid from 8 o'clock this morning. So we walked out and then rang the union.'

Management offered to settle in October by according the women equal bonus rates with the semi-skilled men only; no increase in the basic rate; an increase of 80p in the threshold but with no further payment. The evening shift, which is all women, was to be extended from twenty hours to twenty-one hours so the workers would qualify for redundancy pay. The night shift from 9 p.m. until morning is worked by men. The factory never stops for seven days and seven nights a week.

. . . The days spent occupying the factory and the nights wrapped in blankets, have allowed for an exchange and sharing of the experience of working at S E I. While only individually experienced, the resolution of a revolt takes an uneasy, lonely path into thicker tangles:

'When I first came to S E I I was doing crystals. For six months the machine kept splashing me in the face. The foreman got a new bit put in but it didn't get any better. They look after the men's jobs more. The women wouldn't say anything. They didn't think I'd stick up for myself. He said I was only making trouble. So I went to Personnel and asked for a transfer. The foreman said, "I'll give you a transfer", and he takes me to the other room where his mate is. They get over you and push you round. Mind you, they don't push the men around. It's a woman – Personnel – she's nice. She's not out, she's management. So I moved upstairs. You can make a better bonus on crystals, I got up to 160. The best I ever made on soldering is 60. If you do something wrong on crystals you can get a new one – you just carry on – but on soldering you have to strip it all down and start again. I lost £5 a week through moving.'

She wanted to do karate like her husband, but he reckoned she was too soft. Previously she had worked at a wallpaper factory – another big employer of women round there – and stuck it out for half a day. She described women who could only see themselves from outside themselves. Because the women are constantly an object for others they define themselves by the expectations of others, they are caged by the other's view of them:

'It was awful. You had to grab the paper out and it was burning my hands all the time. I said to one girl what are you working like this for? There's no bonus there. She said they had to get this lot finished. She repeated it. They don't realize that as soon as they get one lot finished, then they have another to do. The more they do the more they've got to do.'

Women are emotionally committed to working long and hard for others. Women's feelings towards loving and women's feelings towards authority are connected, yet this connection is elusive because it is so deep. Its surfacing is hesitant and painful. A way of making the complicated feelings provoked less threatening is to express them as absurd. The reactions of men at home to the strike were discussed amongst the women as a joke: 'I called him a male chauvinist pig last night while he was watching the telly. He said he didn't want me to go to any more meetings.' It's complicated for, after all, 'The men were out for nearly six weeks early this year and they lost £100 in wages.'

While laughter prevents the feelings becoming overwhelming, it also delays a public understanding of the connections. The equal pay demand has torn away at the edges of women's martyrdom at work. Their fears inside can be turned over, the anger incorporated can be directed outside. Yet the process is slow. The women at SEI have been submitting to abysmal working conditions:

'They are at you and at you to get a bit more out of you. I've been here for twelve years. I was working evening shifts because of the kids. Lots of women do. He [management] mythered me until I agreed to work days instead. Mythered? That means pestered. I'd said I'd work till 4 p.m. He carried on about how they needed more help until I agreed eventually to work till 5.20. I said you'd never get me here in the morning till 9 o'clock, what with getting the kids off to school, but here I am now starting at 8 a.m. like the rest.'

Not only can the management wangle more hours spent at work by the women, they can retime the jobs within the factory. An improvement in the efficiency of machinery means an improvement for SEI, not for the women who work the machines.

'If there's anything different in the job they get the rate fixer in. Last time on mounting they cut something out. They altered the jigs. The rate fixer is in APEX. She timed this girl who was faster than the others, so now they can't make even 85 per cent. For ordinary Timing you might be allowed 1 hour 45 minutes for 100 – that's not a bad time. You have to fill out your bonus book and your ticket once a day. Your job number and quantity is on the job ticket. They have it all weighed up. It's all down in the office. They have a list. If your average goes up and down, if you're feeling a bit tired one day, it's in their books.'

Not content with this tortuous way of extracting fast work from the women, competence and efficiency are exploited by the management. The women's skill backfires on themselves:

'The thing is, I get moved about because I'm good. And you forget, when you haven't done a job for a bit, like welding, you lose your speed. The others on it all the time were making £3 bonus and I was only making 12s.'

'What sort of work? Well, in our room there are loads and loads of jobs: etching, orientation, about eight I think, and they're all together. What's finished gets passed on. There's a lot of assembly. For base and cage assembly, you have to tin the wires, then cut them, thread them on the markers, weld them, trim them off, take the bases to be cleaned, then crank them on a machine, the machine bends the wires, thread them through the cage assemblies, weld them on, trim them off and then you take them down to inspection. The finest wire is ·6 millimetres. If you are not careful, you bend it, then it's no use.'

'I do coil winding – it's for telephones – a man couldn't do it, he would not have the patience.'

'I was burning myself soldering. I had marks right up my arm.'

'I used to work at Mutual Mills. My friend lost her thumb there last week.'

'My friend lost the top of her fingers. She's at Middleton. She's a dress cutter.'

'Remember little Maureen here, when the wire snapped and got her in the eye.'

'Have you seen *Shoulder to Shoulder*?* It's just finished on the telly here. Which side have you joined up with? Your women's lib membership? I think if I lived in the time, I would have gone with Sylvia because she's for the working women.'

This article was criticized by Bella Fullard and Julie Lomax, Shop Stewards at SEI because it originally contained criticisms of the AEUW district officials' negotiations for the women to return to work without all their demands being met. They wrote that 'the author throughout the article trivialized the dispute, avoided any criticism of the Employer (who after all was one of the main contestants)'.

These criticisms were taken up, and two subsequent articles followed.

---

* *Shoulder to Shoulder*, historical serial made for British television about the movement for women's suffrage.

*The first gave the economic context of the General Electric Company, the
multinational which owns SEI: 'GEC is the fifth largest company and the
largest private employer in the UK, and the eighth largest of the world
electrical corporations.' The second article was about action taken by
women workers around the country employed by GEC, and put the SEI
equal-pay dispute into a wider context.*

SR.31, January 1975

Grunwick Women

BEATRIX CAMPBELL AND VALERIE CHARLTON

For the last eight years since Jayaben Desai came with her family from
East Africa to Britain she has been watching the activities of trade
unions on television.

'All this time I have been watching the strikes and I realized that the
workers are the people who give their blood for the management and
that they should have good conditions, good pay and should be well
fed. The trade unions are the best thing here – they are not so powerful
in other countries.

'They are a nice power and we should keep it on,' said Ms Desai, the
most vocal of the fifty or so Asian and West Indian women involved in
the eleven-month Grunwick strike which has now exploded into a
national *cause célèbre*.

'We didn't think about trade unions at Grunwick – they harass you
so much there that you couldn't have any idea about joining a union.'

Before Ms Desai began working at the film processing factory three
years ago there had been two attempts to organize a union. Both were
smashed by the same management which is taking union leaders and
government officials to the High Court to stop unionization – all in the
name of freedom of the individual.

After nearly a year of diligent picketing the eighty-five strikers seem
to have been almost obscured by the media mob stories which have
dominated the news for a month, and even by the charisma surrounding
the lions of the Labour movement such as miners' leaders Mick
McGahey and Arthur Scargill, and Hugh Scanlon of the engineering
union, who have joined them on their picket line.

What about the women who have been supported by those men?
What has it all been like for them?

'This dispute is bringing us so many good things,' said Ms Desai.

'Before the mass picketing began in June the issue was not so clear in our community, it was misty before. But now the Asian community sees what we are fighting for.

'And before, the trade unions in this country were feeling that our community was not interested – that was always a gap in our community. But this will bring the distance nearer. We can all see the result – people coming here from all over the country are seeing us as part of the workers now.'

Being seen at all wasn't automatic, however, for the women who make up 60 per cent of the strikers.

'In our community ladies are always obedient,' Ms Desai explained. 'So some had problems at the start. There was some bad feeling. But men know the women are always obedient, and in his heart a man knows he must not disturb a woman.'

Ms Desai felt quite challenging toward what she experiences as glib assumptions among British women about the relationship between Asian men and women, and upholds the culture of her community, young people's respect for their parents and their right to arrange marriages for their daughters.

But what if a husband lays down the law and blocks his wife's independent decisions, like in a Grunwick situation? The woman must make him understand, she replied. Does that mean persuading him? 'No, not persuade. If she feels capable then she should tell him powerfully!'

In the early days of the strike there was a tendency among the young men to assume a division of labour, which often took the form of a protective patronage and which effectively relegated the women, the majority, to tea-making and servicing the picketing men.

Backed by Brent Trades Council, which has been deeply committed to the strike, as it was indeed to the Trico equal-pay strike, the women insisted on taking an equal part on the gates. They have stuck to this despite the ferocity of the management's counter-attack: Ms Desai's foot was run over by a director's Jaguar, two young Asian women were run down at the factory gate by a scab driver, and in the forty-second week, before the mass picketing and its consequent mass arrests began, Ms Desai was arrested on the picketline.

By the fifth week of the strike they came up with a radical device to confront domestic resistance from their husbands. A Sunday was set aside, the young men laid on Indian food and the strikers made their case together in the presence of about forty husbands.

. . . Furthermore, Grunwick deputations to factories, building sites and shipyards up and down the country have included two women and two men. This is adhered to not only for the experience gained by the strikers themselves, but because of its impact on white British workers. The strike committee relishes the image of Clydeside shipyard workers talking with the Grunwick women – men who have minimal political contact with women of their own community, never mind Asian women militants from Brent.

Appalling pay – £25 for 25 hours, and £28 for 40 hours – and the arbitrary imposition of overtime were the immediate grievances that sparked the dispute, which first involved four young Asians and later in the same day Ms Desai herself.

As she left the factory following a row with the management, Ms Desai found them hanging around outside feeling angry and thwarted, not knowing what to do. She argued that instead of doing 'something silly' they should all find out about trade unions. At home that night she talked it over with her husband, also a film process worker in the cine technicians' union ACTT, and he advised her to contact the Citizens Advice Bureau, which eventually led to joining up with APEX, a union for clerical and professional workers.

One of the Asian women who pickets round at Grunwick's Cobbold Road processing factory about ten minutes away from the Chapter Road plant which has been the main action area, explained the particular hardships faced by women:

'What I mean by slave treatment is that if a woman is pregnant, for example, she can't get time off to go to the clinic. The management says why can't we go on Saturdays, but the clinic is not open on that day.

'Many of our women have small children at school or in nurseries. The management tells you halfway through the day that you *must* work overtime that night – but this is terrible because you can't pick up your children and you can't contact your home.'

A constant feature of life with Grunwick, then, was the nightmare of the sack or agony about your children.

The combination of the Trades Council, Brent Law Centre and the strikers has been instrumental in the strike, and in strengthening pressure in APEX, a notoriously conservative union. Possibly feeling against APEX made members of other trade unions a bit tentative about offering support. The hesitancy of the union's general secretary Roy Grantham about the mass picketing was evident in his attempts to placate Grunwick boss George Ward, backed by the extreme right-wing National Association For Freedom. Grantham's appeal to restrict numbers to 500 was rejected by the strike committee.

Media coverage of NAFF's intervention in Ward's courtroom battle against APEX and the government conciliation service ACAS has subtly shifted the whole emphasis of this contest.

After Ms Desai had recruited many Grunwick workers into APEX, George Ward prevented any proper ballot being organized by ACAS to test the feeling of his employees. Subsequently he sued ACAS for not doing a proper survey – precisely the thing he prevented. Ward and NAFF have turned the issue on its head. Instead of being about the right to belong to a trade union, NAFF insists that the dispute is about the freedom *not* to join a union. A freedom nobody at Grunwick was ever denied.

But the media's scare stories obviously got to some of the union leadership, and it was only their first-hand experience of police brutality on 1 July, the day of a crucial APEX executive meeting on the strike, that persuaded them to change their minds and support continuation of the mass picket.

However, there is another important feature of APEX – 50 per cent of its membership is female. Did the union make a special appeal to those members to support their Grunwick sisters, particularly given that much of the Asian women's sense of grievance is against Ward's treatment of them as women? 'No, we hadn't thought of that,' said London APEX chairman Eddie Hayes. 'But you've got a point. You have definitely got a point, maybe it could have been productive to address our women as *women*,' he reflected.

The women's demands that they have equal right to picket took an ironic twist recently when they complained to their Grunwick brothers that they were spending too much time doing the talking and being 'generals' at the strike HQ instead of doing their turn in the picketing rota.

. . . The dramatic turn which the strike took in the last month began on 13 June, the first day of a week of action called by the strike committee. This was planned as a women's day, following talks between the strikers and London Communist Party women, and got support from feminists within the women's liberation movement and from the national conference of the Working Women's Charter, who heard Ms Desai at their rally earlier this year. June 13 was the day when a massive battalion of police waded into the stunned crowd and arrested eighty-four people. After ten months of virtual silence on Grunwick, it hit the front pages of the national press.

'So after ten months we found out about the trade union movement in this country and what a power it has,' said Ms Desai. 'We have the police to thank for that. The police created the Post Office boycott. We had been asking for that for ten months but never got it until then.'

After a week of the mass picket, it was extended in the hope of pulling in sufficient numbers to close the factory. For hundreds of trade unionists throughout Britain, Grunwick became a regular appointment. During one picketline discussion about the risk of APEX selling out, a south coast seaman insisted: 'Grantham can't sell out – Grunwick isn't his property to sell out. It belongs to the whole of the movement now.'

The increased picketing also began to reveal that the dimensions of solidarity were much wider than the gates of Grunwick and the daily ritual of trying to stop the bus carrying scabs inside. Picketing was being stepped up outside scores of chemists still supplying the firm, and solidarity action by trades councils and unions in other cities has stopped supplies from all but fifty out of 400 chemists.

Many feminists who got up every day at 6 a.m. to travel to Grunwick experienced an edgy reserve in encounters with the scabs, for they too were mainly women. And did it work, all that shouting and fist-waving as the crowded coach carved its way through the crowd?

A dozen scabs deserted the company during the first three weeks of the mass picket. One of them was twenty-one-year-old Black office worker Susan Pitts, who started working at the factory two weeks after the strike began last August. She joined the strike a couple of weeks ago after a programme on TV about the strike confirmed some of the reservations which had been growing in her mind.

Inside the factory the strikers were abused and scorned. 'The thing is, you don't hear the truth inside there, it's all verbal manipulation. They call the pickets rent-a-mob and scum. And of course when you arrive there on the bus it does seem a bit like that.' One morning in the beginning of July Ms Pitts missed the scabs' bus. 'This feeling I had about the strike had been accumulating for months, so I decided not to go in. I phoned up to tell them and they kept saying, "Come in, come in". But when I said I wouldn't, they just said "You must be sick. You are sick".'

What had clinched her decision? 'It was when I was walking through Willesden after missing the bus, and I saw some people standing outside Willesden Court. They were a couple of guys who had been going along to the picketline and I got talking to them about it. That was when I finally decided.' The men took her along to the strike headquarters to meet the strikers. 'I was a bit scared at first, but it turned out all right.' Later that day she joined the picketline.

The Asian women also stress that despite the aggravation at the gates, they maintain personal contact with women from their community who are scabbing. One of them was the close friend of Nirmala

Patel. They worked together in Grunwick's office. 'It is very sad,' said Ms Patel, who still hoped that her former workmate would join them. Scabs and strikers came together several weeks ago for a marriage in their community, and for that day tried to forget that they were on opposite sides of the gate.

Sarah Greaves, a feminist who has been supporting the pickets, also said that she felt 'really bad shouting at the scabs. It's awful, you get no chance to talk to them. The police just don't give you a chance, and that's what polarizes the whole thing.'

As for many other feminists, this strike is her first experience of violent confrontation and volatile industrial action. 'I went at the end of the first week, and it was pretty hairy. I was completely taken by surprise. And I was in a state of shock about it for some time.' Before this her contact with politics was 'basically about dealing with personal politics, but I felt I had been bashing my head against various brick walls. I felt a lot of energy to do something more about my oppression as a woman, and about the general political situation. During this I have realized that the situation was very much more serious than I had thought. You see up to then there was a real distance for me between left-wing politics and feminism. It really hit me hard to realize that this whole political thing at Grunwick comes down to a fight in the streets.'

She was wandering round to the back gate with her friends to join the picket. 'Suddenly we were set upon by a huge flying wedge. I was in the middle of it all before I'd had time to make any decisions. I was terrified, absolutely scared stiff. I was done for assault. Couldn't believe it . . . They said I kicked a policeman in the back causing him to fall to the ground.'

One thing the experience has produced is 'a really trusting circle of friends. We meet every morning to go to Grunwick, we support each other – men and women – and now we've built up a support group in West London. I'd felt very isolated for a long time, particularly because I've got a four-year-old son to bring up on my own. But now we are taking turns looking after him so that I can join the picket. It is really breaking down the barriers between what is called personal and political.'

How did she feel about the trade union men? 'I thought they were great. Maybe if you bumped up against some miners in a pub there would be all sorts of sexist stuff. But at Grunwick you thought they had the same feelings that we did.' Other feminists said they were struck by the sense of order and purpose introduced by trade union delegations. At a socialist feminist conference in London on 10 July, women involved in the picketing agreed to try to function as a women's contingent, in order to be more of a presence, and to co-ordinate as a group with the strikers. Many feminists have been picketing regularly, but had not identified themselves with banners.

Gail Lewis, a Black feminist who joined the picketline virtually every day with other feminists, commented that she felt impressed by the trade unionists' 'sense of solidarity and caring in their discipline. They were really caring, trying to see that our people didn't get hurt.' And Maria Duggan, another feminist who suffered a fractured leg when she was stamped on by police, said she felt 'very solid with the support of the men, particularly the miners'.

But they also confronted sexism on the picketline. 'In one struggle with the police you would hear men testing manhood by saying things like "What sort of man are you, hitting a woman?" to the police,' said Gail Lewis. 'So I said "Hey what's this, we are here as part of the struggle and if you are suggesting that women are more feeble then we'll have that out with you here and now." When another woman overheard male pickets complaining that "We'd have got that bus if it wasn't for those silly women in the way", she countered, "Wait a minute, it's those silly girls who have been holding that gate all this time." '

SR.61, August 1977

NEWSHORT

The Grunwick strike is now officially over, after 690 days. The government arbitration service, ACAS, finally gave up trying to get Grunwick boss George Ward to allow a ballot of all the workers about union recognition. The Cabinet put pressure on the TUC and the TUC put pressure on the strikers' union APEX to end the strike. The massive support that came from other trade unionists, from feminists, from students, and the determination of the fifty-five remaining strikers, mainly East African Asian women, wasn't enough to win the strike. And all feminist issues were lost in the top level manoeuvring. Jayaben Desai is now referred to as 'legendary' – safe, saintly and alone.

SR.74, September 1978

Save the Green

BETHNAL GREEN HOSPITAL WORKERS INTERVIEWED
BY AMANDA SEBESTYEN

SCOTTY works in the hospital laundry, NUPE Shop Steward
MYRNA SHAW secretary of the Medical Postgraduate Department,
   NALGO Shop Steward
MARJORIE CHESKIN Sister-in-Charge of the Nurses' Home
EILEEN lives in the area
ELIZABETH works at the London Hospital, Whitechapel, the big local
   teaching hospital where funds are now being concentrated
LYNNE teacher, from the East London Women's Health Group

We know that the Health Service is under attack all over the country,
from our own experiences − longer queues, more medical mistakes,
more harassed staff, less time in a hospital bed, more time looking
after sick people at home. And East London is really in the front line.
With some of the worst medical provision in England, the Area Health
Authority proposes cutting a third of the area's hospital beds. A new
hospital is due for the 1980s − work hasn't even begun on the site yet.

Bethnal Green has an extremely successful small hospital. Last
autumn [1978] the Area Health Authority revealed their plan to close
down all its general services, and convert the wards for geriatric patients.
But the staff and local people had plans of their own. A campaign to
Save the Green started right away, beginning with half a dozen staff and
a local doctor, and growing by Christmas to a meeting of 700.

People are now occupying the hospital twenty-four hours a day to stop
the conversion. Unlike the planners, most campaign members come from
Bethnal Green itself. The staff are not only upset about their jobs, but
about the decline of a community: 'If I had to give up work tomorrow it
wouldn't bother me. But I live in this area, I want to end my days here,
and in the thirty-odd years that I've lived here I've seen this borough go
down.' Women have been in a majority in the campaign.

There was David Ennals on the television saying that the very large
hospitals are a mistake, 'the 300-bedded hospital is the hospital of the
future.' Well, *this* is a 300-bedded hospital. And this is still − or was
before they started running it down − a very busy little hospital. I find
that the smaller a thing is, the better it runs, the far less expensive it is
and a much better atmosphere there is for everyone to work in. *Marjorie
Cheskin.*

   ... I think the London's a good example of how a large hospital

2

218 *Spare Rib Reader*

doesn't work. It's too impersonal, and it's getting larger every day. *Elizabeth.*

. . . There's a woman came up to orthopaedics here and had to be sent over to the London. She's going to have to wait eleven months – that's just to see a doctor, not to get an operation done. *Lynne.*

At the moment there's no fracture clinic locally, there hasn't been for a long while. If you go down to Mile End they just X-ray you and refer you to the London. My daughter hurt her arm on Tuesday, she was sent to hospital Wednesday morning and told it was nothing serious, but she'd chipped a bone or fractured her shoulder. We couldn't go up to the London hospital because it was twelve o'clock, so they strapped it up at Mile End and sent me on Thursday. Thursday they decided it didn't really need plastering, but then again the actual fracture doctor wasn't there, so I had to go back again on Monday. We sat there from about quarter to nine till about ten past eleven to see this doctor, and he said, 'Oh, yes, yes. Yes, we'll leave it wrapped up as it is and we'll see you next week.' *Eileen.*

. . . There's no argument for getting rid of this hospital on health grounds or anything else, it's purely money. This is exactly what the hospital administrator said to us when he was showing contractors around a ward. *Lynne.*

If they want to save money, how can they justify the conversion? Look at all the money they spent here recently on the operating theatre and orthopaedic. Seven or eight years ago, this hospital had everything. *Elizabeth.*

The children's ward went to Hackney Road, the Ear Nose and Throat went to St Leonards. They didn't go in one big lump, they went gradual, but you were always told that something better was going to be put in their place. *Marjorie Cheskin.*

The kitchens here were a showplace. People came from different hospitals all over England to see them, because they were a new design for the National Health Service. *Elizabeth.*

This laundry was going to be the group laundry. We have our own water supply here, we've got room for expansion too. Also we've got much better ventilation than the London will ever have. Am I angry that the laundry's going to be closed down? It's not *going* to be closed down. Because they'll close it down over my dead body. *Scotty.*

. . . We gave the elderly the dignity of being in a general hospital, we didn't stick them in an all-geriatric hospital without the facilities that they've got just as much right to as anyone else. *Myrna Shaw.*

To come out of one ghetto into another – the Area Health Authority aren't doing the old people a favour. *Scotty.*

We're going right back to the very days that this hospital was first built, as a workhouse. I find if you've got elderly people with young people, the young people tend to sort of take them under their wing. But when you separate old people from everyone else, then no one can see what's going on. It just turns into a dump. *Marjorie Cheskin*.

The plan says geriatric for four years, and then closure. So where do people go next? And nobody's asked the old people around here if they want this all-geriatric. They don't. They support us.

. . . For most of the elderly people around here, this *is* their hospital and without it they can't go anywhere for help. We hired a coach for a pensioners' club to come and protest at the Area Health Authority, and they were terrific, singing and dancing and they all had banners. Someone lifted one lady up to the office windows and she was banging on them and saying, 'Come out here, you miserable old gits.' And when the planners' cars drew up for the meeting, another lady was waving her stick in the air and saying, 'If I was younger I'd give you what for!' There were quite a few policemen up there as usual, and one of them said, 'If you younger people were doing what these old ladies are doing, you'd be arrested.' *Eileen*.

Every time a ward gets emptied we padlock it up, to stop any conversions into geriatric. We've got 102 local GPs on our side; we have local residents picketing, and then the dustmen have been coming, and the brewers. *Scotty*.

I think the joint shop stewards' committee is the best thing that's come out of this campaign. But instead of calling an all-London stewards' conference, the leaders of our two main Health Service unions have virtually abandoned us. We think that in return for favours elsewhere they've agreed to keep quiet about our problems.

Four of us on our shop stewards' committee are ladies as opposed to one man. We've been very very active. *Myrna Shaw*.

Eileen: The majority of the people who turn up for the rallies are women.

Elizabeth: I think it's because the men couldn't care where they go, it's the women that have to bring the children and things like that. One Saturday they were due to close Casualty, and we got some leaflets out very quick and went in at the pubs; 'Oh yes, we'll be there' – and yet hardly any of them came, the men.

Eileen: It's nothing to do with the hours, because *I* work during the day.

Lynne: We all do. The only time it's more usually men on the picket is when they stay overnight.

Elizabeth: I think it's because they could probably cope better if there was any violence.

Lynne: I don't feel *I* could cope less than a man.

Eileen: I wouldn't be prepared to stay up here on my own, I would with another girl.

Eileen: We did a leaflet saying, 'Mothers Show Your Power', because there's a lot of people who don't go to work and when they get given leaflets with 'Go to your trades union, Do this and Do that' they feel they're not really involved because they're only a mother. The meeting was in a park which wasn't very dangerous for the road, and it was a time when the children were on holiday.

Lynne: A lot of women objected to it because they said they weren't *just* mothers, they were workers as well and they didn't like being defined like that.

Eileen: Nothing against people working, it was just to try and get some of the mothers who *didn't* go out to work to realize they could still do something.

Another thing we did which I think was good, we asked five local schools if we could put out leaflets. And they all agreed, in fact they gave them out themselves.

In the summer we went to David Ennals's house, which was in a very small block of flats but it wasn't like our flats you know, the door was shut and a porter came out. *Rather* select. And there was all us people shouting 'Up the Green, Up the Green!' and all these curtains were opening . . . And then we went to Downing Street which was also funny because there was a policeman with a walkie-talkie and as the fifty of us walked down towards him he started saying, 'Help, I need reinforcements, I've got a mob assembling!'

And then on the anniversary of the National Health Service there was a protest against the cuts organized countrywide by the Fight Back organization. At nine o'clock you stood outside your own hospital and lit torches, but we turned ours into a singsong. We made our own up: 'It's a long way to the London!' *Eileen.*

Some German people came the other night, and played with their banjos outside the hospital. I was so amazed I almost burst into tears because there was hardly anyone around, and here were these people all the way from Germany come to support us. *Lynne.*

I stood up in the Park and I said, 'You have got to go to council meetings. You have got to be seen there.' Because the council knew that this was happening and didn't bother. If all these people who say they'll help us now had come to our aid when we asked them, we could possibly have halted this from the very beginning. *Marjorie Cheskin*.

At first we were a bit nice, like we wrote a lot of nice letters saying Please could you meet us, and Please produce this. We waited six months once for an answer from the Area Health Authority. We could have been a bit more demanding. *Eileen*.

We should have worked more on getting the Community Health Council to support us, they only came over to our side when it was too late. They're essential for any hospital campaign, they've got the power to hold up closures and get a hearing from the Health Minister. *Lynne*.

You shouldn't just call round the local papers, it's the national press you've got to get to. *Elizabeth*.

To my mind the campaign hasn't involved enough of the ordinary staff in the hospital. I was talking to a Sister today, she said 'The meetings have stopped, haven't they?' and I said 'No – you should come along.' No one had actually asked her. *Lynne*.

. . . I think when you form a committee, you should include someone from outside, like an ordinary housewife. I brought my mother along to the first meeting and they said, 'You shouldn't have. She's not on the committee.' At the beginning they were keeping out the local people, though the attitude's changing. *Elizabeth*.

While I was interviewing Eileen, Elizabeth and Lynne, one of the men on picket duty managed to come into the room four times *with increasingly non-existent excuses.*

That's just typical, that he couldn't leave women alone for five minutes. He had to know what's going on and why. Most of them are like that. *Lynne*.

We were getting ready for a march, and somebody said, 'What shall we do for our last banner, something that's really eyecatching' and immediately a man – obviously – turned round and said 'I know, two women walk topless.' Somebody else who was there done her nut, she said, 'Why must it be women?' and he said 'Oh, well, two men walk bottomless then – it was just a joke.' She said, 'It isn't a joke. We're discussing a campaign for equal people and straight away it's sensational if women walk topless.' *Eileen*.

It's the women who are giving the lead with leafletting and practical things but in all the meetings I've been to they're not listened to so much. The men have more status. *Lynne*.

I've never had any time for unions. I've always felt they did not give you a chance to say how you feel; but now I've joined the Royal College of Nurses for the first time, that's the nurses' organization. And I'm grateful to the other unions for what they're doing. But I've been a little bit dissatisfied because I thought there was far more unity than there actually is. You *could* make these unions work, but only if everybody was to play their part in them. *Marjorie Cheskin*.

. . . I feel I've become more tolerant of people's attitudes, understood that people can change and not to write them off if they seem conservative. *Lynne*.

If it hadn't been the Green, if it had been somewhere up north, I don't think I'd have done anything about it. I'd have just said, 'Terrible, the cuts.' But because this is my local hospital, I've been surprised some of the things I've found myself doing. When we went up to Westminster, we were all militant. I would have thought, Oh David Ennals is a Minister, you can't really go up and see him. But it's your right to go there. Before the campaign I would never have dreamed of it. *Elizabeth*.

Up until I got involved with this, apart from going to work, that was it. I spent all the evenings indoors. I didn't belong to any clubs or evening classes. I come out two or three nights a week now, which I didn't do this time last year.

I think Anne, who does the newsletter with Lynne, said it to me last week, that when you've got children you're always somebody's mum or you're somebody's wife, and when you come somewhere like this you become a person, you're you. My husband and my children, they don't object to me coming, but you know I couldn't drag them up here if I tried. They just say 'Tara, Love'. *Eileen*.

If we win here, I'd join another local hospital campaign, Save St Nick's. *Elizabeth*.

I'd definitely join something else afterwards, because now I've done this I'd find it very hard to just go back. This has got me out of the house, meeting new people, different people. It's been good for me, I don't know about me being good for the hospital but it's been very very good for me! *Eileen*.

. . . It's stalemate. We're stopping the conversion, but now the Area Health Authority are threatening people's jobs. But the staff are really angry because they know the conversion will lose jobs anyway. We're in a stronger position now as ancillary workers in the London and Mile End have promised to work to rule if management moves in. And recently we blocked the main road outside the hospital for twenty minutes to show our determination. *Lynne*.

The Area Health Authority have told us so many bloody lies they don't know which way to turn now. Apparently the Minister has called back the papers to look them over again because he hasn't got the truth from them. Personally myself I think it would be better if we could get an all-London stoppage over all the cuts in all the other hospitals. It's time we all stopped fighting our own little battles and joined together and made the biggest stink that anybody's ever heard. *Scotty.*

SR.77, December 1978

FEMALE AGE 59	MALE AGE 20
FULL TIME	FULL TIME
DOUBLE SEAMER OPERATOR	MACHINE SETTER
GRADE 3	GRADE 5
AVERAGE WEEKLY HOURS 40	AVERAGE WEEKLY HOURS 52
AVERAGE WEEKLY WAGES 25.60	AVERAGE WEEKLY WAGES 41.08

6:00 AM: GET UP, MAKE BREAKFAST	7:00 AM: GET UP, GET FAMILY READY FOR SCHOOL & WORK
6:45 AM: LEAVE HOME	9:00 AM: WASHING, CLEANING
7:30 AM: START WORK, GET LINES READY	10:30 AM: GO SHOPPING
8:00 AM: MACHINES START, KEEP MACHINES RUNNING	11:45 AM: PREPARE MEAL
12:30 PM: LUNCH, RING WIFE	12:30 PM: SERVE MEAL
1:30 PM: START, INSPECTION, GENERAL SUPERVISING, LABOUR, PRODUCTION	2:00 PM: CLEAN WINDOWS
9:30 PM: FINISH WORK	4:00 PM: PREPARE MEAL FOR EVENING
10:00 PM: GET HOME, LIGHT MEAL CHAT WITH WIFE	4:30 PM: MAKE TEA FOR SON
12:00 PM: GO TO BED	4:45 PM: LEAVE FOR WORK
	5:30 PM: START WORK
	9:30 PM: FINISH WORK
	9:45 PM: GET HOME, WASH UP HAVE TEA
	10:45 PM: GO TO BED
CLIFTON McKINSON, AGE 32	EILEEN SZMIDT, AGE 46
1 SON AGE 10 4 DAUGHTERS AGES 7, 6, 4, 2	4 SONS 1 DAUGHTER AGES 25, 24, 21, 19, 14
SECTION FOREMAN	DOUBLE SEAM OPERATOR PART TIME 5:30 PM–9:30 PM

From 'Women and Work: A Document on the Division of Labour in Industry'.

SR.40, October 1975

'It's Really Stirred up the Factory': Trico Women Win

JILL NICHOLLS

After twenty-one weeks the equal-pay strike at Trico's is over. We stood in the rain to cheer the strikers back to work – hundreds of women under umbrellas, jostling on the pavement of the Great West Road, Brentford, at 7.30 on Monday morning, 18 October.

'*We are the champions*,' they sang. A pensioner who had picketed nearly every day started chanting:

'*What have we got?*
Equal Pay
When have we got it?
NOW'

Television cameras glared in the half-light, a young Black woman hustled everyone to get into fours, Bill McLoughlin, local AEUW official, said fall in behind the strike committee – and then they marched through the gates, past the settee they'd sat on all summer, now soaking up rain like a sponge.

The women laughed and waved to the crowd of supporters clustered round the gate – as we cheered and clapped I felt elated yet sad that victory had to mean return to the same old assembly lines.

But so much *has* changed. The women have stuck together, stuck it out and won what they were fighting for – the same rate as men doing the same job. By strike action they have beaten the industrial tribunal that wriggled out of their case for equal pay, and forced the American-owned car component company to give in. This means a rise of £6/ 6.50 each, bringing them up to the same *operational rate* as the men (their *wages* vary according to speed, as they do piecework). On top of that the men and women got the 5 per cent they're entitled to under this round of the government pay deal, and sickness benefits guaranteed.

Full details of the settlement are not publicly available, but the only significant concession seems to be that the rise is not backdated to 1 January when equal pay became law. 'That's because it's a negotiated settlement,' said Sally Groves, an assembly worker at the factory. 'We didn't get it through the Equal Pay Act – you could say we got it despite the Equal Pay Act.'

For weeks the company had used the tribunal's ruling as an excuse, saying that as the women weren't eligible for equal pay, it would go against the pay deal to give them a rise. But as the women and their union didn't go to the tribunal, not trusting it to accept their claim, its decision isn't legally binding. But it does make this a unique situation – even without the full support of the men in their factory, the women have wrung equal pay out of an employer not legally obliged to grant it.

To save face, the company isn't saying it's lost. The official announcement that the strike was over was ambiguously worded: 'Both union and employer agree that the terms of the Equal Pay Act have been complied with'; the company had claimed *that* all along. Apparently the ambiguity was also intended to stop the Department of Employment asking awkward questions about whether this was equal pay or an excessive pay rise.

The women are sure they've won, and want everyone to know it. And they've made other gains – a real community and a sense of solidarity with other workers. On Monday evenings they'll join the picket line at Grunwick's, and they're giving the mainly Asian strikers there half the proceeds of the victory social, and half their first weekly levy of 10p a head; the rest will go into a fighting fund to support future strikes.

And they plan regular factory meetings to support one another. '*Everyone* must come,' said Eileen Ward at the mass meeting where the offer was accepted. 'No one must ever stand alone again.' They have agreed to come out in protest if there's any victimization. 'There's been some aggro since we went back,' said Sally Groves, 'but not as much as you might expect – some of the worst left during the strike.'

'There's heaps of things to sort out now,' she added. 'All the differentials are up the creek, and a lot of men feel hard done by. It's really stirred up the factory.'

It caused quite a stir when two days after going back one woman applied to be a forklift truck driver. Management was horrified – they'd hoped 'women's lib' was left on the picket line. She got the job though, and starts training soon.

The clock-office clerks scored a victory too. They were out all along in solidarity, though they weren't affected by the claim, and as part of the settlement got an extra £1.50 a week. Come pay day, Atkins, the manager, tried to slide out of it, so they threatened to strike next morning. He paid up at once.

A Suspect Statistic: the Trico tribunal is officially listed as a success – because the applicant won!

SR.53, December 1976

Lesbians Ignite

ANNY BRACKX

Louise Boychuk's employers, city stockbrokers H.J. Symons Holdings, sacked her for wearing a 'Lesbians Ignite' badge in the office. She started proceedings against them for unfair dismissal.

The industrial tribunal hearing featured a desiccated panel chairman, who fancied himself as God's judicial administrator; a triple-chinned stockbroker, who consulted a dictionary to find out what a lesbian is; two lawyers in honourable opposition; a roomful of lesbian supporters, badges all over; and Louise, who in vain tried to hammer through to the panel that wearing a lesbian badge was a principled stand confirming her identity.

The tone was set from the beginning: 'Might there have been young girls, aged sixteen, just out of school, working with Miss Boychuk?' The defence avidly confirmed the chairman's suspicions.

It was easy, in this atmosphere of moral indignation, for the defence to put their case: to request Miss Boychuk to take off her badge was reasonable as she was 'displaying a wording at our place of business which is distasteful to others and which could be injurious to our best interests if observed by our clients, whose goodwill results in the earning of large amounts of overseas currencies beneficial to our country'. (Could it be true that lesbianism is tearing down British capitalism?)

Also the fleshy stockbroker didn't want to be 'the laughing stock of the Arab world'. Lending him a hand, in old boys' style, the chairman added that 'any firm is allowed to protect its reputation'.

'Miss Boychuk took no notice of the request,' the defence continued, and kept wearing her badge, even after being warned that she risked her job. As 'reasonable order' had to be maintained in a firm, it was not unfair, under those circumstances, to dismiss Miss Boychuk, the lawyer claimed.

Soon it transpired that Louise hardly ever saw any of the 'overseas currencies' carriers, that nobody in the firm had ever before taken offence at her wearing gay badges, and that there were no complaints about the quality of her work. The whole defence was built on speculation, and when questioned on this the stockbroker had to admit he had expressed 'an opinion'.

He also expressed his opinion on the subject of lesbianism; it is perverted, as confirmed by the dictionary. To leave no doubt about his own 'normality' he said he would not like to sit near a homosexual, while claiming in the same breath that he didn't dismiss Louise because of his prejudice against lesbians.

But prejudice is not the only reason for objecting to gayness, according to the chairman, who before had mumbled that the word 'gay' had been perverted. Referring to Genesis, he informed Louise that the Lord destroyed Sodom and Gomorrah. Fortunately her lawyer pointed out that this went beyond the prerogative of a tribunal and that in fact lesbianism is not illegal in this country.

Louise patiently carried on with her endeavours to explain that she wore gay badges as a symbol, so that people would not assume she was heterosexual and to show 'a real person behind the fearful word lesbian'. But in no way did the chairman see a real person: 'Aren't you really trying to encourage people to become lesbians; bringing other women into the cult?'

At this the audience gave him to understand that he should be practising in a sty, not a court.

Summing up, Louise's lawyer said that sacking somebody because she is openly a lesbian is as unfair as dismissing Jewish employees because of Arab boycotts.

The panel reserved judgement to a later date.

Louise Boychuk subsequently lost her case.

SR.54, January 1977

'We're Not Criminals': Prostitutes Organize

VICTORIA GREEN

Prostitutes in Birmingham are organizing to fight for decriminalization of prostitution [1977]. A group got together eighteen months ago to work out how sympathetic probation officers could be more useful to women on the streets. The prostitutes suggested a drop-in centre for informal advice and meetings. They produced a leaflet, Red Light, *giving legal and medical information and the address of the drop-in centre. Last summer PROS (Programme for the Reform of Soliciting Laws) began its campaign against the prostitution laws.*

'If the law was changed we could work together and be safe from attacks. Blokes think, "She's only an old pro, I can do what I like to her." ' Susan was talking about the dangers of being a prostitute. She has been working with the group since it began: 'I've been thinking about changing the law for years. We're not criminals but the law is always after us. We're picked up all the time, day after day. And now they're thinking of putting the fines up to £100. My friends say "We're on the streets to feed the kids; I can't pay that, they'll have to send me to prison." '

Carol is in PROS; she was sent to prison for three months last summer and her child was taken into care. Louise, who used to work for the probation service, went to see her in prison: 'Carol's a friend of mine and I know she's not a criminal. It enraged me that she was in there.'

Eileen used to be a probation officer, she teaches now. 'We started off trying to see how we could be more useful to the women on the streets. Malcolm, a solicitor, Ann, and four others formed a working nucleus. Ann left the scene after she had been to jail. The drop-in centre has made a lot of difference. The girls come along and we all work out what's to be done to change their situation.'

Susan was part of the group which persuaded the Balsall Heath Association, a local residents' organization, to let them have space to meet. 'They were frightened we'd use it as a brothel and that there'd be knifings or brawls; it's funny how people always think of that sort of thing when they think of us. We had to keep pressing them for months but we got it. Now we go before the Committee every three months to keep the room. And it's working, it's central to where we work and easy to get to. I used to think seeing probation officers was like seeing the headmaster, you'd have to sit up straight and all that. Now we talk about our rights and about how to change things. We're making a video film about our lives to try and educate probation officers and magistrates about prostitutes.'

But the police know about the centre, too. In theory prostitutes are free to meet, leaflet and campaign; but because the law labels them 'common prostitutes', they can be picked up at any time – it's a very unclear and oppressive situation. Susan was going to the centre one night: 'I saw the law outside sitting in its car; their headlights were shining on the door. Another night I left with my mate at about 11.30 and they picked us up after we'd walked down the street a bit. They charged us with "loitering", we pleaded not guilty but we lost. I never used to be charged with loitering, only with soliciting. They're there nearly every night, just driving about or sitting outside. We try to come and go in groups of four or five, but we can't always manage it.'

'It is a problem.' Louise is worried because 'it might put women off coming in. The centre makes the Vice Squad's job easier because they know they'll find prostitutes coming out.' And the group is always worried about losing its members; Susan is under threat of prison now. 'They pick you up a few times, they tot up the number of charges and then you're in court. You stand there while they say it's the eighteenth time. It all goes on your record.'

'The mere charge means you're a "common prostitute", which means you have three previous offences against you.' Eileen points out that prostitutes are the only people who have previous convictions used against them in court. (NB Men accused of rape *don't*.)

'We can't do anything right. If you walk down the road with a boyfriend he's accused of poncing. If you walk down the road alone you're picked up.' Susan has a friend whose husband left her with four children; she's been fined £35 for soliciting. 'Sometimes,' says Louise, 'the law actually forces women on to the streets. That woman is on social security. She has to earn the money for the fine or go to prison.'

We talked about the violence women suffer. 'Anne was beaten up, she had her leg broken. The police did nothing.' Louise thinks the police see violence as an occupational hazard for prostitutes. Susan has been in danger. 'There was this knifer around; in the end he killed Yvonne Kerr, her body was found in the river. Then the law wanted our help, they wanted us to watch out for him and give them information. They left us alone when they wanted us to help them get the bloke. We were terrified and we worked together for safety. I hired a room with some friends and when the law found out they raided us and that was that.'

'We want to publicize what it's really like for girls on the street.' Eileen believes 'the women themselves must do the talking or it's no good. We all take decisions together, it took us months to hammer out our programme. It's what the pros themselves want.'

'It's got to come from us, we know what's going on.' Susan laughs at the way people think about prostitutes: 'If you're a pro, people think you're somehow ill, or you don't wash or something. Blokes ask me, "Why are you doing this?" and I ask them why they drive around Balsall Heath picking us up.' Carol is scathing about liberals who see her as some sort of 'pathetic, stupid victim'. 'I just want to hustle in peace.'

PROS is opposed to any form of licensing system. 'When we were working on our programme, all the pros were against any regulation and against licensed brothels.' Eileen explains that 'they want to control their own lives and work without being intimidated by anyone.'

They are optimistic about the campaign. 'There are groups forming in Sheffield, Leamington and Leicester. They will distribute the bulletin we are bringing out this month. It will be a way for prostitutes to give their own views and we are putting a coupon in for women to send back if they want to join us. The bulletin will come out once a month and carry legal advice, news and medical information.' Eileen described the difficulties they had deciding on an address where they can be reached: 'There will be loads of nuts ready to harass; and of course the police can move in on any place used by "common prostitutes".'

They are all critical of feminists who haven't taken up the issue of the prostitution laws. Eileen and Louise agreed: 'We want women's liberation to think about the whole thing and discuss it, but not just *use* it. They have used the word "prostitute" in a really nasty way – about housewives, to sum up their idea of the exploited situation of women. But we need allies to lobby and to publicize our programme. And we need practical help, centres to meet in and money to run the campaign.'

SR.56, March 1977

Women Farmers in Zambia

BARBARA ROGERS

At the Chapula Irrigation Project in Zambia, the most successful farmers are women. The project's training manager, Margaret Lubinda, is known at the Lusaka headquarters as one of their best project staffers. Increasingly, women throughout the Chapula area are asking for training in the new techniques of food production.

For Zambia, as for practically all underdeveloped countries, the success or failure of these farmers will be crucial. Faced with an acute economic crisis because of falling copper prices, the Zambian government has declared agricultural self-sufficiency to be a priority in future development planning.

In most of Africa, according to studies done by the UN Economic Commission for Africa, the women do the bulk of the agricultural work. Zambia is no exception, and on the Chapula project almost all of those working in the fields are women, even where the primary tenant is registered as the man.

It has not been easy for the women. The first to be trained in the new techniques of irrigated vegetable production was fifty-three-year-old Rachel Mutoba. She told me that she was very proud of having been the pioneer when so many other women were unwilling to try it – others had followed, but only a year and a half later. Even the management had said that women wouldn't be able to do the work, but they had been forced to change their minds because she had done so well. I asked her why she had found the courage to be the first. 'Perhaps I was directed by God,' she answered.

Another of the early participants is forty-five-year-old Alexandrina Mkandu. She was working on her handsome rows of cabbages while I talked to her. She has been on the project for some seven or eight years now, and is quite clear about her ambitions for the future. She uses some of her income from the project to send her children to school, but otherwise every penny is saved. She is planning to buy chickens for a poultry unit and to further expand her capital. Her ultimate goal is to buy an irrigation pump of her own, at which point she will leave the project and develop another plot of her own nearer home, which she will cultivate with her whole family.

These women are fiercely independent: they were adamant that they controlled all the income from their plots, using it to feed, clothe and educate their children, and to send them to school. Alexandrina Mkandu had remarried while working on her plot, after the death of her first husband; her new husband had demanded that she leave the scheme and live off his earnings as a fish-trader. She told him that with eight children from her previous marriage, she simply could not afford to rely on this, and insisted on continuing.

Many of the women I met, both inside and outside the project itself, had no husbands to help them in their work; they were either unmarried or had husbands working in the mining towns of the Copperbelt. These women were not merely supporting their own children, but in several cases their brothers, sisters, parents and assorted other relatives. One project member I saw at her home; Agnes Chembo was supporting about thirty people, both adults and children, while receiving help from only two of them on her vegetable plot. She also built all the houses for them – again, not unusual in the area, where the women do much of the construction and maintenance of the buildings.

The women of the Chapula area are by no means limited to farming: perhaps 90 per cent of all the traders in the near-by Kalulushi market are women. Some are selling their own produce, but many of them specialize in commerce, buying foodstuffs from the Chapula project as well as individual farmers, taking the bus into town and reselling at a profit. I was introduced to two of the most successful traders. One, Lutha Mukabe, had a very impressive set of houses, granaries, chicken coops and her own van, which she drives between the farming area and the market. She supports two 'mothers' (an aunt would be counted as a mother) and employs three full-time workers to deal with her chickens and vegetable fields. She is clearly a successful manager, having started with a government loan for 100 chickens and, after repaying the loan, constantly reinvesting in her farming and commercial business. She had never joined the irrigation project; 'the work is too hard,' she said.

Despite the success stories, the women of Zambia have a long way to go. Though women traditionally work on the land, training in agricul-

ture is still seen as something for men, and women need unusual determination to break into that field instead of the 'home economics' for
which the men – especially international development personnel –
consider them most suited. Margaret Lubinda, in charge of horticul-
tural training at Chapula for people from all over Zambia, told me that
when she trained a few years ago, women in the Natural Resources
Development College had been expected to do nutrition, a 'safer' subject than agriculture; but this was changing now: 'Women are getting
more ambitious: they may be trying to challenge men.'

But the situation in Zambia is somewhat better than other African
countries. In several of the neighbouring countries, where the tradition
of women producing most of the food is at least as strong, there are no
places for them in agricultural training courses and no female agricultural advisers to work with the farmers at grass-roots level. With the
flight of many men to the nearest town – or, as in the case of Malawi, to
the mines in South Africa – the women are left alone to support whole
families. They face blatant discrimination by the policy-makers with
their glib claims to know better than the women where their place is.

SR.67, February 1978

6 EDUCATION

There can be no equality at work between men and women unless
there is equality of opportunity. But our education system offers a
semblance of equal opportunity rather than its reality. It
disadvantages all women compared to men, and it also discriminates
between women on class and race grounds. Working-class girls have
never been encouraged to further their education for the sake of it.
They have always received vocational education at school, which has
been geared to low-paid women's work, or to domestic work, and
only a token number continue into higher education.

In primary school the curriculum on paper may appear to be the
same for all, but teachers' expectations can create subtle and powerful
differences. The general tendency is to expect girls to be conformist,
helpful and to wipe the tables; boys are expected to be independent,
adventurous and unruly. School books offer sharply contrasting adult
models: women seen in a very narrow range of often home-based
activities, men in a wide range of important or exciting occupations.
The most severe difference comes at secondary-school level with the
streaming of boys into science and technical subjects and girls into
arts and domestic sciences. By the time of Advanced level exams,
there are more boys studying than girls, and the boys are taking
exams in more subjects.

When girls leave school, the majority who go into further education
learn typing and office skills. Some working-class girls who reject
this and the alternatives of factory or shop work, are advised to train
as nursery nurses who are lower paid, have longer hours and shorter
holidays than nursery teachers. One young woman who wanted to be
a social worker was told by the careers adviser at her school that she
should be a nursery nurse 'because she was working class' (SR.75).
There are less than a third of girls compared to boys on part-time
day-release or sandwich courses. Of the 5 per cent of girls who obtain
apprenticeships on leaving school, 80 per cent go into hairdressing

where the dropout and turnover rate is high because the apprentices 'are often treated little better than skivvies'. One young woman said in *Spare Rib* No. 68 that her employer seemed to think that because she was on a day-release course, his obligations were met and she received no training at work.

For girls who continue into higher education and academic work, the conflicts between masculinity and femininity continue. Women can feel divided in themselves between their emotions and their intellect, between what seem like feminine feelings and masculine ambitions. They can feel worthless despite their desire to continue learning and find it hard to feel motivated. The idea that women can be assimilated into the system of university education as it was in the nineteenth century when they were at last admitted has been handed down to the present. Its inadequacy is shown by the fact that only one third of university students are women, by the difference between job opportunities open to women and men graduates, and by the crisis in consciousness felt by women students in the sixties which contributed to the beginning of the women's liberation movement. Women have become aware of bias in the way subjects are perceived, structured and taught. Sara Maitland wrote that it was even more important for women to overturn the whole of a subject's perspective in order to see it in relation to women than to try to insert women into the gaps where they had been left out: 'Women's history . . . is riddled with mysteries, inconsistencies and unanswered questions. Even more damning than the unanswered questions are the questions that are never even asked' (*SR.13*). Out of this questioning, women's studies emerged, to research into different areas and to look at women's relation to present society.

Women's studies began outside the state education system, in evening classes and summer schools or informal study groups. They broke from the hierarchy of teacher and taught. Women students had as much to say and explore about what it meant to be a woman as the woman tutor. Expectations were examined along with ideas. The dynamic was away from competitiveness and towards 'an atmosphere that is supportive both intellectually and emotionally'. Women have succeeded in taking women's studies into the university curriculum, but not without a fight. As Mary Moyer wrote: 'Departments and universities have been slow to accept – much less welcome – a development which threatens the traditional approach to learning' (*SR.15*). But teachers of women's studies are now facing the problem of whether their courses, by being incorporated into the exam system,

lose the original aims and become just another subject. Liz Waugh
wrote, 'What are we to conclude if a girl "fails" Women's Studies.
That she's not a good feminist?' (*SR.75*).

Feminist Subversion

MARGARET EDNEY

The John Clark Academy is a summer school for American students. It tries to be a summer school with a difference:

The aim of the JCA Educational centre is to create courses and educational materials which allow the participants to discover for themselves the use of conceptualization, for the understanding of the situations they are in and the phenomena they encounter. The idea is to show conceptions of the world which liberate and add to perception and experience rather than constrain and stultify. Participants are taught how to think rather than what to think; and they are encouraged to become actively involved and utilize a wide range of their talents and skills and perceptions rather than to be passive recipients. For this reason every course includes considerable use of the field seminar which is designed to provoke and then analyse the nature of response. (*JCA Prospectus*)

The scheduled courses are approximately five weeks and are residential. University accommodation throughout the country is utilized since a comprehensive tourist trip of England is part of the deal, although the major part of the time is spent in Yorkshire. Courses in archaeology, architecture, cinema, the mood of the times, the novel, culture and society, etc. are offered and students usually sign on for two or more.

The Academy was started some years ago by some friends who saw it eventually funding a large community project. This year, they decided that liberating experiences weren't quite enough and that some radical content was needed to season the brew. So, partly because they wanted to give some jobs to the girls and partly because it was fashionable and partly because they supported (in a myopic fashion) women's liberation, a course called 'Women in Society' was added to the syllabus. Tricia Langton and I were asked to be tutors for the course and we accepted, knowing that, to some extent, we were being used but hoping that we might also do some using. We wanted to see what could be done in such a short space of time and we had lofty ideas of preparing an all-purpose women's liberation education kit. We also entertained fantasies of self-help clinics and women's centres being part of the eventual community project.

Since the JCA needed a prospectus of the course, our initial approach was formal and we set out a list of seminars as follows:

Seminars 1,2. Introduction. The fundamental questions, who oppresses women? In what ways are women oppressed? Are women the most fundamentally oppressed and hence potentially the most revolutionary group in society? What is women's concrete situation in contemporary society?

Seminars 3,4,5. Historical and cross-cultural study. Case studies including underdeveloped countries: US, Britain, France, Ireland, South Africa, Algeria, Vietnam, China, Cuba and Russia.

Seminars 6,7. Women in contemporary British society. Economic position, ideological position and political roles.

Seminars 8,9. Physiology and Psychology. The female stereotype and its validity. The wife–mother syndrome. The spinster. The lesbian. Alternative roles.

Seminar 10. Women and commercial exploitation. Advertising, TV, and films.

Seminar 11. Woman in control of her own body. Abortion. Contraception. Sterilization.

Seminar 12. The women's movement in Britain and the future. Plus suggested background reading: *Women's Estate* by Juliet Mitchell, *The Second Sex* by Simone de Beauvoir, *Sisterhood is Powerful*, *The Body Politic*, *The Origin of the Family*, *Private Property and the State* by F. Engels, *The Dialectics of Sex* by Shulamith Firestone, *The Female Eunuch* by Germaine Greer, *Women, Resistance and Revolution* by Sheila Rowbotham and *Women and the Subversion of the Community* by Maria Rosa Dalla Costa.

A couple of weeks before the start of the summer school, a planning weekend was arranged and we met some more new members of staff who had been brought in to tutor courses in English education (with emphasis on the open classroom). There were five men and one woman, all much older than us. They were education specialists and had a different conception of, and approach to, learning since they had all spent years as teachers, headmasters, etc. The 'Women in Society' course was a puzzle to them and they were apprehensive about assigning a role to Tricia and me. They alternated between patronizing us and totally ignoring us. At one meeting where the idea of the students meeting immigrant workers (male) as part of their environmental studies was mooted, we pointed out that there were also female immigrants with even more difficult problems. 'Of course, yes, we'll have a woman as well, yes of course, what a good idea – how could we have forgotten it.' For them, our casual style of dress and our independent behaviour were 'such a pity in such nice girls'. Chivalry and protection were their main methods of approach. They rushed to open doors, pay for drinks and leapt to their feet when we entered a room. However when it came to deciding what to do, arranging schedules or discussing projects, all consideration for us fled. They tried to control and dominate. Lip service only was paid to our course. In one breath they would be saying 'how interesting' and in the next calling a girl a nymphomaniac. When the word was objected to they said testily, 'Oh well, replace it with sexually liberated girl then.' We felt we had to assert ourselves since neither we nor the course were being taken seriously. We were fripperies – the icing on the cake. So we became difficult and aggressive to counteract this image, which resulted in us being laughed at as the 'women's libbers', since their desire to categorize us, pigeon-hole us (and then forget us) was so strong. This strengthened our desire to confront and upset their bureaucratic attitudes; we had become stereotypes and had lost our identity. So we rebelled – we went for a walk in the garden instead of going to meetings – we ordered the wildest, most expensive things on the menu – we laughed at them openly – we were generally subversive. 'You have certainly made it clear that you are women', we were told, at the end of the weekend.

Alison Fell, *SR.43*, February 1976

Their over-authoritarianism and their refusal to break down the pupil–teacher relationship provoked us into altering our conception of the course. Total informality was our theme and we now felt it import-ant to relate to all the women in the school, not just those assigned to 'Women in Society'. We would try to make our presence felt at all times and to relate what we were trying to say to all the courses, to weave a contrapuntal, if subversive, theme. After all, this should complement the open education philosophy of the school.

The first seminar was at Oxford. There were over sixty students, mostly women, with an age-range of sixteen to eighty and with very different aims and expectations. Twelve had signed on for the 'Women in Society' course. In the first seminar we discussed endlessly what we thought our approach would be. Firstly, to try and get rid of the desk and chairs, the hierarchical lecture set-up and replace it with a more relaxed grouping. Then to explain that we thought a fairly informal structure would be more appropriate for the course since it would give us space to get to know each other's consciousness. Formal lectures were already assigned, and we would be available at all times for discussion and as potential resource material. We wanted the main emphasis to be on a conscious analysis of one's own direct experience.

It would be patently absurd for two women to sit and lecture another group of women about their role in society. Every waking minute of their lives they experienced the slights, insults, hurts, oppressions (and occasional delights) of being women. By talking together, raising the surface discontents and reactions to each other, and exploring our common experience we could work towards a rediscovery of ourselves. The pupil–teacher relationship would dissolve and with it hopefully the inertia of the passive student who merely takes in and does not give out. They might begin to question what they were doing and what was happening. For example, why were the students mostly women and the teachers mostly men at the Academy? How did the men relate as teachers to the women? What kind of attitudes did they display? What kind of relationship or dynamic was set up? Clearly, this was a bit difficult for the women to adjust to immediately, so for the rest of the seminar, I talked . . . about the lack of female identity, in the sense that it is imposed from outside, about the contradictory images put out by the media – pretty, silly, sexy, childish, inefficient, but also perfect mother; about the family, its relationship to the state and its maintenance of patriarchy. Gradually the women joined in the discussion and the seminar extended as argument raged. 'But I like men opening doors for me,' wailed one woman. 'Well, for every door I've had opened, there've been ten slammed in my face,' retorted another. We had started.

Reasons for coming to the summer school seemed to be varied. They were all teachers or training to be teachers, so it was possible to pick up some graduate credits (which mean salary increments). Some had come for a good time or to pick up an English husband/lover, others to absorb English culture or try a new experience and still others who took the courses seriously.

Jean Gardiner came and gave an invited lecture on Women and the Economy which seemed to shock and horrify a lot of the students who were comparatively well-off. The school then de-camped, first to York University and then to Bradford University. Tricia and I moved in with them for two weeks. The students had a very full schedule, apart from lectures, seminars, education workshops and field trips, there were numerous excursions and social events. We asked the women to try and meet us for a small period each day, apart from our assigned seminars, to assess and analyse our experiences. We wanted them to observe, listen and question, all the time – to become *agents provocateurs* in a sense. Meanwhile, we tried to be always available and always prepared to talk. We kept sherry and biscuits in our rooms so that women could come in for a drink and chat whenever they felt like it. We drove buses, we participated in all the excursions, field trips and social occasions, and we took part in as many other seminars and workshops as possible.

Older married women responded to us immediately and told us of their struggles to keep their jobs and bring up families and their triumph at leaving their husbands to come to Europe on their own. With most of the women of our own age there was a more gradual identification as we tentatively discussed sexuality and emotional problems. They talked endlessly about their oppression in school by a male-dominated staff-control structure. No interest at all was shown by the few women dedicated to the sexual competitive stakes, in fact there was sometimes hostility since we were, in their eyes, potential competitors. We used mealtimes for extra discussion, although hampered by the familiar breakfast scene of some man or other drawing up his chair and saying, 'What women's liberation *ought* to do . . .' or 'I think women's liberation is wonderful but why aren't you thinking about men?' After a week I made a badge saying, 'I eat men for breakfast.' 'Tsk, tsk, how aggressive,' they replied.

Within the university we asked the women to talk to the cooks, the cleaners, and the bed-makers and to watch how they were treated by the men. Also to scrutinize the running of the JCA itself, to notice over-loaded secretaries being asked to dial telephone numbers for men who were idly tapping their own big, strong fingers. On field trips to villages and towns we asked them to try and establish female profiles. Where were the women, what were they doing and what was their relation to the community? The other tutors had asked them to pick up bits of brick and leaves, to do charcoal rubbings of manhole covers and to photograph ducks. We suggested they find out the population, sex, age, class ratios, the recreation facilities, available transport, shops, prices, nurseries, schools, ranges of goods and work prospects. School visits could be used to answer who plays with who, who sits next to who, who teaches who and what is being taught. By the time we visited a Bradford wool mill, there was no need to indicate what to question: the infernal incessant noise, the choking fumes and the appalling wages were all too self-evident.

Our dialogue with the educationalists continued as we moved in on their craft workshops. The general idea was that you used any medium to explore some aspects of the field trips. This was not actually our scheduled province as we were supposed to be using the time to prepare our own seminars. By participating as students with the students we hoped to demystify the idea of us being teachers. Having collected all the local newspapers, we cut out everything we could find about women and made wall newspapers around the themes, work, leisure and home, which tried to point out some of the contradictions (like the part-time jobs offered which were, in fact, a six-hour day). We also made comic strips, diagrams of Bradford facts and figures and a giant cartoon. Surreptitiously, women left their own education project work to help us and when it was finished we covered the foyer of the main dining-room with our efforts. 'Well, you certainly work hard, whatever else . . .' was the male tutor's comment. Later on some of the displays were ripped down although no one would say why.

The film course also provided a forum for discussion. The tutor interpreted the films we watched in terms of Jungian archetypes (man seeking salvation fleeing from devouring mother). This was rejected quite violently by a lot of the women who saw it as women fighting desperately to get out of oppressive material circumstances but ultimately being crushed and destroyed. After much pressure *The Salt of the Earth* was shown. It's about a strike in New Mexico which only succeeds when women join the struggle. Cheers, clapping and stamps of applause went on throughout the film and afterwards the women supported it vehemently against attacks by male students and tutors.

In social situations we made a point of dancing together, of buying drinks, of commandeering buses and cars, of leaving field trips early so that we could go out for tea and buns or of skipping workshops to go shopping instead. This was to show that women could enjoy themselves together and not be dependent on men in social situations. At Batley Variety Club where we were taken en masse for a night out, we had to sit through a cabaret full of sexist and racist jokes. As a reaction we took over the small dance floor and had a wonderful time – sixty slightly drunk and very happy women really bopping and enjoying each other's company.

When the school moved to London we asked Sheilà Rowbotham to talk on the history of the women's liberation movement but to relate it to her own history and to her move from Yorkshire to the south and the differences and problems when encountered. Most of the women said they felt a lot of identification with what Sheila said. They had experienced the cultural and environmental differences between the north and the south but more immediate was their understanding of Sheila's description of awakening sexuality, attitudes to men, and confusion over what society wanted her to be and what she felt she was.

The school was nearly at an end and there was a weekend in which to accomplish whatever project work the tutors required. We suggested a collective attempt at a newspaper which we could print and hand out at the leaving party. It was tackled with great enthusiasm once we had shown them how to lay out etc. and its distribution created quite a stir at the party – 'wonderful' said the women, 'not as hasty as we thought it might be,' said the men.

Was it worth the total exhaustion and shattered nerves we now felt? What had we learned? What had the students learned? Well, there was plenty of response, not just from the women who had signed up for the course but from women throughout the school who felt free to join our seminars and meetings whenever they could. Similarly there was a great deal of social response from everyone and a genuine delight in all female subversive activities. Discussions were intense and when personal histories were revealed a great deal of warmth and solidarity were generated. One student said it had changed her whole outlook on life, others were excited at having discovered collective activity and were making plans to produce their own newspaper in the States and yet others were totally unmoved.

The book list has been a mistake since no one looked at it nor did they use the magazine and pamphlet stall that we maintained. This could have been a reflection of cultural differences which we hadn't really thought out beforehand such as, quite an advanced type of bourgeois-feminist consciousness going hand-in-hand with reactionary social attitudes. A world-view was lacking in their approach to life. Women's liberation had meant to them wild, bra-burning shriekers. They were more at home with NOW (National Organization of Women) which is a liberal civil rights type movement. Our relative gentleness surprised them and made them reconsider their attitudes.

Quite clearly, the internal structure of the course wasn't thought out well enough, although fortunately we were able to learn as we went along and adapt our approach. Women can't just suddenly open up and think creatively or raise their consciousness if they've been educated and trained to keep their minds closed. The balance between formal lecturing and informal discussion has to be carefully worked out. Our fundamental mistake was not to realize that our informal structure had to work within a rigidly formal structure. Our casual attitudes were interpreted as meaning that we were not to be taken seriously. As tutors we were given the worst times in a crowded time-table, the times that nobody else wanted, the times when the students were exhausted. We were given least resources and least consideration. The decision that Tricia and I took to share the course, although it meant sharing the salary, proved to be correct. From the outset, we had insisted that it be a joint venture but the school understood this to be doing half each – in terms of time. We had to fight to be allowed to work together and throughout the course it was vitally important in terms of our solidarity and sanity. We are still receiving letters from some of the women and that in itself makes it worthwhile but I won't forget the huge bunches of flowers they gave us when they left. We both wept.

SR.20, February 1974

NEWSHORT

Seven thirteen-year-old girls at Altwood Comprehensive in Maiden-head raised a 100-signature petition and threatened to report their headmaster to the EOC when he tried to push them out of a car-maintenance class. Headmaster Maurice Edwards claimed the class was over-subscribed but the girls told him 'You have a mixed class or none at all.' He checked the law and gave in – it's large, and mixed.

SR.71, June 1978

Schoolgirls up against Sexism

DEBRA PEART, TWELVE YEARS, LEEDS

I have recently moved to Leeds and am attending a middle school.
During my time here I have been put out a little by the attitudes of
some of the teachers towards the girls. In the games lessons the girls
have a choice: rounders, tennis and sometimes volley ball in the

Caroline Jackson

summer, and in the winter hockey and netball. But the boys have a
much more varied choice: rounders, tennis, softball, volley ball and
cricket in the summer, and rugby or football in the winter. A lot of the
girls fancy cricket and football, and even rugby. The boys laugh at us –
it's not surprising really. They would win in a game because no one
will teach us. My friend and I decided to ask our games master if we
could learn. I saw him in the dinner line, and I asked him about the
girls playing football etc. He gave a surprising answer. 'Have you been
listening to the radio?' 'No,' I said. 'Well, as long as I'm running the

games around here, the girls won't do any of the boys' games.' He then walked off. It's impossible to say anything to our headmaster, as he's a male chauvinist pig as well.

But even if we cannot play football we are expected to read about it. When we were given our class reading book, the class went in uproar – the girls did anyway. The book was called *The Goalkeeper's Revenge*, and when sifting through it, I saw a paragraph saying, 'This book is for boys, about boys. Rugby, fighting, trolley driving and football.' That is typical of my school's opinion on girls – we are classed second, while the boys must have what suits them.

Although there are mixed classes for needlework, cookery and wood-work, the work we do is different. In needlework, the girls have to make aprons, and the boys make ties or cravats. This is stupid, because both boys and girls need aprons for cookery. So when we asked the teacher the reason for this, she replied, 'The girls are willing to stay in at breaks and finish their aprons, while the boys would like to go out and play football.'

I would like the opportunity next year to do all subjects which I am interested in but I am barred from at present. Instead I am being guided towards girl subjects which usually end up in family care and childcare. I know there is a recognizable movement against all these things which degrade us and exclude us. Soon something's going to happen to make it right for us, but it may take time.

JENNY SMITH, FOURTEEN YEARS, MIDDLESEX

I am at a mixed grammar school, and when I first came here, I didn't think it was particularly sexist, as I had come from a very sexist junior school, where girls were taught they should play with dolls, and boys to be Big and Tough (and beat each other up).

So the sexism at my new school did not seem so blatant, because the boys were allowed to do cookery and needlework, and the girls do woodwork and metalwork. However I soon discovered that sexism gets everywhere. In my first week we had a history lesson in which were were learning about Mohammed and Islam. The (male) teacher asked me if I would like to be a Muslim. I said no, and he asked why. Apart from the fact that I am an atheist and saw no reason to change my religion, I said that I did not agree with purdah and male chauvinism. He said, 'Are you one of those women's libbers, then, girl?' I said yes, to which he replied, 'Oh mah gawd, we've got a right one 'ere.' I thought I must be some sort of crank because everyone, including the other girls, laughed. I only had a vague idea of what 'women's lib was, but I knew I supported it because the 'women's libbers' everyone hated were the only people who didn't just want to stop me doing things I considered worthwhile just because I was a girl.

There's a history teacher at our school who never stops insulting women. He says we never stop 'gossiping' – he never shuts up himself. Once in a lesson on Nazi Germany he told us how clever Hitler was to stop all married women from working, because it solved unemployment, and that the British government should do the same thing. Recently he gave us a test, and worked out that the average boy's mark was 1.5 higher than the average girl's. He said this proved that men are superior to women. How stupid can you get?

In an art lesson once the (female) teacher said: 'Today we are going to draw aeroplanes. The ladies [sic] may like to draw birds instead.' I drew an aeroplane. In a geography lesson, the (male) teacher complained about my untidy map, saying, 'I thought girls were supposed to be able to draw neatly.' And there are innumerable examples of teachers making this sort of remark.

At my school the headteacher, the deputy head, and the heads of block are all males. There's a senior mistress, but no senior master, presumably because they think the head will always be a man, anyway. All the senior mistress does is to tell the girls off for wearing the wrong colour blouse or something. Last year, all the fourth-year girls had to attend a lecture on the follies of wearing high-heeled shoes. The boys didn't have to go! To make this even more patronizing, the lecturer was a man. If this happens again next year (when I'm in the fourth year) we shall try to organize a boycott.

Obviously most text books are sexist. I once went through my school physics book and counted eighty pictures of people doing experiments. Only one of these was a girl, all the rest were male. In the series of French books used at our school from first to fifth year, the girls are always shown staying at home helping their mothers with the housework, while the boys are out fishing, and their fathers are at work. Other text books, and teachers, constantly refer to the human race as 'Man'. If you ask why, they reply that it means women too. Of course it doesn't. Man means men, and has nothing to do with the other half of the human race which is female.

There is a great deal of opposition to feminism among the pupils as well as the staff. The boys just laugh at it, and often make it clear that they don't like us trespassing on male preserves like the metalwork room. While the girls are afraid of being ridiculed if people think they are 'women's libbers' – they never say feminist.

When I ask people why they are sexist, they always say that people are different, and if we had equality, everyone would be the same. (The usual Tory line.) They don't seem to realize that the individuality of women – and men too – is suppressed by the sexism which flourishes under capitalism. Obviously at an old-fashioned grammar school like mine, you'd expect to find rigid attitudes, but there is sexism in *every* school. The way it is drummed into us is indeed what some people actually mean by education. Judging by the attitudes of people my own age, and the way we are being conditioned at school, sexism is definitely alive and kicking, and will survive for a long time to come.

SR.75, October 1978

It's Trousers Time!

SUSAN HEMMINGS

The problem at Isabel, Jayne and Sylvia's junior school is basically with a very strict headmistress who doesn't like girls in trousers. If they wear them, she gives them a good telling off. When common sense prevailed on her to let them wear them through the snow to school, she still insisted that when they arrived they had to change into skirts. And if it was *very* cold in school, they could wear the trousers . . . with a skirt over them!

Most of the teachers at this junior school are women, and they wear trousers. They don't want to tell the girls off, but *they'll* get into trouble if they don't make them change. And most of the mothers, too, like their girls in trousers at home, and don't really see why they shouldn't wear them to school, but definitely don't want their girls breaking school rules.

One day this October, Isabel, Jayne and Sylvia decided enough was enough, and made a plan with their friends to all turn up in trousers the next day. They all had sleepless nights worrying if the others would be able to, and, sure enough, several parents put a stop to it. Still, those three and a couple of others managed to wear them, and two of them kept them on all day. 'At lunchtime we felt really sick, because the head walks about then and can see us. We kept behind the other girls. Other children kept saying to us, why are you wearing them? Are we allowed? And we said, we want to. The thing is, everyone is so scared of getting into trouble. Lots of them agree with us – but they won't take the risk of getting told off.' It is difficult in junior schools – especially for the fourth- (final) year students, whose behaviour record goes forward to secondary school and might affect their chances there.

They don't dislike wearing skirts. 'But you can't do so many things in them. You can't run or climb, because you have to wear special shoes with skirts, you can't just wear plimsolls. Skirts blow around in the playground, and the boys are always lifting them up. In trousers you can sit more comfortably on the floor. Your legs are protected when you fall over. You are generally much freer.' They've been told that if they wore trousers, they'd get the hems wet on the toilet floors . . . and that they'd get sweaty . . . 'Well, if all those things are true, boys should wear shorts.'

In any case they don't agree with being told what to wear. 'They're just trying to get us trained for when we have to wear uniform at secondary school, and we don't agree with that either. It's got nothing to do with what you learn or how you behave.' They are considering ways to get more support for their trousers protest, especially from mothers and teachers. 'Even people who don't want us to break rules should see that it's a nonsense rule, and if they don't want it broken, it should be changed.'

SR.89, December 1979

Ten Ways to Counter Sexism in a Junior School

SALLY SHAVE

1 I teach on a one-to-one basis. It's exhausting, but it lessens the need for the children to conform.

2 I dress and behave in school, and use the same language and mannerisms as I do in the community, with parents and friends, hoping to lessen the gap between school and home.

3 I've made sure the school purchased and uses a varied reading scheme consisting of non-sexist books. And we always discuss the sexism in traditional stories, like *Cinderella*, and often reverse the roles in such stories.

4 I never, even for the slightest convenience, divide the children into boys and girls, for any activity.

5 I never co-operate with other teachers' requests for 'Four strong boys to move these boxes, please.' I train the girls to lift and carry – very difficult at first.

6 I introduced and encourage mixed sports. The boys love mixed netball and hate mixed football.

7 In sewing and cookery which the boys do I always oppose suggestions that the boys will grow up homosexual (by parents or children) by asking why this would be such a bad thing anyway.

8 The children change for PE and swimming in mixed sex groups.

9 I encourage the girls to wear jeans and easygoing clothes and to get dirty if necessary.

10 We have discussions on sex, family life, and different ways of life in the community. I never give them the 'beauty of sex and the mystery of life' talk.

SR.75, October 1978

Acting it Out

JASMINE, DIANE, CYNTHIA, LINDA, DAWN

. . . Although we'd noticed sexism, and thought it unfair, it wasn't that which made us angry at first. What really pissed us off, very early on in this school, was streaming. Right from the beginning the teachers started calling us thick. Yes, they tell you outright, to your face. 'Has anyone ever told you you're thick?' Fucking hell! What *is* this? We've been really angry and upset, and this has been going on for five years. And then they have the nerve to write on your report that your trouble is you've no confidence. Well, how the hell could we have confidence? And when we were confident, about the play, they told us off for being big-headed. So it all started with that, with being labelled thick.

Our school has eight streams. When you come into this school, if you're Black, or working-class white, or coloured, or Greek or Turkish Cypriots, you automatically get put into the lower streams. Recently a girl of fourth-year age came back again to this area from spending some time in Jamaica. The teacher said to one of us who is Black, 'What stream are you in?' On hearing it was stream four, he said, 'Yes, that's the one I was thinking of for her', and that was it! Sometimes a Black person, or a white working-class one, might make it into a higher stream. The other children can't believe it. 'What's that thickie doing in here?' Our new headmaster says he's going to end streaming, and we hear people say all the time, 'Thank goodness we're not coming into the new first form. I'd hate to be taught with all the thickies.' And we've got a teacher at the moment who's just told us that people who don't get 'A' levels are boring people.

We've had nothing but this sort of thing all the time – racist comments, thickies, dunces. We reckoned we'd start with a play on sexism, and if we can get that out, maybe it's a start on getting the whole thing out. Sexism, racism, streaming and class – it's all the same system, and it's all got to come out . . .

SR.85, August 1979

No More School Meals

JILL NICHOLLS

. . . The government's Education Bill, published on 26 October and now going through committee, leaves it entirely up to local authorities to decide what meals and milk to provide. All they would have to offer would be a place for children to eat packed lunches. You'll be glad to know that the Bill explicitly states that they 'would not be empowered to charge pupils bringing their own food'. Great!

For children from families claiming supplementary benefit or family income supplement, local authorities would have to 'ensure that any necessary provision was made for them in the middle of the day', free of charge. But this qualifying level is much lower than at present, so half a million children who now get free meals would no longer be entitled to them. And the Bill does not specify what 'necessary provision' is – 'I hope they provide more than a bowl of soup and an apple,' says Mr Carlisle, but his Bill does not insist that they do . . .

SR.89, December 1979

Diary of a Feminist Teacher

KATE ELLIOTT

In May last year, Kate Elliott took on a part-time 'supply' teaching job in a girls' comprehensive school. Much of her work was in social studies, with a group of fourth-year girls waiting to leave. This group disliked school intensely, and were locked in a mutual antagonism with most of the teachers.

Kate decided to keep a diary of her progress with this class, because she felt that the power relationships between herself and the girls were some-thing she wanted to work out within the context of her commitment to feminism. These are some of the extracts from the notebook she kept.

1977 May

The hostility met me like a perspex wall – twenty-three individual versions of it.

Me: I hear you've had quite a rough time this year.

Yvonne: We're the class they all talk about in the staffroom – like that Miss Robinson. We give her hell.

Trisha: No good giving me detentions, I've got ten a week already – can't fit any more in.

Yvonne: Can we stand up in your class? Like we get really bad if they try to make us sit down in rows.

Margaret was combing her hair, her back towards me. Most of the others were talking to each other. So I thought, they're testing me, keep calm . . . but I've done ten years in this job, and what have I learnt? Who am I?

Me: Look, we've got nine weeks together and I've no wish for it to be hell every lesson. Why shouldn't you walk around? I do. Stand on your heads if you need to. We need to talk to each other. We don't know each other.

Although Kate's job was supposed to end after those nine weeks, it was offered again to her from the next September, and so she became their teacher again, this time in their fifth and final year of compulsory schooling. And so she continued her diary.

1977 September

Youth unemployment now began to force its way into the consciousness of the girls.

Eileen: What's the point of doing all this work in school? It isn't going to make it any more likely I'll get a job. I've got three friends with 'O' levels and CSEs who are Black like me, and they're all un-employed. They'll just have me up for an interview with six white girls, they'll see me . . . and it's the Blacks who get no jobs.

It seems to me that the whole 'education debate' has successfully deflected criticism away from who controls industry, and from the economic crisis (of which youth and Black unemployment are two aspects), on to the schools, seeing the blame as the failure of teachers to provide young people with the 'correct' skills and attitudes for the 'needs of industry'.

Streaming divides up the girls in this school in both obvious and subtle ways, and the girls themselves have ambivalent attitudes to it. This group regard the top streamers as foolish, giving too much time and effort to the school. Yet it isn't unusual for bottom streamers to spend whole evenings working on school projects which interest them. Girls in the top stream regard the others as disruptive and unwilling to learn, yet envy them for their time and boyfriends. But for all of them the illusion of choice of employment is maintained, in spite of the fact that neither 'O' levels nor CSEs are guarantees against setbacks and disappointments under the current unemployment situation.

At about this time Kate began to talk to other teachers who might be feeling the same way as she did. Most sympathy was to be found among teachers in the English and Remedial departments, and not insignificantly this arose out of their focus upon *talking* in the classroom.

1977 October

This is an all-girls school, but the girls were always focusing their attention on boys.

Una (while working on a project about housing): Miss, what would you wear to go with a brown pleated skirt?

Me: Why?

Una: There's this dishy boy who's not like the ordinary ones, slobbing around in jeans – he wears suits and he's smart.

Me: Why not dress as you usually do?

Una: I've got to impress him – you've got to catch him first.

Yvonne and Trisha arrived ten minutes later.

Me: Hey, you're taking me for granted because I'm nice to you.

Trisha: What do you mean? Now you look here, Miss. We're only ten minutes late. You should think yourself lucky, we're ever so good to you. Look at all this work – pages and pages.

(*She showed me her project and Yvonne did the same.*)

Me: You mean I'm privileged because it's only ten minutes, and that I should count my blessings?

Trisha: Yes, you expect too much.

I am very aware of the problem of my control over them. I view it as

*part of my work to enable them to make a critical examination of their
position and mine. I don't want them to see me as one of their pals, because
that could blur their awareness of all the structures in school which reproduce power relationships, dominating them here, at home and in their
future work. If you discuss explicit aspects of domination with the girls,
you are immediately viewed as a subversive by the prevailing hierarchy
here.*

1978 January

Elizabeth came boiling into the lesson.

Elizabeth: Miss, did you see *The South African Experience* on TV?
I was so angry. The way the Blacks are treated there. This woman
was given the sack after twenty-three years and no reason, and the
white man in the car factory saying the Blacks live like that. Well, my
mum's a nurse, and she has to bow to the matron above her, treated
like dirt because she's Black, and she's brought me up never to take it.
If I was in South Africa I'd want to fight. I'm not just angry – I can't
explain how I feel. I'd just want to explode. I know not all the Blacks
even want a revolution, but me, I would. I'd want to die for it. But
they wouldn't let me in – they only let whites in. And they put us down
over here as well. I know you shouldn't lump all whites together, but
we're all lumped together, especially here in school. I don't agree with
fighting for the sake of it – you've got to know what you're fighting for.

*This was the first time that she had explained her ideas so strongly and
we met here emotionally and intellectually in a way not previously
achieved. How can I make this happen more frequently?*

*Elizabeth is called the following things in the staffroom: troublemaker,
disruptive, thick, thoroughly unpleasant, remedial, immature. Two weeks
later: Elizabeth is suspended for a fortnight, following an incident of
'unco-operativeness' in another lesson. Her English teacher and I negotiate
on her behalf whenever we can. Decide who you are, find others like you,
and then fight.*

1978 February

Linda: Miss, if one of us was to tell you she was pregnant, what
would you do?

Me: I'd help her all I could. Why?

Linda: Would you tell her parents for her?

Me: Yes, I'd go to the clinic as well. I'd do whatever I could.

Linda: Well, we've been going together for two years. My doctor would kill me, he said to go on the Pill after I was sixteen, but I never did. My boyfriend says he'll stand by me – we're engaged, but . . . I don't know. I just had to tell somebody.

Later: Linda has now found out that she is not pregnant. She left at Easter as she'd already been promised a job as a dental nurse, which she'd been doing on Saturdays for ages. Most of the girls already do a great deal of domestic work, taking a very large part in running the home along with their working mothers. All have a large amount of it built into their lives, and some, like Una, run their homes without a mother. Most are anticipating early marriage and motherhood in spite of the resistance they already feel to these stereotypes.

Eileen: We have lots of housework to do. Every night me and Angela take turns with the washing up. It's me tonight.

Me: Do the boys do it?

Eileen and Frances: No! They don't do anything – we do it all. I often think it's us waiting on them while they watch TV. We've always had to do it.

Now the group is splitting into Easter leavers, and those who are staying to take the June CSE exam. The first group mark time – school is even more irrelevant. They are making some tape recordings about their feelings about school, and what they expect of the future. And the second group are slogging away at revision. This means we are controlled by the imminence of the exam, and have no more time for free discussions.

1978 March

We've got problems over the tape recording. The girls had talked about their past, present and future sexuality and the head has asked me to stop this work, on the grounds that further taping would be construed as deliberately soliciting this material. All radical teachers walk on a tightrope, and feminist teachers trying, like me, to create spaces with young women to talk about our own issues and problems face a particularly painful and exhausting struggle.

1978 May

The revision group is now approaching their exam – it's half term and we're all at screaming point. So we've changed back again to a less constraining content, using role play as our revision method, and this has, on the surface, eased our situation.

Last lesson: a visit to the Old Bailey. And on the steps of St Pauls, they hand me a card saying, 'Remember us? Love from . . .'

1978 June

We are beginning to form a women's group among the teachers here. When we first put up a notice about it in the staffroom, a male colleague replaced it by a clever negative cartoon. One of the men had drawn a picture of a group of women tied on to chairs with books on their laps, with the captions, 'Shoulder to Shoulder' and 'Forced Reading' – there was little doubt who those women were meant to be.

Our group now consists of open and closed meetings. We have designed a liberal studies (women's studies) course which includes the study of misconceptions of women, violence, work, domestic labour, and other cultures. The closed group, of about six, meets for consciousness raising, and it looks as though another parallel group may start.

The girls we have worked with have been crucial in the formation of our group identity – and the contradiction is that these girls are not part of our group. Nor are the other women workers in the school. I want to do something about that. But in any case, we are at the beginning of an exciting new phase.

SR.75, October 1978

[*Kate Elliott now calls herself Caeia March. Ed.*]

Korbet, from 'Women and Education', *SR.67*, February 1978

Working with Girls

VAL CARPENTER

. . . Youth work means working and building relationships with young people, either in particular clubs or premises like schools, church halls, etc., or in places where young people go, like pubs, street corners, or wherever they happen to be. The problem is that not only do girls stay away from youth clubs, they also don't hang around street corners, so they are almost invisible in the youth service.

. . . Once you become a committed feminist, boys start to react to you more aggressively. If you show them your attitude towards their sexism, their knowledge of your feminism can increase the violence you want to dispel. We learnt that the more energy we put into girls, the more the boys and men would feel threatened.

Besides discussing these sorts of problems, we also got down to looking at the ways we were treating the girls. We began to develop an awareness together of how we were neglecting them: when I'd go back from our meetings to the club, I'd be horrified at what I was doing. All my close relationships were with the boys, all my energy and time went to them. With the girls it was just, 'Hallo, how's tricks?' and that's all – nothing. So I made a commitment to get closer to them. At first they just weren't interested, but what I didn't realize was that I wasn't picking up the right signals, or I was ignoring them.

But one night there was a big disco, and I was very busy, whizzing about ensuring that things were running smoothly, and I just put my head around the door of the girls' toilets. My response would usually be, 'What do you want to hang around there for, there's lots of nicer places to be', and try to encourage them out. So crazy: it never occurred to me it was the only place they could be on their own without boys. Anyway, this time one of the girls said, 'Come on, ask her, she'll tell you.' I replied, 'Come on, quick, what?' 'Go on, ask her.' 'No, you.' And they all started laughing, till one of them said, 'Tell us, have we got three holes down there, or two?' I suddenly realized that this was important, and that this sort of thing happened to me countless times, and that I'd been too busy to pick it up. We've been encouraged all our life to put down women's talk – and I'd fallen right into that trap.

Anyway, we had this most amazing talk together. We stayed in there the whole evening, didn't go to the disco at all, talking about so many things. It caused a terrible scene because all the boys were outside wanting to come in – why were there no girls dancing? In the end the caretaker threw us out. It was a school-based club that closed at 10.30, but we were still outside at a quarter to twelve. The girls were avid for information, and wanting to share their experiences.

So that was how girls' work in my club really got started . . .

SR.94, May 1980

Sex with Your Tutor? It's His Fringe Benefit

DEBORAH CAMERON

When I began my university course, the first lecture was given by the professor of English literature, an urbane little man who announced he was pleased to welcome a class of 'such clever young men and beautiful young ladies'. At the time, I gritted my teeth and dismissed the remark as a triviality. It wasn't. On the contrary, the most serious problem facing women at college is the attitude which made that remark possible.

. . . Classroom harassment runs through the whole familiar spectrum, from the uncomfortable feeling you are being eyed up, through suggestive remarks, jokes, groping, to 'serious' propositions of sex. Tutors do not ignore the personal and intellectual qualities of their female students, but these come second to burning questions like, 'Is she attractive?' 'Will she or won't she?' No encounter or assessment remains free from this cattle-market mentality.

. . . It is not unusual for women to sleep with their tutors; I did, and I spoke to others who did. In the 'liberal' ambience of the average university, such involvements are seen as personal matters, and tactfully ignored. But in fact, they arise directly from the attitudes and harassment I have described: sex for some tutors is just another perk of the job. The women I spoke to knew, or had discovered, that their tutors had slept with other students besides them. Reactions varied. When it happened to me, I was inclined to feel that my case was somehow different, but now I admit that I felt depersonalized, devalued and depressed, as if I had come off an assembly line for young, free, subordinate and available females. In effect, that was exactly what happened, but like most other women I suppressed my feelings about it for a long time. I rationalized my relationship because I couldn't bear to examine it in political terms.

For men, all this is very convenient. One of them told me it was a fantasy come true: 'I get older every year, but the girls are always eighteen.' He did not add the all-important point that when they are twenty-one they graduate, and are thus eliminated before they start to make demands.

... It is often said disparagingly of women that they cannot keep their academic and personal concerns apart. A bitter irony, since it is men who will not allow *us* to make the separation. We have to study and be assessed on terms which are not applied to men, but which men define. This state of affairs effectively debars us from full and equal participation in intellectual life.

Recently I have been able to express and analyse my anger at what happens to women students, but I cannot feel optimistic about a solution to our problems. While our educational system is geared to approval seeking, and while men perceive women as they do – in a word, while patriarchy rules – things are unlikely to change much . . .

SR.99, November 1980

7   THE ARTS

Artwork – in pictures, words, music, performance – is a way of making meaning out of life; it asserts values, illuminates and communicates ideas. Unless women are active in the arts, and seen to be active, women's lives are only portrayed from a male point of view. Women have always made art about their lives and their view of the world, no less than men. But their work has often been ridiculed and stereotyped on the basis of their sex, or, more recently, suppressed and kept from the public eye.

Women artists have always painted despite institutional discrimination by guilds and academies; but their work has often been hidden. Women who use fabric and stitches rather than paint, for example, have their work demoted from fine art to craft, with its connotations of out-dated skill, limited imagination and marginal aesthetic value. Although this particular female art is gaining recognition, work that comes from a safe distance – such as the blankets woven by the Navajos – is still more readily exhibited.

Even more than the plastic arts, both theatre and music need the active co-operation of other people. They require performance halls and audiences, as well as a sense within the woman that she can move freely outside the home and domestic responsibility. In *Spare Rib* No. 31 Marion Lees wrote about the composer Ethel Smyth (1858–1944) who had an independent income, along with feminism and a 'hearty' snobbery to propel her past problems. A Mass she composed was performed at the Royal Albert Hall in 1892, thanks to the intervention of Empress Eugenie – 'very few girls live next door to rich Empresses of pronounced feminist sympathies' was Ethel Smyth's ironic comment.

The big orchestras practise discrimination among performers such as advertising for both men and women but rarely auditioning the women who apply (*SR.34*). In 1974 the London Philharmonic Orchestra had seven women out of eighty-nine musicians, the B B C

symphony had sixteen out of 105, and Covent Garden Opera had
twelve out of ninety.

When women in the Musicians' Union had a conference to discuss
discrimination they noted a difference between classical music where
women played lyrical instruments, like violins, cellos and pianos,
and the 'jazz/rock/pop world' where it was 'far more difficult because
they are immediately expected to be the singer – the one who puts
the glamour on the stage' (*SR.36*). When saxophonist Kathy Stobart,
'an inspired jazz player', met a BBC department head to discuss her
band's audition in 1950, she was met with 'Why do you do what you
do?'. Her stunned reaction led to a row and in 1977 Val Wilmer wrote
in *Spare Rib* that 'she has never broadcast to this day'.

In theatre, women's role has been largely confined to that of
actress, often in subsidiary parts to those played by men. Michelene
Wandor wrote that in addition to men having administrative control
in theatre, their judgement of a play's content and form dominated.
Although on the surface they assessed the work in conventional
terms, their bias was towards work that interests men: 'women's plays
are so often rejected as either "not good enough" (artistic grounds)
or "not interesting enough" (often ideological or political grounds)'
(*SR.62*). In film, too, women's opportunities hinge on a sexual
division of labour. Feminists active in the film union, ACTT,
produced a report in 1974 revealing persistent discrimination which
stops women from moving out of traditional areas of work like
research, despite the adoption of equal pay in the industry since the
late 1940s.

The one area where women are acknowledged to have contributed
to the evolution of a cultural form is novel-writing and even this has
been subject to neglect. Mary Moyer in *Spare Rib* No. 15 cited the
number of women writers studied in one university course as an
example – there were seventeen compared to 313 male writers.
Women poets have been the object of the same disappearing tricks.
Cora Kaplan wrote in *Spare Rib* No. 68 that the love sonnets of
Elizabeth Barrett Browning are her only poems popularized this
century and they are made to appear as the 'spontaneous outpouring
of feeling rather than highly crafted poems by a mature poet',
while much of her late poetry that is 'public and political' is ignored.

Feminism in the arts has begun to demystify the concept of the
individual artist, apparently thrown up out of nowhere by the moving
spirit of 'his' own genius. In every form – photography, film, dance,
music, painting, plays, fiction, poetry – women have found it essential
to form groups, not in order to cease creating as individuals, but in

order to have a community in which to discuss and share ideas, and to make room for their work to be seen and heard. This has also provided the strength to oppose the pretence that cultural institutions are neuter and neutral, exposing them as bastions of male power and social privilege. In its demand for space within the institutions, feminism is not asking to be allowed in on the promise of silence, but demanding the right to public speech.

Underground Women

GRISELDA POLLOCK

I belong to a Women's Art History Collective which is working on a feminist critique of cultural history. One obvious project is to find out about women artists of the past and I decided to do some research into Old Mistresses in the National Gallery. With a certain amount of detective work I discovered seven named women painters. This included Katerina van Hemessen (1527/8–66), a fine Netherlandish portraitist, Marie Blancour, a seventeenth-century still-life painter, and Judith Leyster, a Dutch contemporary and possibly rival of Frans Hals. Moving southwards, there was the Venetian Rosalba Carriera, who revolutionized the use of pastel in the eighteenth century, and Elizabeth Vigée-Lebrun, a favourite portrait painter at the court of Marie Antoinette. The National Gallery has two nineteenth-century women painters, Rosa Bonheur, who excelled in large-scale animal paintings, and Berthe Morisot, the impressionist.

There are two other women who sneak in by the backdoor. Sofonisba Anguiscola (1538–1625) was thought to be the author of a *Portrait of a Lady*, but the attribution has since been changed. The catalogue now reads:

Sofonisba Anguiscola,
Attributed
3817 Portrait of a Lady '
Formerly; possibly one of *her sisters* or *Lavinia Fontana*
rather more probable candidate is a *male painter, Bartolomeo Passarotti*.
(My italics)

There is also a large painting of a *Negro Woman* which may be the work of Marie-Guilhemine Benoist (1769–1826), who was the pupil of Vigée-Lebrun and of the neoclassical painter David. This makes a possible total of nine women painters represented by thirteen paintings. Not one of these paintings is at present on exhibition on the main floors of the National Gallery. The first seven are all in the Reserve Collection in the basement; Benoist is in Dublin and Anguiscola in Leeds. Most museums do own more pictures than they have space to exhibit, and the excess is usually stored in some inaccessible basement, attic or suburban depository. Fortunately, the National Gallery Reserve Collection is open to the public. However, pictures 'below stairs' do not get VIP treatment. Instead, they are hung row upon row, screen upon screen, packed on to the walls from ceiling to floor, and more often than not, cordoned off from view. This makes it difficult not only to find them but also to get a decent look at them.

I wrote to the Director of the National Gallery, Michael Levey, and asked why all the paintings by women were in the basement. He wrote back: 'I do not have any policy about the pictures from the point of view of the sex of the painters.' He assured me that paintings moved up and down the stairs continually, but when I asked for exact dates when the paintings by women had been on show upstairs, he replied: '. . . the Rosalba and the Leyster have been on exhibition in the Upper Floor Galleries in comparatively recent years. I think you would give a very misleading impression if you tried to put precise dates on this sort of information.'

I do not doubt Mr Levey's sincerity nor his good intentions, but the fact remains that only two out of a possible nine women have been

The Cigarette – print of a sketch

Marie Bashkirtseff, *SR.34*, April 1975

exhibited with the main collection in 'comparatively recent years'. I don't believe that there is a conscious conspiracy on the part of the gallery staff to keep women out of the limelight. Works by women receive the same treatment that women themselves receive from society at large. Since women are almost universally second-class citizens, their works have second-class status and the National Gallery, probably unthinkingly, perpetuates this state of affairs.

But the point is not just to notice that there are women painters represented in the National Gallery or to complain that all their paintings are in the basement. Even superficial research into the lives and experience of these women provides insights into the social and institutional factors affecting women's chances of becoming artists and enables us to criticize the usual art historical biographies of male artists which ignore the critical economic and social circumstances.

In the time of apprentice systems, all-male workshops and guilds, women had difficulty in obtaining training in their craft, but most of the National Gallery Nine by-passed this because they came from artistic families. Katerina van Hemessen learnt her skills from her father Jan van Hemessen, a successful painter himself. Rosa Bonheur was the daughter of a minor drawing master and had a sister, Juliette, and a brother, Auguste, who also became professional painters. Anguiscola came from a family of five painter-sisters and Rosalba's sisters Angela and Nanetta both became known in the arts.

Berthe Morisot had two sisters, Edma and Yves, and all three showed such remarkable talent as children that their parents were obliged to let them study art. Yves married young and gave up. In 1863 Edma and Berthe went to the studio of the famous landscape painter Corot, who expressed a preference for Edma's work. They continued to work together for six years until, in 1869, Edma married and gave up, confining herself to producing copies of her sister's work. Berthe must have been very determined to continue her work, despite her own marriage in 1874, and her career is remarkable in the light of Victorian attitudes to women, marriage and the pursuit of art. Morisot was up against ideas such as these expressed by Bettina van Hutten, even as late as 1910: 'So long as a woman refrains from unsexing herself by acquiring genius, let her dabble in anything. The woman of genius not only does not exist but when she does, she is a MAN.' . . .

I had not expected to find that so many of these women had had artistically active sisters, but I was even more surprised to find that there were many more women artists in the circles around them. The painting in the Gallery by Rosa Bonheur, *The Horse Fair*, was painted in part by her friend and life-long companion, Nathalie Micas. She was a pupil of Bonheur's but exhibited paintings in her own right. No writer on this fact has commented on the significance of *another* woman who could paint these large animal paintings well enough to pass for a work by Rosa Bonheur.

One of the many copies that we know of the Vigée-Lebrun *Self Portrait* in the National Gallery (itself a copy by the artist of her own original) is by an otherwise unknown Madame Tupier-Lefranc, a painting which is now in the museum at Versailles. Very little is known about this painter, but probably she was a pupil of Vigée-Lebrun since the artist is known to have had many women pupils. Rosalba's leading rival in portraiture was a Florentine woman artist. Two of her best known pupils were Margherita Terzi and Angioletta Sartori, and the latter was a sister of another famous woman artist of the period, Felicita Sartori. There must have existed a lively women's culture which was more or less taken for granted by their contemporaries. There have been good, mediocre and bad women artists and not just solitary figures who rise out of nowhere by magical processes which defy all the social and educational obstacles that we know existed. We don't have to prove that all women artists of the past were great, but we need to know that they were more numerous than we are led to believe if we are to explode the individualistic-genius-will-win-through-myth that abounds today in art history. Moreover I am tempted to see in these family workshops and women's studios a network of support and encouragement which would counter the discrimination they received as women.

The women's studio at the Academy Julian

Marie Bashkirtseff, *SR.34*, April 1975

. . . Bonheur painted *The Horse Fair* in 1855 as a small replica of a very successful and very large painting which is now in New York. She had worked directly from the horses in the Paris horse market. In order to do this in peace she applied to the police for special permission to wear men's clothing while she worked.

. . . *The Horse Fair* went to England where it travelled round the country being exhibited to large crowds. Even Queen Victoria had it brought to Buckingham Palace so that she too could see this famous work. Bonheur and Micas painted a replica one quarter the original size to assist the engraver and it is this version that had the single honour of being the first work by a living artist to enter the National Gallery.

The *Self Portrait* by Elizabeth Vigée-Lebrun was painted in 1782 in Brussels after she had seen the famous painting by Rubens, *The Straw Hat.* Her own painting is an echo of the Rubens and a compliment to it, yet it is very different. In the Rubens, the female who wears the hat of the title is coquettish and painted with all the love of luscious female flesh for which Rubens is renowned. The style of the Vigée-Lebrun owes a lot to Rubens in rich colours and free brushwork. But the woman who looks out at you with a clear gaze is not a pretty passive mannequin for a milliner. In her hands she holds the proof of her activity, her palette and brushes, the tools with which she has just created the image you are now contemplating. Still, it is not a characterful portrait, and it does not convey the dynamic quality of activity. The explanation is in part that women artists are constrained by traditional representations of women in art. Women are rarely the active protagonists of a painting; they are all too often the beautiful objects presented to the spectator for HIS enjoyment. So, when a woman comes to paint herself as a maker of pictures, her active role comes into conflict with the stereotyped images of women which she sees, all around her in the history of her art. This portrait shows Vigée-Lebrun surveying herself as women have always been surveyed in art, rather than analysing her own image in terms of personality, individuality or energy. It is a nice painting with many appealing qualities but I feel that it lacks conviction because of the internal contradiction she experienced as a woman making an image of a woman in a language that has been made by men for men.

This problem did not prevent many of the women I have mentioned from being very successful. Rosalba had a brilliant career, courted by royalty, honoured by the Academy of Clementina at Bologna in 1720 and acclaimed in Italy, Germany, France and England. She was a member of the guild of St Luke at Rome which was the exclusive, professional body of artists. Judith Leyster was a member of the same guild in Haarlem in 1633 and by 1635 had three pupils of her own. Hemessen and Anguiscola went to the Spanish court under royal patronage and the latter was given a splendid dowry on her marriage by Philip II as a mark of his respect. Vigée-Lebrun was a member of the prestigious Académie Royale in France. This body had allowed women in (on a quota system) since its foundation in the seventeenth century, but when it was reconstituted after temporary suspension during the French Revolution, its doors were closed to women.

There was a marked trend towards more overt prejudice and disparagement of women in the nineteenth century. More and more critics are at pains to point out the sex and sexually-determined characteristics of an artist and her work. Morisot exhibited the National Gallery painting *A Summer Day* in the Impressionist Group Exhibition in 1880 where she met with this comment: 'Mesdames Morisot, Cassatt and Bracquemond represent *feminine* impressionism.' A later critic, James Laver, also delights to use this dismissive adjective: 'The lighter palette of the impressionists suited her *femininity* more than the sombre tones of Manet.' It would be interesting to expand that equation of lightness of palette with femininity and talk about the effeminacy of other impressionists, of Monet, or of Renoir who claimed that he painted with his prick.

. . . The purpose of this survey is emphatically not merely to prove that there are women artists in the past. Although their existence is important for our history as women, the Old Mistresses are interesting for what they tell us about art in general; about the conditions necessary to become an artist, to remain at work and to gain recognition and about the ingrained biases against women and when they developed.

There may be only nine women artists in the National Gallery, but it should be enough to make everyone take a new look at the collection and the values on which its exhibition policy is based.

Although I take responsibility for the views that are expressed in the text I would like to acknowledge the group discussions with Rosie, Pat, Tina, Amanda, Alene and Annie.

SR.21, March 1974

American Women's Conceptual Art Exhibition, London

REVIEWED BY ROZSIKA PARKER

... 'Why have an all-women show?' Lucy Lippard suggests the reason why: 'All art no matter how "rational" comes from *inside* the artist and the social and biological experience of any woman is very different from that of any man in this society. Art of course has no sex. But artists do.' ...

SR.25, July 1974

Dedicated to the Unknown Artist

SUSAN HILLER INTERVIEWED BY ROZSIKA PARKER

Feminist artists are working in any number of ways from up-front poster art, to thoroughly researched documentary exhibitions, to avant-garde art practice which is where Susan Hiller's work belongs. She was trained as an anthropologist but in the mid 1960s began working as an artist. She pursues her initial fascination for objects like seaside postcards, fragments of Pueblo Indian women's pottery, photos from automatic machines, analyses them and classifies them. She wants to bring out the cultural meanings hidden within the images, to raise questions about ways of seeing and ordering experience in a patriarchal society.

During April three exhibitions of your work opened in relatively conventional galleries, yet you are highly critical of the 'Art World' structure.

I would say that my using the gallery context at the moment is strategic. I am trying to insert a kind of world view smack into the middle of patriarchal notions of what art is. When I was younger I experienced real difficulty in placing my work within this very hostile structure, but at a certain point you have to face up to the necessities.

If you want to communicate you are impelled to insert your work into the art of your time. I think you have a responsibility towards your work, and it's a heavy burden to have it sitting around unseen by everyone but a few friends. Once you've been working for a fair period, once you feel fairly confident about your work, you have to make a decision about what to do with it. The decision to place your work within the contemporary art context causes incredible stress. I don't know any women artists who are not stressed.

I can understand that putting your work up for public judgement would be stressful, but why is it particularly acute for women?

Well, your work won't be seen properly, it won't be seen clearly. And no matter how much validation I receive from the mainstream, I can only see my presence within it as intrusive. And the difficulties that I get into are, I believe, the difficulties of communication and language based on a totally different perception of the world.

I'd agree that the way people see your work is indelibly coloured by the fact you are a woman, but how does your experience as a woman – your perception of the world – affect your relationship to the male art establishment?

Take for example the arts grant-aiding committee that you and I served on. It had initially been all male but gradually over the years more and more women were invited to serve as members. As soon as there were several women on that panel the language of discussion changed from being the formal and strategic language of the committee room to being a language of feeling and a language of confrontation. Rows broke out that had formerly seethed unmentioned, and those rows were about absolutely basic issues concerning the whole problem of grant-aiding the arts. But they had not been made explicit in all those years of funding the arts in this country. Who made them explicit? The women on the panel.

Don't you think that happened because we were already politicized rather than because we were women?

No. Look, recently there's been a lot of trouble because there are not enough women teaching in art colleges and the students are finally getting to the point where they are demanding that more women be hired. In a staff meeting at the college where I teach I said that this request of the students should be listened to, I think it's important because I respect the students, not just because that specific demand might be in my interest. A male member of the staff stood up after me and said he totally agreed with everything I said, he thought we should have at least 50 per cent women teaching at the college and ended up by saying, 'Of course that would mean the end of art education as we know it.' He's absolutely right (laughter).

But surely a lot of art administrators, people running galleries and so on, are women and they change nothing.

Because administrators who are not feminists are often people who fit themselves into the male structure. They can therefore only give credibility to the existing value system.

. . . When I was talking at Cambridge about the work I showed there, the only hostile member of the discussion was a woman art historian whose speciality was the Renaissance. She attacked me because she said I was calling into doubt ideas about art that she held dear. I was saying that soup ladles were as important as Rembrandts and she didn't think soup ladles were as important as Rembrandts. I replied that in terms of personal meanings to her Rembrandt's work might be more important than soup ladles, but in terms of telling us things about ourselves, soup ladles were just as important. Then she did a sudden about-face, she looked as though she was going to cry. I could see some sort of pressure building up inside and she started to mumble. The mumbling, all the inarticulate stuff, was what she really thought. Suddenly she said, 'You're absolutely right, soup ladles are important,' and dashed out of the room. I never saw her again. One of the reasons she was able to be initially articulate was that she was dealing with the accepted frameworks and categories. It's when we try to deal with the contradictions arising from our experience within these frameworks that we have no language. .

So one of the reasons why I think some women arts administrators – who aren't feminists – are hostile to women artists without recognizing their own hostility is that they resent the fact that there are at least a few women around who are attempting to speak and to create a language in which they feel at home.

How does your work challenge conventional ways of seeing reality?

In the three shows on in April, the components of the works are cultural artifacts . . . postcards, fragments of pottery, photographs from automatic machines and clippings from popular encyclopaedias. Now conventional art materials (canvas, paint) are mute, it's only when work is put into them in terms of presentation and analysis that they say anything. So by extension what I'm trying to do in my recent work is to make articulate that which is inarticulate. I'm interested in these cultural materials for the unspoken assumptions they convey.

. . . When I wrote about one of the pieces I said that to examine the givens of a culture implies to some extent that you are separated from it. Now I didn't say that I am separated from the language of my culture *because* I am a woman. I don't want to make those kind of statements, I want the art to speak. I don't want to label it – here is the work of a feminist artist. That notion has been very much degraded; to call people feminist artists is to box them off into an area which cannot insert itself, cannot contradict mainstream notions of art. Feminists are shunted off to a little side-track called 'Feminist Art'.

And it's characterized as being utterly unconcerned with notions of what art is and only concerned with making strong, direct statements about the position of women in our culture.

. . . *Let's talk about your piece called* Dedicated to the Unknown Artist *in which you collected and presented hundreds of seaside postcards, all titled* Rough Sea . . .

My conviction is that popular formats may well be art. A postcard is after all a miniature picture. In some of the postcards where the original image is photographic, hand tinting has been added. We tend to think of this sort of thing as a mechanical process, but by comparing several examples based on one initial image, it is easy to see that each painter painted the image completely differently. Aspects of imagination, fantasy or whatever enter the process inevitably. Human beings are not machines; they express their creativity in their gestures, in their ordinary, mundane working gestures. And it's those sort of things I am trying to bring out in that piece.

You no longer work collectively but always make it clear how your work depends on other people's, whether it is the postcard artists or the Pueblo Indian women potters whose shards you work with in Fragments. *You point out that the Pueblo women say they draw inspiration from their art history, from a tradition of pottery making handed down for over two thousand years from mother to daughter, as well as basing their painted pots on designs that they have dreamed at night. Are you saying our culture makes too rigid a distinction between rational and irrational thought?*

Yes, our culture more than most makes a distinction between the rational and irrational, between empiricism and intuitive ways of apprehending the world. In my experience those kinds of distinctions don't have any validity. In my work I'm trying to approach a kind of reconciliation of rational and irrational factors which seems to me a lived truth for many people – particularly for women. For myself, speaking as a woman, I can say that this is part of the way that I see things.

It is true that a comparatively large number of women became involved in Surrealism which as an art movement aimed to unite the rational and irrational, conscious and unconscious, and which supported the notion of the artist as medium rather than a domineering, ordering force.

It has been argued that the subjugation of women has strengthened certain faculties because in order to survive women had to develop resources to judge the nature of people and situations. Our culture, however, has laid great stress on the development of rational, thinking faculties in people and dismissed or minimized the irrational, calling these qualities feminine, negating them, calling them *extra-sensory* perception.

Except when male artists draw on irrational mode of thought or dreams and then it's termed inspiration provided by The Muse – the female, silent, representative of the unconscious and the dream.

Yet there are numerous instances in the history of science of great insights coming to people in a way that our culture dismisses. In other words when you study the history of science, you study it as a history of empiricism, experimentation and the formulation of hypotheses, but in fact so many important insights of science have come through what are called irrational means that we have to conclude that the way science describes itself is not value free.

Now I think that because of the situation of women in our society, they may have a kind of privileged access to those ways of knowledge, and I don't see them as antithetical to, or less significant than, the more dominant, rational modes.

SR.72, July 1978

Portrait of the Artist as Housewife

ROZSIKA PARKER

'They had houses, children, lives of habit and habitation. They were trapped in an especially painful way. Their spirits yearning to travel, their bodies committed to men, to children, to houses.'*

Feministo, the women's postal art event, could be described as a lifeline for trapped women. Growing numbers are exchanging small art works through the post.

It began in 1975 when Sally Gollop, isolated on the Isle of Wight,

* *How to Save Your Own Life* by Erica Jong.

and Kate Walker in London started sending each other images which expressed the feelings of women confined by childcare and domestic responsibility. An early work from Sally, for example, took the form of a miniature kitchen dresser with shelves like bars across the window. Cups obscured the view and with the crockery hung hands and a brain.

The two involved their friends and the numbers have slowly increased. Some were inspired to join by shows of the work in England, Scotland and Germany, others heard about it on the radio or answered an invitation in *Spare Rib*.

. . . The significance of Feministo goes way beyond individual art works. Both the *form* and *content* of the art take up many of the criticisms that the women's movement has levelled at established art practice.

It undermines, for example, the idea of the isolated genius (the artist who, whether they wish it or not, intimidates others from producing) by revealing the collective basis of inspiration: 'images are reiterated in different people's work, images and ideas aren't private property.'* And as each woman can reply directly to the work she receives, the division between art producer and consumer begins to be broken down. Art practice becomes a living process – more of a dialogue.

Perhaps because Feministo is like a visual discussion, a long-distance consciousness-raising session, it avoids simplistic polemics. The images are neither idealistic (women are strong, wonderful, invincible) nor

* *Spare Rib* review by Phil Goodall.

despairing (women are helpless, hopeless, victims). Instead the work explores the complexity of our relationship to our sexuality, domesticity, motherhood and romanticism. It's often witty, irreverent and most subversive when, as in a consciousness-raising group, a number of women contribute to the same theme.

The destructive conflict we experience between being a consumer, a commodity and a nurturer is analysed in images of food. A box of Black Magic chocolates opens to reveal fragments of women's bodies symbolizing the way women are portrayed as 'something to be enjoyed', until we too accept our bodies as commodities, seeing ourselves through other people's eyes and believing that parts of our bodies are desirable and other parts are disaster areas. Another box, filled with smiling, pleasing mouths is titled 'Keep Smiling Chocs'.

Then there's the plate of salad with a reclining nude – the image of women which most directly conflicts with their activity as artists – lying instead of ham amongst cucumber, lettuce and tomatoes.

A golden, appetizing, plaster pie bears the words 'The Safe Way Humble Pie', which reading between the pie crust could spell adapt, conform, compromise. The hours consumed by shopping, cooking and feeding are symbolized by strings of knitted zippered sandwiches or a saucepan sawn in half and filled with crocheted cauliflower.

Nearly all the pieces manage to convey both the appeal of domesticity and the bitterness and disillusion. This is part of the show's political strength. Certain images predominate: butterflies impaled or escaping, masks reflecting the shifts of identity daily demanded of women, windows simultaneously forming prison bars and frames for domestic dreams.

I think the same ambivalence is reflected in the materials used. There's nostalgia as well as rebellion in the scraps of cloth, old photographs, packaging and supermarket trays – sterile, depressing yet seductive. The materials also reflect women's limited resources, and in some cases, a rejection of the 'complex technology which has become an integral part of the established art scene'. And because much of the work is flimsy it has an impermanence which the women value. Most want to make statements rather than consumer objects.

Techniques vary. The show contains a great deal of assemblage, some painting and drawing, but a lot is knitted or sewn. On one level the use of craft validates women's traditional skills and emphasizes how much pleasure there is in, for example, crocheting. On another level it draws attention to the way our time and energy has been absorbed by our massive contribution to the domestic economy: knitting, sewing and furnishing the home.

Because all that work was done for immediate use in the home, not for the cultural market – for love not money – its creativity has been discounted. A pink and blue knitted panel, still hanging from the needles, picks up this theme. It reads 'Heart Not Art, Homemade I'm Afraid.'

If craftwork is valued, it's out of nostalgia or out of admiration for an individual skill. The symbolic significance craftworks had or have for women is usually overlooked despite the fact that feminist art historians continue to draw attention to the content and social role of craft production. And like the eighteenth-century women who sent each other Friendship Samplers, the women of Feministo exchange stitched messages, only their samplers read 'Wife is a Four Letter Word'.

. . . By providing audience and feedback, Feministo has given women who have abandoned art the incentive to start again, while women who've never seen themselves as artists gain the confidence to try making things.

. . . Not all the women in Feministo wanted to risk showing the work in public, but most believe it is politically important. They are, after

Salad Plate

all, fighting both the art world and sexism by bringing domestic imagery into the open.

They try to create a new form of exhibition, showing the context of the work by pinning up the letters the women send to each other with the art works. Their aim is to unite 'apparently disparate aspects – the private, domestic and personal with political and social understanding'. Exhibiting homemade works begins to challenge the split between the public and domestic spheres, between 'home and work', validating women's work in the home as 'work'.

Visitors pick up on the protest. 'Miserable bitches,' commented one man. 'Bitter and twisted,' said another. 'I don't see what all the fuss is about.' While North West Arts Association who housed their first show put up a notice reading 'Unsuitable for Children'. That struck the women as particularly ironic. Most of them work on the kitchen table 'in between making the tea and doing the ironing', constantly interrupted by children.

. . . They want to 'develop a visual language that is accessible to women in that it corresponds to their own experience' . . . Feministo steers a course between 'celebrating the area of domestic creativity and "women's world" and exposing it for its paucity'.

With much of the work, the spectator's response will be invoked by their personal experience, their fantasies and their relationship to the family and sexuality. It can be threatening. 'You just want to make people as unhappy as yourselves,' said one woman defensively. It's hard to predict whether feminist imagery will fill a woman with anger and insecurity, or with instant recognition and relief, but no one can remain unmoved by *Portrait of the Artist as Housewife*.

SR.60, July 1977

The Lost Theatre

JULES HOLLEDGE

It was the first performance of a feminist play in the East End of London. Arriving early on Thursday evening at Bow Bath Hall, the actresses arranged the few pieces of furniture necessary for the play and then waited. The hall soon filled with local people. The play, An Englishwoman's Home, *set in 1910, opens with Maria, a young working-class woman, hard at work in the kitchen. Her husband, John, enters drunk.*

John: Britons never, never shall be slaves! (after a pause, cheerily) Well, Maria, 'ere I ham, you see.

Maria: Is females Britons?

John: Females? Of course! Wot do you think? Wot's the good of askin' such a silly question?

Maria: Well, 'ow was I to know what the arrangement was? And if it comes to that, what is slavery I should like to know?

John (pompously): Well, I'll tell yer. If you was a slave you'd have to work for some man without any wages. Just for your food and lodging, like.

Maria: Oh Rule Britannia! Fancy that! 'E would provide my food and lodging!

Maria supports herself, her husband and their child by taking in laundry and renting out a room to a lodger. She is persuaded during the course of the play to go to a suffragette meeting, and in the final scene she demands the vote and forces John to help her with the housework.

The Actresses' Franchise League performed this play in 1911. They were acting real women rather than the simpering debutantes and stereotyped matrons of the West End stage. The story of those actresses and their feminist theatre was pieced together by Jules Holledge from old newspaper cuttings, theatre programmes and playscripts. Jane Comfort, who started her career on the stage in 1909 and retired after her last engagement in The Mousetrap *just eighteen months ago, helped to write 'The Lost Theatre'.*

On 8 December 1908, the Criterion Restaurant, London, was packed with four hundred actresses, actors and dramatists; among them the leading stars of the day, Ellen Terry, Gertrude Forbes Robertson, Decima Moore, Eva Moore and Mrs Kendal. The meeting had been called to form the Actresses' Franchise League, to campaign for votes for women.

It is not surprising that such a large number of artistes were there. That same year nearly a quarter of a million people demonstrated in Hyde Park for women's enfranchisement, and a Private Member's Bill giving women the vote had passed its first reading in Parliament before being killed by the government. It is also not surprising that actresses were forming a franchise league. A successful Edwardian actress was a privileged woman; she was free to manage theatres and control her employment and had some control over her sexuality: an actress could marry, divorce and have numerous lovers without ever becoming a social outcast.

That first meeting was noted more for its theatricality than its political conflicts. Jane Comfort remembers it and how she came to join: 'Gertrude Forbes Robertson came to collect my aunt, the dramatist

Madeline Lucette Ryley, to take her to the meeting, and I was dragged along because wherever my aunt went in those days I went too. I had just left school and I was studying for the stage. I remember on the way home in the car I was terribly excited about all I had heard, and what a wonderful thing it was, and how I wished I could join the Actresses' Franchise League. My aunt said, "You're not eligible to join; you're not an actress!" But Gertrude, who was always ready to help, said, "Why don't you come and walk on in *The High Bid*, at Her Majesty's Theatre." And so I went on in one of the crowd scenes for a guinea a week, and provided my own costume. That was my first appearance on the London stage and as soon as I could say I was an actress I joined the Actresses' Franchise League.'

A Pageant Of Great Women was the first major theatrical event organized by the Actresses' Franchise League. It was performed at the Scala Theatre, London, on 10 November 1909, barely two months after the first suffragette prisoners had been forcibly fed in Winston Green prison, Birmingham. The main character of the Pageant is 'Woman', who demands freedom from 'Justice', while 'Prejudice', a man, argues against her. 'Prejudice's' objection to 'Woman's' liberation is that her innate stupidity makes her incapable of mature thought. This is how 'Woman' answers:

Oh well, indeed, well does this come from you
Who held the body as all, the spirit as nought.
For you who saw us only as a sex!
Who praised a simper far above a thought
Who prized a dimple far above a brain!
So we were trained to simper, not to think,
So were we bred for dimples not for brains!

The language may be unduly formal but the message is clear: if you treat women as sex objects that is what they become. But the Pageant is primarily an excuse to introduce women warriors, artists, scholars, monarchs and saints, who demonstrate the physical, intellectual, creative and ethical strengths of women. Fifty-two well-known actresses were using their skills, probably for the first time in their theatrical careers, to create positive images of women. The Edwardian era had no film stars or professional models so actresses were powerful image-makers. They modelled clothes, posed for discreet pin-ups and post-cards and from the variety halls to the West End stage provided sex symbols for every class. Often they were mistaken for the sexist stereotypes they were employed to portray. The Pageant gave them the freedom to express on stage their own political viewpoint. Because of its importance to both the performers and audience, Ellen Terry described the Pageant as 'the first practical piece of political propaganda'.

Cicely Hamilton, the author, gave up acting to become a playwright, a profession which offered few opportunities to women. Her literary agent advised her to conceal the sex of the author until after the press notices were out, warning her that plays known to be written by women were apt to get a bad press.

The Pageant proved so popular that suffrage societies all over the country performed it. Edy Craig, who directed the first performance, also directed these local productions, and the Actresses' Franchise League provided the costumes and the leading performers. The Great Women were cast from the local suffragettes which, as Cicely Hamilton explains, often caused problems: 'The secretary of the local suffrage movement was furnished beforehand with a list of types required for the various parts; this list I should add, was marked "strictly confidential" – as well it might, considering it contained such items as "need not be good looking" and, in the case of one character whose face was all but concealed beneath her head-dress, "any old thing will do". The extreme popularity of Joan of Arc was on more than one occasion a source of real unpleasantness, when Edy had to deal firmly with some lady of entirely unsuitable appearance who, by sheer determination of the pulling of strings, had got herself cast for the part.'

The Pageant was a success, but it required months of preparation, and every day the League was besieged with requests from suffrage societies for short entertainments, to be performed at political meetings. Some of the actresses in the League tried to meet this demand by preparing short monologues and poems. Jane Comfort was one of them: 'One Friday my dear old uncle was coming home from lunch when a leaflet was thrust into his hand with my name on it, saying I was appearing at the Women's Social and Political Union meeting at the Queen's Hall, Upper Regent Street. He was always interested in what I was doing so he toddled along to the meeting and sat at the back of the hall to see what I was up to. Well I recited my little bit, a prologue by Laurence Housman. It began:

No cause is great that is not hard to gain
No right so clear as not to be denied.
Else in the past no martyrs had been slain,
No prophets stoned, no saints by torture tried.

It went very well and Christabel Pankhurst who was in the chair passed word along the platform: Did I have an encore; did I know "Woman This And Woman That"? I was horrified because Decima Moore always recited "Woman This And Woman That" and I thought it sacrilege for anyone else to perform it. So I felt very foolish and said, terribly sorry, I didn't. After the meeting I sneaked out and went home for tea, and as I put my key in the door, I heard my uncle say, "You silly juggins, why didn't you take a call?" That was the actor speaking, so I said, "How could I take a call? It wasn't a theatrical performance, it was a political meeting, and anyway Christabel Pankhurst is the star of the thing." '

The suffrage societies soon found that feminist entertainment at a political meeting both doubled audiences and was effective propaganda. The demands made on the League provided a strong incentive to develop feminist theatre, and by the middle of 1909 five plays were ready for performance at meetings throughout the country. The informality of the production and performance acted as a stimulus for more women and men to try their hand at writing for the stage, and between 1909 and 1914 over twenty women had their plays performed by the League. Women's groups all over the country wrote and performed their own plays. In 1911 the employees of Selfridges got together a musical comedy called *The Suffrage Girl*, about a general election in a country where women have the vote. The humour of the play lay in the fact that the fate of the candidates was ultimately decided by the heroine's casting vote.

All the plays are in some measure influenced by the contemporary theatre, especially in the representation of working-class characters, who tend to be either desperate suicidal cases or comic drunks. However, these class stereotypes are combated by what can be roughly described as the 'sisterhood is powerful' theme: the solidarity of middle- and working-class women in the fight for their rights. In *The Woman with a Pack*, the middle-class suffragette and the working-class woman fight against sweated labour and prostitution; in *An Englishwoman's Home* they fight against the oppression of the wife and mother in the home; and in *True Womanhood*, the only film the Actresses' Franchise League made, they fight the poor law system and the workhouse.

The appalling conditions of working-class women are time and again used as the dramatic argument in favour of the vote. This is true even in a comic drawing-room piece like *Ten Clowning Street*. It is set in the Prime Minister's home, where he is furtively plotting the death and destruction of the suffragettes. His devilish plan is to put a bill through parliament forcing all unmarried women over twenty-one to go out to work. He hopes this will force all the middle-class troublemakers into repressive marriages or occupy them in exhausting work. He is helped by his three daughters, who are anti-suffragists and who have already found work in a shop, a laundry and as a parlour maid to a Labour MP. The scheme is about to be leaked to the press when the three daughters arrive home furious with their father. They have experienced such exploitation that they want the vote to ensure that working women's conditions are improved. Judith, who has worked in the laundry, is the first to tackle her father:

What do you know about women's work and its conditions? If you did, you have no business to send me off, as you did, in cold blood to that laundry. You know nothing about it, so you have no business to legislate for it. Why, I know a thousand times more than you know . . . I'm thankful I've had my week's misery. It's opened my eyes; taught me what women have to go through when they're not sheltered behind padded doors like ours.

A lot of the preoccupations of the present women's movement were expressed in these plays. One, called *Physical Force*, was concerned with self-defence and even featured a Ju Jitsu display.

The plays were all short, usually between ten and thirty minutes long, and they were performed in virtually any conditions. The women and men who wrote them were not concerned with abstract concepts of the 'well-made play'; they were merely using a dramatic form to argue out topical issues. As a discussion about taxation or the position of married women was taken up by the women's movement, so a play was immediately written, encapsulating the main arguments. In this way the theatre responded to a need and was neither in advance nor lagging behind the movement as a whole.

The Women's Theatre was set up in 1913, as a response to the demand for the League's work. Its one and only season took place at the Coronet Theatre, London, in December of the same year. They performed two full-length plays in repertoire: *A Woman on Her Own* by the French playwright Brieux and *A Gauntlet* by the Scandinavian Bjornsen. *A Gauntlet*, written in 1870, challenges the notion that a woman must have an irreproachable past in order to be fit for marriage, whereas a man may be totally debauched and suffer no recrimination. *A Woman on Her Own* is the story of an upper-class girl who tries to maintain her independence, by earning her own living, in a society which offers no opportunity to women outside the home. She fails, and the play ends with her going to Paris either to become a prostitute or to join her former lover as his kept mistress. Brieux, still virtually unknown in England, also wrote a play advocating abortion on demand. The plans for a women's theatre season in 1914 were curtailed by the outbreak of the First World War, and like so many other activities of the women's movement, failed to re-emerge in 1919.

The Pioneer Players survived until 1920. Established by Edy Craig, they were not a strictly feminist company but were committed to producing progressive theatre. Many of the performers, who worked for the Actresses' Franchise League and the Women's Theatre, also worked for the Pioneer Players. Jane Comfort performed in *The Daughters of Ishmael*, a play about prostitution. A young girl is lured into a brothel, but finds it impossible to live down her past. Jane Comfort remembers how Edy Craig directed the last scene: 'The girl can't get a job anywhere, because wherever she goes some man recognizes her; they know where she's been and she promptly gets the sack. She is literally starving, so she crawls back to the brothel. Edy was so clever with her stage effects. The last scene is the exterior of the brothel. The girl goes up to the door and rings the bell. The madame opens the door and says, "No, you're no use to me, you're all in, dearie," and slams the door in her face. The stage was all dark except for an old-fashioned street light centre stage. At the dress rehearsal Edy noticed Ben Webster, and said to him, "Ben, you'll be at the performance, won't you, you'll be in evening dress; walk across and stop under that lamp and light a cigarette, would you?" That was how she roped people in to do what she wanted in her plays. At the performance Ben was there, beautifully dressed in tails, top hat and everything. He saunters on, stops under the lamp, strikes a match for his cigarette; the girl, who had been sitting on the steps of the brothel, comes up to him and says, "You going home, dearie?"; he blows out the match and passes on.

My aunt told me my uncle left in the middle of the play thoroughly sickened, but as she said to me, "Any man would get upset at the sight of a brothel." '

The Actresses' Franchise League and the Women's Theatre gradually disappeared during the course of the First World War. The organizational resources of the League were redirected into the British Women's Hospital and the theatrical skills into Troops Entertainment. By March 1916, the Women's Theatre Camps Entertainment had performed over three hundred concerts to troops in England and France. Although some of the actresses, like Cicely Hamilton, tried to preserve a feminist perspective in this traditionally sexist form of entertainment, they met with little success. The prevalent attitude was similar to that of Lena Ashwell, the entertainments organizer: 'When it was impossible to find men, the parties were composed entirely of women. One officer complained at the selection we had made. I was persistent, so finally he asked if I realized that there was not a single member of the company who the men did not long to kiss, and he was petrified with horror when I said that that was just why they were chosen. Even a china teacup, a coloured cloth, a coloured stone, a flower, was a gift to those thousands starved of all beauty, all loveliness.'

The actresses were back in their time-worn roles, an image of beauty like a china teacup with sexual overtones. Had they really achieved nothing in the previous ten years? Feminist theatre in 1909 grew out of the demands of the women's movement and served its needs, crystallized its theories, reflected and challenged them, which is true of the best feminist theatre today. The actresses were not isolated artists with an abstract conception of feminist theatre, they were politically active women, who were swamped by the nationalism of the First World War. They achieved a great deal, but their strengths and weaknesses were those of the movement as a whole.

SR.55, February 1977

The Death of Buzz Goodbody

for Buzz-news items in the paper on 18 April —

So the report concludes: these
women were
in much distress, did
suffer, and were most
unhappy women

poets too
can document
peculiar
pain attaching one
warm day in spring
to heads
that push the earth both ways

statistics pin
you bleeding
up against the wall
men's eyes, hands, poems freeze
your body bloom in earth
your pain to one exquisite
second's consciousness

we will execute
your memory thus
as minuet of grief
nor weep in family
allowances: you sister you
a grief specific; we
your sisters also share
your halting
struggle
to be born

(MICHÈLE ROBERTS)

On Saturday 12 April Buzz Goodbody was found dead at her home in Islington. She was twenty-eight. It's hard to face the fact that the possibilities, the contradictions, the light and shade of the life of a sister like Buzz have now, tragically, finished. One's left with only a memory to delineate, a handful of dry facts to state. Many know of her talents and her accomplishments as a director with the Royal Shakespeare Company, but it is in a different context I want to speak of Buzz, the context of women's liberation.

She was one of the founder members of the first Women's Street Theatre Group, which was set up in the winter of 1970. She was dedicated, like all of us, to taking women's political theatre to the places where women were – to demonstrations, streets, shopping centres and markets.

Buzz believed in working collectively. Like the rest of us, she acted, made props, tap-danced, wrote leaflets, laughed, suffered and shared her self-doubts in collective script-writing sessions which often turned into consciousness-raising groups. She shared in the heady hours of the Women's March in 1971, when we burlesqued our way down Oxford Street to the tune of 'Keep Young and Beautiful', and performed our first play in Trafalgar Square.

Despite her individual success in the theatre world, Buzz was too clear-sighted to think that liberation could be achieved in an individual way, by her own, or any other woman's success, and so she put her talents and energies into the fight for the liberation of all women.

We shall remember her as a revolutionary, and a struggling, all too human sister. (ALISON FELL)

Michèle Roberts and Alison Fell both belonged to the Women's Street Theatre Group.

SR.36, June 1975

Anna Wickham and Her Poetry

NAOMI LEWIS

. . . Writing poems was, to Anna's husband, a kind of mental infidelity, which his jealousy could not endure . . .

> The gentleman I married
> Says, I ruined his intelligence
> By marrying him.
> The gentleman I did not marry
> Says, I ruined his intelligence
> By not marrying him.
> I wonder if either of these gentlemen
> Had an intelligence!
> I wonder if marriage
> Is an affair of the intelligence.
> But now, I will borrow a book from a eunuch.
> I begin to be interested
> In my own intelligence.

'Jane and a Dilemma'

SR.9, March 1973

Positive Discrimination

MICHELENE WANDOR

It's always something of a problem to know how to be constructively critical of work (in the arts) produced by people with whom one is in basic sympathy. As we slowly put together the history of women's oppression and suppression, we are also in the process of trying to alter the course of that history. From the beginnings of the women's liberation movement we have urgently demanded of ourselves to make visible what has been suppressed, to encourage each other to produce where we have not produced, and to produce with confidence where we have produced with timidity. It becomes relatively easy for us to encourage each other and to have an initial enthusiasm when we see either an individual woman's name, or the name of a women's group attached to

Begonia Tamarit, *SR.78*, January 1979

work in an area where women have figured relatively little – playwriting and production, for example. 'It's great – it's by a woman.'

And yet I think we're all aware that this is a response which has its own contradictions. The simple *fact* of production isn't enough, and neither is a simple supportive attitude which assumes that anything a woman wants to do must simply be encouraged because she is a woman and women are oppressed. In cultural production women have for so long been objects and concepts in a male-dominated view of the world and in the male-dominated cultural industries, that we have to be critical as consumers, as audiences and producers. Critical response is the lifeblood of further production and development – critical response not passive encouragement.

The need to be supportive to each other as women who share the same forms of oppression, which became a tenet of the small consciousness-raising group, has had its own specific backlash. As a result of this, the initial reaching out uncritical support has made it very difficult to be frankly critical, and when women disagree, as indeed we must and do, both individually and politically, it manifests itself in one of two ways. Either it takes the familiar form of behind-the-back gossip, or the sort of violent emotional outbursts and hatreds which many of us have experienced and/or been part of. It is something which I believe is much talked over informally among women, but remains virtually unwritten about. This uneasy ambivalence – trying to maintain a precarious balancing act between support and 'betrayal' of sisterhood, generated within feminist ideology – is reflected in women's liberation writing, and happens continually behind the scenes in a way which is rarely visible.

. . . In some respects we're beginning to move towards serious criticism as the highest form of encouragement, although there is a big gap between theory and practice. All forms of cultural feminist ideology (radical feminist as well as Marxist feminist) reject the notion of woman as supreme isolated artist, writing or painting from a unique subjectivity. We acknowledge the social sources of both our oppression and our inspiration and must therefore also acknowledge our social audiences and the importance of their (our) response.

Of course, many of these difficulties apply equally to attempts to evaluate work produced by people whose struggle with and through art forms has so far been primarily defined as 'socialist' – though there can't be many theatre groups left who have not in some way looked at the question of sexism as part of the class struggle. But for all artistic work which challenges the dominant ideology (in this case, anything which doesn't fit the demands of commercial West End theatre, or safe repertory), there is always the simple problem of survival, since box office alone isn't enough. Any political theatre group which has been going for any length of time, has managed to do so because of subsidy, however small, and the role of a reviewer or critic can be an invidious one.

Any play, book, film, etc. has had weeks and sometimes months or years of work put into it. A review, political or purely aesthetic, can have a disproportionately powerful effect. A 'bad' review could knock the art-worker's livelihood on the head. People can be put off from going to see a play, arts councils may decide not to subsidize it. Some groups actively try and avoid the dangers of depending solely on publicly available reviews or assessments, by the hard and rewarding slog of doing their own publicity and relying on recommendations of people who've seen and admire their work. A network of contacts such as this takes a long time to build up, and the disembodied 'review' still has an important function, both in telling people what is available and in its attempts to evaluate and assess a particular product in relation to others of the same kind, to suggest what is progressive and what is not. It is important to try and do so without setting up competitive standards which effectively suppress anything which doesn't meet the highest demands, or in a way which serves to demonstrate the superior writing skill of the reviewer as against the reviewed . . .

SR.39, September 1975

Tales I Tell My Mother by Zoe Fairbairns, Sara Maitland, Valerie Miner, Michèle Roberts, and Michelene Wandor

REVIEWED BY KATHERINE GIEVE

These are short stories by a group of five feminists who worked together in a fiction collective, meeting frequently over a period of eighteen months. A challenge to the traditional picture of the artist alone in a room of her own.

The stories, each of which has a single author, are loosely gathered into three sections: feminists confronting the outside world; experience and conflict within the movement; and a world transformed by feminism. There is an introduction to each part crystallizing the discussion within the group and explaining their ideas to us, and particularly why they see fiction as an important part of their work in the women's movement. To this extent the book is vigorous and exciting: the questions in their minds when they write become questions for us to answer as we read.

The force of the collection is an attempt to reclaim fiction and try to make it our own, to use it to explore our consciousness, give an account of our experience, to discuss and to convince. In doing this they are prepared to make explicit the political content of art.

Art and the artist have been mystified, reified and isolated in our society. We are trying to talk about method and process and collectivity. If this fact and our open didacticism make it more difficult for you to read these stories as 'art' in any traditional ivory tower sense, so much the better.

My problem is that the stories *are* made more difficult to read for these reasons. I don't deny that art is political; but it seems that where fiction is dominated by ideas and where characters appear as protagonists in an intellectual argument the power of fiction (as against other literary forms) to move and to transform the imagination and perceptions can be lost. For all that, I did like some of the stories a great deal and for them and for the discussion, this is worth reading.

SR.81, April 1979

Liverpool Worker Writers: War of Words

OLIVE, MARIA AND HELEN, ALL OF WHOM BELONG TO WRITERS' WORKSHOPS, TALK TO EILEEN FAIRWEATHER

. . . *Olive*: But Second Chance, generally . . . it's a lifeline for the working class.

Maria: You don't need any confidence to go on it, and no one's filling you up with anything – you teach each other.

Maria: That's why it's marvellous to go along to a writers' workshop. Maybe we're not very professional, in that we don't criticize much, but just to be able to get people's ideas out of them is enough.

Olive: Because we're *all* capable of putting words on paper – I don't care how simple they are or involved. You don't have to appeal to somebody 'up there' – you've got your own worth. The Arts Council say that our work isn't art, just an 'interesting social exercise'. We don't care if we're not artists – we're craftsmen in our own right.

Helen: When we were at school we were bored to tears by 'accepted' poetry books. But now if one of the men or girls is writing, it's in a language I understand, and I can say *yes*, I identify with that . . .

SR.88, November 1979

Clapperclaw

REVIEWED BY JILL NICHOLLS

Clapperclaw are entertainers. A four-woman band, they sing and they take the piss. They're at their best doing feminist satire: singing very solemnly 'Grandperson's Advice to the Boys', an old Temperance Song ('Everywhere experience shows It pays to be a man'); sending up a very serious number from the 1942 Rochdale and Pioneer Songbook – 'The Girl with a Spanner in the Pocket of her Pants'; taking off Ronny and the Ronnettes – '*I got me a helluva fella – He's got a jaw like a cliff – and he's seven foot tall – the woman they just fall for him – but he went and ditched them all – when he saw* my *face.*' They play on women's supposed bitchiness – '*If I catch any of yous gals – hanging around I'm gonna – get me my big machine gun and – mow you all down*' – but make a huge joke of it as they sidekick, simper and smirk. When I saw them at a left-wing benefit, women in the audience were surer what the joke was, laughing themselves silly; the men looked a little ill at ease. And like all satire, it can be misunderstood; their spoof sexiness has been taken straight.

To 'clapperclaw' means to revile, to scratch and bite, noisily. The noise comes from all kinds of acoustic instruments – clarinet, guitar, kazoo. They scratch at men, at Maggie Thatcher, the dole queue, the jubilee. They do squatting songs – gleefully acting policemen – a few straight socialist songs and some lyrical folk like 'The Ant and the Grasshopper'. 'We need the softer ones too,' says Caroline John, 'or it would be just too raucous. But we're not very good yet at the patter in between. It's necessary because the songs are so different.'

They started last September when one of them put an ad in *Time Out* for 'competent musicians to sing socialist songs'. Only two women answered. This June Caroline joined. Though it was coincidental at first that they were all women, she says it's grown on them now. 'It wasn't a policy decision but it feels right. Men tend to be more strident, harder. We don't want to lecture people.'

SR.65, December 1977

Terri Quaye

INTERVIEWED BY MARION FUDGER

I wasn't born in Africa, I was born here, my father's family are from Accra, Ghana, that's where you get the name Quaye, it's from the Gha tribe. I went there for the first time in about 1970 and they know I sing and play congas, so it was an incredible thing when I went back, 'cos it was like one of their daughters coming home.

A couple of days after I arrived I experienced one of the most frightening things in my life as a musician. A bandleader friend of ours was holding a dance in a big hotel, and he asked if I'd play. So at one point in the evening, they put two conga drums in the middle of the floor and Jerry stopped everything and addressed the crowd in Gha. He was saying 'one of our daughters Naakoshie [my Ghanian name] has come back tonight' and you could tell that people were thinking 'OK so she's here but what are those drums doing there?' I was announced and the family were very proud, I counted the musicians into a pre-arranged number and we roared off. Suddenly the whole crowd went silent and when a few hundred people stop talking, that kind of silence is quite frightening. Nobody was smiling and I thought 'maybe I've done something very wrong' and suddenly one woman got up and started coming at me and about six other women followed her and were running towards me, it was quite a distance. I was in a worried sweat, but kept on playing 'cos I didn't know what else to do and just before they reached me, they burst into smiles and said, 'Play sister play!' The custom there is that if you're really knocked out with somebody, you stick money on their head and I was showered with all this money. As they did that, the crowd roared and I knew it was all right, but for a minute I didn't know what was happening, God was I frightened!

Yeah, I had a good time there. Down town in the poorer sections, people would bring out drums and we'd sit in back gardens or the gutter and we'd just play together in the streets. That was really nice.

Shortly after that, I did a broadcast on Ghana radio which culminated in a weekly broadcast with Ghanian musicians. Women play an important part in music over there, usually as dancers and in some Ghanian tribes as drummers. Music is really the world's ambassador, you can do a lot of things with music, where talking would fail, you can bring more people together with music than with any words.

My whole family is in music, it goes back to my great grandfather, who was a church musician, then my grandfather who was the first jazz pianist to come out of Ghana and then my father who was the top jazz singer in this country for many years. Caleb my brother is a musician, my sister plays guitar, my father's mother was a dancer and my mother was a singer. So it was presumed that I would be in music by the way I related to musicians, though my parents assumed I'd be a singer or pianist. When I chose drums, I wasn't discouraged but I guess they found it a bit strange, though not as strange as it would have been to an unmusical family. I was always banging on the table tops and things, I felt it was a very natural thing. I think I actually started when I was about eleven or twelve but remember drums were always accessible to me. My father was a bandleader, so when musicians left their instruments behind, I'd have a go. They'd rehearse at home, or I'd go wherever they were, I was what you'd call the band boy, I'd clean their instruments for them and carry the music.

There's a lot of difference between bongo playing, conga playing and playing a drum kit. I can't play bongos, though people assume that if you can play one, then you can play the lot. The bongos are a finger instrument, whereas the congas require the whole of the hand, I can't play a drum kit because I can't get the co-ordination together – the arms and legs. You don't need a lot of power from the body to play a drum kit, it's all in the wrists, but with congas, you need a hell of a lot of strength and also inner strength – a very strong mind.

For instance, when I was in New York playing for the dancers (*Syvilla Forte's Afro American Ballet*) there was a woman with a withered arm, who would sit in and play some beautiful things on congas. This is the kind of inner strength I'm talking about, it's the determination that has to come through. Congas aren't given the respect of a separate instrument but no one can dispute that if you add congas to any kind of music, the very nature of the sound lifts the music and musicians and gives the whole thing impetus and drive.

I remember when I was in the show *Catch My Soul*, I never got to meet any of the women in it because being a drummer I was put in the men's dressing room! It was funny, one night, Marsha Hunt was coming up on to the top of the set, where I was playing, to do a long speech and when she saw me, she did a double take, it was a complete shock to her that there was a woman playing drums.

Here unfortunately, women are expected to play games to boost the male ego and I don't go along with that. As far as I'm concerned, I'm a drummer and singer, I don't feel that I have to impress anybody and more than that, I don't feel that I have to play their sexual games because that's what it boils down to. I remember when I had my own show in Germany, one night the band got talking about a woman that played vibes and was getting a lot of work. I was interested in this and tried to find out who she was, they told me that she wasn't that good but she'd bend over and show a lot of cleavage, so she got the bookings. That's one of the games you're expected to play to get work. I've always fought against this and I always will but I must say that it's getting better, things are improving. On the other hand, maybe it's because I'm getting older! Also, you know, if you fight the sexual fight for long enough and you really are determined not to be exploited, then you become a different kind of person, a stronger person and you become looked upon in a different light. I don't want to say I'm still suffering but I'm still struggling let's say, people don't call me 'one of the boys' but you become an individual and people respect you for that.

Look, I'll tell you another story, this is a few years ago when I was doing my cabaret stuff which I've more or less severed now. Anyway, against my will, I was sent by an agent to do an audition at one of the leading clubs in town. There were quite a few other singers there and when we'd finished, the club owner told me that I could have had the job, but the thing that was wrong with me was that I wasn't showing any tit (or tits as I wasn't deformed)! So I told him where he could put his job and he said he'd see to it that I'd never ever work in that club, and that was it. Now, shortly after that, a very beautiful friend of mine was appearing at this club and she invited me down. The time came when she was introduced and the curtains flew open and she was doing the whole thing but the funny thing was, a man sitting in the front row fell asleep.

So, is it the public or is it the clubs that demand this exploitation? The nightclubs here have been meat factories for years and are they ever full? Well, they're not! What keeps them going is their high prices, the escorts they supply and the custom they get from paying off taxi drivers. So let's face it it's not the tits that's pulling them in, is it? I'm saying, things are getting better because you'll find that these clubs are becoming more and more empty. It's not what the public want, it's what they're having rammed down their throats, the oppression lies with the club owners, promoters and agents and it's the same in the pop world. Another thing, if those half-empty clubs put music on for music's sake, they'd double their audience, men and women would come in together, but no woman wants to go to a meat market. It's the old school of thinking and it's dying out because women, whether it's performers or audiences, don't want to be subjected to that.

When I was working in a club in Beirut, the reason they booked me back was because men were bringing their wives in and one day I even achieved a man bringing in his mother! Now remember we're talking about Beirut where most of the clubs are 'girly' clubs and women are ten steps behind the men. So to begin with, men came, then their wives, then wives would bring in their sisters and women were coming in regularly. Well, you can imagine, the whole place changed, and we'd stay behind and get to meet each other and there was no animosity.

SR.56, March 1977

This particular club was where I had to deal with a pianist on the biggest and cruellest ego trip ever, all because he felt I didn't respect him as a woman should. He'd mess up the control desk, night after night, so that I'd have to stop the show and sort out the distortion and feedback. Then when I learned how to work the control desk myself, he threatened to break both my wrists and even when the management restrained him from doing that, he'd sit in the front row during my show and sing out of tune, just loud enough to put me off. Ooh, it got very heavy! But that's what I mean about needing strength.

If you won't compromise and become a sex object then you have to become more confident in what you believe and it stretches to your views on other subjects, i.e. politics. You can't help but combine the two. With Jo'burg Hawk, I sing in two African languages. The base of the group are Black South Africans, I'm part African, part West Indian, and as we've all experienced racism our material is obviously politically biased.

I believe that the music that you play (you can't do it all the time obviously) should reflect yourself and that's the barrier between the pop world and the other forms of music – reggae, jazz, blues and so on. The pop world doesn't reflect the person. Even the way I play drums reflects me completely, your music is everything that you are and the most important thing is to relate to people as people.

Music is my living and I'll keep on travelling because I draw things from new places. But the most important thing of all is that I have complete control over what I do, I insist on it. Maybe you would have heard of me if I'd put my life into someone else's hands, maybe you'd have my records at home. But most probably that person would be a man and no matter how kind or considerate he might be, he would still have been brought up as a man and it wouldn't work. His values would be different to mine, his expectations and his sensitivity would be different to mine so he'd be thinking what a woman should be – which is not the same as what a woman is.

I've been working for a hell of a lot of years and I'm still here, I'm still playing and I'm still my own person. I'm really pleased to be around at this time because I can see the improvement, not just here but all over the world, it's changing every day, women are getting stronger and this is great. It just takes time and also for women who are in the position to – to set a good example, a strong example. When women can fight and men can cry, then we'll be getting somewhere. There, that's ending on an optimistic note.

SR.26, August 1974

Love Music/Hate Sexism

LUCY TOOTHPASTE

Popular music in the sixties often expressed protest and rebellion – against parental authority, an outdated sexual morality, the war in Vietnam, and so on. But the whole thing seemed to curdle in the early seventies: a great gap yawned between the rock stars – wallowing in their fabulous wealth – and their fans, who were actually growing poorer, in the grip of the economic recession and the sudden rise in unemployment. It seemed like a terrible, cynical triumph for the status quo, the system's uncanny ability to absorb any threat and turn it somehow to its own advantage. This disaster seemed to bear out the argument that because rock music is dependent for its existence on the multinational business corporations, it is reactionary by definition and can never successfully challenge oppression. Both musicians and their audiences are exploited financially, and at the same time, the lyrics, full of fantasies and stereotypes of true love, chic rebellion, etc., effectively keep people's brains in chains.

Feminists in particular have objected to rock, which has always been even more male-dominated than other kinds of popular music. The macho posturing and misogynist lyrics of the cock rock bands from the Stones to the Stranglers are notorious. Women artistes have been tolerated as singers, but jeered at as instrumentalists, and the patronizing way women musicians are treated in the rock world must deter all but the toughest (or perhaps the most thick-skinned) . . . All women who make records are under constant pressure from the record companies to agree to sexist advertising campaigns, and the music press reeks of what has now become a very *self-conscious* (as if that excused it) sexism.

. . . In the circumstances it's hardly surprising that many feminist musicians reject rock music, preferring to play jazz or funk or folk or other less macho forms, and also reject the whole commercial music scene, preferring instead to play on the pure but restricted feminist/women-only-event circuit, and record on independent labels.

And yet, there are those of us who still love rock music and believe it does still have an energy and an enthusiasm and an ability to *move* people which is potentially subversive. Two campaigns have come into existence based on this belief, namely Rock Against Racism, and the newly-formed Rock Against Sexism.

Rock Against Racism was formed in 1976 at the end of a hot and hysterical summer. Unemployment had risen to one and a half million, and we were just beginning to feel the effects of the first big public spending cuts. The press chose to divert attention from this by creating the 'Scandal of the Four-Star Asians' (homeless people temporarily housed in a hotel) and by making a hero out of Robert Relf with his famous house 'For Sale to an English Family Only'. Within a few weeks three Asians had died in brutal attacks. Enoch Powell made a speech about 'alien wedges', and Eric Clapton said he agreed that repatriation of immigrants was a good idea. RAR was started by music fans who were indignant that white rock stars, of all people, who owe so much in their music to the influence of Black musicians, could suggest that Black people have no right to live amongst them.

The formation of RAR coincided with a national revival of live music caused by the emergence of punk bands – with their philosophy of demystifying rock music – and homegrown reggae bands. 'Rock Against Racism' didn't have to be just a slogan, because the bands

themselves were writing songs about racism and oppression and boredom and, in the case of bands like X-Ray Spex and T R B, sexism too.
. . . A bunch of intrepid musicians and assorted optimists have been meeting in London since November to get Rock Against Sexism off the ground. The aims are: 1) to fight sexism in rock music, and to use rock music to fight sexism in the world at large, 2) to challenge the stereotype images of women and men and promote a more positive image of women in rock, 3) to attack the exploitation of women in advertising, in the press and on the stage, 4) to encourage women musicians by giving them more opportunities to play, and 5) to assert the right of everyone to determine their own sexuality. Rock Against Sexism intends to book name bands as well as unknown ones, trying to draw in a mixed audience of feminists and people as yet unacquainted with feminist ideas . . . Rock music is such an influential area of popular youth culture that it can't simply be ignored by feminists. What's more, for those of us who actually do love the music, it's worth fighting for the right to express our *own* experience, our *own* hopes and struggles in rock.

SR.81, April 1979

Gynaecocratia: 8 January, Midwife's Day, Greece

MERIEL SKINNER

. . . On 8 January this year, I went to Monoklissia, a village near the town of Serres near Thessalonica, in Macedonia, for the Gynaecocratia events.

Out of Serres, we're approaching Monoklissia. All around there are flat, ploughed fields and tall, thin, bare trees marking the ditches between the fields. White overcast sky. We could be in Essex on a winter day.

I am with four tourists who I met by chance at the bus station. There was no bus, so we shared a taxi.

We are three women and two men. We leave the taxi outside the village, deciding to walk in to see what the reception for the men will be like. We round the bend and are confronted by a lever-barrier right across the road. GYNAECOCRATIA – rule by women – is written on a banner suspended from the barrier pole. Five women in Macedonian costume stand in front of the barrier, defending the entrance to the village. They are full of good humour and we are greeted, 'Welcome! Many years!'

The five are having a great time, singing, dancing and laughing, and spirits are high – though the frost has not long disappeared and it is very chilly standing around in the cold January countryside.

There is a bucket of water at the ready and a pine-frond for splashing the water with. These are the weapons for either 'blessing' you with a light sprinkling of water on the head, or for flinging water at you more energetically, depending on your sex.

A van approaches and has to pull up. The windows must be opened and all the men inside are liberally splashed with water. They must pay a fine before the women let the barrier up to allow the van through to the village. A great deal of horseplay goes on amid gales of laughter. The men show a good sense of humour. They knew what they were letting themselves in for when they came here today.

Every car, van, bicycle and lorry is processed like this, and then a coach draws up. There are women and men in this coach which has come from a village anything up to forty miles away for the day's fun. Karitsa, one of the older women and a key figure in the celebrations, gets on the coach to sort them all out. She takes the microphone and welcomes everyone, and delivers a string of dirty stories, rhymes and riddles. Everyone is laughing by now. One of her stories is about a priest (Roman Catholic not Greek Orthodox) 'who blessed everyone: normally, of course, it's done like this . . . but he did it with something else – well, you all know what it is, and if you don't, you should, so here you are.' At this point, she whips out a plastic doll monk in a brown habit, holds it up to the audience, presses the head and from under the habit out springs an enormously long plastic penis. Everyone is thoroughly enjoying all this. When it is over the coach is allowed through to the village.

At 11 a.m. we go into the village. The main street is wide but not tarmacked. The church is on the left and the town hall and police station are on the right. An area of the road about sixty yards by twenty is cordoned off. This is the village square for the day, and only women and girls are allowed in it. Except for the three-man musical band, men are not allowed in the enclosure under any pretext whatsoever. Dancing and merrymaking go on in the enclosure, while the men look on from behind the cordon. Whole sections of the male part of the crowd move back with a roar, like a wave, following the path of the sprays of water from the pine-frond, and any individual man who enters the area is swiftly attacked with bucketfuls of water.

In the square there are about thirty women of all ages in local costume and many other women from this village or visiting for the day. They are all dancing to the Macedonian clarinet, accordian and drum music, and the atmosphere is really festive and friendly.

One of today's characters is a woman in local costume, with a policeman's sash, belt, purse and cap, and a whistle which she frequently uses to instil order in the crowd. Another woman arrives wearing local costume, and carrying a gun and a rabbit, a dog following at her heels. The hunter saunters along smoking a cigarette. In the countryside the notion of a Greek woman smoking a cigarette is completely unthinkable, and for a countrywoman to do so in public borders on science fiction. (Nevertheless, although hunting is completely a male pastime, the ancient god of hunting was *not* a god. She was a goddess – Diana, or Artemis.)

At midday we all dance and walk around the village, calling in at the houses of two of the oldest women of the village. Perhaps they were the midwives before the law was enforced that only qualified doctors and nurses were allowed to do this work. The first woman is between ninety and a hundred years old – she is not sure exactly – and she is delighted by the crowd of a hundred or so of us who have come to give her festive greetings, many people kissing her hand as they do so. It is the same scene when we stop at the house of the second old woman, who is aged about sixty, and perhaps the next midwife in the village after the older one.

An hour later, we are back at the centre, and while some dancing goes on, most people crowd into the town hall which has been completely taken over for the day, and where a lunch of chicken soup, rice and vegetables is laid on.

'We weren't expecting this number. Last year we had two coaches. This year there are six or seven.' But everyone is fed, and everyone has a good time.

Dancing, talking, laughing, eating and keeping the men wetly in order go on all the time until things are in full swing again after lunch.

All through the afternoon, we dance in the square. We dance in a long line, arms on each other's shoulders, a Macedonian dance in labyrinth fashion, spiralling into and out from the centre. Or we dance in circles of about six. Or we dance in completely unstructured groupings. Sometimes only the women in local costume dance, and when they take over, from time to time there is a lot of clowning around, the leader puffing ostentatiously on a cigarette or drooping a cigarette from her mouth as she dances around.

In the afternoon there are a lot of attacks on the men who get too near the enclosure, or who get pushed into it by their mates. They have to run the gauntlet having buckets of water flung at them or being pounced on from all sides by all available hands. They rush, stumbling, for the nearest exit, speeding like greased lightning as soon as they can get free and helpless with laughter.

At four o'clock, precisely, the chief of the nome (local area) ventures into the enclosure and, after a gentle water blessing, he joins the dance for one lap, being led by one of the women. (Normally, when women and men dance the men always lead at the start of the dance and even a whole line of women doing a women's dance is led by a man.) The chief of the nome does not chance more than one lap of the ring, and then he disappears to the safety of the men's area.

Late in the afternoon the football teams appear. The women who were wearing Macedonian dress are totally transformed, running into the ring in their tracksuits. Although there's a great deal of laughing and shouting it's clear that both sides mean business. The dancing shoes are doubling as football boots now, but despite this, the kicking is really effective, and the goalies are ready to save goals in the most flamboyant manner, landing up full-length in the mud whenever necessary. These are Greek village women of forty and fifty. (The teams are made up of women of *all* ages.) By the time the game is over it's getting dark, and we adjourn to the town hall. It's all over for the men now, as they really are excluded from even observing what goes on in the town hall. The curtains are drawn, and the locked doors are open only to women. The three-man band has done fantastically well, playing all day long and throughout the evening, with breaks from time to time. But the prize must go to Karitsa (aged sixty-five) and some of the other women, who keep on the go non-stop from dawn till night, instigating all the fun, horsing around, dancing all day and throwing the water around.

There isn't a way to describe the time we spend dancing. It isn't just the dancing, it's the beaming faces, the laughing and the spirit overflowing from all the women here. Each instant is as exhilarating as the first moment, for all of the time that we are together like this. It can't go on too long, and you don't realize how long it is going on. Every instant is beautiful.

We three tourists (the other two, being men, are sitting it out in the cafe outside) are hauled into the dancing as we were in the afternoon. Though there's no feeling of competition, good or sexy dancing is appreciated by everyone around and there is a lot of shoulder-and-bust shaking. Some attempt backbends, while shaking their shoulders from side to side, and they are always supported by a helping hand, just in case they go too far.

There are two interludes when Karitsa or another woman takes over the microphone to relate a string of dirty stories and the audience roars with laughter. The men in the band are sent out for most of these story sessions. It is a wonderful sight to see the face of an old woman of ninety, in black from head to toe, her face as wrinkled as the hide of an elephant, completely creased up in laughter at these jokes. During the dancing Karitsa especially would poke her backside out, proffering it to anyone sitting by the dance floor who might be interested; and there was no shortage of fingers eager to poke her.

At eleven o'clock, the amateur dramatics started. In came – The Moor, a traditional character in Northern Greek folk drama. It was one of the women who had been on the go all day and she was wearing what seemed to be half the entire display of local weaving, which had until then been on show in the front room of the town hall. Her outfit was a red rug which served as a fez, a moustache painted on her face, a shirt and a cotton bedspread pinned to make a pair of pantaloons with the crutch somewhere at mid-calf. After a turn around the floor, she went out and came back leading at the end of a string – The Bear. The Bear shuffled in on all fours. It was small but very bulky, wearing an enormous heavy brown overcoat. It kept its head down, so all you could see was a great bear-like overcoat lumbering around on all fours. It was really effective.

The Moor and The Bear paraded around for a while until the excitement had died down a little and then The Bear reared on to its hind legs, to the gasps of the crowd, and somehow started to become 'Man', rearing up at the audience with its arms up, with vaguely threatening, bragging gestures. Then he or it lumbered into the audience and grabbed a victim, flung her on to the floor and leapt on top of her, humping away in a parody of sexual intercourse. There they are, on the floor, falling from full height, without putting out a hand to break the fall, and rolling around on top of each other. They are over sixty, both of them. (The Bear is, of course, Karitsa.)

The Bear attempts attacks on other women and finally turns on its master, throwing her also to the ground, and leaping on top of her, full-length. After this has gone on for a while, The Moor (whose turban has fallen off in the mêlée, and who is therefore now clearly identifiable as one of the women) throws The Bear over, and the humping goes on, with the roles reversed. Everything is so chaotic now, that whatever The Bear or its leader do we are helpless with laughter.

After this interlude, the band starts up again, and everyone dances. But I am told that these are men's dances. Women do not do men's dances. But you wouldn't have known, everyone obviously knows the dances perfectly well. The proceedings wind up at midnight, with a conga all round the hall while pieces of bread, cheese, egg and chicken are handed round.

It has been non-stop action for sixteen hours, and the fun, exhilaration and enthusiasm have not wavered for an instant throughout the day. How they all do it, I really don't know. I was exhausted by just a few dances. The real athletes of the day were undoubtedly Karitsa – with her broad gold-toothed beam always on her face, a large red flower over her ear, and a cigarette usually in her mouth – and a few other women aged forty to sixty; though all ages were involved throughout the day in all the activities . . .

SR.51, October 1976

8   SEXUALITY

If women are to determine their own lives and change their place in the world, they must first know and accept themselves, including their sexual selves. But the interpretations of women's sexuality – the moral and censorious, the prurient and commercial – make it difficult for women to talk about sexuality or even to find the right words without sounding too technical, crude or romantic. Eleanor Stephens wrote that she was aware that the word 'intercourse' described 'a form of sexual activity defined by men for male orgasm and female reproduction' (*SR.48*). And when Nancy Friday asked women about their sexual fantasies, they often replied they didn't have them, only 'sexual thoughts' (*SR.43*).

Fear and repression of women's sexuality is related to women's social oppression. The Victorian double standard which is still an undercurrent in our thinking about sexuality maintained that all men had an insistent drive that they had to be allowed to act on. But a wife should be chaste and obedient to the husband. The 'proper' wife had sex for the purposes of pregnancy, and the 'improper' woman provided sexual services for money. The prostitute was denied dignity and the wife was denied any sexual feeling or self-determination.

The more permissive, promiscuous sexuality following the introduction of the contraceptive pill also brought more sexual mystification and pressures for women. Jo Mattison remembered feeling very isolated in her sexual relationship and wrote: 'I felt I was in a situation where I was expected to behave in an emancipated way but actually felt incapable of doing so' (*SR.29*). Anna Koedt's pamphlet of 1969, *The Myth of the Vaginal Orgasm*, asserted the necessity of clitoral stimulation for women to reach orgasm, and broke with the reproductive view of women's sexuality which centred women's pleasure solely in the vagina and dependent on male performance. This was further radicalized by lesbian women, who brought sexuality between women into the foreground after years of concealment and deeply disrupted the heterosexual hold over eroticism. By presenting a positive alternative, it also made sexual autonomy for all women more possible.

Along with the Pill and the toleration of sex outside marriage came the commercialization of sex and the use of women's bodies to sell goods, which separated sex from relationships and turned it into another commodity on the market. Women's liberation reacted by public demonstrations and protests against beauty contests, pornography and advertising. These brought angry accusations that feminists were humourless and spoiling the fun. The sixties also promoted a new myth of the independent, liberated woman which divorced sex from feeling and encouraged sexual competitiveness. The myth made non-reproductive sex a lonely freedom and idealized young, single women separate from mothers and older women.

Women wanted to reclaim their bodies, to define their own desires, to understand their own needs. They are using self-examination to find out more about their own reproductive anatomy. They have discussed sexuality in its context of personal relationships. The discussions have led to questioning the genital focus of eroticism and to the desire for more affectionate sexuality.

Sex is part of a wider process of women losing their timidity with themselves and with each other. Women need to feel proud of their sexuality without being totally defined by it or by their reproductive capacity. Jo Mattison wrote that 'if you can rid yourself of self-hate then you can see the absurdity of denying your sexuality. You want to allow yourself the creativity which you deny to yourself in being self-hating and self-destructive.'

Going All the Way

SARA RANCE

'Various awful things will happen to you, but never forget, my dear, the men like it.'

Fifty years ago, a middle-aged woman gave her betrothed daughter these words of advice on the eve of her wedding; it was probably her first and last piece of sex education. My friend's mother told her, 'You must be very careful of men now', as she handed her her first sanitary towel. No more, no less.

Today, in addition to euphemistic warnings from mothers, many children receive some kind of sex education in school. Sadly, however, it continues to reflect a double standard of morality for men and women, and does little to encourage girls to take a more exploratory and active view of their own sexuality. It preserves the view that sex is essentially for reproduction, reinforcing romanticized notions about marriage, and perpetuating antagonisms towards homosexuality and masturbation.

Children's sexual attitudes and knowledge are being patterned from an early age, and are moulded as much by the media, their friends, parents, and other adults, as by what they learn in school. However progressive or conservative the teaching, the 'facts of life' are not being written on a blank page: patriarchy has already made its indelible mark. Most girls by the time they are teenagers have learned the ropes of female objectification – spots and fat must be got rid of, periods kept hidden and secret, underarm and leg hair shaved, vaginal smells deodorized. 'Give your eyes a rest and go around for a day or two without make-up. Try it when your fella's not around or he'll get the shock of his life' (*Jackie* magazine). How ironical that within the same magazine's pages anxieties should be created and 'problems' answered. And such problem pages often provide the most important and influential source of information for those girls who receive no sex education in their schools.

Feminists would like to see sex education taking account of all the many factors which condition our attitudes to our bodies, to sex and reproduction. It should provide an opportunity for children to challenge and question the view of women as sex objects, and the stereotypical roles of wives and mothers. But at present school sex lessons reinforce the assumption that biology is destiny.

Sex education in schools crops up in all sorts of guises. It's hard to generalize about a subject which still isn't explicitly taught at all in many schools, and doesn't really exist on any curriculum in its own right. Usually it is incorporated into biology, social studies or religious education. Or it might take the form of an hour-long lecture in a packed assembly hall, given by a marriage guidance counsellor or G P. And what the children are required to study may vary considerably, from the mating habits of Mongolian gerbils to Walt Disney's (only?) war film, *VD Attack Plan*. But where the lessons do not just consist of biological facts, about reproduction in the mammal, they become the scene of moral indoctrination. Government reports on education have repeatedly encouraged the conscious use of sex education to inculcate the values of chastity, marriage and family life. *The Crowther Report – 15 to 18* (1959) said, 'To preserve the family in the future a conscious effort is needed by way of the educational system, on a much greater scale than has yet been envisaged.' And the *Newsom Report* (1963, on 'average and below average' children) suggested that religious instruction should help boys and girls to find a firm base for sexual morality based on chastity before marriage, and fidelity within it, and also suggests that married teachers are best equipped to handle the teaching of sex education.

Many Local Education Authorities have produced similar reports. Some issued guidelines to teachers, in response to the media furore about the rape and murder of a little girl by a twelve-year-old boy – which the papers implied was the direct result of sex lessons at school. 'Boy killed after sex lessons' (*Daily Telegraph*, 29.9.77). Shropshire L E A, for instance, gave a five-point guideline, the top two being that the family is to be regarded as the fundamental unit of society, and that children are to be taught that intercourse should only take place within marriage (*Shropshire Star*, 28.9.77). This particular incident provoked a huge response from parents, teachers and officials. On phone-ins and on letter pages people questioned the need for sex education at all. 'Surely sex is natural instinctive behaviour, like eating, and doesn't require teaching?' A common fear, and perhaps a more reasonable one, was that it was being taught in an impersonal, clinical manner, without any reference to feelings and relationships. This was distorted and sentimentalized by the press and morality crusaders, who claimed that children must be taught how to love: 'Storm over "loveless" school sex . . . sex education which ignores morality and affection' (*Daily Telegraph*, 27.9.77). 'Put love on the syllabus' (*Daily Mail*, 28.9.77). 'The missing lesson was love' (*Evening News*, 27.9.77).

Extreme opponents of sex education, such as the Responsible Society, argue that it depraves and corrupts. They have recently attacked such respectable organizations as the F P A (who are now also

Lesley Ruda

involved in sex education) because they hold special young people's clinics. 'There is a concerted effort by certain organizations to undermine the security of the family.' A prevalent view is that children who are told about sex will immediately experiment, and that the availability of contraception encourages the young to be promiscuous. In the face of attacks such as these, workers in the field are constantly pushed into defensive positions, and it is hardly surprising that so little progress has been made in the content of sex education materials for children, or in the philosophy underlying them. Even the 'progressives' in the field seem constantly at pains to point out their reverence for marriage and the family. The fairly recent introduction of teaching about methods of contraception in a few schools has, like abortion, been justified not from a positive feminist standpoint, a woman's right to choose, but in terms of population control and prevention of unwanted (read 'illegitimate') pregnancy.

These, then, are the attitudes which characterize most recent publications, and school radio and TV broadcasts. Sex educators are still restricting the information they give to children to the life cycle, marriage and the family, possibly with the mention of VD as cautionary advice against both promiscuity and homosexuality (often the *only* context in which homosexuality is mentioned). Even the rare advocate of premarital (note the wording) sex holds marriage as the ultimate goal. At a recent conference on 'accepting adolescent sexuality', the main speaker, James Hemming, said that premarital sex contributes to a 'mature capacity for physical love' which is 'the basis of happy and enduring marriage and the foundation for loving homes for the next generation to grow up in'. But what about those of us who choose to stay single? Who are gay, or widowed, or divorced? Sex educators still leave children to assume that such people have no legitimate outlet for their sexuality.

How pervasive is the view that sex is just for reproduction? It's surprising how many children even today are still under the impression that their parents have only had sex as many times as there are children in the family. For instance, one sixteen-year-old girl, when asked if she had ever seen or heard her parents making love, replied, 'I was too young, there's only me and my brother that are the youngest, all the others are older – so I don't see how I could've.'

Because sex education is so limited to this conceptual framework of reproduction, there is no place within it for basic information (let alone discussion) on such topics as masturbation, female arousal and orgasm, or homosexuality. For boys, it is possible that masturbation is explained as having the physiological function of relieving sexual tensions built up by the production of sperm – the common assumption being that male sexuality is somehow irrepressible. Female masturbation is rarely mentioned, confirming the belief that women have no autonomous sexuality, but are capable only of responding to male initiatives – and yet at the same time engendering (irrepressible) sexual desire in the male. This latter continues to be held against them – the seductress Eve being responsible for Adam's fall. And this 'original sin' is still used to absolve male responsibility for rape, and to counsel girls to be modest. Even the latest Department of Education Report (1977) on Health Education says, 'Girls should also understand that they may inadvertently impose great stresses on boys by arousing sexual reactions in them which they do not fully comprehend and may not be able to control.'

The vast majority of sex education books treat 'sex' as synonymous with heterosexual intercourse: yes, it is necessary for reproduction, and also conveniently well suited to the sexual gratification of the heterosexual male, but female arousal and orgasm may play no part in this process, and hence can be easily omitted, both in the classroom and in bed. It is staggering how many teenage girls are unaware of the existence of the clitoris, or the possibility of female orgasm. Even a book reprinted in 1977 fails to include the clitoris in its diagram of the female sexual organs (K. Elgin, 1977).

The stress on sexual intercourse as the be-all and end-all of sex is not only heterosexist, it also misleads many girls into the expectation that penetration will be their primary and ultimate source of physical pleasure. In fact we know that only a minority of women achieve orgasm during intercourse. And yet millions of us continue to feel confused, guilty and inadequate because we find petting, significantly known as foreplay, more physically satisfying than intercourse itself. In addition to the obvious fear of pregnancy, this may explain why many girls are reluctant to 'go all the way', and may well be very disappointed when they do so. Meanwhile the male interpretation of this reluctance is 'prick teasing'.

This emphasis on heterosexual intercourse as *the* valid sexual activity also leads to a striking silence on the subject of homosexuality, or, in cases where it is mentioned, endless cautions and warnings. The DES (*Health Education Report*, 1977) blatantly encourages sex educators to sweep the subject under the carpet, to deal with it 'in passing, if and when it arises', and definitely not to go into it on a deeper level, except for undertaking the essential task of guiding any wayward youngsters back on to the path to the altar. And can you imagine a sex education book which refers to heterosexuality as a phase which will usually pass as you get older? 'Nobody really knows why heterosexuality develops in some people . . . It's a mistake to assume you're heterosexual on the basis of occasional heterosexual feelings, and it's a mistake to push yourself towards heterosexuality because of them. Wait until you're sure, otherwise you could cause yourself a lot of unhappiness and confusion.' Replace 'hetero' with 'homo' and you have what *Will I Like It?*, published in 1978, has to say on the subject. This particular manual may be a slight improvement in that it no longer describes homosexuality as a sickness, but it's still a far cry from 'glad to be gay'.

Like homosexuality, masturbation is presented not as a valid expression of sexuality in its own right, but as a phase of adolescence, fairly harmless unless it persists into adulthood, when it might begin to inhibit the development of 'healthy' and 'productive' heterosexual relationships. The DES *Health Education Report* (1977) refers to it as 'an inevitable but transient part of sexual awareness', 'innocuous' but 'infantile'. This is in total harmony with these words of comfort offered in *Sex and the Young Teenager* (1978):

'A few simple precautions . . . will help the need pass more quickly.'

'A rugged game of tennis or football . . . will focus your attention elsewhere . . . helping you to get over the more difficult moments.'

Since the so-called 'sexual revolution' of the sixties, the do-your-own-thing approach has occasionally emerged in sex education books. It is a highly questionable approach from the feminist perspective, because although it does acknowledge non-reproductive and extra-marital sex, it tends to glamorize sexual activity and ignore sexual inequality. In advocating the 'free expression' of sexual needs and fantasies, it obscures the fact that most of these are socially constructed and thrive upon the sexual objectification and violation of women. *Will I Like It?* is such a book. 'Something else to treat carefully the first time out is the smash-and-grab approach. If both of you feel like raping each other, fine, if not, an over-aggressive rush by either side can lead to an impossibly tense vagina or a lost erection.' In its eagerness to highlight the pleasures of sex, it becomes glib, misleading and unrealistic. Sex is described as 'the world's most popular indoor sport', and the following statement, too, could only have been written by a privileged male: 'It's a physical fact that from the end of puberty to early adulthood you are at your most sexually potent. Orgasms come thick and fast, and you are capable of a level of sexual activity that is exhausting even to think about when you get older.' Ageist, sexist, inaccurate, and so far removed from the experience of the average teenage girl as to seem quite ludicrous – this is precisely the kind of male attitude which makes women feel despairing and inadequate. Of course it is important that girls discover that their sexuality can be a source of pleasure, but it is unrealistic to expect that this can develop from an understanding of physiology and a grasp of techniques alone. The dependence and passivity which at present characterize female sexuality cannot be separated from women's general lack of autonomy.

So how *do* we get away from the reproductive view of sex? As a general rule it's worth trying constantly to make it clear to children that we have a *capacity* to reproduce, but that's not necessarily what our bodies are *for*.

It's all too easy to slide into 'functionalist' explanations when describing physiology, especially as we often begin to talk to children about sex in response to the question 'Where did I come from?' Another reason is that many girls often receive their first sex education around the time that their periods start, and it's almost impossible to explain menstruation without reference to reproduction! So bearing this in mind, it's good to bring out with children from a really early age the many ways in which we can use, or gain pleasure from our bodies: to work, to show affection, to make love, to make babies, so that reproduction is seen as a choice, and not destiny.

An ideal learning situation is the small informal group, preferably segregated by sex. No doubt segregation is frowned upon by many teachers and seen as old-fashioned, but it leads to a lot more openness and honesty in discussion. It helps reduce the tendency of girls to feign ignorance or innocence, for fear of otherwise 'losing their reputations' and also to reduce the amount of bragging and bravado from boys. Even so, girls are usually reluctant to say anything which might implicate them, and frequently questions will be prefixed by 'my friend wants to know . . .'

Role-playing games are useful in getting children to explore ideas and different ways of reacting to certain situations. You merely provide the bare bones of the situation and get them to improvise. For instance a conversation between a pregnant girl and her best friend, a boy pressurizing his girlfriend to have sex, a girl discovering her sister is a lesbian, a visit to a family planning clinic. Teachers can gauge from the improvisations how much the children know about, for example, the symptoms of pregnancy, and fill in afterwards during discussion.

An idea drawn from experience within the woman's liberation movement is self-examination: encouraging girls to look at their external sexual anatomy with a mirror, explaining the changes that take place during sexual arousal and orgasm and talking about masturbation. Whereas most boys are used to handling their penis when they pee, for girls looking and touching themselves 'down there' is still regarded as 'dirty', so they need some encouragement. However, girls *and* boys need information about female sexual response. The stress on penetration often provokes anxiety in boys about the size of their penis. It's useful for them to discover that this bears no relation to their ability to satisfy their partner, and that penetration is only one way, not the only way, and that the clitoris is far more sensitive than the vagina. It's also this penetration-centred view of sex which creates the mystery of 'what lesbians do in bed', and the feeling of many girls that masturbation, apart from being 'dirty', is a bit of a waste of time. Masturbation is probably one of the best ways that people can learn about their own sexual response, and it contributes to a sense of autonomy to discover that there are many ways of gaining sexual satisfaction. It is a step towards helping people to communicate with their partners, but it should be treated as a valid form of sexual expression in its own right.

As far as girls are concerned, it seems to me that a basic aim of good sex education must be to counter the sense of dependency on boys and men, and to move towards a greater physical and emotional autonomy. Of course, it is very hard to break through the prevailing feelings of romanticism (or cynicism) and emerge with a fighting spirit.

Despite the well-worn feminist slogan 'the personal is political', and the assertion that we must have the right to define our own sexuality, it's surprising how easily the issue of sexuality gets side-stepped even within the women's liberation movement. And yet as women our personal identity and public image is tied up almost entirely with sex and reproduction. We learn that our bodies are our bread and butter, we learn that our capacity to reproduce and provide titillation and sexual servicing are our strongest selling points in the marriage market. Marriage and motherhood are still the 'facts of life' that all girls are required to learn . . .

SR.75, October 1978

Don't Get Too Near the Big Chakra

ANNE SEVERSON

'Gee, I would really like to be in your cunt movie, but mine isn't quite . . .?' Over and over again women who came into the room where I was shooting expressed their anxiety about that most intimate part of their bodies. The 'invisible ideal' I began to call it. Everyone thought there was such a thing as a beautiful cunt – but did they have it? No grounds for comparison. No information. Little reinforcement beyond the occasional assurances of a lover or husband.

I think I first got the idea of making the movie one day in California when my teenage daughter, lounging nude in the sun after a bath, casually exposed herself. I found myself staring at her vagina.

'Mother, for heaven's sakes!'

We both felt a little embarrassed. Later it seemed to me odd that first, I had not looked at that part of her body since she was very small, and secondly, that my curiosity made me uncomfortable. I felt there was something wrong about my interest. I started thinking and realized that I had never seen any woman's body, that is vagina – with the exception of crotch-shots in pornographic films and magazines or close-ups in birth films. I asked my women friends if they had ever looked at

Alison Fell, *SR.42*, December 1975

other women's cunts. One or two, with bisexual experience, assured me they had, others hadn't. Few wanted to pursue the matter.

. . . Diane and I were taking a yoga class together and I was intrigued that the first chakra one gains control of, or 'awakens' in yogic terms, was located between the vagina and the anus. 'Chakra' is Sanscrit for wheels or centres of radiating life force. Joseph Campbell calls them 'centres of consciousness'. There are seven or eight depending upon the system you follow. The first is located at the base of the spine and is the chakra of pure physical being, survival – it's the place where you just hang on.

The second is the centre in which zeal for life is sexually oriented, the level of consciousness where all psychological energy is erotic. I was jokingly calling it the 'big chakra' because we all seemed to be stuck at this level of development. It also seemed to me that the way out of this morass was by transforming some of this energy into a piece of art. In the proposed film I wanted to focus on the same area that our energy was flowing from in the beginning yoga class. I also hoped to creatively release some of this energy for myself and other women in order to move on up the cerebrospinal ladder.

But maybe I was still anxious about this new interest. Anyway, enough people told me it was a terrible idea which I should not pursue under any circumstances that I definitely decided to do it. In the back of my mind was the undeniable realization that, at worst, it was sure to be a lucrative potboiler. The people at the Multi-Media Resource Center, then a branch of Glide Methodist Church in San Francisco, agreed to produce and distribute the film and to help me find women willing to be photographed.

I designed a flyer with a red rose in the centre, a good symbol for the vagina – spiritual unfolding, feminity, fecundity – inviting women to be in a film about 'women's parts'. This phrase seemed evasive but I was still a little uneasy.

On the first day of shooting I was even more uneasy. It seemed likely that none would show up. Then in walked one of my oldest friends, unmarried and three months pregnant. She explained she was early because she was lunching with her parents, up from Los Angeles for a visit, and she didn't want to tell them she was showing her 'pee pee hole' in Anne's movie. With enormous relief I got to the business of shooting.

A steady stream of women followed her. Most were friends or students and former-students of mine from the San Francisco Art Institute where I was filming. A few were strangers who had seen the flyer or heard my announcement at a Multi-Media sex education class. By the time the mother of my friend who had been the first to appear walked in, I was feeling quite confident.

'What's the matter, isn't my vagina good enough for your film?' she said. I was so grateful to her for coming that I almost wept. She was solid middle-class and completely respectable. If she wanted to be in the film, there was nothing for me to worry about.

The atmosphere of the room where I was working was actually very pleasant. Several women told me later that they had come that day to see what was happening, thinking they would decide whether or not to be in the film on the basis of the feeling they had. I had arranged to have a woman from a class of mine whom I felt had unusually calm and supportive vibes to be there to explain to each arrival exactly what was expected. It worked very well. Women came in nervously, talked to her, then to other women who had already been filmed, and decided to sign up.

Everyone wrote down name, address, and birth date. I wanted to know the age range of the women participating and I was also interested in ascertaining if there was a particular astrological spread. At the most banal level of astrological prediction one would expect a high percentage of women with sun in Taurus or Scorpio to appear in a cunt film. Taurus is ruled by the planet Venus, love and beauty. Being an earth sign it is typically sensual, physical, earthy. Scorpio is ruled by Mars, the planet of desire and dynamic energy. It is the sex sign of the zodiac and rules the generative system. As expected, over half of the women in the film had suns in these two signs. Each other sign was represented. The only Gemini was a baby brought in by her Taurus mother.

I noticed a few other amusing astrological relationships. A Leo woman – proud, self-confident – came in with her fiancé who, before she was filmed, took out his pocket comb and carefully combed her pubic hair. A triple Libra, that is, a woman with both sun and moon in Libra plus Libra rising, she had already been in a number of independent films because of her unusual good looks. She was one of the few women who revealed no anxiety about the beauty of her vagina. She was also the only woman who did not wear underpants, which I interpreted as another mark of self-confidence.

A Scorpio woman came in late the first evening with her husband. She had been attending a sex education class which included physical training to develop the muscles of the vaginal barrel and they were both very pleased with the results. She volunteered to demonstrate the movements she had learned for the film. They were remarkable. After filming her I began asking each woman to move and discovered a whole range of personal variations on the basic levator ani contraction.

There were four Virgos involved: myself, a prostitute, a lesbian, and a psychologist who arrived too late, after I had dismantled the equipment. I find this combination difficult to explain briefly. Suffice it to say that we all deviate from the sexual-social norm in some way. The prostitute, in addition to her choice of profession, is distinguished by having had considerable body work done. She had a nose and chin job some years ago, which she now regrets, later had silicone injections in her breasts, and finally had her vagina surgically altered. The clitoral hood was removed to intensify sensation and the outer labia were trimmed to give the vagina a more youthful appearance and to allow deeper penetration. She feels that the vaginal surgery was a good idea and explained to me that it was necessary for her work. I am tempted to go on writing about her since she has been a kind of female guru for me and a lot of other women and men for some years, but I'll just recount one anecdote.

We first met when I was teaching a women's class at the Art Institute in the early days of the movement. It was a touchy situation. I had been maligned by the other faculty in my department, all male, for raising an issue that had no relevance to art. On the other hand, my class had been raided by a group of women radicals from Berkeley because it was co-ed and I had a male teaching assistant. I later discovered that it was one of my hostile colleagues who had turned us in.

The 'hooker', a word she used, had not appeared the week we expected her but we had an exciting session anyway, each of us in the class taking a turn at pretending to be her while the others asked questions. When she arrived the next week I was afraid that we might embarrass or upset her because the questions we had worked up were very personal and direct . . .

The whole cosmos tipped and I saw how a position at the bottom becomes the ultimate strength. During the class meeting she talked about how prostitution cracked and destroyed the egos of a lot of hookers. She also pointed out, and was intensely alive evidence for, the enormous power that comes from doing it the hard way, acting on your impulses, taking the consequences. If you choose to be at the bottom, or find yourself there, ain't nobody can shove you down. I might point out that she has Venus in Leo in the twelfth house: her love nature in the sign of generosity and expansion, in the house of karma and bondage, of salvation and secret undoing. I, finally, have Jupiter in Aries in the eleventh house, an indication of unusual heroes, heroines.

So all together thirty-eight women appeared for the film. The age range was from three months to sixty-three years. There were two Black women, one half-Oriental girl, two lesbians, one prostitute, two

virgins (I think), a lot of mothers, three mothers-to-be, three grand-
mothers, four women menstruating, and one girl who discovered a
week later that she had gonorrhea, and one woman who learned a
month later that she had uterine cancer. All relevant, I believe, because
none of these characteristics is evident in the film – except the women
who are menstruating – you can see their Tampax strings.

In fact, when the first woman having her period came in to be filmed
and casually mentioned that she hoped I didn't mind, I felt mildly
shocked. One more anxiety registered. I realized that I would never
consider being in such a film during my period – an old hangover from
the fifties when the fact of one's period was to be concealed or disguised.
Teenage Kotex terrors. What if someone could *see* the outline! I can
remember my grandmother on the day after the big event occurred for
the first time: 'Your mother told me about it, dear, I'm so sorry.' How
angry I felt. It was bad enough to have to walk around with a soggy
mattress between your legs on the hottest summer day, but why that
vile women's burden attitude?

Anyway, these women didn't seem to suffer from any fears about
menstruation being dirty or a source of shame. They climbed up on
the table and spread their legs, exposing the vagina, menstrual period,
Tampax string and all. One last shudder when I realized that even
during times of casual nudity with my most intimate friends I would
carefully tuck the little string into the vaginal opening so it wouldn't
be visible.

I had just finished writing the preceding paragraph when I opened
Robert Graves's *The White Goddess* and read the following:

The baleful moon-dew used by the witches of Thessaly was apparently a
girl's first menstrual blood, taken during an eclipse of the moon. Pliny devotes a
whole chapter of his *Natural History* to the subject and gives a long list of the
powers for good and bad that a menstruating woman possesses. Her touch can
blast vines, ivy, and rue, fade purple cloth, blacken linen in the wash-tub,
tarnish copper, make bees desert their hives, and cause abortion in mares; but
she can also rid a field of pests by walking around it naked before sunrise, calm
a storm at sea by exposing her genitals, and cure boils, erysipelas, hydrophobia,
and barrenness.

Too bad all that mythic power can't cure the one common female
condition that is so vividly evident in the film. The ubiquitous yeast
infection. Ick. An unattractive, smelly, recurrent nuisance.

. . . I finished editing the film and started showing it. One of the first
screenings was for the women who were in it and their guests. Few
were able to recognize themselves except for one friend who has bright
red pubic hair and the prostitute. She was accompanied by a happy

crowd of intimates who whistled and applauded when her cunt appeared on the screen.

Another male film-maker, Scott Bartlett, was dissatisfied with the editing and volunteered to do another cut for me. I gave him the colour workprint and waited expectantly to see what he would do. Not surprisingly, Scott eliminated all of the sexually irrelevant or, perhaps I should say, sexually distracting details. He edited out all cunts with Tampax strings, all of those with yeast infections. Each shot was shortened. The result is a lot hotter. Short fast shots of beautiful cunts in glowing technicolor. I just looked at it in my viewer to check these impressions. Objectively, I might even say that he made a better film of the footage. His film is erotic, exciting, sexual. My version is gruelling, even tedious, and as far as I know, no man has ever gotten an erection watching it. But subjectively, I am satisfied by my film and not interested in his.

A lot of people have seen the film and gotten angry. Crowds were annoyed at the 1972 Edinburgh Festival, and in a magazine review someone showed me the cunts were compared to 'rashers of bacon'.

When it was shown at the Ann Arbor Film Festival several hundred walked out. One woman was outraged by this response, especially since some of those leaving were making rude and irreverent comments. She chased them up the aisles, bashing with her bag. Later, she explained to me, 'I would kill for your film'.

Another woman walked up to me after a screening in England, and with a very sweet smile, told me she was furious. When I asked why, she explained that her husband had been sitting next to her! I was still perplexed. We took a long walk together. I explained the genesis of my idea and my motivations as well as I could. She explained that she feared that her husband, having been exposed to the horror of the female genitals in such an unequivocal fashion, would never desire her again. We parted sympathetically. I didn't particularly want *Chakra* to turn men on, but it would seem too bad if an unhurried non-sexual view of the human vagina turned them off.

The most candid response was that of an official of the American Embassy in London where I did a small private screening. We were relaxed after a fine dinner with wine and drinks, and more drinks. He would grin effusively at me and slap my back, 'You had the balls to do that! . . . the balls to do that!'

Not at all, I thought, not at all.

SR.20, February 1974

'Readers' Poems'

MARGARET S. CHALMERS

I have never had a climax.
No! I swear!
It's the clitoral truth.

SR.39, September 1975

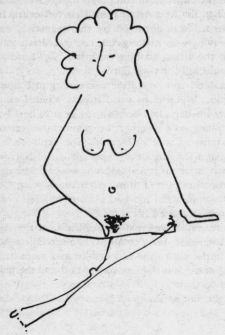

SR.23, May 1974

The Moon within Your Reach

ELEANOR STEPHENS

'The toughest problem to treat is frigidity, some say because a woman's response is so subjective, variable, and vulnerable to so many outside factors. In any case, success depends upon the goals of the patient. Some are happy to be having sex at all. Some want the moon' (FPA doctor, *Sunday Times*, September 1975).

Amongst all the issues raised by the women's movement, the feminist approach to female sexuality is one which has, for many women, completely transformed our feelings about ourselves and our lives. Just as women are questioning many of the institutions, ideas and social relations defined for us by men, so we are no longer prepared to accept traditional sexual attitudes and practices. These attitudes have for centuries kept us in ignorance of our needs and responses, and unequal and passive in our relationships with men.

The implications of taking responsibility for our own sexuality reach into all areas of our lives, giving women a new sense of autonomy and power. Theorists such as Freud, Reich and Marcuse have often connected sexual satisfaction with 'self-actualization' and linked sexual repression with a submissive personality structure. It is time to apply this to women. A feminist psychiatrist, Carmen Kerr, puts it this way:

Taking an active role in making her sex life exactly how she wants it, is the nitty gritty of women asking for what they want in their lives as a whole. For women to feel confident and knowledgeable enough to say 'I want more of that' and 'I don't want any of that, thanks' during sex, and so achieve her demands and needs, is a most immediately rewarding way for her to be able to do the same with other demands in her life . . . In other words, I believe that for some women to break down their sexual inhibitions is a first, indispensable step in claiming power in respect to men, and ultimately the world. (*Women's Orgasm*)

This may sound very high flying and theoretical but, as with many of the issues of the women's movement, the reality on which it is based is profoundly personal. Before each of us can begin to take responsibility for our individual sexuality, we have to discover for ourselves what it is that we want.

My own experience of first discussing sex in a serious and open way, in contrast to nervous giggling with girlfriends at school and embarrassed exchanges with teachers, took place in my women's group in Cambridge (Massachusetts, USA). At that time I was living with a man with our small child and while I was aware of some problems, I was generally happy with our sexual relationship. One small 'problem' which I never thought worth mentioning or seeking 'professional advice' (I'm thankful I didn't) was that I was never sure whether or not I had orgasms. The hot topic of the day was the vaginal versus clitoral controversy, which added to the confusion. It was an extraordinary relief to find that women in my group had similar doubts and confusions. With their encouragement, I taught myself to masturbate, and gradually learned what my body enjoyed and the sensations that I was capable of experiencing. Although it took a long time to share this with my lover, at least I knew what I was aiming at and what I needed. I also realized that I had been defining my satisfaction in his terms, and for me the climax was a feeling of empathy with his orgasm. We accepted this since it seemed that we often achieved the famed goal of simultaneous orgasm, though in fact we were both experiencing his orgasm!

The following year I worked with a group of women teaching the course called 'Women and Our Bodies', the material for which was later published as the book *Our Bodies, Ourselves*. Of the ten topics covered in the course, the three which concerned female sexuality were the most popular. At the end of the last session, a shy woman in her thirties with three children came up to me to tell me how useful she had found this and how much she had enjoyed it. But could she ask me one last question: 'What does it feel like to have an orgasm?' For her, and how many others, I knew that we had failed. Yet we had talked frankly about childhood experiences and attitudes to our bodies, Freud and other theorists had been discussed, the Masters and Johnson work reviewed, extrovert women had compared positions that suited them best, and so on. Yet basically we'd missed the point, and it was very likely that a lot of the women coming to our groups were not experiencing orgasm. (Kinsey's survey of 1938–49 on 5,940 women showed that 55 per cent never or rarely experienced orgasm. The 1972 Playboy Foundation study showed a decrease of only 7 per cent.) Why not and what could be done? While it was important to connect female orgasm with clitoral rather than vaginal stimulation, the crucial point was not 'where does it happen?' but 'what makes it happen?' At that time women were learning all kinds of new practical skills, like car mechanics and self-defence, and it occurred to me that if we could demystify sexuality and think of the orgasm response as a skill then we could begin to help women to learn it. And the simplest way, the way that had worked for me, was through masturbation.

Two years later, in 1973, I went to work in Berkeley, California, and found that this idea had occurred to feminists there and that groups had already begun with the aim of teaching women to reach orgasm through masturbation. (Berkeley, of course, where every flat surface is a notice board, has groups on everything so this was not so surprising.) These groups, which started in 1972 and are going from strength to strength, helping hundreds of women, are called pre-orgasmic women's groups. Pre-orgasmic rather than the medical term 'non-orgasmic', because this approach presupposes that every woman with a clitoris can become orgasmic given the right kind and amount of stimulation. Anyone who can learn to ride a bicycle, and this too can be a slow and fearful process especially as an adult, can learn to have an orgasm. While the term 'pre-orgasmic' may sound pompous, it seems to be accurate; the success rate is astonishing. A minimum of 90 per cent of the women become orgasmic by the end of the ten-week course (through masturbation) and a follow-up study showed that within four months 50 per cent of the women experienced orgasms in their sexual relationships. Many women joined these groups as a last resort having spent hundreds of dollars and hours in conventional psychotherapy, hypnosis, encounter groups, anything that offered hope. And most commonly and sadly, they would go from one relationship to another looking for the right lover who would teach them the secret of sexual satisfaction. This after all is an important aspect of the Romantic Myth of the Ideal Lover, which has prevented women from taking responsibility for their own sexuality, and maintained their dependence on men.

This new definition of the female orgasm throws the clinical concept of frigidity out of the window. At a conference in Berkeley in January, a female therapist from the Women's Sexuality Institute, one of the several organizations that run these workshops, began her speech with the rally call: 'There is no such thing as a frigid woman!' The entire audience, over two hundred men and women, rose to their feet and cheered. A frigid woman is one who has not had an orgasm – yet. This is the simple assumption on which the workshops are based, together with the belief that the key to achieving orgasm is through masturbation, as a Los Angeles therapist explains: 'It's our conviction that a woman must be in touch with her own sexuality and understand her own individual needs before she can effectively communicate to her partner her likes and dislikes, and what she finds sexually exciting. Masturbation is the best way for a woman to learn and teach herself about herself.' By teaching women to give orgasms to themselves, literally to learn to love themselves, the whole process is demystified and orgasm is seen not as something beyond our control, something 'done to us' but something which we can cause to happen. With this confidence, we can then share the experience with a partner when we make love.

How then are the groups or workshops organized? There are several variations but in general they follow a similar pattern based upon the method developed by Lonnie Barbach and Nancy Carlsen, two therapists who worked at the University of California Medical Center in San Francisco. Each group has two co-ordinators who lead the discussions and not more than ten members; they meet for two hours twice a week for five weeks. The women contract to undertake one hour's homework each day, which is essential and involves a heavy time commitment. (Five weeks of intensive work seems to be more effective than a longer period.) The techniques used come from a variety of sources: Masters and Johnson, and Lo Piccolo and Kegel, whose specific exercises for controlling the muscles of the pelvic floor are practised. Relaxation exercises and massage are an initial part of the homework helping women to explore and feel comfortable with their bodies in general, and sexual areas in particular, as a preliminary for masturbation. The first sessions introduce women to the physiological and anatomical aspects of human sexuality, about which many women are ignorant; some feel their genitals are abnormal and it is reassuring to look at pictures and to look at themselves in a mirror.

Detailed discussion of the process of masturbation is introduced through several short films which have been made for this purpose. One shows a woman taking a shower, enjoying soaping herself and touching her body, then going on to masturbate to orgasm. Another film shows a woman using a vibrator. However strange this sounds, in practice the films work beautifully. They are sensitively produced and their explicitness makes them far more useful than books or lectures. (Most young boys have seen each other masturbate, but very few women have ever shared this.) Another film shows a heterosexual couple making love with both of them concentrating on the woman reaching orgasm – by manual stimulation not through penetration which is, incidentally, the most difficult way for most women to reach a climax. In this film the woman has an orgasm and the man does not, and both appear happy and satisfied with this. Women are so used to the opposite situation that it is gratifying to see an alternative. This raises discussion of the problems associated with simultaneous orgasm, a very entrenched myth, and very frustrating to women. Except in the situation where both people stimulate each other orally, it is very hard for partners to give sensitive and rhythmic stimulation when they are on the verge of an orgasm themselves. In most heterosexual situations, the man becomes distracted from the woman's orgasm and the woman gives way to the male orgasm.

Lots of time in each session is devoted to sharing feelings about sex in general and particularly about orgasm. Many women find themselves reaching a block because of all their deeply rooted fears. The fear of being out of control is very common, so that when they feel themselves close to a climax, they deliberately resist the sensations. Some worry about looking funny, or making too much noise, or not enough. Lots of these aspects of self-consciousness are relieved by the privacy of masturbation, and being able to share the worries with others in the group. We all have so many 'shoulds' about sex, so many imperatives which we have been socialized to accept, that it is hard to find out what we are really like. This is the importance of the hour's daily homework; it gives women a chance to explore their own potential for sexual pleasure without pressures to conform to external standards. Many women find it hard to put aside this time for themselves because they feel that they don't deserve the attention. This is why the group structure and the support it gives is so crucial. The process involves so much courage and trust, that without encouragement many women could not continue. The leaders, some of whom have clinical group experience, are all trained and meet together to discuss the progress of their different groups. They bring to each group the experiences of many women they have worked with, and also share their own personal feelings. In the traditions of the women's movement, the groups are non-hierarchical and everybody is encouraged to participate.

The focus of these groups is to teach women to achieve orgasm through masturbation, and only if there is time will the problems of having orgasms with a partner be discussed. (Some women may not currently be in a relationship.) Other groups now exist which deal specifically with this, and lots of women go on to these groups; while it is a great breakthrough to experience orgasm for the first time, it is only a start. Most women want to share this with their lovers. But one problem which is important to confront from the outset, since it can be a huge stumbling block, is that of the woman who has learned to fake orgasm. This is far more common than I ever supposed, though I had been aware of doing it myself on occasion. Betty Dodson, who organizes similar body workshops in New York, describes a woman called Nancy who, after six years of heterosexual relationships, had taught herself to have orgasms using a stream of water from the tap while in the bath: 'Nancy started a new love affair and felt confused about how to handle the sex with him. Now that she knew what orgasm was, should she tell him that she could not come having intercourse. I urged her to get her lover involved in her sexual exploration immediately and stressed the importance of not faking orgasm. Once we do that we are trapped in the biggest collective lie of them all. We must stop sacrificing our own pleasure to protect the male ego or to avoid taking sexual responsibility for ourselves.' Nancy took this advice and fortunately her boyfriend was reassuring and explored her sexuality with her. 'Within a relatively short period of time, Nancy was able to have orgasms several different ways: with water, with the vibrator, by hand, with oral sex, and with intercourse plus the vibrator.'

Nancy's situation was easier, but to confront the fact that one doesn't have orgasms if one has been pretending to do so, takes a tremendous amount of courage. One woman who had been faking for five years finally explained this to her husband. He told her that she deserved an Academy Award for best actress of the century. His response was sympathetic and relevant because many women feel that when they are in bed, they are also on stage, and when the earth doesn't move we believe it is we who have failed.

Several criticisms of this approach are commonly raised during discussion and it may be helpful to try to answer some now:

Isn't all this very unromantic?

Yes, it certainly is. Romanticism is largely responsible for keeping people in ignorance about sex and maintaining many of our most oppressive myths. Women have tolerated miserable sexual relationships, faked orgasms and generally kept quiet about their needs, all in the name of Romantic Love. But I do not believe that it is unromantic, in the sense of unloving or mechanical, to discuss sex with your lover. To plunge into a sexual encounter 'spontaneously' and just let it happen will usually be to the disadvantage of the woman. Ultimately, both people suffer if one of them is not happy and many relationships where strong 'romantic' attractions exist, deteriorate because of fear and ignorance of discussing ways to improve their sexual communication. Nothing in the approach described here is intended to undermine the importance of the human and emotional aspects of sex. It simply supposes that women have the right to enter a relationship on an equal basis with men, with the confidence that both people can and will have orgasms if they wish.

Are you saying that women are never helped by traditional therapy and psychoanalysis?

My own suspicions of psychotherapy are so deeply entrenched since I have known so many women severely damaged by this patriarchal institution, that I would almost never recommend this course. But certainly some women have been helped, although more in the sense of feeling more relaxed and open about sex, rather than in the 'treatment of orgasmic dysfunction' so-called. Some women may be so traumatized by their negative sexual conditioning that they require a great deal of time and attention to work through this. A sympathetic therapist (or a friend) may be helpful. But to turn to psychotherapy as a first, and often a last, resort seems to me to be expensive and usually worthless. Even the Masters and Johnson clinics which are starting over here tend to be far more helpful to men than women. They emphasize the goal of achieving orgasm through intercourse (penetration) rather than exploring the other techniques which are more suited to women's sexual anatomy.

These groups may work for young women who have grown up in a climate of sexual experimentation and whose sexual habits are not so set. Surely older women need more intensive help, or are perhaps beyond help?

The women who attend these workshops vary tremendously in age and backgrounds. It is certainly not too late for older women to learn how to have orgasms; on the contrary, the longer the years of missing out, the stronger the motivation for making changes. Many women in their twenties and thirties are still waiting for their ideal lover to show them how, or just keep hoping that an orgasm will some day happen to them.

The adjustment needed in the sexual relationship may be greater the longer it has continued. When a forty-eight-year-old woman explained to her husband what kind of stimulation she needed to reach orgasm, he objected that he was too old to change. Her response to this, which worked, was to say: 'We've tried it your way for twenty-six years, why not give my way a try?' If this sounds flippant, I would emphasize both the amount of courage it takes to make this change, and the revolutionary effect on the total relationship as a result of the increased competence and confidence the woman feels. For this woman, and for many others, her decision to take her sexual life in her hands marked the start of a new life.

Only heterosexual women have these problems. Lesbians would neither need, nor be interested in these groups.

About a quarter of the women in the groups are lesbian or bisexual. I was most surprised by this since I had accepted the myth that lesbians were by definition terrific lovers with none of my sexual hang-ups. (This made me feel more guilty about not being gay when, in 1970, the pressure was on all 'good feminists' to come out and affirm their sexual allegiance. After all, how could one expect satisfactory sexual relationships with men!) This kind of myth put performance pressures on gay women, many of whom felt insecure and confused about their sexuality and have been delighted to participate in the groups. Since the basic aim of this approach is to encourage each person to take more responsibility for her own sexuality, and to start to define it for herself, women can benefit whatever their sexual bias and way of life. Incidentally, women come together who would not otherwise have occasion to meet, nor to share such personal experiences, so the groups perform a general consciousness-raising function.

SR.42, December 1975

How Did We Get This Way?

SUE CARTLEDGE AND SUSAN HEMMINGS

If you are a lesbian, chances are you've spent a lot of time wondering how you got that way. Heterosexuals rarely give their sexuality a second thought. They may worry about sex and all its complications but it won't usually have crossed their minds to ask themselves why they've grown up heterosexual. And very probably no one has ever asked them to justify or explain it.

This one-sided state of affairs, where homosexuality is seen as deviating from what is 'natural', accounts for the kinds of questions we as lesbians ask ourselves about our sexuality, and the kinds of answers we can come up with. If you have to start by assuming you're the one who is different, even before you can ask yourself why and how, you will come up with different explanations than if you assume you're 'normal'. Heterosexual people could ask themselves all the questions raised here, but they don't. Not unless they're among the handful of feminists who are especially interested in the effect of social pressures on the way we develop our sexual identity. It's not only a climate of 'difference' in which lesbians have to define themselves but one of almost total *in*difference. It's not just, 'Why am I like this?' but, 'Do I really exist at all?' Even when people are *trying* to be helpful, lesbians constantly fail to get a mention: 'We must recognize the fact that love, whether it be between a man and woman, or man and man, can achieve a pure and glorious relationship if it is expressed with restraint and discipline' (Bishop of Southwark, June 1979).

Being able to assert that you're alive and well and lesbian often leads to becoming more interested in why it is that, despite all the counter-pressures, and despite the conspiracy of silence on the subject, you've managed to end up that way. Here are some of the discussions we've had with each other and with friends about the origins of our lesbianism. We looked at the more frequently encountered theories —some of them seem to contain grains of truth, but none are totally satisfactory. They can't be, because they are inherited from a society which classifies us as unnatural and unhealthy.

> So, how did it start, how did it all begin?
> I'm trying, yes, I'm trying hard to find
> My lesbian . . . origin.

Baby Bio
the genetic explanation

The poems which follow are verses from a song, 'Lesbian Origin', which Susan wrote for the Lesbian Left Revue Theatre Group, and the quotations are from conversations with Sue's friends.

> Now what's the problem, sisters?
> I'll tell you what I say –
> It's quite straightforward, the reason why I'm gay:
> Way back in the embryo I was formed that way.

'I knew I was different. I just wasn't interested in the things the other girls were into – boys, clothes, make-up, etc. I was a tomboy. My father kept saying: "It's time you got out of those dungarees and into a skirt." I played a lot of sport specially netball, because I was in love with the netball teacher. I just kept falling in love with women all the time – never with men. I was very isolated. I didn't have any images of lesbians, didn't really know what the word meant. I just knew I was different.'

Many women, both heterosexual and lesbian, remember being strongly resistant to efforts to 'feminize' them when they were younger –and have memories of always being different in their choice of play-things, games or friends. Many had crushes on other girls and women. Lesbians often say that they were aware, as far back as they can re-member, of being strongly attracted to girls and women. But the dif-ference for those lesbians from heterosexual women with the same memories is that lesbians placed an important emotional significance on those experiences. We didn't 'outgrow' it or 'transfer' it on to boys. Lesbians who feel this is specially true of their history often say they were *born* lesbian.

This was the view of Radclyffe Hall, who told the publisher of her book *The Well of Loneliness* (first printed in 1928), that homosexuals, 'being from birth set apart in accordance with some hidden scheme of nature, need all the help that society can give them'. It's an explanation which homosexuals themselves use, when they are putting their trust in the liberal tolerance of the great mass of heterosexuals.

The idea that homosexuality is an innate, inherited characteristic, a

Jo Nesbitt

freak of the genes, has twin advantages. It reassures nervous heterosexuals that they can't catch it: after all, if it's genetic, it can't be
infectious. And it allows us to say that it's not really our fault: after all,
you can't punish us for a handicap. But there are serious and dangerous
drawbacks to this explanation. It can, and has led to the views held by
those who think we should be exterminated. Hitler had thousands of
homosexuals slaughtered along with the Jews and other groups he
considered less than human. Then there is the contemporary research
featured in May of this year, on BBC's *Horizon*. In 'The Fight to be
Male' homosexuality was discussed in these terms: 'Derner is now
studying mothers in the fourth month of pregnancy, the time which he
believes is the critical period . . . He is measuring the testosterone
levels in their wombs . . . He follows the selected children growing up,
to prove low testosterone in the womb leads to homosexuality . . . then
the next step might be to inject [into the womb] more testosterone –
and so prevent homosexuality' . . . and thus breed us off the planet, as
if we were mutations.

At an entirely less objectionable, though still personally painful level,
these genetic arguments lead to the commonly held belief that there are
two kinds of homosexuals: those who were born like it, so can't help it,
and those who were born 'normal' – but are just plain wilful. Mother
of a lesbian: 'You want all the fun, and none of the responsibility.'

Daughter of a lesbian: 'You could at least *try* to find a man. After all, you must have done it at least once.'

It's not surprising that under such pressures, many of us who do not really believe we were 'born' lesbian, often want to claim that we were, just to get the nagging world off our backs. Look, we say, lay off, we can't change just to suit you. But those of us who are feminists, as well as lesbians, have a deep suspicion of all genetic theorists, knowing how often they've used their research to 'prove' that women are born inferior to men, or blacks to whites.

For us, the major drawback of the total dependency biology as an explanation is that it leaves no room for the possibility of changing sexuality, or sexual practice, or attitudes toward these. And it successfully lets heterosexuals off the hook from ever having to explain *their* sexual selves.

> *Psycho-Dyke*
> *theories from your dark past*
>
> 'Please tell me expert therapist
> Why've I grown up a freak?
> I hate being gay
> And I'm going up the creek.'
> 'Your mummy was too dominant,
>   your daddy frail and weak.
> But don't despair, for help is here:
>   your future's not too bleak.
> That's ten pounds fifty please, and
>   I'll see you Tuesday week.'

'When I was five, I can remember walking with my mother down a long, dark lane to our house. And I remember saying to her, "Don't be frightened, Mum." I always felt very protective towards her. My father was away a great deal, and I think that's why I'm a lesbian.'

'Psychological' theories of the origins of homosexuality are perhaps even more popular now than biological ones. In some ways this is progress. At least psychological theories, through their examination of early relationships, pay some recognition to the idea that sexuality may not be 'natural' and God-given, but formed by the society we live in, and by our own particular backgrounds.

Many women have found that exploring the past, through consciousness raising or through feminist therapy, has been enormously liberating, shedding light on murky private fears and lifting the burden of guilt. It has given us the opportunity to make some sense of our personal history, by discovering how much of it is similar to other women's. So exploring our lives in this way has been very rewarding for many women, lesbian or otherwise.

But in the 'common-sense' world outside the radical influence of feminist theory, lesbianism is still seen as a deviation from the norm. Psychology doesn't tell us we are morally reprehensible, but the drift of the explanations it gives us is still negative: 'immaturity' in failing to transfer the early love for the mother on to the father; 'mother-fixation' resulting from a broken home or not enough love and affection in childhood. Psychology may claim to make no judgements. But lesbianism is still seen as a problem to be analysed, often an illness to be treated. In any case we can't win. Even those rare psychologists who don't start off by seeing us as freaks say that the pressures we have to live with will *make* us into freaks. Phyllis Chesler (*Women and Madness*, 1972) describes this trap:

Most psychoanalytic theorists either sincerely misunderstand or severely condemn lesbianism. Some do both. The 'condition', they say, is biologically or hormonally based. No, say others, it is really an environmental phenomenon. In any event all agree, it is maladaptive, regressive and infantile: even if it isn't it leads to undeniable suffering – and is therefore maladaptive, regressive and infantile.

As far as the media are concerned, psychology can be used to explain all female aberrations, not just lesbianism. Women terrorists are depicted as spoilt middle-class malcontents longing to get back at their fathers. Violence among teenage girls is the result of reversed sex-roles, with women's liberation to blame. And psychology is used to predict the dire results of feminism – a generation of farmed-out, nursery-reared children with no sense of security. We are all sick, unless we conform to men's idea of femininity – pretty, passive and unchallenging.

The notion that those of us who haven't conformed are strong and healthy, rather than weak, sickly deviants, hasn't yet gained much popular appeal! Lots of people still believe that lesbians are women who, because they are too ugly to attract men, or because they've had bad experiences with men, turn to each other for comfort. A male Labour MP visiting a Sappho meeting exclaimed with genuine surprise, 'But this room is full of attractive women!' It's true that many of us have given up the search for Mr Right. Is that a weakness? Why potter on with hope in your heart – for what might be a lifetime – looking for that non-sexist dream man? Psychologists have seen us as battle-scarred invalids who couldn't take any more in the rough and tumble of heterosexual competition, rather than as strong-minded realists with a positive preference for women. Lesbians have had to be

Jo Nesbitt

tremendously strong to resist all the pressures which insist that women search out Mr Right. So it's hard to see why the image of us as 'invalids' has survived for so long.

Cupid's Dart
the romantic conversion

> Why do you want to make things so very black or white?
> I'm not an actual lesbian, so don't label me, all right?
> I just met my girlfriend at a party one night . . .
> It's not her sex that matters. It just feels right.

'I think I'm a lesbian because I fell in love with a woman. I suppose I could have fallen in love with a man, and I'd be heterosexual. I don't know, because I've never felt that total emotional involvement with a man. But I didn't think of myself as a lesbian – not until my girlfriend called me a "fucking lesbian". The only images I had of lesbians were of pipes and tweeds, and I knew I wasn't like *that*.'

So does love really conquer all – even the massive edifice of heterosexuality? Certainly most women become lesbian through powerful romantic feelings for another woman. And such feelings (stars crossing, bolts from the blue, chemistry at work . . .) often *seem* to enter our lives from outside, sweeping us off our feet. But it's unlikely that we just happen to fall in love. We create and nurture romantic feelings, consciously or otherwise, partly to give ourselves the chance to make emotional leaps, and to bring about drastic changes in our lives which we otherwise might not dare to make – such as straight to gay.

Heterosexual romance is highly valued but, as yet, gay romance has had a mixed response. In the sex education kit recently published by the Campaign for Homosexual Equality, ideas about 'romance' are used to get the tolerance of the straight teenager. As prime targets for romance propaganda they will *surely* be understanding of the gay teenager who's only asking for the same 'right' of someone to love? But even the romantic explanation has not so far brought us society's indulgence. Maureen Colquhoun's relationship with her lover was presented in that way in a *Woman's Own* article last year: 'It's Marvellous to be in Love Again'. 'It simply didn't matter whether she was a man or a woman,' ran the article. But it certainly did matter to Maureen's political colleagues, who campaigned locally and nationally for her to be removed from her job as MP.

. . . But lesbianism is a wider experience, a deeper commitment than can be contained within one individual and privatized passionate relationship. To represent lesbianism just in terms of one, or even a series, of intense romantic experiences would not account for the loving feelings which many lesbians have for women friends, and women in general. There are many celibate lesbians, who are not just waiting for the next big romance to show up. Heterosexuals do not 'lose' their sexuality when they are celibate. Nor is a lesbian less of one if she is not within a sexual relationship. Sexuality cannot be collapsed into sex, nor can love be contained just within romance.

The Sisterhood Theory

> We came home from the meeting feeling utterly depressed.
> Why can't Arthur Scargill see that women are oppressed?
> Linda stayed all night: in the morning we caressed,
> And I realized all the loving feelings I'd suppressed . . .

'I began being attracted to other women as soon as I started going to women's liberation conferences. I suppose my life had become more and more involved with women, and they seemed far more interesting than my husband, or any men, more exciting, more glamorous. And I certainly saw lesbians as the elite of the movement – as well as being very nervous of them. Looking back now, I suppose I can trace elements of my earlier life which with hindsight could be pointers to lesbianism. I was always very competitive with boys when I was a kid. I never wanted to be like my mother, stuck for years staring across a pile of dirty dishes at the neighbours' side wall. But without the

women's movement, I just don't know if I would ever have taken the
step of becoming a lesbian. The only images I had before were of fat
girls at school with spots who held hands in the back row when we had
a film – I assumed they turned to each other because boys rejected
them. As soon as I heard about gay liberation, and positive images of
gayness, I changed my views.'

This quotation isn't necessarily typical of all the hundreds of women
who've become lesbians 'through the movement'. To many of us, lesbianism contained not so much a glamorous excitement, or a way out
of marriage, but rather an extension of the closeness that grows up
between women working together politically, and depending on each
other, as well as enjoying more relaxed times. A lot of us asked ourselves, 'If I'm feeling all these things for women, why am I keeping my
sexual feelings separate?' It began to seem like a false and unnecessary
separation, forced on us by men.

The history of the women's movement both here and in the States
includes a period when feminists didn't want lesbians to be terribly
vocal, in case it put other women off joining. And such attitudes still
exist. In consciousness-raising groups women exchange anxieties about
lesbianism, and constantly have to deal with boyfriends and husbands
taunting them on the topic. And when two women do decide to become
lovers, enraged husbands and all the local papers scream 'Women's Lib
Turned Her Into A Man Hater'. It's hardly surprising that women prefer
to skate around the issue of sexual preference, except for a brief 'Well, I
don't know, I've just always needed a man in that kind of way.' Lots of
women feel they have cracked sexism in their personal lives, either by
finding a nice man who isn't so hung up on conventional sex roles, or by
training one not to be. But sexism is not just about sex roles and having the
good luck to find your Mr Right won't change a sexist society.

... A lesbian relationship is far more threatening to the status quo
than even the most radically reformed heterosexual one.

'When I first joined the women's movement, as a heterosexual feminist, my women's group spent most of the time talking about sexuality
and relationships. We talked for hours about sex, problems with men,
how we resented sex roles (like how come men have this inability to
clean cookers), how we hated being whistled at in the street, how we
had been shy teenagers, how men had let us down – all those kinds of
things. But we never wondered how we got to be heterosexual. The
question just didn't arise. I suppose, like the rest of the world, we
assumed that was the norm. So all our questioning about why a
woman's role *within* heterosexuality was constructed in such and such
a way, never once extended to questioning heterosexuality itself.'

Jo Nesbitt

But even if you become a lesbian through your feminism – growing to love and trust other women, and choosing your sexuality – you still won't escape the sexologists. It is still biological freaks plus psychological cripples versus the rest. Recent American researchers call the (relatively) chosen homosexuality of women's movement lesbians *pseudo*homosexuality. According to them, if we weren't born this way, or if we didn't get this way because of inadequate parenting, we're just damn phoneys.

So What's the Answer

So, how did it start, how did it all begin?
We're trying, yes, we're trying hard to find our lesbian origin.
If only we could find it, it would be just great –
Then the straights could tell us how they got so straight.
So let's think about it sisters – but where should we begin . . .
Is it a sociological,
Biological,
Psychological,
Astrological, or . . .
Phenomenological
Lesbian origin?

We ourselves find it hard to choose any one particular theory about our lesbianism, especially because they are all far too close, except for the Sisterhood Theory, to the kinds of ideas foisted upon us all our lives by people who wish we'd grown up 'normal'. We certainly reject, as total explanations, all those which end up making us feel hopeless and powerless – like Born That Way, or Psychologically Disordered – because these only serve the purposes of those who would like us to shut up, and put up with our misfortune as invisibly as possible.

. . . So we mainly go along with the idea that sexuality is constructed out of general social conditioning, which men control, and have done for centuries, saying what women may do and how. And within that warping culture, each of us has a particular and personal history. Like heterosexual feminists, we are clear in our minds that heterosexuality, as it is practised in our society, is a key part of the system which always benefits men. Romance, legalization of pair-bonding, raising of children within the enclosed and privatized family, are all bound together in ways which oppress women. It is through heterosexuality that most people see this whole interlinking system as 'normal' and even 'natural', a perception which for most people is so fixed that they can't even question it.

There has been considerable pressure from some gay groups over the past few years to say to the straight world, look, we're just the same as you, we just want equal rights. This has been the main element in the campaigns of gay reformers. In many ways our lives *are* the same. And obviously we can't change everything, even where we'd like to. Yet we ourselves feel that we really are different. We want to take our difference, whatever its origin, and study so we can understand it *in our own terms*. We think it's up to us to say why our difference is important, and how we want to use it. It is not for heterosexuals to contain us within their oppressive and defensive definitions.

Ultimately we do not want to spend too much time in the tunnel of research into our individual pasts – the possibility for changing things lies ahead, not behind. And we've all to some extent now come out of the tunnel with the ability to proclaim, against all odds, the potential of women to love other women, and to include our sexuality within that love. For us, 'How did we get this way?' isn't a little cry of bewilderment in a hard world, but a challenge to everyone who still thinks that sexuality has nothing to do with politics, and that sexual preference is an inherited and unchangeable part of their nature.

SR.86, September 1979

Physical Relationships and the Disabled Woman

JULIE MIMMACK

I am a tetraplegic – paralysed from the armpits downwards with partial movement in my arms and hands. I have some feeling in my legs and torso generally, but no voluntary movement. I am confined to a wheel-chair and am twenty-four years of age. My injury was caused by a car accident seven years ago and although the muscles which function are stronger than before, there have been no other physical improvements.

. . . Social encounters at parties or other functions are obviously varied. But in my experience they do follow certain patterns.

a) Complete Rejection

In such cases even eye-to-eye contact is impossible. People get embar-rassed, but sometimes they're just indifferent – you're written off. I ignore them back or, if I don't like their remarks, I speak back in kind. I've got a loud mouth and I'm not prepared to huddle away in corners. There've been a few feet I've run over with my wheelchair too.

b) Over-Enthusiasm

This may be caused by over-drinking or whatever. You may be treated as a 'plaything' or a 'novelty'. The fact that you may be the only wheelchair-bound guest can draw excess attention, not so much for your 'self' but your 'predicament'. This may only temporarily boost the old ego; if you should so want it boosted!

c) Admiration

This can be beneficial or otherwise. Personally I have found this coming from older men (usually married) and those with heart-rending tales to tell; breakdowns, marital hang-ups, etc. (as if you haven't got enough of your own). Admiration also seems to make the female a target for 'religious salesmen'. Often promises are made at the end of what may seem a fruitful evening. But will you ever see him again? Even if sincere at the time, parties can be a superficial basis for a relationship. There are many obstacles to come.

A sexual relationship can be extremely difficult. Especially if the disabled female lives at home with parents – as I do – and is of the age when hopefully she would be living independently, working and travelling. Parents can be over-protective, especially if you are dependent on them both physically and financially. They may interrogate your partner more than in normal circumstances; after all, you are more vulnerable to maltreatment. Nonetheless, you are unable to create your own atmosphere in such a situation – making coffee, or generally 'moving around'. There is also that first moment when 'bladder management' is revealed. It would seem that this is the real test. How will he react to a mature individual who wears plastic knickers and pads and requires help when going to the loo? Rejection on this count can be very grim and frustrating.

. . . A successful sexual relationship would seem impossible to define (whether disabled or not). If you are praised, there is always a feeling of doubt; no one can really convince you of sexual prowess when half your body isn't really *normal* – however this may be defined. You may also worry about your body-shape. Many disabilities come equipped with drooping breasts, a thin rib-cage, not to mention a lax tum, due to lack of muscle-tone. You may compare your body-shape with how it was prior to disability. And wonder whether your partner is comparing your body to someone else's. In either case, discussion can help.

. . . When/if your relationship passes the 'bladder test' the next hurdle is arranging a private meeting (place and time). 'Time' is a leading factor here because *a*) a considerable amount of physical preparation is required and *b*) unexpected visitors or disturbances are impossible to cope with – the disabled party can't quickly get up, dress, wash. When sexually aroused, the heat can be taken out of the moment when your partner has to help you empty your bladder and carefully clean and position you. This can cause a mechanical barrier. On the other hand things can be taken in a light-hearted manner, which helps. During and after sexual intercourse, over-exhaustion can make the disabled woman feel inadequate. The mind may be very willing to try out new positions and experiences, but the body function can be that much weaker.

. . . 'Is your partner a nurse-cum-nancy?' This concept annoys me on two counts: the way that it is put forward by many people implies a distinct prejudice against homosexuals, and that it is 'unnatural' for a male to take on the 'caring' role – caring goes against the male macho image. It would seem to be a recognized fact, from experience (sorry, no statistics as yet), that disabled women have a greater chance of pairing up with able-bodied men. Hopefully with greater sexual equality, the introduction of more male nurses, and different attitudes, this will no longer be the case.

. . . To conclude I would say that if barriers can be broken down and a relaxed relationship achieved, one of the greatest outcomes is *confidence*. Both in oneself and with others.

S.R.86, September 1979

The Feelings behind the Slogans

EILEEN FAIRWEATHER

'Soon motherhood became a thing to be shunned and feared. I confess that when well-meaning friends said: "You cannot afford another baby; take this drug", I took their strong concoctions to purge me of the little life that might be mine. They failed, as such things generally do, and the third baby came . . .'

So wrote one mother, in *Maternity: Letters from Working Women*. First published in 1915, these statements by members of the Women's Co-operative Guild are a powerful and moving record of their authors' suffering and courage. Denied contraception and abortion by Church and state, and bodily freedom by their husbands, they tell of how, 'practically as soon as the birth is over, she is tortured again. If the woman does not feel well she must not say so, as a man has such a lot of ways of punishing a woman if she does not give in to him.'

Their yearly pregnancies meant terrible injury. Many, of course, did not survive. Only a little over fifty years ago, my own grandmother died in childbirth. 'Puerperal septicaemia' is the recorded cause, a fancy term which says nothing of the conditions she gave birth in. Which was, like most women of the time, in poverty, without the help of midwife or doctor and with a body made weak through undernourishment and overwork. She died having my mother, only eleven months after her last labour. Twins that time, neither of whom lived longer than six weeks. The good old days.

When you wash away the centuries-old gobblygook about sacred motherhood, sacred infancy, the truth – at least in our culture – is that the generation of women now in their twenties and thirties are the *first ever* to be able to view pregnancy with something less than stricken fear. Today, only twelve women in 100,000 die through childbirth, compared with the one in 250 of fifty years ago. Medical men and male legislators would have us believe this is entirely due to their pioneer policies and technology. But whatever women have gained, we have had to fight for it every inch of the way.

The women of the Co-operative Guild had to campaign for decades to win the maternity grant, and statutory maternal care. Birth control campaigners were prosecuted, imprisoned and fined; in the 1880s, Annie Besant even lost custody of her child for the 'obscenity' of providing other working-class women with information on birth control. In the absence of that, many more, nameless women went to prison for helping their sisters procure abortions. The women in the Middle Ages who performed abortions, and helped women bear children less painfully, were known as 'wicca', or wise women; wicca is the Anglo-Saxon for witch, and 'wise woman' is still the French term for a midwife. The Church had nine million of these women tortured and killed.

... The 1967 Abortion Act was a concession of the liberal sixties, granted because over 3,000 women a year were being admitted to hospital with septic wombs. The MPs who voted for safe and legal abortion never realized, however, how great the demand would be. They estimated 10,000 abortions a year; currently, the figure is over 100,000. So now, for the third time in four years, a bill is in Parliament aimed at restricting abortion to the truly 'deserving'. It was drafted by Sir George Crozier, the chairman of the 'Pro-Life' co-ordinating committee, who don't believe any women at all have the right to abortion. They estimate that the bill will reduce successful applications by two thirds.

... While our elected 'representatives' (616 men, 19 women) strain their consciences over abortion, women have already had to cast their vote. From the statistics available on legal and illegal abortion over the past fifty years, probably one woman in six has had an abortion.

Why, then, don't all these women come forward to defend a woman's right to choose? The National Abortion Campaign has initiated a Campaign Against Corrie, new groups are being formed, old ones revived, a petition is being circulated and the T U C have called an autumn demonstration. But for many feminists there's a feeling of déjà vu. Partly, that's exhaustion. More worrying is the number who fear that the pro-choice movement cannot win the support of women overall because it does not actually reflect their experience. The women's movement was still very young when abortion first became a political football. We duly kicked back and, faced with the opposition's set of slogans, defensively came up with our own. In our rush to do that, the complexity of abortion and its emotional significance for women somehow got lost.

A basic feminist idea is that 'the personal is political', but some feminists have taken that to mean that all you can, or should do, is change your own lifestyle – eliminate the worst aspects of sexism from your life and friends. Others have argued that women can never be free on an individual level if they can't, for example, get equal pay, or nurseries for their kids. So these feminists moved into campaigns. Still others have said: and what are women supposed to do while we wait for this 'revolution' or, more likely, a few measly reforms? They therefore set to creating alternatives for women in the here-and-now, such as refuges for battered women, collective nurseries and rape crisis centres.

. . . It is partly from this split that I believe NAC has suffered.

The National Abortion Campaign is the only nationally organized campaign the British women's movement has apart from the National Women's Aid Federation. Although there are hundreds of women's groups scattered over the country, co-ordination is minimal. Formal structures, it has always been argued, would make the movement impersonal and hierarchical. We would become just like the male-dominated Left – capable only of 'responding to issues' and not to the human experience behind them.

But when the James White bill appeared in 1975, many feminists felt the urgency and severity of this threat meant we *had* to fight in a co-ordinated and national way. Women's groups acting in isolation from each other could not organize demonstrations, petitions, lobbies of parliament and publicity in the press. Efforts would be duplicated, some areas left totally untouched, and in the absence of any visible opposition the bill would zip straight through.

Without NAC, I believe that would have happened. But the doubts feminists have about formal structure have in many cases been proved right. My worry is that the critics have never been able to provide any alternative model for effective campaigning.

Instead, women in NAC were accused of being male-identified, for drawing women away from consciousness-raising groups. My reply then was that I didn't want to raise my consciousness if it was only so that I could stay calm on some backstreet abortionist's table. I still feel pretty much the same, except that I acutely regret the polarization was ever necessary. Because political activity without constant renewal of our feminist anger, caring and understanding quickly becomes counter-productive. Yet the women who are left to shoulder the work of meetings and leaflet-writing inevitably have less time for looking at the deeper issues.

One major fear of 'structure' was swiftly confirmed – the Left spotted it and moved straight in. Soon women members of left groups were prominent in NAC. As an ex-member of a left group, I've never found it helpful to witch-hunt along the lines of 'which leftie is really a feminist and which isn't'. What is objectively true is that all left organizations are male dominated, both in numbers and ideas, so even those genuinely feminist women in them are constantly worn down. Traditional socialism claims that economics alone provides the 'real' explanation for women's oppression. Any mention of men, as individuals, benefiting from the subjugation of women, is therefore sidestepped.

. . . Certainly we need labour movement support. Sending giant knitting needles to MPs might stir a few consciences, but relying on the conscience of your rulers is a dodgy thing. I would love to see the day when the enormous power of organized labour works for feminism with, say, an all-out political strike for a woman's right to choose. We'd be hitting where it hurts, straight in the money-bags.

Unfortunately, that day is a long time off. In the meantime, we've got the 28 October anti-Corrie march, the first-ever demonstration called by the TUC in support of a feminist demand. That in itself is a victory. Even five years ago, a woman who raised abortion in her trade union or Labour Party branch would have been greeted with shocked silence or outright derision.

If the ideas of yesterday's 'loony extremists' are now firmly on the political agenda, it is because the women in NAC have worked hard to put them there. But getting those ideas 'taken up' shouldn't mean we also let them be taken over. Whenever abortion is, for example, primarily argued for on the basis of defending 'a woman's right to work', only half the story is being told. Nothing is being said about the effect fear of pregnancy has on women's sexuality; nothing about the power men gain over women through forced pregnancy; nothing about the fact that some women have abortions simply because they don't *want* children. And, every time we look at abortion mechanistically, we risk alienating those who have reason to care about it most – other women.

Anyone who's ever petitioned for NAC knows that the person who practically pulls the pen from your hand to jab down a signature is usually a woman – and an older one. Two minutes later she's back to tell you of her own experience; the pompous doctor who first humiliated then refused her; the breakdown after the child she didn't want; and most horrific of all, the tales of quinine and penny royal, umbrella spokes and needles.

Yet for every woman like this there are many who simply clam up at the sight of our placards and brusquely walk away. They are not openly hostile, so I've often wondered if these are the women who, in a sense, care most passionately about abortion – precisely because they've had one themselves. What we seem to forget is that women in their thousands won't come flocking to our demos when so many have never even *talked* to anyone of their own experience. The antis have 'God and right' on their side; we have a legacy of shame, secrecy, and often pain which goes so deep you can't even bear to think about it – much less fight *back*.

That vital 'consciousness-raising' element is missing from our campaign. When the anti-abortion Lifeline argue that 'each abortion is a defeat', they are right in the sense that it's an experience any woman would rather do without. Our difference would be in arguing that being forced to bear a child against your will is an even bigger defeat. But still it's something of a Hobson's choice.

In our propaganda, however, there is a tendency to pose abortion as though it were an end in itself. 'Free abortion on demand', the second demand of the women's liberation movement, has something of that ring; the trouble with all slogans, of course, is that they are shorthand for something more complex, but I know my 'Abortion – a woman's right to choose' badge always produced more sympathetic chats on the bus. And we're pretty lazy about using the phrase 'pro-abortion' rather than pro-choice.

Our opponents prey upon the emotional effects of abortion, so we play them down. Both sides hurl around statistics about post-abortion depression and, in the process, any feel for what is a unique and solitary experience for each woman is lost. This self-censorship limits our campaigns and, just as importantly, it abuses us. One feminist found herself totally unprepared: 'I was stunned by my reaction. I never thought I'd want kids and I found I wanted this one. When I got home from hospital and my friends had gone I just rolled about the floor howling, "I wanted it, I wanted it." I even phoned the Samaritans. But a middle-aged man, although comforting, took a standard line. "You're not married, you haven't got a permanent job and you didn't feel able to tell your boyfriend. Don't crucify yourself, you have made the right decision." ' But Debbie thinks circumstances made the decision for her, and 'what I feel now almost more than sadness is resentment . . . we've a long way to go before a woman's right to choose can mean anything.'

NAC rightly says that women must have 'access to free, safe birth control; community-controlled childcare facilities; paid maternity leave; increased child benefit and more financial support for single parents . . . to enable a realistic choice'. But this doesn't come out clearly enough in the work of campaign, perhaps because the women's movement as a whole hasn't gone far enough in fighting for motherhood to

be less oppressive than it is now. At the last socialist feminist conference, for example, there wasn't even a workshop on childcare until
mothers themselves organized one.

The antis use such emotive arguments about motherhood and childhood that we again react defensively. They talk of killing life, and
speak of every foetus as a baby. In response, NAC says the foetus is a
potential human life, incapable of independent existence (my italics).
Another much-used slogan is 'An egg is not a chicken, an acorn is not a
tree, a foetus is not a baby, so don't lay that on me.'

Why do we have to make support for a woman's right to choose
dependent on seeing the foetus as no more than a bunch of splitting
cells? In doing so, we lose many potential supporters, and that includes
those women who have had an abortion, but think of it as killing. Some
women experience nothing but relief after an abortion. Others only feel
guilty because they *don't* feel guilty. But for many women, it's not so
simple: 'I love children so much. It makes it even harder when you
already have a child. This time I couldn't help thinking it was a human
being, a living being. If you asked me how I felt about abortion, I
would say I was against it. I feel very hypocritical.'

The 'potential' human life argument implies that she is merely suffering from feminine fancy and sexist conditioning. It may seem the
most 'revolutionary' position, but it is not pro-woman. How can it be,
when it denies women's experience?

According to one Australian study, 60 per cent of women believe life
begins at conception (compared with 36 per cent of men). That doesn't
stop them having abortions. Countering SPUCs quasi-science with
our own quasi-science is, to me, to argue in a very rational, masculine
way. The only way abortion will cease to be each woman's guilty
secret, and become something she is prepared to fight for publicly, is
through our saying, without apology – yes, if necessary, we put women
first.

. . . In our fight for abortion rights, we need to stress continually
that what women really need is safe and adequate contraception – 75
per cent of abortions are due to contraceptive failure. Nominally the
male Left will happily go along with this because, like abortion, it fits
in with their emphasis on fighting cuts and making demands of the
state. Compared to rape or woman-battering, fertility control must
seem a less threatening issue; the implications of sexism can more
easily be concealed. But one important element is neglected – how the
hell do they think women get pregnant in the first place? Increasingly,
women are rejecting the Pill and IUD for contraceptive methods with
fewer side-effects, but more scope for human error. How many men

take equal responsibility in contraception? 'Liberated' men are often the worst offenders. Yet this aspect is hardly ever mentioned in our campaigns.

Is it from fear of being labelled 'man-haters' that we iron out any mention of sexism . . . or is it the effect of working with men? Our interests have too often been opposed by men for us to allow them anything except an auxiliary role in our campaigns. Yet recently a feminist was shocked to find, at a meeting called by Southwark Labour Party to set up a local Campaign Against Corrie, that 'of the sixty-odd people present, about two thirds were men. I sarcastically asked where were their wives – at home looking after the kids? – and, without any irony, a man complacently said he supposed they were.' When she challenged this set-up, and the fact that men were elected on to what she felt should be an all-woman steering committee, she was roundly condemned for seeing abortion as a women's, instead of class issue.

. . . If we do not want our demands to be co-opted, we must battle to change support into the kind we need. Equally, we don't need to be tied by the rules of any new-found friends. With abortion, we could usefully heal the rift between those feminists who put their energies into campaigning, and those who prioritize creating alternatives.

If the laws are changed, we will have no choice but to learn how to perform abortions. The menstrual extraction method, pioneered by American feminists, is performed a few days after a period is overdue, and before a woman can even tell for certain whether she is pregnant.

Learning to perform abortions could also be a major political weapon. One strong reason why abortion was legalized in France and Italy was that women were defying the law en masse, through feminist-organized underground abortion networks.

Feminists have wanted to challenge previous bills with the open threat that, if the law was changed, we'd break it. But it was felt that we should hold that card until our backs were really up against the wall. Which is precisely where we are now.

There are enough nurses and medics who are feminists, or sympathetic to us, for a *safe*, illegal abortion network to be a reality. We have to let our rulers know now that we're prepared to flout their laws if forced. The law is considered sufficiently sacred in Britain for any threat of mass disobedience to be taken very seriously indeed – God knows, it might lead to all other kinds of anarchy.

We must use every weapon we can. That includes petitions, writing to MPs, demonstrating – but it does not have to stop there. Feminists in Italy took over hospital clinics and performed their own abortions; self-help and political protest combined. The suffragettes had even less mobility and independence than us, but they still wreaked havoc through the length and breadth of the country.

To pin all our hopes on persuasion through demonstration would be false. Nonetheless, a powerful feminist contingent on 28 October is vital. We can organize with a sharp eye to publicity, and make it a demo they have to report. Women in Mexico marched in black; around their waists, they wore syringes and catheters, the implements which killed the sisters they mourned. Those feminist actions which have been imaginative and defiant – Reclaim the Nights, the blocking of Fleet Street, the occupation of Westminster Cathedral – have all won considerable publicity.

Obviously we have to find other ways to organize and campaign. If we are prepared to look beyond the slogans, that can only help us. Our commitment to abortion rights should not mean we have to suppress our own or other women's experience. It is, however, maybe worth recalling how we got pushed into that defensive position in the first place:

'The Consultant pulls off his gloves, pulls down my lower eyelids and glares into my eyes.

– There is no medical reason why you shouldn't have this baby. Just because you don't think you want it, why should I have to kill it?

I keep hoping he might notice the look on my face. I live on social security, but have a place in college in September. If I have another child it will mean another five years of just waiting, living day to day . . .

But, he tells me, if I want to live my life so badly I should have made care I didn't get pregnant.

However. There is some hope, as a private patient . . . have I no way of borrowing some money?

I run, sick, disgusted with his fat, well-fed face. Scared I might spit at him or hit out with my fists. He calls me back, but I can't bear it if he sees my tears, coming out of an anger I am impotent to express . . .'

One woman's experience, under the law as it is now.

SR.87, October 1979

If the Cap Fits

ROZSIKA PARKER

'*I hate using the diaphragm. It robs me of spontaneity. It makes me feel self-conscious, over-responsible, messy.*'

That was the response I expected when I asked women to describe their reactions to returning to the diaphragm – a form of contraception they thought they had abandoned years ago, along with roll-ons, sanitary towels and stilettos. But though some said they resented the cap, others welcomed it back. It all seemed to depend on an individual's attitude towards her own body, towards her sexuality and on the state of her personal relationships.

Recent surveys have come out in favour of the diaphragm or cap. Professors Martin Vessy and Richard Doll at Oxford University in a long-term study of contraceptive methods found that the pregnancy rate for the cap was less than one quarter as high as was previously thought and the cap appeared to protect against cancer of the cervix. But that still leaves the Pill as the most secure contraceptive; 0.14 per cent of women on the Pill in their study became pregnant in a year, compared to 2.4 per cent with the diaphragm. But contraceptives carry risks other than unwanted pregnancy. In 1976 Dr Christopher Tietze published the results of a statistical analysis of different methods of birth control based on a mass of recent evidence from the USA and Britain which revealed that women of all ages risk death least by using the diaphragm or condom backed up by early abortion if they become pregnant. However, the women I spoke to switched from the Pill or the IUD not from fear of death but because their contraceptive was disrupting their lives.

Some found that the IUD gave them impossibly long pre-menstrual tension and heavy periods. Some abandoned the Pill because they felt they had interfered with their body chemistry for long enough. Others simply couldn't find a Pill that suited them. Andrea said, 'I tried loads of different kinds but my body always swelled up and I felt terrible. Finally the woman at the clinic said, "You know the answer for you – abstention", and I decided that the time had come for me to demand a diaphragm.' Her sister Lisa had a similar experience on the Pill: 'I felt sick all the time. Nobody at the clinic told me why. They'd just hand me another variety of pill.'

Three million women take the Pill according to the FPA, compared to only a quarter of a million who use the diaphragm. Andrea asked resentfully why *she* should be forced to use the oldest form of contraception on the market. Why wasn't more intensive research being done to develop a completely safe and satisfactory contraceptive?

The cap does have a long history. The spring-ringed diaphragm, invented by a Dutch feminist in 1880, was the descendent of the half-lemons, balls of opium, discs of beeswax, vinegar-soaked sponges and rubber or metal cervical caps with which women had improvised for centuries.

In fact it was the very history of the diaphragm which endeared it to another recent convert I spoke to. She said she identifies with it because 'it was invented to help free women, and distributed among women by women like Marie Stopes.' She sees the Pill, on the other hand, as 'bound up with professionalization and secrecy'.

Getting pregnant is the major worry amongst diaphragm users: 'There's that corner of doubt in your mind the whole time which you don't have with the pill.' The pill is 99.9 per cent reliable, the IUD 98 per cent and cap and spermicide 97 per cent, according to the FPA, but they add that reliability very much depends on whether or not you are a 'regular and practised user'.

Failure is usually due to:

Improper fit

Improper care

Inconsistent use

Diaphragm slipping because of expansion of the vagina during intercourse; too much spermicide on the rim making it slippery; the penis getting behind the diaphragm, said to happen more easily if the woman is on top.

Diaphragm ring bending due to constipation – a Harley Street gynaecologist commented that this caused the only failure he had come across.

The largest contemporary survey of users, carried out in New York from 1971–3, showed that only 2 per cent of more than 2,000 women had an accidental pregnancy. Failure rates were lowest among women under eighteen years (1.9 per 100), and among women aged thirty-five and older there were no accidental pregnancies.

The researchers attributed the success of the diaphragm to the way in which women were taught to use it. Complete confidence with it depended on whether they had been thoroughly informed.

With such a simple technique it would seem almost impossible for women to come away from clinics clutching their diaphragms and a whole lot of unanswered questions. But even amongst the small number of women I interviewed, there were some disturbing stories.

Take the case of Sally. She became pregnant while using the cap due entirely to the casual attitude of the university clinic in Sydney, Australia, which provided her first diaphragm. They gave her an insertor and never told her to check with her finger to see that the diaphragm was in place. They neither supplied her with spermicide nor told her that the diaphragm should never be used without spermicidal cream or gel.

Rachel came away from a London clinic worrying which way up the device should be worn; dome up against the cervix or pointing down.

Most clinic workers say 'dome upwards' but that you can decide which is most comfortable for you.

Alice had a more serious difficulty. Her retroverted womb makes it hard for her to remove her cap. In some women the top end of the womb is tilted so that there isn't a straight passage from the mouth of the vagina to the cervix. The clinic she attended gave Alice no specific advice about this and home on her own she found she couldn't get it out. 'I went back to the clinic and poured out all my anxieties and problems. Eventually they became really clear, treating me like an idiot and saying, "You are an anxious person, aren't you." It's only by being labelled an anxious person that you actually get any communication. They told me to lie in the bath if I had trouble removing it. Wrestling around in the bath with my legs up to the ceiling and using two fingers to hook it down, I can manage to get it out.'

Margaret had a rather bizarre experience when her cap was fitted. She was taught how to insert it but the hurried, overworked nurse checked her anus to see if Margaret had put it in correctly. The nurse was so embarrassed by her error that she never completed the instructions. For three years Margaret was lucky, then she got pregnant.

Of course most fitting sessions are efficient and uneventful. In the USA paramedical staff are being trained to fit diaphragms in women's health centres. Adele Clark writing in *Country Woman*, March 1976, describes the importance of being fitted by her 'friendly paramedic Nancy' at a women's clinic. It shaped her attitude to the diaphragm: 'We tried one kind and it wouldn't fit; we tried another and we both could get it in and out. Success. The word *we* is crucial. I was a participant, not a patient or a victim in this process of fitting my diaphragm, just as I am when I use it to prevent conception.'

I wondered whether a woman's attitude towards her body affected the extent to which the diaphragm is acceptable. Most said yes, it was an important factor; sometimes in perfectly obvious ways, other times in ways they couldn't fathom.

One or two said that attempts to use the diaphragm had been directly hampered by their inhibitions about touching themselves. But women who had masturbated since childhood had no such problems, and Jo said that touching herself 'in order to put it in seemed like part of my history. I suppose your own history reflects the kind of contraceptive you'll find acceptable. I don't enjoy someone watching me put the cap in though and that can be tricky since I would never dream of going to the bathroom to do it – so to some extent it must represent a continuation of the privacy of my masturbation.'

Diaphragm use seems also to be bound up with the self-hatred that for so many women becomes focused on their bodies. Mary tried to express this: 'I see my body as an enemy, an alien area trying to do me down by not conforming to the fashionable shape. When I'm feeling particularly fat, I simply can't put in my diaphragm. I mean how can I prepare my body for pleasure when I hate it, let alone prepare it to provide pleasure for someone else.'

Feminists often feel that the diaphragm enhances their sense of owning their own body – that it exists for *them* independently of bringing pride to their parents, pleasure to their lover or income to an advertising agency. Margaret commented, 'I need to say my body's mine. The diaphragm is a physical symbol of my control of my own life.' This theme is developed in Erica Jong's *Fear of Flying*: 'Pregnancy seemed like a tremendous abdication of control. Something growing inside you which would eventually usurp your life. I had been compulsively using the diaphragm for so long pregnancy could never be accidental for me.'

Insertion can provide a sense of self-assertion which somehow can't be obtained by swallowing a pill. But the emphasis on control carries defensive overtones of fear, both a need for protection and a struggle for independence. Erica Jong continues, 'The diaphragm has become a kind of fetish for me. A holy object, a barrier between my womb and me.'

Most women, far from valuing the diaphragm as a last line of defence, complained that it inhibited their sexual spontaneity. Alice would like for once to be able to 'fall into bed without thinking whether or not I want sex, whether or not he's satisfying me. I want to be bowled over.' The diaphragm interferes with such fantasies and Alice's resentment gets directed towards her partner: 'Spontaneity is allowed to him but not to me. I get strange feelings of anger about preparing myself for his needs. I always have to look after myself – he wouldn't bother. He didn't respond to my heavy hints about sheaths – he didn't like them. I feel men aren't concerned or interested in women's worries about contraception.'

But other women reported that their partners had no objections to sheaths. Some couples share responsibility for contraception by alternating cap and sheath, others use both together for extra security. Alice continued, 'I remember getting angry the first time we slept together because in the morning we started fucking again and I suddenly remembered you have to put more cream in. He didn't remember, or didn't know, so I was the one who had to interrupt the lovemaking to leap out of bed and be embarrassed. Then I couldn't get into it again – thought he'd find me repulsive or something.'

Some women felt that complete openness was a solution. They incorporate the cap into lovemaking, but Sally discovered a drawback: 'You put it in in front of him or he helps you put it in. You both get covered in goo and by then you are so bored with the whole process that all you want to do is go to sleep.'

Not everyone minds the diaphragm's inconvenience. For Jo, the check on spontaneity isn't a problem. Comparing the Pill and the diaphragm she found the Pill 'coercive. It was developed to enable women to be sexual at *any* time, but to me it was like a statement that I had to be sexual at *all* times. The Pill seemed less to do with not getting pregnant than with being sexually available.'

Rosemary completely disagreed. Far from giving her permission to be sexually discriminating, she finds the diaphragm hopelessly limiting: 'You have to decide in advance not just whether you are going to have sex, but what kind of sex you are going to have. Nobody else seems to have a problem with oral sex but I'm not prepared to inflict it on anybody – it tastes horrible. And Delfen made me ill it smelled so terrible.' Margaret, however, 'actually felt touched that he was prepared to swallow mouthfuls of the stuff for my sake'.

It's worth experimenting with different creams or gels (which are more lubricating) to see which you find least off-putting. Some spermicides contain mercury. Mercury can be absorbed through the vaginal walls resulting in damage to the kidneys. So read the label of the spermicide you use, avoid those containing phenyl mercuric acetate (PMA), and stick to those that don't, Ortho Gynol Jelly, Ortho Cream, Rames Jelly and Delfen cream and gel.

None of the spermicides are delightful and women say that we should demand better-tasting spermicides. But manufacturers would probably respond with stereotypically rose-scented or apple-blossom products.

On the subject of manufacturers, Sarah Calvert suggests in the New Zealand magazine *Broadsheet* No. 40 that 'A lot of preconceptions about the diaphragm (it's messy ... it's a hassle ... it's always a failure) are tied to the campaigns by drug companies and others to promote 'easy' contraception. Easy contraception *does not exist*.'

Nevertheless, the basic inconvenience of the diaphragm is inescapable, though *MS* magazine, Vol IV, No. 2, does quote studies showing that reapplication of spermicide and the 'rule' about not putting the diaphragm in more than two hours ahead of time are not necessary as spermicides retain their strength for twenty-four hours regardless of the number of ejaculations. But until the debate is resolved it seems wisest to follow traditional directions.

Lisa suggested lessening the practical inconvenience by leaving an applicator full of spermicide beside your bed at night or keeping your diaphragm in your bag with a generous supply of tissues. And she pointed out that the diaphragm lessens one specific inconvenience – making love with a period.

The cap made some women feel furtive, and they behaved accordingly: 'I can't even bring myself to show him what it looks like,' said Sue, afraid that its functional, clinical character might put off her partner. Mary had similar anxieties with ironic results that left her outraged: 'I groped my way back to bed from the bathroom with damp hands and cold feet only to find him rolled over against the wall, complaining, "It turns me right off when a woman sneaks off to the bathroom to get ready."'

Jo, on the other hand, found that the practical routine of diaphragm use helped to dispel a strong sense of sexual guilt. She felt that 'the cleaning ritual, particularly in a shared living situation, had a very good effect on me. It went some way towards undermining the association of sexual feelings with dirt and mystery. I think this has something to do with the diaphragm being visible and tangible.'

Margaret too sees advantages in the practical routine demanded by the cap. 'It means I have to make a conscious decision as to whether or not I *want* to make love. It makes me feel I control my sexuality.'

Alice is dubious about such decision-making power. Rather than enabling her to express her own needs and desires, having to decide about the cap creates all kinds of fears and conflicts. She admits she wants 'to abdicate from making decisions about whether I want sex or not – it's too loaded. I don't want to say "no, I'm not sexual today" because it might turn out not to be true, and it's risky – you might get rejected for hurting his feelings. Nor do I want to say "Yes, I definitely do feel sexual." I might then be making a demand to be satisfied, taking a very risky initiative. The decision to put in the cap or not comes to symbolize these conflicts.'

Similarly, though Sally has intellectually rejected women's role as the passive person who waits to be asked, emotionally she's immobilized at the prospect of taking the initiative: 'If you reach for your cap it's almost like saying "we are going to fuck tonight" and I find that a pressure.'

Jane felt much the same. The cap makes her increasingly aware of the chasm between men and women that rigid sex roles create. 'I find it really difficult even to take my diaphragm with me when I go to see him. He lacks sexual confidence to the extent that he's immediately threatened if he thinks I'm being sexually demanding.'

Some cap users say these difficulties can be overcome if it's inserted at night automatically 'like cleaning your teeth'. Then the cap gets divorced from sexuality. I heard of one woman who kept her cap in all the time, removing it every 24 hours to clean it.

Most women agreed that the diaphragm is easier to use within a long-term relationship but added that obviously a lot depended on the quality of the relationship. One woman said resentfully that her husband checked to see if she had taken it with her when she went away. Another became convinced that her husband was about to prick holes in her cap. 'When sex goes sour,' Mary said, 'the resentment you feel towards your partner is projected on to your cap.' And Alice, looking back to her marriage, said that the diaphragm made her confront the fact she no longer enjoyed sex with her husband. 'When you're on the Pill it's easier to have sex than not.'

All the women's feelings about their cap were shaped by whether or not they wanted children. 'On the Pill,' Rosemary commented, 'I experienced sexuality as completely divorced from any thoughts of contraception or reproduction. The diaphragm forced me to think about contraception and therefore about whether or not I wanted a baby.'

Pregnancy fears often dominate the sexuality of diaphragm users and the discovery of her lesbianism can represent a woman's first spontaneous experience. 'Making love with women,' Jo says, 'undercuts that memory of my mother telling me not to get pregnant. It was a real delight to be sexual without a contraceptive, a kind of rebellion. Heterosexual sex invokes a lot of emotion about the family which can be hard to deal with. That's one of the reasons why lesbianism has been such a sexual release for me.'

The diaphragm is not 100 per cent effective as a contraceptive. Most of the women quoted here returned to it because an entirely safe, and satisfactory contraceptive hasn't yet been invented and maybe never will be. They've pointed out that the diaphragm demands a sense of responsibility about your body and whether or not to have children. But restrictive abortion laws deny us that responsibility for our own bodies. If we are to use the diaphragm, and it seems many of us *must*, we have to have free, easily obtainable abortion on demand.

9 HEALTH

It is a basic necessity for free and independent individuals to have control over their own physical wellbeing. For women, this responsibility is increasingly usurped by medical professionals and, indirectly, political arbiters. For centuries childbirth, contraception and abortion were part of lay health tradition, usually the concern of local community-based women. They gradually became the concern of professional medicine. Obstetrics were not included in medical training until the late nineteenth century.

Contraception is now provided free on the National Health Service, abortion was made legal on limited grounds in 1967, and childbirth has moved from 85 per cent home births in 1927 to 91 per cent hospital births in 1972. The scientific and technological developments within medicine, including birth control, and the transfer of maternity care and childbirth from the home to the medical system, have been contradictory benefits for women. The medical profession treats processes like childbirth or menopause more in terms of illness than health. Women feel like passive patients who are manipulated rather than responsible people who need information and care to act positively, while reproductive health care suffers from social taboos and ignorance.

The question of women's control over their own bodies, including the right to make informed decisions and to personal knowledge about reproduction, is a political issue. The National Abortion Campaign, which was begun to defend the 1967 Act, calls for women's right to choose for themselves. One woman who signed the petition at an N A C stall in a Bristol shopping centre said, 'I don't believe in women's lib and all that, but I'm fed up with men telling us what to do. Yes, I'll sign it' (*SR.37*). Some doctors and M Ps, as well as right-wing movements which continually organize to curtail the Abortion Act, hold moralistic attitudes. Ignoring the inadequacies of contraception, they view pregnancy as a punishment for illicit sex, and maternity as women's destiny.

The politics and economics of birth control have international ramifications. The injectable contraceptive, Depo-Provera, despite being banned in the United States, is still sold and issued in vast quantities in seventy, mostly Third World, countries. The morality that makes women both the victim and the cause of social problems underlies many sterilization programmes. And still no one method of existing contraception is completely reliable or safe for all women.

Having formed health groups and learned how to give each other internal examinations, women are beginning to break down the power relation between doctor and patient, to bring control and knowledge of women's bodies back to women themselves, and to learn and share information. Women's groups have also explored alternative medicine like acupuncture, homeopathic remedies and naturopathy which don't destroy the body's natural defences and are concerned with the whole body and general fitness.

Feminists have also investigated the blurred distinction between mental and physical illness, and the connection of both with social conditions and expectations. Both self-starvation and compulsive eating, for example, are linked with the feminine role. Rosie Parker and Sarah Mauger wrote that women who starved themselves often strived to conform, to please, to be slim, while underneath they felt inadequate and selfish. The self-starvation of anorexia nervosa was an attempt to take some form of control over their lives, a hopeless gesture of defiance and independence. Susie Orbach, in a group of women who investigated their own experience of compulsive eating, found that being fat was a way of neutralizing the problems associated with feminine sexuality. There was a similar struggle between dependence and independence.

Mental illness, like physical illness, is often treated with pills and technology in ways that encourage a woman's sense of being ineffectual and a victim, rather than helping towards self-understanding and confidence. Women's self-help therapy groups try to counter the idea that anxiety and an inability to cope are only internal and individual problems, or that to admit to needing help is a failure and a weakness. Alison Fell and Rosie Parker wrote that instead of 'an impossible idea of self-sufficiency', we need to 'envisage a society where self-reliance and caring interdependence could co-exist happily. Where help could be sought and offered as just one more way, acknowledged by all, of sharing human resources' (*SR.43*).

Blood Money

AMANDA SEBESTYEN

Most of us are going to menstruate 300 times in our lives. You'd never guess, though. In fact it's one of the world's best-kept secrets. We talk in code: it's The Curse in middle-class boarding schools, Uncle George in the North, Red Sails in the Sunset in Australia. Everywhere, 'women still buy sanitary towels with enormous discretion and carry their handbags to the loo when they only need to carry a napkin' (G. Greer). No wonder one poor woman who asked her husband to bring her sanitary towels and a belt when she was in hospital ended up with a lace suspender belt and a packet of Brillo pads.

The menstrual period's no joke, though. It still means seven days' absolute seclusion for women in Moslem, Hindu and orthodox Jewish cultures. Fear and hatred of the female body are one obvious reason why this is still happening. But there's also a technology of menstruation which we don't think about so often and which has just as controlling an effect on our lives. In some countries women didn't and still don't use anything to soak up the blood. In others they used moss and other natural fibres inside the vagina or wrapped around outside. In Ghana women wrap themselves in red rags – much more sensible than white.

For centuries most European women used cloths; we still use the old words like towel and napkin, and the American expression 'got the rags on'. Some older women can remember using these cloth towels which had to be constantly washed and reused: 'My diapers were made of harsh towelling, and I used to creep into the laundry and crouch over a bucket of foul clouts, hoping that my brother would not catch me at my revolting labours' (Germaine Greer again). Until quite recently women were expected to spend most of their period indoors. These towels are used today in several Third World countries, notably in China where women have to take time off work to visit wash stations and change cloths; this is sometimes given as a reason why Chinese women are still awarded fewer work points than men. Back home in Britain, though we've got disposable towels and tampons, periods are still supposed to make us a terrible job liability.

The first disposable sanitary towel was marketed in 1880 by Southalls but not widely used until much later. At the turn of the century journeys still meant special equipment, because the usual napkins were so hard to change. Soluble towels came in the 1920s, they were a spin-off from the soluble bandages developed in the First World War. Tampax were first marketed in the thirties. This new technology did mean a lot more mobility for women – and that's certainly a message the makers of sanitary protection are happy to reiterate. This is, in fact:

The only promotional style of advertising to women which shows them in athletic, active and energetic roles instead of indulging the typical media woman's bovine leer. One feminist remarked recently that in advertisements for Tampax, you get the only example of women functioning as normal active people at the time, the only time, in the month when they feel least like it. However you look at it, it is strange that at the only time of the month when women have the ultimate reinforcement of their femininity, the marketers are falling over themselves to show women how to indulge freely and fearlessly in the most 'masculine' of pursuits. (Rosemary Scott, *The Female Consumer*)

That's not the only contradiction. We're supposed to buy freedom by acting as a captive market. Two manufacturers – Southalls and Tampax – sell 80 per cent of the sanitary protection in this country. Commercial monopolies usually mean high prices. Southalls and Tampax made nearly £3 million in 1975, the Price Commission found. Towel prices rose by up to 70 per cent between 1972 and 1975, partly because of a rise in the price of cotton. But tampon prices went up at the same time, though tampons don't use nearly as much cotton in manufacture.

Why? Well, Southalls' tampon prices have to be linked to towel prices because the same company makes both . . . The Commission advised an immediate reduction in recommended retail prices – but found two years later that most small chemists' shops had taken to charging over the recommended price instead. Competing supermarkets, on the other hand, will often cut the price of tampons sharply, but even here, the Commission pointed out, 'our samples did not throw up any loss-leaders in sanitary protection. Even the cut-prices yield a reasonable gross margin' i.e. profit. After all, if tuna gets too expensive customers refuse to buy. But if tampons are expensive women don't really have much choice.

The point about the manufacturers' 'new, improved' methods, of course, is that they often do more for sales figures than they do for our health: deodorized towels can cause allergic reactions, tampons are implicated in cervical erosion. And because the market for sanitary protection is more or less constant, the companies can only expand by trying to create new needs like minipads for between periods, and the by now notorious vaginal deodorants. The youngest age group, still hopefully 'brand-disloyal', is of course the most sought after,

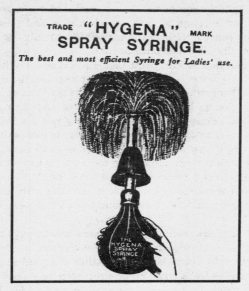

TRADE "HYGENA" MARK
SPRAY SYRINGE.
The best and most efficient Syringe for Ladies' use.

SR.64, November 1977

and firms spend hugely on free samples, information leaflets and talks at schools. The latest youth product is Lillets Mini tampon for teenagers.

The tampon market is, in fact, an area of fierce if limited competition between the two biggest companies – limited because with only one competitor neither can engage in a proper price war. But fierce, because the number of women using tampons is slowly rising (only by 1 per cent a year – apparently those old stories about tampons ruining you for marriage still have a hold). Tampon users tend to be younger than towel users. Lillets Mini are the latest of Southalls' attempts to overtake Tampax, who still have some powerful advantages: they were the innovators and their brand name's become completely identified with the product (like Biro or Hoover), and as an American company they have access to more capital for investing in sophisticated machinery and saving on labour costs. Southalls, though, invested massively in West German machinery to produce Lillets, and they're obviously determined to get their money back. One cut-throat advertising battle has already ended in a draw: 'Lillets are pushing their widthways expansion as opposed to the lengthways expansion of Tampax, a contract which brought the companies to commercial blows in early 1974 when both started sneering at each other's claims and putting out knocking copy to prove it' (*Female Consumer*). Eventually one slapped an injunction on the other's advertisement.

There's another, more secret battle taking place, and it's the period itself that's up for grabs between the sanitary protection firms and the drug companies that market the Pill. The doctors for 'Tampax and Dr Blacks' say that women have always menstruated and can't possibly stop now – besides, every one of us will spend £350 in a lifetime on sanitary protection. The drug companies' doctors say that periods have no function except to keep women fertile – so those of us already taking the Pill could conveniently swallow seven more tablets a month and rid ourselves of 'the Curse' for ever. But we still don't have enough information about menstruation to make a real choice for ourselves. And as usual, these transactions are taking place behind the backs of women.

But there are stirrings within the captive market. In 1975 the Free Sanitary Protection Campaign made a start at confronting the manufacturers directly. It's a pity the campaign didn't last because it's an issue that affects all of us. Women in the street were really enthusiastic about Free Sanitary Protection; one woman on Social Security had three daughters, who all had their periods at the same time. The expense in that week just about wiped out their Giro payment.

Women are now trying out ways of by-passing the companies' monopoly and going back to self-help methods. Bristol Free Sanitary Protection Group 'manufactured' their own tampons at a street theatre and gave them to the audience. But it's even cheaper to use something that doesn't have to be thrown away. Some women have been using their diaphragms to collect the blood – the diaphragm holds a lot more than a towel or tampon. When you think it's full, you remove it, wash it out and re-insert.

Some women in health groups are using menstrual extraction with the Karman Cannula to get their period over in ten minutes instead of five days. Some people say it hurts, though.

Now there's another idea. Small sponges were once used for contraception.

Between the wars chemists sold sponge tampons called 'moisettes', but they were forgotten with the arrival of disposables. Recently, though, women in the States have started using natural sponges again in place of commercial tampons. The sponges are softer, don't irritate the vagina and can be used again and again. Sheffield women's liberation group have been trying out the idea: 'We find that it is more efficient, feels more natural, more comfortable and is certainly much CHEAPER.'

A piece of natural sponge this size absorbs about as much as one regular tampon or towel. Sponges with small holes absorb more. To use the sponge, tie a piece of strong string or dental floss around it or through one end. Dampen it thoroughly, squeeze it out and insert. Whenever necessary, pull the string to remove it, wash with warm water and soap, squeeze out and use again. You can take a clean spare sponge with you in a bag if you can't face washing one out in a public place. But one sponge will last you for several periods. As far as we know it doesn't need sterilizing – towels and tampons aren't sterile either. Just wash and keep till next month. The sponge can also be used to insert yoghurt for a thrush cure.

SR.65, December 1977

'Most of Us Had Three or Four'

AGNES MARCHANT AND HER DAUGHTER SUSAN
INTERVIEWED BY ROZSIKA PARKER

What did you do when you decided that you wanted an abortion?

Agnes: In those days [1951] the problem was not knowing where to go. It wasn't a matter of 'Oh, all right I can go to so-and-so.' You had to be careful who you asked. There were two abortionists in the block of flats where I lived, but I didn't dare go to them though I knew they did it as they'd both got arrested. In fact one had got two years. When she came out she was at it again, but you couldn't knock on her door because she'd tell everybody, 'Guess who knocked on my door.'

So you didn't want people to know that you'd had an abortion.

Agnes: Oh no. It's only now that the law's changed that you can talk about it, and you realize how many did have illegal abortions. People are so much freer now – they can please themselves, can't they. In those days you felt such a hypocrite; you were leading two lives. You couldn't tell anyone at work what was happening to you. You felt really lonely. In the end I spoke to my sister and she said she knew someone.

Why did you want an abortion?

Agnes: I was engaged but I didn't want to rush into marriage. But even if I'd got married the next week, I didn't want children.

Anyway, I went to this woman with my sister. I paid her £10 and she used a syringe and soapy water. Have you ever seen one? They are sold in chemists as enema syringes. There's a long tube with a ball in the middle and nozzle on the end where the water goes in and fills up the ball. You've only got to get an air bubble in and whoosh! you're gone, aren't you.

I've never known anyone who had it come off first time with a syringe. I had to go back to the woman three or four times and pay her another £5 before it came off.

Was it very painful?

Agnes: I was working when I got symptoms. It started at seven o'clock one evening. I was haemorrhaging and losing blood clots. Then twenty-four hours later the thing came away. It was the first abortion I'd had and I thought, 'Well, that wasn't too bad.' But I had pretty awful pain, mind.

Did you think of going to a doctor when the pain got bad?

Agnes: Oh no, oh no. They'd send you straight into hospital where they would try and save it – prop your legs up and give you a few injections. I never went into hospital but I knew people who did and they were given a really rough time by the law. The police would stand by your bed and keep on at you, 'Who did it? Tell us who did it and we'll get your money back for you.'

Did they ever charge the woman who had had the abortion?

Agnes: They'd never have got a conviction.

What was the average sentence passed on an abortionist?

Agnes: It varied from eighteen months to five years. It depended on what the charge was or if a woman had had previous convictions.

You had a second abortion?

Agnes: Yes, the next time I got pregnant my daughter Susan was five and I was divorced and I thought, 'Oh God, I can't . . .' I was pretty desperate. I was on my own and I knew I couldn't possibly manage another. Anyway, this was in 1958, when I had a young doctor who was quite good. He gave me some tablets and said, 'If you're not pregnant this will bring on your period.' I took them. Nothing happened. I went back and he said, 'Well, it's obvious that you are pregnant.

There's nothing I can do, but there are one or two people around . . .'

He mentioned somebody's name. I'd heard of this particular woman and thought that she was wary who she entertained because she'd been arrested a few times. And I'd heard she used knitting needles. 'No, she doesn't,' the doctor said, 'that's just gossip. She uses a syringe and she's quite good. Once it happens, once it comes off, you can call me in and I'll come. I don't mind cleaning up, you know.'

You went to the woman he suggested?

Agnes: Yes. No one knew I was going. If anything had gone wrong she could have just dumped me and nobody would have known. She was – God, she must have been about seventy years old. She had all these Catholic pictures on the walls; big old-fashioned pictures of Our Lord with the lamb and the crook, pictures of the Lady of Lourdes, and rosaries and palm crosses draped everywhere.

She said, 'Well, it's expensive dear.' So I said, 'Look, all I've got is £30.' 'All right,' she said, 'I'll do it.' Later I discovered that she did it for other people for £5.

Her house was none too clean and a bit musty smelling. You sat in a funny, dirty-looking armchair and put your leg over the arm so that she could get into your vagina with the syringe.

Afterwards I waited twelve hours (it comes off within twelve to twenty-four hours after being syringed) but nothing happened. Altogether I went back to her about seven times.

How pregnant were you?

Agnes: Oh, I ended up about three and a half months pregnant. I knew she wasn't really trying so I finally said, 'Look, if you can possibly try and do it I'll see you all right again. I haven't got any money but I'll get some by the end of the week.' Then, as I walked home, so this soapy water started to come away from me. This had never happened before so I thought, well, at least it's penetrated the womb. Before it had just acted like a douche.

Anyway, the next day I woke up with a slight show. I went to work and started to feel a bit queasy. I came home and it came off that night. I didn't have as much pain with that one as I did with the one when I was six and a half weeks pregnant, funnily enough. I had pain for only about two or three hours before the thing came away. Then I thought, well I'll go to bed, but I was frightened to lie down because I felt I'd die if I did. So I propped myself up all night and with the slightest movement of my body I felt all this blood coming away from me. It was, you know, quite frightening.

The next morning, feeling a bit lightheaded, I went to the doctor and he gave me a vitamin shot and some medicine.

Did the woman you went to earn her living by giving abortions?

Agnes: Yes, she used to go out to people – mostly to the West End where girls had plenty of money. This particular old lady, she told me – but whether it was boastful bragging I don't know – she said that she'd been to Belgium and Switzerland to perform abortions. She made a small fortune during the war performing abortions for Americans. She got arrested, thanks to a girl who had it done and had just got to the top of the street when the police picked her up. 'Come on,' they said, 'just take us back and show us the house you went into and we'll get your money back.' She got eighteen months. The local police knew what was going on and she was left alone for quite a while. If she'd stuck to her rich clients she would have been OK – she used to go to their flats. But when she started taking in anyone who knocked on her door . . .

Were there women you knew who gave themselves abortions?

Agnes: One or two girls I knew said they had done it themselves, but those particular girls couldn't even insert a Tampax.

Did your friends' husbands disapprove of their wives having abortions?

Agnes: They didn't like it. Usually they didn't know. So while you are going through the process of the thing coming away and you had pains in your tummy, you had to put on a good front and pretend you were OK.

I suppose many women had children simply because they were scared of having an illegal abortion?

Agnes: Oh yes, no end, because it was frightening. They [the abortionists] didn't tell you what was going to happen. They'd syringe the woman, she would go off, come back if nothing happened, go off again and if she didn't come back the abortionist would think that she was (a) dead, or (b) OK. They never bothered to explain about the afterbirth or anything. Imagine someone home on their own with all that going on.

Were you worried about the notion that abortion was taking a life?

Agnes: Quite honestly, we never even thought about it, it never crossed our minds that we might be taking a human life. Up to a few years ago nobody thought about that – I didn't and I'm sure none of my friends did. It was just a thing there that they didn't want. Anyway

I don't think it is taking a human life – people are only bringing this forward now.

Another thing they are trotting forward is the psychological damage caused by abortion. Well, you might get one or two neurotic girls but if abortion really did cause psychological damage, we – my generation – would all be in the nut-house because we didn't have just one or two, most of us had three or four. Today, with better contraception, girls usually have just one and it's all laid on the line for them, they go in, they go out and it's all done for them. We had to go around looking for somebody and there was all the aggravation of going backwards and forwards, and the worry . . . Yes, if it did upset you psychologically all my generation would be raving lunatics.

Susan: What frightens me about these people who are trying to make abortion illegal is the thought of having to go through what my mum went through. I think every child should be a wanted child. I wasn't wanted and my mum had an awful struggle money-wise.

Agnes: Yes, but I was in love with your father – still am. If I was going to have a kid I'd want his.

Susan: But you must admit it was inconvenient.

Agnes: Oh, goodness me, yes. I tried for a couple of months to get rid of Susan until the woman I went to said, 'No, I can't . . .' But once I'd made up my mind that I couldn't get rid of her, I got on with it. I'm glad I did, of the three I'd have preferred to have her. The others were probably boys – they always say boys come away easier than girls.

Susan: It's understandable. In her situation I'd go for a legal abortion now.

Agnes: When Susan was younger, I used to say to her, 'Look, if ever you get pregnant, don't go and tell your friend's mum or aunt – come to me. Don't go off and buy this and take that when you don't know what's in it.' I knew of cases where people died through taking things.

Taking what things?

Agnes: There were little chemists that sold you pills and things. You'd tell the chemist that you were overdue and he'd say, 'Oh dear, one minute, see if this will help you,' and he'd sell you this pill. You couldn't just go to any chemist, but you'd hear word o' mouth who would help you out. There was one quite near where we lived and my sister bought a tiny pill for half a crown from him in 1953. She took the pill and had this terrific haemorrhage for about two or three days – the toilet was absolutely filled up with blood. Then that packed up and she thought she had miscarried. A fortnight later the haemorrhage started again for three or four days, but she was still pregnant and had the baby after all.

Then there was a friend of mine who took quinine. She drank the stuff by the bottle and today she is almost blind. It didn't help – she had to go and have an abortion afterwards.

Susan: It was all so unnecessary. The men don't understand. They think that if abortion laws are tightened that the problem is going to disappear – that women aren't going to get pregnant. But the problem was always there – people just died quietly in a corner and nobody ever knew it was for an abortion.

Agnes: Yes, they went off and died and nobody mentioned it, or the family would say, 'She died of peritonitis.' So, if it's made illegal again . . .

Susan: Or even if it's tightened up . . .

Agnes: If it's tightened up it's going to give all those crooks scope again. You're going to have all the backstreet abortionists in business again, aren't you.

Susan: Yes, I used to live in a flat over the back of Brixton and my next-door neighbour had girls trooping up, mostly on Sunday afternoons. Nothing was said, but people like her are waiting for trade to pick up if the law goes backwards.

SR.50, September 1976

Visit to an Italian Health Centre

MARIE ARNOLD

I arrived in the street I'd been directed to after a long hot tram ride through the city. The woman who had told me the way didn't remember the number. She said I'd know the *consultorio* when I saw it. This was an old working-class district with blocks of flats and lots of women and kids on the streets.

The first likely building looked a bit official, like a Social Security office, but it said clinic on the door, so I asked the two women at the desk if this was the *consultorio*. They looked at my orange NAC badge which said 'National Abortion Campaign – A Woman's Right to Choose' and asked what it was. When I explained, in my broken Italian, they were all smiles and warmth. 'Ah, you want the *consultorio* . . .

It's not here, it's a bit further down the road. You can't miss it.'

The real *consultorio* was two tiny rooms with a few notices in the window – 'Women's Clinic', 'All Women Welcome'.

The place was crowded that afternoon. Luckily the woman I'd arranged to meet spoke good English. Immediately everyone wanted to know who I was, what my badge was for, how our campaign for free abortion was going.

They showed me their kids, put their arms round me, and pointed out their flats through the window. This was their place. A place for women to come. For most of them it was the only place where they could be together and discuss their problems, husbands, kids with other women.

After a while, I sat down with the woman I had arranged to meet and she told me how the *consultorio* had been set up . . .

Two years ago, several women and women's groups in Turin got together to decide the best way to organize with women. Some were members of left groups, the rest weren't.

After long discussions, some of them decided to set up a women's health centre.

The health system is very poor in Italy. Contraception is expensive and hard to get; abortion is still illegal and in many cases people are forced to pay for their own medicines in full.

The group picked an area with few facilities, old housing and a fairly stable community. They started with a general agreement that they weren't establishing a 'service to the community' – they were fighting women's oppression particularly through struggling for women to be able to control their own bodies.

They had four main principles:

1. To give away contraceptives free and make contraceptive advice central.

2. To try to break down the relationship between doctor and patient.

3. To try to establish a firm relationship with women in the area.

4. Not to do abortions (because it was illegal).

In the months after the *consultorio* opened in January 1975 the last two ideas had to be rethought.

The first to use the centre were feminists from all over Turin, wanting contraceptives and advice. (The *consultorio* still manages to get free supplies from different firms, though they don't know how long this will last.) After six months, the collective called a halt. They said it was a local centre, but local women were being kept away by all these others. Why didn't they set up *consultori* in other areas? (Since then four have started in Turin alone.)

But after this, local women still didn't come, even when all the flats, houses and shops had been leafleted. Quite soon they realized why – local women thought they were do-gooders, but useless because they didn't do abortions.

It's been so hard to get contraception in Italy that women have relied on backstreet abortion. *Three million* illegal abortions *per year* is not an exaggeration. The collective soon realized that it was common for local women to have had three or four.

Eventually they decided they *had* to do abortions too. They contracted a midwife who had learned to use the Karman method (where a small tube is inserted into the neck of the womb and the contents sucked out by an aspirator). They explained how the *consultorio* worked, and she agreed to work with them and keep her prices low. They are also learning to do abortions themselves.

A few days later a woman well-known and -liked locally had an abortion there with the new method. Within a week, the whole neighbourhood had got the word.

A collective of about twenty women runs the *consultorio*. They open up in the mornings, run the sessions, keep the files and have weekly meetings. Two women doctors are part of this collective. (There is also one male doctor, the only man allowed in.)

When someone comes for advice, she is asked to come to the afternoon collective discussion.

This is a first attempt to get women to identify their problems as women together. It is often difficult as few have ever spoken out about their personal and sexual lives. The collective try to draw the new women out. The discussion may be about things in the news like a rape or a demonstration for abortion – or someone may want to ask the doctor for explanations and advice.

The woman I spoke to said this was often difficult: 'When the doctor puts on his white coat, he takes on a lot of authority. The women have respect for him. We have to constantly challenge this. And in many cases, we know more than him now. We're so used to hearing about problems like "Will the Pill affect my liver?" But also we have to learn more ourselves. Some of us are taking courses in health so that we can do examinations too.'

After this first talk, the group usually breaks up into twos or threes. With the women who need internal examination, the *consultorio* tries to avoid individual counselling. They ask one of the younger women, who is likely to be less inhibited about her body, if she objects to other women being present during her examination.

If she says it's O K, three or four women will be asked if they'd like to be present in preparation for their own 'internals'. 'We don't ask everyone, because some would simply be frightened away. We realize that for some women it takes a long time to get used to the idea of even looking at your body.'

So nearly every woman learns in a very practical and *social* way how a woman's body works. When the time comes for her to have an 'internal' (possibly the first she's ever had) it's less traumatic because she knows what to expect. And more important, she *understands* what is happening.

Most of the women didn't previously know much about their bodies. There is a constant emphasis on diagrams, charts and informal chats.

Many of the women then set up their own discussion groups, using the *consultorio* as a place to meet. And they're *all* asked to come back. Without this, it could easily become just a referral service with no continuity.

Other women who had taught themselves to do abortions told me later that they didn't want to run around town with their little black bags, seeing individual women in their kitchens, then disappearing. They wanted a group or a centre to refer to, so that for any woman an abortion would just be the beginning of an involvement with other women. An involvement which could lead to women's power growing collectively and consciously.

I asked about the problems of illegality. They said so far there have been no raids from the police. For security, medical files are hidden elsewhere. But they felt that their strongest defence is that the police wouldn't dare disrupt something which has such strong support and involvement from so many local women.

[*'Marie Arnold' was a pseudonym for Kate Truscott. Ed.*]

SR.51, October 1976

New Zealand Clinic Bombed
NEWSHORT

The Sisters Overseas Service (SOS) in Auckland, New Zealand, is a feminist agency which has helped over five hundred women get abortions in Australia since the New Zealand government passed its extremely restrictive abortion law which even forbids abortion in the case of rape. As well as providing counselling and referrals to sympathetic doctors, SOS accompanies women to the airport, helps them borrow money and provides them with a detailed description of what the abortion will be like and what symptoms to expect afterwards.

This Easter, SOS was burned to a shell – exactly two years after a similar fire destroyed the clinic in Epsom, NZ, which was then performing legal terminations.

. . . The situation in New Zealand has been described by one doctor as 'a tragic shambles which has exceeded our worst fears'. Of the four hospitals in Auckland licensed to carry out abortions, two have no operating surgeons, the third is a private hospital with facilities available only to doctors who regularly operate there, and the fourth has a few doctors willing to perform abortions.

Pressure is building up for a liberalization of the law, but a father of eleven is heading a 'Right to Life' party which intends to put up forty anti-abortion candidates in the general election this year.

SR.75, October 1978

Clinic Bombed, Cleveland, USA
NEWSHORT

An abortion clinic in Cleveland, USA, was firebombed by anti-abortionists on 18 February while a woman was inside having an abortion. Luckily no one was seriously hurt. The 'Right to Life Society' of Greater Cleveland claimed that the bomber must have been a man who was angry because his daughter or wife had chosen not to have a child without asking him.

This isn't the first time health clinics providing abortions have been bombed or burnt in the States – six have been attacked in the last year, and others systematically harassed by anti-abortionist pickets, occupations and even threats on the lives of workers' children. In October picketers of a clinic in North Carolina were acquitted of trespass because the judges believed they had 'a good-faith belief that their actions were necessary to save lives'. But how long will it be before the anti-abortionists manage to burn someone alive in the name of the 'Right to Live'?

SR.70, May 1978

Christine Roche, *SR.39*, September 1975

Puerto Rico: 35 Per Cent of Women of Childbearing Age Sterilized

LYNN DI PIETRO

Puerto Rico in 1975 is an island devoted to tourism, capital-intensive industry, US exploitation of natural resources. 26 per cent of the arable land is occupied by US military bases. The US has succeeded in forcing 40 per cent of the population to migrate to US slums, and has sterilized 35 per cent of the women of childbearing age.

This figure represents the highest incidence of female sterilization in the world. India and Pakistan, which have public sterilization programmes, have 5 per cent and 3 per cent respectively. A 1968 study showed that of all the women sterilized in Puerto Rico two thirds were sterilized between the ages of twenty and twenty-nine years, the average age being twenty-six.

A secret document from an economic policy group commissioned in November 1973 by the Governor of Puerto Rico, entitled *Opportunities for Employment, Education and Training*, sees Puerto Rico's key problem as unemployment. The members of the committee have devised two solutions: one to foster new jobs, and the other to 'reduce the working sector of the population'. The fact that 35 per cent of the women have been sterilized indicates that they have opted for the latter.

The sterilization programme is to be carried out by a network of government agencies: Social Service, Health, Housing. The above-mentioned document sees the potential clientele as all the women of childbearing age not yet sterilized. There are no restrictions as to age, number of children, or marital status.

The sterilization programme in Puerto Rico is a forced one. This does not mean that women are being dragged off the streets and forced to submit to sterilization.

The pressure is much more subtle, and suitably disguised in the rhetoric of health of mother and child: what used to be the Family Planning has now been incorporated into the more comprehensive 'Programme of Mothers and Children', according to the secret document quoted above. 'The programme of mothers and children of the Department of Health is the natural means of attracting the possible clientele. 78 per cent of mothers give birth in hospitals, and 68 per cent in public hospitals.'

In many cases women are approached about sterilization immediately after giving birth, and while still in a weakened state. In other cases they are made to sign documents, often in English – a language which they are unlikely to read – before operations or deliveries, giving the doctor authority to do whatever he or she sees as necessary for their 'physical wellbeing'.

With families receiving state welfare benefits (59.6 per cent of the Puerto Rican population live below the US government poverty level), pressure is brought to bear by the various government agencies on whom they are dependent. Forced into a situation in which they are dependent on local government for a subsistence existence, they are particularly vulnerable. Many accept sterilization without being fully conscious of what they are agreeing to and often after being given the impression that the operation is reversible. Sterilization advice is part of the follow-up to all hospital deliveries.

Thus the very families that are forced into poverty because of a misdirected and profit-oriented economic system are asked to pay a further price by submitting their bodies to government dictates. There is no significant difference in the number of wives of middle- and working-class men who have been sterilized, but the middle-class woman might take the decision to be sterilized because she wants to pursue some endeavour other than childraising, and she has the education and ability to do so. It is the working-class woman, often made to see childbearing as her only contribution to society, who is under pressure to submit.

It is no accident either that sterilization is the preferred and encouraged method of birth control. It is not a case of a woman's right to choose: if this were the case other methods would be encouraged. Only sterilization serves the intended purpose of the whole exercise – depopulation.

It is interesting to note that safe abortions are virtually unobtainable in Puerto Rico, despite a US Supreme Court ruling in January 1973 confirming their legality. In practice abortions are only available in private hospitals, and then at a price of $250 (£110) and up.

Compare this figure with a report in the *New York Times* of November 1974 that nineteen free sterilization clinics have been opened in the San Juan metropolitan area. The clinics have been in operation at a top capacity programme of about 1,000 sterilizations a month.

The object is not to condemn sterilization *per se* but rather to illustrate that sterilization can only be realistically analysed within a social framework.

As women we must take special notice of the sterilization programme in Puerto Rico, as it is indicative of a situation in which a government whose decisions are taken mainly by men has taken upon itself to control our bodies by determining for us when we should not reproduce. While traditionally our ability to have children has been used to create myths about our inferiority in other endeavours, it is enlightening to see that when that ability is economically counterproductive it loses all mystique and becomes a 'function' which must be disposed of.

The US government and the colonial government of Puerto Rico claim that the sterilization programme is meant to be socially beneficial: that it is an attempt to raise the general standard of living and reduce the unemployment rate, estimated at 30 per cent by the Puerto Rican Chamber of Commerce.

However, a brief analysis of the colonial economy of Puerto Rico demonstrates that the social and economic problems of Puerto Rico are not the result of overpopulation, but rather a distortion of the Puerto Rican economy by virtue of its colonial relationship with the US.

Since it acquired Puerto Rico at the end of the Spanish American war in 1898 – an aggressive war waged against Spain in the early days of US imperialism – the US government has controlled the economy of Puerto Rico and developed it according to its own needs and not the needs of the island's people.

Before it became a US colony, the economy of Puerto Rico was an agricultural one in which the country produced coffee, tobacco, and sugar. The first thing the US did was to allow the coffee and tobacco cultivation to decline, and concentrated all investment on sugar – that product which the US needed but did not itself produce.

So from the beginning the Puerto Rican economy took a step backwards, the multiculture agriculture was replaced by a monocultural one. A sugar-plantation economy soon emerged, run by giant members of US sugar monopolies. This economy thrived on abundant sources of cheap labour, and so birth control was not needed.

In the early 1940s the US turned to Cuba, Hawaii and the Dominican Republic for their abundant sugar crop, because of their even cheaper sources of labour. Higher profits could be made elsewhere.

In an attempt to solve the economic problem which it had created, the US government initiated a programme called Operation Bootstrap, designed to create jobs for the Puerto Rican people. Operation Bootstrap coincided with the postwar economic boom when the United States had to supply a war-ravaged Europe with manufactured goods.

Companies were encouraged to relocate in Puerto Rico, the benefits being a source of relatively cheap labour; an up to seventeen-year tax exemption, plus low overheads, expenditures in transport, and a ready supply of cheap energy.

With its agriculture devastated by lack of investment, large masses of Puerto Ricans had migrated to the cities to seek work. Operation Bootstrap failed. When tax exemptions ran out, and Europe recovered from the war, and when it became obvious that a cheaper labour force could be exploited in Asia, US companies pulled out of Puerto Rico. Again, higher profit could be made elsewhere.

The United States was unable to provide an economic solution to Puerto Rico's problems of poverty and unemployment and still reap super profits, the key to all US involvement in the island. The real answer to Puerto Rico's economic, and hence social problems would of

course challenge the colonial nature of its economy, and its total dependence on the US. The US had to avoid recognizing the real cause
of the crisis, and yet still prevent the potential upheaval from the
socially explosive unemployed.

The all-purpose answer was, and is, depopulation. It was during
Operation Bootstrap that masses of Puerto Ricans were forced to
migrate to the US slums. It was during this period, too, that the quiet
beginnings of the sterilization programme were set up.

By 1950, 16.5 per cent of women over twenty had been sterilized. By
1965 the figure had reached 34 per cent. Again there is an economic
explanation for the drastic increase. As Operation Bootstrap was on the
way out, highly mechanized, capital-intensive industry was on the way
in.

Providing jobs is no longer a consideration. A third period of US
exploitation has begun. Huge multinational petrochemical and phar-
maceutical plants have spread over the island. These industries are
noxious and polluting and to avoid outcries by US environmentalists
they are located in Puerto Rico.

While they provide relatively little employment for the people, they
destroy the very basis of their existence – land, water and air. Rich
mineral resources were discovered in Puerto Rico in the early 1960s by
Kennicott Copper and American Metal Climax. Again, these industries
are destroying huge tracts of land in the process, and providing few
jobs.

Major oil interests are eager to build a superport for the refining of
petroleum on the island. This superport has been refused by several
major cities in the US because of pollution and the danger of oil spills.

So the picture becomes clear. US economic plans for Puerto Rico
presuppose depopulation. People are counterproductive to US interests.

All humanitarian rhetoric aside, the sterilization programme does
not benefit Puerto Rican women. It does not benefit the Puerto Rican
people. It benefits multinational companies. It is a genocidal programme aimed at the destruction of the Puerto Rican nation through
the malicious manipulation of women by depriving them of their right
to control their own bodies.

SR.39, September 1975

Breakthrough in Male Contraception
A JOKE

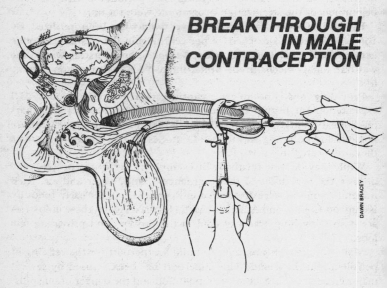

DAWN BRACEY

The newest development in male contraception was unveiled recently at the American Women's Surgical Symposium held at the Ann Arbor Medical Centre. Dr Sophie Merkin, of the Merkin Clinic, announced the preliminary findings of a study conducted on 763 unsuspecting male undergraduate students at a large midwest university. In her report, Dr Merkin stated that the new contraceptive – the IPD – was a breakthrough in male contraception. It will be marketed under the trade-name 'Umbrelly'.

The IPD (intrapenile device) resembles a tiny folded umbrella which is inserted through the head of the penis and pushed into the scrotum with a plunger-like instrument. Occasionally there is perforation of the scrotum but this is disregarded since it is known that the male has few nerve endings in this area of his body. The underside of the umbrella contains a spermicidal jelly, hence the name 'Umbrelly'.

Experiments on 1,000 white whales from the continental shelf (whose sexual apparatus is said to be the closest to man's) proved the Umbrelly to be 100 per cent effective in preventing production of sperm, and eminently satisfactory to the female whale since it does not interfere with her rutting pleasure.

Dr Merkin declared the Umbrelly to be statistically safe for the human male. She reported that of the 763 graduate students tested with the device only two died of scrotal infection, only twenty experienced swelling to the tissues. Three developed cancer of the testicles, and thirteen were too depressed to have an erection. She stated that common complaints ranged from cramping and bleeding to acute abdominal pain. She emphasized that these symptoms were merely indications that the man's body had not yet adjusted to the device. Hopefully the symptoms would disappear within a year.

One complication caused by the IPD and briefly mentioned by Dr Merkin was the incidence of massive scrotal infection necessitating the surgical removal of the testicles. 'But this is a rare case,' said Merkin, 'too rare to be statistically important.' She and other distinguished members of the Women's College of Surgeons agreed that the benefits far outweighed the risk to any individual man.

SR.93, April 1980

Radical Midwives

JENNY SPINKS

The word 'midwife' comes from the Anglo-Saxon 'with woman'. There have always been women who have attended other women in childbirth, and down the ages these women have been under attack. At times they were classed as witches and put to death. Attempts have been made consistently by men in powerful positions, such as priest or medicine man, to destroy the midwife, and take control of the birth process – an essentially female process.

In 1902 the Central Midwives Board (C M B) was set up as a statutory body to supervise the training and practice of midwifery. This board was not run by midwives, but greatly dominated by obstetricians. However, midwifery was recognized as a profession. Once trained and put on the roll of midwives, a midwife became respectable and was a skilled practitioner in her own right.

Meanwhile medical science has become more technical. The whole process of labour and delivery can now be initiated, controlled and completed by doctors and their technology. Control over bodily processes is often substituted for understanding of those processes. Admittedly, many medical advances in obstetrics have helped detect and alleviate problems as they arise. But these successes do not warrant indiscriminate use of medical technology in maternity care. In fact technical interference in the normal physiological process may well carry more risks than advantages to the mother and baby.

The use of a hormone drip to 'accelerate' labour puts the woman at risk of constant strong contractions, which could lead to rupture of the uterus and to the death of the baby due to oxygen deprivation. Monitoring equipment attached to the mother and unborn baby, often used to prevent the risks of accelerated labour occurring, can itself disturb the labour by stopping the mother from making herself comfortable in the position that suits her, and so increasing her need for pain-relieving drugs, which carry their own risks to mother and baby.

These trends inevitably mean the phasing out of basic midwifery skills, such as helping women to cope with the pain of labour, feeling the strength and frequency of contractions, listening to the baby's heart beat, knowing when normal is becoming abnormal. As these skills are phased out, so is the midwife. Instead the teaching hospitals are breeding obstetric nurses to be handmaidens to the obstetricians and their technology.

This means that the choices open to women having babies are becoming narrower and narrower; choices as to where she gives birth, how she gives birth, who is with her, how and when she feeds her baby.

A small group of women, some midwives, others training or about to start training, got together early in 1976 to share their discontent and frustration and their hopes. A few came from the States and Canada, where midwifery was virtually stamped out years ago, though the legal position varies from state to state. In order to learn the skills they had to come to Britain. They were shocked to find that here too midwifery was dying a slow death and that maternity care was becoming very similar to the dehumanized treatment the other side of the Atlantic.

Gradually the group grew by word of mouth and we began to meet every six weeks in different parts of the country. At first our weekends were filled with 'horror stories' (as we call them). But we'd be relieved to see each other and know we were with people who felt the same. For a weekend we were no longer isolated; we could shout and scream and laugh and bawl about our situations.

Midwives are employed by the Area Health Authorities and paid by the NHS. They are trained in schools of midwifery attached to maternity units, in the same way that nurses are trained, but with a period of time working on the district with a district midwife.

Once qualified you can be a district or a hospital midwife, though generally you are required to gain some hospital experience before going on the district. District midwives are given the rank of 'sister'. In hospital you are not made a 'sister' until you have gained some experience as a 'staff midwife'. A midwife who has just been made a 'sister', either on the district or in hospital, is paid £2,706 plus an extra £312 a year and a yearly supplement of 5 per cent.

In 1976–7 there were 21,000 midwives who notified the CMB of their intention to practise. (Every midwife has to do this at the beginning of each year.) They may be practising full- or part-time. In 1975 there were 3,600 full-time district midwives.

Midwives work with women through pregnancy, labour and for twenty-eight days following the birth. If it were possible for midwives to follow the same woman right through the process, midwives would get more job satisfaction and, we think, women would have far better care.

However, as a hospital midwife, you work in either ante-natal, delivery or post-natal; you very rarely see one woman through all three. As a district midwife, you may give some ante-natal care with a GP if s/he holds an ante-natal clinic. You may be lucky enough to do one or two home deliveries or do some deliveries at a GP unit or even in a consultant unit. But most of your work is post-natal care, visiting women who have come home from hospital. These visits are required by law to be done daily for ten days after delivery and then up to twenty-eight days if this is felt necessary by midwife and mother.

Post-natal work can be very rewarding but, on its own, not as satisfying as giving continual care. The district midwife was once described as someone who is invited to a party just to do the washing up!

District and hospital midwifery is supposed to be being 'integrated'. This seems to mean that district midwives are being assimilated by the hospitals. Hospital midwives are hardly ever known to do any work on the district.

Within the hospital there is a career structure with different rates of pay through which a midwife can rise, ending in teaching and administration. We are critical of the fact that beyond a certain point you can climb no further up the ladder without ceasing to practise midwifery.

For those of us who were direct entry student midwives – i.e. with no previous nurse training – to come into midwifery was like going back to school. On the very first day, you put on your uniform and are called nurse so and so. Immediately your identity is taken away and you assume a submissive role in the hierarchy.

The course, which lasts two years for direct entry students, one for SRNs and one and a half years for SENs (though it's about to be lengthened), is organized so that you spend a very short time on each ward. So by the time you have adjusted to the ward staff and their particular routine and are beginning to feel confident in what you are supposed to be doing, you are whisked off somewhere else, just as you feel ready to start making constructive criticism or allowing your personal feelings and views to be known.

But obviously the main barrier against self-expression is the constant threat of not getting qualified – we need that qualification to be able to practise legally.

Those of us who already had nurse training were used to the hierarchy. We'd learned to fear the consequences of standing up for ourselves. But training as midwives, many of us thought, we would acquire a skill of which we were 'practitioners in our own right', not just helping out doctors. It was soon apparent that we were not going to be taught how to take responsibility and make decisions for ourselves, or how to treat our 'patients' as healthy women, not as sick people totally dependent on us.

Student midwives are deliberately deprived of knowledge and power. They are frequently refused entry to medical students' lectures and even to hospital libraries. One student midwife wished to report a midwife who had treated a woman violently during labour. The midwife had in fact had nine previous complaints against her – this one would have brought about her dismissal. But when the student reported it to the nursing officer above her she was not informed that for her complaint to be acknowledged she had to hand in a written report within seven days. So no action was taken and the student was herself ostracized by the rest of the midwifery staff.

Having gained a midwifery qualification, we are kept very much in the confines of NHS bureaucracy. It is difficult to get jobs on the district. In hospitals we are immediately given administrative tasks on the wards and have little time to practise our new skills and little

consistent contact with childbearing women. In ante-natal clinics we are given the joyful job of chaperoning the obstetricians – rushing women in and out of cubicles and taking their blood pressure. The rest is left to the obstetrician, even in many cases where there are no abnormalities in the pregnancy.

So care is fragmented and the midwife's fragment is seen by all concerned as insignificant. The midwife's confidence in her own skills is undermined. The mother is made to feel she is merely an appendage to her uterus, which is proceeding through the hospital on a conveyor belt. If on the other hand midwives could take total responsibility for more women, the doctor would have more time to see any women with complications.

For the more experienced midwife, the labour ward is a humiliating place where she must take orders from inexperienced house doctors. If district midwives are invited into hospital to do a delivery, they are usually interfered with so that now many refuse to take on hospital deliveries.

One district midwife attending a woman in hospital left her for half an hour while she went for lunch. She was quite satisfied with the woman's condition. When she returned, 'someone' had decided that the labour was taking too long (the woman herself had not complained) and had set up a hormone drip to 'accelerate' labour. So the midwife was no longer attending a normal labour: she was now nursing a high-risk patient, and all without any consultation or respect for her own judgement. This is ironic as labouring women in the care of the hospital obstetric services are much more likely to be left alone than those in the care of the district midwife.

It is upsetting and exhausting to have to stand powerlessly and see women deprived of the information and choices that are their right. In the labour ward, it sometimes becomes difficult for the midwife herself to remember that this woman is experiencing something unique in her life and that she has a life and home, family and friends. Too often childbirth becomes a routine procedure, monitored on graphs, unrelated to the world outside. On the post-natal ward everything is still beyond the woman's control. One wanted to feed her baby during the night, but in that particular hospital it was not policy for women to feed their babies on the first night after they were born – they should be asleep. She was told by the auxiliary nurse (evidently in fear and trembling of her superiors) that she couldn't because it would 'upset sister'. Who was most upset we wonder?

Women who can't stand being in hospital any longer find it hard to discharge themselves. Dire warnings are usually given about the possible consequences to the baby and the guilt the mother would feel for the rest of her life. This, despite the safe and adequate care available from the district midwifery service and local GP.

Once home and in the care of the district midwife, it becomes clear what sort of ignorance women are kept in. One woman was so thankful that she'd had her baby in hospital; otherwise, she thought, she might have died. In fact it turns out she might have died *because* she was in hospital under the care of the doctors.

She had had a Caesarean section with her first baby. They induced labour for her second pregnancy. (That is risky in itself because hormone-induced contractions can be very strong indeed and so be dangerous to the scar on her uterus from the Caesarean section.) They also gave her epidural anaesthesia. (This meant that she could feel nothing at all from the waist down, and so would not be able to inform the staff if she felt anything going wrong.)

Anyway, they began to think that something was up and took her to theatre. As they cut through her skin and muscle layer, they saw the uterus rupturing along the scar line and were just able to save the baby and the woman. And this woman was *grateful* to the doctors and the hospital. They had blinded her with science and covered up their complete blunder and mismanagement of her labour.

Gradually we became frustrated with hearing over and over again the horrors of maternity care. We wanted to decide what to do about it. Previously we had described ourselves as a study and support group, but now we had business matters that required time for decision making.

We finally decided to call ourselves the Association of Radical Midwives. (The initials A R M in obstetric terminology stand for artificial rupture of membranes – with obvious implications for getting things moving and stirring them up.) In January 1977 we structured our six weekly meetings to which about twenty people come. Friday evenings (and every opportunity between sessions) are for reunions and 'horror stories'. Saturday is a day of study, when we share practical skills and open discussions on different topics. Sometimes we have outside speakers. We have covered such subjects as breastfeeding, psychoprophylaxis, active management of labour, the use of ultra sound, infant awareness and blood taking. Sunday, our business day, has become more and more hectic.

Early on we discussed the directions we could go in. Did we want to set up an alternative birth centre? Or were we going to be a more general pressure group? Or could we take on both? The birth centre project seems to have been shelved for the moment. Our main problems were how to fund it and how to be alternative and yet within the National Health Service.

In the summer of 1977 an article about us appeared in the *Sunday Times*. The response was quite overwhelming. We were certainly not prepared for dealing with over a hundred inquiries. At our next meeting after that article was published, we had to set out the nitty-gritty of our aims and how we were going to organize. We decided: we aim to restore the role of the midwife for the benefit of childbearing women and their babies.

Our objectives are:

To re-establish the confidence of the midwife in her own skills.

To share ideas, skills and information.

To encourage midwives in their support of a woman's active participation in birth.

To reaffirm the need for midwives to provide continuity of care.

To explore alternative patterns of care.

To encourage evaluation of developments in our field.

The group felt we should avoid any hierarchical structure or elite executive. We wanted our organization to be on womanly lines and not to fall into the pitfalls of male-dominated organizations, such as unions or churches, that are bogged down with bureaucracy and power at the top. We decided that as an organization of midwives for midwives we did not need full-time employees. We would rather work slowly, but with the support of the whole group, than quickly and 'efficiently' without grass roots participation.

So we set up autonomous regional groups and decided to maintain

our six weekly meetings as the national policy-decision-making body.
We hoped to have an annual national conference which would be a
general meeting place and platform for ideas, but not responsible for
making decisions. Meanwhile it was still necessary to have a secretary,
treasurer and publicity co-ordinator. These three are answerable to the
whole group and if problems come up between meetings, they can
consult with the regional group contacts.

Recently we have been struggling to define our political position.
People question our label 'radical'. The Central Midwives Board (the
statutory body responsible for midwifery) felt unable to send a representative to our recent conference on 'Midwives and the Law', not
wanting to be 'partisan'. The Royal College of Midwives (the
midwives' professional association) has some other excuse. It was
apparent that without us outlining our position, or even consciously
having a position, the establishment had decided what our relationship
to it was.

There were fears that we might be alienating whole groups of midwives
and missing important opportunities if we were to stand outside or
against the Royal College of Midwives. Nonetheless, general consensus
was that we are 'radical' in that we are a grass roots organization, wanting
to restore the roots of midwifery, and that we are 'feminist' in that we are
doing this for all women to have the right of control over their bodies in
pregnancy, labour and the post-natal period. We also feel we are more
likely to gain support through involvement in the trade unions (in our
case, NUPE or COHSE) than in the Royal College of Midwives.

It seems that we have taken on quite a struggle and that to restore
the role of the midwife is a hard task. Jobs for midwives are becoming
fewer, especially on the district, where they do have a certain amount
of autonomy. Many Area Health Authorities have definite policies to
phase out the district midwife.

As the national policy is towards 100 per cent hospital confinements
(despite reassuring noises from Ennals) the district midwife is not
needed for delivery. Also much of the ante-natal care is being undertaken in hospital. The post-natal care, it is argued by administrators
and some health workers, could be shared by district nurse/midwife
and health visitors.

We must fight this trend. Childbearing women need the continuity
of care that district midwives can give. Direct entry training for student
midwives (starting to train as a midwife without previous nursing
training) is also being phased out, the excuse being to bring us into line
with the EEC. But in Holland, for instance, all midwives are direct
entry and have a three-year midwifery training. Without direct entry,

women who really wish to become midwives are denied the option unless they are prepared to go through nurse training first.

The struggle of midwives to have their skills recognized is part of the increasing awareness amongst women of their oppression. We need to keep and add to our store of knowledge of normal birth processes before it is too late – to add to our woman-tending, not machine-tending skills.

Student midwives are conditioned to doubt their own skills and accept an inferior status to doctors. This conditioning is easy since, as women, we are all conditioned and trained to be supportive to others (especially men – our boyfriends, husbands, children) and not to re-cognize the potential of our own talents.

If midwives and nurses are to challenge the medical establishment, student midwives and other trainees need support so that they can take back the power of their own knowledge and skills.

With thanks to everyone who talked about it, especially Mavis Kirkham, Pippa Mackeith, Chris Allen and Caroline Mackeith.

SR.73, August 1978

"the breaking of the waters may come as a considerable rush"

Pen Dalton, *SR.34*, April 1975

'My World Became the Size of the Baby'

CATHERINE BALLARD AND HILARY HACKETT

I was alone in the house. The baby was asleep upstairs and I had lots of ordinary things to do. Suddenly I was totally overwhelmed by feelings of panic and terror. My feelings both mental and physical were as if a tiger had walked in the door, so that I was alerted, panic-stricken and in complete turmoil. I had this terrifying sensation that I had somehow snapped.

About 80,000 women every year seek help from their doctors for emotional disturbances of varying intensity following childbirth. This whole area of disturbance, not clearly understood, is usually loosely labelled 'post(after)- partum(birth) depression'. Yet it may not necessarily take place in the immediate post-partum period, nor take the form of depression, nor include feelings of aggression towards the baby, as is often supposed:

If I had felt more obviously miserable or had begun to dislike my child, something might have clicked for us all about what was wrong with me. (Mother of five-month-old baby diagnosed as having 'severe post-partum depression'.)

What then is post-partum depression? According to a consultant gynaecologist:

It's all bunkum and baloney . . .

But a consultant psychiatrist said:

Bloody gynaecologists and midwives fill my wards with desperate women.

The period following childbirth is necessarily one of adjustment to great change in a woman's view of herself and in her relationships. Many women we talked to said that they felt themselves to be in a fog of exhaustion and doubt. Doctors 'comfortingly' reassure them that after about six weeks or 'when the cycle re-establishes itself' – things will 'sort themselves out'. They ignore the terrifying feelings some women have: shock, insecurity, inadequacy, confusion and resentment; fears about their ability to love or look after the child; inexplicable states of tension and difficulty in relaxing and sleeping; sensations of having lost their 'real selves'; new and unpleasant feelings about their bodies and sexuality; guilt feelings sometimes associated with disappointment about the child's sex or looks; loss of concentration and appetite; an obsession with the baby and its routine.

One afternoon the baby was asleep in the other room. I fell into a deep sleep and after about ten minutes he began to cry. I went to the cot and shook him and shouted 'Shut up for God's sake!' I felt I *had* to sleep and sleep. That was the most important thing, he yelled so much and I was shattered.

The day I came home from hospital, I realized that I'd never be able to follow my own line again.

Immediately after Joanna was born I felt really sexy, but by the time the stitches had healed I couldn't face it. The baby seemed to take all my energy. I couldn't have cared less about him and his demands.

I felt fantastically happy with the baby and also with Jonathan, my first child. I didn't particularly want my husband near me, in fact I got him to sleep downstairs. I can remember feeling tremendously happy in the bedroom with the two children, because Jonathan came to sleep with me as well, which my mother didn't approve of.

I was shocked to see myself in the mirror. My body looked flabby and worn out. I couldn't imagine anyone ever wanting me again. Worst of all, I still couldn't wear anything but my maternity clothes.

The man I was living with was so battered by the change the baby made to *his* life that we actually sat down one night and contemplated separating. But the next morning it all seemed horrible and ridiculous.

At this point [after birth of second child] I stopped having any ambitions about finishing my research. I gave up completely. I found that I had less and less to talk to Alan about, apart from the children, that was our shared life. After this our sex life was less good, our marriage rests very much on the children now.

Such feelings may come and go during the first few weeks of the baby's life and then disappear completely. Or they may be, or may become, more intense and begin to swamp a woman. She may be quite unable to 'snap out' of her moods which might continue for a year or longer.

Sometimes feelings of inadequacy and resentment develop into real depression: total inability to face even the easiest day, to perform simple jobs or make decisions, and perhaps self-hatred or hostility towards the baby. Tension and irritability become physical and mental panic: trembling, dizziness, morbid horrors of sickness and death, phobic anxieties about going out, being alone or talking to people. Moods may swing between euphoria and despair, between over-protectiveness to the baby and lack of interest in it. A woman in this state may well not realize that she is disturbed; each of her feelings will probably seem real and reasonable to her as she experiences it. Other people will find it difficult to understand even if she can explain. One woman, who went through many anxieties, realized that she had struggled alone to rationalize them:

. . . it was the weather, or it was anaemia, or it was going back to work, or else it was my relationship with Paul. I had reasons for everything: it was my lack of routine or my personality, but never that it was something to do with post-natal depression. I never once *dared* to admit that. I don't know why I was so frightened of it, that would have been an admitting of failure I suppose.

It is often difficult for a woman who has post-partum depression to imagine what she was like before it began – the change in herself has taken place so suddenly. One woman explained her shock at a sharp return to a normality which, although an immense relief, was different from the way she felt before she conceived:

One morning, when he was about six months old, I just woke up feeling different. It was right from the start, I recognized myself. I kept waiting for this happiness to slump back, but it didn't. What it was was just ordinary, everyday O K, different to when I had been pregnant and before, and from then on I was feeling really great.

Perhaps one or two women in 1,000 become seriously psychotic after childbirth, and may have to be admitted to psychiatric wards straight from the maternity hospitals. This can happen to women who have no known history of emotional disturbance and in most cases the outlook is very good and recovery complete. Psychotic mothers may refuse to acknowledge that the baby is theirs, revert completely to childlike behaviour or experience paranoia or hallucinations.

All this, from the long-lasting anxiety state to severe psychosis is a far cry from the 'third day blues', that period of weepiness which the baby manuals predict will hit most mothers 'when the milk comes in', and after which they are expected to cope, to be themselves again, serene, capable and cosy. Yet . . .

One morning I bathed the baby and did everything, saw that everything was in order, and I can just remember having the feeling that they'd all be better off without *me*, because I'm finished. And I took an overdose, a very bad overdose. (Woman describing herself as she was when her baby was six weeks old.)

It is just not known why some women break down under the stress of the particular changes of childbirth, while for others the problems do not become serious.

The most usual explanation for post-partum depression is 'hormone imbalance' but reports of depression in fathers and adoptive mothers indicate that the causes are not purely physical. Nevertheless insufficient research has been done on hormone levels following delivery and on the connection between hormone levels and mood states. The information that is available seems to be contradictory and has aroused little interest in a male-dominated profession. It is also argued that it might be the state of anxiety and depression which 'unbalances' the hormones, in the same way that anxiety is known to disturb the menstrual cycle. In any case, it is absurd that so little research has been done and that there is still no widely accepted hormone treatment for post-partum depression when a link has been recognized for many years. However, to attribute the whole phenomenon to hormones is to miss the vitally important question of how *different* women will react to a life-crisis which is psychological and social as well as biological.

Recently a lot of publicity has been given to another explanation – the birth situation. Research has centred particularly on the psychological effects of induction of birth, the use of pain-relieving drugs, the separation of the mother and baby following the birth and the effect which this has on their relationship. While it is very clear that a bad birth experience may adversely affect the mother's feelings for her baby and may also cause more general depression, this too does not provide the whole answer. The actual experience of birth is of crucial importance to the mother and it will remain clearly imprinted on her memory for the rest of her life, but some of the mothers to whom we talked had become depressed after really good home births. For example, both these women had easy deliveries at home:

It wasn't panic about can I look after the baby, or the family, or the house. I was perfectly confident. There was no rational explanation for it, it just happened. Just terribly panicky and Oh God, *how* am I going to face the day, how am I going to get through it, and there was absolutely nothing happening in the day, nothing to frighten me at all.

When the baby was about five weeks old I quite suddenly started getting these panics and I felt depressed and tense and exhausted and completely cut off from people and reality. And above all feelings of terrible inadequacy started coming over me in great waves, as though I'd never be able to manage anything. I couldn't understand it, I'd felt so marvellous for the first few weeks, and that's the hardest time.

Other women have become depressed after the birth of each of their children, even though the births had taken place in very different circumstances, some 'good', some 'bad'. Organizations like the National Childbirth Trust and the Association for Improvements in the Maternity Services can do a lot to help us regain control of our bodies during pregnancy and birth and to secure the best possible circumstances for delivery. But for most women the reality is, and is likely to remain, impersonal ante-natal check-ups, classes to learn a few 'relaxation' exercises and how to bath a baby, a hospital birth with drugs and then home with a screaming infant and a tin of National Dried.

A more general explanation is that of conflict with the false ideal of glowing motherhood and the perfect baby, perpetrated by women's literature and lore, which influences most of us however realistic we think we are. There is a conspiracy of silence over this: other women, even close friends and neighbours, *seem* to be coping and they throw our (imaginary) inadequacy into relief. And because they (and we) struggle to keep up the front of competence, the myth that any woman can cope is perpetuated and it becomes very hard to discuss real feelings and anxieties with other women.

I persevered with breast feeding, not because I gained satisfaction but because of propaganda, especially among the women I go round with.

Conversations often stop at the level of the baby's development and the mother's health. However comments like these cropped up again and again in our interviews:

Even now, after three children, I can feel very detached and strange about it. I often get this impression that perhaps I'm only playing with dolls after all and that it isn't really true and that one day I'll wake up and I'll be twelve years old and they are dolls.

I remember shutting myself in the kitchen with the radio on, so that I couldn't hear the baby scream. I guess I must have been depressed.

I remember knowing that I loved the baby, but I just couldn't feel anything.

Often it was only in retrospect that these feelings could be acknowledged.

Our impression is that although all these explanations are important, the over-riding and under-emphasized factor is the identity crisis and dislocation of self brought about by childbirth, which most of the women we talked to were grappling to describe in their different ways. Puberty, establishing important relationships and the menopause are all seen as unavoidable stages of maturation, but in these we are primarily responsible only to ourselves. Childbirth is perhaps a greater crisis than those others in that it involves the creation of a dependent, separate being which *demands* radical changes in the mother's personality and relationships.

I feel spread thin, like peanut butter. You *can't* bring up three children and still remain the same.

Even when she's at Nursery, and I'm working, I find it hard to shut her right out of my mind.

Our research so far seems to show that there is a much higher incidence of admission to mental hospital following childbirth among working-class mothers. They may often have very little support from men and nowadays less from other members of their families or neighbours. The main problems are isolation, exhaustion and confusion:

I can remember watching the woman next door through a gap in the curtains. She was hanging out her nappies and I used to wait for her to go back inside before I hung out mine, because I didn't know what to say to her. I felt so down.

I already had four kids when Tom decided to take on the greengrocery business, then I fell on with Sean. After he was born, business got very bad, I was so desperate I couldn't take any more. I wanted to leave Tom but I couldn't. I was worn out but I used to have terrible dreams about mountains of rotting oranges.

I felt like a child. I wanted to run home to my mother and father and be a little girl again. I felt I was caught in a web, I didn't know how to look after them all.

If people around the woman are insensitive to her feelings then she may have to resort to totally bizarre behaviour to express her distress. Such women have been picked up by the police, doggedly pushing the pram around the centre of the city after dark; or have broken windows or smashed up their most prized possessions. They may then be hospitalized, labelled 'disturbed', and only then, if they are lucky, will they have the chance to sleep enough, eat enough, get to know themselves and (if there are nursery facilities available) their babies, and to think things through.

Many middle-class women, by the nature of their education, have been conditioned to believe that they should be able to cope alone, with ease, in all situations. They expect and are expected to play the superman role as mothers, continuing to succeed professionally at the same time as being 'good' mothers. Although they may be able to analyse and articulate their feelings and so may avoid hospitalization – perhaps because they can approach their GPs with confidence – nonetheless they may find themselves in equally frightening situations:

I really was in an awful state and for days and days all I could concentrate on was a game called 'Chinese Chequers'. Nick, God knows how he went through it, and I just played this child's game over and over again.

I became agoraphobic, it really undermined my personality, but I was able, by bits of strategic planning, to go out occasionally with someone else, and for a long time nobody knew.

I was somehow behind a black curtain. We thought it must just be the culmination of overwork and exhaustion. And when I saw the doctor he was completely thrown by this ranting and raving middle-class woman.

Such a woman can neither easily accept guidance from traditional sources nor from people who formerly gave her support:

I was in a consciousness-raising group and I used to go and they'd say 'How are you feeling?' and I'd say 'Oh, OK', and leave it at that. What had I got to say? I was just in a muddle and you can't talk about a muddle to people, can you?

How then can a woman assess when things have got too much for her to bear, admit this to herself and to others, and find support and help?

For dealing with the immediate problem, either a good GP or other women who are able to step out from behind their own façades can be very helpful in explaining that feelings of conflict and inadequacy and other, stranger, psychological symptoms are not as unique to her as she thinks they are. Unfortunately, few doctors are sensitive enough, or have the time, to give support to the woman and those around her over possibly a long period, reassuring her that her feelings are not unusual, 'wrong' or 'mad'.

All the psychiatrist could tell me was that my problem was 'trying to be a woman in a man's world' and that I should 'settle down with my baby'.

The *time* necessary for every mother's adjustment to her new situation must be recognized with patience by those around her and particularly by the woman herself. The new physical demands on her are stressful and at the same time she will be working through great personal change often in a state of heightened emotional awareness. This makes her very vulnerable to pressures from other people, such as criticisms about the way she looks after her baby, suggestions that she is too preoccupied with it and has cut herself off from her old life and become a different person. It can take many months even for a strong and self-aware woman to feel really competent to care for her baby, to become immune to other people's conflicting advice, to come to terms with herself and to feel ready to return to her social life and her job.

It is very important that, while accepting this, she makes every effort not to isolate herself, arranging support and help in looking after the baby, and learning to trust her own judgement. Ideally both men and other women should give their time and practical help to the new mother, and it is necessary for her to become less precious about doing everything for the child herself. Of prime importance is the relationship with husbands, closest friends, mothers and so on. A depressed and 'irrational' woman usually arouses sympathy in the first instance, particularly where there is an obvious reason for her state. However, when depression has become chronic the initial sympathy may fade – the woman should 'pull herself together', she has 'added responsibilities now' and 'cannot go on like this much longer'. These attitudes are not necessarily aggressive nor do they indicate that a relationship has broken down. It is essential that a woman shares her real feelings with others: if you have a good GP let him talk to your husband, mother or whoever else thinks that your distress is trivial. You need space and freedom from pressure. Make yourself known.

We have found in our research that many women who experienced post-partum depression failed to recognize their symptoms or were extremely afraid of them. But it is difficult to know just how much heavy publicity about the possibility of depression a pregnant woman can take. Nevertheless, those of us who have been depressed should not be ashamed to talk of it openly, and at last the baby manuals are becoming more realistic about how a mother will feel after the birth of her baby. For example:

A feeling of anti-climax follows the first overwhelming sense of achievement and excitement and all of a sudden she's at rock bottom, and left wondering why.

In a very few cases a mother may develop a severe post-natal depression. She loses her ability to cope. She may reject her baby. This has very little to do with a passing black mood. It's no good jollying her along, telling her to take it easy and it will pass. She needs sound medical advice and help . . .

. . . Some days may go like a dream. Others may seem hellish. You're cross with your husband. You can't stand his mother's advice. You're over-tired. You hate the baby. It seems to cry non-stop. You're overwhelmed and feel you can't cope . . .

(From *New Baby*, a Health Visitors' Association Publication 1975 – handed out free at clinics.)

It is to be hoped that this is a sign that Health Visitors are becoming aware of the need to look out for symptoms of depression for a long time after the birth.

Many other societies – and our own until a few decades ago – have social mechanisms to effect the transition into motherhood openly and smoothly, giving the individual woman a pattern to follow and protecting her from stress and isolation. Rituals are performed involving the whole family or community to mark the birth and events such as weaning, first haircutting, first tooth and so on. The birth of a child is not treated as a private act of production but as an event which concerns and changes the *whole* social group. However, in such societies, unlike our own, extended family relationships are still strong.

In our culture, celebrations as part of an outward sign of caring and an acknowledgement of achievement are in short supply. Flowers, congratulatory cards and presents are pleasant, but in a way distant, depersonalized and soon over. Apart from the Christening service, which is much less common than it was, the only public 'ritual' is the post-natal examination at six weeks which puts the final seal on having had the baby.

Until then you are allowed to feel vaguely poorly, but after the 'Right, fine, well done!' you are publicly given a clean bill of health and that's it.

Modern European society tends to promote the ideal of the lone, independent and self-determining individual. The responsibility for personal and psychological adjustment is placed squarely on the shoulders of the individual woman at a time when she is most vulnerable. One way out of the loneliness and strangeness which childbirth inflicts on us today is to share the experience with other women. Kate, whose baby is six months now, still meets three women from her ante-natal class every day. 'We would have been friends anyway – we share a lot of interests.' They babysit for one another and generally give each other support.

Mary describes how she and a group of women used to 'coincide at the Welfare Clinic'. It was years before the growth of today's women's movement and it never occurred to them to meet consciously as a group. She says, 'I never knew if the other women were depressed too. We'd moan a lot about our husbands – "them" – it was therapeutic. But we were very competitive, always eying each other's babies.'

Looking back she believes it would have helped her enormously if they had had the confidence to meet on a regular basis, perhaps discussing books or articles they had all read, particularly those which emphasize the mother's point of view. She suggests that women stick up a notice in their Welfare Clinic inviting others to form a group:

You've got to try and feel some connection with the outside world, with adults, otherwise you lose touch with your adult self. I think that sort of all-encompassing world that you slide into when you have a baby is dangerous because you become paralysed and dependent. Meeting other women, reading and talking weans you.

A group of women of Hackney, London, decided last year to meet regularly once a fortnight after their babies were born. Joceline describes how the group helped her:

I thought my life wouldn't be changed much by a baby. It took me over though – a child really brings out your deepest anxieties. I started relating differently to situations – everything became difficult, problematic; cleaning the house, washing nappies, even drinking a cup of tea. I also felt differently towards people, but my friends related to me as if I was the same and I tried to live up to their expectations. I couldn't; I freaked out, got paranoid and became a recluse with my baby and my world became the size of the baby. Then I started getting together with a couple of other women with young babies. 'I just scream into my pillow at night and sometimes feel like killing myself,' one of them told me. I felt a shock of recognition. Every time we meet now we check out what we have gone through, compare, analyse and feel a lot of mutual support.

Finally then, a willingness to step out of our own image consciousness, giving consistent care and support, and recognition that looking after a baby is hard, life-changing work, are some ways in which we can all make the post-partum period positive rather than destructive. We would then be helping each other towards a creative acceptance of

our own identities and of the interdependent and always growing identities of our children.

ŞR.47, June 1976

"there is no need to be
alarmed or embarrased
at these examinations"

Pen Daulton, *SR.34*, April 1975

Agoraphobia

HILARY WILCE

At sixteen Carolyn Maniford became a patient in a psychiatric hospital
because she was too frightened to leave home, even to go shopping or
to travel to work. Carolyn's situation is extreme but her case history is
similar to that of many agoraphobics. There are quarter of a million
known agoraphobics in this country, the vast majority of them women.
The actual number of sufferers may well be nearer half a million for
the apathy and intolerance of many doctors cause too many other
agoraphobics to keep their bewildering fears a shameful secret.

Agoraphobia is commonly known as a morbid fear of public places.
Sufferers often prefer to define it as a fear of any situation in which
they feel trapped. Neither definition gives any indication of the true
misery of people made prisoners by their fears. Isolated, they live in a
twilight world of panic and apprehension, where a train journey is a
total impossibility and the corner shop might as well be on the other

side of the world. And they live alone with their fears because, as one agoraphobic says: 'How *do* you explain to anyone the terror you feel at the thought of walking down your own street? It would almost be easier to have some sort of obvious, physical disablement.'

Like most illnesses, agoraphobia varies in type and intensity. At one end of the scale is the girl who occasionally feels unable to face travelling on the Underground; at the other end is the housebound housewife who never, ever goes out, who cannot bear to stay on her own and who is perhaps too frightened to take a bath or wash her hair.

But the varied fears of agoraphobics refuse to fit neatly into one phobic slot. If someone is terrified of crowded lifts or crowded trains, are they agoraphobic or claustrophobic? The answer is probably, both. Agoraphobia can also be accompanied by specific phobias – a dread of heights, bridges, clouds – and anxiety and depression states are common among sufferers.

The majority of cases of agoraphobia develop when people are in their mid to late twenties. For some, the fear builds up slowly over a number of years, gradually becoming more and more unbearable. Twenty per cent of agoraphobics were also school phobic when they were younger. Other people find themselves suddenly, and for no apparent reason, experiencing a full, phobic panic.

... At seventeen Carolyn Maniford is a patient in Goodmayes Hospital, a grim-looking psychiatric hospital in Essex. She is an agoraphobic and has been in hospital for three months.

'It started for me when I was eleven and at secondary school. I found it difficult to mix and would get into corners all the time. Then it got worse and when I was fourteen I found it difficult to go to school. I had to run all the way because I couldn't face walking. I thought everyone would know how I felt and laugh. When I got to school I'd hang round outside the classroom plucking up courage to go in.

'In my last year I played truant a lot and would lock myself in the house. Then I left school and I found I couldn't mix at all. I couldn't travel on trains, buses, tubes, anything. I had ten jobs in six months – I just kept taking new ones to see if I could stick them out. My last job was on a farm. I liked that. I used to feed the chickens and it was really peaceful. But it was a long bus journey and the psychiatrist I was under withdrew my tranquillizers to see if I could manage without them and I just couldn't get there any more.

'So then I stayed in the house for several months. It was awful. I became scared stiff of my parents and kept the curtains drawn because I couldn't bear daylight. I came in here then.

'I don't like being here but I can't get home. There's no one there all day. I'd be completely on my own and if there was no food in the house I wouldn't be able to go across the road and get some.

'I can talk to my dad but I can't seem to get through to my mum. I'll sit for hours explaining how I feel and then she'll just say something that goes against everything I've been trying to say. Last Thursday I went for her. She said I'll end up properly mad, I'll end up in the main block here. I can't bear people saying that to me. So I hit her about the head and my dad had to pull me off. Now it's at the back of my mind all the time.

'We don't do much in here. I walk up and down the corridors or sit and think for hours on end till I get really depressed. If I need something from the shop at the gate I force myself to go out but I have to take a bag to grip on to and I feel really awful. I go for walks round the grounds with a girl here but only because she wants to, and because I can't tell her I'm terrified.

'I see a psychiatrist here, but only for a few minutes at a time. The other one I was under left suddenly. We didn't know he was moving. Quite honestly, I've been pushed around so much by psychiatrists that I couldn't care less about them any more.

'Apart from that we have meetings every day when we're meant to talk about our problems. Everyone sits round the room in silence at first. I don't talk much because once you've said what your problem is there isn't much else to say.

'I don't talk to anyone on the ward much. They're all older. One old woman just keeps muttering something about Chelsea Town Hall. It drives me mad. I can't seem to settle down here. Not like everyone else.

'I like art and I've thought about doing nursing or heavy work, like on the farm. But I don't think I'll ever get better. Sometimes I think I'm in here to get worse.' . . .

SR.3, September 1972

Liz: Alcoholics Anonymous

INTERVIEWED BY MARSHA ROWE

. . . My mother used to give me hot toddies to comfort me when I was sick or upset. When I left school I joined the Young Socialists for a while, but none of it made much sense to me and I left it when I got to University. I really enjoyed drinking, it got me over my shyness when

I went to parties. But I couldn't afford to drink that much on a grant, I didn't go out to get drunk then. Bob and I got married when I was in my third year. The rationalization for it was that we weren't allowed to live together because of college regulations which was a hassle. I brought to the marriage all the preconceptions about wanting it to be forever and always and a great relationship. I remember saying I don't want to get divorced and his saying, 'That's bloody ridiculous.' We've rather changed roles now.

I don't think I can honestly say I ever needed to go to pubs in order to meet people. Not like some of the others in AA, people who've obviously done all their socializing in pubs. When I got married I was still hung up on this being taken out for nice meals bit. I thought that was the height of sophistication. In fact, I always had this thing, that I would really have arrived the day I had a well-stocked cocktail cabinet and could say, 'What would you like to drink?' It never arrived, and it never will, because every time I bought anything I drank it as fast as I could.

Then we came to London and that was a sort of nadir of my life. I'd wanted to be an actress and I was very involved with Bob. I still think I'm good on stage but I haven't the inclination to uproot myself and go anywhere at any time twenty-four hours a day. I started supply teaching and I got pregnant.

. . . I thought I'd have perhaps three at the time but when I did I found it was ghastly. Two kids are just a hell of a lot of work, they get jealous of each other. I remember I began to have morning drinks to sort of anaesthetize the mid-morning feed because it was such a strain having to cope with a bawling child while the other was feeding. Then I'd get sloshed you see, and it really used to be quite nice once I was sloshed, the housework and the children were all quite bearable. This was not drinking to get drunk, it was drinking to get into a state where I didn't mind things too much. I don't know whether Bob noticed. I think I told him. He took a very cavalier attitude to the whole thing.

But then I remember I stopped. There was half a bottle of whisky left and I thought, 'I've got to stop because I'm never going to do anything except look after the children and get sloshed,' and then I started painting. That was the first time since being an adolescent. Then I thought, 'Well, that's all right. I've stopped for three months and I've got it under control.' So I started drinking again just in the evenings, but there were days when I got very sloshed because I remember once being very, very drunk on a bottle of Greek sherry and weeping to a friend that I couldn't go on. That's when we moved to where we live now. I know every off-licence in the area, the hours they're open, every single one. I can tell you where to go at what time of day and I'd do the rounds so none of them would know about my drinking. But then there's the problem of empties, that's ghastly. You buy all this stuff, usually in quarters or halves. I was topping up bottles by this time to make it look I hadn't drunk much. I drank anything I could lay my hands on, but mainly whisky. We always had a joint account so it came out of 'housekeeping'.

By this time it began to get ugly. I've always lost my temper easily when I drank a lot, and Bob and this other guy who was living with us would come home and suggest we go out for a drink. I would have a couple of drinks with them on top of all the other drinks they didn't know about. Then I would suddenly snap and all this shit would come out and later I felt dreadful about it. Bob used to hate the rages but I think he quite liked comforting me through the hangovers.

Then we went abroad for a year. I was pregnant again. It's interesting the way one has all these mechanisms towards good health built in because I couldn't drink the last three months of my pregnancy. I'd get this terrific heartburn which was very painful. Although I got plastered the day we left because there was a hell of a lot to do. After we arrived there was no money to spare but then a cheap gin came on the market and I got stuck into that. That was about four months after we left England, and I was discussing women's liberation then. I do think it is a terrible indictment both of me and the group I was in that I didn't talk about it all with them. It wasn't a proper consciousness-raising group, it was sort of half consciousness-raising and half study. Drinking escalates very quickly. Well, it was only 11s a bottle, a small bottle would fit into my bag. It smelled foul. And brandy, I drank, and beer, in the morning or at lunchtime. Then I'd take the kids out in the afternoon to the swimming pool and I'd be pretty plastered then usually. I dunno.

I don't think I showed that many signs of it. Yet I would not remember things. I started having these memory lapses, blackouts they're called, and I didn't know who I'd been talking to or what I said and sometimes I wouldn't know how I got from A to B. I'd lose twelve hours, that's when it starts getting frightening. Bob would notice and I would ask the kids if I'd put them to bed the night before. I was scared I'd leave the kids in a locked car or something.

It's a nightmare because nobody understands. People say drink less, that's the usual. But the minute I've had one drink it's just not enough. By this time I was saying to people on an individual basis I've got a drinking problem, I'm an alcoholic, but nobody knew what to do. I tried to stop drinking again as a result of being involved with somebody else. I remember on the tail of a really awful hangover him saying you've got to stop drinking. I couldn't keep going round with half my brain knocked off, and feeling so ill. I said I wouldn't have another drink, which I'd said frequently before. Next time I was with him I said, 'Right, I'll have a beer.' He said, 'No, you won't.' I was absolutely livid, really furious. I flounced out of the flat and that was the first time anyone had stopped me taking the first drink. He didn't know about alcoholism but he said you are psychologically dependent on this thing and you've got to break this dependency, and that means coming off alcohol for quite some considerable time, like six months. And I thought I'll show you mate, and after this initial thing of flouncing off I thought, he's right, I won't drink for six months. I still haven't made it six months without a drink but I didn't drink for about six weeks after that.

The first thing that happened when I stopped, it was awful, it was really awful, like hanging on a cliff. I really didn't think I could manage it, I hadn't got any A A philosophy at this stage, knowing that you're only supposed to try and cope with a day at a time. It was six months here we come, which is a terrible mistake. After about three or four weeks I was feeling better, not suffering gastritis, and I didn't have cramps in the night, visual disturbances and I didn't get up vomiting. I could remember there were good things about not drinking. I'd remember what I said to people, I hadn't hit anybody and forgotten about it. But I was living on a knife edge.

Then things began to go wrong. He broke off the relationship. But somewhere, deep down, I knew I mustn't drink then; that I had to stay stopped, not to show him, but myself. I was only able to sustain that a couple of weeks. Then I was off on these periodic benders. First I wanted oblivion, then I'd think, 'Oh well, I haven't really stopped at the moment', and have another drink. It's like snakes and ladders.

A A groups help because people have been through the same thing. In terms of character types, I think there are a lot of people who've been very shy, self-conscious, inhibited, often really successful but inside just a quivering mess. There are probably a lot of people around like that who are not alcoholic. Nobody knows how many alcoholics there are, except there must be some people suffering with nobody knowing anything about it, realizing they've got a problem. Women are reputed to be more difficult to treat than men. They are more secretive as drinkers, and I think, because of the economic facts of life, women stick by alcoholic men longer than men stick by alcoholic women. And women usually drink in their home environment, which means that they are back in the drinking environment as soon as they leave hospital or whatever, it's not like the pub, which a man can just avoid. At first, I got into a terrible state about the spiritual side of AA, but I think maybe if I've got to depend on something, it's better to depend on a belief which may or may not be false than to depend on alcohol.

Some people say the power of the group is the higher power, the power of AA and it's true that it works.

So I've stopped thinking of myself as the centre of the universe which I always did before, or I'm trying to stop. If somebody was angry before, I always assumed they were angry with me. I mean, people can be irritable about anything totally different, and just to get over that, and not see everything hinging on proving yourself, just see yourself as an ant essentially, one of the people and part of the universe. There are some people in AA who are atheists, but most people in groups revert to something like a god we were brought up with.

It's very weird, because now I can go around thinking bloody men, they're always putting me down, and look at the differential between my earning power and that of Bob's, and the fact that I look after the kids and nobody ever counts that in an incremental scale. It's all bloody unjust and I could go round feeling that and get myself into a terrible state over all sorts of things. I learned to switch really, and think well, I've got the kids and I know where the next meal is coming from and you know, I'm bloody lucky, and I've got somewhere warm to live. I feel this is difficult to discuss with some women in the movement. You're not supposed to take one step back. Well, I don't think that's true, in order to survive with any sort of equanimity at all. This whole thing AA has about resentment. In a women's liberation group, you're looking at the things you're feeling angry about and validating your anger really, saying, 'Yes, I'm right.' But, in the end, unless you can actually go and change a situation, do something, you have this cancer inside you eating you away. It's not the man who's put you down, or won't give you a job, who's discriminating against you, who's suffering, it's you. Unless you can actually take action. AA has this prayer: 'God grant me the Serenity to accept the things I cannot change, Courage to change the things I can and Wisdom to know the difference.' It seems to me that what's crucial is the wisdom to know the difference, because I differ from a lot of people I've met in AA about what that is – perhaps I've just been unlucky.

I don't have a straight environmentalist line about alcoholism. There are alcoholics, I'm sure, in every society. I really feel I ought to stay in AA but I feel pulled in two directions. What do I do when somebody makes a joke at an AA meeting, like I'd rather be watching a Miss

World competition on the telly than being at an AA meeting. I don't ever say anything in these situations. I'd be odd and isolated and I don't fight it because it just upsets me, because I need to be there. I'm a socialist but one doesn't talk about politics at AA, it's all on this personal level and I suppose I feel isolated because I do connect the personal with the political and nobody else does. Anyway political arguments upset people and so it's an area that isn't discussed and the connection isn't made. I really do feel I'm picking up where I left off about twelve years ago, before I started drinking. I've anaesthetized myself. There's this terrible wilful bit you can't control. When I'd go shopping, I'd walk straight over to the drinks counter in the supermarket, the number of times I've said half a dozen Coca Cola and a quarter bottle of whisky, and it's just been out, just like that, and I feel this part of myself, reason has nothing to do with it. It might have rational beginnings, but now it's totally irrational. Alcoholism is the third biggest killer. Society keeps bloody quiet about it, look how much money they're making out of it. They put a government health warning on cigarettes, but they don't on alcohol. It really is the opium of the people . . .

SR.22, April 1974

Stretched to Breaking Point

ROZSIKA PARKER, JANE WILSON AND ALISON FELL

. . . *Almost half the patients leaving hospital in 1972 had been patients for less than a month. However, for many long-stay patients, hospitals live up to their name – bins, society's dustbins. In the 1971 Census of Psychiatric Hospitals 65 per cent of patients had been in for more than two years and 29 per cent for twenty years or more.*

. . . *The women's sense of self-respect and their ability to help themselves were eroded. Patients, like children, are given no say in the running of their 'home' and no power to shape their own day. But what else does it mean to be treated as a child? They were constantly watched, ordered about one minute and patronizingly indulged the next. They had no rights and worked for nothing. If they inquired about their treatment they were met with 'Because I say so'. Their descriptions of their feelings and experiences were discounted. And other people were licensed to punish and bribe them into 'acceptable' behaviour . . .*

Elaine

... 'I went around to a heck of a lot of different nurseries and foster homes and ended up in a kid's home where I stayed for about seven years.' After such a childhood Elaine needed time to herself, a space to discover what she wanted and respect for her privacy.

The mental hospital where she went with heroin addiction provided neither peace nor privacy. She felt watched, manipulated and invaded.

Here she compares the hospital to the therapeutic community where she finally came off drugs and where no coercion was used on the patients: 'You could do what you wanted to do, go when you wanted to and sort things out for yourself with the help of other people.'

Elaine can't remember how many times she has been in mental hospital. Aged fifteen she was addicted to heroin.

'I first went in after I'd been using it for about five months. I was living at my boyfriend's place. We got really bad, we'd just be lying around fixing and watching T V all day. And the heat – it was a centrally heated place so we'd turn it right up. We never did anything round the house and in the end Kevin's father got really sick of it. You know, he was going out to work and paying our board and lodgings, yeh, he got tired of us.

'So Kevin went up there and pushed to get himself admitted. Then I went up because I had nowhere else to go – I couldn't have stayed with his father.

'At first you're really just sort of quiet. You don't know what is going on. You're nothing. You just sit and wait for the next meal.'

Elaine was the youngest patient in the mental hospital. It didn't bother her unduly but she was upset by the way the staff treated the elderly women. 'Nothing was done for them apart from dressing them, feeding them, chasing them up and down the corridor or getting them back when they ran away.

'For a few people that place worked. It seemed to work for the housewives who came in for a nervous breakdown leaving six children at home. When they first came in they'd be put on pills and stuff. They'd rest and find people in the same situation who would sit around with them, knit and talk.

'When I first went in there it was pretty easy for me to leave again because people didn't know me. But after a while I was stopped from leaving on the dot. They'd cut me down gradually. Once I was down I'd say, "I'm leaving, I'm going," and so they'd put me to sleep. One

Raspberry

Ayme Rosenberg, *SR.34*, April 1975

time they gave me sleep treatment for a fortnight. When I woke up I still kicked up and wanted to leave.'

She fought to leave because she was frightened of group therapy. 'There was no support in the group, nobody knew what they were doing. The stronger people would always pick on the ones who were quiet. There was no way you could get out of it and it completely broke me up. I used to sit there terrified that somebody would speak to me or ask me a question.

'Once I managed to get out of hospital I just forgot about the unit and started fixin'. Then we'd go in when we were fixin' so much that the stuff ran out. You know, we'd still be withdrawing and we'd realize that we'd have to go in otherwise we were going to be really ill. You'd have to say that you really did want to come off and that you were really going to try – this time.'

Elaine loathed the sensation that she was being controlled and constantly observed. She particularly resented the idea that she was being noted down and filed away: 'All my life I've had a file behind me that I've never been allowed to see. I was in a kid's home where they kept a file on me for seven years – annual and bi-annual reports. At the hospital they'd have staff meetings to read the cases. You'd walk past the office, see them chatting and think, "I hope that it's not me they're talking about." Then they'd all come out and you'd know that they'd been told something about you.'

Elaine rebelled. Perhaps it made her feel like somebody. 'I was always a trouble maker. I used to disrupt everything and really was quite a nasty person. The staff said that as soon as I began to get on with them, I'd turn round and kick them in the teeth.

'When I went in I'd soon get together with a guy which in the end would turn out to be a right disaster. I didn't think women liked me. The doctor said it was because they were shit scared I'd take their man away.'

Eventually she was sent to a small therapeutic community in the country where she lived with about eight other addicts and 'a guy called Simon who was more or less one of us, although he hadn't used drugs.

'There you didn't get hassled. You were just treated as someone who had a problem. You were sort of on your own and you had plenty of time to think – that was the main thing.

'In the summertime we'd just get up and lie out on the lawn and in winter we'd sit by the fire and play records. The people in the village called us dirty junkies. They'd stare at us through the gates – that brought us together. You didn't have to go to group therapy and try to think of something to say. The only meetings were to decide who was going to cook, wash up and clean the front room. People would stay there for about six months and then just sort of leave and get a job. I did.'

Susan

Susan went into hospital feeling depressed, isolated and defeated. She wanted somewhere to escape to and she needed people prepared to 'work' with her through her problems. It was a relief to be committed – to cease to be a capable person, but she was still ashamed of being unable to cope.

With these mixed feelings she came slap up against the authoritarian structure of hospital life; the rules and the petty indignities. Her depression gave way to fury. It was a familiar pattern with her.

Instead of allowing her to use or express her anger, the hospital tried to threaten and dope her back into passivity. They gave her no chance to work through her feelings. They no longer defined her as 'sick', but as a 'trouble maker', disrupting the carefully controlled fabric of the institution. Looking back she feels that nothing positive came of her rebellion: 'It was just me against the system, as usual.'

For two years Susan had been a social worker; slowly the barrier she had erected between her own problems and those of the women she worked with broke down. 'Instead of being the social worker, the responsible figure, the one who made the decisions, I completely crumbled.'

Comfrey

Ayme Rosenberg, *SR.34*, April 1975

Six months previously she had got married. 'All my life I had had this big thing about getting married. There's always been *that* to look forward to. Eventually someone was going to come along and love me. Then, when it happened . . . he's a really great guy and all that, but wasn't there something else? Wasn't there a bit more?

'I had absolutely no friends except for Tom who I leaned on heavily. He worked in the evenings and anyway I wasn't usually home until two or three o'clock in the morning.

'Then in the space of about two days I just completely closed off. I just went right inside. I just wasn't connecting at all. Tom phoned the doctor. She just took one look at me and said that I should go inside to protect me from myself. I'll never forget it – the sense of relief, the almost immediate sense of ease. It was kind of letting it all out, it was over, I was going in, I was going to get fixed, I was going to get cured.

'I arrived there and I stood still in the hallway – it was just a big room and there were all these terrifying people. I knew I was sick, but I wasn't . . . there were old men urinating and playing with themselves, there were young men – dossers come to dry out, there were women who were . . . who just kept trying to kill themselves.

'I just wanted to hide but they made me go in and sit in the room with all those people. I couldn't stand it. I was crying and I said to Tom, "Please I don't want to stay here, please take me home with you." He started crying and he said, "Please, I can't help you, let the doctors try and help you, please stay." '

Like Elaine, Susan felt dazed and stupefied at first. Her bed was the only place where she felt secure. 'All I had was this bed.' But the staff wouldn't let her stay on her bed, they continually urged her to 'sit with the others'.

Gradually, her stupor gave way to fury: 'I thought, they've no authority over me, these little girls in their pin stripes, they've no experience of what I'm feeling and yet they think they are above me. They were so patronizing and condescending. I could wear it a bit from the doctor but I couldn't wear it from those little nurses. I was no feminist then. They were a thorn in my side. You'd queue for your pills, stand there in front of them and swallow so that they could check you had taken them. Within a week, far from being depressed, I was the angriest person in the world.'

Susan soon learned that the hospital operated on a system of punishment, threat and reward. 'I was basically a tough person but I still got really knocked under. You see I knew that if I screamed or broke a window they would just shoot me in the ass with largactil and drop me in my bed. Then there was the whole blackmail thing of "How dare you question what we're doing. You've come here completely broken to pieces and we're putting you together again our way. If you don't like it you can go, there are plenty of people queueing up to be admitted." '

As well as the staff/patient power structure, Susan was aware of the rigid hierarchy amongst the staff, with the consultants at the top and female Black student nurses at the bottom. Attitudes of the women on Susan's ward towards the staff on the lower rungs of the ladder varied: 'People had contempt for them or liked them simply because they had no authority – no power. It was always the student nurses who made contact with you. The rest of the staff had no time to sit and chat because they all had administrative work. If you tried to talk seriously to the students about their lives or your own, they got nervous. Maybe they felt that kind of talk was the doctor's job.'

Susan echoed others' criticism of the doctors; they had no respect, they didn't listen. However, she says she saw the doctor more than most of the women in with her. 'I know lots of women who didn't get to see their doctor after they were admitted. I did – perhaps because I was more vocal or perhaps because my husband was middle class and

Marshmallow

Ayme Rosenberg, *SR.34*, April 1975

could speak their language. Anyway, in two short sessions the shrink put together a file on me, had me sussed out and this was me – an alcoholic who was very anti-authority.

'The most humiliating thing was the Wednesday morning meet-the-chief session. It was a massive power trip for the consultant. He never knew any of the patients but once a week you'd be called in to see him and he'd go through your file. You'd be a jittering bundle of nerves all morning; you were afraid of what decisions he was going to make about you when he knew nothing about you except what was written on the file or what the other staff told him.

'It was like a magistrate's court with all the staff who wanted to learn the tricks of the shrink trade sitting in. He doesn't even know your name. He pulls out your file and flicks through it. "Mmm, I see you are anti-authority and have an alcohol problem." I said, "You don't see or know anything." "Yes," he said, "the file's correct, isn't it."'

The staff objected when Susan built up a group of friends: 'They didn't like it. You see, we were supporting one another. We'd go on strike; wouldn't go to Occupational Therapy, wouldn't go to bed when lights went out and wouldn't eat shitty food. I got dragged out of bed one day by one of my friend's shrink. He asked, "What's the story with this little group?" He was very cool and trendy and actually treated me as if I had half a brain. It turned out that he was worse than my straight shrink – he just wanted to get into my knickers. I was just a fun fuck.

'I thought it was the screw of the century. It was me fucking the hospital, getting my own back, because it gave me a hold on him.'

SR.43, March 1975

With a Little Help from Ourselves

CAROL MORRELL

Re-evaluation counselling – more often called co-counselling – is perhaps the most radical of the radical therapies: it is peer group therapy. You work on what is important to you, and at your own pace. Nobody directs you or analyses what you say. This allows you to be in charge of your emotional life. You are not regarded as 'helpless'. Especially for women, taking our therapy into our own hands is the first step towards self-realization.

The theory of re-evaluation counselling, as developed over the years by its founder, Harvey Jackins, is deceptively simple. The genius of the idea is in practice more than theory. Jackins noticed, as many others have, that the functioning of society (including behaviour, roles, values) depends on the systematic and forceful repression of emotions. Take a small child. When it feels sad or happy, it expresses those feelings, usually loudly. This is the healthy thing to do; the child doesn't need to be taught that. When the emotion being expressed is anger or fear or tears, it is immediately cut off by the parent. The adult was stopped too, as a child: the sound of her own child crying reminds her how painful it was to stop crying herself. She is 're-stimulated' and must stop that noise: and she must repeat the way she was brought up to behave. 'Shush shush darling, don't cry', or 'Boys don't take on so. You're a little man now': familiar comments. The child soon learns to apply that outer restraint to itself, stops shouting and crying, and we say 'how grown up he/she is getting', admiringly.

But with the stifling of feeling goes the inability to function well, perhaps even to think. If a child is allowed to express its fear, until it spontaneously stops shaking and perspiring, the immediate result is a happy smile and renewed interest in the world around. The situation has been coped with in a healthy way. The next time a fearful situation arises, the child will again experience being afraid. But it will not experience being afraid for the last event and the time before that, on top of the present fear. The surest way to train up a child into a fearful adult is to refuse to let it express feelings of fear.

Emotions, if not expressed, gradually tighten inside until we *cannot* express them. Worse, the events that produce emotion still occur, have a tendency to set off the same sort of emotion, which adds to the original feelings, the whole mass of which becomes more and more tightly repressed. So we can keep functioning. But now, as a result of repressing 'undesirable' feelings, we function in a highly patterned, unintelligent manner. We never do anything new. Instead of responding to a situation, or a person, we avoid what is likely to be emotion-producing or act in a repetitive way. In order to cope. All the time. Noticing these patterns in other people is easy, once you adjust your vision that way. We often say, 'That's her way' or 'I know what his response to that would be': we think of patterns of behaviour as personality, but the personality, the individuality, is hidden beneath the pattern. It's much less easy to see what our own patterns are, because part of the necessity to stop up emotion includes the necessity to not know, consciously, what troubles us or how we put the feelings out of sight. We just do it, repetitively, machine-like.

The theory continues on to suggest that the only way to end senseless and repetitive behaviour is to get in touch with those painful feelings, to find out what causes them, and to 'discharge' or express them in a supportive context. The context is first the group, then a counselling partner. We will avoid facing alone the accumulation of pain and anger we all carry around, fearing that if the barriers are let down, heaven knows what will surge up, or for how long. Re-evaluation counsellors believe that once a certain amount of this hidden emotion is expressed, and some of the causes and results are understood, a 'mental clearing' happens which enables us to begin to break unwanted patterns and to function in more self-fulfilling ways.

To co-counsel effectively, various skills must be acquired. Usually, a group of people meet with an R C teacher for a period of forty hours, spread out over perhaps two months. Between group meetings, people get together in pairs to practise what they've learned. Finally, you meet your partner once a week to carry on. Counselling is thought of not as a short-term therapy, but as an ongoing process through which we can become more conscious, more independent, more free from patterned behaviour.

There are many techniques, none of which are difficult to learn. I'll mention three that are especially relevant to women's self-realization process. First, new counsellors are asked to build up a new habit of thought, by remembering what's been good and new in the past few days. Many women, when asked this, really can't think of a single good incident. By noticing things that are good and pleasurable, we can break the depressed habit of being conscious only of what's wrong. Another important technique to learn is 'free attention'. We all do a lot of listening, but how valuable is it? In co-counselling, you learn to listen with all your attention, not planning responses before the speaker has finished, not groping around, while she's talking, for helpful advice to give. While we're doing all that, we're not listening. Not judging, commenting, sympathizing, or giving advice means that your partner has a 'free space' in which she can hear herself, and come to her own conclusions. Which are the only valuable conclusions anyway.

A third technique is 'self-validation'. This means liking yourself, and appreciating openly what you like best about yourself. One of the most pernicious ways in which women are kept from developing their individual potential is the subtle invalidation we receive daily. Just as harmful, is being appreciated for all the wrong reasons; for instance, being told how marvellously well we fulfil roles we haven't really chosen and don't especially like ourselves in. One woman was always told, 'What a good listener you are'. Fine, except she often wanted those ego-tripping people to stop and listen to her once in a while. Better, she wanted more about her to be appreciated than her ears and ability to sit patiently still for hours. Her self-validation and direction for the future is, 'You've got an hour to talk, because I like you. Then we do what I want.'

Change is a slow process, perhaps because we can't know what end-result we want when we begin. We have an idea, but it will be modified in time. So we vacillate, go back on our best intentions, then take a couple of important steps forward, only to sidetrack once again. It's useless to expect society or ourselves to pursue a straight line to a pre-determined goal: that's not an organic process. Change is better seen as the unfolding of real individual potential; and discovery, as the potential becomes apparent, of what we want it to accomplish in our lives. Re-evaluation counselling's most important premise is that *we* can achieve that realization and put it to our own best use . . .

SR.15, September 1973

Opening Myself to Change

FRANCES SETON

This article has been very difficult to write. I have had to try and explain how psychotherapy, which has helped me enormously, can be justified as an option for women within a feminist perspective. This has meant not only describing my experience as a patient in therapy, but dealing with the anti-psychiatry arguments of feminists, radical psychiatrists and the friends who have helped me write this.

I have been in therapy with a woman psychotherapist for about eighteen months. Psychotherapy is one of the many forms of help available, along with psychoanalysis, co-counselling, encounter, psychodrama, to name but a few. Many people are confused about the distinction between these forms of help. In psychotherapy you visit a therapist once to three times a week for a fifty-minute session when you sit and face your therapist, though some people choose to lie on a couch. Psychoanalysis differs in theory and in practice; you go five times a week for up to seven years and usually lie on the couch speaking to the analyst indirectly. Psychoanalysis is nearly always Freudian or Jungian while psychotherapy draws on many schools – Freudian, Jungian, Gestalt, Transactional and Behaviourist are the most common. Many therapists use a combination according to the needs of the patient. It is important to know about this and feel free to explore the kind of therapy and therapist you want.

I found my therapist through my University Health Service where the GP referred patients only after discussing the individual's case with the staff therapists and selecting the most suitable combination.

When I first started psychotherapy I encountered opposition and discouragement as well as support and understanding. The most immediate support came from friends who had been in therapy (I had initially got the idea from them) and from two close friends who had recently started themselves. It was really helpful to share this rather alarming process with others who were familiar with the jargon of patterns, syndromes and neuroses.

Other friends were frankly horrified or embarrassed by what seemed an admission on my part of a terrible disease, or deforming blemish.

We are all expected to cope, and not to admit failure, although I am sure many of us have sufficient pressures in our families, relationships and work to make it very difficult to function well. Unhappiness bordering on depression or intense anxiety is seen as shameful or as a kind of illness. It's repressed lest our admission of it threaten everyone else's precarious façades of coping. However, I must admit I did see my decision to go into therapy as an admission of weakness. I was ashamed that I could not work things out for myself or within the structure of a women's group.

By admitting my need for some sort of help I began to learn important things. In the first place I had always appeared to others as strong, productive and together – a competence which was rather daunting. Once I was able to admit my own vulnerability to myself, many relationships became more equal. No longer did I always put myself into the unconsciously superior role of supporting others, instead we were able to share both our strengths and our weaknesses. I believe that women are conditioned into two conflicting roles; one tends to dominate and dictate the nature of relationships. There is the Big Mother role or the emotionally dependent Child. I had been trying to be the first and forcing close friends into the second. With my image of myself as a strong type, I experienced shame in having to admit need and dependence. We are all distorted by the inherent contradictions of these exclusive roles and a lot of work needs to be done to understand the way women relate to each other.

In the second place I learned that to seek help was not an admission of abject failure, but the first step towards taking responsibility for myself, and freeing myself (and others) from the tyranny of my past. It was a matter of coming to a realistic assessment of my capacities and recognizing my healthy need of others.

It requires strength to go through therapy and abandon all such defence mechanisms and behaviour patterns which had got me through in the past. Opening myself to change required an often painful process of self-discovery. I had to come to terms with feelings from which I had hidden – like fear of abandonment and strong self-hate – as well as those I could not allow myself like happiness, the capacity to love others and myself, and the expression of my sexuality.

I was afraid of asking for help because it felt like reverting to childlike dependence. It was a realistic fear in view of the traditional image of therapy in which the woman goes as a patient to an omniscient professional who will make her better.

Feminists have exposed the power structure in the patient–doctor relationship of psychoanalytic (Freudian) theory which is the basis of all other theories. The feminist critique is twofold: psychoanalytic theory propounds the idea of femininity as biologically/psychologically determined. Women want to be mothers and wives, argue the theorists, thus maintaining the role of women as reproducers of the labour force, servicers of workers and children, by making women believe that this is all a healthy, normal female should desire.

Secondly feminists have attacked the patriarchal character of a therapeutic situation in which a desperate woman goes to a male counsellor and enters into a dependent relationship which repeats their social, emotional and often economic dependence on fathers, husbands, boyfriends and bosses. In *Women and Madness* Phyllis Chesler not only exposes the actual sexual content of many therapeutic relationships, but also the use of class power by middle-class white men and 'menwomen' who inflict treatment on working-class, Black and lesbian women. Thus the theory and practice of much psychological counselling seems to reflect the power relationships of patriarchal/class society.

Juliet Mitchell in *Psychoanalysis and Feminism* has tried to reassess the value of psychoanalytic *theory*. Instead of attacking Freud, as many other feminists have done, for being prescriptive, i.e. telling women how they ought to be, she argues that his theory of the unconscious and the Oedipus complex describe the precise mechanisms whereby individual males and females are socialized into their respective roles within a patriarchal society.

She also exposes the inadequacies of the radical psychiatrists' arguments that it is the institutions of society which cause problems and that it is enough to attack them. One must also fully analyse the workings, origins and inter-relationships between the internal structure of the mind and external social structures. In a theoretical form she shows how the personal is political and how the material structure of social relations is placed in the structure of personality.

To sum up – as I see it, in feminist and other radical critiques, psychology is seen to propound an idea of women that is false, oppressive and closely related to the maintenance of patriarchal society. But I don't think we necessarily have to be manipulated by psychology, we can use it for ourselves. The discovery of the unconscious and the recognition of how it can be manipulated paradoxically provides us with the means to escape from socially imposed structures and to work towards new ones. So we can reassess the value of psychological theory to some extent, and I would like to argue that feminist criticism of the practice can also be challenged.

In the light of the feminist condemnation of the whole process, how could I justify my choice to engage in personal therapy? In the first place the actual distress I felt was not at all relieved by the recognition that it had a social origin. When I decided to do therapy I was depressed, withdrawn and sexually frigid. And although I'd tried very hard talking, thinking and reading about it, I could do absolutely nothing about it. At one point I had even managed to make a list of eight possible explanations, but I was absolutely trapped and controlled by something that I did not understand and could not alter.

I read all I could about psychology, which only provided me with a series of labels to describe my state and, more seriously, literally to hide behind. (A criticism I have of psychology and indeed medicine is that it gives problems a concrete existence separate from their origins.) Even when I read Karen Horney's *Feminine Psychology*, which provided illuminating and basically feminist analyses of frigidity in the reproduction of the family structure in adult couple relationships, I did not find the *means* to solve those well-documented problems that I was so intimately experiencing. But I did find a spurious comfort in describing my situation in terms of psychologically validated 'problems'. It was only when I went to a therapist with my neatly labelled 'problems' that I discovered I could no longer hide behind them. The pain was real and the labels irrelevant. I had to react to my pain either with masochistic self-pity or with a determination to change. I had to decide to go through to a new future or submit to the tyranny of my past and present.

My University Health Service GP was surprised when I specifically asked to see a woman therapist. This was partly because I could not really talk to a man about sexual problems, and partly out of simplistic feminism. I had not really appreciated that within an essentially patriarchal institution, the presence of individual women do not necessarily, if at all, effect the nature of the institution. However a female therapist was in fact helpful because an important source of my distress was an unresolved grief, anger and resentment at my mother's death which I saw as her abandoning me. In therapy I was making a relationship with an older woman, who was an authority figure in the situation, and on whom I felt dependent and needy. Through this I was able to exorcize the ghost of my real mother. I don't think this is important only for people whose mothers have died. In the family, the mother wields enormous power by virtue of her role as socializer, sole nurturer, giver (and withholder) of love. Working with a woman therapist helped me to begin to break the power of the figure of The Mother that I had internalized.

How that came about is simple to explain but hard to understand without actually experiencing it. Basically the present replaces the past. My therapist avoids talking exclusively about my childhood because she feels that explaining the cause of particular feelings does not necessarily alter them (and as I found out for myself, it sometimes does the opposite). But by emotionally recognizing that the way I feel and act today are programmed reactions set up in childhood, I have the possibility of changing how I feel and act now – of making new programmes.

For instance I reacted to my mother's death by totally suppressing my genuine reactions – I was brave, I coped remarkably well, while I really felt abandoned and rejected. And since I could not bring myself to blame her for abandoning me, I came to feel that it was my fault; I was unworthy of love or had done something to drive her away. Three patterns emerged: I was terrified to love anyone for fear that they would leave me, I clung desperately to my friends and lover by looking after them and winning love by being kind, and I took responsibility for anything that went wrong in any relationship. I was, therefore, dependent in a covert way, manipulative and riddled with guilt.

I cannot isolate one dramatic moment that changed all this, but I came to trust my therapist. On a conscious level I was in a willed, self-chosen relationship with someone I came to trust. Unconsciously I was transferring to her some of my feelings about my mother.

When my therapist was ill and then almost killed in a car crash, I dealt with that virtual repeat of my past differently. I did not identify her potential demise as abandonment nor did I blame myself. Of course, she didn't in fact die, but had she died making some of the original feelings of guilt and abandonment emerge, they would have been exposed for my conscious recognition of their source and function. I realized that even someone on whom I felt very dependent did not have the power over me to damage me in the way my mother's disappearance had. Thus therapy has worked for me by virtue of the very fact that it restages the authoritarian structure of the family in which personality formation takes place.

The only way that I can explain that process is by saying that I have come to accept the existence of the unconscious. I knew about it intellectually but had never really experienced its effect. Moreover the idea of something over which I had no intellectual control was very threatening to me. All my education had taught me to be profoundly suspicious of such an irrational force as the unconscious. It took me a long time in therapy to stop myself from trying to 'solve the problem', to forego my educated inclination to give the 'right' answer. Analysis, explanation, understanding as rational activities do not touch the range of emotions that profoundly affect one's life and to some extent actually dictate one's intellectual outlook.

I see therapy as a means to bring the unconscious and conscious into closer communication by a twofold process. I describe the first as falling through layers to profounder levels of consciousness; the second as a floating up of the buried unconscious to the surface.

At the beginning of therapy I could not face the idea of making love to anyone – I had no sexual feelings at all. I responded so intellectually and 'rationally' to the situation that I could objectify that paralysis of feeling as 'frigidity'. While many women argued that my 'frigidity' was caused by X number of reasons in my living situation and past, their suggestions simply could not touch me. I was so out of touch with my feelings that the contradictions in my feelings could only manifest themselves to me by a specifically sexual block.

It is possible to unblock through a *structure* in which you have a time and place where you are committed to experience your feelings. But beyond that, the structured time and place serves as a focus for a *process* of recognizing, examining and living your feelings that should go on all the time. This basically means bringing the conscious and unconscious into closer communication. But the unconscious is beyond conscious control by definition and cannot be forced by either therapist or patient. Therapy only provides the opportunity to work things out for yourself. It does not work for everyone because patients can resist deliberately or unconsciously, often out of an unwillingness to change, or a desire for the therapist to confront their feelings for them.

Because the real area of change has to be in the relationship between the unconscious and the conscious, I do not believe that consciousness raising alone can or should provide the same opportunity for psychological change. I was doing consciousness raising for the first six months of my therapy. It was a very politicizing process, one which I believe is crucial to the woman's movement, enabling women to discover the common patterns of being female in this society by sharing personal experience. Up to a point it can duplicate the *structure* of the therapeutic session – a place to explore feelings. But because of the group's democratic structure, it cannot reproduce the authoritarian nature of the family and society which I have argued is an essential part of the workings of therapy. Indeed the consciousness-raising group valuably tries to counter it with a collective model. It applies none of the pressure necessary to shake up the unconscious, and does not provide one figure to whom you relate so strongly that, if you want to, you can change the deeply rooted unconscious patterns of relationships. It is essentially, and usefully, *consciousness* not *unconsciousness* raising.

A process of unconsciousness raising necessarily takes a long time. Therapy does not merely aim to analyse and relieve specific problems, but attempts to remove constrictions on the individual created by past experience, in order to make choice possible. My own therapy fell into two distinct phases. The first six months were goal-orientated and relieved my inability to function sexually. The second phase has been much longer and has made me think in terms of a *process* of permanent revolution that will continue beyond the end of structured therapy.

Having begun to trust the process, to understand the workings of the psyche and how to use the tools of therapy, I can continue to work at it on my own and apply it to a larger social sphere. It is not a matter of cure, there can be no complete cure within a sexist, capitalist society. To be happy is not to be cured but to be or want to be self-determined versus patterned, autonomous versus dependent, to be able to make decisions versus being blocked, to accept vulnerability and needs versus false strength. And to be able to see oneself as separate and ultimately alone yet able to relate within society.

But this is impossible for men and women within our society because we are divided and categorized into masculine (strong, decisive, rational and competitive), and feminine (emotional, indecisive and dependent). Through psychotherapy I have begun to free myself from the crippling effects of my past and have gained the means to explore the kind of social relations through which human potential can be realized in our society.

I am not arguing for personal solutions – I'm all right, Jill – because I have been in therapy. I have found that the therapeutic process has given me a greater appreciation of political issues and motivation . . .

SR.44, March 1976

How to Run a Health Course

BRENT WOMEN'S CENTRE

Organizing a women and health course turned out to be really easy and exciting for our group. We'd like to share our experiences in the hope that it will inspire and help others to set up their own courses.

The ten-week women and health course was organized by women from the Brent Women's Centre with the help of two feminist workers from Brent Community Health Council. We decided to try and get a health course together so that we could gain knowledge about our bodies, our health rights and the facilities available to us. Because all women have so much contact with the health service – for ourselves and for our children and relatives – we felt that discussing health would be a good way of bringing women together.

Women are always on the receiving end of male-dominated health care, for period problems, birth control, pregnancy, childbirth, menopause and depression. When women talk about how they feel about going to doctors, hospitals or clinics, they speak about feeling vulnerable and not knowing or understanding what is happening to them. If they do

Jo Nesbitt

question anything they may be labelled as neurotic or trouble makers. Too often we have no control over our bodies, and no power over what happens to us. Either we are sick and so feel dependent, or are well and made to feel as if we're ill. Surely as women we are the best people to define our health needs and determine the kind of health care we want.

Brent is an area in north-west London which suffers from over-crowding, poor housing, huge council estates with few facilities and high unemployment. It already has had severe cut-backs in its health services. Brent Community Health Council offered us their premises which are very central and easily reached by public transport. Not all CHCs are as open or involved in the local community as ours but it's certainly worth encouraging yours to help out. We hoped that by joining the CHC we'd attract both feminists and women who were interested in health but not familiar with feminism.

. . . When we started planning the course we felt a bit apprehensive. We thought we might need the help of someone with experience, so it was exciting to realize that we could handle it ourselves. This is, after all, what the course was about – the breaking down of the mystique of medical expertise, of our dependency and so-called ignorance. *We* could decide what we wanted to talk and find out about from our own experiences as women. *We* could find women who had expert know-ledge about a specific topic who were willing to share it with us.

As soon as we started talking about the course, ideas just poured out. In the end the subjects we chose for the course were:
WOMAN'S BODY AND HOW IT WORKS · CONTRACEPTION · ABORTION · SEXUALITY · MENTAL HEALTH · CHILDBIRTH · MENOPAUSE AND AGEING · HEALTH AND SAFETY AT WORK · NUTRITION AND SELF-HELP.

The order of the topics evolved, but with care. For instance we gave a lot of thought to where to put Sexuality. Many of us aren't used to talking about sexuality; we had to get to know each other first and gain confidence before that discussion. We deliberately followed Sexuality with Mental Health, which we felt to be linked with sexual oppression. In retrospect we felt that Mental Health should have come towards the end of the course, as it became clear that it was linked with everything we discussed. Our last topic, Nutrition and Self-help, we saw as a positive end – in fact a beginning of taking some control over our own health. Of course we could only cover each subject briefly, and we emphasized throughout that each evening was an introduction and hopefully a springboard for more detailed discussion in follow-up meetings and courses.

Each of us took responsibility for organizing the topics we were most interested in. We invited speakers on each subject, but were always careful to create a balance between women with expertise in certain areas and women familiar with those areas through their own experiences. For example, in the session on childbirth we invited a midwife and a local woman who had recently had a baby. For the session on ageing we invited a social worker from a local geriatric unit and a member of a local pensioners' organization. The speakers were all women who were eager to share their knowledge, and did not create the 'professional' barriers that we usually meet within the health service. The speakers introduced their topics and then encouraged and participated in the general discussion. A measure of the success of this was that the discussion always flowed freely with women eager to share their experiences and views.

To get speakers, we first contacted local women we knew who were particularly knowledgeable about any of the topics. A local women's centre, women's or community groups should be able to help with this information. Where we could not find local women to speak, we used contacts to give us suggestions.

We were very anxious to reach out to women who don't usually go to meetings and courses, and hoped that the 'right' publicity would help. We also wanted it to be a local course, and so kept outside publicity to a minimum. We were lucky to have a sympathetic journalist on the local paper; she did some articles for us, advertising the course. We also produced a leaflet which we distributed through all the local community organizations, tenants' associations, clinics, playgroups, doctors' surgeries, health visitors and social services departments. Two local librarians organized a display for us in the libraries and produced a booklist for the course. We also used the women's centre mailing list, and spread information by word of mouth. None of us had ever experienced such widespread and enthusiastic feedback to any projects we had been involved in before.

Even though we did not have to pay for the premises, we reluctantly made a small charge of 25p a session or £1.50 for the whole course to cover speakers' expenses, printing costs and tea, coffee and biscuits. There was no charge for claimants. We didn't expect the amazing turnout (averaging fifty a session) and so unintentionally ended up with a profit! This was given to the women's centre for future activities.

A measure of our success was that we drew in women not usually involved in local campaigns or groups. But most were younger women in their twenties or thirties. We now see that this may have been because a large part of the course dealt with women in their 'childbearing' years. This was one of the limitations of the course; we were reflecting society's attitude that women cease to be important when they are no longer fertile. The other major frustration was the lack of time at each session. We weren't able to cover any of the topics as fully as both we and the speakers would have liked.

Although women could come to individual sessions, most came often or even for the whole course. The final sessions had no topic, but in spite of that we had a large attendance to discuss future activities. We kept a list of names and addresses, which has been added to the mailing lists of the women's centre and the CHC. Many women from the course were actively involved in the local campaign against the Corrie Abortion Amendment Bill, and in the campaign against Depo Provera (a long term contraceptive injection with dubious side-effects).

Also, as a direct result of the course, a new consciousness-raising group is meeting regularly, a successful pensioners' health course has been organized by the CHC, and one woman is organizing a pregnant women's support group. The course also gave women from a community centre in a neighbouring borough the confidence to set up a course of their own. Other ideas that came out of the course were for a workshop on childbirth, and a project for teenagers on sexual feelings and birth control.

We were very excited by the course, particularly the feeling of support and caring throughout. The learning was a two-way process between those who 'organized' and spoke and those who came along each session. Discussing the course as a whole, a woman who had not previously been involved in an event for women only said, 'The most important thing about the course was the warmth and supportiveness of the group. When you are involved in organizations with men they always seem to be competing with each other.' Having it for women only helped provide a relaxed atmosphere in which to express our thoughts and anxieties, to talk openly and not feel threatened. Some women had previous experience of the women's movement and were familiar with criticisms of doctors and the NHS. Others had not questioned why they always felt inadequate in their dealings with the NHS or why they had an expectation of 'suffering'. Women said that through the course they had discovered that their individual experience of the health service had many common features. Our discussions helped us all develop the awareness to question, and the courage to criticize the treatment we received – it raised our consciousness.

Health courses have an amazing potential for bringing women together, and increasing our knowledge and confidence to strive for the kind of health care that *we* need. They help us understand the society we live in and give us a glimpse of a different society where we will have control of our health, our lives.

SR.94, May 1980

'To Lose a Breast Seemed More Terrible than Dying'

LIN LAYRAM

When I finally made up my mind to leave my husband after a ten-year relationship I was twenty-eight and childless. Within a few months I was beginning to adjust optimistically to a new kind of life. I began a stable and interesting relationship with the man I now live with and for the first time experienced that a sexual relationship was a possible source of happiness. The hang-ups I had built up over years began to get resolved. For the first time I began to feel a pleasure and excitement from my own body that was not tied up with guilt. At this point in my life I discovered that I had cancer of the breast, and the breast had to be amputated (a simple mastectomy). The feelings I experienced are obviously a result of my personal situation, but may strike a chord for other women in the same situation, so I am recording what happened to me in as much detail as possible. I hope that it may help other women to be relieved of some of the unnecessary hurt and humiliation which I felt at the time.

It was my boyfriend who first noticed the lump in my left breast. He persuaded me to visit a doctor which I did, albeit reluctantly. I did not however really believe at this stage that much serious could be wrong since I assumed (an assumption apparently shared by some of the medical profession) that breast cancer is a disease of middle age.* The local, male GP was reassuring. He examined my breasts, said that it was a swollen gland common among women taking the Pill (which I had been on for seven years) and told me not to worry. He did not refer me to a hospital for tests but did mention in passing that I should call in again if the lump didn't disappear. Over the next weeks I was relieved to find that the lump did seem to reduce in size. Looking back, I wonder how much of this was wishful thinking and imagination – difficult to tell with a lump that size – contained within a breast duct above the nipple and probably no bigger than a pea. Shortly after this visit to the GP I moved house and didn't have any official doctor for around four months. It didn't seem necessary as although I was often tired and suffered badly from headaches I had no definite symptoms of distress or illness.

After this period my boyfriend and I moved back to North London. I made a routine visit to the FPA clinic to collect my contraceptive pills. At my visit I mentioned to the doctor that I had a small lump in the breast. She did not seem keen to examine me but finally agreed to look at it as it was time for an annual check-up anyway. After examining both breasts she said that she had found nothing. Feeling over-anxious and fussy I began to question her further. She replied by reassuring me that if I had a 'cyst' she wouldn't be giving me the pill. As she said this she signed me up for a six-month supply.

I should say that I am now 'contra-indicated' as regards the Pill. The hormones have a very bad effect on accelerating cancer of the breast.

As I stood in the queue to collect supplies I decided to take out my treatment card and see what the doctor had written. To my bewilderment I read the words 'Nodule in left breast'. I still find this incident inexplicable. The clinic doctor should have informed me, told me to contact my doctor at once and have ceased to supply the Pill. She did none of these things. I couldn't face going back in to confront her so I

---

* Most breast cancers appear after forty, but something like 18 per cent of cases are in women under forty-five.

collected the pills and went home feeling very shocked and puzzled. I picked up a leaflet as I went out which proclaimed 'Don't gamble with breast cancer!' The leaflet informed me that early treatment was essential and that anyone finding a lump should see a doctor immediately. The doctor had perhaps not read this leaflet! In my experience it was the doctors who 'gambled', not me.

When I look back on these incidents I feel furious with myself for my spinelessness. Yet if the doctors would not take the lump in my breast seriously it was a great temptation for me to take their reassurances at face value. What woman does not dread that a lump will turn out to be cancer and that she will lose her breast and with it her sexual identity. These deeply repressed fears prevented me from fighting the apathy I encountered as I should if I were fighting for a sister in the same situation. I think this may be an important point in helping other women get treatment fast – to recognize the reluctance to fight an issue like this.

Diagnosis of breast cancer in my experience cannot be made by your average or even better than average clinic doctor or GP. It can only be confirmed by a biopsy report and women should insist on this as soon as possible – or other women should insist on their sisters' behalf.

It would seem to me that because of my age the doctors I saw discounted as statistically improbable the diagnosis of cancer and therefore did not even bother to investigate further, even though a woman's life was at stake.

A month or two after the clinic incident my breast began to actually hurt and throb (probably as an effect of the hormones in the Pill which I was still innocently swallowing down every day?). I had to hold my breast tightly in order to relieve the pain and in this state I felt compelled to again visit a doctor. My new GP actually took me seriously as I apologetically repeated my litany and after an examination she referred me to a consultant at the local hospital.

As it was Christmas an appointment couldn't be made until 1 January. At a party during that period I got drunk and broke down sobbing and hysterical with anxiety. Only at that point did I realize how my underlying fears were being repressed and how depressed all the foregoing experiences were making me.

On 1 January the specialist examined me in Out Patients. I was also examined (without my permission being asked) by a male medical student.* I was told I had a small cyst and that it would be wise to remove it. This could be done in three days in hospital. I was studying at the time so arranged my admission for a fortnight hence. I left feeling relieved. Everyone in my house was happy for me that things

---

* Doctors are required to ask permission and you have the right – if you dare – to refuse.

would soon be sorted out. My boyfriend was loving and supportive but I became depressed over the next week. I was feeling tired and ill and finally went down with gastric flu. I still went into hospital on the admission date of 19 January as my GP was afraid I would lose my place in the queue if I didn't. I stayed in the hospital for three days but was not operated on after all because the anaesthetist said I was too weak from the flu to work on. They sent me home and readmitted me again the following week. I was diagnosed as having fibrokinosis (thickening of the fibrous tissue). During the few days that followed I was upset that the lump which was extremely tender and painful was continually handled by long queues of male medical students and housemen. Never was my permission sought and I experienced for the first time what it is like to lie and be an object while jokes are made over your head, and remarks exchanged between consultant and respectful housemen, which do not include the patient as a feeling human being. (Incidentally, *Our Bodies, Ourselves* argues that potentially cancerous growths should be handled as little as possible.)

The operation was fairly untraumatic although I was at the end of the queue and the pre-med had worn off by the time I got into the theatre. The lump was excised and a biopsy done. The stitches were neatly sewn around the nipple so as to reduce the scar. During this period I met women in the ward who were cancer and mastectomy patients. I was struck by their courage, their ability to make jokes. I was also shocked by the sight of one woman waiting for her wound to be dressed after a radical mastectomy and looking to me like a hot cross bun. To me to lose a breast seemed a thing more terrible than dying. Amputation of any kind had always filled me with pity and disgust. The last day I was in the ward the Australian houseman, shouted across the ward loudly as I chatted quietly by someone's bed. His words caused a pit in my stomach. He said 'It looked pretty bad for you, but path. lab. (pathology department) says it's O K – you can go home today.' At that moment I had a glimpse into the future and was flooded by unspoken fears. However I pushed down what he had said back into the deepest layers of my unconscious and 'forgot' it.

I was discharged that day and returned three days later to have the stitches taken out (as an out-patient). The nurse was gentle and didn't hurt me at all. She and I were both pleased at the neatness of the stitches which ensured that no scar would spoil my beauty! I went home and took up life as usual. I remember that I even scrubbed the kitchen floor that day. I didn't feel too great. My arm was aching but I was so relieved to be home and to be in a warm bed with my boyfriend again after the chilly isolation of hospital.

The next day we invited some friends round for a meal to celebrate my triumphant return. I cooked chicken and pineapple I remember and I was just about to take it in to serve it when a knock came on the door. To my indescribable shock I found my husband standing there. (I hadn't seen him for almost a year.) He told me that the hospital had rung him, and asked him to take me there the following morning. The biopsy report had been 'wrong'. (Needless to say when I went into the hospital I had filled in all my details in triplicate, was accompanied by my boyfriend, etc. The administration had got hold of my old admission card and rung a number eighteen months out of date.) I burst into tears, I got rid of him, shut the door, went back upstairs and somehow in a daze we served and ate the meal I'd prepared. The night was endless. I lay in my boyfriend's arms and cried. We tried to comfort each other but it was difficult. In the morning we got up and went together to the hospital.

When we arrived the sister of the ward was expecting us and we were hurried into a private ward off the main ward where she explained that there was a 'mistake' and they now 'wanted to take a bit more tissue away'. Several kind and sympathetic nurses came in and out during the next thirty minutes or so as we waited for the consultant to make his round, bringing paper handkerchiefs to mop up my tears, coffee and tranquillizers. I was totally unable to talk or communicate with anybody. I felt only that I was in a nightmare, perhaps under an anaesthetic still in the first operation and soon someone would wake me up and it would all be unreal. (I still have this feeling occasionally and I have to touch myself to check that my breast really isn't there any more.) As we waited I stared out over a filthy courtyard with a fire escape thinking how it symbolized everything about our society. I felt trapped. I wanted to run from the hospital. I drew on the dirty pane of the window with my finger 'This is the way the world ends – not with a bang but a whimper.' The great man finally arrived. It seemed hours that we had waited in silence though it was probably only a short time. What followed were the most terrible, endless minutes of my life.

I'll just report it as it felt. My boyfriend was sent out of the room (Why?) and I was left with the sister although my memory is that I was alone. Perhaps this is because I felt alone. The consultant had with him around eight white-coated male acolytes. The room seemed to be filled with them. I sat sobbing uncontrollably as he told me he would like to amputate the breast and give me a 'normal life'. I could have an 'appliance'. He told me that there was no other form of treatment. All that I was aware of during this speech was my complete humiliation as a woman under those seemingly dispassionate many pairs of masculine eyes seeing me as 'woman, twenty-eight, carcinogenic', disassociating me from their reactions to women as people, or even women as desirable, warm and human. After the speech was over I stuttered out between sobs that I would not have the operation as I could not bear to be mutilated in that way. He did not argue much but told me that he hoped I would change my mind. Outside the door the Australian houseman (who presumably was responsible for what had happened since he gave me the wrong biopsy report) said to the ward sister 'Why do you British women make such a fuss about a non-functional organ? Women don't behave like that in Australia.'

Needless to say I was persuaded by the nurses, the sister and the other women in the ward to think again and I went into the operating theatre again as the first patient the following morning. I was offered a private ward but chose to go back into the public ward as I valued the support and companionship of other women. The nursing staff helped me a great deal by their sympathy, and by letting me 'talk it out' over several days. The male doctors were brisk and impersonal. There was no psychological follow up on a formal level whatever, either after the operation or on discharge. I find the period around the actual operation difficult to remember. I was very heavily drugged for days afterwards until I asked them to reduce the dose as I felt tired and muddled all the time. I was only in hospital for ten days during which time the stitches were removed, and a bottle taken away which had drained off excess fluid. I didn't suffer any loss of arm functions, just a little stiffness. I felt quite weak for a few weeks (not surprising having had two an-aesthetics in such a short period). The psychological effects are much more difficult to cope with and still persist to a greater or lesser extent.

It is very hard to be a woman with a scar instead of a breast in a society where everywhere you look there are pictures of idealized, beautiful and well-developed bodies. It is very hard not to feel put down and ugly and undesirable. I am very lucky in that I have a loving relationship but even so I found it difficult to adjust and to feel relaxed again without clothes on even when alone. I still feel uneasily that somehow it is a punishment for my sexuality and pride in my body in that period before the operation – that short guilt-free interlude. The prosthesis (false breast) provided on the NHS is relatively good – air-and fluid-filled plastic (some hospitals still don't provide these – Northampton Hospital for example gives out such antiquated old-type prostheses that women buy their own, if they can afford it). I received no follow-up advice on the NHS other than a physical check-up every three months and examination for secondary growths. I found out where to buy special swimwear (made by a mastectomy patient) by reading the *Sunday Times*. Since I had the operation I have given birth to a daughter after a normal pregnancy. In spite of the fact that I couldn't breast feed, and they knew why, health visitors, relaxation instructors were all pleased to point out the disadvantages of bottle feeding – including the prevalence of cot deaths. Etc.

I would therefore end this article by commenting that the lack of concern for and sensitivity towards women in this situation is a result of the hierarchical and male-dominated structure of medicine. Not only the physical mutilation but the fear of death is something that has to be learnt to be lived with and perhaps groups could be set up for women to support each other in this respect by talking these fears out. The psychological aspect needs a great deal of research particularly in regard to the seeming prevalence of the development of breast cancer after periods of great mental stress. It may be coincidence that three women I know contracted breast cancer after the break up of a marriage, and emotional crisis may play some as yet unknown part in acting as a trigger mechanism in the breakdown of immunological defences. This was suggested to me by a sympathetic male registrar at the Whittington.

Much is said about the importance of educating women to seek advice early. I would say from my experience that the medical profession also needs education in this respect and should be discouraged from making dangerous assumptions on the grounds of generalized probabilities. Improving the standard of aftercare is a priority. Mastectomy patients unite – we have nothing to lose but our fears!

SR.37, July 1975

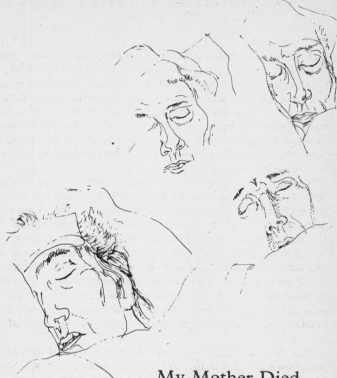

My Mother Died
Two Years Ago

NORMA PITFIELD

These drawings, made as I watched
and waited with her,
are almost too agonizing to show.

She was a strong fine woman
Whom I loved very passionately.
I want to show the drawings now
because they say something
about death.

That's a subject
we don't care much to look at.

SR.73, August 1978

Joan Scott: Living Her Dying

ANN SCOTT

Joan Scott, who reviewed a television play about breast cancer for *Spare Rib*, died last June. The play had been controversial within the BBC on the question of patients being withheld information, and Joan was one of several women asked to read the script before transmission. 'I would not only argue,' she wrote in the magazine, 'that one has a right to such vital information about one's own body, but also that one develops strength to face it. To deny a fellow human being the opportunity of finding and working on inner resources is to belittle and underestimate her/him.'

With her characteristic sense of purpose she wrote that review during one of many hospitalizations for bone cancer. She sat up with her glasses and her biro, writing and rewriting, asking me to read each draft, angry when the nurses got her painkillers wrong. DF118, Distalgesic, she always knew the names and had preferences.

'It is not enough that when we are having surgery we are suffering and scared. We must also rally our wits and defend ourselves against the consequences of other people's incompetence, uncaring attitudes, or reluctance to face our needs. When we can get out we can start/ resume agitating for a better health service; but while "in", if we want to take responsibility for "our bodies, ourselves", we can't afford to be passive.'

That familiar slogan, originally the title of a North American book about women's health, had a particular meaning for Joan. She was in her late fifties when she got involved in women's liberation, a couple of years after her marriage ended. She was sixty-two when she died; and that meant childhood after the First World War, adolescence before the Pill or any ideology of sexual emancipation.

In an essay written for a Workers' Educational Association summer school four years ago, Joan described 'Three Generations of Women': her mother's, her own and her two daughters'. 'There had been a son before me, but he had died. Three more daughters were born in an effort to replace him, and a family legend, no doubt founded on fact, is that the doctor (also a friend) reproached my father when delivering the youngest: my mother was over forty by then. Of course he had never been able to give them any contraceptive advice: in those days, at any rate in Guernsey, it was abstinence or nothing.'

Joan's subsequent experience of a marriage in which domesticity was the only socially acknowledged role for women like her – educated women, genteel women who might go to the theatre – made women's liberation an imperative. Silenced by the demands of her class and sex, she had lived as a competent housewife. 'I put up with the usual domestic oppression, blaming myself for resenting it. When my first child was born I gave up paid work and became a captive wife and mother. I knew it was foolish, and resolved that next time I would go out to work and pay someone to look after the baby. But when the younger one was born I had so internalized the maternal duty that I could not bring myself to hand her over to a stranger, and stayed where I was.' She did volunteer work for the Family Planning Association, entertained neighbours and her husband's friends. Never showing anger. Rarely laughing. Rarely time to read.

She had been active in the pacifist, almost conventionally feminine setting of the Women's International League for Peace and Freedom. It was when she began living on her own that she felt a need to act fast. 'I must look for an outfit working to change the society,' she wrote me in 1971. She would look for women's liberation and socialist groups 'as near home as possible, and latch on to them', urging me, too, to 'develop some empathy towards a woman who is only now, in middle age, struggling to be liberated'.

She stopped wearing her wedding ring, she bought her clothes in boutiques, went to women's conferences. 'The Anti-Discrimination Bill comes up in the House of Commons tomorrow evening and once more we rally to the lobby,' she wrote early in 1973, ending with the casual postscript: 'Now I'm going to do about a fortnight's dishes.' But she was conscious of her age and full of doubt about her worth; she was glad when the women's group met at her flat, for touches like this made her feel accepted. Feminism came to have a real relationship to everyday experience: she had some people to dinner; the men talked, the women fell silent. I was much more critical of the men than Joan was, and she wrote to me the following week: 'I have thought a good deal, intermittently, about the dinner party . . . Your observations on it have made me aware that I can and should do something, even in what appears to be a minor and purely superficial setting, to bolster my sisters' egos and raise the consciousness both of them and of their men.'

Not everything could change, and I think there was always a tension between the demands of her generation and those of the movement. She had learned to be polite, and caring, and discreet; to gauge her meaning as a person by her success as a woman. Irony was possible; convalescing after her mastectomy she wrote: 'Today we have had fun watching the Queen's [wedding] anniversary celebrations and toasting her in vodka and orange juice, wondering how many other middle-aged women whose marriages had gone awry were doing exactly the same thing! . . . From which you will see that I am coming back to life.' And shortly before her bone cancer developed, she laughed when she described her fantasy of opening an FPA sex education seminar with 'Well. One of my daughters is a lesbian and the other's an unsupported mother.' She was discovering defiance.

But there was always a poignancy to her freedom. However much she knew that her needs had been shaped by the culture ('I was thankful to be married – to "fail" to "get" a husband would have been intolerable'), she had been a wife and mother far too long to discard that culture without unease. If she rejected femininity, wasn't she also rejecting years of her own experience, of her sense of herself? In Joni Mitchell she found a singer who spoke to her condition, but inspired her to go on letting go:

> Papa's faith is people
> Mama she believes in cleaning
> Papa's faith is in people
> Mama she's always cleaning
>
> Mama thinks she spoilt me
> Papa knows somehow he set me free
> Mama thinks she spoilt me rotten
> She blames herself
> But Papa he blesses me
> It's a rough road to travel
> Mama let go now
> It's always called for me

The sadness of Joan's cancer was that it interrupted the delicacy of that transition. Letting go became more and more difficult as illness undermined her independence. To find her own autonomy, then, to be her own person, she took responsibility for her body. She fought for control in the only territory that was open to her: her relationship to her illness, her hospital's relationship to her.

It was a very definite fight. 'I had to make clear that I was determined to know everything,' she wrote in reply to Gill Loveday's 'Facing up to death', a letter in *Spare Rib*, 'and that I wanted my daughters to know too. They were interviewed separately [by her doctor and social worker] and since then there are no secrets.' Access to information gave her a way of affirming herself within rather than against her cancer; it was her only defence against the bitterness and humiliation of dependence. She experienced the loss of self-esteem that goes with eating from a feeding bowl with a spout because she had to lie flat on her back for a week. She wished she could walk to X-ray: it felt 'psychologically damaging' to go on a stretcher day after day. She was often too depressed to talk, let alone to cry.

Six weeks later she had learned to walk, first with a frame, then with a stick. She felt there was a bit of a future, the possibility of pleasure. 'It's bone cancer now,' she wrote to her sister-in-law in Vienna, 'and yet, strangely, if one must have cancer, there's something to be said for this brand. Soft tissues rotting mean surgery, whereas I'm treated with radiation and hormones, and the race is on between the disease and the steroids that are being packed into my bones to strengthen them . . . I'm resigned to having no long term – perhaps a couple of years – but I'm just speculating. The excellent people here can't commit themselves. As Dr Johnson said, it [the prospect of death] concentrates the mind wonderfully.'

Leaving the hospital was quite hard. 'I felt so odd driving away,' she told me the day after her discharge. She had been in for two months. 'I knew the nurses would set to, scrubbing my room – they'd soon forget me – and somehow I had to live in the real world.' That determination gave way to despair, anger and loneliness. Joan had deposits at the base of her spine and couldn't bend. She couldn't stand or walk for more than a few minutes. Cooking and cleaning were impossible. She hadn't the strength to go in to work more than two or three mornings a week. 'How I wish I could help you,' her letter to Gill Loveday continues, 'but how right you are when you say what a debilitating disease cancer is and how one's own need is *for* support from others, there's no surplus energy to give. I live on a razor's edge, trying not to conceal this from family and friends, and yet at the same time trying not to be a drag on them and make them feel that I'm a hardly bearable burden.'

The sense of that razor's edge is explicit in two descriptions of the same week. To her sister-in-law she writes: 'I have had to devise occupational therapy for myself – I now *knit*, I who was utterly handless, because I was almost literally twitching as I sat listening to the radio or "relaxing" in some other passive way . . . So you can picture me sitting like a Madame Defarge, feverishly clicking away with big needles.' My own account is rather different. 'My mother knits long scarves as therapy. Fingers shaking, sits watching TV programmes she's not interested in. Is irritated by her listlessness, is pernickety and fastidious, has no pain, wonders whether she'd be better dead. And we have cathartic talks where we cry and hold hands.'

The loss of energy – 'I haven't the physical or psychic energy to initiate anything' – contained an ambiguity for Joan. It was a release from trivia – at times of relative calm she would remind herself of Dr

Johnson – and an opportunity to discover what really mattered: to talk to friends, to read when her concentration allowed it, to be active where it was physically possible. Three weeks before her death she was planning to go to the London Region women's liberation conference; had she gone it would have been her first excursion in three months.

But that loss also meant abdicating her ability to control her environment. Her women's group organized a rota, 'so that there is always someone at the end of the telephone ready to come, do anything, spend the night, simply provide moral support – or drive me somewhere if I need to go.' And yet it was very hard for her to acknowledge the extent of her needs: 'To have to be on the receiving end all the time isn't always easy after learning to be independent.' At times when I would have liked to sit and talk she would force herself to put the dishes away. It was a way of establishing herself as competent. But living on her own had to change, and a friend of mine suggested that Joan have her own flat in the house we were going to buy. We asked her what she thought of this and she burst into tears. But that same day she talked about a holiday in Italy a few years before; she could link her past with a possible future.

It was when the illness was weakening her and she became susceptible to infections like pleurisy that Joan began to talk more about dying. She was in hospital last March; I remember her floral nightie and an angora shawl. She was writing in her notebook when I went in. She lay musing for a while. She had been thinking about a memorial meeting for herself.

She mentioned the song 'Bread and Roses' and a poem of my sister's. She wanted statements to be made about her work in the Family Planning Association and the women's movement. She moved her hands a little, stared ahead of her. 'And there are some lines from Keats's "Ode to a Nightingale",' she began, 'though lots of it isn't relevant, of course . . . "To cease upon the midnight with no pain" . . .' And then, faltering: ' "I have been half in love with easeful death" . . .'

We cried for a while. Then we laughed when I teased her for deciding what people would say about her in advance. She wanted to give her body to a medical school and enquired placidly about the students' work: did they need both breasts? I mentioned the dissection room in Cambridge where I had begun to study medicine. No, you often saw bodies where surgery had been done. She nodded. Thinking all the time.

Darkling I listen; and for many a time
I have been half in love with easeful Death,
Called him soft names in many a musèd rhyme,
To take into the air my quiet breath;
Now more than ever seems it rich to die,
To cease upon the midnight with no pain,
While thou art pouring forth thy soul abroad
In such an ecstasy!

That deep sadness, that recognition of loss could find expression only in metaphor. By remembering the poem Joan was able to externalize her fear, to find acceptance of her death in a kind of magic outside herself. But those meetings of ours had to be ephemeral, almost invisible. The acknowledgement of imminent severance created the very intimacy that would have to be loosened if her death wasn't to become a struggle against itself.

A month later Joan was barely able to move. She was losing her resilience, feeling sick from the painkillers. 'I don't know how much longer I can go on being ill like this . . . I don't know how much the human frame can take.' I helped her to get undressed. There were her bruised arms, her scar, the pain on moving, the nervousness when she cleaned her face, the anxiety when she looked in the mirror. She started to cry. 'It's so hard for you,' I said. 'For you, too,' she replied. 'Why for me?' She sobbed louder – at first her words were indistinct, and then: 'It's so hard for you to see me like this.' She looked at me, as though she were terribly ashamed of herself. And then I understood how hard it was for a mother to be a child, to let her daughter look after her, and how hard Joan had battled to let me go.

She still planned to go to Vienna for a fortnight. Her doctor told her that if she felt as weak when she came back, she should come straight into hospital. She spent that time in Vienna in bed and went into hospital the day after her return, too tired to talk. But a couple of days later she was cheerful again: she'd been told she'd had a mild viral hepatitis. A tangible illness, it seemed to explain everything – the loss of appetite, the depression, the loss of weight.

In fact Joan was dying. The cancer had spread to her liver, and as her next of kin I had been told. It was a real betrayal. Had they forgotten that she was 'determined to know everything'? By deceiving Joan they were denying her right to live her own dying.

A hospital will tend to deny the reality of death and dying so long as medicine's social role is defined as one of curing disease. 'The current culture of the hospital, which emphasizes the disease process and the diseased organ, is counterproductive to the needs of the dying

patient.'* In the work of dying† there is no need for the very resources – technical knowledge, diagnostic and therapeutic procedures
– which legitimate medicine's control of physical experience. The
dying patient, then, represents a particular kind of threat.

The medical management of death itself creates estrangement. 'The
patient's alienation from his own body is increased at just the time
when it needs to be broken down: since medicine defines dying as a
doctor's failure, not a patient's task, the dying person is prevented
from accepting death and allying himself with it,' David Ingleby
wrote.‡ 'As in childbirth, mind and body are disconnected by drugs,
machines and social pressure . . . and as in childbirth, nothing could
guarantee a worse outcome: only those who can let themselves go *with*
the natural process of dying are able to find in death a completion of
life.'

But a denial of death also undermines the kind of therapeutic communication that can go on between people when both know that one of
them is dying. When the patient is ready to accept the reality of dying,
those around her must show they are ready to share her acceptance.
But the dying person's acceptance exists alongside envy and resentment
towards those who will go on living, however much support they have
given; there is also guilt at 'leaving people behind'. Nor does acceptance
cut out fear. What matters is that communication be allowed to go on;
that the dying person experience that ambiguity, that it be acknowledged as real; that the feelings related to death be accepted.

Joan herself understood this. 'One is overwhelmed with sorrow for
Simone's mother,' she had written me five years before, after reading
de Beauvoir's *A Very Easy Death*, 'and at the same time one enters
utterly into Simone's conflict of feeling, so lucidly expressed, between
suffering and the detachment that the living must feel for the dying.
And an added pang for me, as perhaps you can imagine – twenty years
on, will it be you and Miriam and me?'

There was a great deal of conflict over the handling of Joan's last

* Hans O. Mauksch, 'The Organisational Context of Dying' in (ed.) Elizabeth Kübler-
Ross, *Death, The Final Stage of Growth*, Prentice Hall, 1975.
† See Sigmund Freud: 'Towards the actual person who has died we adopt a special
attitude: something like admiration for someone who has accomplished a very difficult
task,' in 'Thoughts for the Times on War and Death', 1915.
‡ 'The Politics of Depth Psychology, Part II – Nature, Culture and Capitalism', Unit for
Research on Medical Applications of Psychology, University of Cambridge, 1976. You can
check out the analogy with childbirth in Ann Oakley, 'Wisewoman and Medicine Man:
Changes in the Management of Childbirth', in (eds.) Juliet Mitchell and Ann Oakley, *The
Rights and Wrongs of Women*, Penguin, 1976.

illness. The hospital staff kept saying different things. Her doctor: 'It's the disease, you see. Patients do change. I see a lot of patients who say they want to be told everything; and they *don't*.' Her social worker: 'I've never lied to my patients and I'm not going to start now.' Her ward sister: 'She's so calm now. It would be a tragedy to make her distressed.' And in the middle of it all was Joan herself, irritated that the nurses kept measuring her fluid intake, but confused by her own behaviour: sometimes relaxing with *The Times*, sometimes dissolving in tears. She rang me one morning: 'Oh . . . I feel so limp; I can hardly rise from my chair – the nurses keep telling me I'm doing very well . . . but I wonder whether they say that to everybody . . .'

I was very angry. I asked to see the medical team together – consultant, senior house officer, house physician, social worker – to discuss Joan's rights in the situation. How much did they think she knew? What did they think she thought they knew? What would her needs be? How could we co-operate better in meeting them? What was the physiology of dying? We went through the ways in which I felt she was being deceived. Her consultant asked me whether I'd thought of the possibility that she herself knew she was dying, but wasn't yet ready to communicate it. 'She isn't asking us any questions about her illness, you see,' he said, 'and she always has – always.' No, she wasn't on the sort of euphoriant dose that would confuse her. I began to see that I had to show her I could let her die.* 'If she asks you a question that you don't feel you can answer, come and ask us to help you.' Apparently it was the first time a relative had challenged the department like this.†

A couple of days later, then, I took her a volume of Keats's poems. Joan looked at it, sighed, and began to cry. I asked her what she was thinking about. 'The process of dying . . . is this it?' she whispered. 'Is it here one minute and gone the next?' I asked her what kinds of anxieties she had about dying; she hesitated – stayed silent.

'You might think I'd be too frightened to talk about it,' I said. 'But I'm not.' It seemed to reassure her; then I said, 'Do you have other anxieties?'

'Yes.' But she couldn't say them.

* Elizabeth Kübler-Ross illustrates the complexity of this exchange in *On Death and Dying*, New York, 1969. The seminar on the psychology of dying that she initiated in Chicago ten years ago has involved doctors, nurses, medical students, social workers, physiotherapists and chaplains. It is an attempt to 'refocus on the patient as a human being, to include him in our dialogues, to learn from him the strengths and weaknesses of our hospital management of the patient. We have asked him to be our teacher.'
† A couple of weeks after her death Joan's consultant wrote to me: 'Did our meetings before she died help? I do hope so. I think we all came to understand things a little better.'

'That you'd be on your own?' She nodded, closing her eyes.

'But you won't . . . because I'll stay with you.'

She looked at me, smiled, held my hand; there was the relief of openness but an agitation too. She said she was scared that she wouldn't be able to breathe. I suggested she talk to her doctor the following morning.

When I saw her the next afternoon, she was much weaker but seemed less anxious, almost unselfconscious. She told me she'd had 'a good long talk' with her doctor, but then she started to drift. 'People keep asking me what my feelings are . . . I wish I wasn't the focus of people's attention . . . I just want to be left alone.'* Joan was separating herself now, and she died the following day.

'An added pang for me,' she had written five years before. 'I want to concentrate on the main impression [de Beauvoir] has made on me – that when one is in one's terminal illness it is too late to talk about one's feelings, past and actual – one is simply too tired to bother . . . one is sunk fathoms deep in self-absorption – it takes a long time "to come to the surface of one's eyes" – as Simone describes her mother doing, and *see* the people around, who once were all-important to one.'

The night before she died the woman who had suggested she live with us came to see her. 'Cathy's here. Will you see her?' Joan smiled with great joy. Cathy came behind the curtains. There was a scent of summer flowers, a feeling of peace. Joan lay her arm on the table; it was a languid gesture – her death was very close, for her body was getting colder. She tilted her head to one side – said Cathy's name – looked up – and towards Cathy again; and that moment, which was one of the sweetest, was soon gone, for Joan was weary. Too weary, as well, to say more, to respond or withdraw. Limbs thin with cancer have a quietness which can be calming.

We held her memorial meeting on Midsummer's Day. Of the letters that I got afterwards, one caught its meaning exactly. 'I was especially glad that you talked about Joan's feelings about having such an illness and preparing for death. Like most other people I find it all very frightening, and it is a great help forward to hear people who have been very close to the experience being able to talk about it . . . as you did. I suppose that is what I meant by consciousness raising, because it is in

---

* 'When our patients reached the stage of acceptance and final decathexis [detachment], interference from outside was regarded as the greatest turmoil and prevented several patients from dying in peace and dignity. It is the signal of imminent death and has allowed us to predict the oncoming death in several patients where there was little or no indication for it from a medical point of view' – Kübler-Ross, *On Death and Dying.*

an ever-present way a component of so much of my thinking – that hope and desire that when it comes one may be able to die among friends and struggle through to an acceptance of what is happening. So though perhaps it is paradoxical, I had a lovely time.'

A month after she died I was looking through Joan's copy of *Away with All Pests*, Joshua Horn's account of his work as a surgeon in People's China. The custom of holding memorial meetings for rank and file comrades who die while serving the revolution, Horn wrote, started in Yenan in 1944 when Mao Tse-tung made a speech at the funeral of a charcoal burner named Chang Szu-teh. Memorial meetings should be held so that what was worthy of study could be brought out and placed before the people and so that they could express their love, their gratitude and their sorrow. 'In his speech Mao quoted a Chinese historian who, two thousand years before, had written: "Though Death befalls all men alike, it may be weightier than Mount Tai or lighter than a feather." He said that the death of anyone who had truly served the people was weightier than Mount Tai.' Joan had underlined those words.

The title of this piece comes from Living Your Dying *by Stanley Keleman, an American bio-energetics therapist (Random House, 1975). Joan's review of* Through the Night *appeared in* Spare Rib *No. 45, April 1976.*

SR.57, April 1977

10 VIOLENCE

New ideas about womanhood question old assumptions about
manhood. Once women challenge their subordinate relation to men,
they dissolve the notion that a harmony exists between the two sexes
who occupy separate but complementary spheres. The opposition and
hostility underlying the relationship of domination and submission
between men and women is then revealed.

Both women and men can have equally violent emotions but 'masculinity' makes it legitimate for men to express aggression outwardly,
while 'femininity' does the opposite for women. Women frequently
turn their anger and aggression against themselves, expressing these
feelings as self-hate, fear, guilt or depression. Male violence against
women takes forms of sexual harassment, rape, physical assault and
battering. It is both public and private. It expresses contempt for
women as the subjugated sex.

The public violence of pornography has become more respectable
because it now appears in all media, including women's magazines.
Thus the representation of women as submissive has escalated. By
intruding more into daily life it reinforces the idea that women
are vulnerable, need male protection, and desire to be overpowered.

Because the family is the centre of personal relationships, the
frustration and distress of economic hardship and emotional strain
from the world outside the home can be unleashed inside its privacy.
During the firemen's strike, Jennifer Duggan, one of the firemen's
wives who demonstrated in support of their husbands, talked about
the effect of her husband's work: 'I can't talk to my husband when he
gets in – the job makes him so tense and ill. When I tell him his
dinner's in the oven or something, he often just tells me to shut
up' (SR.66). Violence under stress is seen as men's birthright. For
women who work a ninety-hour week at home and outside, retaliation
is forbidden.

But now we are fighting back. Starting with lessons in self-defence, the women's liberation movement has gone on to set up Rape Crisis and Women's Aid centres. Their way of organizing allows women independence in deciding about the future, whether a married woman wants to leave her husband or a raped woman will choose to prosecute the man. They aim to help women overcome the sense of themselves as victims. Women are often made to feel that they bring violence on themselves, that they 'ask for it', or even enjoy it. They need, therefore, to share their sense of shame and suffering in order not to be trapped by guilt. The centres offer the protection which can sustain women through the process of recovery and the means to transform a self-destructive response into self-renewal.

Police in *Spare Rib* No. 77 said that reported rape incidents were twice that of the previous year, and that 'now they get one rape every thirty hours and four indecent assaults a day'. Violence as a form of social control by men over women is reflected in misogynist police and judicial procedures. In 1976 the Sex Offences (Amendment) Act allowed raped women anonymity. But rape is still legally defined as vaginal penetration although it often entails worse physical mutilation and damage; it is usually a premeditated crime and is primarily an act of aggression rather than the release of sexual frustration.

Sexism and racism are connected. When Judge Sutcliffe presided over a trial of five Moroccan teenagers who raped a girl in London, his 'chivalry' disguised male property rights over women, and cloaked his racism. Victoria Green wrote that the media attitude was 'righteous fury characterized the criticism of the [light] sentences: "*Our* women are being ravaged" ' (*SR.53*).

Racist attacks by white youths and men on Black women (as well as on Black men) are on the increase but are often not publicized. Whereas when Black people retaliate or organize for their own safety and protection, they encounter suspicion and hostility.

Sex education needs to change so that boys see through the social myths about sexuality. And, on a private level, men need to scrutinize the violent feelings they harbour against women – such as those discovered by one of the men's groups formed in response to feminism, 'Fears of being devoured, possessed, weakened or contaminated by women suddenly poured out of a lot of men' (*SR.10*).

Leeds: Curfew on Men

EILEEN FAIRWEATHER

Scarcely a day goes by without women in the North of England being reminded of the existence of the man police call the Yorkshire Ripper; '*All women are now at risk*' is a fairly typical headline. In the past three and a half years the Ripper has murdered eleven women – seven of them in Leeds – and attempted to kill four others. Vicars' prayers for the victims are reported in the press; the public conscience appears outraged.

Or is it? Read beneath the headlines and you find comments like 'even prostitutes don't deserve to die like this'. And the *Yorkshire* and *Evening Post* (who have jointly offered a reward of £5,000 for information leading to the Ripper's arrest) have yet to mention that the Ripper killings are, as feminists in Leeds point out, only 'at the extreme end of the scale of the violence women face every day; from being touched up in the street at the "frivolous" end of it, through to battering and rape.' In the flood of Ripper publicity, this connection is rarely if ever made.

Instead the press, both locally and nationally, has focused attention on the 'virtue' of the victims. This also, of course, routinely happens in rape cases. In this way, attention is drawn away from who is to blame for these attacks; men, not women. Nine of the Ripper's eleven victims have, in fact, been prostitute women. Or, as the *Daily Mirror* chose to describe them, 'good-time girls offering sex for sale'. Jane McDonald, by contrast, was described as 'an innocent sixteen-year-old shop assistant' and, when Josephine Whittaker was murdered this April, the West Yorkshire Assistant Chief Constable explained how 'It would look as if in this case, as with Miss McDonald, he [the Ripper] made a mistake. Miss Whittaker, a building society clerk, was a perfectly respectable girl.' The implication is that the other women who were also sexually mutilated and murdered somehow 'asked' for it – they were non-innocent, non-respectable.

Magda, of the Leeds Rape Crisis Centre, did not consider the Ripper had killed the non-prostitute women 'by mistake': 'When you hate women as much as he must, *any* woman will do. Prostitutes are simply more vulnerable targets.' She also felt that the enormous publicity given to the women's prostitution had probably hindered catching the Ripper: 'Hundreds of people have phoned with information about the women who weren't prostitutes, but the police themselves say they have had very few offers of information with the other women. The attitude seems to be that prostitutes just don't matter.'

The Yorkshire press and police feel they have proved their concern for 'ordinary' women by constantly warning them to stay indoors after dark. Whether it is the Ripper murders or the 'normal' rapes which take place every night throughout Britain, it is men who are violent yet women who are expected to take responsibility for this, by accepting an unofficial curfew on the times they may safely walk the streets. Apart from the fact that women want the right to move freely, many have no choice about being out late. The women at the *Evening Post* who deal with the adverts for the Rape Crisis Centre, and who work for a paper which is instructing women to be indoors by nine o'clock, themselves finish work at 9.30 . . .

SR.83, June 1979

Siân Thomas, *SR.74*, September 1978

'He's Got to Show Her Who's Boss'

NATIONAL WOMEN'S AID FEDERATION

Mrs X was kicked downstairs.

Miss B's 'husband' switched off the heating and locked away the food whenever he left the house.

Miss C was kept short of money.

Mrs A's husband forced her to have sex with his friends.

These women are being battered and come to Women's Aid refuges.

The battering they receive within their particular relationships is an extreme form of the battering we all receive as women in this society.

Because battering has only recently become 'An Issue For Public Concern', people are trying to find ways of understanding it which fit in with traditional ways of seeing and treating women, whilst ignoring the unequal nature of the society in which it takes place.

'She must have done something to deserve it.'

'She must enjoy it although he probably goes a bit far sometimes.'

'It's a man's right to keep her in her place – he's got to show her who's boss.'

'Only working-class women get battered – it's part of their way of life.'

'All batterers must be mental or alcoholics.'

These are all common reactions to women who are being beaten or mistreated, both from people who haven't really thought about it and from those who have done 'research' into the 'problem'.

. . . About seven years ago women's liberation groups all over Britain, who had been discussing the different ways women are oppressed, began to realize that women were suffering at the hands of the men they were living with. The most immediate need of women who were being mentally and physically battered was for somewhere safe to stay away from their men so that they could think about what to do.

The first refuge, in Chiswick, has stayed outside the Federation, as have others set up by social services. They don't see battering as a women's liberation issue, nor do they recognize its relationship to the general oppression of women. Instead they think that individual family circumstances cause battering and therefore that members of the family have to be treated.

Feminists wanted to set up refuges in a way that didn't limit and oppress the women who came to them. Once these refuges opened, two general rules were developed from the ideas and experience of women involved. The first is that any woman who asks for refuge should be immediately accepted. She should not be asked to prove she is battered – or battered 'badly enough' or without 'cause'. To be able to do this the Federation operates a national open door policy – if one refuge is overcrowded a place will be found in another refuge.

The other 'rule' is that women have the right to self-determination. This means that it is the women living in the refuge who run it with help from the support group – a group of people committed to keeping the refuge going and offering support to the women in the house. We don't have wardens and those of us in support groups try not to act as informal wardens.

Christine Roche, *SR.91*, February 1980

Both these rules bring difficulties as well as advantages. They sometimes clash. When a group of women has been in a refuge a while they tend to forget the desperation they felt when they first phoned for help. They are also under the emotional strain of living in a nearly always overcrowded house, as well as having to make major decisions about their future. So when a woman rings up asking for refuge they may resent having yet another person to deal with. As it is the women who decide who comes into the house, they might sometimes refuse refuge when they could make room.

Most groups have at some time experienced this clash between the principle of self-determination and that of the open door policy. The only effective way of dealing with it is by working it out with the women in the house. It solves nothing in the long term for the support group to take over admissions.

Refuges are generally less tidy and clinically clean than hostels, which can cause friction amongst the women because everyone has different ways of living. But in coming to an agreement about such things a lot is learnt about living with other people and about developing ways of living which are practical and fit in with our own ideas of how we want to live; we can stop failing to live up to someone else's image of the perfect housewife.

Any group-living situation brings problems and this is especially true in a refuge where the women haven't chosen to live together. But in spite of this women living in a refuge give and gain a lot. They have all had similar and horrific experiences which many have never before been able to share with anyone, and they face the same difficulties in the refuge, with the children and in dealing with Social Security, social workers and so on. Links formed in this way are often strong and supportive and sometimes friendships carry on after women have left the refuge. This would probably happen more if they didn't have to cope with being a single parent or being rehoused in different areas of town.

... As a Federation we contain different political views. When women in refuges begin to take part in the work of the Federation they obviously bring to it their own understanding of the world, as do people in support groups. This means there is much heated discussion, with groups and individuals continually learning from each other. But the general outlook is feminist and against capitalism.

Obviously as a national organization we have to work at various levels – local, regional and national, but our strength is local and regional. Everybody in Women's Aid – workers in the national office, women in refuges and support group members – is involved to some degree in their local group, and all national decisions are taken by voluntary representatives of local groups and the regions. We want the structure to be flexible, open to any woman wanting to take part, and the work and information to be shared widely.

In practice women in refuges are less involved in the campaigning and co-ordinating side of Women's Aid at regional and national levels. There are two main reasons for this. Firstly women come to refuges because they need to and generally stay for a short time, whereas women in support groups and paid workers have chosen to make a commitment to Women's Aid and are likely to get involved for longer. It is always difficult for new women to get involved in an established group where other women have more knowledge and experience. The other reason is that most women in support groups and most paid workers are middle class and women who come to refuges tend to be working class. (We are using the terms middle class and working class to describe different experiences and don't see one as better than the other.)

Working-class women are more likely to come to refuges because they have less access to money, other accommodation and information about the law and so are in greater need of practical help. Middle-class women often live in more self-contained homes where battering is more hidden and it is harder for these women to admit they are battered. And if middle-class women leave home they have more to lose in terms of money, status and a financially secure future for their children.

Some Women's Aid groups were started by women involved in the women's liberation movement, which tended to attract mainly middle-class women, without appearing to offer much that related to working-class women's experience. Others were started either by social services, or by middle-class women with the 'helping attitude' which is a sort of tradition among them. Some groups which didn't start with feminist ideas but were prepared to accept the aims of the Federation, are affiliated. None of the social services' refuges are. Most affiliated groups contain different attitudes which are changing with experience. As a Federation we are working towards a more feminist approach and at our last conference we included the six demands of the women's liberation movement in the guidelines to our aims. There is ever-increasing discussion of feminist ideas in Women's Aid.

More women who are or have been in refuges are now involved in local groups but their involvement at other levels of the Federation is very low. Language is a major reason for this; middle-class women tend to use academic language, long words as a sort of shorthand for whole ideas (for example – 'agenda' instead of 'list of things to be discussed'). This puts off women not used to this way of talking.

The same problems apply to the structures we use. In January we held a conference to discuss the structure of conferences and of the Federation as a whole. There was a workshop just for women who were or had been in refuges, so that middle-class women would not inhibit them with their relative confidence and language, which stop working-class women getting what they want from conferences. Women from this workshop got very angry and challenged the general running of the Federation, and many things done unthinkingly which put women down, and which are the hardest to tackle. There was also a strong feeling that Women's Aid should be working towards being an organization for battered women, composed solely of women who are or have been in refuges. Women from refuges felt there should be similar workshops at the next national conference.

As well as seeing class as an important issue, we, as members of support groups, are also becoming more aware of ageism – the problems of older and much younger women – of racism and of sexuality. We are tentative about tackling these issues because we are frightened of our own unthought-out prejudices and of being patronizing. We might feel we have to set up something – a project or campaign – for women who are not 'young', middle class and white and make sure this succeeds – by our own 'young' middle-class white values! Our own fear of failure – from years of learning that women aren't meant to succeed – makes us fear for others. In trying to protect other women from repeating our mistakes we also stop them learning from their own experience.

Class is an issue in the whole women's liberation movement. As more working-class women get involved, established ideas and practices are challenged. Hopefully this will produce a feminism which will make sense to all women.

As well as the contradictions we face within the Federation, we have to deal with many outside bodies; this is the hardest area of work to resolve because we have so little control. Local groups receive grants from different sources – Urban Aid, Job Creation, direct grants from social services and recently under the new Housing Act, as well as rent income from the Department of Health and Social Security. We rent houses from local authorities. Because we depend on local government for money and houses they have some control over us, although we are not usually seen as important enough for them to bother too much. But when they do, there are many legal ways for them to affect the way Women's Aid groups work or stop them working altogether. This happened in Bradford recently when the local authority made it impossible for Bradford Women's Aid to run the house, and effectively deprived them of their government grant (which the local authority controlled). Groups are aware of the pressure to compromise and have to continually discuss this and decide where to draw the lines.

We don't like being answerable to anyone outside Women's Aid, but if we don't accept government money, we will continue to exploit women as they have always been exploited doing voluntary work. Often groups with no official funding still have to be careful as they then depend on fund raising, and can easily lose their sources if they are seen as too 'extreme'.

Social workers often try to use refuges as 'dumping grounds' for women who slip between other more regulated institutions. We realize

448   *Spare Rib Reader*

that all women are battered by society and that these women need our support and yet our resources won't stretch to support *all* women.

Legislation brings conflicts too – we can campaign for laws which will bring small but immediate relief to some women but don't change the real situation of all women. Or we can say that the work this involves isn't worth the small benefit it brings. Because we are dealing with people's lives, and a process of change, we have to use the means available to us now to work towards long-term aims. The Domestic Violence Act was welcomed as a solution to the legal problems facing battered women and some still see it as this. In fact it has brought few benefits but its failings can be used to raise consciousness about the needs of battered women and attitudes to women in general. The limitations of the new Housing (Homeless Persons) Act can be used to expose the extent of homelessness and show how little is being done about it.

Women's Aid is sometimes dismissed by feminists not involved because of the compromises we have to make. One reason for this is the way we are presented in the press. For example, however much we stress that we work collectively the press still insists on using names and titles – 'Miss X, leading committee member of the National Women's Aid Federation . . .' Also, there are groups which call themselves Women's Aid but are not part of the Federation. The publicity these groups get affects the way we are all seen. 'Don't believe all you read in the press' is obviously true, yet feminists don't seem to apply it to Women's Aid.

Some feminists also see Women's Aid as do-gooding social work on the cheap. Rape has been taken up as a 'real' feminist issue, perhaps because all women know they could be raped. Just as all men are potential rapists, all men are potential batterers. Perhaps feminists relating to 'nice', 'considerate' men forget that these men have the power to choose not to be so nice.

We are aware of the compromises we have to make but also of the real advantages of combining a service with our feminist aims. We try to be a support organization – not where 'we' help 'them', but where everybody supports and learns from each other. We ask for criticism from feminists outside as well as inside Women's Aid, but that criticism is only useful if it recognizes the situation we are working in and looks at realistic ways of moving forward.

We believe that real revolutionary change must come from a broad base of anger at society and a willingness to change. In Women's Aid we are reaching women who otherwise would have only the media image of women's liberation – which is enough to put anyone off!

Together we are questioning our lives and the way this society works. Because we are trying to use communal caring ways of living in a competitive society with all the contradictions and confusion that brings, we are forced constantly to question our ideas, to see how they relate to the experience of all women. We mustn't stand back and say we can't work in this society so we'll work on a perfect plan for 'After the Revolution'. We may get bogged down in the day-to-day practical work, but along with other organizations, like the Rape Crisis Centre and Rights of Women legal collective, we are working to build mass support for feminist ideas and a mass feminist movement to change society.

SR.69, April 1978

Three Battered Women Face the Future

STEPHANIE MARKMAN

. . . The three women share a view of themselves and their futures which is strikingly confident and optimistic. They all emphasize one thing which is hardly ever taken into account in the welter of academic writings on this subject. 'It needs courage to break away from your home after all these years, especially if you've got a family,' points out Agnes. 'It takes courage to lift the phone.' And Jenny says, 'Women have already had to think for themselves, to even get to a refuge. They're not helpless, driven, beaten-down women.'

And they have developed particular strengths since then. 'I feel very vulnerable, easily hurt, but also strong,' says Jenny. 'I've become much stronger, much less conventional, in the sense that I've been forced to communicate with women at a very deep level very quickly.' Chris thinks that she's changed: 'I can stand up for myself a lot better. I'm more outspoken than I've ever been. I can see different people's lives more quickly, understand them better. I've got more time for people, as well.'

For Agnes, 'the greatest thing is having peace of mind. To put your head on a pillow and know you're there for the night. To be able to lock your door. It's not lonely. You know you're safe. My kids used to be in the street with me at all hours of the night, sleeping under trees, in the park. It's the greatest thing that can happen to a woman who comes to a refuge, and it costs nothing.'

Chris, too, stresses that. 'I don't feel lonely. I don't miss having a man around. I've got the peace of mind, not waiting for him to come in drunk, waiting for the key to turn in the lock, not living in fear.' Jenny speaks also of another kind of freedom: 'I can do some writing, or real thinking, or reading. I get much more sense of self-value, I rediscover my confidence, I get mental energy. My husband would never let me do anything; he felt threatened. Most of my time was spent getting away from him.'

All three women see their future in positive terms. 'I used to sit and worry about my future, but now I just take the days as they come,' says Chris. And for Agnes the way forward is simply 'to go on doing what I'm doing, to help others the way I've been helped. I'd like to see all the social workers out and the battered women in. I get the biggest pleasure out of helping the other women.'

Jenny, on the point of moving to a far better house next door to her closest friend from the refuge, is particularly optimistic. 'I feel I've come through the worst. I've had to learn to cope with problems on my own, I've learnt how to deal with my child, with welfare agencies. I know where I'm going and what I want to do. I almost never get depressed.'

Pornography: Between the Devil and the True Blue Whitehouse

RUTH WALLSGROVE

I find pornography disturbing, chilling – even sometimes physically disgusting. Must I then be a killjoy, a frustrated prude, secretly longing to write articles on porn so that I can sneak a look while publicly tutting?

I have been, and am still, confused by the distance between my reactions to pornography and the debates carried out in the press about it. Mary Whitehouse and the Festival of Light seem as opposed to what I want for the world as do pornographers. And liberal men who proclaim that the Sexual Revolution has already occurred, and who contend that not only is porn a necessary expression of freedom of speech, but also that it is part of a new freedom of sex, certainly *live* in a different world to me. Freedom of speech? – almost anyone can speak in our society, but only those with money and power can make themselves heard. And sex – they all say pornography is to do with sex, but

Begonia Tamarit, *SR.75*, October 1978

I feel immediately that it has more to do with power and violence. I like to be sexually aroused, but I don't like pictures of women handcuffed, submissive and inviting the reader to be brutal with them.

Pornography presents women as willing victims, as objects to be used, bodies created for the sole purpose of pleasing men. Even when the women in the stories are acting out lesbian or masturbation fantasies there is never any doubt that they are really performing for the reader – a man. And when they 'speak' they perpetuate all the old myths of female sexuality. The rough fuck is what they want, none of this boring foreplay or – worse – affection or communication. They are just holes asking to be humiliated and hurt. Magazines present rows and rows of exposed and disembodied vaginas. And this is just *soft* porn. Sadomasochism and child pornography are becoming ever more common, perhaps because men are becoming satiated with straightforward Page Three of the *Sun* spreads at the family breakfast table.

Men must be pretty sick to enjoy fantasizing about hurting another human being. But perhaps porn is only fantasy; perhaps men do not act on it. Statistical studies do not show a direct link between porno-

452   *Spare Rib Reader*

graphy and rape. Rapists don't read significantly more porn than do other men, and the incidence of rape seems unaffected by trends in pornography. There is no evidence that porn causes rape directly, and there may be no *causal* link. But they are linked in spirit. Both are manifestations of the same attitudes towards women and sex – of a desire to avoid interaction with a woman as another human being, to have complete control over sex, at best. At worst, to feel and maintain power oneself by making women powerless. Both are elements of the ideology of the Patriarchy.

So does porn matter? Does it have any effect on me, or other women, or girls, that my local newsagent stocks twenty varieties of porno-graphic magazines, set out in the doorway, with twenty varieties of simpering, undignified nudes in full colour on the covers? Does it make the men who buy them despise women . . . any more than anything else in our society that degrades women? Pornography can be seen as merely an extension of images of women in adverts, as shiny decorative objects.

But adverts themselves become more and more pornographic. Fashion photographers now take classy porn photos, and the seedy, ludicrous publications in backstreets shops are being superceded by glossies that hold press receptions to announce their first issue. Pornography becomes more intrusive and more threatening in its view of sexuality as it becomes respectable, and as the women in it become glamorous. Perhaps I am missing out on life not having such round breasts and such perfectly symmetrical labia, and not having a macho bloke around . . .

Even if porn were not harmful to women in the street, what of the women who are paid to appear in pornographic films and magazines? It is generally agreed that child – 'chicken' – porn exploits and abuses the child models, that children cannot be said to be choosing freely to appear in pornography, and that the experience could seriously mess up a child's sexuality. But the women in porn are freely consenting adults, aren't they? Do they believe in pornography and the view of women's sexuality portrayed in it – or do they just do it for the money? Are they sisters, forced through lack of positive alternatives as women in our society to find employment and importance in porn – or are they traitors, colluding in the degradation of all women for a few quick quid? And what does it do to them? Georgia Stark, an actress in blue movies, was quoted in *Newsweek*:

The first film I made was really a downer. Afterwards I started to think about suicide. But after a while I got so I could do the Eleanor Rigby thing – you know, leave your mind in a jar by the door. Then I'd know I'm just an animal and they are taking pictures of an animal.

I don't like porn. How then do I differ from Mary Whitehouse? She like me finds porn degrading; in her terms it is anti-love and anti-sex, much of which I disconcertingly find myself in agreement with. She claims to enjoy sex, in its proper place. The reason I believe she and I are fighting on different sides is that she focuses her attacks on things that are not to my mind pornographic at all, but that are worthy, if not entirely successful, attempts to educate or explore. She is not solely concerned with images that distort, but also with those that try to describe sex as it actually happens. She vehemently attacks sex education in schools, but is quieter about hard porn in corner newsagents (although she is beginning to campaign against child porn). She became apoplectic over swear words on the Wednesday Play series on TV, some of which plays were remarkably sharp comments on our society. She finally managed to get *Gay News* prosecuted for 'blasphemy' because she could never prove it was obscene; there are many 'obscene' male homosexual magazines, but she concentrated on non-pornographic *Gay News* because it threatened to make homosexuals feel all right about being gay.

She, and others like her, indicate to us the dangers of legislating against pornography. It is not only the most degrading pictures of women that would be banned, but also things that are trying to question or change society's view of women and sex. Contraception information was illegal because it was considered obscene up until the 1930s in this country; and *Spare Rib* itself was banned in Eire this year as 'usually or frequently indecent or obscene' – for demonstrating to women how to examine our breasts for cancer. Censorship laws are always used against those who attempt to inform women about the basics of their reproductive organs, let alone their sexuality, while backstreet blue movies always find a way to survive.

Mary Whitehouse's reason for attacking pornography is precisely the opposite to mine. She wishes to maintain the sexual status quo, to preserve the stunted roles of women in our society. She is fighting to keep women divided into madonnas and whores, to keep sex disgusting and hidden, to keep women from self-knowledge. She claims to attack porn to protect women, but she does so in the name of the nuclear family and the sanctity of marriage – institutions that oppress women.

I do not know if pornography and the Festival of Light are different sides of the same coin. Certainly both elements have co-existed as far back in society as one looks. It has often been argued – by liberal men – that wherever there is a restriction on acceptable sex, as in monogamous marriage, there will be a need for safe illicit outlets for men's free-ranging sexuality. A case of men having their cake and eating it.

Women, of course, have always had to choose one or the other, between the two male-defined views of their sexuality – between having no sexuality and putting up with sex as a wifely duty, and being defined totally by sex, as a 'good time girl'. I myself feel caught up in this dichotomy still in my head; between feeling sex is unimportant and unnecessary, and seeing sex as a Life Force, underpinning my every action.

But maybe Mary Whitehouse is losing, and pornography flourishes and grows. Maybe we should all now have the mentality of a golden-hearted whore, who loves like a man, within marriage, buying our husbands *The Joy of Sex* for Christmas. Or perhaps porn has got too big for its boots, and is actually undermining marriage; porn is now big business, so perhaps sex itself is becoming capitalistic, moving out on to the market place – with women's bodies as commodities. What then will become of us?

'All the flacks make contracts. Contract sex. It means you agree to put out for so long for so much. You know? Like I have a two-year contract. Some girls got only a one-nighter or a monthly, that's standard. You can be put out on your ear at the end of the month with only a day's notice. That's no life. Course once in a while some real bulger, she ends up with a ten-year contract. I never met one, but I heard of them.'

'What happens when your contract runs out?'

Gildina shrugged nervously. 'Sometimes they renew. The first time I was on a yearly I got renewed by that flack – he was a lower-level ground transport smasher. If you're dropped, sometimes you got a prospect. Sometimes you get by on one-nights or weekends till you turn up a prospect. But it drains you. Always worrying about maybe you'll end up in a knockshop. Sometimes you can't keep maintaining, and then your chances of getting even a lower-level flack run down.'

(One possible future from Marge Piercy's *Woman On The Edge Of Time*.)

I don't want to choose between Mary Whitehouse and the producers of *High Society*, between two equally unacceptable alternatives – between censoring all mention of sex through vaguely-worded laws that will be applied by men, and allowing pornography to invade my life at an ever-increasing rate, on Radio One and in packets of bubblegum, and even in the radical press. I believe we should not agitate for more laws against pornography, but should rather stand up together and say what we feel about it, and what we feel about our own sexuality, and force men to re-examine their own attitudes to sex and women implicit in their consumption of porn. We should talk to our local newsagents – many of whom feel pressured into stocking porn – or picket porn movies, or walk down Oxford Street with our shirts off. We must make it clear that porn is a symptom of our sexist society, a reflection of its assumptions; that it is violent and misogynistic, and nothing to do with the free expression of 'healthy' sex, but rather the truly 'perverted' desire to trample on another human being. We must choose the third alternative – women's liberation.

Love and thanks to Roisin McDonough and Vanessa Coode, and all who helped on their way past my kitchen table.

SR.65, December 1977

Talking with an Egyptian Feminist: Nawal el Saadawi

JILL NICHOLLS

. . . *Is clitoridectomy [physical removal of the clitoris] a common operation?* Yes, especially in the rural areas where it's 90 per cent. In the cities it's about 50 per cent. But you know this female circumcision, it's not related specifically to Islam, but to the patriarchal class system. Female circumcision is the remnant of the chastity belt, it's trying to diminish female sexuality to fit it into monogamous marriage. Patriarchy based itself on monogamous marriage for women. If a woman has two husbands, fatherhood will never be known. So they diminished female sexuality physically by clitoridectomy or the chastity belt, or psychologically, because Freud in fact made what I call psychological clitoridectomy! . . .

SR.78, January 1979

Action on Clitoridectomy

JILL NICHOLLS

Clitoridectomy was the main issue discussed at a recent World Health Organization seminar on traditional health practices, held in Khartoum in Sudan. This was a real breakthrough as WHO has always been wary of taking up the subject.

Representatives of seven countries including Egypt, Somalia, Nigeria and Kenya recommended that the operation (still widespread in Africa) be abolished in all its forms. These are 'sunna' circumcision, where the tip of the clitoris is removed; excision/clitoridectomy, where the entire clitoris and labia minora are removed, and sometimes part of the labia majora; and infibulation, where the two sides of the vulva are sewn up after excision.

They want each country to form a national commission to find out how widely this is practised and to co-ordinate efforts against it, campaigning in the media and among midwives, traditional and modern doctors.

Some of the doctors present wanted the operation to be 'cleaned up' and carried out in modern hospitals as an intermediate step, but all the women thought institutionalization was a real danger . . .

SR.82, May 1979

How Can We Support Our Sisters?

EDITORIAL

If we are allowed to hear of clitoridectomy at all, it is as the custom of faraway tribal people. Our horror and anger are set at a distance; we are taught to see 24 million circumcised women as victims living in some unimaginable Dark Age, not sisters in exploitation. Yet the last known clitoridectomy in the West was performed as recently as 1953, in Kentucky, on a girl of twelve. The operation was popularized in the nineteenth century by a British doctor, Baker Brown, as a cure for 'hysteria' – autonomous sexual desire, leading to every other form of rebellion and 'moral leprosy' in a woman.

. . . Today the same doctors might be performing brain surgery. Chemical and physical lobotomy are our cures for female 'hysteria'. In Arab societies, the word is 'fitna' – sexual disruption – and the cure is clitoridectomy. The West has its purely sexual mutilations too: almost half the hysterectomies in the U S are now performed not from proven medical need but 'in case' something might later go wrong with a womb that is seen as disposable. (One quarter of all North American women over fifty have lost their wombs.) There are also the routine episiotomies to facilitate a quick convenient delivery for the doctor, often with horrible side effects which last for years; the 'voluntary' facelifts, and the breast implants that have caused women's deaths.

. . . These are our modern, progressive versions of clitoridectomy . . . new aspects of that long hatred of women's bodies stretching back to our segregation in the tribal menstrual hut and the Christian churching services to rid us of the 'filth' of childbirth.

In finding parallels, we are not saying that oppression is everywhere

the same. We do not suffer the agonies of a Sudanese woman undergoing circumcision, but we are part of the same system. When we met
Nawal el Saadawi last year, she spoke about what she called the psychological clitoridectomy of women in the West: 'Sometimes you think
you are free, but still you are not free' – how many Western women do
not even know that they *have* a clitoris? Some of the feminists she'd
met abroad had seemed to miss connections – not only between Arab
women's oppression and their own, but between Arab women's oppression and the conditions of their countries as a whole. Women like
Saadawi cannot afford to separate their fight against clitoridectomy
from the deliberate 'underdevelopment' and near-starvation of most
communities where it's practised. Nor should we . . .

SR.92, March 1980

To School with Fear

POLLY TALKED TO TOM COTTLE

*Polly, a small West Indian girl of thirteen, has lived with her family in the
Brixton area of London for seven years. It's a poor area compared with
the rest of London: housing is worse, schools are overcrowded, and there
are less jobs. The family had to move several times. Polly's father works on
building sites and needs to live close by. But they are also constantly
looking for a better place to live. Polly doesn't mind moving too much but
feels badly each time she has to leave an old set of schoolfriends. She does
well in her schoolwork, and works extremely hard. But each new school
gets more demanding than the one before. She always makes sure to choose
a best friend in her new school, but she likes to be friendly with all her
classmates – she hates fights and arguments. And the racial aspect of the
fights only makes her feel that much more upset and confused. One
Wednesday evening, she was assaulted and raped by three boys, none of
whom she claims she knew, although she is certain they attend her school.
Admitted as an emergency case to a hospital several miles from her neighbourhood, she talked to Tom Cottle, a friend of her family, who recorded
what she said.*

I ask myself, what is it about it? And I'm not the only one, you
know. Many people feel like me. But I can't keep going, not when you
hear all the things they're saying to you every day. Then, you know,
two people will have a fight and it will never end, and everybody round
it is part of it. If you want one person to win and you tell this to the

wrong person then you lose some more friends. It keeps going like this too. It's not only black against white, but mostly that's what it is. That seems to be all that's happening in school these days. You can't tell the teachers about it. Of course they know, but if you tell them the other kids think you're weak, or scared, or not loyal to them. No one is allowed to tell anybody they're afraid. I tell my best friend Jessie, but I wouldn't tell anybody else. Some days I get so scared before I have to go to school I feel like I'm going to, you know, throw up. I run into the bathroom but nothing happens. I know it won't because it's nerves.

Rachel Dougherty

Every day I walk by this long brick wall. You have to go through this little passageway to get to school. There's usually a cat there climbing around. When I see him I tell him, bring me good luck. He usually runs away, which I tell myself is a good sign. Then I tell myself, no matter what anybody tells you, don't be upset, don't be afraid. Sometimes it works, but most of the time it doesn't, especially if Jessie isn't with me. It's better when she's with me. I rather have someone yell out, there goes two nigger girls, than have me be there all by myself. You don't know what they're going to do next when they do it, and it's always happening. You don't know what's the best thing to do either. Like they'll say, Hey, you short nigger, what are you, some kind of a pygmy? That's my own special name because I'm short. Aren't they clever! I never know what to do. Some people say you shout back at them so they won't do it again. But I couldn't get myself to do that. What am I supposed to do when it happens, like, when we're on the playground or the stairs? Or in the class too? It happens in class too. Hey, pygmy, you read the lesson for today? What am I supposed to do? Jessie says I should keep my mouth shut and tell one of the boys, like, the biggest person I see, that kid over there called me a pygmy. That's what she says to do because she says if we don't start fighting back they'll never stop doing it to us. Maybe she's right, but I can't see myself going up to some guy and telling him what someone said to me.

The boys tell us too, to tell them. They say they'll go after anyone we want them to, that they're not afraid of a single person in the school. I can't believe what's going on. If you tell someone you don't know what kind of trouble you may be starting, and if you keep your mouth shut, you know what you're letting go on. But everyone keeps saying, they aren't going to hurt you, they aren't going to hurt you, nothing will happen. But I don't see why they should be allowed to call me things that has to do with my being coloured, and that's mostly what they yell. Everybody fights about it. Even Jessie's been in some fights. I didn't see her, but I did see another a few months ago. I got so frightened *that* time I did throw up. One of the worst things was what I was thinking about, how, like, at first I was afraid she would get hurt and I started to cry, and then, without even thinking about it, I found myself hoping she would kill this white girl. I was crying but I wanted her to kill the white girl. I think mostly because the girl was white and because of what she said. She called Jessie some horrible name, I didn't even understand it at first. Jessie didn't either, but you could tell it wasn't a compliment.

Then, you know, when they fight, everybody crowds round and then they start fighting, like they did this one time when Jessie fought this girl Shea. They were all fighting, and I ran away because I got scared. That time I told my mother, which I usually don't do. My mother told me she was going to school to see what was happening. She went too, but the master told her there was nothing the school could do if children fought before or after school; it wasn't their responsibility. He didn't think the fighting was all that bad. Kids have always fought, that's what he told my mother. He said he was surprised she would find all this new. Didn't she have fights in her neighbourhood where she went to school? That's what he told her. I mean, that's what I know he told her, because some of the other things she wouldn't tell me, but she told my father. I know one of them was that I was supposed to be known as a little bit of a baby, that's what the master said; that just because I was a girl didn't mean I shouldn't have to fight and protect myself. He said he thought coloured people were teaching this to their children. She said she thought he was prejudiced, and he told her our kind is too sensitive about all this stuff. Besides he said, he did a special favour for us letting me into the school when we moved here because he could have said no because the classes were so big. My mother told him no one in this country does any favours for us and he told her she was wrong; that's all coloured people do is ask for favours. Anyway, he said there's nothing that could be done about the fighting. It was happening in the school, sure, maybe once a week too, which is a lie because it happens all the time, but the problem isn't the school, it's the country. So my mother said, you mean it's all *our* fault and he said, you said it, Mrs Davies, I didn't.

I was surprised too, because I thought the master was a real nice man. At least *I* never saw him do anything bad to anybody. I don't know all that much what the other kids think of him. Jessie hates him because he blamed her that one time for starting the fighting which she didn't. I know, because I was there. But I always thought he liked us. Like, Mrs Brainaird likes us. She's always asking me how I'm doing and if I have problems. I don't talk to her, but maybe I could. You can't tell with some of these people, like, how they're going to be if they have to take a side. I think a lot of the teachers would like to take our side once in a while, but they're afraid what the master or the assistants might say to them. Lots of them aren't much better off than we are, I guess, although they don't talk about it with us. Well that's not completely true, because Mrs Strandy, she told Jessie and this other girl how she was afraid to teach in the school with all the fighting, so she was looking for a new job. They had a long talk about it. Jessie told her maybe she could do something to make it better, but she said, no, she was leaving, even if it meant she wouldn't be able to find another job. She'd rather go on the dole than teach here. That's what she said. Then she told them, it was better before they let all the coloureds in. Can you believe her saying this to Jessie, who's coloured! She didn't even realize what she was saying. She told them, it was better before they let the coloureds in. So Jessie said, well, Mrs Strandy, if you haven't noticed yet, *we're* coloured. So Mrs Strandy said, of course I know you're coloured, but it's not the children I'm talking about it's their parents! It's all your fathers who don't work and don't want to, and all your mothers having all these children. That's what the matter is. It's never the children's fault. So Jessie just looks at her and says Oh! That's all, just oh!

Doesn't my school sound like a wonderful place? Now do you know why I don't like going around there, no matter how much I might learn, which I don't think is all that much. Most of the time all I learn is that a lot of people in my school think I'm a coloured pygmy, but I ought to be learning a little more than that. And another thing, if these people, like the master and Mrs Strandy, have all these feelings about us, I would like to know how they can be allowed to stay in the school, and some of those people have the most important jobs over there, you know. They make the decisions and they have all these ideas. That's all we hear from them: it's the coloureds. Pretty soon, it will get bad for me and I really will be able to throw up before I walk to school, instead of just thinking that I do. Like, right now, telling all of this to you gives me the same feelings I have before I walk there in the morning. It's like I need my lucky black and white cat to tell you what I *think* about school, and we aren't anywhere near school now, are we? I'm not sure where we are here, but it feels that we're a long, long way from school. At least I hope it's a long way from school. I know this isn't really a holiday but I'm trying to pretend it is.

SR.62, September 1977

'They're Killing Us in Here'

PERMINDER DHILLON

The morning after the first national demonstration organized by Afro-Caribbean and Asian women, I went into work and a white man asked me, 'But what is it you are fighting against? I thought you were feminists. What's this about police brutality?'

That is the sort of question Black feminists get asked. Why did Black women organize a demonstration against police brutality and immigration harassment? What happened in Southall on 23 April might give the answers.

That was the day that the National Front held their electoral meeting in Southall town hall. They had been given permission to bring their racial hatred right into the Black community. The people of Southall decided they would sit down peacefully outside the town hall, stopping the Front from holding their meeting by their sheer numbers, and they obtained police permission to do this. Nearly everyone in Southall from the Afro-Caribbean and Asian communities came out to take part. But as early on as 2 p.m. people were being arrested for trivialities like crossing the street, or refusing to move instantly when told to do so. A hundred such arrests were part of deliberate provocation by police, and set the tempo for what was to follow.

After 3 p.m. Southall had become a town under siege. People were not allowed in or out of buildings. Police with dogs roamed the streets. Around 5 p.m. a group of us Asian women were finally allowed out of the building in which we'd been stranded all afternoon. We joined the crowd behind a cordon of police, who were protecting the side entrance to the town hall. All streets leading to the building had been cleared of demonstrators. No one was allowed to leave, to go home. 'It's for your own protection,' they told us.

Women of Southall know what police protection means – being beaten with their truncheons, while a few streets away a Black sister is sexually assaulted by white youths.

At 6.30 the police began to show their force: mounted police, police with dogs, and the special patrol group with riot shields and truncheons laid into them, forcing them to run into the near-by park. Hitting out, pulling off the turbans of Sikhs, dragging them along the ground by their hair – while women suffered racial and sexist abuse. They were grabbed by their breasts and told, 'Move, you black whores!' Some older women who could not climb over the rails into the park were dragged away and arrested. The group I was in, young and old women, linked arms, and in this way managed through our combined strength to drag ourselves free from the police.

Then the SPG, three with shields and three with truncheons in a special pyramid formation, chased people into 'People Unite', a cultural centre, which has long been the target of police harassment. A Black sister described what happened: 'Everyone rushed upstairs, and the police followed breaking down the door. We ended up in the top room. They shouted to us to come down, women first, and that there'd be no trouble. But when we came down they started kicking us. I was hit on the head and my friend, in the face and head. She lost two teeth.'

An Afro-Caribbean sister ran towards us in the park crying and shouting, 'They are killing us in there!' What could we tell her? That this was nothing for any Black woman? How many Black people have been killed by the British state – through police brutality, through gross neglect in hospitals, or out of grief over families divided by immigration laws?

. . . Around 10, many of us gathered to watch the news at a restaurant, where Rock Against Racism and Indian music had been blaring out all evening, drowning out the National Front speakers inside the town hall. Their wounds still bleeding, people saw the Commissioner of

Police, the Home Secretary, and other 'experts' on the Black community defending the right of the NF to hold their meeting, and condemning the people of Southall for their unprovoked attack on the police! As usual, only pictures of injured policemen were shown – nothing of the pregnant women being kicked and the countless other police assaults. The next day I saw a film crew, apparently from the BBC, selectively filming broken windows of white-owned shops. When I asked why, I was told, 'Fuck off! We know all about thugs like you!'

But the next day the tone of the Prime Minister and so on quickly changed when it became clear that Blair Peach – a white male – had died. Then with the hypocrisy typical of the Labour Party, they called for a ban on NF meetings. But even this did not deter Ealing council from passing a motion commending the police for their 'courage and patience'. Beatrice Howard, leader of the council commented, 'It was surprising that women were on the streets that day. It was inviting trouble.'

SR.84, July 1979

Nuclear Weapons: Stay Home and Die

LUCY WHITMAN

The threat of nuclear disaster looms over us, the ultimate symbol of our powerlessness in an ask-no-questions-and-you'll-be-told-no-lies society.

The government wants us to retreat into our nuclear families, get under the table, shut our eyes and hold our noses while the world outside falls to pieces. We're supposed to keep the radio tuned for government instructions, which will no doubt be interspersed with smash hit singles such as the Electric Light Orchestra's 'I'm alive!' or 'There's gonna be a party all over the world'.

What has nuclear war got to do with women? It certainly wasn't our idea. Yet however peacefully most of us – Margaret Thatcher excepted – want to live our lives, we will all be targets if there is a nuclear war. Even so, isn't it really a 'human' issue, not intrinsically connected to feminism?

I think there *is* a connection. Like a lot of other feminists, I am convinced that nuclear weapons and nuclear power are in fact the most brutal manifestation yet of the murderous patriarchal system which has brought about so much misery throughout recorded history.

. . . A male-dominated society divides people up very rigidly according to whether they are women or men, divides up work and feelings and types of behaviour into those more 'appropriately' masculine or feminine, and *persistently undervalues the work, feelings and behaviour associated with women*, the 'weaker' sex. Men are supposed to be tough, active, inventive and cool-headed, and women are supposed to be loving, yielding, supportive and emotional. Housework and childcare are not even recognized as *work*, and although romantic love and motherhood are sentimentally idealized, compassion, consideration for others and other 'feminine' attributes are held in scorn in the 'real' world of industry and international relations. Ruthless business deals are applauded however much suffering they may cause, and war is glorified as it gives men an opportunity to demonstrate just how *manly* – i.e. competitive, cruel and uncompromising – they are.

Men in our society are encouraged to look on war as a thrilling adventure, as any glance at the sickening quantity of war films and war comics and toys produced each year will show.

I don't believe that 'human nature' accounts for men's aggression any more than it accounts for women's pacifism and/or passivity. If it did, there would be no need to make such strenuous efforts to crush any spontaneous demonstrations of tenderness and gentleness in boys, taunting those who will not conform to the hard-hitting 'norm' by calling them cissies and softies . . .

. . . Of course there are many individual men who are passionately dedicated to the cause of disarmament, and I do not mean to sneer at them or suggest that they should be excluded from the struggle. But I do believe that patriarchy as an institution, the deliberate subjection of women to men, is ultimately responsible for producing a culture which can countenance the nuclear arms race.

SR.99, November 1980

'The Primary Purpose is to Help Raped Women Regain Their Strength as Individuals': Crisis Centre Opens

VICTORIA GREEN

A Rape Crisis Centre has opened in the London area to help women who have been raped. The counsellors provide sympathetic, non-judgemental support; they offer advice and information on police and legal procedures to those women who choose to report the rape; and they will accompany victims to the police station if their help is needed.

The majority of rapes in this country are never reported, probably because the victim quite realistically dreads the experience of police interrogation and the ensuing trial. The Centre does not see itself as a means of increasing the number of convictions for rape but believes it can best help the victim by providing the sort of support which will enable her to choose about prosecuting or not.

Many rape victims find their whole lives are disrupted by the experience and need to express their fears and reactions to someone who understands their situation. Women often suffer for years after a rape; Crisis Centres in the USA have had appeals for help from women raped ten years previously. Often the main problem is the victim's attitude to herself, and talking it over with people who might have had the same experience is an important step towards re-establishing her sense of self.

The Centre in London is run on a collective basis; the idea for a twenty-four-hour emergency service came up in November 1974. Initially the service was limited but it now provides support on a variety of levels at any time of the day.

Registered as a charity, the group has applied for Urban Aid and other government grants. So far it has received grants from two trust funds and is able to rent office space and pay two full-time members of staff. The counsellors are voluntary and the ultimate aim is to have enough people to provide for two women on duty at the centre all the time.

Counsellors go through a training system involving an introductory meeting with the collective, who describe the Centre's outlook on rape and the function of the Centre. They are given a reading list on the subject, they observe a rape case at the Old Bailey and go to a VD clinic to familiarize themselves with the procedures.

The Centre emphasizes that it is there to provide support for victims and not to direct them. Counsellors will go to a victim wherever she is if that is what she wants. She can go to the Centre when she needs help and can rely on sensitive, supportive comfort from the women there. The primary purpose of the collective is to help raped women regain their strength as individuals.

Any woman needing assistance at the police station will be accompanied there and will be made aware of her rights during the proceedings. For example, counsellors can ensure she knows she is entitled to be examined by her own doctor rather than the police surgeon. Counsellors will go with victims to VD clinics and help offset the trauma of that experience so soon after the rape. They provide women with information on the law and will help them through the trial itself.

Education is also an important function. Police stations, hospital casualty departments, community health centres and VD clinics have been sent circulars describing the Centre. The collective intends to publish information sheets and give talks explaining its service in an effort to educate those groups who come into contact with rape victims. It also plans to produce and disseminate leaflets and posters advertising its work.

Ideally, there should be a network of small groups all over the country providing the service offered by the London centre. Some groups are beginning already: Newcastle-on-Tyne should have its own Rape Crisis Centre soon and there have been inquiries from other areas. The London Centre has been putting women in touch with each other and will help them to start operating on their own.

Reactions to the Centre have been varied. The police are wary though fairly sympathetic. They are worried that the service might discourage women from reporting rape. The police feel it is easier to get victims over the hurdles in the system when they are ignorant of what is involved. The police are mainly concerned to catch rapists and feel women will not come forward if they understand the difficulties facing them within the legal processes.

The collective has found that women police officers are often more sympathetic towards rape victims and are themselves sceptical of the official line that the police do not harass rape victims. The Home Office recently issued a five-point directive on police procedure relating to the treatment of rape victims. Intended to ensure that women reporting rape are treated with more gentleness and respect, it is not statutory and its implementation is left to the police discretion.

The forthcoming Private Member's Bill to reform the rape laws does not, the Rape Crisis Centre says, do much to improve the position of the rape victim in court. The definition of rape remains unchanged. Vaginal rape – the penetration of the vagina by a penis – is the only form of rape under the law. A large number of rapes are committed with bottles, sticks or some other object; anal rape and fellatio are common assaults and no less damaging and humiliating than vaginal rape, but are treated as indecent assault and seen as less important.

The collective believes the Bill's well-publicized proposals for changing the laws of evidence are meaningless. The introduction of evidence on a victim's previous sexual history should be ruled out altogether, but the putative law leaves that decision to the discretion of the judge. If the judge decides such evidence is relevant the jury must leave the court and so the victim is automatically cast as provocative.

As the Centre points out, the legal profession is more or less indifferent to the situation of the rape victim. This was made clear by the Haldane Society – a collection of liberal lawyers – who voted to support last year's Law Lords (Morgan) ruling. Only three members opposed the ruling, and they were the only women in the group.

Clearly, it would be good if all rape victims brought charges against their attackers but in the present legal climate it is a big price for women to pay. A victim must face interrogation about her character and sexual history, without the right to call character witnesses in her own defence. She is seen as a witness at the trial and therefore in no need of legal representation or witnesses of her own.

The rapist, meanwhile, may call character witnesses and the law does not allow any evidence of his previous sexual history to be used against him. In his evidence he may, and most often does, attempt to impugn the reputation of his victim and thus establish a case for 'honest' belief in keeping with the Morgan ruling.

Rape victims can only hope for justice when the case is judged on its own merit without recourse to the traditional smear tactics allowed under the law; nor will women see the point in bringing charges until the testimony of the victim is accorded equal value to that of the rapist. 'Honest belief' on the part of the rapist is impossible to prove or disprove. The sexism of the Morgan ruling shows the rape victim that her attacker will not be convicted unless she gets herself beaten up and manages to see a doctor immediately after the rape.

The Rape Crisis Centre does not believe it should try and persuade women to press charges under these circumstances. Quite often the due process of law manages to more damage to the rape victim than did the assault itself.

The Centre will not allow its address to be published. Nor will it fulfil the prurient expectations of the press by giving out information about the cases it deals with. Since it started operating on 15 March, journalists from the national press have tried to break in and take photographs, and there have been requests from journalists wanting to sit in on the work of the Centre. Others have wanted a series of case histories. The women running the Centre are desperate to keep the address secret and already they have had to appeal to the Attorney General to prevent its publication in a national daily.

The day the telephone number was published the lines were kept busy by men ringing with obscene threats; one rang every ten minutes for thirty-six hours. Recently in Australia, the Sydney Rape Crisis Centre was attacked with a bomb.

To be effective the Centre must provide a quiet, supportive environment for the women who go there. They must feel secure in the knowledge that their experiences are treated with respect. For this reason the collective feels its policy towards the media is absolutely justifiable.

SR.46, May 1976

Defending Ourselves

ALISON FELL

After the meeting Janey dropped me at Euston. 'Sure you'll get home OK from here?' 'Oh, I'll be fine, I'll jump into a taxi.' So I stood on the kerb staring up the roaring vista of the Euston Road while the green Volvo swung right down Gower Street. I waved cheerily. Bravely.

Euston was a hell of a place to drop me. I was an idiot, I should have made more demands, showed more of my fear and reluctance. But I felt I'd already exposed more than enough feelings in the meeting. I'd imagined Euston Road would be bright and brimming with lights, loud with the rumble of trains disgorging solid travellers into creeping ranks of taxis. But the station was so dull, so black; only a few lights as dim as gas lamps burned along the top. The drunks were lurching in the park where the grass – always foul and flea-filled – had dried to bone-yellow in the drought. I stood well out on the kerb to avoid the shadow of the scrubby hedge which borders it, and peered back into the oncoming three-lane traffic surge for a taxi's light. Not many taxis, and all of those full. I paced along to the traffic lights. No police cars, either.

I wore flat childish sandals, black blouse – on the prim side – and a knee-length cotton skirt. My hair lay flat, a bit sweaty from the endless heat and the stresses of the meeting. I glanced down Gower Street – perhaps Janey and the others had thought better of it, perhaps they were parked there, craning to see me jump, safe and serene, into a cab? No. I was alone with my pluck. It was nearly 1 a.m.

There were no women in sight – except the delectable Morgan's Rum girls displayed on the hoarding opposite – and there were no couples. Euston Road was the domain of men only.

Was I safer standing still? Was it then *perfectly obvious* that I was intent on hailing cabs? Or did I look more purposeful walking, not waiting? I walked a bit. A man was coming in the opposite direction – a teacher, I thought – bearded and a bit portly. He carried books, well, that was O K, it was useful to have types like that around if things got heavy; he came level; he was almost past; he made smacking, kissing noises with his fat lips.

I started towards the kerb again and stared back into the traffic flow. Immediately a light-coloured saloon veered in from the middle lane and slowed, one man at the wheel. Youngish, I registered, flashy *Playboy* clothes. I turned away from the kerb and sped off towards King's Cross again. He drove on a little way and drew in. I stared straight ahead at the Shaw library and willed my trembling legs to walk straight and sure, willed my hips to rivet like a well-corseted grand-mother's, willed them not to sway an inch. I sensed him lean across and wind the window down: 'Wanna lift babe?' he slurred. I walked faster, hatred raging in my veins – shaking, not looking at him, I flapped my hand in a sort of 'Get Thee behind me, Satan' gesture and yelled 'SOD OFF, SOD OFF!'

Another man was approaching from King's Cross direction. He wore a suit, he looked working class, oldish. This time I wasn't going to risk hearing the obscene invitations when I passed, so as I came level with him I went back out to the kerb, looking back slightly (the other bastard was still kerb-crawling me, ahead) and waved desperately at nothing on the dark road. A mistake. The guy in the suit took this as an invitation and turned after me, and followed me, he was lighting a fag and preparing to make an approach. I started to walk again, faster and faster. I was beginning to pant with terror and disgust. But still he caught up with me, and muttered something in that vile prowler's hiss – they move their lips – in contempt, or self-contempt, who knows? Little eyes flashing in the dark. I don't remember what I shrieked at this one. Meanwhile, another guy had stopped in his tracks, circled back and was crossing the road towards me.

This time I knew I couldn't stand it any longer, they were closing in and Euston Road was like a chasm with me at the bottom, wounded panicking prey; cars were slowing for the lights so I raced out into the road and yelled at a cab, 'Get me off this bloody road, for Christ's sake!' The cab wasn't actually for hire but he said, 'Only to Highbury? Oh, O K then.'

I fell inside and collapsed on the seat like a rag doll. 'Did you have a hard time then, love?' the driver inquired sympathetically. 'Terrible,' I blurted. 'They just won't leave you alone, one after the other, it's just bloody dreadful, I couldn't bear it.' I looked down at my hand, which lay white on the black plastic seat. It was feeble, quivering. The skirt felt stupidly floppy and insubstantial – I needed boots, mail on my fists, and a weapon in my bag, not leaflets. Soft belly, soft breasts, jelly legs.

'Smoke, love?'

'Got one, thanks.' I memorized the taxi number. 5495. Then I said to myself, 'Who's in a bad state of paranoia, then? Just because he's being sympathetic.'

No lights on in the house – it looked deserted. I jumped out of the cab and searched for cash.

'You wouldn't be thinking of puttin' the coffee pot on for me, now love?' I think I went into shock then, because all I could manage was a 'No' that was positively demure. I gave him a tip. And a stiff little smile with it.

(And people are *surprised* that we're ambivalent about our sexuality and our womanhood?)

VICTORIA GREEN AND ROZSIKA PARKER

Any woman walking alone late at night shares Alison's experience. Her fear – our fear – of violence is rational. A woman had been raped on the Euston Road only weeks before Alison's journey home. Yet the effect that threatened violence has on our lives far outweighs the actual incidents of public assault. For example, we would avoid the Euston Road (at night) even though we're aware that most violence happens at home between people who know one another.

Walking through cat-calls we expect violence. It marked us from the moment our mothers said, 'Don't talk to strange men.' We began to see ourselves as weak, vulnerable beings in a world which values strength and courage. 'I looked down at my hand which lay white on the black plastic seat,' writes Alison. 'It was feeble, quivering.'

The threat of male violence is one reason, paradoxically, why women remain dependent on men. In terror Alison looked for a protector: 'A teacher . . . he carried books, that was O K. It was useful to have types like that around if things got heavy.' And remember Judge Morris at the Brixton mugging trial in October, who suggested the need for 'some form or other of vigilante corps comprised of citizens concerned for the safety of lone women'.

If men are seen either as rapists or bodyguards, a woman on her own is obviously 'asking for it' – she's fair game. Our usual defence is to deny our sexuality: 'I willed my hips to rivet like a well-corseted grandmother's.' It doesn't work; we stay scared and they keep whistling. But what if we learn to defend ourselves physically. If we appeared self-confident and self-possessed, would men then be different?

The roots of violence and the reasons for the harassment of women in the streets are too complex for such an immediate strategy to be a real solution. Perhaps, instead of individual women learning to defend themselves, we should be organizing against the violent society. But we've got to deal with the fears we have today. At least by taking responsibility for our own safety at a day-to-day level, we might feel less hedged in by fear, more self-confident, and able to change things.

Spare Rib talked to women who have deliberately stepped outside the 'weaker sex' role – strengthening their muscles, learning to kick, punch and block, and run very fast. We asked women karate students whether learning self-defence had lessened their fears. Did they see themselves differently and had men's attitudes towards them changed?

Most karate classes last roughly two hours and are divided into two sections. The first half is taken up with rigorous exercises to strengthen and loosen muscles: push-ups, back and neck exercises. They include katas – a series of rhythmic, controlled movements necessary to fighting – the fighting stance, kicking, punching and blocking.

The second half consists of fighting. People are paired off according to their level of competence and the fighting is tightly disciplined – punches and kicks are pulled back so that you don't hurt your opponent. Achievement is marked by examinations and you earn coloured belts as you become more proficient – the final stage being the black belt.

The atmosphere of classes is intense and serious, the only noises are the thumps of bare feet on the floor and the voice of the teacher directing the class. The most traditional classes are very hierarchical with much bowing to the instructor who maintains rigid discipline. Others are less formal, but still retain some bowing and the teacher keeps close control.

A karate green belt (2nd grade on) who has been going to classes in King's Cross, London, told us that when she started two years ago she was 'often the only woman in the class. Today more and more young working women are joining though we are still a minority.' What do karate instructors think about the influx of women – do they believe women can use unarmed combat effectively? Do they treat women in their classes in the same way as men?

John Anderson of the Budokwai club in London thinks women suffer from their conditioning: 'They are not used to hard exercise and they are not as aggressive as men.' But he thinks women have better bodies for karate because they are more supple; once they have learned to discipline themselves they can become very good. His women students do all the same work as men, taking the same examinations, but they don't do the hard fighting demanded of the men in the higher grades.

Mr Chang of the Wu Shu Kwan kung-fu club in London says that he treats women in his class with greater care because they are not as tough as men, they are more motivated to learn self-defence but are less aggressive. He too remarked that we are conditioned against sustained physical effort. His solution is to 'give a little more freedom to women – let them get used to the atmosphere. They have freer expression of themselves at first. At the moment men have a higher achievement than women but the gap is narrowing.' In Mr Chang's class beginners only fight with experienced students who teach them how to punch, kick and block.

An instructor at an all-woman class, Pauline Fuller, who teaches karate at the Women's Free Arts Alliance, disagrees with both men. She thinks that women should be pushed just as hard as men and that they should be forced to bring out their aggression. 'I used to think women were naturally less aggressive than men, but now I don't think so. In my class I make them work, I don't let them rest when they are tired; they have to learn that they can't just give up because they are women. Mixed classes are no good for women because then they take on the feminine role and don't push themselves. The men indulge them and they just don't take it seriously. In my class the women understand they have to keep going no matter how bruised or tired they are – surprisingly none of them have dropped out yet.'

One woman we talked to felt that karate classes, by encouraging competition and shows of strength, promote machismo amongst men, making them patronizing towards women learning to fight. In her experience women were either ridiculed as butch or discouraged by not being taken seriously. But other women disagreed, insisting that the men were not hostile, just bewildered at the prospect of fighting women. And as more women join classes and gain competence, attitudes towards them are changing.

Why did you learn self-defence?

Most of the women we questioned said they had taken up karate partly for self-protection and partly to keep fit. Sue is thirty-five, small and slight. She felt that she had gone to pieces physically after having two children but it wasn't until she visited China that she started karate classes: 'It seemed obvious that Chinese women were keen on being strong, to be able to use their strength if they needed it. So I thought of strength, not just in terms of being able to fight but in order to work – to lift heavy boxes, pick up heavy objects. I had always been seen as someone who was frail. I remember my father saying to my husband that I was frail and needed looking after, although I was very seldom sick.'

The practical and symbolic importance of being strong for Sue is clear. But Mary is a tall, strong woman of thirty – why did she take up karate? She explained that she lives alone in a flat where she used to be too petrified to undress and go to bed at night, and having a bath was unthinkable. On long winter nights she'd sit rigid, listening for The Rapist to start breaking down the front door. 'I was never afraid in the streets, only when I came home and sat in the flat. I knew that karate was something I needed for self-protection.'

Other women never felt vulnerable at home, only in the streets. 'I disliked my own nervousness in the street,' Anna told us. 'I went to Paris with my sister; we were hassled. I said to one of the men, "I'll hit you", he said he'd love it. I slapped him and he kicked me in the belly. Then it became a complete brawl. Luckily his friend didn't join in but I fought badly, ineffectually. Eventually he ran away, dropping his packet of Gauloises. We had a moral victory at least.' Anna is thirty-six, with two children; she began to consider karate but it was six months before she joined a class.

Her daughter started karate when she was eleven, 'because Anna did it and I was already being whistled at in the street. It was a glamour thing, too. I didn't like my school and I thought they would hate me less if I could say I learned karate.' There are a number of girls between seven and fifteen in Mr Chang's classes. They want to learn to defend themselves against bullies.

Barbara, aged twenty-five, plays in a rock band. She told us that she needed karate for the life she leads, and she has to be strong to carry the group's equipment: 'I was really surprised when I saw how much I could carry and feel annoyed that I wasn't taught to use my muscles. It's an attitude, I just carry things now.'

Has karate lessened your fears?

All felt it had, but Mary, previously the most beset with fears, was loudest in its praise. Once too frightened to undress at night, she now sits comfortably at home listening to music instead of waiting, ears peeled, for the sounds of the front door shattering. She thinks it's because karate has taught her control over her body. Maggie Lomax (*SR.16*) described the key to karate: 'It puts greatest emphasis on a supple body and an alert mind. The moment you stiffen up your impetus stops, and the essence of Shotokai (karate) is that you're always ready, moving in your mind even before your body sets off.'

But why should learning to control her movements and sharpen her responses have eased Mary's fear? She explained that she now comes forward to face confrontations instead of panicking and freezing like a frightened rabbit. 'It stopped me being so numb. I feel more able to withstand a situation where I feel I might get hurt.'

Feeling sceptical we reminded her of her fear that somebody might at any moment break down the door of her flat. 'What would I do? I'd be able to move into action immediately. Although one obviously has inhibitions about phoning the police – that's what I'd do.'

Practical hints

We think that karate is the ideal form of self-defence for mind and body. But it takes time to learn the techniques and absorb the attitude, so meanwhile here are some instant hints for defending yourself. Obviously violence shouldn't be used indiscriminately. It isn't always the solution any more than is compliance or, as Cosmo advises, 'treating your rapist like a human being', but it's important to have every option at your fingertips.

1 If you think someone is about to attack you, start running suddenly and shout (don't scream, which is the expected response). Break a window or something that makes a lot of noise to attract attention. Carry a whistle or a small siren which you can use to make a lot of noise.

2 If you are grabbed and held from behind, concentrate on kicking him. Kick low and hard from the knee, aim at his shins and kneecaps; kneecaps are sensitive and can be dislodged by hard kicks. And stamp hard on his instep. Better still – though this requires practice – bend your knees, lowering yourself until your bottom is at least as low as his groin, then bend right forward and jerk your hips to one side, flinging him off.

If he's got his arm around your neck, choking you, turn your head into the crook of his elbow so that you can breathe. Kick his shins, stamp on his instep and bring your elbows back hard into his ribs.

If he is strangling you from behind with his hands, grab his little fingers and pull them back hard; at the same time scrape your heel down his shin on to his instep.

3 If he is facing you and trying to hit you, turn sideways so there's less of you he can hit.

If he grabs you from the front, bring the heel of your palm up under his chin or nose – hitting his nose will at least make his eyes water and force him to loosen his hold on you.

If you are pushed up against a wall, use your knees to kick his groin and your feet to kick his shins.

4 If you do get thrown to the ground, roll on to your back, it's then easier to defend yourself against someone standing up.
If he attempts to rape you, bend one knee to get your foot flat on the ground and, using your leg and pelvis as a lever, throw him off with a sudden movement.

Always try and keep your balance when attacked. You must break his hold on you to get away, so keep kicking and hitting him until he lets you go. Make a lot of noise all the time, he expects a passive victim and may panic if you resist noisily. Try to keep in mind an avenue of escape while you are fighting and when you get free run for it, shouting for help.

There are books which give fuller descriptions. We took some of the methods from *Against Rape* by Andrea Medea and Kathleen Thompson (Peter Owen, £3.60) and *The Politics of Rape* by Diana E. H. Russell (Stein & Day, £2.60).

Her new confidence has changed her relationships: 'I confront people much more. I have much more straightforward relationships, less messy.' And it's affected her attitude towards her body. Like many large women she felt pressured into hiding her size, stooping and suffering, resenting her height, scrupulously avoiding skirts and things she thought looked incongruous on her. 'Karate teaches you to accept what you are and to make the most of it. The extraordinary thing is that now I accept and use my height, I no longer feel tall.'

Remembering Alison's comment, 'And people are surprised that we're ambivalent about our sexuality and our womanhood,' we asked Mary if she felt different about her sexuality. 'I really do – you know that feeling women have that they are dirty? I don't have that any more. Quite often when I wear a skirt I don't wear knickers. I don't like the idea of my skirt blowing up and the world seeing – but there is something about it that is sort of exhilarating. And I feel much more confident about making love. I can ask for what I want and express pleasure – that takes a lot of doing. You feel so vulnerable. But once you have started to value your body, you imagine that other people will as well.'

A lot of women were strong, confident children who, only in adolescence, learned that women were supposed to be weak. Valuing physical fitness begins to reverse that conditioning. But getting fit is hard work and karate requires real commitment.

Does self-confidence stop verbal assault and harassment in the street?

'It's good to be hostile and confident, to express opposition instead of fear. An initial response of confidence is vital. You walk differently when you are confident. You are more relaxed and at home with your body,' said Anna. And Barbara added, 'I feel renewed after karate classes so I don't notice the hassles so much when I'm bicycling home.'

But our general impression is that though women feel more secure, men remain much the same. 'Last night I was walking down the street in one of those huge plastic bicycle rain capes,' said Sue, 'and still a man stuck out his hand as I was going by.'

Do you feel you can physically defend yourself if you're attacked?

Pauline Fuller, aged thirty-one, and a black belt, was attacked at night in Nottingham. One of a group of five men pushed her into a doorway where she was trapped. But, she says, 'I dropped him and his friends were so surprised they did nothing to help him. As I ran away I heard one of them say, "Did she hit you?" ' Pauline has been doing karate for fifteen years while the other women have been going to classes for about two years. We got the impression that karate had not yet equipped them with an infallible weapon but rather with attitudes which protected them from fear. They no longer feel completely powerless so street hassles are neither as frightening nor as infuriating. They've had some experience of fighting – it's no longer a foreign country.

We asked Anna what she'd do if she was attacked: 'Well, it would depend on the circumstances, whether they were really aiming for you or just anyone. I have threatened people. I was walking with a friend in Shaftesbury Avenue just talking when two blokes blocked our path and tried to pick us up. I took up a fighting stance and said, "You're in our way." They moved. But sexual innuendo is sometimes just a ritual and it makes me very uncomfortable about reacting aggressively.'

Sue is not at all confident that she could defend herself in all situations. 'But I do know that I wouldn't hesitate to kick hard. I used to lose my temper when I fought, charge in, head down, flailing in a classically female way. I never thought of kicking, except with vicious little kicks from behind. Now I would raise my knee and kick hard, straight on – much more effective.'

A real problem is assessing the situation facing you – fast – and deciding whether or not it is a case for self-defence or a sprint out of danger. Margaret abandoned karate when she realized that she couldn't distinguish between real and threatened violence. 'I was in Paris. A guy came up and grabbed my breast. Instantly I slammed him across the face. He would have flattened me with one blow. To fight back inadequately when faced with real violence can be just dangerous. There should be far more discussion amongst women learning karate about the difference between real danger and muscle flexing, swaggering.'

Mary thinks she'd always 'get away as quickly as possible' knowing that she was fit and well shod enough to run very fast. Her response is in line with the central philosophy of karate that you 'gradually rid yourself of your ego, that part of you that makes you want to stand and fight to prove you're stronger than your opponent'.

Barbara, however, did use what she learned in class. Her band was playing in a pub when a man began trying to distract them and make trouble: 'You've got power when you are on stage, all that amplification makes you much stronger than them. The men who hassle us do it because they are angry at seeing women with that sort of power, and this one was angry. He punched a woman in the mouth and then started boasting about it, so I punched him to the ground.'

Are you worried about aggression in yourselves?

We noticed that once women learn to use their bodies as weapons, they respond in ways that could be called male. For example, they assume the dominant role of protector. On late-night tube trains Mary finds herself slipping off her rings when she senses trouble, in anticipation of fighting off attackers for her friends. We see this not as role-reversal but as essential defence. But men – and other women too – would characterize Barbara and Pauline as 'aggressive women'. It's as if a woman can only gain approval by remaining helpless – start looking after yourself and you're an aggressive woman. Inevitably, fear of being labelled aggressive makes women hesitant to take up karate.

What does it mean to you to be fit and strong?

When Mary began to get fit she gave up smoking and started to eat sensitively. Looking back on how she used to treat her body she feels it was almost masochistic: 'Today I feel I am indulging myself in a way I really need to be indulged when I do karate exercises.'

As we talked to the women, we began to see that getting strong has radically changed how they feel about themselves, greatly increasing their self-assurance. However, when we visited classes and women said to us, 'OK, try and move my arm,' holding out a rock-hard limb, our envy was mixed with disquiet. Were women going to become as anxious and obsessive about developing their muscles to protect themselves as they had been about keeping their figures to obtain a protector? Would they adopt typical male vanity about rippling muscles and superior strength?

But we realized that learning karate doesn't build a Charlotte Atlas physique, it strengthens the muscles you have. Most of the women we saw were lithe, and some said with pleasure that karate had fined them down. And anyway, women don't get strong in order to be one up on other people, but for practical purposes and to deal with their fears.

We began to see that we were ambivalent because we still found it difficult to believe that our bodies, which always seemed to invite trouble, could protect us. We slowly understood that karate breaks down the division between body and mind. As Maggie Lomax writes: 'Karate gives you a positive attitude towards your body as something to use *with* your mind.'

We asked the women whether they worried about displaying and experiencing anger and aggression. One or two said that it had taken them at least a year before they could actually fight and even then they had immense inhibitions at sparring with other women in case they hurt them.

But the point about karate is that it both releases and focuses anger and energy. Mary described how before karate she rarely directed her anger at the cause of her fury: 'If someone irritated me I'd take it out on everyone else – often quite unaware of what I was doing. Now I recognize my anger and concentrate it.'

Barbara agrees, saying that since learning karate she has actually fought less. 'Karate makes you feel confident you can deal with a violent situation without becoming aggressive. The emotions don't come into karate; it's like mathematics. When you fight you work out clinically the best way to immobilize your opponent.'

Once women start externalizing and focusing their anger, their fantasies change. 'It's good to imagine what you'd do in a fight,' commented one woman who fantasizes about defending herself instead of being injured or raped. But for women who've always seen themselves as receptive and generous, this can be disturbing. 'It's horrible to be confronted with what feels like sadism in yourself,' says Margaret. 'Women doing karate really need to do consciousness raising on the existence and implication of such fantasies – at least then they'd know they weren't alone.'

But if women fight back will violence escalate? It's hard to generalize but a doctor writing in the *Medical News* tells a story which shows that effective self-defence can reduced violence. He prescribed self-defence for battered women who came to him for tranquillizers. Far from escalating domestic violence, the 'bewildered' husbands never bashed their wives again.

SR.55, February 1977

11 STATE

Ideas about a woman's place in the world are not merely outdated prejudices and fancies lurking in the minds of individuals. They are enshrined in Acts of Parliament, the actions of local government, in welfare legislation and they are enforced through the courts, the police, the army. Women's domestic and subordinate role in the family is clearly assigned by the mass of systems that make up the state.

The development of the British welfare state shows this clearly. National Insurance benefits (for which all who work pay) and Supplementary Benefit, the safety-net system for those whose needs are not met by a wage, accrue to the man as head of the family. A married woman cannot claim supplementary benefit in her own right since she is expected to be supported by her husband. Where there is no 'proper' family the woman is penalized by benefit geared to subsistence level and by humiliating pressures, as in the case of Carol Geddings, reported in *Spare Rib* No. 73, who was divorced from her husband and had her benefit cut off 'because her husband was visiting the house – because he had legal access to the children!' The cohabitation rule assumes that a woman who has a sexual relationship with a man is his financial dependant and is therefore not allowed benefit.

This state of affairs is not static and has been challenged repeatedly throughout the seventies. The state branches into so many areas which affect women, either through public financing or through the law, that women have come into political confrontation with its processes. Some confrontations have been a direct result of the women's movement, like the refuges which establish a centre for women in the community and point to the lack of adequate protection for women under the law. Some engage women as consumers, such as the protests over withdrawing free school milk, or in direct action, as in the housing movement in which unsupported mothers or women living in collectives squat empty houses. Women have been especially involved in the mushrooming of Claimants' Unions, since three out of five

claimants are women. Women social workers have helped to pinpoint
the inconsistency of state policy which views the family as 'natural'
and eternal and, at the same time, needing to be fostered and
encouraged to stop it disintegrating. They have questioned their own
role in obscuring the stop-gap role of welfare where, in Jo Bock's
words, 'Living conditions, financial and employment problems were
regarded as excuses rather than explanations for "problem" families'
(an early *SR*).

In other countries where the patriarchal family holds sway through
religious institutions which are more intertwined in government and
the state judiciary, feminist campaigns have often centred on sexuality
or rights in matrimony. The Italian divorce referendum in 1974 raised
the whole question of the structure of the state and its links with the
power of the Church. An act to legalize abortion brought 50,000
women marching through Rome in 1976, while the Catholic Church
threatened to excommunicate anyone from social worker to doctor
who helped in an abortion after it was legalized in 1978. Public
demonstration has often been crucial, as in the case of Maria Benito in
Spain, who was saved from five years jail and a £450 fine for adultery
(*SR.54*). By 1978 adultery had moved out of the Spanish criminal
law bracket and into civil law, along with women's right to divorce,
contraception and abortion, thus loosening the feudal hold of men
over women which had been legally entrenched in the Franco regime
and upheld by the religious moral code.

In liberation wars, either against an imperialist power or a
repressive national government, women's militance is often inspired
by their role in the family. In Chile, women relatives of 'disappeared'
prisoners formed an alliance after 1974 and, in this case, with the help
of the Catholic Church, focused protest against the military
dictatorship. Similarly the patchwork protest pictures made by
women in the shanty towns around Santiago illustrate the vitality of
kinship and community in sustaining political resistance. Women have
been in the forefront in movements arising out of civil rights, as in
Ireland or the Black movement in the United States in the sixties, yet
their political role is often trivialized. National liberation movements
have also intensified conflict over women's traditional role. In *Spare
Rib* No. 66 Rosemary Sayigh described how the Palestinian concepts
of male honour and the protection of women were challenged by
young women 'undertaking direct political action, leading in some
cases to imprisonment, torture, rape and death'.

Netherley United

MARIA O'REILLY

The government has just spent four years and two million pounds on a
report which 'reveals' that inner areas of Liverpool are poverty-stricken
and deprived, and that the slum clearance programmes of the past were
'a brutal uprooting of people and communities'. Defensively, councillors
call for a Dunkirk spirit – and continue to cut back on housing. Only
thirty-seven new council houses were built in Liverpool in 1976, though
there are thousands homeless.

Netherley, a huge council estate on the southern edge of Liverpool,
was part of those slum clearance programmes. 22,000 people live there,
half in flats, half in houses. 'It's Colditz or the concrete jungle,' says
Dot, a flat-dweller. 'It is. I don't know how they could put people in
here to live. The woman who designed them is supposed to have got a
medal. I bet she wouldn't live in them rent free.'

The design is bad, the building, the drainage. So there's a high inci-
dence of diarrhoea and dysentery on the estate, and mental-illness figures
are very high, especially among housewives and mothers. This sub-stan-
dard property is let to what the council consider sub-standard people –
the homeless, social services cases, people with no bargaining power. At
least half of the men are unemployed. There are many single mothers
and twice the city norm of pre-school children – with very few facilities
for them.

. . . I suppose it would only be fair to start off by describing myself
in some loose terms.

I'm a housewife with three kids. I'm twenty-eight and live with my
husband. I'm also tall, thin, part-time barmaid, with the sort of teeth a
dentist would be sued for insuring. I'm basically optimistic, a terrible
gabber. Oh and I'm a woman, making a valiant attempt to write this article
for the fourth time. I've decided before I give up totally I'll try questioning
and answering myself, with fingers crossed. I hope I don't develop
schizophrenia because the odd valium I take won't cure that. Here goes:

When did you first get involved in tenants' work, Maria O'Reilly?
Well, it all started in 1973 after a near fatal accident in the block of
flats where I live.

These flats are an overspill development – huge uniform lines of
flats and houses, a concrete city, city being a poor word really because
it implies some kind of facilities. But facilities here are non-existent. It
wasn't till two years after the first houses were opened that any shops

were built – there was only a mobile one. And you still have to go 1½ miles by bus to do any real shopping. In most cases the accommodation is unsuitable. The landings are draughty, offering little opportunity for socializing. The overall emotion here is usually isolation and despair, closely followed by apathy.

After I'd lived in the flats for a few months it became obvious that the council's policy was one of total indifference. Lifts are constantly broken down. Structural defects are apparent. The leaking roofs for example make your home life intolerable.

Christine Roche, *SR.28*, October 1974

Much of our community comes from slum clearance areas, friendly communities where people had their own front doors, with more space for the kids to play out. Life in the flats for those with kids was totally alien and the kids' response to their environment is graffiti and vandalism.

All the feelings of discontent came to a head in the demonstrations which followed the child's accident. An ambitious toddler had climbed the three foot six balcony to have a peek at the world below, but leant too far out. The housing department were reluctant to rehouse his family, reluctant to set a precedent, a precedent in humanity. It was only because we demonstrated and began to organize ourselves, that anything happened.

I got involved because I wondered how many would be interested in improving things by forming an Action Group, instead of grumbling in groups on the way to the shops or the rent office. The response was encouraging – over 100 came to the first meetings, over 300 of us blocked off the roads. We wanted to organize around housing allocations, repairs and the general conditions on the estate. The system by which people are allocated new housing had not been reviewed for ten years. It's assessed on points -- supposedly based on living circumstances – not on individual needs. One way of getting out of the Netherley flats is to have a medical certificate. But as a doctor here said, you need to have no legs and no head to get a house in Netherley if you're a flat-dweller!

But how were we to get the City Council to take notice of our demands?
We decided on a demonstration to the town hall with the total conviction in our hearts that the Lord Mayor would sort out the City Housing Department for us (he left by the back door when he heard we were in the foyer!). We presented a petition to his secretary who very efficiently steered us to the door. We then decided to march to the Housing Office. It was teeming down and we all got soaked.

Next we took over the Housing Information Office and refused to leave. The best aspect of the whole thing was that all the mothers and kids who were down there that day were in the same boat, all wanting to be rehoused . . . but their main concern was for the woman whose kid had been hurt. They wanted her and her kids to get rehoused. It was a tremendous show of human concern, considering the difficulties all these mothers had and the premium on rehousing.

We managed to get a list of our complaints to the District Housing Manager, trusting him to deal with them. We heard nothing. So we decided to block the main road in Netherley. This was a strategic move as it is the main road to Widness and very busy at peak hours. It was a frightening step to take. We realized we would upset a lot of motorists, besides – and most seriously – the local police. Ironically they turned into our most lenient allies. They dealt with us with an expertise lacking in the housing department, and asked what our demands were. By now I'd realized it was best to climb to the top of the ladder, though harder. We asked for a meeting with the Director of Housing. With the help of the police this was promptly arranged.

Two of us were chosen to represent our case to him, but we also needed an official name. We called ourselves the Netherley Flatdwellers Action Group. We set off apprehensively for our destination. The office was impressive enough. There were eight of them and three of us, including the mother of the child who was injured. I had to take my baby with me and they were quite considerate, even giving her some milk for her bottle.

What they thought of us I don't know. I secretly quaked in my shoes. But we were convinced we had right on our side. A local newspaper had printed a satirical article I had written about the flats, which helped us a lot since it was an obvious embarrassment to the housing officials. When we'd presented our case, a list of complaints and a threat to occupy the office until the mother was transferred, they relented. She was given a place, and an agreement was made that officers from the different departments concerned would walk around the estate to check our more general complaints about conditions. This was progress. We had shown we were concerned about our environment and were beginning to get organized. We were determined that our protests should result in concrete benefits for everyone on the estate.

They then set up a Liaison Committee with various officials and ourselves on it. Attending these meetings was a trial in itself since they were on *their* ground – in the city hall with its endless meeting rooms, all huge and intimidating. To me it was another world. Armed only with a Woollies notebook, a list of complaints, packets of cigarettes and a brazenness begotten by fear, I confronted the officers as the meeting progressed, feeling an undercurrent of hostility from them. After over a year of attending these meetings I realized why. To them I was an unpolished opponent, totally ignorant of procedure, with no knowledge of building, planning and allocation, a council tenant and *most of all a woman* amongst a group of men. What a cheek I appeared to have telling them where they had gone wrong. They with their huge salaries and diplomas and years of 'experience', some having worked the whole of my lifetime in their particular field. No wonder they were patronizing and refused to understand any points I made. And they didn't like it when I told them the only way they could understand just how bad Netherley was would be by living there themselves.

We made some progress and won some small victories. Next we wanted to change the allocations procedure, and decided to prepare the case on behalf of *all* flat-dwellers with families, not just those in

Netherley. So we went round conducting surveys, collecting cuttings from newspapers. I read all I could get my hands on about housing. Finally, in 1975, we prepared a report and sent a copy to our MP with the hope that the Minister of Housing might read it.

(In November 1976 the council did eventually pass new allocations proposals though they don't go far enough – they won't help people in ground-floor flats [like myself] or one-parent families. We've drafted our own suggestions for 'points' – we say people who spend two years in the flats should be automatically rehoused.)

Meanwhile things had begun to move. The council agreed to move out families with three children and those with children of opposite sexes, because they need more bedrooms. We felt elated, but it wasn't enough – *any* child is in danger in the flats. Slowly the decanting began, but at present it's virtually at a standstill because of the cuts. Also the city council have decided to build all new council houses for sale not for rent, and this is a city where there's not enough housing to go round as it is.

The past years of fighting round housing have been fascinating. I have faced male chauvinism I failed to see existed before. As a representative of the other women I always tried to present our case forcefully. The councillors had their salaries to rely on; I only had the other women's trust. Sometimes our faith failed us. Four years is a long time when progress is slow. An opponent once said to me, 'You never give up do you?' Well we haven't, though we're not naive enough to think that the fight is over. We've been offered a tenants' co-operative which we think is a form of buck-passing. We wouldn't be allowed to use the rents for house building and would inherit the mess of bad planning. In fact we'd just be unpaid rent collectors and eviction squads for all the real managing of the estate we'd be allowed to do.

One of the difficulties, and one of the strengths, of our campaign is that we are nearly all women with kids. Taking the kids on demos and to meetings was a drawback when you never knew how long you'd be out. We tried to get round this by organizing babysitting rotas. This wasn't really satisfactory because the women who had to mind the kids in their homes, no matter how earnestly they believed in the cause, were dampened in their enthusiasm by hordes of toddlers clambering all over the furniture. With no community centre at that time there was no alternative, and we also had to organize the meetings in our own homes. We never minded this as it gave more women with kids a chance to discuss their problems and come out of their isolation, drawing strength from one another. Some mothers were keen but didn't think it was quite nice to go on demonstrations, so they helped with the propaganda work. You see, we didn't have any money so it was hard to produce leaflets; so news of the time and place of meetings had to go by word of mouth.

We did paste posters up by the lifts. They often got torn down. We thought the council employed special leaflet-tearer-downers! They certainly spied on us to see how many turned up to the meetings.

I've known our group to club together out of their own pockets to stop gas being turned off and people being evicted, sometimes out of their own rent money, getting into arrears themselves. We contacted all the major companies that directly affect our lives – electricity, gas – and we fought them all.

We have met interesting people over these years, people we wouldn't have met otherwise, people with strange ideals none of us were used to. We learned to accept people as they really were, not by what they had or whether they were dirty or poor. We came to understand politics, usually thought of as a man's world, and expected more of ourselves – knew more about what we could and couldn't do for ourselves. People now call us women's libbers. I never realized but we must have become just that, though we're not all aware of it. Of course some of the men around regard us suspiciously and think that we hold ritual bra-burning sessions to which we might invite their wives.

Then there are the vultures, those who consider us a bit crackers, the 'you'll never get anywhere' brigade, who sit back and reap the benefits of our efforts. There are those who don't care for us and are rude about us until they have a problem themselves. We don't care though, it's nice to think that despite what they say they trust us enough to ask for our help when they need it. If we can give it we will, and we're not resentful of the 'vultures'.

One of the things that became apparent over the years was the isolation people felt. They always compared their lives and homes to the old days, yearning after the old community. But why wouldn't people do anything? Why all the apathy? It was obvious that without a fight things would get worse. We had managed to confront some of the council's apathy and indifference, but you can't demonstrate against your own kind.

I sensed they felt Netherley didn't really belong to them. True, it doesn't, but while we live here we belong to it. You can't expect people to fight for or demand something they don't even feel exists. That's why we organized the Carnival.

What started out as an idea snowballed from a pathetic beginning to a week-long event involving thousands of people. Flat-dwellers, house-dwellers, people who'd been poles apart in understanding one another's problems, mixed freely in one week of fun and activity. At the first meeting three of us stood for two hours waiting for someone else to turn up. We were just about to go when three girls came. That saved the Carnival.

The idea caught on and soon the meetings were attracting sixty people at a time. Street committees were organized, street parties, day events. The estate was decorated like a May horse. One wholesaler said he'd never heard of Netherley until we started coming in for the crêpe paper! On the parade that preceded the Carnival over 4,000 mums and dads, kids, grannies, aunties and uncles turned out in fancy dress. They were marching round the corner twenty deep and that's when we realized we'd won. Every organization on the estate was involved. Schools, the community centre, the judo club. It must have been something people were waiting for and waiting to do or it wouldn't have come off. We found organizers and people with skills they never knew they had. We couldn't solve everyone's problems, people with little or no money or whatever, but we hoped people would have a happy week, something to smoothe over their wounds, a week when they'd say bugger the problems, bugger the rent and spend it on themselves and the kids having a good time.

After the Carnival a big lorry driver came into the pub for a pint. He didn't know me but had seen something about me in the local paper. He simply said, 'Well, when are we going to start organizing next year's Carnival?' Then I realized we had reached our goal. Unity. People had become Netherleyites. They had stopped saying 'When are *you* going to . . .'

I was at home the night the Carnival ended, exhausted, wondering if it had all been worth it. An old lady knocked on the door – you see her often on the estate, she's always asking for ciggies; she and her husband look really down and out. What she said to me convinced me more than anything else that we'd succeeded. In stilted speech she asked me to thank all the people of Netherley for the lovely week they'd had. 'Everyone has been so friendly and happy,' she said, 'and my husband says Netherley isn't such a bad place to live after all.'

SR.56, March 1977

Dependence and a New Political Consciousness

KATHERINE GIEVE

In spring this year at the Oxford Women and Socialism Conference on the Demands of the Women's Movement a new demand was put forward. It was proposed that we should demand an end to women's position as dependent persons, and that this should be brought forward for adoption at the national conference in Edinburgh at the end of June. A group of us in Oxford have been working on a paper for the conference and felt that people who couldn't go to Edinburgh, or who are not actively involved in the movement, should know something of the proposal.

A married woman is a dependant of her husband, much in the way his children are. This dependence is expressed in numerous different rules and regulations. It is one of the first principles of social welfare legislations, it affects pensions, taxes, student grants, unemployment, sickness, and supplement benefits; in terms of common practice though not of laws, it affects business negotiations such as HP and mortgages.

Nor does it confine itself to married women, the principle is clearly shown in a rule which relates particularly to unmarried women: the cohabitation rule. When a woman lives with a man, they are treated as man and wife, and the woman loses her right to claim supplementary benefit as a single person. The man she lives with has an obligation to support her, she becomes a dependent person whether she likes it or not.

The demand is not intended to be merely a legal one. We want to challenge the idea of dependence as well as the laws. For this reason we would like to group the campaigns together under one general demand rather than fighting separately on each question. The new demand would embody important ideas not expressed in the four demands as they stand. Though these demands are concerned with ways in which women can gain control over their lives, and so become independent, they do not directly attack the presumption of women as dependent persons, nor do they attack the crucial role of the state in creating and re-creating this dependence.

Thus the new demand would represent an important long-term goal. From it would flow a variety of different campaigns centred around women's immediate needs. There campaigns need by no means all involve parliamentary lobbying, but could be conducted in various

Posy Simmonds, *SR.6*, December 1972

ways: women at work could fight for better pensions; discriminating
business practice could be exposed in local areas; women could add
their active support to the Claimants' Union campaign against the
cohabitation rule, perhaps by supporting individual women who are
trying to make claims. These campaigns should appeal to diverse
groups of women, and might have the advantage of introducing into
the movement more women who are angry about particular practical
questions.

There will certainly be problems in making our demands. One general one emerged from our discussions: that of how to break the
vicious circle of dependence. Women are treated as being dependent
on men; because of this they do not seek equal pay, unemployment
benefits, pensions, etc. It is therefore difficult for them to be independent, hence they need the benefits of their position – for example, the
right of a woman to get support from her husband. We are faced with
the question of how far we should try to preserve these benefits, or
how far we can preserve them, while fighting dependency. This remains a problem even though many women do not benefit at the
moment anyway. There does not seem to be a general solution, and we
will have to work out the answers in the context of particular campaigns.

It is clear that we will not succeed in changing the attitudes of men

towards women, nor women to themselves, just by changing the laws.
But the laws do contribute to maintaining women's inferior position,
and we hope that, by working to change them, women's material conditions will be improved, and that the campaigns will give rise to a new
political consciousness in thinking about the state and the family.

SR.25, July 1974

Mice in Manchester

ROSE ADES AND ELEANOR STEPHENS

The Equal Opportunities Commission (EOC) was set up in 1975
under the Sex Discrimination Act (SDA) as a testament to the
Labour Party's continuing concern about the position of women. Its
overall brief was to abolish discrimination against women and to promote equality. For a kick off, the government gave them a budget of
over a million pounds for the first year (which they didn't manage to
spend), three floors of a shiny new office block in Manchester and a
staff of about a hundred seconded civil servants. They're headed by
fifteen commissioners appointed by the Home Secretary who meet
once a month to make all policy decisions.

While not expecting revolutionary action from a government body,
and accepting its own definition of itself as a 'middle-aged
Establishment pressure group', we did expect to see some results after
a year and a half. The EOC does, after all, have formal powers of
investigation backed up by legal sanctions, no shortage of things crying
out to be investigated and, unlike women's liberation groups, easy
access to government and the power to ai. nd legislation. Yet they've
made very little impact: as one feminist, he self involved for years in
bureaucratic struggles, put it, 'They crept off like mice to Manchester
and we've hardly heard a squeak out of them since.' Why not?

The Chairman (she insists on this title) is Betty Lockwood, appointed to the Commission in return for nearly thirty years of service
to the Labour Party, the last eight as Chief Women's Officer. Similarly
experienced in party politics, and also a committee woman, is her
deputy Lady Howe, married to the Shadow Chancellor. This political
balancing act is unique among statutory bodies – maybe they'd have to
change places under a Tory government! Certainly it's a factor in the
Commission's obvious difficulties in reaching decisions, taking actions
and making swift public statements on relevant issues. (Lockwood and
Howe are the EOC's only public voices.)

Three of the commissioners are nominated by the TUC and three by the CBI. They tend to act as a block to maintain the status quo and guard their own territory of traditional bargaining. Do they see themselves as accountable to the bodies they represent or to the Commission? These roles often conflict and neither of the TUC women, Ethel Chipchase and Marie Patterson, are known to represent women except in a token way.

The other 'independent' commissioners were chosen from the official civil service lists of The Great and The Good (these lists exist!) and they represent, among others, Education, Scotland, Wales and the Law. As far as we could discover none had been at all involved in pushing the anti-discrimination laws through or in any other women's rights groups – though one had written speeches for Roy Jenkins, the then Home Secretary. Several women's groups and agencies like the National Council of Civil Liberties (NCCL) had put forward well-qualified feminist candidates but none were chosen, although similar bodies like the Consumer Council do have 'interest groups' represented on them. At the moment there is a vacancy to be filled, but there's no way of finding out on what grounds the Home Office will make the appointment. Last week this question was asked in the House of Commons and the answer was a predictable example of parliamentary evasion.

Among the commissioners only Caroline Woodroffe, head of Brook Advisory Centres, a family planning agency, has any obvious professional involvement with women and, from talking to her, some sympathetic awareness of their needs. On the whole they are competent professionals of the 'I did it myself and so can you' school. Two women involved in campaigning for the legislation told us: 'It was such a shock when we saw who they'd appointed as commissioners. We knew then that the whole thing was going to be a farce. We had never really discussed the role of the Commission but we knew it could only be as good as the people on it. We needed people committed to women with the will to fight for changes.'

So what has the EOC been doing? Despite their full co-operation we found this hard to discover: when we asked commissioners and staff members what they had been working on and what were their immediate priorities, we were nearly always referred back to the EOC's *strategic role* (a phrase used again and again in press releases) and the importance of doing nothing which would jeopardize long-term strategy. What is this strategy? This, we were told, would have to wait upon their present efforts to discover the extent of the problem. As Betty Lockwood told us: 'We haven't yet defined what we're going to have to look at.' Were we being impatient or impertinent to expect more than this after a year and a half and a million pounds?

The EOC has wide powers to investigate discrimination and promote equality. Under the SDA it has to work in three main areas: Goods, Facilities and Services; Employment; and Education. As well as making sure that everyone is aware of her rights and his obligations (!) it has a duty to see whether these laws are strong enough, to suggest improvement and to look at areas like taxation and social security not covered by the act.

So what happens when evidence of discrimination is brought to the EOC's attention? (In general it doesn't go out to find it.) Believing that it's basically in everyone's interests not to discriminate against women, the EOC likes to use Softly Softly methods of persuasion. Betty Lockwood and most of the Commission seem genuinely to believe that no one really benefits from the exploitation of women – they only need to be shown that discrimination is bad for business or the labour movement, and then they'll automatically shape up: 'If we're going to succeed in any area we've got to have the goodwill and co-operation of *all* who are involved; there's no point our being involved in a head-on clash.' This political viewpoint is at the root of their failure to recognize the vested interests involved in keeping things the way they are and that, to have any effect at all, they'll have to take a much stronger stand. We looked at how they've approached the three main areas.

Their preference for working behind the scenes with informal fix-it-up tactics ('We have to see what the other chap's afraid of,' we were told) has had some success in consumer service areas like hire purchase and credit – particularly with trade associations and central management whose business depends on good public relations. But even if, after letters, phone calls or visits, Head Office agrees to co-operate, local branches are not obliged to stop discriminating unless someone takes them to the county court. So far only five cases have been brought under this section of the SDA and three of these are still waiting.

The county-court system costs money and is so unwieldy that you'll almost certainly have to stay angry about being refused a pint, or a cup of coffee after ten at night, for at least a year! But until a case is won no legal precedent can be set, so the EOC are keen to support women in bringing cases, especially since at the moment they won't issue non-discrimination notices on their own initiative. Its attempts to persuade Local Authorities to stop discriminating against women on housing matters have been almost entirely ignored.

In education the emphasis has also been on high-level consultation but it's even harder here to see any concrete results. We do know they took the initiative in getting quotas abolished, like the Open University quotas, some of which had had the effect of positively discriminating in favour of women. As for the Tameside investigation into the selection of grammar school places, it's generally agreed to be a complete red herring.

Some interest was expressed in setting up a working party to examine sex stereotypes in school textbooks, but they've already made it clear that they wouldn't dream of using any legal pressure to change it – 'This would be censorship,' said Eileen Byrne. They aren't even planning to issue guidelines to publishers, but they have given a little money to Spare Rib and Virago to produce educational materials. Some staff members are very keen to see the E O C take action on day care and a working party has just been set up to look into this. We certainly hope they'll make some headway, and not accept the Cuts as an excuse for government inaction.

Everyone we spoke with admitted that the employment section has been fraught with difficulties – 'A complete non-starter,' said one staff member – and several new staff, including the head of department, have just begun work. Given the crucial importance of this area for women – 'This is our main thrust,' said Betty Lockwood – their almost total inactivity here beyond answering enquiries is pathetic. Not only have the Cuts and unemployment hit women hardest but the difference between men and women's average hourly earnings has actually increased in the past two years.

We were told by the legal officer, Jennifer Corcoran, who monitors all the tribunal results on equal pay, that 'some companies have ten cases clocked up against them, but we were hesitant to recommend that the employment section responded to this as we felt it was more important that they should work out their own emphasis and areas to work on.' This may be sensible in theory but in fact they still haven't decided what these areas are. Until February 13 this year they hadn't used their powers of formal investigation at all, and they only started to investigate Electrolux after a pep talk from the Home Secretary and a specific request from Justice Phillips, president of the Employment Appeals Tribunal. This investigation is still in progress and they have no idea when it will be completed.

Legally the E O C can conduct a formal investigation wherever discrimination is suspected (it's hard to think of anywhere this would be inappropriate!) and if this results in issuing a non-discrimination notice with legal sanctions, the offender(s) have to change their ways whatever the cost or they can go to prison. This would give us something comparable to America's very powerful 'class action suit' whereby a group can take a case – though with British laws, we still couldn't get such huge sums in compensation. So what stops the E O C using this, their most powerful weapon? Apart from their fear of combat and terror of making themselves unpopular, they treat formal investigations as mammoth two-year projects only to be used with extreme caution as a last resort. There's no reason why this should be: given that things are getting worse all the time for women, investigations should be swift and sharp. It's not essential to have a complete dossier, with every extenuating circumstance, before issuing a non-discrimination notice. If the E O C was known to move quickly, this could make them a force to be reckoned with, rather than weakening their behind-the-scenes bargaining position as they fear.

As it is, their main achievement has been to post a letter to 500 employers asking them about their policies and practices for promoting equal opportunities. No one has to answer it (several companies have told them to get lost) and they are not going to be investigated further. There is no way for the E O C to know whether the versions they receive from the employers tally with what the workers would say, if asked, unless someone happens to make a complaint or goes on strike for equal pay! In fact the E O C sent one of these November letters to the Laird Portch company in East Kilbride, where the women have recently come out on strike for Equal Pay. There are plans to use the answers to these letters as the basis for their long-awaited guidelines of best employment practices. Unlike the statutory code they originally planned, it has no legal force but can be more outspoken. As the E O C has so far taken little initiative itself in the area of employment, everything depends upon cases being brought to tribunals by individuals with the help of their unions, the N C C L or the E O C.

Betty Lockwood has tried to influence the composition of the industrial tribunals and offered training for their members, but the Chairman of the Council of Industrial Tribunals has turned her down: after all Equal Pay cases are only 6 per cent of the total. But it's extraordinary that the E O C has made no public statements criticizing these decisions, and remained silent over the five-month Trico strike. It's very fortunate for women that Justice Phillips, head of the Appeals Tribunals and an expert in Inland Revenue law, has chosen to base his judgements on the spirit of the law. So the appeals results are a great improvement.

The Commission does claim considerable influence at government level, which lies beyond the scope of most women's groups. They've submitted evidence to the Department of Education on student grants, and recently to the Royal Commission on Distribution of Wealth, showing both how women suffer economically from their dual role and the hidden poverty of married women. They also sent a deputation to the Chancellor attacking the sexist basis of personal taxation.

Two reports have just been published evaluating the Manpower Services Commission (MSC) and the Job Creation Programmes. Since the 16–19 age group is one of the EOC's stated priority target areas, we expected to see signs of their influence here. Betty Lockwood told us: 'We have a considerable influence in the MSC and quite frankly I would like to establish a real power base there.' The House and Commons Expenditure Committee report showed that three quarters of the jobs go to boys, with girls still channelled into traditional slots like typing and laundry work. It pointed out that some of this can be explained by the fact that the Area Organizers, nominated by the TUC and CBI, comprise two women and sixty-five men. It deplores the discriminatory practices of these schemes and makes proposals for improving them. If the MSC *is* an area of EOC influence, perhaps the time has come to start using this influence.

Their role in influencing government and exerting pressure from the top down was often emphasized as the main reason for their lack of militancy, their desire not to be identified with 'irresponsible elements' and their fear of being partisan. ('We might gladden the hearts of thousands of women, but this could lead to a backlash,' we were told.) So far, there's little evidence that this sacrifice has been worthwhile.

While the EOC's existence has had some consciousness-raising effect on women's expectations and is an acknowledgement of the extent of the discrimination that needs to be tackled, it had no publicity campaign in 1976. Because of confusion over its desired public image, its first Press Officer, Sandra Oliver, who lasted six months, wasn't allowed to spend any of her budget. Finally in February this year there was a one-day national press campaign costing £56,000 to advertise some of the smiling faces at the EOC. They now agree that this wasn't the right emphasis, and that subsequent campaigns will have a wider perspective. We're not quite sure what this will be: 'The Commission has accepted at a recent meeting that the image that the Commission wishes to project will change from time to time. Sometimes it will be low profile, sometimes a persuasive one and sometimes a much sharper one,' was Betty Lockwood's statement when we asked her about this.

Obviously the EOC's most effective publicity comes from what it does and its own public statements. While it issues frequent and lengthy press releases, usually based on speeches by Lockwood and

Howe, these are rarely taken up because they're not newsworthy. (On two issues where the EOC's voice might have had some impact – Child Benefits and the Benyon Bill – they said nothing.) The Press Officer's job is not a happy one.

Many of the problems and criticisms we've raised have been put down to teething problems and of course some are to be expected in any organization. But despite all the talk of new initiatives and improved working relationships between staff and commissioners, there's little evidence of any real change in attitude or a greater understanding of the power struggle involved. It's true that some of the staff are increasingly committed to what they're trying to do but this only adds to their frustration when so much of their ideas and work is ignored or blocked at the top.

Even more depressing, the EOC may actually be doing more harm than good. Without the courage and the will to battle for changes, it takes the heat off other institutions and serves to keep people quiet and things as they are. We certainly hope that now its teething problems are over things will change dramatically. Otherwise its real problem can only be the fear of showing any teeth at all.

SR.60, July 1977

Christine Roche, *SR.86*, September 1979

In on the Act

JILL NICHOLLS AND RUTH WALLSGROVE

An appeal tribunal has said that cases of dismissal for pregnancy cannot be heard under the Sex Discrimination Act – because there is no possible comparison with a man. They ruled that Kim Turley was not dismissed from Allders Department Store because she was a woman, but because she was pregnant! She had no case under the Employment Protection Act either, because she'd been working there less than a year.

On the other hand, a contract excluding illnesses connected with pregnancy from provision for sick pay has been found unlawful under the Equal Pay Act.

Three women clerical workers at Sim-Chem Ltd are appealing to the House of Lords about a job evaluation scheme. They are claiming that they should get equal pay backdated to the day when their jobs were rated equivalent to men's. At the time of the evaluation, there was a voluntary – not statutory – pay policy in Britain, and the company did not implement the scheme because the necessary salary increases would have been in breach of the pay code . . . Even more pathetic than their excuse is that the lower courts have ruled that the women are *not* entitled to back pay.

Lord Denning has ruled that it is not unlawful for a company to select women's jobs for redundancy if it can show that it is in those jobs that work is diminishing. But of course service and unskilled jobs are usually thought to be less 'important' than skilled or heavy manual jobs which, not by accident, are seen as men's work.

The Equal Opportunities Commission has won its first case against advertising that discriminates against women. Trago Mills had placed eight unlawful ads in West Country newspapers. They were trying to claim exemption from the Act because their staff have the legal status of being 'self-employed'. Another ridiculous excuse. (NB Only the EOC can take discriminatory advertisers to court.)

June Quinn has lost her case under the SDA against a Williams Furniture store. They refused her credit facilities unless her husband acted as a guarantor – even though they told her that her husband would not have needed a guarantor if *he'd* applied for credit. A county court judge ruled that she was discriminated against not because she was a woman, but because she had a low-paid job. Pretty much the same difference! Her appeal will be important as this could be a large loophole in the Act.

The EOC backed all these cases.

SR.96, July 1980

Pay Figures Fall

JILL NICHOLLS

Women's pay is falling again in relation to men's, and we are suffering more from unemployment, says the Equal Opportunities Commisssion's fourth annual report, a much stroppier document than they usually produce.

This growth of unemployment amongst women, combined with the dramatic increase in the rate of inflation has, in our view, contributed to a growing sense of uncertainty and insecurity among women. Taken together with the view, increasingly openly expressed, that the place of women is in the home, this has had the effect at once of encouraging an inclination to shelve equal opportunities policies as a luxury the nation cannot afford, and to increase the sense of frustration and resentment amongst many women.

The report also complains of the demoralizing effect on people of having an EOC 'set up to promote the principle of non-discrimination when other government policies appear to run contrary to that principle' – referring in particular to government proposals on immigration and maternity leave.

The widening gap between men's and women's earnings in the last year indicates, they say, the failure of the Equal Pay Act. The situation won't improve until the Sex Discrimination Act is forcefully implemented. They criticize the constraints of the EPA, 'which insists on the existence of a definite male comparison, does not allow comparisons of equal value in the absence of job evaluation schemes, and does not recognize the concept of indirect discrimination'.

They also acknowledge that the EPA is useless for women 'segregated in jobs traditionally performed by women and where there are no men engaged on like work . . . There is no remedy in the EPA for complaints from highly qualified secretaries seeking to compare themselves with more highly paid but unqualified clerical staff.'

SR.98, September 1980

NEWSHORTS EDITORIAL JILL NICHOLLS

All our worst nightmares of what a Tory government could mean seem
to be coming true. Even we had not foreseen that the Tories would cut
social services spending so far that they look likely to become the party
to kill off many old people – providing no help or meals for the homebound, and fewer places in homes. They're considering cutting pocket
money for old people in homes and slackening the fire regulations.
They want to close hostels for the mentally handicapped, hand hospitals over to voluntary organizations, charge for the use of public
libraries ... the government is cutting £300 million nationally this
year. For 1980–81 the cut is 7½ per cent.

And how much worse it is to know that a woman is presiding over
the carnage. As we predicted, women are bearing the brunt of the cuts:
it is we who have to stay at home to care for the elderly and disabled,
we who have to give up work when nurseries close, or if the school-
day is shortened. The Tories are even considering cutting our right
to maternity leave, not because it costs very much (last year's budget
was underspent by 50 per cent) but because filling jobs on a temporary
basis is inconvenient to employers. Perhaps what they are really
saying is that women shouldn't expect to be able to have children *and*
jobs. The proposed abortion-law changes fit neatly into this scheme
too.

SR.86, September 1979

Harassment at Heathrow

JILL NICHOLLS, ANGELA PHILLIPS AND
RUTH WALLSGROVE

The outcry over the case of the Indian schoolteacher who arrived at
Heathrow as the fiancée of a man living here and was subjected to a
'virginity test' by immigration officials, has forced the Home Secretary
to ban such tests in future. It is not clear though how the government
intends to enforce such a ban, as they claim not even to have known
that the tests were going on. They must either admit that the immigration service is out of their control or accept responsibility for it.

... It's quite outrageous that anyone should have to go through a
medical examination to see if she's lying – in this case pretending to be

a fiancée not a wife. And of course you can't prove virginity by sticking
a finger up a vagina – not every woman has a hymen. And even if you
could, not being a virgin does not mean you are married. The whole
disgusting exercise is an extreme stage in the humiliation and harassment of Black immigrants – like the equally pointless X-ray tests on
children to 'prove' whether they're telling the truth about their age.
This woman says she was stripped, refused a dressing gown and
examined internally by a male doctor, though she asked to see a woman.
She was frightened that if she made a fuss she would be sent back. 'I
have been feeling very bad mentally ever since,' she says. 'I was very
embarrassed and upset. I had never had a gynaecological examination
before.'

A female fiancée has a legal right to come to Britain without an entry
certificate – she gets a three-month visa and if she marries in that time
she gets permission to stay permanently. But wives wanting to join
husbands here have to go through an extremely lengthy clearance procedure in their country of origin. Given the racist assumption that the
worst thing that could happen to Britain is for one more Black person
to get in than absolutely necessary, it becomes natural, as the JCWI
say, 'for an immigration officer to strive to ensure that all his errors
consist in excluding genuine claimants and not in admitting spurious
ones – and to be prepared to go to any lengths to attempt to detect the
latter'.

SR.78, January 1979

Immigration Tests in Britain

JILL NICHOLLS, ANGELA PHILLIPS AND
RUTH WALLSGROVE

The uproar over the harassment and humiliation of Black immigrants
may be dying down in the press, but Black people's organizations are
determined to keep the protests going.

The Asian women's group AWAZ (which means 'voice' in Hindi)
organized a demonstration at Heathrow airport on 10 February, calling for a public inquiry into the workings of the immigration service:
'But there'd be no point in another Select Committee behind closed
doors. What is needed is something completely open to the public, so
that people can understand the *meaning* of these outrages.' It is not just
a question of winning concessions – getting virginity tests or X-ray

tests banned – though these would be important steps. The demonstration also demanded that the ministers and immigration officers responsible be made accountable for their actions, and asked whether the Labour government condoned the present police-state situation where people have to show their passports to get medical treatment, to claim welfare benefits, even to send their children to school . . .

SR.81, April 1979

One Wins, One Loses

PAT FITZSIMONS AND KATH MCKAY

The daily newspapers reported the decision on 30 July to allow Nasira Begum, an Asian woman threatened with deportation because her British husband deserted her, to remain in this country. They failed to report another case being announced on the same day by the adjudicator which did not have such a happy ending. Anwar Ditta, a British-born Asian woman, was refused permission to bring her three children from Pakistan to join her here.

Anwar and her husband entered Britain under the wrong procedure, though both were legally allowed to enter. The Home Office had never previously raised the issue of their entry and does not dispute their right to stay. In his decision, the adjudicator took these irregularities as the sole reason for disbelieving that the children are Anwar's, despite the substantial evidence put before him that they are hers.

Sushuma Lal, Anwar's solicitor at the Manchester Law Centre (which also handled Nasira's case) believes the authorities did not think it wise to refuse both applications, and so chose to allow Nasira to stay as it would have been more difficult to deport her than it is to refuse Anwar's children entry. Sushuma believes the two cases were purposely juxtaposed to soften the blow: Anwar's decision was held up an unusual two and a half months until Nasira's was heard.

Anwar's only recourse is to take an appeal to a tribunal, if she is given leave to do so. But as Sushuma says, that would entail convincing three people instead of just one, and they are all of the same 'persuasion'.

SR.98, September 1980

Inside

MAUREEN REYNOLDS INTERVIEWED BY
ROZSIKA PARKER

Maureen Reynolds was sent to prison for violence. Only 3 per cent of all 'serious offences' committed by women over a year involve violence against others. Like the vast majority, Maureen's 'crime' was unpremeditated and committed in the home under extreme emotional pressure. She should never have been sent to prison. Neither should all the other women prisoners whose 'offences' are reactions to the female role, or ways of dealing with the demands of being a woman in the face of poverty, poor housing and ill health. Most women are sentenced for petty theft (shop lifting to feed and clothe a family), prostitution, or receiving stolen goods (helping and supporting a husband or lover).

Maureen was a battered wife, but in 1968 when she was sentenced, battered wives were still hidden behind their front doors. Would she receive the same sentence today now that the context of her 'crime' is public knowledge? Would she be sentenced at all?

Prison is destructive. Many women find it impossible to cope with the shock of institutional life. Others adapt all too easily, and with their feelings of dependency and inadequacy drastically increased, they become hopelessly institutionalized and incapable of surviving outside.

Prison is supposed to 'encourage them [the inmates] to lead a good and useful life'. Maureen was sent to prison because she once expressed the violence that, until then, she had turned against herself. Yet as the Radical Alternatives to Prison Group points out, 'the very act of shutting people up in a closed institution creates more violence.' Maureen's story speaks for itself.

I was charged with wounding with intent, but there wasn't any intent. It was completely out of my control – I just reacted immediately to the situation. That's what used to bug me in there, thinking about it – I could so easily have been doing life.

My husband was very violent – I was battered stupid for ten years. It got to the stage where there was nowhere I could run to because the police got fed up with me, and my husband would come and smash the windows wherever I stayed – my mother got sick of having her windows smashed. It went on and on and on. I tried to commit suicide twice. Then one day they sent me home from work because I was ill. All I wanted to do was lie down, I went upstairs, walked into the room and he was with this chick on the bed. I didn't have anything against the girl, she was just the latest in a long line, but I went . . . and I just picked up . . . I didn't even know if it was him or her . . . it all seemed to be coming out.

I was on £20 bail for three months, everybody told me that getting £20 bail meant that it wasn't serious, the police said I wouldn't go down because they knew I'd had a lot of aggravation with my husband. Still, I realized I needed a solicitor so I walked along the street near the law courts where there are a lot of solicitors and I went into the first one I came to. I only saw him twice in the three months, and I saw the barrister twenty minutes before I went into court.

Normally if violence, which can attract high penalties, is involved in a case, a solicitor will arrange at least one conference between the barrister and the defendant. It will be particularly important when the defendant's personal history is so relevant. Maureen was on legal aid and payments are not likely to encourage barristers and solicitors to do more work than they might be remunerated for.

Yes, the first time I'd ever set eyes on the barrister was sitting outside the Assizes. I felt so alone and I was terrified. In those days there weren't any women's groups or anything like that, and none of my family were up, they didn't even know about it – I didn't want anyone to know.

You go in and there they are, all in their gowns with the bloody judge sitting up there in his big wig. There was one woman on the jury, *one*. Thinking back, I realize I should have said this, should have done that, but they are throwing questions at you, and you're in that witness box . . .

There is a right of challenge that a barrister can use to have seven members of the jury changed, although they can be replaced only by other potential jurors who have been summoned for service at the same time. 'An inexperienced defendant is at a disadvantage in court even if well educated and articulate, but for those who have little education, who are scared or nervous and unable to express themselves in the kind of language they believe is expected of them in court, the handicap can be crippling, particularly if they wish to deny the offence or plead mitigating circumstances' (Susanne Dell, *Silent In Court – a study of the legal representation of women who went to Holloway*).

I was the only witness for the defence, and the judge threw the police evidence out of court because it was contradictory. First of all this sergeant came on, and he was asked if I'd seemed upset when I was at the police station after it had happened. He replied that I'd been perfectly calm. Of course I'd been in a terrible state, crying and really sort of gone.

And then this other policeman came in and he was terrified, you could see he was awed by the whole thing, he was only young. He was

asked, 'Was she crying? Was she upset?' 'Yes,' he replied. The judge
turned round to the jury and said, 'I want you to ignore the police
evidence, I'm not going to allow it.' But what the sergeant said about
me had already been pretty damaging. He claimed I'd said, 'I did it
'cos she was messing about with my old man.' That's just not something I'd say.

We suggest Emergency Legal Advice Services attached to police stations and
available night and day to people held in custody at the station. (This was
recommended to the Widgery Committee on Legal Aid and rejected.) Advice
centres attached to police stations have been shown to work in Holland. (RAP)

In fact all I could say at the police station after it happened was 'my
little boy', 'my little boy'. Steve was at home on his own, I was
worried he'd wake up and wouldn't find me there in the morning –
he'd been through so much. That's all I kept going on about.

In the court they wanted to discredit me as an honest witness. They
wanted to bring up in court, in front of the jury, in the middle of the
case, that I had had a previous conviction – one for selling drinks
without a licence, and one for being involved in a theft which meant
I'd received something when I was seventeen (a long time ago). So
they sent out the jury while they debated this point, well the jury must
have known that something was going on. The judge then decided to
allow my previous convictions, and the prosecutor tore me to pieces,
'How can a woman who has been involved in all this be an honest
witness' – you know.

On the last day of my trial the judge had me remanded in custody.

Fewer remands in custody will also reduce the number of women and girls
subsequently sentenced to prison as there is strong evidence from this country
and America that apart from any other considerations, the mere fact of being
remanded in custody rather than on bail significantly affects (adversely) both
the finding of guilt and the sentence. (RAP)

I went all the way from Birmingham to Holloway for the night, and
came back next morning shattered – and then back to Holloway again
– I got three years. The judge had made a big statement a few days
before about the rise in violence and the need for law and order. And
anyone who came into his court . . . I only got that judge at the last
minute, it was a switch, just pure luck (or bad luck).

I was taken from Birmingham to Holloway and arrived at reception
with quite a few other women. There you are put into a box, we call
them horse boxes though they are not as big as horse boxes. They each
contain a little seat and if you sit on it there's about a foot between you
and the door and the walls. You strip and put on a dressing gown; the

only thing you are allowed to keep on is your wedding ring, if you've got one, and anything else that won't come off. They couldn't get my bracelets off me. Then you are taken to where they check your clothes in. They make you take the dressing gown off, weigh you and search you all in front of the screws and the prisoners who work in reception.

I was numb, I couldn't believe that it was happening to me. After you are convicted the change in people's attitudes towards you is, well, extraordinary, and suddenly you have no control over anything – they are all in control of you.

After you've had your clothes checked in you're taken back to the boxes where you sit and wait for anything up to four hours to see the doctor. He says, 'Had any serious diseases? Got anything wrong with you? Are you on drugs?' And you say, 'Yea, I'm on this or that', and he writes it down and gives it to you as long as it's not heroin or anything. Then you go to see the nurse, you take off your clothes again and she searches you for crabs, and you're back in your box again till they take you to whatever room you've been assigned to.

I was given a great bundle of blankets to carry with my clothes and everything I'd got. It was like nothing I had ever experienced. It was just like you see in the pictures, all those landings, you know – and the smell. There are all the bogs out on the landings, it's what they call the recess, a row of sluices where you sling your slop – you know, you sling it out in the mornings.

I went to get my jug of water, and that's it – you're just locked in. I couldn't believe that, could you? I thought they must let you out again, for something, a class – but no, it wasn't until 8.00 the next morning. I kept waiting all night. And you hear the voices, all calling to one another from window to window. They scream abuse at the male screws going round with dogs, patrolling the grounds. They must have been really thick, really thick skinned to take that, because I couldn't take all that abuse. But I think they are thick skinned – they stop thinking of you as people. That's the only way they could do it.

The screaming. I couldn't sleep for smashing windows. Every night women slash their arms in the windows, often because their best friend has been moved away from them or because they are awaiting trial and haven't heard from anybody. The windows are often not mended and it's right draughty. You stick your jumper in the holes.

In the morning, on a security wing, first thing you do is empty your pot or bucket, get your water and have a wash. You try to get the tap first because the water is cold by the time the last woman gets there. Then you get your tin tray and your mug, and march downstairs to what they call the 'ones', the 'twos' and the 'threes' – all those landings

– then you get breakfast (sometimes porridge, sometimes cornflakes and occasionally an egg). You take it back upstairs to your cell. After breakfast you go straight to work.

It's the little things that get you down, like not being able to walk through a door and make a cup of tea. And their attitude towards you; you hear them talking about you as if you're not there, 'how to lock *them* in', 'how many have you got out', etc. And the sound of the keys all the time, when I came out I really missed that, you know, because that's what you've lived with. A lot of the screws, the older ones, have got something wrong with their hands, after all those years of having to pull it and turn it, they get arthritis. The keys are on their belts and when they are opening the door it looks as if they are attached to the door. And they sort of swing their keys as they go along. It's weird because prison is their whole life too. After they lock you in, you see their eye at the spy hole. The screw on duty at night has no keys. To get them she has to go the centre and come back with another screw who has the keys after the day screws give them in. If it was a real emergency you'd be dead by the time they reached you.

I lost my appeal, they refused my appeal, and took sixty days waiting time off me as well. It took me nine months before I realized what had happened to me, then I got really depressed. Before that – it is such a funny feeling to explain – it was like a dream really. I knew it was all happening but I just seemed to be going through all the motions and not being there. What did worry me was that for two weeks I didn't know where Steve was, he was eleven at the time. Eventually I stood on the wing and just screamed for the welfare person. They are so overworked – they have to deal with the whole bloody prison.

After six months I was sent to Askam Grange, an open prison which I could not stand. I think it was partly because you could just walk out – the gate was wide open. I couldn't stand the other women there either. Most of them are stars – first time in nick – they just sit around – they're really sort of brainwashed. They are like robots sitting there knitting. A lot of them were middle-aged ladies, who had just done a post office book or a cheque. They were good ladies, just dying of shame at being in there. All the best prisoners are sent to Askam Grange, or prisoners who have been in a long time.

What I really minded was that it was too far for my mother to bring my son to see me. You were allowed a monthly visit from your family and there was a welfare visit every three months when the authorities had to bring your child to see you.

Today women in open prisons and stars are allowed fortnightly visits.

I asked twice to go back to Holloway but they said no. I said, O K I'll go myself, and I did. Two of us came out, but I didn't want to stay out because I figured they'd get me in the end and anyway I could never go home and be with my Steve. We had a couple of days out, and then went and knocked on the gate at Holloway. They wouldn't let us in. 'Visiting time is over,' he said. 'Oh, well, please yourself,' I said.

I went up in front of what they call a V C – a visiting committee of magistrates – for escaping from Askam Grange. You are marched in, and stood in front of these lady magistrates with a screw on either side of you – up close to stop you attacking somebody.

They called me by my number, 89745, Reynolds, have you anything to say – and it freaks you out the way they say that. I just said that I'd wanted to be in London so Steve could be brought to see me. 'Right,' they said, 'twenty-eight days loss of privileges, twenty-eight days behind the door, twenty-eight days loss of remission and twenty-eight days loss of pay.'

I couldn't believe it. That was another twenty-eight days, on top of the six weeks they had taken off me on my appeal. It was the same sentence as someone who had been out for six months and had been caught by the police. I was fighting mad, certainly not numb any more.

I was in solitary for a month.

I think a lot of women get used to it, because it is usually the same women who go there, you know, the people who won't co-operate. And sometimes it seems to me that the more they do to you the more you sort of fight. I found that, anyway, the more they came down on me.

You only come out of your cell to go to the bog, and that is when everyone else is locked up, so you don't have contact with anyone. You are in artificial light all the time – there is opaque glass in the window and a dim bulb. There is no heating and the ventilation is fixed. At first you are given no bedding, just a mattress with a strip cover and you put on a strip jacket which is made of thick cotton to prevent people tearing it and committing suicide, I suppose.

. . . One day they told me I was going to Styal in Cheshire the next morning – I was fighting mad and told them that if they wanted me there they'd have to drag me.

Well, they have got these two men who work on the hospital wing and walk around with white coats on, they are supposed to be for people who are troublesome. They are the ones who strip you naked and throw you in the padded cells. You know, if you are playing at not coming out of your cell or something. Anyway, they came for me next morning, and they got the men, and they just stuck something in me, I

Pat Arrowsmith

don't know what it was but I was just like a zombie – all the way to Styal I didn't know where I was.

Women in Holloway are heavily tranquillized: valium, nuactil and largactil are the drugs most frequently used.

I've seen people come in there just full of life, really full of life, and been sort of vegetables when they go out. I noticed it when I went to Styal and came back down to Holloway for my divorce. A girl who had been a real sort of rebel just a few months before, when I came back she was just sitting on the stairs. I couldn't believe it. I was told she'd had E C T. It was unbelievable, it was like it wasn't the same person.

When I arrived at Styal I went in front of the board, it consists of the governor and the assistant governor, priest, welfare and somebody else. I was screaming and shouting, 'I'm not fucking staying, I'll get out of here.' So then I was on escort which means that everywhere you go you've got a screw with you, even when you go to the bog.

They put me in where they make the grey jumpers the men wear in prison. Those machines were going all day long and I just sat and stared into space. Some women love the job in the machine shop top line because you can get 90p a week instead of 30p, but you have to put up with the noise and the intensity. I was quite lucky because the screw was really nice, she was really beautiful, she shouldn't have been there. She became quite concerned as I looked a bit of a mess; I was very pale and sort of half dead. So they put me on an outside working party where I was a bricky's labourer – mixed cement and carried bricks.

Styal is a security prison which used to be a children's home, then a refugee camp. There are all these big red brick houses with names like Elizabeth Fry – that's the long-term house. Styal has got the biggest turnover of staff of any prison because they hate it being bound by the petty rules and regulations as much as the prisoners. For example you can lose three days' remission for smoking in the wrong place.

They had these patrols at night; they go round in stockinged feet with gloved keys to see who is in bed with anybody else. If they caught you out of bed you'd go straight down to Bleak House for the night – that's the punishment block. Every night they would have a sort of swoop, and you know you would stand at the bars in your nightie looking down at some other poor soul being escorted down the block. Every little thing that happens is a talking point for days – 'they are raiding Sarah Martin House tonight, oh, there's so and so, and so and so.'

They'd be put in solitary and go in front of the governor next day, and lose a week's pay. You have 30p a week, and out of that you have to buy tobacco, shampoo, matches, letters. You are entitled to one free letter a week and you could buy one more out of your wages. It's hard for a woman whose family is in Jamaica.

. . . In Holloway women make bags – they're called dollybags – to carry round their valuables like mascara and soap – because the cells are open during work hours and things get nicked. Toothpaste is considered valuable because you only get tooth powder in there.

Each house at Styal had a different library day. It's quite hard to get an exercise book, you have to say exactly what you want it for and why it's necessary for you to have it. You are not supposed to use it for anything except study. You have to promise faithfully that you won't write in it about yourself, or about your crime, or about the prison or about other prisoners. Then if you want to take it out with you, you have to give it to the governor a month before you go. I started to get books and things and read a lot. It kept me sane. A lot of women inside can't read. For those who can't read well they have these big books with huge print. They are like kids' books which is ridiculous, just because people can't read small print it doesn't mean they want Mary-went-down-the-road-to-get-mummy's-shopping sort of books. The classes are terrible at Styal. It's compulsory to go to two – it's nearly all needlework, dressmaking and cooking.

There are lots of prison lawyers, you know, people telling you what to do and how to go about this or that. In Styal I was in the long-term house where it was more or less a dog-eats-dog situation. People become very possessive about little things. If you're doing a long time you are allowed to have your own tea cup, some had a whole fucking tea set. Some would kill you for their own tea cup and their footstool – you know, respectable-type ladies with their little possessions and their little rooms, they feel secure and can't survive outside. A lot of the women I was with had been coming in all their lives. They started off when they were twenty, got nine months, and then got eighteen months. They were usually the people who did fraud – cheques – and ended up doing five or six years.

You even get a sort of upper-class distinction thing where the long-term prisoners in for classy crimes sort of look down their noses on the bed and breakfast prisoners.

It's the privileges which divide the women because they are so dead scared of losing them. What they do is to make someone house leader who is meant to be responsible and to see that everything goes quietly at night. Divide and conquer. The only place where there's any solidarity is on the punishment block.

Still, you do make real friends because you go through so much together. I made one friend who I still see often. She helped me inside because she was into Buddhism and things like that, and I got interested. I gave her one of my bracelets – the ones they couldn't get off me in Holloway. You aren't allowed to give things away, and she got caught wearing it. She was given twenty-eight days behind the door (solitary) because she wouldn't say who had given it to her. I owned up and got seven days.

There are endless little rules like that. You are not allowed to have a photograph of yourself in there – in case you remember who you are, I suppose – but you can have a picture of your family. You are never allowed to take your tights off even if it's boiling hot. And you're not supposed to talk about the prison – of course you talk about nothing else. Even at the group therapy sessions you are not allowed to complain about the prison, so you complain about each other.

Every so often magistrates come round and they say, 'Have you got any complaints?' But if you do complain there are all the repercussions after they've gone. You are hauled up in front of the governor. 'Why did you complain? If you have anything to complain about, why didn't you complain to me?' Anyway, as a prisoner your word is nothing – nothing you say is ever believed. If you have got a complaint against a screw, you know before you go into the governor that you have got no chance at all.

I always thought that prison would never affect me. I always said that I wouldn't let it affect me when I came out. But you've had time to think in there, and I became much more tolerant of other women – you start to look for the reason behind people's actions – but I also realized what people could do to other people, things I'd never have believed, and I ended up thoroughly disillusioned with so-called justice.

Suddenly you are shoved outside when, for three years you haven't had to think. You don't make decisions there at all. Then you're out and you've got to find somewhere to live, you've got to find a job, you've got to start taking care of your kid again who has become a little stranger – it's really scary.

So much seems to have changed and there is nobody you know any more. You've been through something they haven't, that's the thing; a lot of people can only relate to people who have been inside as well. Then there's the fact that you are alone. You know I had a bad relationship with my husband, but at least it was a relationship. I did live with someone for all those years, and suddenly I was totally alone – while you are in there you are sort of safe and secure. I had my mother outside otherwise I don't know what I would have done. It leaves a mark, obviously it does.

SR.33, March 1975

Living with the Army in Your Front Garden

MARY MCKAY

From the press and television it is easy to get a bundle of glib ideas about the situation in Northern Ireland, which assume that it is much like any other part of the UK, and could be normal, peaceful and democratic if only the population weren't stuck in religious fanaticisms of a bygone age: a sectarianism associated on the Catholic side with a romantic nationalism, harking back to generations of Irish heroes; and on the Protestant side with a backward-looking loyalty to British historical victories irrelevant to the days of the EEC.

If only, the story goes, people in Northern Ireland would take up more modern ideas, the Protestants would have no *real* reason to keep rights from the Catholics, and the Catholics would happily get on with life in an integrated Northern Irish state and stop worrying about Irishness.

According to this picture, the Catholics were quite justified in demanding civil rights in 1967. Britain sent the troops in to protect them from the bigoted Protestant refusal. But then the Catholics too became unreasonable: their demands went beyond civil rights to nationalism, so the troops had to move against them too.

This popular view of the N. Ireland situation leaves people here in Britain feeling befuddled about why the war goes on, and what they are fighting about now. And most of all, people here do not see why the Catholics want so passionately to get Britain out. To many people here it looks as if the British army is left in the middle trying to keep the extremists apart, and aiming to bring back conditions in which 'ordinary people' can get on with their lives – their homes, jobs and families.

But this bewilderment and impatience in Britain comes from an ignorance of what life in N. Ireland has been since long before 1967. The fact is that everyday life for Catholics in Ulster never has been the 'ordinary life' of an average English family of the last thirty years. The essential feature is *not* the peculiarly intense religious differences that persist there, but that ancient economic and social privileges are overlaid on this religious divide, and still exist. They penetrate every aspect of daily life, and it is this that has drawn whole communities of Catholic men, women and children into political activity.

I understood the part played by women very much in the context of a whole community's resistance on a street level to the grinding discrimination in their basic conditions of life.

On a short visit you have to peer through the dramatic details of the war situation to catch hints of what the place is 'normally' like. Once I had got over the shock of the foot patrols among the prams and shopping, the iron-grilled shopwindows, the overhead helicopters, the kerbsides lined with petrol drums against car-bombs, the Union Jacks waving outside concrete-barricaded Protestant villages, the house-high wall paintings of republican lilies – I became aware of the underlying poverty of N. Ireland: the railway stations, small, grey, bedraggled and dowdy; the narrow streets in the centre of town, and their meagre shops; the old cars, the tiny shoddy houses. N. Ireland is an underdeveloped region of the British Isles, economically drained, like Glasgow and the north-eastern counties of England.

Without even considering sectarianism, N. Ireland is getting a bad deal. It has always had the highest unemployment, lowest wages, worst housing, crummiest schools, highest emigration. This affects the whole working class, not only the Catholics. The average wage in Ulster is 88.3 per cent of the British male average, 79.5 per cent of the female. Unemployment is usually twice as high. Over 19 per cent of inhabited houses are officially uninhabitable, as compared with 7 per cent over Britain as a whole.

But Ulster differs from the other underdeveloped regions in one crucial way: in these conditions of all-round scarcity, one group had the power to monopolize what little there was. The Protestants had all the key posts in public and private industry and government, nation-ally and locally. They used this to give all the jobs, houses and social amenities to the Protestant working class. This has created in N. Ireland a working class divided into two layers: 60 per cent Protestant, with relative privileges, and 40 per cent Catholic, discriminated against in an apartheid type of situation, to the extent of living in fairly separate enclaves of the cities.

This isn't so hard to imagine: the same thing happens to Blacks in parts of Britain, and to immigrant workers from southern Europe who come to work in Switzerland, France and Germany, to do the worst and poorest paid jobs, with very much second-class civil rights.

N. Ireland is special only because the hierarchy in the working class is so highly organized into a system of Protestant *political* power.

Women in N. Ireland suffer from the general pattern of deprivation. Their conditions as women are even worse than in the rest of the U K. Thirty-six per cent work outside the home, and they are even more confined to traditional women's work in textile and service industries. The main firms, like the cigarette makers Gallaghers, engineering works and shipyards, advertise specifically for boys. Women can't be postmen, and only very recently bus conductresses. The Sex Discrimination Act does not apply at all in N. Ireland. The Equal Pay Act is so watered down as to be useless: there is a special clause for N. Ireland that allows employers to keep special grades for women's work – in an area where women's pay is on average £16.73 a week, com-pared with £36.37 for men.

In recent years government-sponsored industry has been aimed at providing jobs for men rather than women. In 1972 it was claimed that 6,242 jobs were created for men, but only 622 for women.

In industry as a whole, plant and conditions are out of date, par-ticularly in the mills where women are concentrated. A woman from Newry told us that when her mother worked in the local mill only twenty years ago, the mill girls had to work in nineteenth-century conditions, standing barefoot in water. The mill horn had called the women to work from their factory-owned houses. Her mother had died giving birth to her ninth child. The daughter spent much of her life in England because the Catholics in Newry, an overwhelmingly Catholic town, could get factory work or no work. She went to London to work in an office.

With such high overall unemployment, it isn't a simple matter of women finding it even harder to get work. Where work is so tight you often find women taken on instead of men, because they can be paid less. This has been the pattern in some parts of industry in N. Ireland, especially in the linen factories in Derry.

We met women in the Catholic ghettoes of Derry, the Bogside and the Creggan, who had work in the local shirt factories when their husbands had none. There's a song with the lines:

> In the early morning the shirt factory horn
> Calls women from Creggan, the Moor and the Bog . . .

This must have affected men and women's feelings about each other. The song goes on:

> While the men on the dole played a mother's role,
> Fed the children and then walked the dog . . .

but a couple of women told us that the women normally did the wife's job as well, to 'compensate' the men for their feeling of uselessness during all those years out of work. Often the women had no choice anyway: their husbands went away to England for work, for whole stretches of their married lives, sending home money and returning only for the holidays, so the women *had* to keep house as well as do paid work.

These conditions foster the strength and independence you'd expect, but even so we spoke with one woman whose husband, a long-distance lorry driver in England, said she wasn't to go out in the evening while he was away. (She did though.)

In fact, on our first evening in Derry, she was one of a group of women friends who took us to a social club. Between the four of them they had thirty-five children, which was quite typical. With all these children, living in tiny two-up, two-down terraces, the women keep a closeness to one another that has been lost in most English housing estates today. We hadn't time to find out many facts about how women informally help each other nor what formal arrangements there were, like playgroups, but we had a glimpse.

We turned up at the house where we stayed in the Creggan at about five in the afternoon. Maureen and a neighbour, Anne, were sipping tea and doing each other's hair. As soon as we arrived, Maureen ran out for a couple of other women across the road, and soon there were seven or eight of us in Maureen's sitting room, talking as evening fell. Children came in and out; all ages play together in the street, so they can look after each other a lot of the time. We parted only when the women went home to get tea and smarten up to meet again later to go out together to a club.

These Catholic women were in their mid-thirties and upwards. Talking with them about contraception, we found they were reluctant to use it themselves – 'It would seem wrong' – and anyway they loved all their children and would have liked more. But they wished the young girls luck. Mary, who was about fifty-five, said that the teenage girls dressed and acted like boys (Bay City Roller pants were the rage), and were very free and brave. Sometimes they were mistaken for boys and picked up by the army. But it was a great pity, she said, that they married so young, often well before twenty, and changed, settling for a life of kids and domestic cares, just as she had done.

The Catholic ideology is not solely responsible. There are real material pressures to marry early. A boy and girl never have much privacy, living in large families. Marriage is the only chance to move out. There is even more severe overcrowding since the 'troubles' because many Catholic families have left unsafe areas and crowded into the ghettoes. The householder voting qualification has also made Protestant-controlled councils unwilling to build more houses for Catholics. This was one of the chief grievances in 1967 when the Civil Rights Movement began.

There are other restrictions too. Law relating to women in N. Ireland is backward: the liberalization of the British divorce laws doesn't apply there, and neither does the Abortion Act of 1967 – it is almost impossible to get an abortion in N. Ireland.

So although there is an obvious delight in the children, there are resentments too, often unvoiced. For the woman from Newry whose mother died in childbirth, time spent away in England has made it easier to say how she resents, even rejects, the church, for her mother's early death.

The Catholic church is bound into the life of the people and has an enormous influence on them, not least through running all the schools that Catholic children attend (all education is religious in N. Ireland, Catholic or Protestant). Church attendance is very high. The Catholic hierarchy of N. Ireland is known in the Catholic world as particularly orthodox and conservative on religious and moral matters.

Maureen said that as a young girl she thought the clergy must always be right. Since the troubles she has thought more for herself and is less subservient to the priests, though this hasn't affected her faith. She said that some of the young are much more critical of both the clergy and the faith than she is, and there have been instances of open hostility to the local church when the priests did not show enough solidarity with what militants were doing.

These women spoke a lot about their closeness and courage since the troubles. This must be partly as a result of long years of police repression and intimidation. Such deliberate discrimination needs a back-up of force. This is provided by the Special Powers Act of 1922, which gives the government unlimited powers to proclaim an emergency 'whereafter it can make whatever regulations it deems necessary'. The act has been used throughout the century to intern Catholics without trial.

While the Catholic and Protestant people of N. Ireland to some extent share the burdens of unemployment and poverty, it is the Catholics who are the main victims of the police. The Royal Ulster Constabulary, an armed elite police force almost entirely Protestant, spread fear among the Catholics. They always had some excuse for harassment in a state whose laws make it an offence to interfere with the display of the Union Jack, while the police confiscate any other emblem – such as the Irish flag – if they think it could cause a breach of the peace.

The RUC was backed up by a part-time volunteer force, also armed, the B Specials, who acted like an official Protestant sectarian gang for forty years. Their disbanding was one of the first things demanded, and won, by the Civil Rights Movement. The woman from Newry told me of her memories of her childhood there: the 'big Special', who might be a grocer or a builder by day, who would shove you around with his gun, ask you where you came from, abuse you as a Fenian and tell you to get back to the ghetto where you belong. She remembered the time an armed Special came into a Catholic classroom to question a child about her parents' activities.

Out of this experience of life in Ulster the Catholic opposition arose. The particular kind of protest meant that women became very active. This protest didn't take the conventional channels of Parliament or the trade unions. Although union membership is quite high (54 per cent of working people), in general the trade union movement has avoided the political issues of sectarianism, and the Catholics have not been organized as an oppressed minority in the unions. Nor have they had economic leverage there, as the Ulster Workers' Council strike of May 1974 showed – Protestants in key industries stopped work in protest against any possibility of 'power-sharing'. Catholics have not been working inside the heavy industry, skilled trades and power stations where trade unionism is traditionally strongest and strikes can have most effect. The working lives of Catholics have been continuously fragmented and disorganized by unemployment, emigration, casual work and unskilled demoralizing jobs.

In the local government and Parliamentary sphere Catholics have been effectively barred from influence. Council elections have always given a Protestant majority. At Stormont any efforts by Catholic MPs to change things were always frustrated by the unity of the Protestant majority against them. By the 1960s Catholic politics were at a low ebb: the parties representing the Catholics were demoralized, and the Irish Republican Army was no longer a real force.

All this is the background to the types of action the Catholics undertook in 1967–8: the Civil Rights Movement which began the process of bringing people out of their shells to take initiatives like civil rights marches and demonstrations, sit-downs, rent and rate strikes and boycotts of local elections. Eventually, after their marches and mass meetings had been attacked by armed police and Protestant gangs, communities organized barricades and 'no-go' areas. These were Catholic areas where people began to run their daily life and defence *themselves*, through street committees and other grass-roots bodies in the locality.

A woman I spoke to in Derry, an active community organizer, said that before the troubles people had been very depressed and demoralized, after all those years with no jobs and nothing happening. It had been hard even to get a tenants' association going. Now people were doing a lot more together, socially as well as politically, especially women. Anything that had been done in the community in Derry, she said, had been done by the women above all.

In Derry and Belfast we heard of projects run by women, like social clubs, a food co-op, committees to help people forced to flee from their houses. These kept up a network of social contacts. There was nothing much like them before the troubles. But these forms of protest and organization seemed limited as the need for military defence of the areas grew. It also became more difficult to meet and organize in this way once the army moved in. It was the Protestant backlash to the Civil Rights Movement which carried the Catholics' protest to armed defence, in which many women took part.

The Protestants had something real to defend. Giving way to Catholic demands wasn't just a case of a few reforms here and there. It would mean a total reorganization of the structure of the society, down to the smallest local institution, and it would mean a real redistribution of resources in a province with small enough resources anyway.

Protestant fury is expressed through the symbols of their historic victories over the Catholics. They parade on 12 July in celebration of the Battle of the Boyne. They parade on 12 August, the date of the

Siege of Derry in 1689, when the Protestant apprentice boys held the town against the Catholic James II.

The Protestants came from England and Scotland as settlers of land cleared of native Catholic gaels by the invading English armies of Elizabeth I and Cromwell. This past lives on because the same competition goes on today. The descendants of the apprentice boys, organized into the Orange Order, still hold the citadels of Derry, still run the town, and the Catholics still live outside the city walls, in the Bogside, on the economic margins of society, on the dole. These apprentice boys now march with their drums and flags along the old city walls overlooking the streets of the Bogside, flaunting their supremacy.

Sectarian violence has always flared up most when the Protestants have felt most threatened in their privileges. In the late 1960s they were threatened by the Civil Rights Movement. But a deeper fear was that the new Common Market conditions were eroding Britain's interest in a divided Ireland, and that Britain would withdraw economic and political support for the Protestant supremacy.

Loyalist gangs attacked and burnt Catholic homes, setting in motion the train of events leading eventually to the direct occupation of the Catholic areas by the British army, and the internment of hundreds of men and boys.

You have only to go to their houses to see how greatly this occupation has affected the lives of the women. Rooms are decorated with pictures and ornaments made by men inside: pictures of the 'cages' themselves (the Nissen huts inside the prison camps), wooden plaques with pictures of Connolly, leading republican and socialist shot after the 1916 rising. Holy pictures and photos of killed relatives and friends hang on the walls. Some women have leather purses made by internees, with republican slogans and symbols on one side and the woman's name on the other.

Of the women we met, several had husbands in Magilligan and Long Kesh, and visited them every week in special coaches laid on by community organizations run by women. Food parcels are taken every week, costing over £6 a time. It takes a lot of a woman's income, and some have more than one male relative inside, as well as a daughter in Armagh jail. Women also organize relief committees to help financially the families of internees, or generally, families whose homes are destroyed or relatives killed.

The experience of the raids and arrests has given women a lot of courage, out of anger. As mothers, they have had to watch twelve armed men tear up the stairs at four in the morning and pull their kids out of bed, herd the whole family into one room, and search the house. Each time the identity of everyone in the family has to be established.

The army in Ulster now has detailed files on the domestic situations and personal life of almost every Catholic. A woman in Derry showed us a brown envelope on which she had noted down the ages and dates of birth of her fourteen children. She just hands it over each time the army comes.

Women have themselves been involved in the republican organizations, but I am speaking here only of the way the mass of women have been involved as a community. For example, in Derry, we heard that when the army first came in 1971, they took a school as their base. It was the women who got up a march and picket to move them out of the school.

It is very much as *mothers* that women are moved to action against the army. This shouldn't make us over here too sceptical. The Catholic Church and economic underdevelopment do make the family conservative and cohesive in N. Ireland, and this obviously does circumscribe the part played by women in current events. But because so much of the action has been in the communities, where whole families are involved together, domestic life and family relationships have been opened to change. For instance, our friend Jane has a poster in her window supporting the Catholic Social Democratic and Labour Party; her twelve-year-old son has put up beside it the Sinn Fein slogan 'Boycott the election'. The politics and discussion in their daily lives gives parents and children new responsibilities to people outside the family. This changes their relationship to one another. In this situation the family is not just a conservative force: it is also part of the network of solidarity in the community.

EMPLOYMENT FIGURES 1969	PROTESTANTS	CATHOLICS
Population	66.6%	33.3%
Civil Service Administration	93%	7%
Local Government	94%	6%
Health Service Administration	92%	8%
Police	90%	10%
Courts	86%	14%

AREAS OF EMPLOYMENT
(1) Shipbuilding and linen
These traditional industries are declining. The Harland and Wolff shipyard in Belfast has a 90% Protestant workforce. The 10% Catholics are all in low-paid, unskilled jobs.
(2) Civil Service and local government
Public employment has risen since the 1950s. It is highly discriminatory, only for those 'loyal' to the state. In Derry, where Catholics outnumber Protestants 2:1, only 26% of public employees are Catholic. There are equal numbers only in labouring. In

Fermanagh, a predominantly Catholic county, Catholics have 32 out of 370 local government jobs.

(3) Agriculture

10% of the population work on the land, mostly in small uneconomic farms which need subsidies and reorganization. Government planning projects are leaving farming to stagnate. This means higher unemployment for Catholics, who can't turn to public employment.

In Antrim, mainly Protestant, 8.23% are employed in agriculture, and 5.9% are unemployed. In Tyrone, mainly Catholic, 23.5% are employed in agriculture and 13.45% are unemployed.

['*Mary McKay*' *was a pseudonym for Sue O'Halloran. Ed.*]

SR.43, February 1976

Women in Chile:
A Year after the Coup

TRACY ULLTVEIT-MOE

According to Mirtal Vidal, national staff member of the United States Committee for Justice to Latin American Political Prisoners (USLA), 'Among the worst victims of the junta's repression are a group of women being held at two detention camps in Chile – El Buen Pastor (the Good Shepherd) in Santiago and the Tejas Verde concentration camp.' The latter is possibly now closed. Ms Vidal was speaking at a press conference held in New York on 5 June to make public a document recently received from Chile, but the evidence produced at the conference is simply the latest in a series of reports which have documented the torture and indignities inflicted upon women arrested in Chile since last September's coup.

According to material now available from several sources, political prisoners, both male and female, have been subjected to icy baths, hung by their hands or feet or tied to chairs for days on end without food or water, brutally beaten and whipped, and in methods apparently 'imported' by Brazilian experts, interrogated with the 'aid' of lighted cigarettes and electric shock equipment applied to the nostrils, eyelids, anus and genital organs. Psychological torture, such as threats to the victim's family, accompanied by recorded cries allegedly made while relatives were undergoing interrogation and torture, is also used.

And, as we have all too sadly seen again recently in Cyprus, women in time of war or civil upheaval are also vulnerable sexually, whether they are politically suspect or not. Instances have been reported of

SR.45

arbitrary arrests of women, who have been released without interrogation after repeated rapes by drunken soldiers, while a recent report,
submitted to the United Nations Committee on Human Rights and the
United States Senate by a six-member delegation of the US branch of
the Women's International League for Peace and Freedom, presents
strong evidence that sexual abuse has apparently been adopted in
interrogation centres as a standard technique in the questioning of
female suspects. The victim is blindfolded and stripped in front of a
roomful of men; she is then thrown from man to man until she falls.
Multiple assault then follows. Cases of male prisoners forced to rape
female prisoners under threat of further torture for one or both, have
also been reported.

The WILPF delegation collected its evidence during a visit to

Chile in January and February of this year; surprisingly they were permitted a short visit to the Buen Pastor prison referred to above. Authorities maintained that the approximately ninety-five women held at the prison were largely prostitutes or thieves, but the nuns running the centre told the delegates that in fact almost all were political prisoners. The detainees, almost all of whom were still uncharged, were initially afraid to speak to the W I L P F group, but when they learned the purpose of their visit, the prisoners crowded round, many with heads shaved or nipples burnt from electric shock treatment, and reported that prior to their transfer to Buen Pastor only two amongst them had not been raped.

According to the prisoners, some women had had mice and insects inserted in their vaginas; pregnant women had been beaten until they aborted. In another case, the foetus carried by a woman subjected to electric shock treatment is still considered viable, but the prognosis is that the child will be born with severe brain damage. Other horror stories tell of prisoners being forced to eat excrement and semen.

The women at Buen Pastor prison have improved the dirty, pest-infected centre since they arrived, but nutrition remains inadequate, and their most appalling complaint still stands; women who were re-peatedly raped by unknown assailants and now find themselves preg-nant have been refused abortions. When they requested a doctor, only an ear specialist was sent, and the women were told that they should be proud of 'what they had in their bellies'. The psychological effects of such treatment can well be imagined and are already evident amongst many women and children.

The W I L P F delegation also saw children who bore scars and had required hospitalization due to beatings they had received from soldiers who were intent on using any means available to locate the children's relatives; they visited poor areas in Santiago and heard testimony concerning the hardships the poor were undergoing due to sky-rocketing inflation and the dismantling of welfare programmes, free milk schemes and health facilities initiated under the Allende government. Women told the W I L P F delegates of the typhoid epidemic affecting their children because authorities intent on keen surveillance in working-class areas had forced the removal of all latrines to the centre of the community.

W I L P F also learned that other women whose husbands had been killed by the junta often could not leave Chile or obtain any sort of social assistance without a certificate attesting to their husband's death, a document which was impossible to obtain in many instances where the junta denied that the deceased spouse had in fact ever been arrested. Other women have been stranded for months in foreign embassies where they had taken refuge following the coup. Junta officials refused to award them 'safe conduct' passes in cases where relatives were still being sought.

With a fascist twist to a typical sexist technique, a pro-junta Santiago newspaper *La Segunda* resorted to ridicule as a means of diminishing the impact of WILPF's report on its visit to Chile. The newspaper's article on WILPF's findings was headlined 'Majaderia Internacional' (perhaps weakly translatable as 'International Jackassery') and scornfully reported that the 'little old ladies' carried notebooks filled with appointments and asked questions about just how many litres of blood had been spilled in post-coup Chile.

Nonetheless, the allegations by WILPF that women in Chile have been subjected to vile degradations as human beings and as women have been supported by countless other bodies, including the Chicago Commission of Inquiry, the International Federation of Women, Amnesty International and legal and medical groups which have visited Chile in the last year. Courageous Chilean women have done their best to make these facts known abroad; the prisoners in Buen Pastor prison, for example, who risked further torture in order to tell their story, did so, they said, in order to protect the others, who are daily being brought to interrogation centres in Chile.

SR.28, October 1974

Dora Tamana

ROSALYNDE AINSLIE

Dora Tamana lives in a four-roomed house in Nyanga, an 'African township' ten miles outside Cape Town. Her home has no bathroom, no floors, no ceiling, no internal doors (Cape Town Municipality provides these for its Coloured – mixed race – tenants, not for Africans). But the walls are decorated with family photographs and coloured pictures cut from magazines, and children run in and out.

Dora describes Nyanga as 'a place of persecution', the houses 'surrounded by dirt and filth, overflowing dustbins, flies and smelly lavatories – each used by two to three families'. Many of the houses are merely corrugated iron 'pondokkies', burning hot in summer, freezing in winter. The whole estate is surrounded by a high wire fence, with only one entrance that everyone must use. A police van guards the gate

526   *Spare Rib Reader*

and residents are constantly searched for illegal liquor and their passes (permission to be in an urban area and to seek work, permission to work, tax receipts) are checked.

In any case the township is gradually being converted, following government policy, into a barracks town for migrant male workers, who must leave their families behind in the homelands. Few of the little 'family' houses like Dora's remain. Over the years many of her women neighbours and their children have been deported from the city. The police still raid Dora now and then, demanding yet again her pass with its precious permanent residence permit, in case she should feel just a little secure in the city where she has lived for forty-five years. She is now seventy-four years old.

Dora was born in 1901 at Gqamakwe in the Transkei, the poor but still beautiful area of the Eastern Cape that is all that is left of the land of the Xhosas. Her father had no formal education, and taught himself to read and write, but her mother reached Standard IV at school (roughly equivalent to the fourth year in an English junior school), and Dora was able to do the same. She was brought up like every African village girl – she tended the poultry, sold eggs and chickens in the local market, learned to care for babies, to cook and sew, to clean the house with mud and wash the clothes with clay.

In 1920, when Dora was twenty, came the first violent event that was to change her life. A 'prophet' named Enoch Mgijima had acquired a following in the area. He preached that Armageddon was coming, and called upon the people to join the Israelites, the Church of God, and to celebrate Passover once a year near his home at Bulhoek. People came from all over the Transkei, some from as far away as the Transvaal, built huts and stayed for seven days. But this year, at the end of the Passover, they did not go home.

'When the authorities found the people still there,' writes Dora, 'the clash began. Enoch Mgijima replied to the government messages saying, "I have no right to disperse them because they are here by the will of God." At the same time, he told his followers of the coming of *i kongolosi* [Xhosa pronunciation of the word Congress – the African National Congress was formed in 1912], telling them to support activities in the outside world, like the Kadalie strike [Clements Kadalie was the organizer of a nationwide African trade union, the Industrial and Commercial Workers' Union, which grew rapidly during the 1920s]. But this was like a dream to me – a sweet dream. He said these people were fighting for our rights . . .

'They had a hymn that said "There is a great destruction coming in our land upon all those who won't obey the Lord. They will be running to the rocks and mountains, saying Hide me from the face of an angry God."

'Eventually the government gave the prophet an ultimatum. His people must disperse by dawn on 24 May 1921. The day before we heard that the soldiers had come, led by General Smuts [later to become Prime Minister of South Africa and Britain's ally during the Second World War], and instead of Church service that evening it was a meeting of men only.

'In the morning the men waited in groups for what was going to happen. About 11 a.m. a voice came from the soldiers, "Put down your swords and sticks, otherwise we are shooting." Oh, the people were shot dead. Nearly 200 of them died on that sad day. After the shooting, the soldiers marched to the "Holy City" of Natabelanga with their guns on their shoulders. They told the women to take water to the wounded men, lying in the bushes. The women carried the wounded in blankets. It was a sad scene. My father, Joel Ntloko, was among the dead, and his two brothers. The prophet Enoch Mgijima and the rest of the men were arrested, and the wounded taken by wagon to Queenstown Hospital and some to the Military Hospital at Wynberg, Cape Town.

'Mgijima was sentenced to six years. The elders and evangelists received three years each, and the ordinary followers, called "saints", one and a half years, under the Riotous Assemblies Act.'

Dora herself helped to carry the wounded from the battlefield. She had lost her father and two uncles, and within a year her mother was dead. She and her sisters went to live with one of their widowed aunts, a schoolteacher, whose brother was also an Israelite, imprisoned at Takai, near Cape Town.

Among the wounded at Bulhoek had been a young man, John Tamana. After his discharge from hospital he returned to the Transkei, and in 1923 he and Dora were married. 'He was working in a private house,' she says, 'for £1.10s [£1.50] a month. Between 1924 and 1930 I had four children, and three of them died – of starvation and tuberculosis and meningitis. I had to leave a baby of only a month with my ten-year-old sister so that I could go out to work for one shilling and sixpence [7½p] a day. In 1930 we moved to Cape Town, in the hope that our children might have a chance to survive.

'My husband found work as a labourer in a timber yard, for £1.4s [£1.20] a week, and we stayed in a stable, paying eight shillings [40p] a month rent. Then he learned to be a driver, hoping to earn more, and in 1931 we got a house in Langa township [an African area just outside the city] for fifteen shillings [75p] a month.

'My husband looked for a job. He was nearly four months without work, and I had somehow to find something for the children to eat every day. Langa Administration hired him as a driver, but he had to work so hard for £3 a week that he gave it up, and looked for another job, up and down, up and down. We couldn't pay the rent, so we were put out, and moved to town again. My husband found work as a driver, and we saved a little money. Then he decided to buy a car and set up in business on his own.

'We were not agreed that the money we saved should buy a car, but he told me I couldn't rule his money, and bought the car. Soon enough it broke down and could not move. So the hardship was on me.

'After that my husband began to drink. Then he said he couldn't save money with me and the children there, so he sent me back to Queenstown – me and six children, five of them our own and the sixth the orphan of my dead sister – the tears running down my cheeks.

'Within six months two of the children died, we were starving, and the children coughing. When my husband heard this, he came in his car to fetch us, and I was very glad to get back to Cape Town where I could make a living of some kind myself.

'All through 1937 my husband drank heavily, sometimes disappearing for days at a time. He paraded his girlfriends and his car in front of me, leaving me with the children, and nothing to eat. I struggled very hard.

'My husband became more and more difficult. He told me what I must do and how I should do it, what clothes I should wear. He tried to beat me, and to stop me going to meetings (I was taking a part in township political life by then). He told me to go to church instead. Then one day he said he wanted to give up drinking.

'And he did. But it was horrible. We had more arguments than ever, and once a real fight. At last one day in 1938 he took all his belongings –his clothes, a suitcase, his blankets, saw and hammer – and went away, to another woman.

'Somehow, among all our sorrows and difficulties, I never thought he could leave me.'

But by now Dora had concerns beyond her personal anger and grief. She had been drawn into the problems of the women around her – working mothers, abandoned mothers, children who had no one to care for them, children with nothing but rags to wear and never enough to eat. She knew that the misery of the man who can never earn enough to support his family is an old misery. John Tamana was but one of thousands who stopped struggling, who drank to find, just for a little while, the illusion of lost manhood, who deserted their families when they could no longer bear the face of failure. Her anger began to be directed against poverty, the root of misery, and the racialism of a society that created poverty.

Her political awareness was awakened during the war, when African and left-wing political activity were intense, and speakers addressed meetings every Sunday on the Grand Parade (Cape Town's Trafalgar Square). They spoke of the struggle against fascism, alliance with the USSR, and the paradox of a white South Africa that fought a war in the name of democracy, and oppressed its Black majority in the name of greed.

Dora describes these meetings, where speakers talked of ways the people might free themselves from oppression, the pass laws, the 'chains of slavery' and the loss of the land. 'I recalled Enoch Mgijima's dream of "i kongolosi".'

During the war food was scarcer than ever. Some of the more politically aware in the African townships and Coloured slum areas out on the Cape Flats began to organize self-help groups: the Women's Food Committee and the Cape Flats Distress Association, which operated mobile food vans and won some support from city charities. But Dora felt that her main concern was the children, and education.

'I worried that the children of working mothers had no one to teach them,' she says, 'and to look after them during the day.' She heard a speaker at a political meeting describe the USSR, where every mother could leave her child in a creche or nursery school when she went to work. Dora decided she too would set up a creche.

She accepted twenty babies, from six months to five years. The youngest she tied on her back. Old soap boxes were used as cots. Each child was bathed daily, although water cost one penny a four-gallon tin and had to be fetched and carried across the sand. The children were fed as well as possible on the 6d [2½p] a day that every mother paid. Although Dora herself was trying to raise five children on 30s [£1.50] a week, she made no profit from the creche. It was her gift of service to the community – and she taught what writing and arithmetic she could, drawing with a stick in the sand.

When after the war Dora moved to the new house at Blaaulei (also on the Flats) she once again ran a creche, and this time she began to win public support. A training college for (white) nursery school teachers became interested, as did a welfare society run by university students. A committee was set up to raise funds and, once government permission had been obtained, a fine new building was constructed to accommodate forty children and a trained nursery school teacher. The children even had toys! Dora was triumphant.

Then suddenly, within a year, Blaaulei was declared a Coloured Area under the Group Areas Act, which zoned all urban areas for exclusive occupation by a particular racial group. The Africans were given notice to quit. They lost their homes, their jobs – and the nursery school, achieved after so many years of struggle. Dora merely commented that Coloured children needed nursery schools as much as Africans did, and they could use it until the day came – and it would – when African, Coloured and White children could use it together.

The creche was not Dora's only educational venture in Blaaulei. Around 1950, together with three friends, she started a school. Official figures numbered less than 50 per cent of school-age African children in the Cape accommodated in existing schools. They built, with their own hands, a hall of ironed-out petrol drums, their classroom for thirty youngsters. By 1953 the government was obstructive again – new legislation made it an offence for an African to run a school (even to teach a group of children informally) unless that school was registered with the Bantu Education Department, and thus run in accordance with the government's apartheid principles.

Throughout the early 1950s Dora became increasingly drawn into political action: she helped campaign to restore to African children the school feeding scheme; she was a member of a protest delegation to the Minister about the increase in bread prices; she became secretary of the local branch of the African National Congress; was active in the Communist Party and the Peace Committee; and supported the 1951/2 Campaign of Defiance of Unjust Laws, when thousands courted arrest by deliberately defying the racialist laws. She was a leader of the campaign against the removal of Africans during the mid-1950s from the Western Cape, and against the extension of passes to women.

'This is something that touches my heart,' she told a meeting called by the African National Congress in 1953. 'Who will look after our children when we go to jail for a small technical offence – not having a pass?' And indeed in subsequent years thousands of women went to gaol, and thousands of children were left uncared for.

In November 1954 Dora was elected National Secretary of the South Africa Women's Federation, a non-racial (and therefore, in South Africa, highly exceptional) organization campaigning against the worst effects of apartheid on women. The following year she was chosen, with Lilian Ngoyi, to attend a World Congress of Mothers in Lausanne.

But passports were denied to people with political records, in particular to Blacks. The notorious Suppression of Communism Act of 1950 had made the issue of a passport not a right but a 'privilege'. New legislation was already under way to make it a punishable offence to leave the country without a passport.

So, as Dora puts it, 'It was a very hard journey when I went overseas in 1955 with my friend Mrs Lilian Ngoyi from Johannesburg.' It was doubly difficult, for Dora, now in her mid fifties, was suffering from a chronic heart condition.

Their first attempt, by mailboat, using tickets bought in the names of white passport-holders, failed. Dora and Lilian were dragged out of the women's toilets just before the boat sailed. The gangplank was again lowered and they were put ashore. They stood on the dockside and watched the ship move away, 'Lost,' says Dora, 'and disappointed.' But the next attempt, this time by air, succeeded, although they were nearly deported by officials in Rome because they had no passports.

Unhappily, Dora's health deteriorated when they reached Europe, and she missed the Lausanne Congress. But both women were invited to visit China, Mongolia and the Soviet Union. This trip, with its revelations of the possibility of revolutionary change, she has remembered in the minutest detail. What impressed her most, in all the socialist countries she visited, was the standard of child care, especially the provision of creches and nurseries for the children of working mothers. The children, she keeps insisting, were *happy*.

The opportunities for women, particularly in China and Mongolia, for centuries underdeveloped agrarian countries, delighted and amazed her. 'It was a great surprise to see the women being doctors,' she writes. 'They are magistrates and lawyers. In factories the women are leading ... I saw old Chinese women with tiny feet which had been tightly bound up when they were little girls, and this was a custom, like the Xhosa who cut their finger, first or second finger. But in these days the customs are rejected, they are things which weakened the people, for the Chinese women who had their feet bound walked like cripples.

'Others told me that in former times they were beaten by their husbands; yet today they do not feel the pangs of childbirth.

'Women in China are taking part in the government. And the Chinese are non-whites!'

On her return she summed it up: 'When I saw these things, different nations together, my eyes were opened and I said, I have tasted the new world and won the confidence in our future. This has been one of the wonderful, great experiences of my life.

'I came back to the country of my birth.'

Dora's political activities had drawn attention from the political police for some time, and she was harassed in a thousand small ways. On her return the persecution became serious. She was served with a notice under the Suppression of Communism Act ordering her to resign from a long list of organizations (including, of course, the African National Congress), and prohibiting her from attending any gathering (defined as more than two people) for the next five years, under penalty of imprisonment. Demands for her 'permit' to remain in Cape Town (she had lived there continuously since 1930, and was one of few Africans with a right to permanent residence) escalated to a campaign of harrassment. She describes one of the police raids:

'One morning, early, I dressed in my national costume to go out to collect for our nursery when a European policeman arrested me, and drove me in a van from Retreat to Langa. But when I came there I was allowed to go free – because the pass laws for women were not yet gazetted! So that day I couldn't do a collection for the nursery. That is the Africans' life, in the country of their birth, waste of time, waste of energy, waste of money – under the low wages!'

Again, a policeman came to Dora's house demanding her pass. 'I told him I was not carrying a pass. He pushed me into the van. I had Elizabeth, the baby, on my back. But a group of women came out to protect me: "If you arrest Dora we are all going too." They surrounded the police van, singing.' Two white policemen left the van to demand passes from other Africans. In their absence the African policemen who arrested Dora decided to let her go. 'So they let me go free. The women shouted: "We don't want passes. We want university education!" '

Later, when she was living in Nyanga, 'the police came to my pondokkie searching for passes. They found a bottle of methylated spirits, which they claimed was illegal liquor. Two African policemen took me to the van. I told them not to hurry me, I am taking all my grandchildren – there is no one else to care for them. I did not know that the children had their toys with them until we got to the police station. They sat on the floor, playing. The youngest, Benjamin Nqaba, was on my back. When we came before the Sergeant, the African policemen picked up all the children and set them on the counter and pointed to Benjamin Nqaba on my back.

'He said, "Look how old is the mother!" I was then sixty-one years old. And I was freed. I heard a European policeman arguing with the others, saying that methylated spirits is for lighting our primus stoves, and there is no offence in having it. I told the police to take me home with my children. They said to wait until a van is going to that area. So I went on my own in the bus.'

On two occasions Dora was imprisoned. The first was in April 1960, when the government declared a State of Emergency after the massacre at Sharpeville. Some 20,000 people of all races were arrested and detained for four months. Not one was ever charged.

'I stayed in jail for four months and twelve days,' writes Dora, 'and these were hard days. Lying on cement floors with one grass mat. In the morning mealie [maize] porridge, lunch-time mealies. Meat once a week. Supper, porridge again. The cell had no window, no toilet but the open bucket which we covered with a bag. The drinking water in an open dish near the bucket, because there is no space. When we sleep, it is close to each other.'

In 1963 she was arrested again, charged, as a 'named Communist' under the Suppression of Communism Act, with failure to notify a change of address. This was the most trivial of technical offences. To comply with government policy she had had to move to Nyanga, and there from one address to another in the same street — it was this change of address which she failed to report. She was sentenced to one year's imprisonment, all but one month suspended for three years.

'When I was in jail I learned more about the pass laws. Some of the women came twice in one month to jail, most of them young women and girls who hadn't had their passes brought up to date. The jail is full of victims of the pass laws.

'When I finished my sentence my ten grandchildren, left in the care of a fourteen-year-old girl, were in a bad position, sick, and of five at school three had stopped going.'

Yet she said afterwards that she was glad she had had the opportunity of serving her sentence: there was so much that she could teach the women she met inside.

Dora has brought up her own five children, ten grandchildren, and is now caring for a great-grandchild. Of her own children, only one daughter remains near her mother. The youngest son, Benjamin's father, was drowned in 1962; and Bethwell 'disappeared' in 1963.

For nearly five years Dora heard nothing of Bethwell. Then in November 1967 a letter came from Salisbury prison, Rhodesia. He was under sentence of death as a freedom fighter. 'From the day that letter arrived, I prepared to go and see him,' writes Dora. After much effort and help from many friends, she and her eleven-year-old grandson finally set off by train from Cape Town in December 1968. It was a journey of over 2,000 miles, and took nearly three days.

'The teacher with whom we stayed in Salisbury took us to the jail. We saw detainees waving from a gallery, raising hands and fists, and we heard them shout "Amandla" ["Power to the People", the slogan of the freedom fighters]. Then we went to the other side of the prison, to the condemned prisoners. That is the day I saw my son through a thick wire, hardly able to see him, asking him to turn this way and that, move back a little bit, and we were talking and laughing, speaking about preparations for Christmas Day.'

The relatives prepared Christmas food for the prisoners. 'A teacher who had a brother in jail with my son killed a goat for the prisoners. His wife baked cakes and fried chickens. We bought oranges, peaches, bananas, tooth brushes and paste, cigarettes and sugar.

'We went to the jail. We could see the prisoners waving to us, and they sang a song: "Oh so great my case is promoted to stand before the Judge's bench!"

'But we were disappointed. We were not allowed to see the men, and we went away with the meat, the chickens, oranges, cakes, peaches, bananas, tooth brushes, cigarettes and sugar.'

Eventually, after intervention by a lawyer, they were permitted to give the non-perishable foods to the prisoners; and Dora's grandson was finally allowed to see his father. 'I spent a month in Rhodesia and was permitted to see one prisoner a week, and I managed to see four South African prisoners through a wire net.'

Bethwell's sentence was commuted to life imprisonment by the Smith government after an international outcry following the execution of several freedom fighters in 1968. And since then, every Christmas, Dora has managed to obtain permission to leave South Africa for Rhodesia and the two half-hour visits with her son.

Her going is a gift.

SR.39, September 1975

Women against the Shahs

RUTH WALLSGROVE AND SUSAN HEMMINGS

It was the present Shah's father, Reza Shah Pahlavi, who in 1935 ordered Iranian women to take off their veils. He sent his soldiers into the streets to tear them from women's faces – not because he believed in women's freedom, but because Iran had, and still has, an acute shortage of skilled labour, and he needed women workers. The veil, a *chadoor*, is not just a small piece of cloth. It's a semi-circular piece of black material that covers the whole body and has to be held in place over the mouth, or at the throat, by one hand – impossible for women working in fields or factories. His decree worked; immediately after it there was a sharp rise in women in important industries such as textiles.

The present Shah has told women, 'If you don't wear the veil, you're liberated,' and makes much of the 'progressive' nature of his dynasty. But under his regime women are still barely people in the eyes of the law, and their day-to-day living conditions have remained constrained and impoverished. And women who don't wear the veil now in Iran have come to be associated with his rule – with the 'westernization' that has led to poverty, corruption and terror.

Some of the many women who don't normally wear the veil are now choosing to put it on for demonstrations against the Shah, to show their unity within the broad opposition – which includes conservative and anti-women religious groups. These women feel that the veil, and all it represents in terms of its mistrust and suppression of women, should not be argued about at this time: the important thing is to depose the Shah. They say that the veil disguises them from SAVAK, the Shah's secret police, and makes it easier to approach other women in the street on the same footing. In other words, it's a tactic. It doesn't represent a return to religion.

There are still many women demonstrating who disagree with wearing the veil, however. But the western press only picks up on the image of seas of black-robed women holding placards with quotes from the Koran, the Islamic holy book, on them. We see nothing of the other women, nor do we hear about women's campaigns in the past.

. . . The influence of the religious groups grows because there isn't any strong alternative. The Left and feminists, illegal for years and harassed by SAVAK, are frightened to speak up until after the Shah goes. The danger is that unless they put forward an alternative, the mass of people – who are fighting repression and exploitation – may only see the religious groups opposing the Shah, and feel that the Left has nothing to offer them.

. . . Some believe that now is not the time for Iranian feminists to make their demands – that women are not ready, and that there will be time after the Shah has been deposed and a liberal democracy instituted, to raise the consciousness of women. But will there? Already the Shah is making concessions to the religious groups – ending the conscription of women, and on 14 December repealing the abortion law that at least allowed some women abortions.

In Algeria women did raise their demands at the time of the struggle against the French, and were granted many of them by the nationalist forces; but as soon as the French had been kicked out, the women were pushed back into their homes again. There too the veil has been a symbol of resistance.

SR.79, February 1979

Iran: Women for Freedom

RUTH WALLSGROVE

Tens of thousands of women marched for their rights in Iran on International Women's Day, 8 March, and during the following week. Photos showed women massed to the horizon, angry and unshakeable – even by the flashes, knives and guns of men who attacked them.

Women were enraged at the apparently blithe assumption that now that the Shah was gone, and the 'revolution' here, they would all want to return to the veil and to their husbands' custody. 'On the dawn of freedom, there is no freedom,' they shouted. The Ayatollah Khomeini had proclaimed that 'women must not come naked into ministries' – women clerical workers and secretaries were turned away by gangs of men when they arrived at work in 'western' dress. As one said, 'We hoped this would be a revolution for all the people. We did not expect to be harassed because we were without a veil or scarf.' . . .

SR.82, May 1979

United Nations Notices Women

JILL NICHOLLS

The United Nations – the name suggests the shadow boxing it will be. Disunited nations with disputed territories, armies of occupation, warring world views, unequal economies, sit in wide semicircles so they never have to see eye to eye, or even answer each other's questions. 'I want to thank the distinguished People's Republic of X warmly for his most gracious statement and I now call on the distinguished delegate from the Democratic Federation of Y to take the floor.' 'I wish to thank Madame Chairman very kindly for her gracious invitation and to congratulate her on her election to this most high office of the conference . . .'

Western capitalist democracies, socialist centralized economies, fascist military dictatorships sit side by side, in alphabetical order – Algeria, Angola, Argentina, Australia ... Behind sit the UN bodies, big names like the UNDP (United Nations Development Programme) and the World Health Organization – dominated by the USA because countries are represented on them according to how much money they put in. Behind them the translators, a lot of press, a little public (corralled, contained, sworn to silence).

The governments try to reach a consensus that can't last outside the sterility of the conference centre; they argue over amendments to a document that bears little or no relation to reality. And as this is a conference on women – mid way through our very own decade – some countries have sent teams of talking women. Some haven't bothered – the Soviet bloc for instance: men and women now being equal, what difference does it make if a delegate is male or female? As if to prove impartiality, most East European voices are male.

The 'General Debate' lasts two weeks – the time it takes 136 representatives of governments, four observer delegations and several representatives of UN bodies to read out lists of their achievements. At half an hour each, that's about twelve speeches a day, with a right of reply before home-time if you're lucky.

The only surprises here are the walk-outs (by other Arab nations when Madame Sadat of Egypt stood to speak) and the break-ins (someone shouting about the women living in their own shit in Armagh jail; anti-nuclear campaigners unfurling a banner). Spectacular sparks within this frozen spectacle.

... The World Plan of Action is actually quite a radical document, if a bit vague. Were it implemented, the world would be unrecognizable. All the rights, opportunities and sharing of work demanded by the western women's liberation movement in the late sixties and early seventies are covered. Its big weakness as a feminist programme is that there is no mention of sexuality (aside from the need for contraception, sex education and free choice of marriage partner), no mention of lesbianism, domestic violence or rape. Male power as such is not confronted, only 'discrimination on grounds of sex'. And a movement of women to liberate ourselves is neither seen as necessary nor acknowledged as already existing and being the main reason a conference like this was thought to be necessary. The best we get is a passing reference to 'encouraging women to develop confidence in themselves and in other women, and a sense of their own value and importance as human beings'.

Still, did you know that in 1975 Britain agreed to:

Recognize the economic value of women's work in the home, in domestic food production, marketing and voluntary activities.

Re-evaluate and where necessary rewrite textbooks and other teaching materials to ensure they reflect an image of women in positive and participatory roles in society.

Strengthen international peace and disarmament and combat colonialism, neo-colonialism, foreign domination and alien subjugation, apartheid and racial discrimination.

Ensure, along with employers and trades unions, the right of all women workers to maternity protection, including maternity leave with a guarantee of returning to their former employment, and nursing breaks.

And look at this one:

Special attention should be given to ways of facilitating the combination of family and work responsibilities, such as: a general reduction and/or staggering of working hours; flexible working hours; part-time work for men and women (with governments and trade unions ensuring the full protection of the rights of part-time workers); childcare facilities and childcare leave systems to assist parents; communal kitchens; various facilities to help parents cope with household tasks more easily.

Sound like Britain 1980? Or what Patrick Jenkins, Secretary of State for Social Services, thinks he's working towards?

Ireland also signed the World Plan: 'All legislative, social or financial obstacles to the dissemination of family planning knowledge, means or services should be removed.'

India signed: 'The same right of women and men to have free choice of spouse and to enter into marriage only with their free and full consent should be ensured.'

They all signed: 'The principle of equal rights and responsibilities means that during marriage both partners should perform an active role in the home, taking into account the importance of combining home and work responsibilities and sharing jointly decision-making on matters affecting the family and children.'

Some sections sound like the Scandinavian ideal of clean nuclear equality, especially with action proposals like these: 'labour-saving interior finishes and surfaces conducive to comfort and hygiene.'

Tell that to a Bedouin Arab, who might not want a dream kitchen. Or to a Kampuchean refugee, who hasn't a hope in hell of getting one . . .

MEANWHILE BACK AT THE FORUM...

Radical, political, world-encompassing feminism was not easily created either at the forum – the parallel conference organized by Non-Governmental Organizations with an advisory status at the UN.

... An amazing 8,000 women and a scattering of men did turn up representing traditional women's organizations, population control agencies, national liberation movements, women's professional associations, women's liberation campaigns and publications, church groups, development organizations, their governments – or simply themselves.

... The conflict between world politics and women's issues was not confined to the official conference, though the unofficial forum put the questions differently. Debate here was less rhetorical – and often more openly angry. Most women spoke from their lived experience, saying how sexism and imperialism, for instance, interacted in their lives. 'We women from the developing countries have been accused by some women of bringing politics into the forum,' said an Iraqi woman at the first plenary. 'But in our countries, politics is a matter of life and death. We see ourselves as women and also as fighters for the liberation of our country – these are not separate.'

... Speaking itself was, sadly, another point of conflict at the forum. There were no translation facilities, except at the formal panel sessions. In the workshops, the dominant language was English, with occasional contributions in French or Spanish – usually obligingly translated into English, though no time was made for translating the English into French or Spanish! It was as if English was invisible, natural, while the other languages were 'foreign'. An Iraqi woman said, 'What happens in this forum is a reflection of the outside world. We are not being given a voice. We are made into a minority again.'

Domitila de Chungara, active in the Bolivian Miners' Wives' Union and author of *Let Me Speak*, a political autobiography, struggled hard against being silenced by what she called the 'barbarous discrimination' of this language barrier: 'Nothing at this conference is written in Spanish, so we don't know where to go to discuss important political issues. We can't read any signs, it's not even clear where the toilet is. It makes it hard for us to participate in the conference, as much as we'd like to.'

Ironically, Domitila ended up making probably more impact on the forum than any other individual. On the Friday of the first week came news of a fascist coup in Bolivia. About a hundred people from the forum – Bolivians and their supporters – hurried to the Bella Centre where the UN conference was taking place. Some sat in shouting 'Domitila with us', 'Imperialists out', 'No to the Bolivian coup', while outside with a megaphone, Domitila said, 'We've come to a women's

conference to talk of women's problems. We were invited to come –
they must listen to us. Why did they ask us if they don't want to
hear?' . . .

SR.98, September 1980

12 WOMEN'S LIBERATION MOVEMENT

The women sewing machinists at Ford's, Dagenham, who went on strike for parity with men in 1968, brought the issue of equal pay back into public awareness. Women who had become involved in the radical politics of the sixties through student activism, university sit-ins and protests against the Vietnam war and who were in socialist groups concerned with these issues, found that they were expected to take a back seat to men, to do the dogsbody work and were excluded from political debate. At the same time, women who had their job expectations raised by the opening up of mass higher education found that they were discriminated against in favour of men when it came to career and job prospects. For the women who met at the first British women's liberation conference at Oxford in 1970 these various issues were not isolated from each other. The discrimination against women at work was linked to the responsibilities women had at home in caring for children. The way men dominated political or trade union meetings reflected the way men expected women to be submissive in private life. A movement for women's liberation had to recognize that the split between personal relations and the more public world of work and politics is artificial.

Women began to meet in small groups in 1969 to talk about their lives. The process of exchanging experience was called consciousness raising. It enabled women to see that attitudes and feelings were shared, not simply confined to the individual, and from there a group could draw out connections between their common experience and women's social conditions. Sharing personal experience also released strong emotions which had been held in check, especially anger at the way women are treated. Women recognized that when they internalized the social view that men were more interesting or more important, they also felt contempt for themselves and for other women. By excluding men from their meetings women could see how much energy went into vying with each other for male attention and approval. Women needed to have time and space away from men to recognize these feelings and to learn to trust and value each other. This autonomy from men was the necessary basis on which women could develop their ideas, learn confidence and create a political movement for women's liberation.

Grouping together as women means that political action is not taken on behalf of someone else. It is to overcome your own oppression in conjunction with that of other women. The experience brought by each woman is valid. The idea that 'the personal is political' has been developed by the women's movement to encompass various political tendencies which stem from particular needs and interests. The women's movement has a multiplicity of political approaches, both in what changes are desired, in methods to achieve those changes, in its internal politics, and in its approach to traditional political areas. However, the majority of the new feminist theories, despite differences, go beyond demanding equal rights with men to argue that the whole of society must change to alter existing power relations and to achieve women's liberation.

The women's liberation movement has placed as much emphasis on its ways of organizing as on its aims. Because women had been silenced by sexual hierarchy, we have tried to avoid hierarchical ways of working. The idea of the small group for democratic discussion is the basis of the movement's structure, as is the idea of working collectively so that everyone will shape the outcome of a project. When large conferences are held to pool ideas and experiences, the decisions are made at a plenary session from ideas brought back from small workshop meetings. The movement has also had to become alert to the informal ways people can dominate – by talking all the time, not explaining theories, by emotional pressure – but these sorts of difficulties are secondary to the movement's need to remain open and flexible, to allow for differences. The women's movement is more than a political party or pressure group. It is a social movement which springs from women recognizing their oppression and gathering together so they can work to overcome that oppression wherever they find it in their lives.

Adam's Knobby Rib

SHEILA ROWBOTHAM

The arguments for and against women's liberation are much older than you'd think. Chaucer makes his wife of Bath protest against the Church's treatment of women. The clergy had a monopoly over communications.

> My God, if women hadde written stories
> As clerics hav with-inne hir oratories,
> They wolde han written of men more wicked verse,
> Than all the mark of Adam may redress.

Old sayings, too, indicate that men felt women presented some kind of threat. 'A woman, a dog and a walnut-tree, the more you beat them the better they be.'

Controversy about women's liberation was expressed in religious terms. People took texts from the Bible to argue in support and in opposition. An old pro-feminist ballad used the story of Eve's creation to argue for female equality.

> She was not made out of his head, Sir,
> To rule and to govern the man,
> Nor was she made out of his feet, Sir,
> By man to be trampled upon,
> But she did come forth from his side, Sir,
> His equal and partner to be;
> And now they are coupled together
> She oft proves the top of the tree.

But Eve's temptation and fall could be used by others to show the weakness and wickedness of women.

In the seventeenth century the question of women's place came up in the context of religious conflict and revolution. The Puritans challenged the authority of king and priest, saying a man's own conscience should be his guide to interpreting God's will. But most of them regarded the authority of the father over his household, children, wife and servants as still sacred. They wanted liberty for the male property owner not his dependants. Economic changes in the organization of work were driving women out of some of the trades where their position had been protected by guild regulations. The Puritans had a strong suspicion of female sexuality. In the seventeenth century men thought women were lascivious and hypocritical – 'Saints in the Church, angels in the streets, devils in the lecturn and apes in your bed'.

However, there was another side to Puritanism. Women began to argue that they too should follow their consciences and interpret God's will for themselves. Why couldn't women become prophetesses? Small Puritan sects developed, all believing that they were absolutely correct. Women sometimes differed in their allegiance to these from their husbands. When it came to a conflict between the husband's authority and the dictates of conscience some chose to follow the latter. Women, too, started to take more public political action. They petitioned Parliament in 1642 against popery and justified themselves by explaining that Christ had come to save them as much as men and that they had had to suffer from popery as much as men. By 1647 they were more confident in asserting their rights.

'Would you have us keep at home in our houses while men are fetched out of their beds and forced from their houses by soldiers, to the affrightening and undoing of themselves, and their wives, children and families . . . shall we sit still and keep at home?'

In 1651 they gave voice to their powerlessness and grief in the Civil War. 'We have for many years chattered like Cranes and mourned like Doves.'

A strong anti-feminist tendency appeared in contemporary pamphlets. In response 'Mary Tattlewell' and 'Joan Hit-him-home' spinsters produced one called 'The Women's Sharpe Revenge', defending woman on the old grounds that she came out of Adam's side and was therefore meant to be man's equal and companion.

Thirty years later the debate was still going on, though the grounds of feminist defence had shifted to the more regular argument of natural rights. The anti-feminists were far from defeated. In the mid 1670s 'The Women's Fagaries', showing the great endeavours they had used for obtaining 'the Breeches', supported male domination against their sex which had been made out of a 'knobbly crooked rib', and took a firm give 'em an inch and they take a mile, feminists under the bed line on female aspirations.

'When Men unto their wives make long beseeches, the women domineer who wear breeches, their tongues, their hands, their wits to work they set. And never leave till they conquest get . . . Nothing will serve them when their fingers itches. Until such time they have attained the Breeches.'

Three hundred years later Adam's knobby rib is still struggling and the monstrous regiment has grown and multiplied.

SR.1, July 1972

'A Serious Proposal to the Ladies'

SHEILA ROWBOTHAM

In the last quarter of the seventeenth century several feminist women of letters appeared. The early connection of women's rights with the puritan revolution disappeared and feminist arguments took shape in a new context. Women like Hannah Wooley authoress of *The Gentle Woman's Companion* in 1675 and Mary Astell who wrote *A Serious Proposal to the Ladies* in 1694 argued for a useful place for women in the new world of commerce, science and the professions. They wanted to be accommodated in the emergent capitalist society as equals to the men in their class, not as dependants.

Hannah Wooley criticized men for thinking women were merely intended for propagation and household tasks, 'had we the same literature they would find our brains, as fruitful as our bodies.' Education seemed to be the reason for women's inferiority. As formal education and the teaching of specialized skills became the mark of sex and class privilege to those who were excluded, women and 'the inferior sort of people' struggled for knowledge as a means of breaking down the division of labour which made women of the upper classes spend their life in helpless leisure and exhausted the poor in ceaseless toil.

Picking up on a remark of Pope's comparing women to tulips, Mary Astell asked: 'How can you be content to be in the world like tulips in a garden, to make a fine show and be good for nothing?'

In the new world usefulness and business went together resulting in power but women were content to accept a position which was only decorative. She assured men that they could only benefit from women's improvement. 'The men if they rightly understood their own interest, have no reason to oppose an ingenious education of the women since it would go a great way towards redeeming the men.'

The scheme of ingenious education was a kind of Protestant convent 'rather academic than monastic' on Church of England principles. She saw this as filling the gap in female education since the closing of the Catholic convents at the Reformation. She imagined the growth of a new learning in a place where 'ladies nauseating the parade of the world' could pursue knowledge in cloistered academic solitude.

She gained some support in court circles, raising money from aristocratic women like Lady Elizabeth Hastings, of whom the journalist Steele had said 'To love her is a liberal education.' Even the Queen wanted to give £10,000 but was persuaded not to by a bishop on the grounds that it would lead to the dreaded popery.

Inevitably Mary Astell was opposed on anti-feminist grounds as well. Swift satirized proposals for a women's college in the *Tatler* in June 1709, by inventing a correspondent called Charles Sturdy who was being rejected by an intellectual 'Platonne'. Sturdy announced:

'It is my misfortune to be six foot and a half high, two full spans between the shoulders, thirteen inches diameter in the calves, and before I was in love, I had a noble stomach and usually went to bed sober with two bottles.'

Swift advised him to woo her with flattery and told an imaginary tale of the visit of a group of gentlemen to an academy of 'Platonnes'. Amongst the visitors was a well-known rake who flattered the women by saying he wished 'men might rise out of the earth like plants, and that our minds were not of necessity to be sullied with carnivorous appetites for the generation, as well as support of our species'. By devious means the gentlemen in the story get their way. 'There was hardly one of them but was a mother or father that day twelve-month.'

In September Swift returned to the attack and ridiculed the presumption of women who would reject 'Scissors, needles and samplers' for 'pens, compasses, Quadrants, books, manuscripts, Greek, Latin and Hebrew' and military exercises.

These two themes of anti-feminist attack were to be replayed many times. Feminists were portrayed as blue-stocking celibates swelling with suppressed desire or absurd Amazons aping men.

Defoe however was more sympathetic to the idea of a female academy than Swift, perhaps because he was from a dissenting family and had experienced discrimination. He had been educated at a Nonconformist academy in Newington Green, North London. In 1698 in his Essay on 'Projects' he wrote:

We reproach the sex every day with folly and impertinence; while I am confident had they the advantages of education equal to us, they would be guilty of less than ourselves ... The capacities of women are supposed to be greater, and their senses quicker than those of men; and what they might be capable of being bred to, is plain from some instances of female wit, which this age is not without. Which upbraids us with injustice, and looks as if we denied women the advantages of education, for fear that they should vie with men in their improvements.

He did not believe in 'female government' but thought women should be fit companions for men. This was the new ideal of marriage as a relationship between companions which had first appeared in the puritan movement and was to challenge the authority of aristocratic property marriage in the eighteenth-century novel. The right to a marriage of conscience had already been hinted at in the dissenting tradition which asserted the equality of conscience and the right of improvement, spiritual, intellectual, social and economic of all, regardless of sex or station.

SR.2, August 1972

Women against the Demon Drink

AMANDA SEBESTYEN

What was the biggest feminist organization a hundred years ago? With 30,000 members all over the world, fighting around everything from the vote to prostitution to lynching to child labour to kindergartens to dress reform? Who was its charismatic leader, the most famous woman of her place and time?

The organization is long forgotten: *The Women's Christian Temperance Union.* 'It is probable', their leader the American Frances Willard once remarked, 'that if a passer-by were asked why we are gathered here, he would exclaim, "Because they are a lot of cranks and fanatics, who do not know what they want, except to take away the poor man's glass of beer and spoil his hours of recreation." ' That judgement has come down to us to this day. But there was a time when temperance (or teetotalism, or Prohibition) was part and parcel of every struggle for women's rights.

Bars, after all, were and are male territory. A 'Masculine Republic' – or, in the words of a modern feminist, 'tavernacles invulnerable to female intrusion, an extension of the buddy system, a place where men get away from their wives'.

'They tell me,' said Frances Willard, 'that the saloon is the poor man's club. When I hear that, I often say to myself, "What is his wife's club, I wonder?" ' Alcohol primed male violence, then as now. (In 1976 the National Council of Women interviewed battered women in a northern hospital: '70 per cent were assaulted on Friday or Saturday nights or Sunday lunchtime by their husbands on their return from the local pub or club.')

The fight against 'King Alcohol' became a metaphor for the sex war. Drink gave a reason for finding men unbearable and justified withdrawing from them. Drink and tobacco were 'the great separatists' between the sexes, wrote Frances Willard.

. . . Violent anger and physical disgust at men, otherwise tabooed, could be expressed in the temperance cause. 'If I were a young woman,' Carry Nation exploded, 'I would say to the men who use tobacco and who would wish to converse with me: "Use the telephone, come no closer!" I would as soon kiss a spitoon as kiss such a mouth.'

Like the campaigns against slavery in the USA, and 'white slavery' – state-organized prostitution – in this country, the temperance movement was a training ground where women learned to speak and organize. It was seen as the equivalent to a union: 'One drunkard's wife prostrate beneath his hobnailed shoes can do nothing but moan and agonize, but if she joins herself to the great groups of women who have banded themselves together to work steadily on to avenge the indignity under which she suffers, this indignity will cease.'

Again, like the movements against slavery and the 'regulation' of prostitutes, the temperance struggle brought women up against the organized power of men from the ruling class downwards. Josephine Butler, leader in the fight against prostitution and also a member of the flamboyant Good Templars, saw slavers, white slavers and drink dealers as part of the same 'privileged and protected class whose interests are opposed to the best interests of the mass of our people'.

. . . The temperance movement was part of a humanitarian wave opposed to child labour, capital punishment, blood sports (the movement's first lecture theatre was a converted cockpit), and for universal suffrage. The radical teetotallers campaigned for drinking fountains and libraries, and for galleries and entertainments to open on Sunday. As the prices came down, they set up coffee houses with papers and space for meetings. They needed – and made – a whole temperance subculture to support themselves.

Though history records the pioneer teetotallers as 'The Men of Preston', a very high proportion of the movement were women. From the start we hear of incidents like the women's teetotal picnic in Wychwood Forest, broken up when 'drunkenness, ignorance and brutality, in the shape of men from the neighbouring village, surrounded the platform'. The reasons for the antagonism are clear. 'Every pay day the pub was besieged by wives desperately anxious to feed and clothe the family' (*Drink and the Victorians*). In most parts of the country it was impossible for women to earn a living wage outside of prostitution. The pub was also the local brothel, with rooms upstairs for the poorest prostitutes and small huts close by for the better-off. The barmaids themselves – 'white slaves of the bar' – were still working ninety hours a week by the end of the century, on wages so low that alcoholism seems to have been a happy relief. Radical and Chartist women were

sure of a big response to speeches which brought temperance together
with the rights of women and sometimes even birth control.

In America, the founders of the women's rights movement were also
in the New York branch of the women's temperance organization.
Susan B. Anthony had begun her public career with a group called
the Daughters of Temperance; the first feminist magazine, Amelia

Bloomer's *Lily*, was originally 'Devoted to Temperance and
Literature', moving on to become 'a monthly journal devoted to the
Emancipation of Woman from Intemperance, Injustice, Prejudice and
Bigotry'. For these early feminists the central temperance issue became
women's right to divorce from drunken husbands. Elizabeth Cady
Stanton was even more outspoken: drunken husbands raped their
wives. 'Alas! Alas! Who can measure the mountains of sorrow and
suffering endured in unwelcome motherhood in the abodes where
terror-stricken women and children are the victims of strong men
frenzied with passion and intoxicating drink?' The most fundamental
of women's rights, said Stanton, was 'the right to her own body' – the
right to refuse. Shocked audiences correctly interpreted this as an
attack on the heart of the marriage institution. Susan Anthony, as a
spinster, was torn apart by the press for daring to urge women not to

let drunkards father their children. Less daring feminists like Lucy Stone admitted in letters that 'the abuse in question is perfectly appalling', but felt that 'premature' discussion would 'frighten women away'. Perhaps she was right – there was a conservative takeover of the New York branch after Stanton's declaration on divorce at the 1852 Temperance Convention. The radical feminists withdrew to concentrate on the vote, though they remained temperance advocates all their lives.

... In November 1874 Frances Willard founded the Women's Christian Temperance Union. Their programme was 'destruction of the liquor traffic, a living wage for all workers, an eight hour day, equal civil rights and equal moral standards'. Over the next twenty years, in fact, votes for women and Prohibition became almost synonymous. The Prohibition Party was the first to promise women's suffrage, and it was accepted that wherever women got the chance they would vote the towns dry. At any state referendum on women's suffrage the brewers would line up all the barkeepers to keep the women out.

There was one other goal that all the feminists agreed on. They called it by the daunting name of Social Purity. But what they wanted, like us, was an end to the sexual coercion of women. Frances Willard defended the unmarried mother: 'a phrase that we must chase out of the dictionary of common speech is the phrase "an illegitimate child". No such child was ever born. The only illegitimate factor in the problem is the father.' The WCTU's Social Purity Department demanded harsher penalties for 'white slavers', rehabilitation centres for prostitutes who wanted to find other work, and an age of consent fixed at eighteen (in twenty of the states it was ten). There was a White Shield department of men who promised never to exploit women sexually. The WCTU campaigned against insulting advertising images:

A woman sees a poster on the hoardings that by the exhibition made in figure and attitude painfully impresses her sense of self-respect; but [alone] she can do nothing to banish the billboard ... Organize that woman into a group with others who have felt the same sense of degradation, and something can be done.

It was a life-sized Cleopatra in a Kansas hotel that started Carry Nation on her one-woman war: 'It is very significant that pictures of naked women are in the saloons. Women are stripped of everything by them. Her husband is torn from her, she is robbed of her son, her food and virtue, and then they strip her clothes off and hang her up in those dens of robbery and murder.' Carry Nation smashed a bottle over the picture and returned next day with several rocks and a steel rod to sweep the bar clean. A maverick never quite disowned by the WCTU, she travelled alone through Kansas, Illinois, Ohio and on to New York, paying for her cart full of brickbats and axes by sales of her *Smasher's Mail* and souvenir hatchets in cardboard. At over six foot, she had all the makings of a folk heroine.

In the meantime Frances Willard was notching up her twentieth year as president, averaging 20,000 miles a year and one speech a day as well as all her writing and lobbying. She was widely regarded as a saint, or 'the uncrowned queen of American womanhood'. Strangely enough this immense fame and her personal power over the WCTU's huge membership don't seem to have stopped her learning and growing. She herself became more and more radical.

It was only our ignorance of the condition of the industrial classes that magnified a single propaganda and minimised every other so that Temperance people in the old days believed that if men and women were temperate all other material good would follow in the train of that great grace. But now we know that . . . there are millions of men and women in Great Britain and America who would gladly work, but the pitiless restraining hand of invention and monopoly hold them back . . . For myself, twenty years of study and observation have convinced me that poverty is a prime cause of intemperance.

She called her new position 'gospel politics'. At the giant St Louis People's Convention in 1892 Willard tried for a merger between the WCTU, the Prohibition Party (which had just polled its highest-ever 270,000 votes), the woman suffragists, the Knights of Labor, the Federation of Organized Trade and Labor Unions, and the radical farming Granger and Populist parties. She failed; both temperance and feminist movements entered a very conservative period, lobbying to get laws passed from above not by grass roots action. The initiative passed from the WCTU to the male 'Dry Boss' leaders of the Anti-Saloon League.

. . . The British Women's Temperance Association had been inspired by the Women's Crusade and by another remarkable American organizer, Mother Stewart, who had the marvellous idea of using the law to help drunkards' wives sue the saloonkeepers for damages. She met and impressed a Scottish organizer, Mrs Parker, at the Chicago Temperance Conference, and was invited over to inaugurate the first British women's temperance conference in Dundee in 1874. The new Association's paper, *The White Ribbon*, steered clear of open feminism but made a strong plea for women's right to go out into the world – in the interests of the home, of course:

The cold-hearted critic may make his strictures, and tell us that our sphere is in the kitchen or the parlour but not the public platform . . . We shrink from public interest and popular gaze, but the true wife and mother cannot be content to merely shut down the windows and bolt the door of her house to secure her own safety so long as the tyrant alcohol prowls around her home, stealing her sons and daughters the moment they cross the threshold.

BWTA speakers linked temperance to the Factory Acts against child labour, the repeal of the Corn Laws, the abolition of slavery, even dress reform – but not to the vote.

Then in 1890 the Association elected a new president. Lady Henry Somerset was a suffragist and a radical, a 'traitor to her class' who mounted platforms beside dockers and miners. She was a sexual outcast who'd dared to leave her husband after years of misery and to sue for custody of the children. Her meeting with Frances Willard in 1891 began 'the most beautiful friendship that has ever blessed my life'. The two women's politics were close, and when Isabel Somerset took over the *Women's Signal* she hoped to embody Willard's conception of the temperance movement as 'a clearing-house for reform'.

Some of the longstanding BWTA workers took a more doubtful view of 'the do-everything policy of our American friends'. They were afraid of 'saddling our Association with so thorny a subject [as votes for women, thought one] which most of us as individuals cordially approve'. They were reluctant to work around prostitution: 'If the association adopts this line of work, mothers will feel unable to bring their daughters to our assemblies, for it is the subject of all others unsuited to young minds.' Above all, they disagreed with the new president's 'gospel politics', her view of alcoholism as a disease caused by social conditions, and statements like 'we are too prone to say that all poverty comes from intemperance.'

The new magazine may have been a shock to the hardliners – who called for 'more Gospel Temperance matter' – but it was a wonderful read. There were interviews with novelists like Sarah Grand, artists like Rosa Bonheur, suffragists like Millicent Fawcett, trades unionists like Amie Hicks; pieces of feminist history like the winning of the Married Women's Property Act; theoretical articles by Josephine Butler; discussions of Froebel infant teaching.

Social Purity campaigning was a central theme, for as the music hall and the mass circulation daily developed they brought with them Victorian equivalents of the strip show and the Page Three Girl – favourite subjects were women posing in pink tights for 'The Turkish Bath' and 'The Greek Slave' (complete with manacles). The *Signal* gave warm support to the women picketing music halls and denouncing sexist covers and advertising images. At the same time – and unusually – the magazine supported women art students who'd been refused the right to draw male nudes, taking a clear line against 'amusements that degrade women for the purposes of gain' and not nakedness itself. Isabel Somerset herself was not a complete Prohibitionist. 'She believed that, if the claws of the trade were cut, wine-drinking might be as innocent a pleasure in England and America as it is in France.'

The BWTA committee was made of sterner stuff. The final straw for them was probably the *Signal*'s serial, an advanced story of professional women with one heroine breaking off her engagement after a night at Ibsen's *Doll's House*, and the other falling tragically in love with a married man. A majority of the committee voted that the president should resign. Instead, she asked for a vote from the rank and file, and at a special conference the local branches supported her new policy. The committee resigned and formed the British Women's Total Abstinence Union. To them, the decision looked like a victory for Isabel Somerset's personal charisma over political principle. But I'd like to think the majority of the temperance women were casting a vote for feminism and not just a glamorous new leader.

The *Signal* went on from strength to strength, edited by Florence Fenwick Miller, the only woman leader writer in the national press (are there any now?) and the first woman in England to follow Lucy Stone's example and keep her own name on marriage – simply changing from 'Miss' to 'Mrs' Fenwick Miller. The *Signal* retained its liveliness, with debates on 'Should Women Play Football?' and dress reform. It was better organized, with more subscribers and advertisers. But in 1897 another split occurred, and feminism and temperance never came together so closely again in this country . . .

SR.100, November 1980

Jessie

EDITED BY SUZIE FLEMING AND GLODEN DALLAS

'*You're a bonny fighter, Jessie, but you've got the wrong name. I think we should call you Battling Bella.*'

Thus, as Jessie Stephen says, does the labour movement coin nicknames for those it really respects. Jessie is now eighty-one. A socialist and pacifist all her life and, before the First World War, a militant suffragette – a political connection which she remembers as typical of many women's experience at that time – she is still now involved in trade union work and is a fierce believer in full and genuine equality for women. She was the first woman president of the Bristol Trades Council, an office she only gave up a couple of years ago.

The eldest of eleven children of a caring, though overworked mother, and of a skilled tailor, who was nonetheless quite often out of work, she was brought up in some poverty. From an early age Jessie took various jobs after school hours to help keep the family going. Her father was, from the beginning, a member of the Independent Labour Party (I L P), which was established in 1893 specifically to work for parliamentary representation for, and by, the working class, but which in practice in its early years encompassed a wide range of labour and socialist opinion and activities.

Here Jessie's early political career is told in extracts from her unpublished autobiography and from recorded conversations with Susie Fleming and with Gloden Dallas, who edited and annotated the material.

Good gracious, when I was fourteen my father gave me Darwin to read. It was double dutch to me then, but when I was a couple of years older I did read it and appreciated it. He used to read all the Rationalist Press publications and stuff by Engels and Tom Paine, though he left school when he was eight.

I was a member of the Socialist Sunday School. My dad insisted on us all going there, and what we learned was in no way inferior to the ethics taught elsewhere. We had all sorts there – we had Catholics, Protestants, Jewish children. We all went in it together. Two of our family were christened there. There were about fifty to sixty boys and girls every Sunday morning, but in the afternoon I had to go to the ordinary religious school because Mother was very devout in that respect. She was C. of E. and Dad, of course, was agnostic, more or less, and when the parsons used to come and visit us, there'd be quite a set to.

Jessie did well at school and won a scholarship, but felt that without a regular wage she would only be a burden on her family. So she became a domestic servant and started trying to organize her fellow workers 'below stairs'.

At fifteen I became a pupil teacher and was much elated, for it had always been my ambition to teach. Unfortunately for my dreams unemployment became worse so there was nothing for it but to leave school. I had to choose between taking jobs which ran between half a crown and four shillings a week, and the prospect of domestic service where board and lodging helped the money wage. And it was my experience that there were far too many employers who treated their domestic help as slaves. And the sons of the house, they thought they had a right to walk into your bedroom – that's a fact. If a girl got pregnant they sacked her, and if a son was responsible they sent him away. But the girl never got any money. If she couldn't go back to her family there was nothing else she could do but go on the streets, and a lot of them did, sometimes girls of fourteen and fifteen.

And these domestic servants, they were much more intelligent than people gave them credit for at that time. Employers used to talk about them being ignorant Highland so-and-sos. They weren't so ignorant. When I began to think about ways and means of organizing my fellow servants and started to canvass in my spare time, I was really encouraged by the interest the girls showed. I tried to get their support for a trade union. And this work was beginning to get results in recruitment of members of the new Scottish Domestic Workers' Federation, subscription three halfpence weekly. I used to go round the back doors of big houses, getting the girls to join the union.

About the same time, in her late teens, Jessie was much involved in socialist and suffragette agitation in Glasgow. It was through these activities that she was brought in touch with John Maclean, perhaps the greatest of the Clydeside socialists and also with Helen Crawfurd, a Women's Social and Political Union (WSPU) militant and socialist who was, like Maclean, an uncompromising opponent of the Great War.

Well, I got my political training when I was only twelve years old. I was selling the *Labour Woman* outside the St Andrew's hall, Glasgow. That was a very small magazine, they only paid a ha'penny for it in those days. Keir Hardie was the speaker, and when he came out and saw me – I was very tiny then – he said, 'Ah, that's all right, lassie, ye'll be a real credit to the movement yet.' I was so proud of this I ran all the way home and told my dad, and he says, 'Maybe you will, maybe you will.'

I became vice-chairman of my local ILP branch, Maryhill, when I was sixteen. That was the youngest age you were allowed to join as a full member and, around that time, I became a member of the WSPU in Glasgow and attended branch meetings and demonstrations whenever I could. It must have been when I was in service. I know that because that's how I was able to drop acid into the postal pillar boxes without being suspected, because I walked down from where I was employed in my cap and apron, you know, muslin apron, black frock, nobody would ever suspect me of dropping acid through the box.

Mind you, we in the WSPU attacked property but never life. As far as the more violent things were concerned, I don't think the ordinary working woman was quite so anxious to be in that sort of thing. They didn't mind the smashing of plate glass windows but they felt the other things, for instance the burning down of castles, were risking human life and they were against that. You could see that there was a sort of dissent to the widening of the violence.

We had these regular meetings, open air and indoors. And we used to get big meetings. It wasn't a question of hole in the corner. And for women to come out like that, and with the Liberal Party doing practically everything they could to smash the whole idea of what the women stood for. I know the Liberals are always claiming to be progressive, but they were our bitterest enemies. They could've given us the vote way back in 1910, but they wouldn't do it and we had to wait till the end of the war, and then got it at the age of thirty instead of twenty-one.

All kinds of people came to our big meetings, working women, even working men, and I think the idea of the middle-class men was that this must not be allowed to continue, and this was why we had all the interruptions at the meetings and so on. That one was pretty violent when Mrs Pankhurst was on, and she was released under the Cat and Mouse Act. That was pretty violent that night because the police had been so careful – they were on the roof, they were in the hall, all over the place – to see that she didn't get into the hall. Then when the chairman announced that she had the greatest pleasure in announcing the arrival of her respected and beloved leader – because you used very emotive words – everybody thought it was a joke. But we didn't because we knew that something had happened. We had all the platform with barbed wire around it, with bunting over the barbed wire, with flower pots and all sorts, and one woman had one of those revolvers with blank shot. And when Mrs Pankhurst stepped forward, you should have seen the faces of the police. They couldn't believe their eyes.

Nobody told them how she got in there, but we were told afterwards that she came in the Corporation laundry basket. The WSPU organizer got in touch with some of our Labour councillors – well, they were ILPers in those days – they were very good. Well, when the police tried to drag poor Mrs Pankhurst away, they rushed forward to the bunting and got their hands all lacerated. We were throwing flower pots, there were all sorts banged at the police. You didn't think about it being violence, you only wanted to protect the woman you'd brought there. The police were absolute bullies in those days, and the *Daily Mail* and papers like that were working up some sort of agitation; we were having the clothes torn off our backs, the hair torn out of our heads before we'd ever been violent. Some of the ordinary men were even worse than the police. They threatened to throw me in the river once and I said, 'Well, if you throw me in, I'll take you with me.' And that was trying to be brave but, you know, you were scared to death.

To counter such hostility the Glaswegian suffragettes, and similarly those in other provincial cities, could rely on a network of support, much of which came from within the local socialist movement.

Och, yes, there were my comrades in the branch. There were three or four of them who were dockers who were really keen I L Pers, really keen. They certainly passed the word along, and when the meeting took place there they were, lined up against the walls. Nobody suspected, of course, that there'd be anybody there to help these poor, weak women. Weak is right, too. Yes, we had quite a lot of help from ordinary working men and women in those days. Then there was Mr Austin who had a chain of tea rooms, the ordinary cheap tea rooms in the city and he used to give me the free use of them for my meetings. That's the kind of help we used to get.

Mary Miller, who was the woman editor of the *Glasgow Herald*, was very sympathetic to the socialist movement and also to the domestic servants. She believed in the work of the W S P U although she couldn't declare herself. We had a curious combination. You had very wealthy women, upper-class women, and the ordinary working woman, but we got on well together. I remember Helen Crawfurd who was an I L Per. She went to gaol for breaking windows, and was gaoled during the war, as was John Maclean. Good old John, I knew him well because he used to come and speak at some of our meetings and demonstrations. They treated him cruelly. He was held in very high regard in the socialist movement, no doubt about that.

Jessie's feminist convictions kept her loyal to the militant policy which pursued in such a single-minded way the achievement of the vote as a panacea for all the ills inflicted on women. Her socialism, and feelings of the 'ordinary' women whom, by the nature of her work and social background, she met day to day, convinced her that the vote alone was no solution to the problems which women were having to face.

There was a lot more than the vote. You see, most of these books – I've read a good few of them at different times – they don't really go very deep. They don't talk about the discussions we used to have, the aspirations the ordinary member of the W S P U was thinking about. These were about jobs, about wages, about the present matrimonial laws. All that sort of thing used to be discussed by us. I didn't know a lot about it, but some of these women did. One of them was a divorcee – a socialist, mind you – and a very hardworking woman, and she used to bring up things like this which were interesting to people who knew something about it.

And those of us who were socialists were far more interested in economics than they gave us credit for. Some of these women who were really active in the WSPU had deep convictions about the economic state of society, and there was the question of housing, and the question of making life easier for the woman in the home, and maternity benefits. The vote was only the means to an end, to a new state of society where women could be treated as human beings, not as second-class citizens.

Largely as a result of her political activities, Jessie found congenial work hard to find in Glasgow. She went to London, where she made contact with the English Domestic Workers' Union and, with their aid, found a job with people who did not object to having a trade unionist maid.

After the outbreak of war she returned to Glasgow, and did various jobs which, until then, had been regarded as men's work, just as hundreds of other domestic workers had been tempted to try their luck in wartime occupations. It was during this time in Glasgow that Jessie met Sylvia Pankhurst who was campaigning for adult suffrage and an end to the war.

Naturally I introduced myself to Sylvia. She asked me what I was doing and told me a lot about her work with the Workers' Suffrage Federation (WSF) in London. As I moved away she said suddenly, 'How would you like to come and work for me?' I said I would like to come to London but I did not have the fare and would have to ask my father first. Dad was pessimistic. He told me not be foolish and to stay where I was, but Mother was more sympathetic. One night she handed me some money when we were alone and said I wasn't to tell anyone where I had raised it. Till now I have kept the secret of how I raised my fare. In Bow, where Sylvia had her headquarters, she had established a creche and a clinic and, though her strong pacifist views were not very popular, her work in this district was highly regarded and she herself almost worshipped.

When Sylvia decided that Jessie had had enough experience in organization and propaganda in London, she was sent to the provinces to start new branches of the WSF and to raise money for the work in Bow.

There were two of us, Mrs Boyce, a working woman who'd brought up a family of twelve kids and was going round the country, just like me. She gave me lots of hints as to what to do. She says, 'Always take with you a pound of candles because you'll find in some places no light, when you'll want to read in your bed and you can't.' She was a lovely old soul, I must say. She'd been in the WSPU and, of course, she was a socialist as well. She was a fine worker. She was fifty. I think of some of those women there in the East End.

When I was working for Sylvia I got thirty bob a week and it wasn't enough sometimes to pay my digs when I was travelling through the country. But I used to go to the ILP branches as well – freelance, of course, because none of us were on a salary – we just had to depend on the branches to pay us what they could. They might manage to give you £3 one week, but others couldn't raise that. So they gave you hospitality and expenses.

You couldn't buy new clothes on that. In fact, I went to Burnley market once and bought a remnant there for 6d to make myself a blouse. My first stop on the WSF tour was Sheffield where I was lucky enough to find lodgings with Mrs Manion. The friendly atmosphere helped me enormously in this first provincial venture. The author Edward Carpenter lived just outside Sheffield and Mrs Manion told me of her interest in his books. Her favourite was one whose title I can't remember now, but I think it was *The Coming of Love* [*Love's Coming of Age*]. Over this she would enthuse and recite passages from memory. In the socialist movement it was very widely read.

Jessie was very successful as a fund raiser, due in part to her capacity to get on with, and through to, 'what they call the lower echelons of labour'. Her usefulness didn't prevent, though, a few rows with Sylvia who could 'charm when she liked, but at the core was inclined to be as autocratic as her mother and her elder sister, Christabel'.

She continued to work for the WSF until spring 1917, when she was chosen as an ILP organizer for Bermondsey, in which branch the leading figure was a Quaker, Dr Salter.

The doctor felt we must attract the women and girls in local factories – in short, I was to act as industrial organizer as well. But because the ILP saw my industrial work was putting burdens upon me, it was decided to appoint two other women to help build up the political organization.

Eventually I had two ex-suffragettes, Mary Richardson, who slashed the Velasquez painting, and Ada Broughton. Between all my other activities, I stood outside factory gates, handing out union literature. Success did not come at first, though a wage increase won for leather workers had aroused much attention. But by autumn 1918, over 5,000 girls had been recruited [into the National Union of Women Workers].

Most of Jessie's life since that period has been spent as a political and trade union organizer, with particular concern for the problems of women. In the twenties she was active in the Workers' Birth Control movement.

I've had people coming up to me at my meetings, asking my advice because they knew I belonged to that group and, you know, you listen to some tragedies. It's not because they wanted children but they didn't know how to stop them. The Workers' Birth Control people really were pioneers. They used to hold propaganda meetings and issue little pamphlets.

Curious thing, when I was secretary to Leonora Eyles who wrote for *Women's Own* when it was a 2d magazine, if she ever had an article on birth control, do you know, we'd be flooded out with letters of inquiry for weeks later.

The methods were a bit crude then. There was either what they called the 'cage' in those days or, apart from that, there was a fine sponge with a silk thread attached to it, soaked in quinine and olive oil, or quinine and linseed oil, but preferably olive oil because it didn't smell so. They had to insert this, and immediately after intercourse, they pulled this down because they'd impregnated the womb with this stuff and that prevented conception. You know, my mother used to speak to me, being the eldest, you see. She'd say, 'I don't know, I wish I didn't have all these babies.' I said, 'Why don't you ask Dad to do something about it?' She says, 'Oh no, he says it's not natural.' A socialist, mind you, and he hadn't learned enough about that. It so happened that, a few months later, I came across a book which gave all the information and I handed it to my mother. I said, 'Now, Mother, here's your chance, read this.' She was forty-two at the time and she didn't have the menopause till she was fifty-four. She had no more children though. That's what you call teaching grandma to suck eggs.

For a young girl of her time, an independent and unconventional life like Jessie's can have been neither personally easy nor readily acceptable to society at large. What were its difficulties and rewards?

In those days it was unusual for a woman, especially a young woman, to lead an independent life. And a woman speaker was fair game as I learned in the days of the suffrage campaign. One heckler in Sheffield shouted, 'Would you rather sleep with a woman or a man?' Remembering a somewhat similar question put to a prominent suffragette and her reply I said, 'A woman, wouldn't you?' There was a burst of laughter at this and he silently stole away.

Some of the women lived together but of course the ordinary working girls never got to that stage. They hadn't got the philosophy to start with and they couldn't have afforded to live like that. It's still true. There isn't the money there. They might be prepared to experiment if they had the means. There was also a cult of free love in the socialist movement in my youth but we won't go into that too deeply.

As to my public political life, my dad was quite proud of it as a matter of fact. He used to come to meetings with me and all that sort of thing, but Mother wasn't so keen on it. You know, she says to me, 'You ought to be thinking of having a home of your own instead of rushing about all over the place.' And later on in life she used to say, 'Look at all your sisters, what lovely homes they have' and so on and so on. My dad was with me then. 'What's wrong with this home?' he says. 'She's got a lovely flat here, nice furniture all on her own. I wish I'd been able to do what she's done.'

The curious thing about my mother, even though she was so quiet and the very opposite of my dad, when the deaconess came up to her once and said, 'Oh, Mrs Stephen, you must be so hurt over your eldest daughter and her brother', preaching peace you see. She says, 'When the country's at war they should be doing their bit.' And mother says, 'I'm not ashamed of my boy and girl. They're doing what they were taught by their father when they were youngsters. I'm very proud of them. I wish all my boys and girls had taken that stand.' And the next May Day procession, there was mother. She'd never gone on a May Day procession in her life, and with a little pennant, marching.

It would be inaccurate and unjust, by concentrating on the events of more than fifty years ago, to give the impression that Jessie in any way lives in the past. She was the first woman president of the Bristol Trades Council, an office she only gave up a couple of years ago, and is still active in the TUC. How does she estimate the progress of women since the winning of the vote?

Most of my public work has been concerned with the organization of women and advocacy of their claim to equal status with men. Too many assumed that the victory on women suffrage would bring other benefits automatically. When the women were glorying in this new-found so-called freedom, we were only just beginning. For those of us who looked ahead, it appeared to be the beginning of the real fight and so it has proved to be, despite the small gains made on the way. Take the myth about bra-burning fabricated by the American press. Such an incident never took place and yet male journalists and radio and television broadcasters continue to repeat the lie every time they find an opportunity to sneer at women's liberation. Truly, you need seven-league boots to catch up with an untruth. For me, and others who share my views, this is another example of the prejudice that dies hard in our menfolk.

SR.32, February 1975
[*Suzie Fleming is a member of the Wages for Housework Campaign.*]

Nine Years Together
BELSIZE LANE WOMEN'S GROUP

The London Women's Liberation Workshop – a network of small groups with an information service – was the first organization of the British women's movement. The Workshop in its original form no longer exists. A Woman's Place has taken over as an information centre, local centres have mushroomed, groups like Women's Aid and the National Abortion Campaign have developed along separate feminist lines.

But the small local women's groups which used to be the backbone of the Workshop are still alive: Belsize Lane was one of the first. They are still meeting after nine years.

At the peak of the Workshop there were seventy small local groups. When the Belsize Lane group began in 1969 there were only two or three other groups. We were very conscious that the Workshop's structure was completely different from the traditional Left from which many of us had come. Our women's groups were deliberately small and federated to avoid the pitfalls of centralization and hierarchy. We wanted to redefine the meaning of politics to include an analysis of our daily lives, so although we discussed feminism in other countries like Vietnam and Cuba, and read feminist literature from Europe and the States, we concentrated on who we were and what we could do now in our own country.

We wrote a statement called 'Our Point of View' which became the basis for the Workshop Manifesto reprinted in each issue of *Shrew*. *Shrew* (begun in 1969 and briefly called *Bird* and *Harpie's Bizarre!*) was the Workshop's monthly magazine. Each issue was as different as the group which produced it – political discussion, poetry, personal exploration, psychology, Third World. *Shrew* was '6d for women and 9d for men until equal pay'. In May 1971, the Belsize Lane group produced an issue of *Shrew* on the family. It was the first time most of us had ever written or produced anything collectively. We began nervously and ended with a real sense of achievement.

Most of what we wrote in those days seems more angry and passionate than articles in feminist magazines today. Do women entering the movement now, when feminist ideas have become fairly common currency, experience the same sense of revelation and exhilaration that we did then?

Certainly the ridicule and cruelty we received from the press helped our own solidarity. Our views and activities were misrepresented by all the papers – particularly in relation to: 1) leadership (they couldn't understand our non-hierarchical structure); 2) attitude to men (they thought we wanted to devour them for breakfast); 3) bra-burning (that one died hard). We insisted on being interviewed by women journalists only, but of course this was no guarantee that we would be taken seriously or that there would be no editorial intervention. For example,

Jill Tweedie wrote a mocking article on the Tufnell Park group in 1969 and the *Sketch* did a two-page spread with plenty of pictures headed 'Inside the Sex Revolution Headquarters: Sketch exclusive on a plot to destroy the masculine ego'!

Mary Holland's article on the Oxford Conference was sarcastic and patronizing: 'Hell Bent On Women's Liberation'. But a growing number of women journalists, these among them, though derisive at first, later joined the movement or at least became close sympathizers.

The movement was growing so fast that by the beginning of 1970 we felt confident enough to hold a national conference. Three hundred people were expected; six hundred arrived. Women, and some men, came from all over Britain, and a few from Europe, to Ruskin College, Oxford.

The groups and individuals who came had never met as a body before and although there was often strong disagreement among us we all felt an exhilaration *knowing* that we were at the beginning of a new movement. There were proposals that we research into women's history; that we lobby for a Sex Discrimination Act; that we campaign for free contraception and abortion on demand; that we study alternatives to the nuclear family and childrearing. Though many women at the Conference did not have children, questioning their assumed role of motherhood was a dominant theme. Several sympathetic men organized the first movement creche – now a commonplace, but then a total innovation. Ellen and Sue from Belsize Lane were in Liberation Films which organized a crew to film the conference. *A Woman's Place* was finished a year later.

In the autumn of 1970, Carole represented our group on the committee which organized the first national women's demonstration since the suffragettes. Thrashing out the four demands, even organizing the practical jobs proved surprisingly difficult. The Ministry of Works didn't help either, refusing our request to use Trafalgar Square for fear we would do something obscene. Angrily we announced we would march there anyway, and permission was finally granted.

The weather on the day of the demonstration – 6 March 1971 – was unbelievably cold with sudden bursts of snow, but a massive crowd of women, men and children gathered at Speaker's Corner. Down Oxford Street we went with floats and badges, and placards listing the finally-agreed four demands: 'Equal Pay Now; Equal Education and Job Opportunities; Free 24-hour Nurseries; Free Contraception and Abortion on Demand'. All the way there were chants: 'Out of the office; Out of the home; Out from under; Women unite!' The Women's Street Theatre Group, with grotesquely made-up faces, danced the whole way to the music of an Eddie Cantor song: 'Keep young and beautiful; it's your duty to be beautiful; keep young and beautiful, if you want to be loved.'

After presenting a petition at Downing Street, the march arrived at Trafalgar Square where there were speakers on the four demands, a play performed by the Street Theatre Group and a collection taken up which vastly exceeded our expectations.

In the weeks following the demo, the Workshop was suddenly enlarged by fifty new groups bringing the total to sixty-six. The growth was so sudden and enormous the Workshop could hardly cope with it.

1969–71

After the march we got involved in a wide range of activities, sometimes as a group, and at others only a few members. We were invited, as most groups were, to speak all over London – to schools, colleges, trade unions, women's institutes – and we went in twos to show that, though we were in common agreement, no *one* person could represent the movement. A few of us were involved in the demonstrations against the Miss World Contest and the subsequent trial of some of the demonstrators. But many of us felt critical: the protest created mis-understandings and an image of the women's movement which took years to dispel. It allowed the media to ignore the other important women's issues such as abortion, equal pay, sexuality, the family.

1972 Wimpy Bars

'No unaccompanied woman will be served after 11.00 pm.' We staged a late-night protest at the Finchley Road Wimpy. The staff were friendly; the manager absent. Later that year other groups organized a more comprehensive campaign and the ruling was changed.

1971 Feminist Film Workshop

Some of our group when in the original Tufnell Park Group had made a ten-minute silent film: *Women, Are You Satisfied With Your Life?* Using stills from magazines it showed the complicity of advertising in idealizing woman as housewife. We all recognized the power of media images and the potential of film for radical organizing. Many women, even in the movement, had never seen the films available on feminism, so we organized the Workshop to show as many of these films as we could (in those days still most films were from the US) and teach anyone who wanted to learn how to project films for themselves.

We showed rushes from *A Woman's Place*, the documentary about the Oxford Conference and 1971 women's march which two of our group were editing. And proceeds from the Film Workshop went to Sue towards making *One, Two, Three* about the Children's Community Centre.

1971 Children's Community Centre onwards

Our groups campaigned for play centres for after school and in the holidays, to be run on more radical lines than the few centres that actually existed. There were several meetings with local parents, leaf-lettings and discussions but people lived quite far away from each other and the activities drifted.

Two of us from Belsize Lane began organizing in greater earnest for better pre-school provision. With five other women, only one other in the movement, we chose a redevelopment area, Highgate New Town, near where one of us lived and got to know each house as it became, or was about to become empty.

After eighteen months' hard work we finally opened a nursery, the Children's Community Centre. It has a man and a woman worker, is co-operatively run, is as non-sexist as possible and publicly funded . . . though money has always been a problem. The council has finally given permanent premises at The Children's Community Centre, 20 Lawford Road, London NW5. These kinds of activity meant that some of us were spending less time with our specific women's group and more time applying feminist politics in community action. All of us continually took the ideas and projects back to the group for discussion.

Audrey Battersby, age 42; Student Counsellor; also involved in Abortion/Contraception Campaign; kids: Ben, 15; Anna and Frank, 13.

Sally Belfrage, 41; Writer; Eve, 11; Moby, 9.

Sue Crockford, 35; Youth Centre leader; also involved in Children's Community Centre and One Two Three Films; Barnaby, 8.

Carole de Jong, 41; Potter; in Women's Art Group, Nightcleaners' Campaign; Max, 9.

Nan Fromer, 37; Editor for educational film-strip company; was in Women in Media; Jenny, 12; Megan, 7.

Mica Nava, 38; Research Student at Institute of Education; previously in Women's Theatre Group, 1973–76; Zadoc, 13; Orson, 11; Jacob, 8.

Carolyn Roth, 31; Nurse.

Dinah Brooke, 41; Writer; previously with Women's Street Theatre Group and Women's Psychology Group; Emily and Felix, 12.

Judith Brandt, 32; Psychotherapist; was in Women's Psychology Group.

Sally Fraser, 28; Acupuncturist, photographer; previously involved in Claimants' Union and Women's Newspaper.

These last three are in India with Bhagwan Shree Rajneesh.

The present Belsize Lane group was formed in 1970, after the first Women's Conference at Oxford. But many of us had been going to meetings since 1969, at Tufnell Park, Belsize Lane or elsewhere. We had become involved for broadly similar reasons, but there were certain doubts that persisted in the early stages.

Nan: Like many experiences that have shaken me to the core, my initial involvement was largely accidental. Late in 1969, a woman I barely knew invited me to a woman's meeting in Tufnell Park. 'They call themselves revolutionary socialists,' she said. Without a second thought I accepted, secure in the knowledge that, whatever their aims, attending this meeting was bound to be an improvement over plopping my weary pregnant body in front of the telly in our freezing sitting room for yet another evening.

Fifteen minutes after our arrival, I was aware that I would not miss another of these weekly meetings if I could help it. If it did not provide me with instant sanity, it did provide assurance that I need no longer consider myself a candidate for the 'funny farm', since so many of the women arrayed in that small sitting room, despite their surface differences, seemed to share what for so long I had believed to be my own idiosyncratic suffering.

Sue: I resisted joining the women's movement for a few months. I was told it would divide the Left. And it took me some time to acknowledge that ordinary daily events could be political. How could the solidarity of 16 million Vietnamese struggling and winning against 200 million Americans compare with the underachievement of women?

But I'd been teaching, and I'd become very conscious of how girls seemed to lower their sights in early adolescence. I had a son I delighted in, but I couldn't reconcile myself to a life restricted to four walls. I found I could neither be comfortable in a purely private life nor easy in formal left-wing groups: I found them competitive and lacking in humour. It was really through discussion with Sheli Wortis, for whom I had a deep affection and respect and who was in the same Vietnam

Solidarity group I was, that I overcame my fears that to meet as a group of women somehow wasn't serious enough.

Mica: At eighteen I vowed never to marry. Before I was twenty-four I spent years in New York and in Mexico: I was independent and active. By the time I was twenty-nine I had married and had three kids.

Before the first, I was aware and afraid of what motherhood might bring: I wrote in my journal that I wanted to avoid the trap of obsession with petty housewifely concerns. Yet I chose to have a child because I felt it would be as 'creative' as finishing the novel I had started – and easier. I was Earth-Mother: home births and breast-feeding and all that. I felt enriched by babies. But in patches I also felt unproductive, depressed and increasingly conservative.

After the second child I started teaching, and I felt justified in using my wage to pay someone to help look after the kids. During the political fever of '68 I wanted desperately to find a space in which I could be active and involved. My husband spent weeks at the Hornsey College of Art occupation; I felt strongly about Vietnam, about the May events in Paris; yet there seemed no way for me to be involved without feeling somehow fraudulent. Besides, I had to look after the kids, didn't I?

A few weeks after my third kid was born I went to my first women's meeting with the Tufnell Park group, in September 1969. Initially I resisted a good number of the new ideas presented there because they represented a direct attack on much of the way I'd been living – but all the same I went assiduously and was very excited.

The next year or so was probably the most explosive and passionate of my life. We had embarked on the long and difficult task of 'Changing The Way We Lived', which meant endless battles about the trivia of sharing daily domestic responsibilities, as well as the struggle with issues of sexuality, possessiveness, living in groups, property . . .

Audrey: I first became involved in the women's movement early in 1969 after two of the most difficult years in my life. My marriage broke up in 1967 leaving me with three small children, one of them brain-damaged by whooping cough vaccine, to bring up alone. The feelings of despair, failure, anxiety about the children (how could I cope?) were almost overwhelming.

Predictably, I leaned heavily on a few women friends and we spent many, often happy enough, hours looking after each other's children and belly-aching about men, clothes, menstruation, and wondering where it all went wrong. Why did marriages fail? Why didn't we feel fulfilled by motherhood? We tried to analyse the problems, even held meetings to discuss childcare and education, but we never made the links between politics and our individual feelings of disillusionment and discontent.

Then an old friend and I attended a short course run by Juliet Mitchell on 'The Role of Women in Society' at the Anti-University, and we began to read people such as Betty Friedan, Hannah Gavron and Shulamith Firestone. Then the bells rang and the connections were made and there was that feeling of excitement, a dawning sense of militancy that I'd never experienced before despite involvement in various left-wing groups. I was no longer alone, but part of a movement which was primarily political but could be personal to me.

But I also suffered at first from reservations – a hangover from male-dominated left-wing groups? I was worried about separation, revisionism. What had Miss World demonstrations got to do with revolution? I didn't want to be seen as an angry, castrating 'Women's Libber'.

Slowly, however, reservations faded as the sense of group solidarity and support grew. The group has caused us all to change and see our lives in a different light: in bad times it gives us courage and optimism; we are critical and loving.

Discussions in the early meetings were deliberately and excitingly personal, but they were also quite structured and productive. We would take a topic and at the end of the meeting try to draw out general principles.

Nan: Among the many early discussions, the ones which most radically altered the course of my personal life were on the family. Disenchantment with the existing nuclear structure was not a new idea introduced to me through women's liberation, but our discussions brought it into much sharper focus. Perhaps the single most important idea that emerged for me was that the way you live your life is a political statement. In terms of the evils we had discovered in our dissection of the family, this came to mean for me a commitment to trying to find a viable alternative in communal living.

Mica: Another important area of discussion was childcare. In the winter of 1969/70 we had read and talked about a paper written by Sheli on maternal attachment, first delivered at the Oxford Conference. It was a critique of Bowlby's hypothesis (subsequently popularized by Dr Spock) which suggested that children separated from their mothers were likely to suffer permanent emotional damage. Sheli's paper also examined how these theories had been used as justification for keeping women at home (in their place!). She pointed out that there was evidence to indicate that what kids needed was a stable, stimulating and caring environment and that this could be provided just as well by the father as by the mother, or in fact by several people – 'in certain societies multiple attachments were the norm'.

In the political and intellectual environment of today it is hard to imagine the impact that this paper had on some of us with young kids. I had accepted without question (but over the years with increasing disquiet and resentment) the idea that the care of kids was mainly my responsibility, and like others of my generation I was wracked with guilt about the harm I could do my children through absence. So this paper was, for me at any rate, perhaps the single most significant and liberating experience of the early movement.

Sally: We began as fragments, guilt-ridden, inadequate as people (because mere women – no, not women, we were only *girls* then, whatever our ages); and by bringing our depression to each other like a gift, an offering of pain, we gradually drew each other out of our isolation. At any given time the change didn't seem so remarkable, though it was becoming apparent that life could be confronted, we could get up in the morning and bit by bit even enjoy what followed. And Monday nights became a treat, an addiction. There was always one beautiful and strong woman in every meeting. Sometimes she remained the same person for weeks; as often she shifted. She was her, or her, or them, or me. It taught me new ways to love myself, by loving all of us.

The group served as stretcher and crutches to those of us limping out of our relationships (the big ones, the children ones). At the start, all but two of us were in a similar predicament, mothers of small children with no one to turn to for help but their fathers, and then not even them as the bottles started falling off the wall. The first step was finding reliance and support in each other to combat isolation, finding the muscle to stand alone and bear the weight of self and of children, the courage to try new work, and finally to correct the warps and distortions in our relationships.

Sally: We have a peculiarly protective, even suspicious, set of feelings about each other's mates. We know the pain of these romances better than the bliss: no one has bothered to reproduce the emotions that got her into a marriage (though short-term affairs are happily discussed and in a way renew us all) but we've learned vicariously as well as on our own about the fears of living with male incomprehension, callousness, cruelty, possessiveness. Familiarity with what is by its nature a one-sided case about the man of one woman can make it hard to understand what she sees in him at all, and when a specimen has had the nerve to show us his face I'd often sooner punch it than embrace it. (This usually comes as a great surprise to him, whoever he is.)

To redress the imbalance we've gone to each other's parties, had picnics, even tried inviting them to meetings. And they've been human enough, even if you sometimes can't avoid that German-soldier feeling (kind to their mothers no doubt; can they help it if they just followed orders?). It's unfair: very. But they've been unfair to us: verier. Let a few of them feel what it's like, ignorant prejudice based on species, not character. They've all survived it, anyhow, even if they didn't learn anything much. (That wasn't the primary purpose of it, after all.)

Sue: The very strength of the group can affect a sometimes fragile relationship with a man. I sometimes feel conflicting loyalties. Mostly I feel completely open to discuss a particular man with the group. Sometimes I don't – either becaue I think he'll feel betrayed or because I know myself to be in a suggestible frame of mind and because the group knows me and not him, so I'll be the one to receive support and understanding and the situation will be unfair.

At one meeting we sat in a circle and each of us spoke for ten or fifteen minutes as if she were the person on her left and described the reasons why she was with her particular sexual partner. It was eye-opening, and for me, with no experience of encounter groups or psychoanalysis, these were the stimulating and original meetings; I took political discussion and plans of action for granted. For others in the group, the revelations were the other way round.

Sally: The women's mags would say we'd failed, denying our children the live-in dad. But what the children have instead is honesty: they've witnessed our efforts to overturn the false premises of our and their existence, and what they've lost in fairytale stability – so often just a pantomime for the neighbours and relations – they've gained in being part of building something true and real. Maybe it's only an easy way out to claim they're better off, but the only available evidence tangibly supports it: our children are all extraordinary people. (A case of so far so good? Well, typing on paper *is* knocking on wood.)

We had enormous problems about the size of our 'small' group. Sometimes fifty or sixty women would arrive; each week six to ten were new. We had already talked through many problematic areas and wanted to move forward together; yet the group was becoming unmanageable, even disintegrating as women left it in frustration at the increasing numbers and the necessity to return to issues that the core group had already explored. Eventually we decided to close the group to newcomers. We were accused of elitism, but we felt the group would collapse otherwise. In retrospect, we think we were right.

One way of resolving the problem was to 'foster' new groups: two or three of us would meet with a new group for several sessions, until it was on its feet as it were; in this way we spawned the Daleham Gardens and Chalk Farm groups. Looking back our action seems paternal/maternal . . . but we were ourselves threatened and that seemed the only way out.

Even after the group was closed, it took a few years to shake down to its hard core. Some original members – Sheli, Carolyn, Laura, Ellen – went back to North America (though Carolyn returned); and perhaps because they were particularly strong and active, their loss gave the slightest hint of disaffection in others exaggerated weight. Thus, when Michelene left she couldn't merely say 'So long, I'm moving on'; the event became a major drama.

Michelene was brave to face up to it. She felt 'the defensive nature of the small women's group had been superseded by a much more general climate of discussion about sexism in our society, and this undermined the political importance [of such groups].' She recognized the value of the support we could give each other, but wanted us to be more than that: 'I had recently joined my union at work, was getting interested in discussions among feminists of the need for political study groups, and felt impatient at the apparent lack of interest from other women in the group at these things.'

In the context of her own political development, Michelene's decision made a certain kind of sense. But perversely, her position helped solidify the very tendency of which she had complained.

We became not more but less politically active, and this led to Sally Fraser leaving too. While we talked about putting ourselves on the line, Sally wanted to do it. Of course we had children, we rationalized, and couldn't take mad risks; but all the same we were devastated by her decision. Were we really becoming the people we'd warned ourselves against?

Our spirits sagged and, for weeks turning to months, meetings were irregular, people coming late or later, and it was less than ever possible to redeem our lost group-confidence by organizing energetic political pursuits when nobody was around anyway and whoever was felt despair at the desertions, which now extended to Sheila, whose symbolic importance as the face on the big demo poster had been matched by her strenuous efforts on behalf of the Family Allowances Campaign; and by Liz, who with Sheila appeared in the feminist **drama** *Holocaust*. Imogen left for a group at LSE.

Mica: 1971 was the year when Michelene and Sally Fraser left us; by then the group had started to become a little less central in all our lives. The first flush of passion had died, and it was at this point, I suppose, that the rest of us reconciled ourselves to a change in the quality of our involvement with the group.

In 1973 or '74 we started to meet about every two weeks for dinner in each other's houses. We were no longer politically active as a group, although several of us were active as individuals or with other groups. What we could provide for each other was a crucial network of affection and support within which we were able to sort out our political ideas and personal problems.

Audrey: Even when we'd opted out of the Workshop and felt we'd lost our political perspective, the group still didn't break up. It continued to live an organic life of its own – we needed each other to feel complete.

I remember one summer, '73 I think it was: we had a long break for about three months. And I became aware whilst I was away on holiday that I still related to the group as a kind of alter-ego – never to any individual woman but always to the group, as if it had an existence, an identity, greater than the sum of its parts.

Our next problem in division started when Dinah announced that she was visiting an ashram in India.

She returned dressed in orange and wearing a picture of Bhagwan Shree Rajneesh around her neck.

As she increasingly exemplified the 'surrender' that Bhagwan advocates, Dinah was loath to meet us and our barbs. Eventually, however, she came to a meeting with Judith, whose own sympathies were coming round to Dinah's. The meeting became a passionate discussion of death.

Dinah had just witnessed a friend's terminal illness at the ashram, and participation in the Indian rites had been revelatory for her: she no longer feared death, she said, but was learning to see it as part of an inevitable cycle of birth and rebirth. She met with outraged argument: how, as a feminist only recently aware of the myths put upon us by men, could she accept a rationale which so obviously suited the Indian ruling classes? The quarrel seemed to evoke the bitterest passions and had obviously touched a deep anxiety in us all.

Since then, Judith and Sally Fraser have also gone orange; all three are at Poona at this writing, with their new names and preoccupations: a source of wonder to some of us, and anger to others.

But the threat of death . . .? We'd always made brave noises about ageing, but how ready were we for old age, let alone death? The idea arose (broached with the sort of phoney bravado that disguises the greater panics) to stay together and to help each other to die as each wished, with informed support based on a thorough understanding of our needs and wants. We drew calm immediately from the idea. It has given us a renewed sense of continuity and value to each other; we've got a renewed sense of security in the knowledge that we're together, in greater or lesser numbers, to share the rest. And so, it appears, we have a future.

Carole: The most profound effect of the movement has been on ourselves. We can look back over eight years to some external reforms in our society, but not nearly enough and not in the revolutionary way we at first envisaged. Sad too is the fact that most men, on a personal level, have been totally unaffected by the movement. We have left them behind. But as for the group, there are now such feelings of warmth and trust between us that I can hardly imagine my life without the presence of these women.

Mica: Whether or not this can still be called a 'political' group is an issue which remains unresolved and is an example of the type of disagreement that exists within the group. Although most of us have kids, are more or less of the same age and have known and loved each other well all these years, we are not more similar to each other now than we were. There are important differences of interpretation about the history of the group and there are political differences (some of these have been thrown up by the writing of this article, the first 'action' taken collectively by the group for many years). We see each other infrequently as individuals between meetings; on the whole we are *not* each other's everyday friends. Yet there exists a commitment to each other and to the life of the group itself which is powerful and which includes an understanding that it will continue.

Nan: To have the positive conviction that a communal environment might make possible less anxiety and more variety in human relationships is one thing; to live it out is quite another. For a time it appeared that we as a women's group, with our kids and our men, would embark on this experiment together. With the disappointing recognition that this was not going to happen began a long period of communal experimentation, for me, with other people (which still continues). It was an absorption which gradually began to cut me off from the others. Ironically, it was the group which had largely spawned my ideas about communal living; but now, when I came with my 'new' problems it seemed largely incapable of responding to them as it had to

Workshop Manifesto

Women's Liberation Workshop

believes that women in our society are oppressed. We are economically oppressed: in jobs we do full work for half pay, in the home we do unpaid work full time. We are commercially exploited by advertisements, television and press; legally we often have only the status of children. We are brought up to feel inadequate, educated to narrower horizons than men. This is our specific oppression as women. It is as women that we are, therefore, organizing.

The Women's Liberation Workshop questions women's role and redefines the possibilities. It seeks to bring women to a full awareness of the meaning of their inferior status and to devise methods to change it. In society women and girls relate primarily to men; any organization duplicates this pattern: the men lead and dominate, the women follow and submit.

We close our meetings to men to break through this pattern, to establish our own leaderless groups and to meet each other over our common experience as women. If we admitted men there would be a tendency for them, by virtue of their experience, vested interests, and status in society, to dominate the organization. We want eventually to be, and to help other women to be, in charge of our own lives; therefore, we must be in charge of our own movement, directly, not by remote control. This means that not only those with experience in politics, but all, must learn to take their own decisions, both political and personal.

For this reason, groups small enough for all to take part in discussion and decisions are the basic units of our movement. We feel that the small group makes personal commitment a possibility and a necessity and that it provides understanding and solidarity. Each small group is autonomous, holding different positions and engaging in different types of activity. As a federation of a number of different groups, Women's Liberation Workshop is essentially heterogeneous, incorporating within it a wide range of opinions and plans for action.

The magazine, SHREW, is produced by a different group each month. Thus, to a certain extent, it reflects the preoccupations of the group producing it. WLW meets monthly, the small groups weekly. We come together as groups and individuals to further our part in the struggle for social change and transformation of society.

those individual problems we all more commonly shared.

However, one definition of a *creative situation* is that it simultaneously provides individuals with enough freedom to be able to take a leap into the unknown, and enough security for them to want to take those risks. The group has fulfilled that function for me. We have all frequently referred to Sally B's idea that the group has served each one of us as a kind of collective super-ego: could we live up to the ideals of the group conscience from one week to the next? It is, of course, a question which can be asked the other way around too: can the group live up to each of our individual expectations? Happily, for those of us who have stayed with it and in it, the answer to both questions is *yes*.

SR.69, April 1978

Womanweb

ALISON FELL

In September the women's liberation movement's first official national information service will go into operation in Leeds. A bi-monthly newsletter will be available at a cost of £3.00 a quarter to groups and £3.00 a year to individuals. The information centre will answer postal and telephone inquiries from women in the movement and those who don't yet know about it: on the action groups, resources and campaigns of the movement. The newsletter will publicize events, conferences, provide report-backs and keep up the flow of information and debate between different groups all over the country.

In building the women's movement we have always had to handle a double task – on the one hand we had to work out how to make the movement's resources public and available to isolated individual women, and on the other, how to keep up the level of communication between existing groups. At different times, one aspect has been more difficult than the other. For instance, when the movement was just beginning and the Women's Liberation Workshop set up a London office, there were only a few groups to co-ordinate. But daily the workers faced a barrage of phone calls. Inquiries about every aspect of women's lives, calls for advice and help which came directly from the many needs that women were discovering and starting to voice. It was heart-tearing, frustrating, not having the answers, knowing how much needed to be done, knowing we didn't yet have the resources.

Now, things have changed. There is hardly a single aspect of women's existence without a study or action group investigating or campaigning around it. So when we at *Spare Rib*, in the bustle and hurry of producing the magazine, get a call asking what stage the Anti-Discrimination Bill has reached in Parliament, or where the best place is to find women's plays for a Further Education drama class, at least we can rustle through some files, or ask each other 'Does anyone remember where . . .?' Because we know what the Women's Liberation Workshop office workers of 1970 didn't – we know that the relevant group or individual who can answer these questions *does exist*, somewhere. So gathering together the strands into a web of information has become a priority.

In 1972 the Leamington group made a brave attempt to set up an information service and newsletter, but this floundered through lack of money and publicity, and indifference – certainly from London groups already kept in contact with each other through the Women's Liberation Workshop newsletter. Now, once again, the initiative has come from women in the provinces to set up a workable national service, one which will not only solve communication problems for groups outside London, but which we can all benefit from.

Because, just as the woman isolated at home, for instance, feels little identity of her own, so we as a movement hardly know who we are. To be able to look around and say with certainty 'These are my sisters, they are doing this here and that there and in a year we have together won those things' – this is a great strength. Much of the work of women's liberation groups – from battling with a local authority for more and better nursery care to setting up women's therapy groups – has been so dispersed as to be invisible to all but those directly involved. All of us need to become acquainted with our achievements and keep ourselves informed about them and begin to assess them. A well-subscribed and supported newsletter would go some way towards this.

What women trade unionists are fighting for at work is clearer, less dispersed, and the traditions longer, yet it's often difficult to see how many struggles are going on nationally, and where support and solidarity could come from. Difficult, also, to see what other women are fighting for outside the workplace, to appreciate and draw strength from the sheer breadth of that fight. How many women's struggles at work might receive support from women's liberation groups if there was a constant flow of information about them? How many women trade unionists might put their weight behind women's struggles in the community if they knew about them?

Being in the women's movement may mean that we 'carry a new world in our hearts', but the old one has its place in our heads. Faced with practical organizing tasks, we often feel a certain inertia, an inability to take ourselves seriously. It's hard to remember that that new world has to be organized for concretely if its continuity and durability in a hostile environment is to be assured. The Leeds women responsible for the main work of the Information Service are doing just this, grappling with finance, constitutions, leases, administration, legal safeguards. Strictly limited functions of information and communication have been laid out for the service – it has no power to make policy for the movement. The workers will have their jobs clearly outlined by an office collective, and may be recalled by a monthly meeting which is open to all women's liberation groups. But all these carefully devised structures are useless unless women follow through in concrete ways the decision they made to give support to the service, unless they send lists of all groups and activities locally, subscribe, publicize the W L M N I S and be ready to send regular news.

Organizing against women's oppression is such a vast affair that sometimes it has that quality found in dreams – a feeling of walking slowly and heavily forward through a swamp. No doubt the mud will be sucking at our feet for a long time yet. But sturdy projects like the Women's Liberation Movement National Information Service hold the promise of firmer ground for all of us to move on.

Subsequently this became the Woman's Information, Referral and Enquiry Service (WIRES).

SR.38, August 1975

Women Together: Edinburgh Sixth National Women's Liberation Conference

NORTHERN WOMEN'S LIBERATION ROCK BAND

. . . We had worked quite hard to get things together for Edinburgh; it was to be our debut and we were looking forward to it but we couldn't have anticipated the experience itself; it was incredible. The power and energy generated at women's conferences is almost too much. That is why all women's socials are as important as the workshops – to capture the spirit of the conference.

Too often the sexism of popular and progressive music invades and insults the occasion, marring the experience of just being with other women. We felt the need to use music as a force for us to express the new feelings, relationships and attitudes towards each other that we are trying to create in the women's movement.

We collected together and worked on a few songs that had some meaning for us, like Jimmy Cliff's 'You can get it if you really want', as well as some songs that have come out of the movement, like Susan Straightarrow's 'Marge's Song', and some that members of the group have written themselves. We were trying to develop a sound that was strong but not heavy.

Up on stage we felt tentative – it was our first major performance and we were not confident about how things would go down. After the first number we could feel the audience really with us: we were infected by their enthusiasm: together we seemed to create an atmosphere that was electric, indescribable. We felt really happy. The music was no longer merely ours in the group, it was everybody's and we all wanted it. Looking out over the hall all we could see was a forest of waving hands and the applause and general din was terrific. Energy and enthusiasm seemed to be pouring out of people.

How did we feel? We shared that specially elated feeling that we all seemed to get from that social because this time the music was completely created by women; the music was ours, we weren't dependent on sounds created by men. We also got a lot of satisfaction after all the work we'd put in, knowing that it had all been worthwhile.

But the experience was also in some ways bewildering; for the rest of the time we'd just been taking part in the conference like everyone else, anonymous figures milling around and now there we were, part of the social, part of it in a particular way. We could see our friends dancing but we weren't dancing with them because we were playing. At times it felt as if all the forces generated at the social were focused on us and it was a bit overpowering. Since then, in order to cope with the experience, we have felt the need to assess our relationship as a group to the people for whom we are playing. In the world of pop, performers are idealized as superstars, in turn they look down on and manipulate the audience. Out of the movement we hope that a new type of relationship is developing in which there is no alienation between group and audience. We don't want to be performers, we are really only women from the movement: the movement has created us and the music we make: we have merely worked on it and play it.

SR.27, September 1974

SR.72, July 1978

Going Back to the Beginning

JILL NICHOLLS

The gap between national campaigns, and the way we tend to organize for them, and informal local groups, was a main theme of the seventh National Women's Liberation Conference in Newcastle on 23–25 April.

How can we make national structures reflect local activity? How does our local campaigning reflect our personal and sexual politics? There was talk of 'reclaiming' the campaigns into women's liberation, of expanding the demands and drawing out their implications, of the need to restate constantly and publicly the feminist content of the demands – so that we don't lose our energy and imagination in an effort to come over as 'respectable' and get things done.

Must the movement organize differently to be more accessible to new members, especially to working-class women? Is feminism just a question of women struggling together? Do feminist ideas emerge spontaneously when women fight in whatever way to take control of their lives? Or do feminist ideas need to be discovered and developed in consciousness-raising and study groups?

The standard split between 'activism' and 'consciousness raising' was discussed in a new way, with both 'sides' seeing *both* as necessary and inter-related.

We reaffirmed the need for an autonomous women's movement,

rooted in the struggle against sexism. We talked of 'going back to the beginning', combatting everyday manifestations of sexism in the media, advertising and stripshows.

As well as a whole afternoon discussing the direction of the movement, there were dozens of workshops.

Women's burden of housework was discussed in a workshop round a Brighton paper, which suggested we needed a seventh demand and campaign around the sharing of domestic labour and care of dependants. It was agreed that the demand as stated in the paper was too muddled to be proposed at the moment, but that it was certainly a priority to organize publicly about housework in a way which brought out what the women's liberation movement wants to do about this drudgery – to minimize it by fighting for more socialized facilities, and to raise consciousness about sharing it (rather than to demand wages for it).

More work needs to be done on how we fight around this and the childcare demand.

A workshop on socialism discussed why the 'Women and Socialism' conferences had collapsed in sectarian squabbles. They decided on a new regional structure, dividing the country into eight areas. Each will have a one-day conference soon, on a theme relevant to the area.

Information was exchanged about how to set up courses on self-help health and services such as pregnancy testing in the health workshop, which also faced the problem of how much to create alternative structures and how much to put pressure on the NHS to provide what women need.

Women met to discuss hospitals – as workers and patients. Someone from Liverpool said that when she was in hospital having her third baby, a younger woman in the ward was having trouble breast-feeding. She went over to help her, showing her how to hold the breast back so the baby could suck the nipple without suffocating. The Sister came in and screamed, 'How dare you touch another woman's breast!'

After the workshops, the plenary. We decided that International Women's Day should be organized locally, not from London, and that local groups should decide how to celebrate. We voted to support WIRES, NAC and Women's Aid, and to hold the next national conference in London.

The plenary petered out after confrontation by a group of lesbians who said they'd felt oppressed all weekend by heterosexuals. Other gay women had found the conference very open, and disagreed with that group's tactics – shouting their anger from the stage.

The rushed voting began to seem pointless, and many sisters were setting off home, so we all disbanded.

Nearly one and a half thousand registered at the conference. Fifty children were looked after by fifteen men in a creche nearby. We had a whole toy-town to play in – a college campus empty for Easter, but for a rugby team stomping back to base late on Sunday afternoon.

All weekend we saw films – including *We're Alive*, an amazingly militant film made by women in an American prison, and *To the People of the World*, with Laura Allende and Carmen Castillo talking about resistance in Chile. We bought books, made posters, made friends. On Saturday night, we danced to the Stepney Sisters, sang to each other. We left feeling stronger, recharged.

SR.47, June 1976

Women's Liberation 1977

NEWS ROUND-UP

The National Women's Liberation Conference is the only time in the year that so many feminists are together and you get a sense of the movement as a whole. For this year's conference, 2–3 April, we used the City of London Poly. Three thousand women discussed in small groups (workshops), danced to women's music and on Sunday brought ideas to a mass meeting. Spare Rib 'interviewed' some women before they went home and invited everyone there to write down their impressions. Here they are – not comprehensive, but a selection of what we received.

• • •

NAC – a feminist campaign

Angela Phillips (London)

As usual there were problems of what to discuss. The majority wanted to consider the relationship between the National Abortion Campaign and the women's movement and therefore necessarily the difficulties of operating alongside members of left groups. Some others considered such theoretical discussion a waste of time which should have been used discussing action, and a small group of women afterwards expressed annoyance that the discussion hadn't centred around viability and positive legislation.

The discussion did reveal the degree of frustration felt by women's liberation feminists who are, or have been, organizing around the abortion issue. In spite of attempts to prevent the naming of names, the

Socialist Worker Party came in for considerable criticism for their insensitive tactics of flooding small groups, alienating the non-aligned women, engaging in a few rounds of sectarian in-fighting and then disappearing for months leaving the group fractured and often unable to reorganize. Unfortunately no members of the SWP were there to answer this criticism.

Feelings were relieved and suggestions aired for a slightly different orientation to the campaign, bringing in the broader aspects of the slogan 'A Woman's Right to Choose' and engaging in more imaginative direct action rather than the perennial demonstrations and meetings. The relatively small size of the workshop was perhaps the biggest indication of the movement's reluctance to engage seriously in the abortion campaign at present. We can only hope that the mass meeting's vote to support the demonstration against the Benyon Bill will prove to be an expression of concrete support rather than a meaningless raising of hands.

. . .

Revolutionary feminism

Sheila Jeffreys (London)

I asked to have a workshop entitled 'The Need for Revolutionary Feminism – against the liberal takeover of the women's liberation movement', as a result of my growing feeling of alienation and isolation within the movement. I had been unable to discover a *political* feminism. There was sex-rolism, lifestylism, and socialist feminism. I was in a desperate search for radical feminist theory which talked of the power of men and how to take it from them. Politics was taken to mean socialism, and theory the extension of Marxism. I was terrified lest I grew to hate my sisters because of the frustration and anger I felt at so many meetings, workshops and conferences where no one spoke of power, but of campaigns or sexuality or structure, etc. I could not imagine that I was the first or only person saying these things, and I felt that I daren't write them down because they must already be written somewhere, but I couldn't find them. So eventually I had to do it myself.

I expected twelve to fifty women to come to the workshop and had no idea whether they would come to criticize or support, and I was very nervous. About two hundred women came and were tremendously supportive and enthusiastic. I was not only not alone but had struck gold . . .

. . .

Age

Anna Briggs (North Tyneside Coast Women's Group)

'Sister, you too will grow old, learn to love it!'

This was one of the messages from the workshops on older women's issues. Fifty women attended, most armed with a conference paper on 'ageism' in society – the sexual and financial position of older women, and the fact that 'community care' means women, especially older women, looking after dependent relatives.

This is what emerged:

Older women often have more conditioning to unlearn and it's difficult to 'pull the rug' from under them after years of rationalizing their oppression, or kidding themselves they are personally liberated.

Do 'older' women need separate consciousness-raising groups as their problems are different, or should women of all ages give each other mutual support?

Male colleagues find success in older women very threatening.

Widowhood is a traumatic time when people could benefit from positive feminist support.

Will the movement 'grow older' or will older women leave and be replaced?

We talked of the problems older women face, wanting to urge younger women to look at their own attitudes to age and to reassess their campaigns, demanding daycare for dependent relatives as well as nurseries. And we talked of the identity of women as they grow older, particularly centering round the failure of mother/daughter relationships: could mothers and daughters join the same group? How did a mother's illness or death affect the daughter's self-perception?

Women there from the south-east decided to convene meetings. Other women will keep in touch by newsletter, and hope to develop the issue in *Spare Rib*, etc.

A woman from Leicester Women's Liberation

I went to the older women's group – it really brought home to me the problems of forty to fifty-year-old women coming into Women's Liberation, how they feel excluded: Jam Today, for instance, is great, but it's rock and not all women want that kind of thing. In a way older women are the pioneers for us later.

I've lost a lot of energy lately, I've been in the movement four or five years. The same things are coming up all the time, and they're important every time but I've lost energy to discuss them. This was the only issue that sparked off new thought for me, something new to work on.

I've just moved to Leicester from Leeds. I was surprised how many women I knew, who've been really strong in the movement, haven't come. It's not just that they couldn't make it this week – it's not important to them any more.

. . .

Class

Working Class Women's Liberation Group (London)

Many working-class women realize that through our contact with the women's liberation movement we have access to new skills, ideas, etc. We see this as positive; a good education, however you define it, should be available to all of us. But as soon as we begin to use the facilities of the women's liberation movement we are told we are middle class. This makes us invisible and allows the middle-class women, who dominate the movement, to go on saying that we're all middle class. It's a way of keeping power. Also middle-class women expect us to adopt their 'culture', before we can use those facilities. We object to the assumption that everything middle class is better than everything working class. That perpetuates the male class system within the movement.

Middle-class women must begin to understand and criticize their own attitudes and standards.

In our workshops on classism there were working-class women from all over Britain, and of all ages, with different kinds of education. A lot of us talked about the confusion of being in a movement that has tried to cut us off, perhaps unconsciously, from our backgrounds and our experience. We want classism talked about – but we don't only want talk, we want change.

Three women, two in Big Flame (Liverpool)

Vera: I've never been to one of these in my life – just to see so many women together is great. It's broadened my mind. I live on an estate on the outskirts of town – I'd come again. You feel like you've got someone behind you when you see this – I've just started living alone with my kids and I don't feel so lost any more.

I got that drunk last night, it was more excitement really. It's not like when you go down the pub with all the fellas staring – I felt really relaxed. It's brought me out a bit – I used to freeze when anyone talked to me.

Agnes: Three of the workshops I went to were around working-class issues. I feel women's liberation is progressing, it's getting broader, people are willing to talk about class now too.

Jill: The 'How dare you assume I'm middle class' workshop was supposed to be for working-class women only, but it didn't really go into problems of being working class without an education. It was mainly women who've had middle-class education but working-class backgrounds and don't know where they are now. I was a bit upset by that, I didn't really feel I could join in.

Vera: One girl got upset because she didn't know what class she was and someone said: 'that's your problem' and she ran out.

Agnes: I think women in the women's movement are feeling a bit stagnant and want to break out.

Vera: I was shitting myself before I came, looking for all kinds of excuses. But now I'd love to see more women from my street come. Some of them got scared of me because I was going round with the Big Flame girls – they thought I had all the answers.

Jill: It's not a question of what's the best way to get 'ideas' across to working-class women like some people here think – it's not that we're ignorant or stupid, all we need on say abortion are facts.

SR.58, May 1977

Consciousness Raising: Back to Basics

GILL PHILPOTT DESCRIBES HER EXPERIENCE

In the early days of the women's liberation movement, groups *were* consciousness-raising groups, though they didn't always call themselves that. Small groups of women met regularly to talk about their personal experiences as well as take other forms of action. As the movement grew, a split developed between 'campaigns' and consciousness raising – between those who felt they should be doing things 'out there', and those who thought it was essential to talk together as women. The phrase 'consciousness raising' itself has come to be thrown around without anyone stopping to explain what they mean by it – or how you go about it.

. . . Are consciousness-raising groups still important for the women's liberation movement? Is it possible to be in a group with women who are very different from you? Is CR something you do when you're new to feminism, but that you grow out of? Is it necessary to be in a group at all to raise your consciousness?

I went into a consciousness-raising group expecting to sort something out about myself, and came out instead questioning everything.
None of us had been in a CR group before and our opinions on what
we were supposed to be doing varied widely. Some wanted intellectual
stimulation and looked forward to discussing articles, whilst others did
not really know why they were there, except that they wanted to talk
about themselves. We held a meeting on 'Why I feel I need a CR
group', and talked about ourselves and experiences that had led us to
join. I explained that recently I had found it more and more irritating
to be with men I knew, and had worried that the difficulties were in
myself, in not being able to take a joke, being too serious, easily upset,
touchy – I found myself half believing the remarks the men made with
such simplicity and ease. However, I had grown very close to another
woman who also disliked these comments; we joined the group in need
of support, hoping to find other women who were also unhappy with
the explanations, and were looking for alternative ones.

It had not been comfortable for any of us to talk so personally, but
we agreed to continue. Over the following weeks we acknowledged
many important parts of ourselves and our lives as women. We spoke
of our families, childhood, friends, colleagues, lovers, our painful experiences, fears, secrets and happy times, our future dreams and plans
. . . all of which sparked off talk on many other subjects. We were
continually surprised, encouraged, and excited by the similarity of our
experiences, and as this sharing went on many of us found the confidence to do things that really mattered to us, however trivial. We were
able to make important personal changes, in both self-image and
lifestyle; decisions we had previously avoided or ignored. Through
consciousness raising there is the realization that you are no longer
alone. What you are voicing is no longer anger at yourself and what
you took to be personal failings, but rather at a society which continues
to oppress us all as women in it.

Of course, CR doesn't just happen. It's something you have to work
at. Not all groups work. The one I was part of did. Primarily, I believe,
because we *did* all think it important – we weren't ashamed of being
serious about it, even to the extent of having fixed issues for discussion,
especially during our first few meetings. We never abandoned the idea
of writing down general points that were made in the group. We had
fun, too, and sometimes went out together or supplemented the group
with donations of food and drink. Looking back, though, the most
amazing outcome was that we didn't stop at coming to know one
another and helping each other to make changes. We felt we owed
something to all women, and so our group would regularly be re-

sponsible for producing the local newsletter and would be invited to meet with other groups to feed back information, and more importantly, to offer help to new women in search of a group. This all seemed to work because the city we lived in was fairly small, with only one women's centre, which helped co-ordinate all the CR groups. New women wishing to form or join groups had a specific place to go to where contacts could quickly be made.

I don't know how far CR can go in bringing all women together regardless of say, age, colour or class. For instance, in my group we were roughly the same age, all white, all had higher education and similar work situations. However, we were not all feminists, or married, or mothers, or lesbians. CR surely should be a way of releasing us, not tying us to such labels.

CR does not mean an end to women being oppressed. It's simply the beginning. It does bring an awareness of political as well as of our personal situations. And that kind of knowledge leads to challenge, not compliance.

SR.92, March 1980

Why Socialist Feminism?
Gatherings in Paris and Amsterdam

MICHAEL ANN MULLEN

Two socialist feminist conferences were held in Europe recently – one of about 4,000 women at Vincennes University in Paris on 28–30 May [1977], the other of 250 in the 'Vrouwenhuis' (women's house) in Amsterdam on 3–5 June.

'Socialism is a pre-condition for women's liberation . . . Socialism though is not a guarantee for women's liberation' (Feminist Socialist Platform in the Netherlands).

Women have arrived at a socialist feminist perspective from two different directions. There are those who began to become politically aware through their involvement in the women's movement, and have been led to identify the growing pressures on women with the capitalist society in which we live. And there are those who were first aware of capitalist exploitation and later of their oppression as women, through involvement in the women's movement.

Few feminists who, over the last five years, have sought socialist/ revolutionary groups to work with have found one with a theory and practice which deals adequately with the specific oppression of women in the patriarchal tradition of which capitalism is one expression.

Many women whose first involvement was with left groups have also become aware of these limitations. For traditional socialist groups have a theory and practice which deals with capitalism only. They continue to operate within a patriarchal tradition. Feminist socialists are groping towards a theory and practice which deal with both patriarchy and capitalism.

In December 1975 a group of French women sent an appeal for an international gathering of women trying to come to grips with these problems. At the first two planning meetings there were no major disagreements, but at the third, in London in October 1976, differences in emphasis manifested themselves, because a wider range of political tendencies was represented.

We need to understand the differences if the evolution of Socialist Feminism is not to be weakened by fragmentation.

The split seems to have taken place over two specific issues. The first was whether the women's struggle should be viewed as *within* or *alongside* the class struggle. The second was whether discussion at the proposed conference should centre around Women and Work or be more broadly based and include issues like sexuality, abortion, the position of women in the home, in the community . . .

It is unfortunate that these issues led to the calling of two separate conferences. They could have been better considered at the international conference itself . . .

SR.61, August 1977

Germany: Reclaiming the Night
NEWS FEATURE

On the night of 30 April, women demonstrated in towns all over West Germany against being barred from the streets at night, against the way we're hassled, abused and raped. In most towns the procession went through the bleak area round the station, past men's nightclubs, pubs and sex shops. In Berlin the route we'd planned was too short for us – we ran on down the Ku-Damm, the main street, pushing the police before us.

Some women had painted themselves and were 'armed' with flour bags, water pistols, spray cans and dyes; they'd brought along saucepan lids, drums, pipes and bangers to make a noise. We didn't want a funeral march – we wanted fun, strength and solidarity.

When women then looned around in circles doing May dances, raced, screeched, shouted for joy in city squares otherwise commanded only by cars, I felt funny about it. I preferred the full-blooded, aggressive shouts, loaded with our fear and rage, though these too always ended in laughter. We literally made an uproar.

I thought of processions to drive out evil spirits, I heard the all too seldom expressed cries of fear and experienced this 'disturbance of the peace' as a conscious attack. Yet our protest remained 'feminine'. Women scream, men hit out. In Frankfurt a woman was badly injured. A man had thrown flower-pots down on the demonstrators.

In Hanau women were beaten up. When men hurled abuse at them, they'd tried to talk with them (!). The men's answer: blows and insults. In Cologne a woman was so badly beaten she had to go to hospital. In Berlin there were men who simply couldn't understand that our demonstration wasn't the place for them. They wanted to be in solidarity – such solidarity that when Brigitte G. pushed one out he broke her fingers.

If women were attacked by men, the whole procession stopped – a few blokes were thumped and cuffed, had flour poured over them, were sprinkled with lemonade, coloured with dye and scared with bangers. Sex shops were sprayed with women's symbols and sexist posters ripped off walls. We all had plenty to do and felt strong – as long as we stuck together. Speeches, songs, colours, recitations, the light of torches, shouts: against contempt, brutality and male violence, which we still don't know how to resist when things get serious.

From Courage.

SR.61, August 1977

Black Women Together

ORGANIZATION OF WOMEN OF AFRO-CARIBBEAN AND ASIAN DESCENT

For us Black women, the National Black Women's Conference held in Brixton, London, on 18 March this year was an historic occasion. For the first time nearly 300 Black women got together from places as far apart as Birmingham, Brighton, Bristol, Coventry, Leeds, London, Manchester and Sheffield, to discuss some of the many issues which concern us because we are Black, female, working class or all three.

. . . The conference marks an important stage in the development of an autonomous Black Women's Movement in Britain. It was a living witness to our conviction that, if the voice of Black women in this country is to be heard, we need to set up a separate and independent organization of Black women in which we ourselves lead a struggle against the specific type of oppression that we face. For too long the fact that as Black women we suffer triple oppression has been ignored – by male-dominated Black groups; by white-dominated women's groups; and by middle-class-dominated left groups. This continual lack of interest in the situation of Black women created a vicious circle, so that many of us who wanted to speak out were reluctant to do so. But by contacting each other, and working together, we have now broken this circle.

Moreover, the fact that the conference took place testifies to our belief that our common experience as second-class citizens in contemporary Britain, as well as our joint history as victims of colonialism and imperialism, represents a bond between us which far outweighs ethnic and cultural differences which may exist . . .

SR.87, October 1979

We Will Walk without Fear

LEEDS RECLAIM THE NIGHT GROUP

'I never dared go out alone after dark. When I saw the leaflet about the night demo I knew I had to go but I was so scared. I was even sick before going out but I did and it really changed how I felt. I'm not alone. I know that now. It's wonderful.'

Alison Fell, *SR.16*, October 1973

Women unite, reclaim the night! 130 Leeds women congregating in City Square, torchlit figures shouting in the windy darkness, and suddenly we're in a big circle holding hands. Voices hoarse from singing rise again in memory of the walk down to town from Woodhouse, where rapists lurk on the moor, or Chapeltown, Ripper '77 territory. Strong, knowing our sisters all over Britain are marching tonight too.

City Square is a wild spontaneous women's takeover, singing, dancing, a speech – 'We've got this space but it's not enough. What are we going to do to take more?'

MANCHESTER: MARION BOWMAN

Over the Pennines about 400 women had turned out, marching in from their local areas. 'We wanted to show that it's not just the city centre where women are attacked, it's in the local streets that you live on,' said Lesley Merryfinch.

The planning group in Manchester decided not to contact the police beforehand. In their leaflet they said, 'The police attitude is "Stay at home" which means we're imprisoned in our homes to avoid attacks, while the men who might attack us can walk around freely. We want to say we've had enough of male violence and male justifications for it. We're walking together tonight in the streets because we've got a right to be here. It's men's violence that's got to stop. We agree that men's attitudes won't change overnight, but at least we're showing that we're no longer content to accept this situation and we're angry about it.'

On the night the police turned up at the meeting points, but after some discussion agreed to put policewomen on the escort. 'They did show some tact,' said Lesley.

We met in Piccadilly Gardens and stood under the statue of Queen Victoria, some women speaking out about why we were marching: 'People try to pin attacks on sex fiends. But it's not just that, it's the ordinary man in the street.'

It was the night before Armistice Sunday. We stood in silence for two minutes in remembrance of all women who've suffered at the hands of men, then went on our way to the new women's centre singing 'The Women's Army is marching, O, Sisters, don't you weep.'

LONDON: PAT MOAN

This is the best high-flying demo I've EVER been on! Hundreds of women wailing and dancing through the streets of Soho. 'Sexist crap, sexist crap, SEXIST CRAP!' startling bystanders.

The manager of The Pussy Parlour tight-jawed, face flesh quivering as he scrapes stickers off his windows. 'What does this *mean*?' he hisses

at me as I take his picture. 'Can't you read?' I say. THIS DEGRADES
WOMEN, THIS EXPLOITS WOMEN.

One woman is running ahead squirting windows with water, followed
by others slapping stickers on with such exuberant violence you think
the windows must break, and hope they will.

A man steps out of fluorescent-lit doorway and gets his chest squirted
then slapped with a sticker.

Not like any other march. No stewards, cowed by police, cajoling
people to keep the ranks. No. We are all over. Humming, buzzing,
shouting. A real woman's march – a rampage. Surging, droning, chanting. Women Fight Rape.

> Yes means yes
> No means no
> However we dress
> Wherever we go.

Flame-lit faces of people who have found the spirit to fight a mammoth war. One woman stops another to get a light for her torch. A
young black man comes over, blows out the torch and turns to run off
to his smirking mates. She belts him over the back with it and it
reignites, burning a hole in his jacket. Women's laughter in the torch-
light. Men looking at the jacket under the streetlight.

It is a measure of how confident men feel of their unconditional
right to abuse women that so many of them step into our group and
smugly insult individual women. Sometimes other women rally round
in defence and the men wander off.

One delightful woman has a bag of maggots for sprinkling on the
offending males.

It is so fluid this 'march' – very fast at times, running around, at,
over cars, stopping traffic. I think police are not used to running. They
come along behind ripping down stickers, muttering comfortingly into
radios – little gestures, by stiff spectators.

Around the event, before and after, there are objections: that it
should have been held locally, not in Soho; that it might be confused
with a Mary Whitehouse-type campaign; an ex-prostitute told me she
didn't agree with it because she thought it would be bad for the business
of the prostitutes in Soho. I'm sure there were more that I didn't hear.
But this event isn't the be-all and the end-all, the definitive perfect
demonstration. It should be a starting point, an inspiration, a learning
experience, a step forward. It does not preclude other actions. Women's
liberation is about supporting other women. Let's do it.

Whatever politicking went on to do with the organization of it (and I wasn't in on it) it was a blow-out to be there. It was wild. There. There, where normally we walk silently, stewing inside, keeping our disgust to ourselves. It was exhilarating just to MOVE, express our feelings, instead of the eyes-down-look-like-you're-going-somewhere walk, the woman-alone walk. We ran and jumped, and argued and stretched ourselves.

At the end we meet in Leicester Square. And all the piggy men. I sense a sporting violence from them.

'Wot you doin' 'ere? You ain't even ugly.' (This man got bopped in the face.)

'I should come here to pick up my chicks.' (A denim-clad slickster.) Horrible, slimy men.

May the day come when sex-shop owners and strip-club owners can't buy insurance, are afraid to do business for fear of their plate glass being smashed, for fear of their plushy interiors being messed up, for fear of their own crummy lives. I saw fear in the eyes of those traffickers. They are afraid of our rage. They should be.

LANCASTER: LANCASTER WOMEN'S LIBERATION NEWSLETTER

We met in the Women's Centre and left in procession, twenty-seven of us, at 11 p.m. We started out slightly hysterical, giggling our way along but we calmed down fast enough when we started getting abuse from men.

The centre of Lancaster seemed to be crawling with police . . . It was very noticeable that in the areas immediately outside the centre, in the places where women are most likely to have trouble, there were no police present at all.

The best thing was the constant warmth and support we got from other women. There was no arguing about us being 'extreme' or 'crazy' or 'anti-men'. They knew exactly what we were shouting about and shouted their support back. These contacts made all the wind and the wet worth it.

BRIGHTON

Women walked all over the town, giving out leaflets, banging saucepan lids, blowing whistles and singing. Many wore white make-up or had women's signs painted on their cheeks.

BRISTOL

The police were very unwilling to let the women march through the city-centre, so there was a silent torch-lit procession through dark residential areas, where there have been several sexual assaults. 'It was too cold to wear anything fancy! But we had lots of placards, and the Bristol Women's Liberation Group banner in front.'

YORK

About eighty women sang and danced round York, and had a party afterwards. 'It was amazing to be able to walk through the street singing at the top of your voice, but we needed more songs to sing!'

NEWCASTLE

A hundred women turned up equipped with homemade torches, and the demonstration ended with an impromptu party and meeting.

How did it all start?

Leeds women formed a Reclaim the Night Group after reading the report of the night demos in Germany (*SR.61*) and discussing action against male violence at the 'Revolutionary Feminist' conference in Edinburgh in July. 'We were particularly concerned because there'd been a series of women murdered in West Yorkshire,' they explained. 'There'd been a need for a new area of action radical enough to really fire people.'

They decided to fix a date for a march which they published in WIRES, the National Women's Liberation Newsletter. They also sent letters to women's centres and publications calling for support. The idea caught on.

Locally they distributed 1,700 leaflets in offices, factories, hospitals, shopping centres and pubs. 'Just doing that was in itself consciousness raising,' said Magda Yates. They co-ordinated national publicity, spending a lot of time and money contacting the national press (who gave some coverage) and the BBC (who weren't interested). They did manage to get on local radio to explain what they were doing . . .

SR.66, January 1978

Finding Each Other at School

NAOMI, PETRA, JANE, JULIE, RACHEL, KATE, JANE, LUCY, NICOLE

Ours is a large mixed comprehensive school with quite a big sixth form. There's been a woman's group here for three years, though of course with people leaving and new ones coming into the sixth form, it restarts every year.

... We decided to start off with a few consciousness-raising meetings, closed to boys, to exchange experiences. For example, a Greek girl told us about her problems over wanting to have a boyfriend, and how she was being made unhappy by her family's restrictions.

... One of the real problems with school groups is getting somewhere regular and comfortable to meet. Your life is governed by rules, bells, timetables, and generally uncomfortable conditions. In an average comprehensive school, younger students are particularly discriminated against in this way. They are virtually locked out of rooms except for lesson times, and have nowhere to go except crowded, cold, noisy places, or just to wander around. As sixth formers, we are privileged: We've been given a special building and made an elite. We're lucky – but this effectively cuts us off from the rest of the students, and we are sure that there are many girls like us, only a bit younger, who'd like to come to meetings.

... We've also discussed quite a lot whether teachers should be in the group, and on the whole we think not. However friendly teachers are, however supportive, however similar in their politics, in the end they remain a teacher, and in any discussion they have power over you whether or not they use it. You can never be absolutely sure they won't say things later in the staff room. They also basically have more power than us to push their views, even though these are built on greater experience. We think it's best for women teachers to form their own groups, and for us to have ours, and of course for the groups to meet and work together.

... We realize we are lucky to have this relative freedom – a fairly relaxed school, with several feminist teachers and many special sixth-form privileges. But basically we are still very restricted – everything to do with our meetings has to be checked out first, and even the contents of this article have to go through the headmistress before it can be published. There's really no school with girls and women in it which doesn't need a women's group. When you find each other it's such a relief.

'We are All Criminals':
Women's Liberation in Spain

ANITA BENNETT AND JILL NICHOLLS

'We are all adulteresses' read the placards on the largest women's liberation demonstration in Spain ever. By their hundreds women took to the streets – in Barcelona, Zaragosa, Madrid, Valencia, Seville – to protest the charge of adultery against Maria Angela Munoz. Her husband, Ramon Soto, went to the judge to gain custody of their small child, Yolanda, whom he had abandoned two months after her birth. 'A Father Who Wants His Daughter Back' read the male-dominated press. A father supported in his claim by the Spanish state and the Church. In Spain, as elsewhere, women are property, mere breeders of children. Under the Penal Code women can be prosecuted for adultery, for any sexual relations outside marriage. Men can be charged only when they have it off within the four walls of the matrimonial home. And few would be so foolish as to pursue their affairs (*asuntos*) at home.

Spanish prisons are full of women incarcerated for 'crimes' such as prostitution and abortion. In fact, one half of the women now in prison are said to be charged with either having had or performed an illegal abortion. The Pope still feels it his duty to define for women everywhere the meaning of the 'right to life', and the Church in Spain wields considerable influence.

While thousands demonstrate for the release of all political prisoners, for a total amnesty, the burgeoning women's liberation movement is demanding that their sisters too be recognized as *political* prisoners. One of the most famous women prisoners in Spain, psychoanalyst and author Eva Forest, has recently been released from the women's prison of Yeserias where she was held more than two years without trial and subjected to brutal sexual torture. Lidia Falcon, a feminist lawyer from Barcelona, was arrested with her friend Eva but released in the summer of 1975. The publicity given to Eva's case by the international women's liberation movement was instrumental in her release as well as in the lessening of her torture. The international movement has also contributed considerably to the growth of feminist consciousness inside Spain.

Women were active in Spanish politics long before the women's movement, but they are only now beginning to organize autonomously, around their own issues. For example, the Communist Party's *Associacion Democratica de Mujeres* in Madrid has worked since 1970

SR.69, April 1978

for the release of their (mainly male) relatives and friends. They have demonstrated, petitioned, published underground bulletins. However, Lidia Falcon, concerned for the forgotten female prisoners, criticized the *Associacion*'s food march at Christmas 1975. 'They brought food and placards to the men's prison of Carabanchel, the best known. But they forgot the women political prisoners sitting in Yeserias. No one cares about the women, they're not considered to be "political"! Yet some of the women in Yeserias with me were charged with "terrorism". Some had tiny children, no exercise, fewer visits. In the Barcelona women's prison the situation is even worse because the place is run by repressed nuns.'

The male torturers inside the prisons cannot be totally divorce from the men outside. Brutality, sex warfare is waged against ever woman who walks the streets. The degree of oppression often depend on the class into which a woman is born. A friend from a village i Andalucia once said, 'I remember when one of the women in th village committed adultery. She was paraded through the village an stoned by all the villagers.'

The sexism is deep-rooted. But the most encouraging sign for chang is the feminist movement – which has exploded on the scene since th death of Franco in 1975. Before that, any oppositional organizatio was underground. Even over the last year and a half the movement ha been semi-clandestine. In May/June 1976, 4,000 women gathered fo four days in Barcelona for the first national feminist conference, th first public meeting of any kind since Franco's death. Here they gav further impetus to an independent women's movement and elaborate some basic demands – on pay, abortion, contraception.

Some feminist groups want to be legalized, especially those involve with specific campaigns; the Barcelona divorce groups were legalize on 19 May. The radical feminist groups feel their goal goes beyon legalization; they don't feel they could integrate their fight with th 'democracy' available in Spain. If a group is not legitimized, its meet ings can be forbidden – 'But we go ahead anyway, and don't ask fo permission.'

Perhaps because women have been so oppressed for the last fort years, their movement arrives with a greater force and seriousness tha in any other European country. 'Feminist' is becoming a househol word: magazines, newspapers, television and, yes, even men, pay li service to the women's movement.

In Palma de Majorca, the newly formed women's groups have both news column in the island's major newspaper and their own weekl radio programme. 'It consists partly of news reports and partly o interviews,' explained Leonor Taboada, one of the group. 'For instanc women talk about their sexual lives from the very beginning – how they lost their virginity, what kind of orgasm they feel. One woman talked about getting an orgasm at last by going off with another mar after being married eight years. The radio station turned the sound down very low – so we wrote it up in the newspaper instead!'

Women of all ages and classes have begun to approach the feminists – they are sick of being treated like cattle. Leonor said with great glee that she and another sister were driving along the main strip on the waterfront when some men accosted them: 'I started honking the horn, telling them to go home and teach their fathers to drive a car, to go cover their cocks. They were so surprised they didn't know what to do at first, then they got really angry and started to chase us.

'Things are moving fast in Majorca,' she added, 'though we have a lot of trouble with the Left. We had a conference on women and our bodies in Palma on 6 May, and wouldn't let men in because we were showing how to use speculums [instruments for spreading the vaginal walls while examining the cervix]. The men were fighting women outside because they couldn't come in. Many women bought speculums and were rushing round the main square that night clacking their speculums!'

One of the most active tendencies in the movement is the *Colectivo*; founded in Barcelona by Lidia Falcon, it now has nationwide co-ordination, with occasional conferences to work out their line. Although their membership is small, the impact of their ideas has helped shape the new movement. Lidia and a couple of other women from the *Colectivo* work on *Vindicacion Feminista*, a monthly magazine with a circulation of about 30,000. It is not the official journal of the *Colectivo*, who as a whole don't feel represented by it.

Past experience coupled with the present political practice of left groups has convinced many women of the need for a specifically feminist revolution. They, like radical feminists in other countries, view women as a distinct social class and see men as the primary oppressors of women. Most of the women in the *Colectivo* have been Marxists of one sort or another (Lidia was in the Spanish Communist Party – PCE). However, they now view Marxism as totally incapable of bringing about the liberation of women. They concentrate very much on theory, holding small group discussions and writing.

Their experiences in Leninist-type parties, however distorted, have led them to function rather like one themselves. Because they think women constitute a *class* which must overthrow the patriarchy, they want their own feminist, democratic centralist party. Women who belong to other political parties are not permitted to maintain *doble militancia* (double militancy), that is, dual membership of the *Colectivo* and another organization, on the grounds that it wouldn't be clear where their 'real' loyalties lay – to women or to the men in their left groups. They can have 'double militancy' for a trial period, but then have to choose.

One must be *elected* into a *Colectivo*. From this and their dogmatic line many problems have arisen. Recently Lidia Falcon, her daughter Regina and Any Estany, who all help publish *Vindicacion*, were expelled from the Barcelona *Colectivo*. This feud was instantly lapped up by the press, anxious to discredit the movement. Others in the group accused these three of being 'elitist, egotistical, dictatorial'. The *Colectivo* criticized them on twenty points: one concerned an article which Lidia had published on domestic labour, roughly corresponding to the Wages for Housework position – should she have signed it personally or credited it to the *Colectivo*? Was it the 'correct line'?

A difference in strategy as to how to approach the national elections on 15 June, the first held in Spain for forty years, caused further divisions in the national *Colectivo* network, and in other sections of the women's movement. Lidia believes that women should boycott the elections since participation means acceptance of the 'democratic farce' and de facto recognition of the monarchy. She argues that 'Women have more to gain from the Republican form of government. Under the Republic, women could vote, own property, have abortions. Women in Catalonia today want to get similar benefits to those they had during the Republic. But some of the *Colectivo* want to put up feminist candidates in the elections. There's also conflict within the movement as to whether or not to vote, and whether to give support to left-wing parties.

Nationally, the women's movement is held together by a co-ordinating body, the *Coordinadora Estatal*. Locally, there are co-ordinating networks such as the *Coordinadora de Barcelona*, which has representatives from a number of women's, trade union and neighbourhood organizations. Rosa Franquet, invited by the National Abortion Campaign to the 14 May demonstration against Benyon's Bill, is an active member of the Sants neighbourhood women's group – a *Vocalia de Mujeres*. During the Franco dictatorship, these neighbourhood committees worked for local reforms, such as better street lights. (Regina Falcon once accused these women of 'having street lights instead of vaginas'.) Now the neighbourhood groups are becoming more radicalized and feminist, attracting women in left groups and trade unions, and local women who've had no previous contact with the women's movement.

There are too many groups to list – some that have split from the *Colectivo*, like a lesbian group in Valencia, and the Majorca group 'Pelvis' who objected to the *Colectivo*'s hard line; and others, like ANCHE in Barcelona, once an open group of about 150 socialist feminists, now split into radical feminists and those on the left. The movement's main concerns are broad political issues and health; groups are always in flux, and will be even more so after the 15 June elections.

Theoretical differences between the groups have very practical consequences. Rosa Franquet, for example, argues for the necessity of a single issue campaign on abortion and contraception. Both are illegal; women with money can get abortions in London, but poorer women have to find other ways. In one recent case a teenage girl, aided by her boyfriend, sought an illegal abortion on the resort island of Ibiza. The female abortionist is reported to have injected hot beer into the woman's uterus, provoking a severe haemorrhage. When the girl and her boyfriend sought medical advice, they were turned away for lack of money (15,000 pesetas or £125). The girl died four days later. Her boyfriend, the abortionist and even her small child remain in prison for conspiring to abort. Feminists protested, and now the doctor who refused to give treatment is on trial for malpractice.

Given this atrocious situation, for some the priority is to change the law. A group in Madrid for example is working for legal contraceptive clinics. Women in political parties are trying to get their organizations to take up the fight for contraception and abortion – abortion is obviously the more controversial.

The radical feminists tend to leave the hard grind of campaigning for legal change to the 'reformists'. A self-help collective in Barcelona tries to spread 'counter-information' – they assume that contraceptive clinics will come, and want to make sure that women have the right *kind* of contraception. They do realize that abortion on demand won't come so easily.

The *Colectivo* argue that sex with men is always an act of aggression, and unnecessary because women can have orgasms without penetration. They agree in theory with a woman's right to choose, but put no energy into building a campaign involving all women against the abortion laws.

In Barcelona there have been large meetings on the right to divorce, which does not exist under the present civil law. The Communist and Socialist parties, and those to their left, tend to at least mention this issue in their election propaganda. 'This is hardly surprising,' Rosa Franquet explained; 'It is very likely that the government is going to have to give in on divorce, since many of the *progres* [trendies] are campaigning for it. It is an important issue, but not as central as abortion and contraception.'

The radical feminists are against marriage and the family, so for them divorce is only part of the problem. 'We have to support the campaign for divorce,' says Leonor, 'but we are trying to open women's minds about what it means to be married.'

Splits in the women's liberation movement showed clearly this year on May Day, which happened to coincide with Mother's Day. May Day, a traditional international trade union celebration, was particularly significant in Spain this year. In Madrid and in the Basque country (*Euzkadi*), demonstrations were brutally repressed by the police. Some feminists in Barcelona argued for joining the main trade union demonstration outside the city, as a separate women's contingent.

Others objected, and instead of joining the massive May Day march, women from the *Colectivo* and from LAMAR ('the sea', a very active radical feminist grouping), took up the issue of Mother's Day. They held a picket outside the 'Maternidad' (maternity) hospital, the biggest in Barcelona. In particular they protested the situation of unmarried mothers. In Spain these women are criminals – many are forced to put their children up for adoption. But the children are not even legal human beings. They are 'illegitimate' – without a father they are quite literally not recognized by Church and state. Without a man, a woman is 'illegitimate' – *that* is what the feminists are challenging.

SR.60, July 1977

From 'Lotta Continua', *SR.51*, October 1976

Decades: Talking across the Century

GAIL LEWIS AT THIRTY
TALKED WITH CAROLE SPEDDING

How did you first become interested in feminism?

Well, I first got involved in the women's movement in about 1974 after having been active in other political campaigns and thinking about feminism a lot. Then, after a while, I met a group of white women with whom I became friends and we started working together, politically. It was a very close and supportive time for me. But then, after the high of all this had worn off, I started to understand that the specifics of my life, as a Black woman, weren't really being dealt with. That was true on two levels really – the more general level that reflects the differences between Black and white women in Britain, and on a more personal level, the way that those differences can influence your personal relationships. For example, there may be some white women with whom Black lesbians can feel closer in terms of racial aspects because those white women, due to past experiences in their own lives, may be more conscious of the way in which racism affects people on a day-to-day basis.

I found that many of the women with whom I had felt close before just couldn't understand this. At some level they had incorporated the idea prevalent in the women's movement that feminism made a total, absolute bond between all women.

So where did you go from there?

In order for me to feel that the issues that affected *me* were being tackled I then had to join a Black women's group. This was important because not only did it deal with *my* personal things, but being involved in a Black women's group meant that the general issues that affect all Black people in this country, and the development of a Black feminist politics were taking place side by side. This involvement has helped me to crystallize my criticisms of the women's movement in England – and has led me to understand that it is important to make a distinction between feminism and the women's liberation movement.

What do you mean?

That it's important that feminism, which leads us to a greater understanding specifically of women's position but more generally of the workings of capitalism, must then be fed into a socialist analysis. But the women's movement in this country, by and large, has reflected the white middle-class women's privileges that are now under threat. For me, it's important that feminism in England (a country that has been *made* on the backs of Third World countries) challenges the ideology and structures of British imperialism. Only when the women's movement comes to grips with this will it even be able to *begin* to address itself to the position of Black women (after all, we are only here because of imperialism in the first place). So unless the women's movement develops an anti-imperialist perspective, issues like Ireland and racism will never be able to be dealt with.

HAZEL HUNKINS HALLINAN AT NINETY TALKED WITH AMANDA SEBESTYEN

Becoming a feminist was a change in my life, completely. When I graduated from college I got a job teaching chemistry at the University of Missouri, and everything was going beautifully. My mother got ill, and my brother thought that I – being the daughter – ought to come home and take care of her. It was a long hard illness, but she got well; and in the meantime I'd given up my job!

I wrote all the summer, 1916, trying to get practical research work. I got a stack of letters that high from firms and corporations, and every single letter said, We do not employ women. No reasons at all – we don't; it's a man's job. So I taught at the local high school for a while, and it just killed me. I was just about ready to commit suicide! My goal was closed to me and the only things that were open to me were things that I didn't want to do . . .

Along came a girl to see me. Alice Paul, the leader of the National Women's Party, had sent her out to Montana to organize the women's movement there; and she just converted me hook, line and sinker. She asked me to a conference at Colorado Springs, where I got another full-sized dose of what I ought to have known long ago.

I've been in the women's movement ever since.

I came to England in 1920, just after Lady Rhondda had established the Six Point Group. Lady Rhondda's idea was: We've got the vote, now we've got to do something with it. But the Six Points were welfare matters, they were not universal freedom clauses. Along in the 1930s we changed the aims to 'Equality for women politically, occupationally, morally, socially, economically and legally.'

My interest today is in what the Equal Opportunities Commission does *not* touch. Domicile, nationality, immigration, Social Security and taxation. That's quite a lot. They're difficult things; and we have a weak Commission. I grant that it's a difficult period of time, but some-how or other we've got to get around it.

... I had a considerable fame at one time by backing the women's liberation movement – nobody else would at the start. Germaine Greer's book does me proud on the first and second pages, thanking me for backing the movement when it was so unpopular. I thought – and I still think – that consciousness raising was a very important part of it. It was something everybody laughed at, but I think it was a good thing.

... I haven't seen a copy of *Spare Rib* for ages. The last time I saw it, it was much bigger and not as sophisticated. But why, oh why, do you have such small type that old ladies can't read? You ought to be more strict with your editing ...

Well, well, well. I really didn't know *Spare Rib* had grown up so.

SR.100, November 1980

Afterword by the *Spare Rib* Collective

Around the time of *Spare Rib*'s 100th issue – as good a time as any to take stock of what we were doing at the magazine – the collective sat round a table and each of us scribbled down what we thought the aim of our work was. Did we still feel we had a vision beyond the practical details of producing and selling a magazine every month? And if so, did we have a *shared* vision in spite of all our differences? Going through our notes together, we were struck by the similarity of what each of us had noted down and by the passion with which we'd expressed it.

Underlining everything we'd written was the continuing belief that *Spare Rib* could reach all women – that we wanted it to be challenging in its content yet accessible in its form and available in every newsagent. We had no doubts about it being a women's liberation magazine, about it being part of the process of women working together for fundamental change. Our emphasis was on making changes from the bottom, not on getting to the top. We wanted *Spare Rib* to take the women's liberation movement to women who'd never encountered it, and involve them in it. We also wanted to be exciting and challenging for women already active in the movement.

Spare Rib aims to reflect women's lives in all their diverse situations so that they can recognize themselves in its pages. This is done by making the magazine a vehicle for their writing and their images. Most of all, *Spare Rib* aims to bring women together and support them in taking control of their lives. If there is one thing that sums up that common vision it is the letter that comes from Shropshire or Swansea or South London: 'I thought I was the only woman in the world who felt as I did until I read *Spare Rib* . . .'

That letter arrives all the time. But of course there are problems too. In trying to stimulate a wide range of readers, do we settle for a blandness that satisfies no one? We're variously accused of being too

Spare Rib Reader

lefty/not lefty enough, too man-hating not man-hating enough, too parochial/too international, or, most commonly of all, too internal to the women's movement totally out of touch with feminist debate. However contradictory these criticisms may seem, we often find ourselves agreeing with all of them. Despite our need to produce a magazine which is fulfilling to us, as well as attractive and challenging to readers, we rarely feel totally satisfied. We know how complex the struggle for change has to be, on how many fronts, and over what a long period of time.

The sheer volume of work astounds us. Despite the depressing conditions of the recession, the women's movement is expanding; this means that more and more ideas for articles and requests for information and help arrive at our office every day. We are publishing more about racism, violence against women, and militarism than ever before. As fast as we try to update our coverage on one major area of struggle, another area emerges. More groups of women are demanding the right to speak – Black women, older women, young women, women with disabilities. We're bursting at the seams and thinking of increasing the pages of the magazine yet again.

Whilst absorbing all these changes, we want to support each other in working effectively as a collective – this often means political and practical upheavals in our working day. And yet we still want to find time to be involved in other feminist actions – and fun – outside the magazine. High expectations on low pay!

Something like sixty women have worked on the *Spare Rib* collective since its first issue ten years ago, and many hundreds more have written, drawn, photographed, designed and helped out in the office. In these ten years, the way the magazine looks and the issues it covers have changed in as many ways as the women who make it, on and off the collective, have changed. And with another 100 issues it will be different again. But we think whichever women come together to bring out *Spare Rib*, and whatever the limitations of the vision we've all shared, they will still be saying, this magazine is for women, directed towards changing all our lives.

November 1981

Index

Note. Figures in italics indicate an article written by the person named in the index.

More about Penguins and Pelicans

OUTSIDE IN ... INSIDE OUT
WOMEN'S PSYCHOLOGY:
A FEMINIST PSYCHOANALYTIC APPROACH
Luise Eichenbaum and Susie Orbach

Susie Orbach (author of the world-famous *Fat is a Feminist Issue*) and Luise Eichenbaum together set up The Women's Therapy Centre in London. Drawing on their experiences and their work there, the authors propose here a new developmental model of women's psychology which is different from current and accepted (and usually male-dominated) thinking. From its radical reappraisal of the mother–daughter relationship to its conclusions on gender identity and object theory, *Outside In ... Inside Out* is a stimulating and exciting contribution to the field of women's studies.

THE SCEPTICAL FEMINIST
A PHILOSOPHICAL ENQUIRY
Janet Radcliffe Richards

Janet Radcliffe Richards's analysis leads her to considerable criticism of many commonly held feminist views, but from it emerges the outline of a new and more powerful feminism which sacrifices neither rationality nor radicalism.

'Intellectually sober and politically practical, yet gay, witty and dashing at the same time ... It's a model of how to write a book on *any* topic; on a contentious subject like this *it's a triumph*' – *Sunday Times*

THE FEMININE MYSTIQUE
Betty Friedan

First published in the sixties *The Feminine Mystique* still remains a powerful and illuminating analysis of the position of women in Western society.

'Brilliantly researched, passionately argued book – a time-bomb flung into the Mom-and-Apple-Pie image ... Out of the debris of that shattered ideal, the Women's Liberation Movement was born' – Anne Leslie

A choice of Penguin Fiction

FALLING IN PLACE
Ann Beattie

It's a hot, sullen summer on America's East Coast. As John and Louise Knapp bicker at their weekend marriage; as twelve-year-old Parker makes another trip to the shrink in New York; as Cynthia the English teacher clings to her freaky lover Spangle – Ann Beattie invades Updike and Cheever territory to give us a cinematic, brilliantly comic view of America's affluent hell.

'Wonderfully funny' – *The Times*

MOTHER'S HELPER
Maureen Freely

The Pyle-Carpenter household comes complete with three children who can do what they like as long as they have Thought It Through, an intercom that never turns off, with Weekly Family Councils and with the television padlocked into a bag. Like Kay Carpenter herself, it was a totally liberated, principled, caring, warm, nurturing nucleus ... And at first, Laura was completely fooled.

'A novel to weep over or laugh with. Whichever will stop you going mad' – *Literary Review*

DAUGHTERS OF PASSION
Julia O'Faolain

Anger, passion, tenderness ... nine evocative stories from the author of *No Country for Young Men*. Julia O'Faolain never falters as she moves through situations both strange and familiar – the seduction of a lonely nanny in Paris, a family embarrassed by an unwelcome guest, the sharply focused memories of an imprisoned hunger-striker under pressure to eat. It is a brilliant, compulsive foray into a landscape of passion from a writer at the height of her powers.